New Online Biographical Resource from African American Publications

We're pleased to introduce the *Reference Library of American Men* and a wonderful, new online biographical resource. This online Web enhancement brings you extended coverage of notable individuals featured in the *Reference Library of American Men*, as well as coverage of other prominent male figures not found in the print publication.

We're pleased to remind you that you have been **automatically authorized** to access the site. Just follow these simple instructions:

• Locate the Web address card in the front matter of Volume I of this publication

• Go to **www.americanmenpubs.com** and simply access the Registration page

• When registering, be sure to include your invoice/access number

Your students are sure to enjoy these easy-to-read online essays that offer extensive insight into the lives of *hundreds* of fascinating American men.

Thank you for your interest and enjoy this terrific online biographical resource!

www.americanmenpubs.com

African American Publications
Phone: 215-321-7742
Fax: 215-321-9568
E-mail: afriampub@aol.com

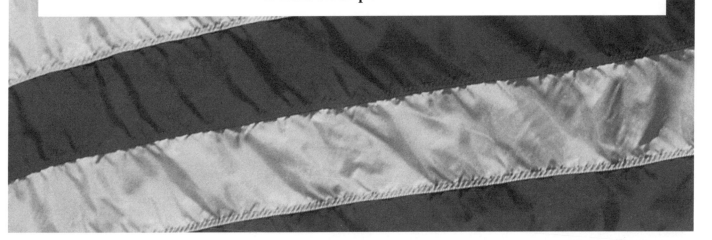

*Reference
Library of*

AMERICAN

MEN

Reference Library of

AMERICAN

MEN

VOLUME **II**

E-J

REFERENCE LIBRARY OF AMERICAN MEN

Staff

Editor: Jennifer Mossman
Managing Editor: Bridget Travers

Permissions Manager: Maria L. Franklin
Permissions Associate: Shalice Shah-Caldwell

Manufacturing Manager: Dorothy Maki
Production Manager: Evi Seoud
Buyer: Rita Wimberley

Product Design Manager: Kenn Zorn
Graphic Artist: Mike Logusz

ISBN 0-7876-6259-3 (4-volume set)
ISBN 0-7876-6260-7 (Volume 1)
ISBN 0-7876-6261-5 (Volume 2)
ISBN 0-7876-6262-3 (Volume 3)
ISBN 0-7876-6263-1 (Volume 4)

Printed in the United States of America

10 9 8 7 6 5 4 3 2 1

CONTENTS

INTRODUCTION

The *Reference Library of American Men* provides a unique, comprehensive source for biographical information on 650 men who have gained international recognition for their enduring contributions to human culture and society. Entries in this four-volume set have been culled from Gale's extensive biographical database. Both contemporary and historic figures covering a wide range of occupations or fields of endeavor can be found. Featured are such renowned contemporary personalities as Muhammad Ali, Woody Allen, Bob Dylan, Bill Gates, Steven Spielberg, and Tiger Woods. Important historic figures include presidents George Washington, Thomas Jefferson, Abraham Lincoln, and Franklin Roosevelt; writers William Faulkner, Ernest Hemingway, Herman Melville, Edgar Allan Poe and Mark Twain; industrialists Andrew Carnegie, Thomas Edison, William Randolph Hearst, Henry Ford, and John D. Rockefeller; and musicians Louis Armstrong, Duke Ellington, Elvis Presley, and Frank Sinatra. Biographical information can be found for the many social or political activists who have organized movements to demand equal rights for all American citizens, such as Martin Luther King Jr., Malcolm X, and Cesar Chavez. Others have made major contributions to the arts, business, education, journalism, religion, or science.

Format

Arranged alphabetically, each authoritative article begins with a brief descriptive paragraph that provides a capsule identification and a statement of the man's significance. Birth and death years are included. Often this is all the information required. This useful feature allows you to determine at a glance whether you need to read further. For example:

The second president of the United States, John Adams (1735–1826) played a major role in the colonial movement toward independence. He wrote the Massachusetts Constitution of 1780 and served as a diplomatic representative of Congress in the 1780s.

The essays that follow are generally about 800 words in length and offer a substantial treatment of the men's lives. Some proceed chronologically, while others confine biographical data to a few paragraphs and then move on to a consideration of the subject's life work. When very few biographical facts are known, the article is necessarily devoted to an analysis of the subject's contribution to society and culture.

Following the essay is a "Further Reading" section and, when applicable, a list of additional sources providing more recent biographical works. Bibliographic citations include books, periodicals, and Internet addresses for World Wide Web pages. This feature will be especially helpful to students, who are frequently required to consult multiple sources when compiling a report or preparing a classroom presentation.

Additional Features

Images. Portraits accompany many of the articles and provide an authentic likeness or representation of the biographee. For historic figures, there are depictions from coins, engravings, and sculptures; for the moderns there are many photographs.

Indexes. Two indexes have been included to help researchers identify the men by name and occupation.

A Valuable Resource

Biographical information on internationally renowned men is always in high demand. The *Reference Library of American Men* can meet this need by presenting lively and informative essays on 650 men whose contributions have earned them a place in the annals of human history.

ACKNOWLEDGMENTS

Photographs and illustrations that appear in *Reference Library of American Men* were received from the following sources:

Aaron, Hank, photograph. National Archives and Records Administration.

Abernathy, Ralph, photograph. The Library of Congress.

Acheson, Dean, photograph. Archive Photos, Inc. Reproduced by permission.

Adams, Ansel, photograph. AP/Wide World Photos. Reproduced by permission.

Adams, Hank, photograph. AP/Wide World Photos. Reproduced by permission.

Adams, John, painting by C. W. Peale. National Archives and Records Administration.

Adams, Samuel, portrait by John S. Copley. National Archives and Records Administration.

Aiken, Conrad, photograph. The Library of Congress.

Ailey, Alvin, photograph. The Library of Congress

Ali, Muhammad, photograph. UPI/Corbis-Bettmann. Reproduced by permission.

Allen, Woody, photograph. United Artists.

Alvarez, Luis, photograph. The Library of Congress.

Armstrong, Edwin Howard, photograph. The Library of Congress.

Armstrong, Louis, photograph. AP/Wide World Photos, Inc. Reproduced by permission.

Armstrong, Neil A., photograph. U.S. National Aeronautics and Space Administration (NASA).

Arnold, Benedict, painting. The Library of Congress.

Arthur, Chester A., photograph. The Library of Congress.

Ashe, Arthur, photograph. AP/Wide World Photos. Reproduced by permission.

Asimov, Isaac, photograph. The Library of Congress.

Astaire, Fred, photograph. AP/Wide World Photos. Reproduced by permission.

Astor, John Jacob, painting. The Library of Congress.

Audubon, John James, engraving. The Library of Congress.

Balanchine, George, photograph. Archive Photos, Inc. Reproduced by permission.

Baltimore, David, 1975, photograph. AP/Wide World Photos, Inc. Reproduced by permission.

Banneker, Benjamin, engraving.

Baraka, Amiri, 1994, photograph by Christopher Felver. Archive Photos, Inc. Reproduced by permission.

Barnum, P. T., photograph. Archive Photos, Inc. Reproduced by permission.

Barthe, Richmond, photograph by Betsy G. Reyneau. National Archives and Records Administration.

Basie, Count, photograph. The Library of Congress.

Beadle, George W., Chicago, 1965, photograph. The Library of Congress.

Bell, Alexander Graham, photograph. U. S. National Aeronautics and Space Administration.

Bellow, Saul, photograph. The Library of Congress.

Bennett, William, photograph by Ira Schwarz. Archive Photos. Reproduced by permission.

Berg, Paul, photograph. The Library of Congress.

Berlin, Irving, photograph. The Library of Congress.

Bernardin, Joseph Cardinal, photograph. The Library of Congress.

Berry, Chuck, photograph. The Library of Congress.

Bieber, Owen, photograph. UPI/Bettmann Newsphotos. Reproduced by permission.

Bird, Larry, photograph. AP/Wide World Photos. Reproduced by permission.

Blanc, Mel, 1980, photograph. AP/Wide World Photos. Reproduced by permission.

Bluford, Guion, S. Jr., photograph. U.S. National Aeronautics and Space Administration (NASA).

Boeing, William E, photograph. AP/Wide World Photos. Reproduced by permission.

Bogart, Humphrey, photograph. Springer/Corbis-Bettmann. Reproduced by permission.

Bond, Julian, photograph. The Library of Congress

Boone, Daniel, photograph. The Library of Congress.

Bradbury, Ray, photograph. The Library of Congress.

Bradley, Ed, photograph. AP/Wide World Photos. Reproduced by permission.

Brady, Mathew B., photograph. The Library of Congress.

Brandeis, Louis, photograph . The Library of Congress.

Brown, James, photograph. The Library of Congress.

Brown, John, illustration. National Archives and Records Administration.

Bruce, Blanche Kelso, photograph. U.S. Senate Historical Office.

Bryant, William Cullen, photograph. The Library of Congress.

Buchanan, James, painting. The Library of Congress.

Buchanan, Patrick J., photograph. The Library of Congress.

Buffett, Warren E., photograph. AP/Wide World Photos. Reproduced by permission.

Burbank, Luther, photograph. The Library of Congress.

Burger, Warren E., photograph. The Library of Congress.

Burns, George, photograph. The Library of Congress.

Burroughs, William S., photograph. AP/Wide World Photos. Reproduced by permission.

Bush, George, photograph. The Library of Congress.

Bush, George W, photograph by Adrees Latif. Reuters/ Archive Photos. Reproduced by permission.

Bush, Vannevar, photograph. The Library of Congress.

Byrd, Richard Evelyn, photograph by Underwood and Underwood. The Library of Congress.

Calder, Alexander S., photograph. The Library of Congress.

Calhoun, John Caldwell, photograph. The Library of Congress

Calvin, Melvin, photograph. The Library of Congress.

Campbell, Ben Nighthorse, photograph. AP/Wide World Photos. Reproduced by permission.

Capone, Al, photograph. Archive Photos, Inc. Reproduced by permission.

Capote, Truman, photograph. The Library of Congress.

Carmichael, Stokely, photograph. The Library of Congress.

Carson, Johnny, photograph. The Library of Congress.

Carson, Kit, painting. The Library of Congress.

Carter, Jimmy, photograph. The Library of Congress.

Carver, George Washington, photograph. The Library of Congress.

Cash, Johnny, photograph. The Library of Congress.

Chamberlain, Wilt, 1991, photograph. AP/Wide World Photos. Reproduced by permission.

Charles, Ray, photograph. The Library of Congress.

Chavez, Cesar, photograph. The Library of Congress.

Chavez, Dennis, photograph. Library of Congress.

Chavis, Benjamin Franklin, Jr., photograph. AP/Wide World. Reproduced by permission.

Chief Seattle, photograph. The Library of Congress.

Chomsky, Noam, photograph. Archive Photos. Reproduced by permission.

Christopher, Warren, photograph. Archive Photo/ Popperfoto. Reproduced by permission.

Cisneros, Henry, photograph. AP/Wide World Photos. Reproduced by permission.

Clancy, Tom, photograph. AP/Wide World Photos. Reproduced by permission.

Cleaver, Eldridge, New York City, 1968, photograph. AP/Wide World Photos. Reproduced by permission.

Cleveland, Grover, photograph. The Library of Congress.

Cleveland, James, photograph. AP/Wide World Photos. Reproduced by permission.

Clinton, George, painting . The Library of Congress.

Clinton, Bill, flanked by Vice-President Gore and Attorney General Janet Reno, 1993–95, photograph. The Library of Congress.

Cole, Nat King, photograph. The Library of Congress.

Colt, Samuel, illustration.

Coltrane, John, photograph. The Library of Congress.

Compton, Arthur Holly, photograph. The Library of Congress.

Coolidge, Calvin, photograph. The Library of Congress.

Cooper, James Fenimore, drawing by C. L. Elliot. Source unknown.

Copland, Aaron, photograph.

Coppola, Francis Ford, photograph by Frank Capri. Archive Photos, Inc. Reproduced by permission.

Cosby, (Bill) William Henry, Jr., photograph. The Library of Congress.

Coughlin, Charles E., photograph. AP/Wide World Photos, Inc. Reproduced by permission.

Crane, Stephen, photograph. The Library of Congress.

Cray, Seymour, photograph. AP/Wide World Photos, Inc. Reproduced by permission.

Crazy Horse, photograph. The Library of Congress.

Crichton, Michael, photograph. AP/Wide World Photos, Inc. Reproduced by permission.

Cronkite, Walter L., Jr., photograph. The Library of Congress.

Cummings, E. E., photograph. The Library of Congress.

Cuomo, Mario, photograph. Archive Photos, Inc. Reproduced by permission.

Cushing, Harvey Williams, photograph. The Library of Congress.

Custer, George Armstrong, photograph. The Library of Congress.

Darrow, Clarence Seward, photograph. The Library of Congress.

Davis, Jefferson, photograph by Mathew Brady. National Archives and Records Administration.

Davis, Miles, photograph. The Library of Congress.

Davis, Richard Harding, photograph. The Library of Congress

Goodyear, Charles, sketch. The Library of Congress.

Gordy, Berry, Jr., photograph. AP/Wide World Photos. Reproduced by permission.

Gorgas, William Crawford, photograph.

Gould, Stephen Jay, photograph. AP/Wide World Photos. Reproduced by permission.

Graham, Billy, photograph. The Library of Congress.

Grant, Ulysses Simpson, photograph. The Library of Congress.

Greeley, Reverand Andrew, photograph. AP/Wide World Photos, Inc. Reproduced by permission.

Greenspan, Alan, photograph.The Library of Congress.

Gregory, Dick, photograph. The Library of Congress.

Griffith, David Lewelyn Wark, photograph. Archive Photos, Inc. Reproduced by permission.

Grisham, John, photograph by Capri. Archive. Reproduced by permission.

Grove, Andrew, 1997, photograph by Russell Boyce. Reuters/Archive Photos, Inc. Reproduced by permission.

Guthrie, Woodrow W., photograph. The Library of Congress.

Halberstam, David, photograph by Bernard Gotfryd. Archive Photos, Inc. Reproduced by permission.

Haley, Alex, photograph. AP/Wide World Photos, Inc. Reproduced by permission.

Hamilton, Alexander, portrait by John Trumbull. National Archives and Records Administration.

Hammer, Armand, photograph. The Library of Congress.

Hancock, John, painting by John Singleton Copley. National Archives and Records Administration.

Handsome Lake, drawing by Jesse Cornplanter. The Library of Congress.

Handy, W.C., photograph. The Library of Congress.

Harding, Warren G., photograph. The Library of Congress.

Haring, Keith, photograph. Archive Photos, Inc. Reproduced by permission.

Harris, Joel Chandler, photograph. The Library of Congress.

Harrison, Benjamin, photograph. The Library of Congress.

Harte, Bret, engraving. The Library of Congress.

Hawthorne, Nathaniel, photograph.

Hay, John Milton, photograph. The Library of Congress.

Hayes, Rutherford B., photograph. The Library of Congress.

Hearst, William Randolph, photograph. The Library of Congress.

Heller, Joseph, photograph. AP/Wide World Photos. Reproduced by permission.

Hemingway, Ernest and Elizabeth Hadley, photograph.

Hendrix, Jimi, photograph. AP/Wide World Photos. Reproduced by permission.

Henry, Joseph, photograph. Corbis-Bettmann. Reproduced by permission.

Henson, Matthew A., illustration. The Library of Congress.

Hershey, Alfred D., photograph. The Library of Congress.

Heschel, Abraham J., photograph. The Library of Congress.

Hickok, Wild Bill, photograph. National Archives and Records Administration.

Hiss, Alger, photograph. The Library of Congress.

Hoffa, Jimmy, photograph. Archive Photos, Inc. Reproduced by permission.

Hoffman, Abbie, photograph. The Library of Congress.

Holmes, Oliver Wendall Jr., photograph. The Library of Congress.

Holmes, Oliver Wendell, photograph. The Library of Congress.

Hooks, Benjamin L., photograph. The Library of Congress.

Hoover, Herbert, photograph. The Library of Congress.

Hoover, J. Edgar, photograph. The Library of Congress.

Hope, Bob, photograph. UPI/Bettmann. Reproduced by permission.

Hopper, Edward, photograph. AP/Wide World Photos. Reproduced by permission.

Horowitz, Vladimir, photograph. The Library of Congress.

Houdini, Harry, photograph. Archive Photos, Inc. Reproduced by permission.

Houston, Charles H., photograph. UPI/Corbis-Bettmann. Reproduced by permission.

Houston, Samuel, drawing. The Library of Congress.

Howe, Elias, photograph. Archive Photos, Inc. Reproduced by permission.

Hubble, Edwin, photograph. The Library of Congress.

Hughes, Howard, photograph. The Library of Congress.

Humphrey, Hubert H., Jr., photograph. The Library of Congress.

Iacocca, Lee, photograph. The Library of Congress.

Irving, Washington, painting. The Library of Congress.

Jackson, Andrew, drawing. The Library of Congress.

Jackson, Jesse L., photograph. The Library of Congress.

Jackson, Michael, photograph. AP/Wide World Photos. Reproduced by permission.

Jackson, Reggie, photograph. AP/Wide World Photos. Reproduced by permission.

Jackson, T.J. (Stonewall), print.

James, Henry, photograph. The Library of Congress.

Jefferson, Thomas, engraving. The Library of Congress.

Jobs, Steven, photograph. Archive Photos/Reuters/Sell. Reproduced by permission.

Joffrey, Robert, photograph. AP/Wide World Photos. Reproduced by permissions.

Johns, Jasper, photograph. Corbis-Bettmann. Reproduced by permission.

Johnson, Andrew, photograph. The Library of Congress.

Johnson, Earvin "Magic", photograph. AP/Wide World Photos. Reproduced by permission.

Johnson, Jack, photograph. The Library of Congress.

Johnson, James Weldon, photograph. The Library of Congress.

Johnson, John H., photograph. The Library of Congress.

Johnson, Lyndon B., photograph. LBJ Library Collections.

Jolson, Al, photograph. The Library of Congress.

Jones, James Earl, photograph. The Library of Congress.

Jones, Quincy, photograph. The Library of Congress.

Jones, Robert T., photograph. The Library of Congress.

Joplin, Scott, illustration. Corbis-Bettmann. Reproduced by permission.

Jordan, Louis, photograph. The Library of Congress.

Jordan, Michael, photograph. Reuters/Corbis-Bettmann. Reproduced by permission.

Julian, Percy Lavon, photograph. The Library of Congress.

Kahn, Louis, photograph. AP/Wide World Photos. Reproduced by permission.

Kelly, Gene, photograph. The Library of Congress.

Kemp, Jack French Jr., photograph. The Library of Congress.

Kendall, Edward C., photograph. The Library of Congress.

Kennedy, John F., photograph. The Library of Congress.

Kennedy, Robert, photograph. John F. Kennedy Library.

Kerouac, Jack, photograph. Archive Photos. Reproduced by permission.

Kessler, David A., photograph by Dennis Cook. AP/Wide World Photos. Reproduced by permission.

Kettering, Charles Franklin, photograph. The Library of Congress

King, B.B., photograph. AP/Wide World Photos. Reproduced by permission.

King, Dr. Martin Luther, Jr., painting by Betsy G. Reyneau. National Archives and Records Administration.

King, Stephen, photograph. Archive Photos, Inc. Reproduced by permission.

Kinsey, Alfred, photograph. The Library of Congress.

Klein, Calvin, photograph. AP/Wide World Photos. Reproduced by permission.

Koop, C. Everett, photograph. Archive Photos. Reproduced by permission.

Kornberg, Arthur, portrait. The Library of Congress.

Kroc, Ray, photograph. The Library of Congress.

Kubrick, Stanley, photograph. Archive Photos. Reproduced by permission.

LaFlesche, Francis, photograph. The Library of Congress.

Land, Edwin H., photograph. The Library of Congress.

Langmuir, Irving, photograph. The Library of Congress.

Langston, John Mercer, photograph. The Library of Congress.

Lardner, Ring, photograph. The Library of Congress.

Lauren, Ralph, photograph. Archive Photos, Inc. Reproduced by permission.

Leary, Timothy, photograph. Archive Photos, Inc. Reproduced by permission.

Lederberg, Joshua, photograph. The Library of Congress.

Lee, Bruce, photograph. Archive Photos. Reproduced by permission.

Lee, Robert E., photograph by Mathew Brady. National Archives and Records Administration.

Lee, Spike, photograph by Chrystyna Czajkowsky. AP/Wide World Photos. Reproduced by permission.

Lee, Tsung-Dao, photograph. The Library of Congress.

Lewis, Carl, photograph. AP/Wide World Photos. Reproduced by permission.

Lewis, John L., photograph. The Library of Congress.

Lewis, John Robert, photograph.

Lewis, Meriwether, painting. The Library of Congress.

Lewis, Sinclair, photograph. The Library of Congress.

Libby, Willard F., photograph. The Library of Congress.

Lichtenstein, Roy, photograph. AP/Wide World Photos. Reproduced by permission.

Lincoln, Abraham, postcard. The Library of Congress.

Lindberg, Charles A., photograph. The Library of Congress.

Lipman, Fritz, photograph. The Library of Congress.

Lippmann, Walter, photograph. The Library of Congress.

Little Richard, photograph. AP/Wide World Photos. Reproduced by permission.

Little Wolf, photograph. The Library of Congress.

Locke, Dr, Alain, photograph. The Library of Congress.

London, Jack, photograph. The Library of Congress.

Long, Huey, photograph. Archive Photos, Inc. Reproduced by permission.

Longfellow, Henry Wadsworth, photograph. AP/Wide World Photos. Reproduced by permission.

Love, Nat, photograph. Denver Public Library.

Luce, Henry R., photograph. The Library of Congress.

Madison, James, portrait by Stuart Gilbert. National Archives and Records Administration.

Mahan, Alfred Thayer, photograph. The Library of Congress.

Malamud, Bernard, photograph. The Library of Congress.

Malcolm X, photograph. AP/Wide World Photos. Reproduced by permission.

Mamet, David Alam, Rebecca Pidgeon, photograph by Jose Goitia. AP/Wide World Photos. Reproduced by permission.

Marshall, George C., photograph.

Marshall, John, illustration. Source unknown.

Marshall, Thurgood, photograph. The Library of Congress.

Massasoit, engraving. The Library of Congress.

Masters, William, photograph. AP/Wide World Photos. Reproduced by permission.

Mather, Cotton, drawing. The Library of Congress.

Mather, Increase, engraving. The Library of Congress.

Maury, Matthew Fontain, photograph of engraving. The Library of Congress.

Mayo, Charles Horace, photograph.

Mays, Benjamin E., President John F. Kennedy, photograph. John F. Kennedy Library.

Mays, Willie, photograph. Archive Photos, Inc. Reproduced by permission.

McArthur, Douglas, photograph. National Archives and Records Administration.

McCarthy, Senator Joseph, photograph. Archive Photos. Reproduced by permisssion.

McCormick, Cyrus H., engraving. The Library of Congress.

McKinley, William, photograph. The Library of Congress.

McNamara, Robert and John F. Kennedy, photograph. Photograph No. ST-A26-23-62 in the John F. Kennedy Library.

McNickle, D'Arcy, illustration by Francisca Bollez. The Library of Congress.

Means, Russell, photograph. AP/Wide World Photos. Reproduced by permission.

Melville, Herman, photograph. The Library of Congress.

Mencken, Henry Louis, photograph. The Library of Congress.

Meredith, James, photograph. The Library of Congress.

Merrill, James, photograph. AP/Wide World Photos. Reproduced by permission.

Metacom, engraving. Archive Photos, Inc. Reproduced by permission.

Mfume, Kweisi, photograph. AP/Wide World Photos. Reproduced by permission.

Michelson, Albert, photograph. The Library of Congress.

Milk, Harvey, photograph. AP/Wide World Photos. Reproduced by permission.

Miller, Arthur, photograph. The Library of Congress.

Miller, Henry, photograph. The Library of Congress.

Millikan, Robert A., photograph. The Library of Congress.

Mills, Charles Wright, photograph. The Library of Congress.

Momaday, N. Scott, photograph. AP/Wide World Photos. Reproduced by permission.

Monk, Thelonius S., photograph. The Library of Congress.

Monroe, James, drawing. The Library of Congress.

Montana, Joe, Tim Grunhard and Glenn Montgomery, photograph. AP/Wide World Photos. Reproduced by permission.

Montezuma, Carlos, photogrraph. Source unknown.

Morgan, Garrett A., photograph. AP/Wide World Photos. Reproduced by permission.

Morgan, J. P, photograph. Archive Photos. Reproduced by permission.

Morgan, Thomas Hunt, photograph. The Library of Congress.

Morse, Samuel Finley Breese, painting. The Library of Congress.

Muhammed, Elijah, photograph. Archive Photos. Reproduced by permission.

Muller, Hermann Joseph, photograph. The Library of Congress.

Murrow, Edward R., photograph. The Library of Congress.

Nader, Ralph, photograph. The Library of Congress.

Nash, Ogden, photograph. AP/Wide World Photos. Reproduced by permission.

Newman, Paul, photograph. Archive Photos. Reproduced by permission.

Newton, Huey, photograph. AP/Wide World Photos, Inc. Reproduced by permission.

Niebuhr, Reinhold, photograph. The Library of Congress.

Nirenberg, Marshall Warren, photograph. The Library of Congress.

Nixon, Richard M., photograph. The Library of Congress.

Noguchi, Isamu, photograph. AP/Wide World Photos. Reproduced by permission.

Norris, George W., photograph. The Library of Congress.

Noyce, Robert, photograph. AP/Wide World Photos, Inc. Reproduced by permission.

O'Neill, Eugene G., photograph. The Library of Congress.

Onsager, Lars, photograph. Archive Photo/Express News. Reproduced by permission.

Oppenheimer, J. Robert, photograph. The Library of Congress.

Osceola, a Seminole chief, photograph. National Archives and Records Administration.

Parker, Charlie, photograph. Archive Photos, Inc. Reproduced by permission.

Parker, Quanah,, photograph by Lanney. National Archives and Records Administration.

Patton, George Smith, Tunisia, 1943, photograph. The Library of Congress.

Pauling, Linus, photograph. The Library of Congress.

Peary, Robert Edwin, photograph. AP/Wide World Photos. Reproduced by permission.

Peltier, Leonard, photograph. AP/Wide World Photos. Reproduced by permission.

Perot, Ross, photograph. Archive Photos, Inc. Reproduced by permission.

Perry, Bishop Harold, photograph.The Library of Congress.

Perry, Matthew Calbraith, engraving. The Library of Congress.

Pershing, John J., photograph. The Library of Congress.

Pierce, Franklin, photograph. The Library of Congress.

Pike, Zebulon M., illustration. U.S. Army Photographs

Pinchback, Pinckney Benton Stewart, photograph. The Library of Congress.

Pincus, Gregory, photograph. AP/Wide World Photos. Reproduced by permission.

Plenty Coups, photograph by Edward S. Curtis. The Library of Congress.

Poe, Edgar Allen, photograph.

Poitier, Sidney, photograph. The Library of Congress.

Polk, James Knox, photograph. The Library of Congress.

Pontiac, painting.

Porter, Cole, photograph. The Library of Congress.

Pound, Ezra, photograph. The Library of Congress.

Powell, Adam Clayton, photograph. The Library of Congress.

Powell, Colin L., photograph. AP/Wide World Photos. Reproduced by permission.

Powhatan, engraving. The Library of Congress.

Presley, Elvis, photograph. AP/Wide World Photos. Reproduced by permission.

Puente, Tito, photograph by Bruno Bernard. NYWTS/ The Library of Congress.

Pynchon, Thomas R., photograph. UPI/Corbis-Bettmann. Reproduced by permission.

Quayle, Dan, photograph. The Library of Congress.

Randolph, Asa P., photograph. The Library of Congress.

Rauschenberg, Robert, photograph by Felveregi. C. Archive Photos, Inc. Reproduced by permission.

Reagan, Ronald, photograph. The Library of Congress.

Red Cloud, photograph. National Archives and Records Administration.

Red Jacket, engraving. Archive Photos, Inc. Reproduced by permission.

Reed, Walter, photograph. AP/Wide World Photos. Reproduced by permission.

Reeve, Christopher, photograph by Gary Hershorn. Reuters/Archive Photos, Inc. Reproduced by permission

Remington, Frederic, photograph. The Library of Congress.

Revels, Hiram R., drawing. Harper's Weekly.

Revere, Paul, illustration. National Archives and Records Administration.

Richards, Theodore William, photograph. The Library of Congress.

Richter, Charles, Clarence Allen, photograph. AP/Wide World Photos, Inc. Reproduced by permission.

Riordan, Richard, photograph. AP/Wide World Photos. Reproduced by permission.

Ripken, Cal, Jr., photograph. Archive Photos, Inc. Re-

produced by permission.

Robertson, Pat, photograph by Steve Jaffe. Reuters/ Archive Photos, Inc. Reproduced by permission.

Robinson, Frank, photograph. Archive Photos. Reproduced by permission.

Robinson, Max, photograph. AP/Wide World Photos. Reproduced by permission.

Robinson, Smokey, photograph. AP/Wide World Photos. Reproduced by permission.

Rockefeller, John D., photograph. The Library of Congress.

Rockwell, Norman, photograph by Underwood & Underwood. The Library of Congress.

Rodgers, Richard, photograph. The Library of Congress.

Roebling, John Augustus, photograph. The Library of Congress.

Rogers, Will, photograph. The Library of Congress.

Roosevelt, Franklin D., photograph. Franklin D. Roosevelt Library.

Roosevelt, Theodore, photograph. The Library of Congress.

Ross, John, lithograph. The Library of Congress.

Rowan, Carl T., photograph. The Library of Congress.

Rustin, Bayard, photograph. A. Philip Randolph Institute.

Ruth, Babe, photograph. The Library of Congress.

Ryan, Nolan, photograph. UPI/Corbis-Bettmann. Reproduced by permission.

Sabin, Albert, photograph. The Library of Congress.

Sagan, Carl, photograph. The Library of Congress

Salinger, J.D., photograph. The Library of Congress.

Salk, Jonas, photograph. The Library of Congress.

Sandburg, Carl, photograph. The Library of Congress.

Schlesinger, Arthur, Jr., photograph. Corbis-Bettmann. Reproduced by permission.

Schulz, Charles M., photograph. The Library of Congress.

Schwarzkopf, Norman, Colin Powell, photograph by John Gaps. AP/Wide World Photos. Reproduced by permission.

Scorsese, Martin, photograph. Archive Photos/Popperfoto. Reproduced by permission.

Scott, Dred, illustration. The Library of Congress.

Scott, Winfield, photograph. The Library of Congress.

Seaborg, Glenn T., photograph. The Library of Congress.

Sequoyah, painting. The Library of Congress.

Seward, William H., bust. National Archives and Records Administration.

Shapley, Harlow, photograph. The Library of Congress.

Sharpton, Al, photograph. Archive Photos, Inc. Reproduced by permission.

Sheen, Fulton J., photograph by Louis Fabian Bachrach. The Library of Congress.

Shepard, Alan, photograph. The Library of Congress.

Shockley, William, photograph. The Library of Congress.

Siegel, Benjamin, photograph. AP/Wide World Photos.

Reproduced by permission.

Simon, Neil, photograph. AP/Wide World Photos. Reproduced by permission.

Simon, Paul, photograph. The Library of Congress.

Simpson, George Gaylord, photograph The Library of Congress.

Sinatra, Frank, photograph. AP/Wide World Photos, Inc. Reproduced by permission.

Sinclair, Upton, photograph. AP/Wide World Photos, Inc. Reproduced by permission.

Singer, Isaac Bashevis, photograph. UPI/Corbis-Bettmann. Reproduced by permission.

Singer, Isaac Merritt, illustration.

Sitting Bull, photograph. National Archives and Records Administration.

Slater, Samuel, engraving The Library of Congress.

Smith, Joseph, illustration. The Library of Congress.

Smohalla, photograph. The Library of Congress.

Sondheim, Stephen and Richard Rodgers, photograph.The Library of Congress.

Spielberg, Steven, photograph. Archive Photos, Inc. Reproduced by permission.

Spock, Benjamin, photograph.The Library of Congress.

Stanley, Wendell Meredith, photograph. The Library of Congress.

Steinbeck, John, photograph. The Library of Congress.

Steinmetz, Charles P., photograph. The Library of Congress

Stone, Oliver, photograph. AP/Wide World Photos. Reproduced by permission.

Stuart, Gilbert, engraving. The Library of Congress.

Sullivan, Leon Howard, photograph. The Library of Congress.

Sullivan, Louis Henry, photograph.

Sutter, John Augustus, photograph. The Library of Congress.

Taft, William Howard, photograph. The Library of Congress.

Tanner, Henry O., photograph. UPI/Corbis-Bettmann. Reproduced by permission.

Taylor, Zachary, photograph. The Library of Congress.

Teller, Edward, photograph. The Library of Congress.

Theiler, Max, photograph. The Library of Congress.

Thoreau, Henry David, drawing. The Library of Congress.

Thorpe, Jim, photograph. National Archives and Records Administration.

Thurber, James, photograph by Fred Palumbo. NYWTS/The Library of Congress.

Townes, Charles H., photograph. NYWTS/The Library of Congress.

Trudeau, Garry, photograph. The Library of Congress.

Truman, Harry S., photograph. The Library of Congress.

Trump, Donald, photograph. Archive Photos, Inc. Reproduced by permission.

Turner, Henry McNeal, engraving.

Turner, Nat, engraving. Corbis-Bettmann. Reproduced by permission.

Turner, Ted, photograph. Archive Photo/Malafronte. Reproduced by permission.

Twain, Mark, photograph. The Library of Congress.

Tyler, John, daguerrotype by Mathew Brady. The Library of Congress.

Updike, John, photograph by Wyatt Counts. AP/Wide World Photos. Reproduced by permission.

Urey, Harold, photograph. The Library of Congress.

Van Buren, Martin, photograph. The Library of Congress.

Von Neumann, John,, photograph. AP/Wide World Photos. Reproduced by permission.

Vonnegut, Kurt, photograph. AP/Wide World Photos. Reproduced by permission.

Waksman, Selman A., photograph. The Library of Congress.

Wallace, George, photograph. The Library of Congress.

Wang, An, photograph. AP/Wide World Photos. Reproduced by permission.

Warhol, Andy, photograph. The Library of Congress.

Warren, Earl, photograph. The Library of Congress.

Warren, Robert Penn, photograph. The library of Congress.

Washakie, photograph. National Archives and Records Administration.

Washington, Booker T., photograph. The Library of Congress.

Washington, George, painting by Stuart Gilbert. The Library of Congress

Waters, Muddy, photograph. Archive Photos. Reproduced by permission.

Watson, James Dewey, photograph. The Library of Congress.

Webster, Daniel, painting. The Library of Congress.

Webster, Noah, engraving. The Library of Congress.

Westinghouse, George, portrait. The Library of Congress.

Westmoreland, William, photograph. AP/Wide World Photos. Reproduced by permission.

Whipple, George Hoyt, photograph. The Library of Congress.

Whistler, James McNeill, drawing. The Library of Congress.

White, E.B., photograph. Corbis-Bettmann. Reproduced by permission.

White, Walter Francis, photograph. The Library of Congress.

Whitney, Eli, engravings. The Library of Congress.

Wiener, Norbert, photograph. The Library of Congress.

Wiesel, Elie, photograph. AP/Wide World Photos. Reproduced by permission.

Wilder, L. Douglas, photograph. AP/Wide World Photos. Reproduced by permission.

Wilkes, Charles, engraving. The Library of Congress.

Williams, Roger, photograph. Archive Photos, Inc. Reproduced by permission.

Williams, Tennessee, photograph. The Library of Congress.

Wilson, August, photograph. AP/Wide World Photos. Reproduced by permission.

Wilson, Woodrow, photograph. The Library of Congress.

Wolfe, Thomas, painting. The Library of Congress.

Woods, Tiger, photograph. AP/Wide World Photos. Re-produced by permission.

Woodson, Carter Goodwin, photograph. AP/Wide World Photos. Reproduced by permission.

Wyeth, Andrew, photograph. The Library of Congress.

Yeager, Charles E., photograph. The Library of Congress.

Young, Andrew, photograph. The Library of Congress.

Young, Brigham, photograph. The Library of Congress.

Zah, Peterson, photograph. UPI/Corbis-Bettmann. Reproduced by permission.

Zindel, Paul, photograph. AP/Wide World Photos. Reproduced by permission.

E

Charles A. Eastman

Charles Eastman (1858–1939) was the first Native American physician to serve on the Pine Ridge Reservation and a prolific author of works about Indian life and culture.

Born near Redwood Falls, Minnesota, of mixed Santee Sioux and white parentage, Charles Eastman was much influenced in his distinguished career as a writer, physician, and Indian spokesman by two of the last bloody Indian-white conflicts on the North American prairies and plains. He published two autobiographical accounts of his youth—*Indian Boyhood* and *From the Deep Woods to Civilization*—which were widely credited with raising white awareness of Indian issues.

His parents were Jacob Eastman ["Many Lightnings"], a Wahpeton Sioux, and Mary Nancy Eastman, a mixed-blood Sioux who died when he was a baby. His maternal grandfather was artist Seth Eastman. The youngest of five children, and given the name Hakadah ["The Pitiful Last"] because of his mother's early death, Eastman fled with his family from Minnesota to British Columbia following the Sioux Indian Uprising of 1862. Ten years later, after thorough training as a hunter and warrior, he was reclaimed by his father, who had been in prison during most of that time for his part in the uprising.

At his father's insistence, Eastman enrolled in the Flandreau Indian School and thus was abruptly introduced into an alien society that he would struggle to understand for the rest of his life. Eastman went on to study at Beloit College, Knox College, Dartmouth College (where he earned a bachelor's degree in 1887), and Boston University (where he received his doctorate in 1890). In his first position as government physician at Pine Ridge Agency in South Dakota, he treated the survivors of the Wounded Knee Mas-

sacre. There he also met—and the next year married—Elaine Goodale, a poet, educator, and reformer.

A succession of positions followed with the YMCA and the Bureau of Indian Affairs, and he was much in demand in America and England throughout his life as an authority on Indian concerns. With his wife's assistance, Eastman began his career as a published author in 1893 with a series called "Recollections of the Wild Life" in *St. Nicholas* magazine. Over the next 27 years he gained increasing fame as America's distinguished Indian writer with many more articles and ten books, one of them written jointly with his wife Elaine. In addition to collaborating as writers, the couple produced six children. In 1933, Eastman was recognized by the Indian Council Fire, a national organization, with its first award for "most distinguished achievement by an American Indian."

Throughout his life, Eastman's reputation as a writer, speaker, and advocate of Indian rights rested largely on the fact that he had made the dramatic transition from the life of a traditional Sioux Indian in the wilds of Canada to the drawing rooms and lecture halls of white America. As an articulate and accomplished physician, with a dynamic wife who spoke Lakota like a native, Eastman amazed many auditors and readers. Even some Congressmen were startled, as Rob Eshman points out in the *Dartmouth Alumni Magazine*. From 1897 to 1900 Eastman was a lobbyist for the Santee Sioux Tribe in Washington, D.C. Following one presentation before a Congressional committee, the only responses from the Congressmen were, "Where did you go to school? Why are there not more Indians like you?"

Began Literary Career with Autobiography

Eastman's literary career began in earnest in 1902 with the publication of *Indian Boyhood*. He had previously pub-

lished a handful of short pieces, mostly in *Red Man* and *St. Nicholas* magazines, but this autobiography—dedicated to his son Ohiyesa the second—appealed to a wide non-Indian public with its depiction of "the freest life in the world," as Eastman called it. It consists of his earliest recollections from childhood; tributes to Uncheedah, his paternal grandmother who reared him, and to Mysterious Medicine, his uncle who taught him the lore of a life lived close to nature; and a moving conclusion that recounts the return of his father, just released from the federal penitentiary at Davenport, Iowa.

Of his grandmother, Eastman wrote, she "was a wonder to the young maidens of the tribe." Although she was 60 years old, she cared for Eastman as if he were her own child. "Every little attention that is due to a loved child she performed with much skill and devotion. She made all my scanty garments and my tiny moccasins with a great deal of taste. It was said by all that I could not have had more attention had my mother been living." For his uncle, his father's brother, Eastman had the greatest admiration. He characterized the warrior as "a father to me for ten years of my life," a teacher with infinite patience who knew his subject—nature—thoroughly. Said Eastman, "Nothing irritated him more than to hear some natural fact misrepresented. I have often thought that with education he might have made a Darwin or an Agassiz." But Mysterious Medicine also realized that the things he knew and taught would soon lose their value. After telling Eastman the story of one of his most exciting hunting adventures, he concluded: "But all this life is fast disappearing, and the world is becoming different."

The world became shockingly different for Eastman when his father sought him out in Canada in 1873 and returned him to the United States, to Flandreau, Dakota Territory, where a group of Santees lived as homesteaders among the whites. "Here," wrote Eastman, "my wild life came to an end, and my school days began." It was an ironic reunion and return, for Eastman had thought his father dead, had pledged himself to take revenge upon the whites for that death, and now would be living among them with his father and adopting their ways.

Eastman would go on to publish the sequel to *Indian Boyhood* in 1916, when *From the Deep Woods to Civilization* appeared. In it, as Raymond Wilson concludes in *Ohiyesa: Charles Eastman, Santee Sioux,* Eastman presents a more realistic picture of the white world, "openly attacking the evils of white society and lamenting the sorrows Indians encountered as a result of cultural contact. . . ." In particular, his versions of the controversies in which he was embroiled at Pine Ridge and later at Crow Creek are clearly presented in a one-sided way. In addition, the pervasive tone of innocence in *Indian Boyhood* is now replaced by one of frustration, expressed in its most ironic form by his comment on his years at Dartmouth College: "It was here that I had most of my savage gentleness and native refinement knocked out of me. I do not complain, for I know that I gained more than their equivalent." Above all, Eastman was profoundly depressed by the failure of Americans to practice the Christianity that they professed, so that the meek might inherit the earth and "the peacemakers receive high honor." Instead, he wrote in *From the Deep Woods to Civilization,* "When I reduce civilization to its lowest terms, it becomes a system of life based upon trade. . . ."

All told, Eastman wrote ten books, and they established him as the leading apologist for his people and a storyteller of historic significance. Other titles include *Red Hunters and the Animal People* (1904), stories and legends for youth; *Old Indian Days* (1907), divided into stories about warriors and women; *Smoky Day's Wigwam Evenings: Indian Stories Retold* (1910), written with his wife Elaine; *The Soul of the Indian* (1911), the most fully developed statement of his religious beliefs; and *The Indian Today: The Past and Future of the First American* (1915), a review of Indian history, contributions, and problems. Eastman's last book was *Indian Heroes and Great Chieftains* (1918), a collection of short biographies of Sioux leaders written for young people.

Throughout the years that Charles and Elaine Eastman lived together, she served as his editorial assistant in all of his writing. Although on occasion Eastman resented some of Elaine's rewriting, she seems to have been essential to his publishing success, for after their separation in 1921 he published nothing more. What he had done by then was to contribute substantially to a better understanding by whites of Indians in general and the Sioux in particular. For Sioux readers, Wilson explained, Eastman's books "provide a bridge to self-respect . . . expressing their stories, beliefs, and customs in the language of White men." As a cultural bridge builder in the early twentieth century, Eastman was unequaled.

Served Sioux People in Other Capacities

Throughout his career as a writer, Eastman also served his people and the larger society in a variety of roles. His training as a physician he used on the Pine Ridge Reservation (1890-1893), in private practice in St. Paul, Minnesota (1894-1897), and at Crow Creek Reservation in South Dakota (1900-1903). While in St. Paul he began to work for the YMCA, organizing chapters around the country, and from 1897 to 1900 he lobbied for the Santee Sioux. For seven years (1903-09) Eastman was engaged, at Hamlin Garland's urging, in a BIA project to re-name the Sioux, giving them legal names in order to protect their interests. In 1910 he began a lifelong association with the Boy Scouts of America, and from 1914 to 1925 he and Elaine operated a girls' camp near Munsonville, New Hampshire. In 1923 he entered the Indian service for the last time, working until 1925 as an Indian inspector on and off the reservations. The last years of his life, until his death in 1939, Eastman devoted principally to lecturing.

In the last analysis, Charles Eastman's most important contribution to American letters is as a writer of autobiography and as a preserver of Sioux Indian legends, myths, and history. As autobiography, his *Indian Boyhood* is without equal. As William Bloodworth concludes in *Where the West Begins,* nearly all other life stories by his contemporaries consist of "coup stories, stories that explain an individual's name, and narrative elements in oratory and prophecy." Moreover, Eastman is the most prolific teller of Sioux Indian myths and legends. In her essay for *American Indian Quarterly,* Anna Lee Stensland concludes that despite our uncertainty over which stories are tribal legends and which are Eastman's own creations, and to what degree Eastman's Christianity led him to modify incompatible Indian concepts, Eastman is still the George Bird Grinnell and Stith Thompson of his people: "In the prolific writings of Charles Eastman there is probably more Sioux legend, myth, and history than is recorded any place else."

Further Reading

Copeland, Marion W., *Charles Alexander Eastman,* Boise State University Western Writers Series, 1978.

Eastman, Elaine Goodale, *Pratt, The Red Man Moses,* Norman, University of Oklahoma Press, 1935.

Graber, Kay, editor, *Sister to the Sioux: The Memoirs of Elaine Goodale Eastman, 1885-91,* Lincoln, University of Nebraska Press, 1978.

Hassrick, Royal B., *The Sioux: Life and Customs of a Warrior Society,* Norman, University of Oklahoma Press, 1964.

Meyer, Roy W., *History of the Santee Sioux: United States Indian Policy on Trial,* Lincoln, University of Nebraska Press, 1967.

Mooney, James, *The Ghost-Dance Religion and the Sioux Outbreak of 1890,* Chicago, University of Chicago Press, 1965.

Prucha, Francis Paul, editor, *Americanizing the American Indians: Writings by the "Friends of the Indian," 1880-1900,* Cambridge, Harvard University Press, 1973.

Riggs, Stephen R., *Mary and I: Forty Years with the Sioux,* Chicago, W.G. Holmes, 1880.

Utley, Robert M., *The Last Days of the Sioux Nation,* New Haven, Yale University Press, 1963.

Wilson, Raymond, *Ohiyesa: Charles Eastman, Santee Sioux,* Urbana, University of Illinois Press, 1983.

Alexander, Ruth, "Building a Cultural Bridge: Elaine and Charles Eastman," *South Dakota Leaders,* edited by Herbert T. Hoover and Larry J. Zimmerman, Vermillion, University of South Dakota Press, 1989; 355-66.

Alexander, "Finding Oneself through a Cause: Elaine Goodale Eastman and Indian Reform in the 1880s," *South Dakota History,* 22:1, Spring 1992; 1-37.

Bloodworth, William, "Neihardt, Momaday, and the Art of Indian Autobiography," *Where the West Begins,* edited by Arthur R. Huseboe and William Geyer, Sioux Falls, South Dakota, Center for Western Studies Press, 1978; 152-60.

Eastman, Charles Alexander (Ohiyesa), "A Canoe Trip among the Northern Ojibways," *The Red Man* 3, February 1911; 236-44.

Eastman, Charles, "Recollections of the Wild Life," *St. Nicholas: An Illustrated Magazine for Young Folks* 21, December 1893-May 1894.

Eastman, Charles, "Report on Sacajawea," *Annals of Wyoming* 13, July 1941; 187-94.

Eastman, Elaine Goodale, "All the Days of My Life," *South Dakota Historical Review* 2, July 1937; 171-84.

Eshman, Rob, "The Ghost Dance and Wounded Knee Massacre of 1890-91," *Nebraska History* 26, January 1945; 26-42.

Eshman, Rob, "Stranger in the Land," *Dartmouth Alumni Magazine,* January/February 1981; 20-23.

Fowler, Herbert B., "Ohiyesa, The First Sioux M.D.," *Association of American Indian Physicians Newsletter* 4, April 1976; 1, 6.

Holm, Tom, "American Indian Intellectuals and the Continuity of Tribal Ideals," *Book Forum* 5.3, 1981; 349-56.

Johnson, Stanley Edwards, "The Indian Ohiyesa," *Dartmouth Alumni Magazine,* June 1929; 521-23.

Milroy, Thomas W., "A Physician by the Name of Ohiyesa: Charles Alexander Eastman, M.D.," *Minnesota Medicine* 5, July 1971; 569-72.

Oandasan, William, "A Cross-Disciplinary Note on Charles Eastman (Santee Sioux)," *American Indian Culture and Research Journal* 7.2, 1983; 75-78.

Stensland, Anna Lee, "Charles Alexander Eastman: Sioux Storyteller and Historian," *American Indian Quarterly* 3, 1977; 199-207. □

George Eastman

By mass-producing his inventions, the American inventor and industrialist George Eastman (1854-1932) promoted photography as a popular hobby. He was also a benefactor of educational institutions.

George Eastman was born in Waterville, N.Y., on July 12, 1854, and educated in Rochester public schools. He advanced from messenger to bookkeeper in the Rochester Savings Bank by 1877. Frugal with money—his only extravagance amateur photography—he spent his savings on cameras and supplies and went to Mackinac Island. When photographic chemicals ruined his packed clothes, he became disgusted with the wet-plate process.

In the 1870s American photography was still slow, difficult, and expensive. Equipment included a huge cam-

era, strong tripod, large plateholder, dark tent, chemicals, water container, and heavy glass plates. Eastman experimented with dry-plate techniques. He was the first American to contribute to photographic technology by coating glass plates with gelatin and silver bromide. In 1879 his coating machine was patented in England, in 1880 in America. He sold his English patent and opened a shop to manufacture photographic plates in Rochester. To eliminate glass plates, Eastman coated paper with gelatin and photographic emulsion. The developed film was stripped from the paper to make a negative. This film was rolled on spools. Eastman and William Walker devised a lightweight roll holder to fit any camera.

Amateurs could develop pictures after Eastman substituted transparent film for the paper in 1884. Flexible film was created by Hannibal Goodwin of New York and a young Eastman chemist, Henry Reichenback. The long patent dispute between Goodwin and Eastman was the most important legal controversy in photographic history. A Federal court decision on Aug. 14, 1913, favored Goodwin. Goodwin's heirs and Ansco Company, owners of his patent, received $5,000,000 from Eastman in 1914.

In 1888 Eastman designed a simple camera, the Kodak (Eastman's coined word, without meaning), which was easy to carry and eliminated focusing and lighting. With a 100-exposure roll of celluloid film, it sold for $25.00. After taking the pictures and sending the camera and $10 to the Rochester factory, the photographer received his prints and reloaded camera. Eastman's slogan, "You press the button, we do the rest," was well known.

Anticipating photography's increased popularity, in 1892 Eastman incorporated the Eastman Kodak Company. This was one of the first American firms to mass-produce standardized products and to maintain a chemical laboratory. By 1900 his factories at Rochester and at Harrow, England, employed over 3,000 people and by 1920 more than 15,000. Eastman, at first treasurer and general manager, later became president and finally board chairman.

Daylight-loading film and cameras eliminated returning them to the factory. To Eastman's old slogan was added "or you can do it yourself." A pocket Kodak was marketed in 1897, a folding Kodak in 1898, noncurling film in 1903, and color film in 1928. Eastman film was indispensable to Thomas Edison's motion pictures; Edison's incandescent bulb was used by Eastman and by photographers specializing in "portraits taken by electric light."

Eastman's staff worked on abstract problems of molecular structure and relativity, as well as on photographic improvements. During World War I his laboratory helped make America's chemical industry independent of Germany, and finally the world leader.

Concerned with employee welfare, Eastman was the first American businessman to grant workers dividends and profit sharing. He systematically gave away his huge fortune to the University of Rochester (especially the medical school and Eastman School of Music), Massachusetts Institute of Technology, Hampton Institute, Tuskegee Institute, Rochester Dental Dispensary, and European dental clinics.

After a long illness the lonely, retiring bachelor committed suicide on March 14, 1932, in Rochester. He had written to friends, "My work is done. Why wait?"

Further Reading

The best biography of Eastman is Carl W. Ackerman, *George Eastman* (1930). Robert Taft, *Photography and the American Scene: A Social History, 1839-1889* (1938), places Eastman in perspective in the evolution of photography. Mitchell Wilson, *American Science and Invention: A Pictorial History* (1954), is also helpful. □

Clint Eastwood

Clint Eastwood (born 1930) ranks among the world's best known and most successful movie stars. Most of his films have done well at the box office and he has established himself as a director of note.

A 1971 *Life* magazine cover carried his picture with the tag line "the world's favorite movie star is—no kidding—Clint Eastwood." After that he continued to win box-office and financial success—as well as increasing critical acclaim—well into the 1990s. Born Clinton Eastwood, Jr., on May 30, 1930, in San Francisco, California, he had a tough childhood because of the Great Depression, as his parents moved frequently in search of work, finally settling in Oakland. There he went to high school, graduating in 1948. Striking out on his own, he held various menial jobs before being drafted into the army. Discharged in

1953, he enrolled in Los Angeles City College as a business administration major, supporting himself with various odd jobs which included digging swimming pool foundations.

Bit Parts in "B" Movies

Army friends in the film business urged Eastwood to try his luck. He did, was screen-tested by Universal, and on the basis of his good looks was hired as a contract player in 1955. His salary was $75 a week, and his assignments included minuscule roles in forgettable movies, including *Tarantula* and *Francis in the Navy)*. After Universal dropped him in 1956, the roles briefly got bigger but not better: Eastwood has described the 1958 *Ambush at Cimarron Pass*, in which he had a substantial part, as "maybe the worst film ever made."

Notwithstanding an occasional unimpressive role in television series such as "Highway Patrol," by 1958 Eastwood found himself again digging swimming pools for a living. As the result of a chance meeting, he was chosen to play Rowdy Yates, the second lead in the CBS television series "Rawhide." Characterized as "an endless cattle drive," the series lasted seven years (1959-1966), owing much of its success to Eastwood's popular "punk ramrod."

Gains Stardom with "Spaghetti Westerns"

During a hiatus from "Rawhide" in 1964, Eastwood filmed *A Fistful of Dollars* in Spain for Italian director Sergio Leone. Eastwood portrayed a hired gun, a nameless man, who successfully manipulates—and then ruthlessly kills—rival gangs of bandits. The film catapulted Eastwood from a

dead-end television career to stardom in the movies. Over the next two years, Eastwood returned to Europe to film two equally popular sequels, both also featuring the "Man with No Name": *For a Few Dollars More* (1965) and *The Good, The Bad, and The Ugly* (1966).

These films defined the Eastwood screen persona which, as *New York Times* reporter John Vinocur pointed out, was "a western hero without the westerner's traditional heroic characteristics." Eastwood's character was callous, violent, cynical, tough. Facets of that character were present in his best westerns, such as *The Outlaw Josey Wales* (1976) and *Unforgiven* (1992), both stark bloody films about an outsider.

The same toughness also characterized many of Eastwood's non-western roles. His appeal lay (to use Eastwood's words) in his ability "to hack his way through" because such a person "is almost . . . a mythical character in our day and age" as everything "becomes more complicated." That capacity underlay what has been described as one of Eastwood's "enduring screen figures"—Harry Callahan, a contemporary San Francisco detective who roams the city defying a legalistic bureaucracy and practicing a vigorous populist brand of justice. Callahan was introduced in *Dirty Harry* (1971), which critic Pauline Kael found imbued with "fascist medievalism."

No matter what the critics thought, the American public flocked to see *Dirty Harry,* and the role was reprised in 1973, 1976, 1983, and 1988. All but the last did well at the box office, if not critically, because they (in the words of one writer) seized "the mood of many Americans frustrated by . . . an ineffectual law enforcement system."

His career, which by 1997 encompassed almost 40 roles, was not without weak spots. He co-starred with an orangutan in the critically attacked comedies *Every Which Way But Loose* (1978) and *Any Which Way You Can* (1980), among Warner's highest grossing films in those years. Less successful theatrically but critically well-received was *The Beguiled* (1971), a Gothic tale about a crippled Union soldier murdered by southern school girls. Critics and moviegoers both agreed the musical *Paint Your Wagon* (1969) wasted his talents. He had flops in 1989 (*The Pink Cadillac*) and 1990 (*The Rookie*).

Eastwood made a striking comeback with *Unforgiven* (1992) and *In The Line of Fire* (1993), a taut tale about a Secret Service agent and a potential presidential assassin. Both films won critical plaudits and were among their years' highest grossing films. *Unforgiven* won Eastwood numerous directing and acting awards, including Oscars for best picture and best direction and a nomination for an Oscar as best actor.

Begins Directing

Eastwood's interest in directing reached back to "Rawhide," but CBS allowed him only to direct trailers. He made an auspicious directorial debut in 1971 with *Play Misty for Me*, a thriller about a psychotic obsessed woman. It received good notices and did well at the box office, as did many of the over one dozen films he directed after it. Most starred him, but one of his finest efforts did not: *Bird*

(1988) dealt movingly with the downbeat life of the jazz great Charlie Parker. Eastwood was a life-long fan of jazz, and jazz music and songs have been a frequent presence on the soundtracks of many of his films.

Eastwood's direction has been described as "a lean location sense of realism"; his technique shows economy, vitality, imagination, and a good sense of humor. In 1993 he said that "favorites among his own films" were *Play Misty for Me, The Outlaw Josey Wales, Unforgiven,* and *Bronco Billy,* a sweet 1980 movie about an ex-shoe-salesman from New Jersey (played by Eastwood) who has formed a wild West show with a group of misfits.

Finally Earns Critical Acclaim

From the early 1980s. the critical community began to reassess Eastwood's contribution to cinema. Open hostility turned to grudging acceptance and finally to admiration. More and more people began to appreciate Eastwood's contribution as producer and director, especially in his smaller, more personal films, including *Play Misty for Me* and *Honkytonk Man.* While Eastwood told the *New York Times Magazine* that he "never begged for respectability," he nonetheless flew to Paris in 1985 to accept the honor of Chevalier des Arts et Lettres, a French national award.

In 1992, with *Unforgiven,* Eastwood finally won his first Academy Award. After the ceremony, Eastwood told reporters that the wait for the award had been worth it. "I think it means more to me now," he was quoted as saying in the*Philadelphia Inquirer.* "If you win it when you're 20 or 30 years old, you're wondering, "Where do I go from here?'. . . You learn to take your work seriously and not yourself seriously, and that comes with time." Three years later, at the 1995 Academy Awards, the film community reaffirmed its respect for Eastwood's body of work. The Academy bestowed upon him the Irving G. Thalberg Memorial Award, which is given to producers or directors for consistently high quality of motion picture production.

Eastwood has not, however, rested on his laurels. In the summer of 1995, he directed and starred in *The Bridges of Madison County.* The film, based on the best-selling novel by Robert James Waller, follows a National Geographic photographer as he is sent on assignment to photograph covered bridges in Iowa. While there he has a passionate three-day affair with an Italian-born farm wife, played by Meryl Streep. The film enjoyed success as a classic "three-handkerchief weepie." It also received favorable notices from critics. Many praised Eastwood's even-handed and sensitive depiction of the brief affair and, especially, of the farm wife, who came across as much more realized character on screen than she did in the novel.

Absolute Power released in early 1997, was less of a triumph with the pubic and with critics. Eastwood once again directed but played a less romantic lead. His character, an aging Washington, D.C. burglar, accidently watches the president of the United States kill a woman during a sexual tryst.

Seeks Privacy in Personal Life

"Not a Hollywood type," as a 1993 profile explained, Eastwood has made his home in Carmel, California, far from filmdom's party circuit. There he lived a private life, spending time with friends who were not involved in the entertainment industry. And he is known as a loyal employer whose production crew included people who had worked for him for 15 years.

Politically conservative, Eastwood was several times approached by the Republican Party for various positions but he eschewed any public political stance except for a two-year term (1986-1988) as mayor of Carmel. Eastwood sought the position because he disapproved of zoning laws in the village. After serving one two-year term—and changing the laws—he stepped down with no regrets.

Eastwood married Maggie Johnson in 1953; they had a son Kyle (born 1968) and a daughter Alison (born 1972). They separated in the late 1970s, and the marriage ended in 1984, with Maggie Johnson reportedly receiving a settlement of $25 million.

After separating from Johnson, Eastwood spent more than a decade living with actress Sandra Locke, who appeared in many of his films. That relationship broke up acrimoniously at the end of the 1980s, resulting in a palimony suit eventually settled out of court at a cost to Eastwood of more than $7 million. He then established a relationship with Frances Fisher, an actress who appeared in *The Pink Cadillac.* The two had a baby girl in August 1993, whom they named Francesca Ruth.

In April 1993, Eastwood was interviewed by Dina Ruiz, a television news anchorwoman in Los Angeles, California. Three years later, in March 1996, Eastwood, then aged 65, married Dina Ruiz, 30, in a small private ceremony at the Las Vegas, Nevada, home of gambling casino magnate Steve Wynn.

By 1997, Eastwood had appeared in more than 40 motion pictures and directed 19 of them himself. Over the years his talents, both in front of and behind the camera, have been reevaluated. He won newfound respect for his talents as actor and director. He remained a potent force in the film industry through the 1990s, and for the public he became (to use *Newsweek's* phrase) "An American Icon."

Further Reading

For additional reading about Eastwood see Boris Zmijewsky and Lee Pfeiffer, *The Films of Clint Eastwood* (1993), which provides an up-to-date overview of Eastwood's career; C. Frayling, *Clint Eastwood* (London, 1992), a better than average popular biography; and Paul Smith, *Clint Eastwood* (1992), a somewhat overheated attempt to deal with Eastwood's impact on American culture. There is a fascinating interview with Eastwood in *Focus on Film,* #25 (Summer-Autumn 1976), undertaken when Eastwood talked with almost no one. There are also useful and interesting articles such as Bernard Weinraub, "The Last Icon," *GQ* (March 1993); and John Vinocur, "Clint Eastwood, Seriously," *New York Times Magazine* (February 24, 1985). An intellectual approach with some good Eastwood quotes is Richard Combs, "Shadowing the Hero," in *Sight and Sound* (October 1992).

Bingham, Dennis. *Acting Male: Masculinities in the Films of James Stewart, Jack Nicholson, & Clint Eastwood* (Rutgers University Press, 1994). Clinch, Minty. *Clint Eastwood* (Hoder & Stoughthton, 1995). Gallafent, Edward. *Clint Eastwood: Filmaker and Star* (Continuum, 1994). Knapp, Laurence. *Directed by Clint Eastwood: Eighteen Films Analyzed.* (McFarland, 1996). Munn, Michael. *Clint Eastwood: Hollywood's Loner* (Parkwest, 1993). O'Brien, Daniel. *Clint Eastwood Film Maker* (Trafalgar Square, 1997). Schickel, Richard. *Clint Eastwood: A Biography* (McKay, 1996). Tanitch, Robert. *Clint Eastwood* (Studio Vista Books, 1995). Thompson, Douglas. *Clint Eastwood: Riding High* (1992). □

Thomas Alva Edison

The American inventor Thomas Alva Edison (1847-1931) held hundreds of patents, most for electrical devices and electric light and power. Although the phonograph and incandescent lamp are best known, perhaps his greatest invention was organized research.

Thomas Edison was born in Milan, Ohio, on Feb. 11, 1847; his father was a jack-of-all-trades, his mother a former teacher. Edison spent 3 months in school, then was taught by his mother. At the age of 12 he sold fruit, candy, and papers on the Grand Trunk Railroad. In 1862, using his small handpress in a baggage car, he wrote and printed the *Grand Trunk Herald,* which was circulated to 400 railroad employees. That year he became a telegraph operator, taught by the father of a child whose life Edison had saved. Exempt from military service because of deafness, he was a tramp telegrapher until he joined Western Union Telegraph Company in Boston in 1868.

Early Inventions

Probably Edison's first invention was an automatic telegraph repeater (1864). His first patent was for an electric vote recorder. In 1869, as a partner in a New York electrical firm, he perfected the stock ticker and sold it. This money, in addition to that from his share of the partnership, provided funds for his own factory in Newark, N.J. Edison hired technicians to collaborate on inventions; he wanted an "invention factory." As many as 80 "earnest men," including chemists, physicists, and mathematicians, were on his staff. "Invention to order" became very profitable.

From 1870 to 1875 Edison invented many telegraphic improvements: transmitters; receivers; the duplex, quadruplex, and sextuplex systems; and automatic printers and tape. He worked with Christopher Sholes, "father of the typewriter," in 1871 to improve the typing machine. Edison claimed he made 12 typewriters at Newark about 1870. The Remington Company bought his interests.

In 1876 Edison's carbon telegraph transmitter for Western Union marked a real advance toward making the Bell telephone practical. (Later, Émile Berliner's transmitter was granted patent priority by the courts.) With the money Edison received from Western Union for his transmitter, he established a factory in Menlo Park, N.J. Again he pooled scientific talent, and within 6 years he had more than 300 patents. The electric pen (1877) produced stencils to make

copies. (The A. B. Dick Company licensed Edison's patent and manufactured the mimeograph machine.)

The Phonograph

Edison's most original and lucrative invention, the phonograph, was patented in 1877. From a manually operated instrument making impressions on metal foil and replaying sounds, it became a motor-driven machine playing cylindrical wax records by 1887. By 1890 he had more than 80 patents on it. The Victor Company developed from his patents. (Alexander Graham Bell impressed sound tracks on cylindrical shellac records; Berliner invented disk records. Edison's later dictating machine, the Ediphone, used disks.)

Incandescent Lamp

To research incandescence, Edison and others, including J. P. Morgan, organized the Edison Electric Light Company in 1878. (Later it became the General Electric Company.) Edison made the first practical incandescent lamp in 1879, and it was patented the following year. After months of testing metal filaments, Edison and his staff examined 6,000 organic fibers from around the world and decided that Japanese bamboo was best. Mass production soon made the lamps, although low-priced, profitable.

First Central Electric-Light Power Plant

Prior to Edison's central power station, each user of electricity needed a dynamo (generator), which was inconvenient and expensive. Edison opened the first commercial electric station in London in 1882; in September the Pearl

Street Station in New York City marked the beginning of America's electrical age. Within 4 months the station was lighting more than 5,000 lamps for 230 customers, and the demand for lamps exceeded supply. By 1890 it supplied current to 20,000 lamps, mainly in office buildings, and to motors, fans, printing presses, and heating appliances. Many towns and cities installed central stations.

Increased use of electricity led to Edison-base sockets, junction boxes, safety fuses, underground conduits, meters, and the three-wire system. Jumbo dynamos, with drum-wound armatures, could maintain 110 volts with 90 percent efficiency. The three-wire system, first installed in Sunbury, Pa., in 1883, superseded the parallel circuit, used 110 volts, and necessitated high-resistance lamp filaments (metal alloys were later used).

In 1883 Edison made a significant discovery in pure science, the Edison effect—electrons flowed from incandescent filaments. With a metal-plate insert, the lamp could serve as a valve, admitting only negative electricity. Although "etheric force" had been recognized in 1875 and the Edison effect was patented in 1883, the phenomenon was little known outside the Edison laboratory. (At this time existence of electrons was not generally accepted.) This "force" underlies radio broadcasting, long-distance telephony, sound pictures, television, electric eyes, x-rays, high-frequency surgery, and electronic musical instruments. In 1885 Edison patented a method to transmit telegraphic "aerial" signals, which worked over short distances, and later sold this "wireless" patent to Guglielmo Marconi.

Creating the Modern Research Laboratory

The vast West Orange, N.J., factory, which Edison directed from 1887 to 1931, was the world's most complete research laboratory, an antecedent of modern research and development laboratories, with teams of workers systematically investigating problems. Various inventions included a method to make plate glass, a magnetic ore separator, compressing dies, composition brick, a cement process, an all-concrete house, an electric locomotive (patented 1893), a fluoroscope, a nickel-iron battery, and motion pictures. Edison refused to patent the fluoroscope, so that doctors could use it freely; but he patented the first fluorescent lamp in 1896.

The Edison battery, finally perfected in 1910, was a superior storage battery with an alkaline electrolyte. After 8000 trials Edison remarked, "Well, at least we know 8000 things that don't work." In 1902 he improved the copper oxide battery, which resembled modern dry cells.

Edison's motion picture camera, the kinetograph, could photograph action on 50-foot strips of film, 16 images per foot. A young assistant, in order to make the first Edison movies, in 1893 built a small laboratory called the "Black Maria,"—a shed, painted black inside and out, that revolved on a base to follow the sun and kept the actors illuminated. The kinetoscope projector of 1893 showed the films. The first commercial movie theater, a peepshow, opened in New York in 1884. A coin put into a slot activated the kinetoscope inside the box. Acquiring and improving the projector of Thomas Armat in 1895, Edison marketed it as the Vitascope.

Movie Production

The Edison Company produced over 1,700 movies. Synchronizing movies with the phonograph in 1904, Edison laid the basis for talking pictures. In 1908 his cinemaphone appeared, adjusting film speed to phonograph speed. In 1913 his kinetophone projected talking pictures: the phonograph, behind the screen, was synchronized by ropes and pulleys with the projector. Edison produced several "talkies."

Meanwhile, among other inventions, the universal motor, which used alternating or direct current, appeared in 1907; and the electric safety lantern, patented in 1914, greatly reduced casualties among miners. That year Edison invented the telescribe, which combined features of the telephone and dictating phonograph.

Work for the Government

During World War I Edison headed the U.S. Navy Consulting Board and contributed 45 inventions, including substitutes for previously imported chemicals (especially carbolic acid, or phenol), defensive instruments against U-boats, a ship-telephone system, an underwater searchlight, smoke screen machines, antitorpedo nets, turbine projectile heads, collision mats, navigating equipment, and methods of aiming and firing naval guns. After the war he established the Naval Research Laboratory, the only American institution for organized weapons research until World War II.

Synthetic Rubber

With Henry Ford and the Firestone Company, Edison organized the Edison Botanic Research Company in 1927 to discover or develop a domestic source of rubber. Some 17,000 different botanical specimens were examined over 4 years—an indication of Edison's tenaciousness. By crossbreeding goldenrod, he developed a strain yielding 12 percent latex, and in 1930 he received his last patent, for this process.

The Man Himself

To raise money, Edison dramatized himself by careless dress, clowning for reporters, and playing the role of homespun sage with aphorisms like "Genius is 1 percent inspiration and 99 percent perspiration" and "Discovery is not invention." He scoffed at formal education, thought 4 hours' sleep a night enough, and often worked 40 or 50 hours straight. As a world symbol of Yankee ingenuity, he looked and acted the part. George Bernard Shaw, briefly an Edison employee in 1879, put an Edison-type hero into his novel *The Irrational Knot:* free-souled, sensitive, cheerful, and profane.

Edison had more than 10,000 books at home and masses of printed materials at the laboratory. When launching a new project, he wished to avoid others' mistakes and to know everything about a subject. Some 25,000 notebooks contained his research records, ideas, hunches, and mistakes. Supposedly, his great shortcoming was lack of interest in anything not utilitarian; yet he loved to read Shakespeare and Thomas Paine.

Edison died in West Orange, N.J., on Oct. 18, 1931. The laboratory buildings and equipment associated with his career are preserved in Greenfield Village, Detroit, Mich., thanks to Henry Ford's interest and friendship.

Further Reading

A good biography of Edison, filled with human interest, is Matthew Josephson, *Edison: A Biography* (1959). Biographies emphasizing his inventions include William Adams Simonds, *Edison: His Life, His Work, His Genius* (1934), and H. Gordon Garbedian, *Thomas Alva Edison: Builder of Civilization* (1947). There is more emphasis on industry in John Winthrop Hammond, *Men and Volts: The Story of General Electric,* edited by Arthur Pound (1941). See also Charles Singer and others, eds., *A History of Technology,* vol.5: *The Late Nineteenth Century* (1958). □

Dwight David Eisenhower

Dwight David Eisenhower (1890-1969) was leader of the Allied forces in Europe in World War II, commander of NATO, and thirty-fourth president of the United States.

Dwight Eisenhower was born in Denison, Tex., on Oct. 14, 1890, one of seven sons. The family soon moved to Abilene, Kansas. The family was poor, and Eisenhower early learned the virtue of hard work. He graduated from West Point Military Academy in 1915. He was remarkable for his buoyant temperament and his capacity to inspire affection.

Eisenhower married Mamie Doud in 1916. One of the couple's two sons died in infancy; the other, John, followed in his father's footsteps and went to West Point, later resigning from the Army to assist in preparing his father's memoirs.

Army Career

Eisenhower's career in the Army was marked by a slow rise to distinction. He graduated first in his class in 1926 from the Army's Command and General Staff School. Following graduation from the Army War College he served in the office of the chief of staff under Gen. Douglas MacArthur. He became MacArthur's distinguished aid in the Philippines. Returning to the United States in 1939, Eisenhower became chief of staff to the 3d Army. He attracted the attention of Gen. George C. Marshall, U.S. Chief of Staff, by his brilliant conduct of war operations in Louisiana in 1941. When World War II began, Eisenhower became assistant chief of the War Plans Division of the Army General Staff. He assisted in the preparations for carrying the war to Europe and in May of 1942 was made supreme commander of European operations, arriving in London in this capacity in June.

Supreme Commander in Europe

Eisenhower's personal qualities were precisely right for the situation in the months that followed. He had to deal

with British generals whose war experience exceeded his own and with a prime minister, Winston Churchill, whose strength and determination were of the first order. Eisenhower's post called for a combination of tact and resolution, for an ability to get along with people and yet maintain his own position as the leader of the Allied forces. In addition to his capacity to command respect and affection, Eisenhower showed high executive quality in his selection of subordinates.

In London, Eisenhower paved the way for the November 1942 invasion of North Africa. Against powerful British reluctance he prepared for the June 1944 invasion of Europe. He chose precisely the day on which massive troop landings in Normandy were feasible, and once the bridgehead was established, he swept forward triumphantly—with one short interruption—to defeat the German armies. By spring 1945, with powerful support from the Russian forces advancing from the east, the war in Europe was ended. Eisenhower became one of the best known men in the United States, and there was talk of a possible political career.

Columbia University and NATO

Eisenhower disavowed any political ambitions, however, and in 1948 he retired from military service to become president of Columbia University. It cannot be said that he filled this role with distinction. Nothing in his training suggested a special capacity to deal with university problems. Yet it was only because of a strong sense of duty that he accepted President Harry Truman's appeal to become the first commander of the newly formed North Atlantic Treaty Organization (NATO) in December 1950. Here Eisenhower's truly remarkable gifts in dealing with men of various views and strong will were again fully exhibited.

Eisenhower's political views had never been clearly defined. But Republican leaders in the eastern United States found him a highly acceptable candidate for the presidency, perhaps all the more so because he was not identified with any particular wing of the party. After a bitter convention fight against Robert Taft, Eisenhower emerged victorious. In the election of 1952 he defeated the Democratic candidate, Adlai Stevenson, by a tremendous margin.

Eisenhower repeated this achievement in 1956. In 1955 he had suffered a serious stroke, and in 1956 he underwent an operation for ileitis. Behaving with great dignity and making it clear that he would stand for a second term only if he felt he could perform his duties to the full, he accepted renomination and won the election with 477 of the 531 electoral votes and a popular majority of over 9 million.

The President

Eisenhower's strength as a political leader rested almost entirely upon his disinterestedness and his integrity. He had little taste for political maneuvers and was never a strong partisan. His party, which attained a majority in both houses of Congress in 1952, lost control in 1954, and for 6 of 8 years in office the President was compelled to rely upon both Democrats and Republicans. His personal qualities, however, made this easier than it might have been.

Eisenhower did not conceive of the presidency as a positive executiveship, as has been the view of most of the great U.S. presidents. His personal philosophy was never very clearly defined. He was not a dynamic leader; he took a position in the center and drew his strength from that. In domestic affairs he was influenced by his strong and able secretary of the Treasury, George Humphrey. In foreign affairs he leaned heavily upon his secretary of state, John Foster Dulles. He delegated wide powers to those he trusted; in domestic affairs his personal assistant, Sherman Adams, exercised great influence. In a sense, Eisenhower's stance above the "battle" no doubt made him stronger.

Domestic Policies

To attempt to classify Eisenhower as liberal or conservative is difficult. He was undoubtedly sympathetic to business interests and had widespread support from them. He had austere views as to fiscal matters and was not generally in favor of enlarging the role of government in economic affairs. Yet he favored measures such as a far-reaching extension of social security, he signed a law fixing a minimum wage, and he recommended the formation of the Department of Health, Education and Welfare. After an initial error, he appointed to this post Marion B. Folsom, an outstanding administrator who had been a pioneer in the movement for social security in the 1930s.

Civil Rights

But the most significant development in domestic policy came through the Supreme Court. The President appointed Earl Warren to the post of chief justice. In 1954 the Warren Court handed down a unanimous decision declaring segregation in the schools unconstitutional, giving a new impetus to the civil rights movement.

Eisenhower was extremely cautious in implementing this decision. He saw that it was enforced in the District of Columbia, but in his heart he did not believe in it and thought that it was for the states rather than the Federal government to take appropriate action. Nonetheless, he was compelled to move in 1957 when Arkansas governor Orval Faubus attempted to defy the desegregation decision by using national guardsmen to bar African Americans from entering the schools of Little Rock. The President's stand was unequivocal; he made it clear that he would enforce the law. When Faubus proved obdurate, the President enjoined him and forced the removal of the national guard. When the African Americans admitted were forced by an armed mob to withdraw, the President sent Federal troops to Little Rock and federalized the national guard. A month later the Federal troops were withdrawn. But it was a long time before the situation was completely stabilized.

The President's second term saw further progress in civil rights. In 1957 he signed a measure providing further personnel for the attorney general's office for enforcing the law and barring interference with voting rights. In 1960 he signed legislation strengthening the measure and making resistance to desegregation a Federal offense.

Foreign Policies

In foreign affairs Eisenhower encouraged the strengthening of NATO, at the same time seeking an understanding with the Soviet Union. In 1955 the U.S.S.R. agreed to evacuate Austria, then under four-power occupation, but a Geneva meeting of the powers (Britain, France, the U.S.S.R., and the United States) made little progress on the problem of divided Germany. A new effort at understanding came in 1959, when the Russian leader Nikita Khrushchev visited the United States. In friendly discussions it was agreed to hold a new international conference in Paris. When that time arrived, however, the Russians had just captured an American plane engaged in spying operations over the Soviet Union (the Gary Powers incident). Khrushchev flew into a tantrum and broke up the conference. When Eisenhower's term ended, relations with the Kremlin were still unhappy.

In the Orient the President negotiated an armistice with the North Koreans to terminate the Korean War begun in 1950. It appears that Eisenhower brought the North Koreans and their Chinese Communist allies to terms by threatening to enlarge the war. He supported the Chinese Nationalists. Dulles negotiated the treaty that created SEATO (Southeast Asia Treaty Organization) and pledged the United States to consult with the other signatories and to meet any threat of peace in that region "in accordance with their constitutional practices. . . ." This treaty was of special significance with regard to Vietnam, where the French had been battling against a movement for independence. In 1954 Vietnam was divided, the North coming under Communist control, the South (anti-Communist) increasingly supported by the United States.

In the Near East, Eisenhower faced a very difficult situation. In 1956 the Egyptian dictator Gamal Abdel Nasser nationalized the Suez Canal. The government of Israel, probably encouraged by France and Great Britain, launched a preventive war, soon joined by the two great powers. The President and the secretary of state condemned this breach of the peace within the deliberations framework of the United Nations, and the three powers were obliged to sign an armistice. These events occurred at a particularly inauspicious time for the United States, since a popular revolt against the Soviet Union had broken out in Hungary. The hands of the American government were tied, though perhaps in no case could the United States have acted effectively in preventing Soviet suppression of the revolt.

In the Latin American sphere the President was confronted with events of great importance in Cuba. Cuba was ruled by an increasingly brutal and tyrannical president, Fulgencio Batista. In 1958, to mark its displeasure, the American government withdrew military support from the Batista regime. There followed a collapse of the government, and the Cuban leftist leader, Fidel Castro, installed himself in power. Almost from the beginning Castro began a flirtation with the Soviet Union, and relations between Havana and Washington were severed in January 1960.

In the meantime the United States had embarked upon a course which was to cause great embarrassment to Eisenhower's successor. It had encouraged and assisted anti-Castro Cubans to prepare to invade the island and overthrow the Castro regime. Though these plans had not crystallized when Eisenhower left office in 1961, it proved difficult to reverse them, and the result for the John F. Kennedy administration was the fiasco of the Bay of Pigs.

Assessing His Career

It will be difficult for future historians to assess Eisenhower's foreign policy objectively. Ending the Korean War was a substantial achievement. The support of NATO was most certainly in line with American opinion. In the Far East the extension of American commitments can be variously judged. It is fair to Eisenhower to say that only the first steps to the eventual deep involvement in Vietnam were taken during his presidency.

One other aspect of the Eisenhower years must be noted. The President's intention to reduce the military budget at first succeeded. But during his first term the American position with the Soviets deteriorated. Then came the Soviet launching of the Sputnik space probe in 1957—a grisly suggestion of what nuclear weapons might be like in the future. In response, United States policy was altered, and the missile gap had been closed by the time the President left office. Unhappily, the arms race was not ended but attained new intensity in the post-Eisenhower years.

Few presidents have enjoyed greater popularity than Eisenhower or left office as solidly entrenched in public opinion as when they entered it. Eisenhower was not a great orator and did not conceive of the presidency as a post of political leadership. But at the end of his administration, admiration for his integrity, modesty, and strength was undiminished among the mass of the American people.

Eisenhower played at times the role of an elder statesman in Republican politics. His death on March 26, 1969, was the occasion for national mourning and for world-wide recognition of his important role in the events of his time.

Further Reading

Works written by Eisenhower are *Crusade in Europe* (1948) and his account of the presidency, *Mandate for Change, 1953-1956: The White House Years* (1963) and *Waging Peace, 1956-1961: The White House Years* (1965). For a brief summary of Eisenhower's early career see Marquis W. Childs, *Eisenhower, Captive Hero: A Critical Study of the General and the President* (1958). For the war years see W. B. Smith, *Eisenhower's Six Great Decisions* (1950). Eisenhower's election to the presidency is covered in Arthur M. Schlesinger, Jr., ed., *History of American Presidential Elections* (4 vols., 1971). Very important is Sherman Adams, *Firsthand Report: The Story of the Eisenhower Administration* (1961). The most illuminating discussion of the President is Emmett John Hughes, *The Ordeal of Power: A Political Memoir of the Eisenhower Years* (1963). See also Robert J. Donovan, *Eisenhower: The Inside Story* (1956), and Merlo J. Pusey, *Eisenhower the President* (1956). □

Thomas Stearns Eliot

Thomas Stearns Eliot (1888-1965), American-English author, was one of the most influential poets writing in English in the 20th century, one of the most seminal critics, an interesting playwright, and an editor and publisher.

On Sept. 26, 1888, T. S. Eliot was born in St. Louis, Mo., a member of the third generation of a New England family that had come to St. Louis in 1834. Eliot's grandfather, William Greenleaf Eliot, Unitarian minister and founder of schools, a university, a learned society, and charities, was the family patriarch. While carrying on a tradition of public service, the Eliots never forgot their New England ties. T. S. Eliot claimed that he was a child of both the Southwest and New England. In Massachusetts he missed Missouri's dark river, cardinal birds, and lush vegetation. In Missouri he missed the fir trees, song sparrows, red granite shores, and blue sea of Massachusetts.

Eliot Family

Henry Ware Eliot, the father of T. S. Eliot, became chairman of the board of a brick company and served the cultural institutions his father had helped found, as well as others. He married an intellectual New Englander, Charlotte Champ. After having six children, she turned her energies to education and legal safeguards for the young. She also wrote a biography, some religious poems, and a dramatic poem (1926), with a preface by her already widely respected youngest child, Thomas.

Eliot grew up within the family's tradition of service to religion, community, and education. Years later he declared, "Missouri and the Mississippi have made a deeper

impression on me than any part of the world." The Eliots also spent summers on Cape Ann, Mass. These places appear in Eliot's early poetry, but in the *Four Quartets* of his maturity his affection for them is most explicit.

Education of a Poet

In St. Louis young Eliot received a classical education privately and at Smith Academy, originally named Eliot Academy. He composed and read the valedictory poem for his graduation in 1905. After a year at Milton Academy in Massachusetts, he went to Harvard in 1906. He was shy, correct in dress, and intellectually independent. He studied under such versatile men as William James, George Santayana, Josiah Royce, and Irving Babbitt. He discovered Dante and heard talk of reviving poetic drama. Among such student personalities as Walter Lippmann, Heywood Broun, Conrad Aiken, and E. E. Cummings, Eliot made a modest impression as a contributor and editor of the *Harvard Advocate.* He was quietly completing his bachelor of arts degree in 3 years and was hard on the track of a new poetic voice. In 1908 he discovered Arthur Symons's *The Symbolist Movement in Literature,* and through it the French poet Jules Laforgue. From the example of Laforgue, other French symbolists, and late Elizabethan dramatists, he began to develop the offhand eloquence, the pastiches and discordant juxtapositions, the rhythmic versatility, and the concern masked by evasive irony and wit that would soon dominate the American-British renascence in poetry.

Eliot's stay at Harvard to earn a master of arts in philosophy was interrupted by a year at the Sorbonne. He returned

to Harvard in 1911 but in 1914 he went abroad again on a Harvard fellowship to study in Germany. When World War I broke out, he transferred to Merton College, Oxford, and studied with a disciple of F. H. Bradley, who became the subject of Eliot's dissertation. Ezra Pound, the young American poet, discovered Eliot at Oxford. Though they were quite different, they shared a devotion to learning and poetry. After Oxford, Eliot decided to stay in England and in 1915 married a vivacious Englishwoman, Vivienne Haigh Haigh-Wood. He taught at Highgate Junior School for boys near London (1915-1916) and then worked for Lloyd's Bank. While teaching, he completed his dissertation, *Knowledge and Experience in the Philosophy of F. H. Bradley.* The dissertation was accepted, but Eliot did not return to America to defend it so as to receive his doctorate. His study of Bradley, however, contributed to his thought and prose style.

Early Poetry

When the United States entered World War I in 1917, Eliot tried to join the U.S. Navy but was rejected for physical reasons. That year his first volume of verse, *Prufrock and Other Observations,* appeared and almost immediately became the focus for discussion and controversy. Eliot's abruptly varied rhythms and his mixtures of precision and discontinuity, contemporary references and echoes of the past, and immediate experience and haunting leitmotifs spoke to the distraction and alienation that World War I had intensified in Western civilization. This quality was most effective in the ironically titled poem "The Love Song of J. Alfred Prufrock," in which the Victorian dramatic monologue is turned inward and wedded to witty disillusion and psychic privacies to present a dilettante character fearful of disturbing or being disturbed by anything in the universe. Prufrock moves through a dehumanized city of dispirited common men on an empty round of elegant but uncommunicative chitchat. The many voices within him, speaking in approximations of blank verse and in catchy couplets, contribute to what Hugh Kenner, the American critic, called an "eloquence of inadequacy."

Critic and Editor

As literary editor of the *Egoist,* a feminist magazine, from 1917 to 1919, Eliot began the editorial and critical careers that would continue until his death. The back pages of the *Egoist* were entrusted to a succession of young poet-editors, and here, with the aid of Ezra Pound, the new poetry and criticism got a hearing. Eliot was also writing anonymous reviews for the London *Times* and publishing essays that announced the appearance of a sometimes pontifical but illuminating critic. In 1919 two of his most influential pieces appeared. "Tradition and the Individual Talent" advocated the "depersonalization" of poetry and a redirection of interest away from the poet's personality to the poem, the process, and the tradition to which the poem belonged. "Hamlet and His Problems" defined "objective correlative," a term soon to achieve wide currency, as a particular object, act, sequence, or situation which the poet infuses with a particular feeling in order to be able to call it up economically by mere mention of the thing or event. In this essay Eliot demonstrated the need to cut through received opinion to the literary work itself. He declared that the "primary problem" in *Hamlet* is not the character but the play, because the character has to bear the burden of an "inexpressible" emotion "in excess of the facts as they appear."

In his early critical essays, collected as *The Sacred Wood* (1920), *Homage to John Dryden* (1924), *Selected Essays: 1917-1932* (1932), and *The Use of Poetry and the Use of Criticism* (1933), Eliot pointed to the poets, critics, and cultural figures who had been helpful to him and might assist others in adjusting 20th-century experience to literary and cultural tradition. Eliot was drawn to precision and concreteness in language, seeking "to purify the dialect of the tribe," as he later put it. He called attention to thematic or musical structure for communicating complex psychological experience, to past mergers of thought and feeling that could counteract the modern "dissociation of sensibility," and to the "mythical method" of James Joyce's novel *Ulysses* and of his own poetry—a method that contrasts the balance and sanity of masterpieces and the ages that produced them with the contemporary deracination that isolates individuals culturally and psychologically. With learned understatement he also assessed critics from Aristotle to his Harvard teacher Irving Babbitt. He found creative guides in 19th-century French symbolists; the 17th-century man of letters John Dryden and his predecessor John Donne; the Jacobean dramatists; and beyond them Dante, a bitter exile who created a serene master-piece.

A rising poet and critic, Eliot made his way into elite British circles. The Bloomsbury group led by Leonard and Virginia Woolf welcomed him; as a somewhat British American, both conservative and liberal leaders could accept him; and young writers on both sides of the Atlantic offered respect and affection. When restless Pound left London for Paris in 1920, Eliot quietly assumed the leadership of England's young intelligentsia.

In "Gerontion" (1920) Eliot offered a shorter, less fragmented perspective on Prufrock's unfocused world, resorting again to the interior monologue, this time spoken by a despairing old man who did not believe or act passionately in youth and now regrets the spiritual waste of his life.

The Waste Land

While convalescing from exhaustion in 1921, Eliot advanced his diagnosis of war-enervated, spiritually moribund Europe with a draft of *The Waste Land*. This was to become, after publication in 1922, the most influential and controversial poem of the century. Eliot corresponded with Pound about the poem, and Pound's drastic editing compressed it, no doubt unifying and sharpening it. Eliot acknowledged Pound's help by dedicating the poem to him in Dante's words as "il miglior fabbro," the better maker.

In *The Waste Land* Eliot defines alienation and also indicates a remedy. Voices such as Prufrock's and Gerontion's are still heard, but Eliot's spokesman is now a mild Jeremiah, a lonely prophet or pilgrim who seeks spiritual regeneration in person and in thought throughout a corrupt city and across a disoriented continent. Spring is no longer

the joyous season of renewal: "April is the cruelest month," for it calls unwilling people to physical and spiritual regeneration, to leave off unsacramental sex and materialistic busy-ness. Eliot had intensified and extended the varied rhythms and montages of his earlier interior monologues and now organized them in a five-part structure deriving from Beethoven's late quarters. While sordid and distracted images still abound, hopeful ones have increased, and a greater tension exists between the two. Social disintegration is equated with a shattered wasteland, but the poem's central consciousness is nevertheless alert to the possibility of recreating personal and communal wholes out of the present and the past, of fertility rites, Christianity, Indian philosophy, and Western literature and art: "These fragments I have shored against my ruin."

Also in 1922 Eliot founded the *Criterion,* an influential little magazine that appeared until 1939, when he discontinued its publication. In it he stressed learning, discipline, and the constant renewal of tradition in literature. The magazine also reflected his growing religiousness and his devotion to the idea of a culture stratified by class and unified by Christianity.

As author of *The Waste Land* and editor of the *Criterion,* Eliot assumed a dominant role in literature in America and in Great Britain. He left Lloyd's Bank in 1925 and joined Faber and Faber, Ltd., a publisher, eventually rising to a directorship there.

Meanwhile Eliot was crossing a divide in his career. He ended his preoccupation with one kind of alienation in "The Hollow Men" (1925), where the will-less subjects of the poem cluster in a dead land, waiting like effigies for a galvanic revelation that does not come. They comment on their lot in a spastic chorus that includes a children's game song, a fragment of the Lord's Prayer, and a parody of "world without end" and other expressions from the Bible and the Book of Common Prayer.

"The Hollow Men," "Gerontion," and *The Waste Land* compose a triptych that delineates the estrangement of the self in a society fallen into secularism, with the central panel, *The Waste Land,* suggesting the possibility of salvaging the self by reconstituting culture out of its scattered parts.

Religious and Cultural Views

In 1927 Eliot became an Anglo-Catholic and a British citizen. With the heightened social consciousness of the worldwide economic depression, a reaction set in against his conservatism. It grew more difficult to explain away on literary grounds the anti-Semitic references in several of his poems. In *After Strange Gods* (1934) Eliot took the literary ideas of his "Tradition and the Individual Talent" and made them apply to culture. He also declared that too many freethinking Jews would be a detriment to the kind of organic Christian culture he proposed. This work, along with *The Idea of a Christian Society* (1939) and *Notes toward a Definition of Culture* (1948), indicated Eliot's stand against the pluralistic society of most Western democracies. Without a reconstruction of Christendom, the alternative, he felt, was paganism.

With *Ash Wednesday* (1930), while the literary tide was flowing Leftward, Eliot emerged as the sole orthodox Christian among important Anglo-American poets. The title of this six-part poem refers to the beginning of Lent, the most intense season of penitence and self-denial in the Christian year. The poem's central consciousness is an aging penitent closer to the convert Eliot than his spokesman in any previous major poem. Like his antecedents, the penitent is alienated—but from God, not from society or nature; and following the precedents of Dante and St. John of the Cross, the 16th-century Spanish mystic, he sets out to draw near the divine presence. The poem is his interior monologue narrating his progress and praying for guidance. The tone of unbroken sincerity and passionate yearning, of anxiety and some joy is new for Eliot. The penitent desires to abandon ambition, his fading powers of expression, the enticements of the world, and all that may prevent his mounting the turning stairs toward salvation. Though his longing for the vision of God known in childhood is not fulfilled, he progresses toward it, and he will persist. American critic F. O. Matthiessen remarked how Eliot with "paradoxical precision in vagueness" used wonderfully concrete images to convey the mystery of a spiritual experience.

In 1934 Eliot published *After Strange Gods* and also brought his religious and dramatic interests together in *The Rock*. This pageant mingles narrative prose with poetic dialogue and choruses as part of a campaign to raise funds to restore London's churches. Eliot's speakers ask for visible gathering places, where the "Invisible Light" can do its work.

In 1935 *Murder in the Cathedral*, perhaps Eliot's best play, was produced at Canterbury Cathedral. It has to do with Archbishop Thomas Becket, who was assassinated before the altar there in 1170. Its theme is the historical competition between church and state for the allegiance of the individual. Its poetry suggests blank verse with deviations. Becket prepares, like the penitent in *Ash Wednesday*, to accept God's will, knowing that "humanity cannot bear much reality." After his death, the chorus, speaking for humanity, confesses that "in life there is not time to grieve long," even for a martyr.

Four Quartets

In 1936 Eliot concluded his *Poems 1909-1935* with "Burnt Norton," the first of what became the *Four Quartets,* an extended work that proved to be his poetic viaticum. "Burnt Norton," in which Eliot makes vivid use of his recurring rose-garden symbolism, grew out of a visit to a deserted Gloucestershire mansion. This poem engendered three others, each associated with a place. "East Coker" (1940) is set in the village of Eliot's Massachusetts ancestors. The last two quartets appeared with the publication of *Four Quartets* (1943). The third, "The Dry Salvages," named for three small islands off the Massachusetts coast where Eliot vacationed in his youth, draws on his American experiences; and the fourth, "Little Gidding," derives from a visit to the site of a religious community, now an Anglican shrine, where the British king Charles I paused before he surrendered and went to his death. Here Eliot asks forgiveness for a

lifetime of mistakes, which no doubt includes his possible anti-Semitism of the years before the war. Each of the quartets is a separate whole but related to the others. All employ the thematic structure of music and the five movements of *The Waste Land*. The theme, developed differently, is the same in each: a penitential Eliot seeks the eternal in and through the temporal, the still dynamic center of the turning world. One may seek or wait in any place at any time, for God is in all places at all times. The theme and method continue those of *Ash Wednesday,* but the feeling in *Four Quartets* is less passionately personal, more compassionate and reconciled. The verse is serene, poised, and sparsely graceful.

Midway in his composition of *Four Quartets,* Eliot published *Old Possum's Book of Practical Cats* (1939). Here Eliot the fabulist appeared, and the humorist and wit resurfaced.

The Playwright

The Family Reunion, the first of Eliot's four plays for the professional stage, appeared in 1939. He later observed that its hero was a prig but its poetry the best in any of his plays. This play, like the other three, employs the familiar conventions of drawing-room comedy to encase religious matters. *The Family Reunion* and *The Cocktail Party* (1940) both involve analogs with classical Greek dramas. *The Confidential Clerk* (1954) and *The Elder Statesman* (1959) even employ potentially melodramatic situations, although they are not developed popularly, for Eliot is preoccupied with individual religiousness and the self-revelations and mutual understandings it effects within families. In fact, *The Elder Statesman,* the last and simplest of his plays, contending that true love is beyond verbal expression, is dedicated to his second wife, Valerie.

The most successful of these plays, *The Cocktail Party,* enjoyed respectable runs and revivals in London and New York. It puts the tension between the temporal and the eternal in more effective dramatic terms than do the other plays. By means of the familiar, a cocktail party, Eliot involves the audience in the unbelievable, a modern martyrdom. He contrasts lives oriented to the natural with that of a martyred missionary devoted to the supernatural. At the same time he parallels a Greek drama more subtly than he did in *The Family Reunion.*

Eliot's drawing-room plays, however, have only a limited appeal. The poetry in the last three is unobtrusively effective, carried by voices moving naturally along the hazy border between poetry and prose. They are not so much powerful plays as suggestive ones.

Honor and Old Age

Following World War II there were important changes in Eliot's life and literary activities. In 1947 his first wife died. Suffering from nervous debilities, she had been institutionalized for years, and Eliot had visited her every Sunday and kept his suffering and deprivation private. In 1948 he received the Nobel Prize and the British Order of Merit, and the list of his honors continued to grow. Publishing no important poetry after the *Four Quartets,* he devoted himself to the poetic drama, the revitalization of culture, some new criticism in *On Poetry and Poets* (1957), the readjustment of earlier critical judgments, and the editing of collections of his poetry and plays. In 1957 he married his private secretary, Valerie Fischer, and enjoyed a felicitous marriage until he died on Jan. 4, 1965, in London. In accordance with earlier arrangements his ashes were deposited in St. Michael's Church, East Coker, his ancestral village, on April 17, 1965.

Many poets and artists paid final tribute to Eliot, including Pound: "A grand poet and brotherly friend"; W. H. Auden: "A great poet and a great man"; Allen Tate: "Mr. Eliot was the greatest poet in English of the 20th century"; Robert Lowell: "He was a dear personal friend. Our American literature has had no greater poet or critic"; Robert Penn Warren: "He is the key figure of our century in America and England, the most powerful single influence." Avowedly Christian in a secular age, Eliot tried to revitalize the religious roots of Western culture. His career recalls the versatile man of letters of the 18th century.

Further Reading

An edition of Eliot's work is *The Complete Poems and Plays of T. S. Eliot* (1969). Donald C. Gallup, *T. S. Eliot: A Bibliography* (1952), lists Eliot's writings through 1951.

The literature on Eliot is extensive. Herbert Howarth, *Notes on Some Figures behind T. S. Eliot* (1964), provides biographical information. Hugh Kenner, *The Invisible Poet: T. S. Eliot* (1959), is probably the standard work on Eliot. Francis O. Matthiessen, *The Achievement of T. S. Eliot* (1935; 3d ed. 1958), provides a balanced introduction. Russell H. Robbins, *The T. S. Eliot Myth* (1951), primarily because of Eliot's conservatism, offers a negative view. Other studies include Elizabeth A. Drew, *T. S. Eliot: The Design of His Poetry* (1949); Helen L. Gardner, *The Art of T. S. Eliot* (1949); and D. E. S. Maxwell, *The Poetry of T. S. Eliot* (1952). George Williamson, *A Reader's Guide to T. S. Eliot: A Poem-by-Poem Analysis* (1953; 2d ed. 1966), is a helpful reference work.

Collections of critical estimates of Eliot are Balachandra Rajan, ed., *T. S. Eliot: A Study of His Writings by Several Hands* (1947); Richard March and M. J. Tambimuttu, eds., *T. S. Eliot: A Symposium* (1948); Leonard Unger, ed., *T. S. Eliot: A Selected Critique* (1948); and Neville Braybrooke, ed., *T. S. Eliot: A Symposium for His Seventieth Birthday* (1958). Studies of particular works include Raymond Preston, *"Four Quarters" Rehearsed* (1946), and Robert E. Knoll, ed., *Storm over the Waste Land* (1964). □

Edward Kennedy Ellington

Edward Kennedy Ellington (1899-1974), certainly America's most brilliant jazz composer, was considered by many to be one of the great composers of the 20th century, irrespective of categories.

On April 29, 1899, Edward Ellington, known universally as "Duke," was born in Washington, D.C. He divided his studies between music and commercial art, and by 1918 establishing a reputation as a bandleader and agent. In 1923 he went to New York City and soon became a successful bandleader. In 1927 he secured

an important engagement at the Cotton Club in Harlem, remaining there (aside from occasional tours) until 1932.

Ellington's band made its first European trip in 1932. After World War II it toured Europe regularly, with excursions to South America, the Far East, and Australia. One peak period for the band was from 1939 to 1942, when many critics considered its performances unrivaled by any other jazz ensemble.

As a composer, Ellington was responsible for numerous works that achieved popular success, some written in collaboration with his band members and with his coarranger Billy Strayhorn. The Duke's most significant music was written specifically for his own band and soloists. Always sensitive to the nuances of tone of his soloists, Ellington wrote features for individual sidemen and used his knowledge of their characteristic sounds when composing other works. His arrangements achieved a remarkable blend of individual and ensemble contributions. However, because most of his works were written for his own band, interpretations by others have seldom been satisfactory.

With *Creole Rhapsody* (1931) and *Reminiscing in Tempo* (1935) Ellington was the first jazz composer to break the 3-minute time limitation of the 78-rpm record. After the 1940s he concentrated more on longer works, including several suites built around a central theme, frequently an aspect of African American life. Always a fine orchestral pianist, with a style influenced by the Harlem stylists of the 1920s, Ellington remained in the background on most of his early recordings. After the 1950s he emerged as a highly imaginative piano soloist.

Throughout his career Ellington was the recipient of numerous Grammy Awards, and in 1959 he was awarded the Springarn Medal from the National Association for the Advancement of Colored People (NAACP). He was nominated for the Pulitzer Prize in 1964. The City of New York gave him a prize and Yale University awarded him a doctor of music degree in 1967; Morgan State and Washington universities also gave him honorary degrees that year. On his seventieth birthday Ellington was honored by President Richard Nixon at a White House ceremony and given the Medal of Freedom. In 1970 he was elected to the National Institute of Arts and Letters.

Ellington continued to compose and perform until his death from lung cancer on May 24, 1974, in New York City. His band, headed by his son Mercer, survives him, but as Phyl Garland, writing in *Ebony* magazine, put it, the elder Ellington will always be remembered for "the daring innovations that came to mark his music—the strange modulations built upon lush melodies that ramble into unexpected places, the unorthodox construction of songs . . . ; the bold use of dissonance in advance of the time."

Further Reading

Peter Gammond, ed., *Duke Ellington: His Life and Music* (1958), contains some first-rate essays on Ellington. See also Barry Ulanov, *Duke Ellington* (1946), and George E. Lambert, *Duke Ellington* (1961). Gunther Schuller, *The History of Jazz* (1968), includes the most perspicacious and scholarly study of Ellington's recordings of the 1920s.

James Lincoln Collier, *Duke Ellington,* Oxford University Press, 1987.

Stanley Dance, *The World of Duke Ellington,* Da Capo, 1980.

Duke Ellington, *Music Is My Mistress,* Doubleday, 1973.

Mercer Ellington, and Stanley Dance, *Duke Ellington in Person,* Houghton Mifflin, 1978.

Ron Frankl, *Duke Ellington,* Chelsea House, 1988.

Derek Jewell, *Duke, A Portrait of Duke Ellington,* Norton, 1977.

Ken Rattenbury, *Duke Ellington: Jazz Composer,* Yale University Press, 1991.

Duke Ellington, *The Beginning,* Decca.

Duke Ellington, *The Best of Duke Ellington,* Capitol.

Duke Ellington, *The Ellington Era,* Columbia. □

Ralph Waldo Ellison

American author Ralph Waldo Ellison (1914-1994) wrote "Invisible Man," a classic 20th-century American novel. He was an early spokesman among African Americans for the need for racial identity.

Ralph Ellison was born in Oklahoma City on March 1, 1914. His father, a construction worker, died when Ellison was 3, and his mother stretched a meager income as a domestic worker to support her son. He studied music at Tuskegee Institute from 1933 to 1936. He worked on the New York City Federal Writers Project, contributed stories, reviews, and essays to *New Masses,* the *Antioch Review,* and other journals (these

writings have not yet been collected); and in 1942 became editor of the *Negro Quarterly.* He met Richard Wright and Langston Hughes during these years; both had a major influence on his work, along with T.S. Eliot, Ernest Hemingway, and the Russian novelists.

After brief duty in the U.S. Merchant Marine during World War II, Ellison won a Rosenwald fellowship to work on the novel which brought him instant recognition and the National Book Award, *Invisible Man* (1952). The story of a young man's growing up, first in the South and then in Harlem, it is sensational, brutally honest, and graphic in the humiliating, often violent treatment the nameless hero suffers at the hands of the Southern white men who "educate" him and the Northern black men who "use" him. But Ellison reminds the reader that he "didn't select the surrealism, the distortion, the intensity as an experimental technique but because reality is surreal." When, at the end of the novel, the hero creeps into an empty Harlem cellar to escape from the world, it is only the last of his many bouts with "invisibility." The life of a African-American has always been relentlessly unreal, and his search for identity endless. But what Ellison's novel illuminates is the common plight of all human beings in the confrontations between dream and reality, light against darkness, idealism smothered by disillusion, injured psyche, adopted personae. In 1965, in a poll of 200 writers and critics, they voted *Invisible Man* the most distinguished novel published between 1945 and 1965 in America.

Ellison's *Shadow and Act* (1964) is a collection of 20 essays and 2 interviews. He contributed to *The Living Novel*

(Granville Hicks, ed., 1957), *The Angry Black* (John A. Williams, ed., 1963), and *Soon One Morning* (Herbert Hill, ed., 1963) and to numerous literary journals. He lectured at the Salzburg Seminar in 1954; taught Russian and American literature at Bard College from 1958 to 1961; was visiting professor at the University of Chicago in 1961 and visiting professor of writing at Rutgers University from 1962 to 1964; and in 1964, became visiting fellow in American studies at Yale University.

Ellison died on April 16, 1994, in New York City, leaving his second novel unfinished. His influence on American literature has been tremendous, and the loss of this second work is a bitter pill. According to Ellison himself, it was to be a work which would "[equal] his imaginative vision of the American novel as conqueror of the frontier and [answer] the Emersonian call for a literature to release all people from the bonds of oppression."

Further Reading

Perceptive critical comment on Ellison is available in Robert Bone, *The Negro Novel in America* (1958; rev. ed. 1965); Ihab Hassan, *Radical Innocence: Studies in the Contemporary American Novel* (1961); Marcus Klein, *After Alienation: American Novels in Mid-century* (1964); Jonathan Baumbach, *The Landscape of Nightmare* (1965); and Seymour L. Gross and John Edward Hardy, eds., *Images of the Negro in American Literature* (1966).

Ralph Ellsion, *Invisible Man,* Random House, 1982.

Ralph Ellison, *Shadow and Act,* Random House, 1964.

Ralph Ellison, *Going to the Territory,* Random House, 1986.

Kimberly W. Benston, editor, *The Black American Writer,* Everett Edwards, 1969. □

Lincoln Ellsworth

Lincoln Ellsworth (1880-1951), American adventurer and explorer, became the first man to cross both the Arctic and the Antarctic by air.

The son of a wealthy businessman and financier, Lincoln Ellsworth was born in Chicago on May 12, 1880. Graduating from preparatory school in 1900, he briefly attended Yale and Columbia universities, but his real interest was in outdoor life. He traveled extensively, working in Canada and Alaska as a railroad surveyor and mining engineer. He then formally studied practical astronomy and surveying in preparation for realizing his lifelong ambition—polar exploration.

A true adventurer, Ellsworth participated in the Canadian government's buffalo hunt of 1911, prospected for gold, spent 3 years with the U.S. Biological Survey on the Pacific coast, and volunteered for service in World War I, training as a pilot in France. Following the war and a protracted illness, Ellsworth in 1924 joined a geological expedition to Peru.

The following year Ellsworth joined and largely financed the expedition with Roald Amundsen, the Norwegian explorer, that initiated Arctic exploration by air. Flying from Spitsbergen for the North Pole in two planes, the party

of six reached 87° 44′N before being forced down with engine trouble. One plane was badly damaged during the landing, and it took 3 weeks to get the other plane off the polar ice pack. They returned to Spitsbergen to announce that no land existed on the European side of the pole. In 1926 Amundsen and Ellsworth returned to the Arctic, this time with a semirigid airship, the *Norge*.

Ellsworth concentrated on geologic work in the American Southwest for several years, although in 1931 he represented the American Geographic Society on the Arctic flight of the *Graf Zeppelin*. He undertook the exploration of Antarctica by air in 1933. In 1935, on his third attempt, Ellsworth and his pilot crossed Antarctica, landing 16 miles short of Richard Byrd's abandoned camp at Little America, where they were rescued. On this and a subsequent flight in 1939 Ellsworth discovered and claimed for the United States 377,000 square miles of land.

Ellsworth was a bold, imaginative, superbly conditioned man. He died in New York City on May 26, 1951.

Further Reading

The only books dealing with Ellsworth's life were written by the explorer himself: *The Last Wild Buffalo Hunt* (1919); two books written with Roald Amundsen, *Our Polar Flight* (1925) and *First Crossing of the Polar Sea* (1927); *Exploring Today* (1935); and the autobiographical *Search* (1932) and *Beyond Horizons* (1937). *Air Pioneering in the Arctic,* edited by Ellsworth (1929), is a collection of articles on his expeditions. □

Ralph Waldo Emerson

Ralph Waldo Emerson (1803-1882) was the most thought-provoking American cultural leader of the mid-19th century. In his unorthodox ideas and actions he represented a minority of Americans, but by the end of his life he was considered a sage.

Though Ralph Waldo Emerson's origins were promising, his path to eminence was by no means easy. He was born in Boston on May 25, 1803, of a fairly well-known New England family. His father was a prominent Boston minister. However, young Emerson was only 8 when his father died and left the family to face hard times. The genteel poverty which the Emerson family endured did not prevent it from sending the promising boy to the Boston Latin School, where he received the best basic education of his day. At 14 he enrolled in Harvard College. As a scholarship boy, he studied more and relaxed less than some of his classmates. He won several minor prizes for his writing. When he was 17, he started keeping a journal and continued it for over half a century.

Unitarian Minister

Emerson was slow in finding himself. After graduation from Harvard he taught at the school of his brother William. Gradually he moved toward the ministry. He undertook studies at the Harvard Divinity School, meanwhile continuing his journal and other writing. In 1826 he began his career as a Unitarian minister. Appropriately, Unitarianism was the creed of the questioner; in particular it questioned the divine nature of the Trinity. Emerson received several offers before an unusually attractive one presented itself: the junior pastorship at Boston's noted Second Church, with the promise that it would quickly become the senior pastorship. His reputation spread swiftly. Soon he was chosen chaplain of the Massachusetts Senate, and he was elected to the Boston School Committee.

Emerson's personal life flowered even more than his professional one, for he fell in love, deeply in love, for the only time in his life. He wooed and won a charming New Hampshire girl named Ellen Tucker. Their wedding, in September 1829, marked the start of an idyllic marriage. But it was all too short, for she died a year and a half later, leaving Emerson desolate. Though he tried to find consolation in his religion, he was unsuccessful. As a result, his religious doubts developed. Even the permissive creed of Unitarianism seemed to him to be a shackle. In September 1832 he resigned his pastorate; according to his farewell sermon he could no longer believe in celebrating Holy Communion.

Emerson's decision to leave the ministry was the more difficult because it left him with no other work to do. After months of floundering and even sickness, he scraped together enough money to take a 10-month tour of Europe. He hoped that his travels would give him the perspective he needed. They did, but only to the extent of confirming what he did not want rather than what he wanted.

Professional Lecturer

However, the times were on Emerson's side, for he found on his return to America that a new institution was emerging that held unique promise for him. This was the lyceum, a system of lecturing which started in the late 1820s, established itself in the 1830s, and rose to great popularity during the next 2 decades. The local lecture clubs that sprang up discovered that they had to pay for the best lecturers, Emerson among them. Emerson turned the lyceum into his unofficial pulpit and in the process earned at least a modest stipend. He spoke to his audiences with great, if unorthodox, effectiveness. They saw before them a tall, thin Yankee with slightly aquiline features whose words sometimes baffled but often uplifted them. After a few seasons he organized his own lecture courses as a supplement to his lyceum lectures. For example, during the winter of 1837-1838 he offered the Boston public a group of 10 lectures on "human culture" and earned more than $500. Equally to the point, his lectures grew into essays and books, and these he published from the early 1840s on.

Emerson's Creed

As a transcendentalist, Emerson spoke out against materialism, formal religion, and slavery. He could not have found targets better designed to offend the mass of Americans, most of whom considered making money a major purpose in life and church and churchgoing a mainstay and, until they faced the hard fact of the Civil War, either supported slavery or were willing to let it alone. But Emerson spoke of slavery in the context of the Fugitive Slave Law

(1850), saying, in one of his rare bursts of profanity, "I will not obey it, by God."

Emerson, however, was not merely *against* certain things; he both preached and exemplified a positive doctrine. He became America's leading transcendentalist; that is, he believed in a reality and a knowledge that transcended the everyday reality Americans were accustomed to. He believed in the integrity of the individual: "Trust thyself," he urged in one of his famous phrases. He believed in a spiritual universe governed by a mystic Over-soul with which each individual soul should try to harmonize. Touchingly enough, he believed in America. Though he ranked as his country's most searching critic, he helped as much as anyone to establish the "American identity." He not only called out for a genuinely American literature but also helped inaugurate it through his own writings. In addition, he espoused the cause of American music and American art; as a matter of fact, his grand purpose was to assist in the creation of an indigenous American national culture.

Publishing His Ideas

His first two books were brilliant. He had published a pamphlet, *Nature,* in 1836, which excited his fellow transcendentalists; but now he issued two volumes of essays for a broader public, *Essays,* First Series, in 1841 and *Essays,* Second Series, in 1844. Their overarching subjects were man, nature, and God. In such pieces as "Self-reliance," "Spiritual Laws," "Nature," "The Poet," and "The Over-soul," Emerson expounded on the innate nobility of man, the joys of nature and their spiritual significance, and the sort of deity omnipresent in the universe. The tone of the essays was optimistic, but Emerson did not neglect the gritty realities of life. In such essays as "Compensation" and "Experience," he tried to suggest how to deal with human losses and failings.

Whether he wrote prose or verse, Emerson was a poet with a poet's gift of metaphor. Both his lectures and his published works were filled from the first with telling phrases, with wisdom startlingly expressed. His next book, after the second series of essays, was a volume of his poems. They proved to be irregular in form and movingly individual in expression. After that came more than one remarkable volume of prose. In *Representative Men: Seven Lectures* (1850) Emerson pondered the uses of great men, devoting individual essays to half a dozen figures, including Plato, Shakespeare, and Goethe. *English Traits* (1856) resulted from an extended visit to Great Britain. In this volume Emerson anatomized the English people and their culture. His approach was impressionistic, but the result was the best book by an American on the subject up to that time.

Meanwhile, Emerson had been immersed—sometimes willingly, sometimes not—in things other than literature. He had found a second wife, pale and serene, in Lydia Jackson of Plymouth. He had married her in 1835 and got from her the comfort of love, if not its passion. They had four children, one of whom, Waldo, died when he was a little boy; the others outlived their eminent father. As Emerson's family life expanded, so did his friendships. After leaving his pastorate in Boston, he had moved to nearby Concord,

where he stayed the rest of his life. In Concord he met a prickly young Harvard graduate who became his disciple, friend, and occasional adversary: Henry David Thoreau. Emerson added others to his circle, becoming as he did so the nexus of the transcendentalist movement. Among his close friends were Bronson Alcott, George Ripley, and Theodore Parker.

Emerson's public life also expanded. During the 1850s he was drawn deeply into the struggle against slavery. Though he found some of the abolitionists almost as distasteful as the slaveholders, he knew where his place had to be. The apolitical Emerson became a Republican, voting for Abraham Lincoln. When Lincoln signed the Emancipation Proclamation (Jan. 1, 1863), Emerson counted it a momentous day for the United States; when Lincoln was killed, Emerson considered him a martyr.

Last Years

After the Civil War, Emerson continued to lecture and write. Though he had nothing really new to say anymore, audiences continued to throng his lectures and many readers bought his books. The best of the final books were *Society and Solitude* (1870) and *Letters and Social Aims* (1876). However, he was losing his memory and needed more and more help from others, especially his daughter Ellen. He was nearly 79 when he died on April 27, 1882.

America mourned Emerson's passing, as did much of the rest of the Western world. In the general judgment, he had been both a great writer and a great man. Certainly he had been America's leading essayist for half a century. And he had been not only one of the most wise but one of the most sincere of men. He had shown his countrymen the possibilities of the human spirit, and he had done so without a trace of sanctimony or pomposity. The *Chicago Tribune,* for instance, exclaimed, "How rare he was; how original in thought; how true in character!" Some of the eulogizing was extravagant, but in general the verdict at the time of Emerson's death has been upheld.

Further Reading

Emerson's *Journals* were reedited with care by William Gilman and others (7 vols., 1960-1969). Also valuable are *The Letters of Ralph Waldo Emerson,* edited by Ralph L. Rusk (6 vols., 1939). The best biography is still Rusk's *The Life of Ralph Waldo Emerson* (1949). The best critical study of Emerson's writing is Sherman Paul, *Emerson's Angle of Vision: Man and Nature in American Experience* (1952), which concentrates on Emerson's principle of "correspondence." Stephen E. Whicher, *Freedom and Fate* (1953), is also valuable; it is called an "inner life" of Emerson and concentrates on the 1830s. The only treatment of Emerson's mind and art as they relate to the transcendentalist movement is Francis O. Matthiessen's superb *American Renaissance: Art and Expression in the Age of Emerson and Whitman* (1941). □

John Franklin Enders

The American virologist John Franklin Enders (1897-1985), a leader in modern virology, cultivated poliovirus in tissue cultures of human cells and developed an attenuated live vaccine for measles.

John Franklin Enders was born on Feb. 10, 1897, in West Hartford, Conn. After serving from 1917 to 1920 in the United States Naval Reserve Flying Corps, he achieved his undergraduate degree at Yale University. In 1922, he earned a master's degree in English at Harvard University. But before completing doctoral work he became attracted to the study of bacteriology under Hans Zinsser, with whom he developed methods of synthesizing anti-typhus vaccines. He was married to Sarah Bennett in 1927, with whom he had two children; she died in 1943. In 1930 he received his doctorate in microbiology. He then embarked upon a remarkable and productive career as a member of the faculty of Harvard Medical School. During World War II, he was a civilian consultant on epidemic diseases to the Secretary of War, and after 1945 was affiliated with the Civilian Commission on Virus and Rickettsial Disease until 1949. He became head of the Research Division of Infectious Diseases of Children's Hospital, Boston, in 1947. In 1951 he married again, this time to Carolyn Keane.

In the late 1930s Enders focused on virologic problems. His first major breakthrough was the development of techniques for detection of antibodies to mumps virus; he and others subsequently showed that the virus could be grown in chick embryos and tissue culture. On the basis of this work the immunology and epidemiology of mumps infection could be studied, a skin test was developed, and it was shown that the infection frequently was inapparent. Finally, the studies provided the basis for the development of preventive measures against the disease, which now include an attenuated live-virus vaccine.

While Enders and his colleagues, Dr. Frederick Robbins and Dr. Thomas Weller, were continuing the study of mumps and chicken-pox viruses, various types of human cells in culture were being used. Enders suggested that some of the cultures be inoculated with poliovirus, which at that time could be studied only with difficulty in a few species of expensive experimental animals. The poliovirus did propagate in one type of culture made up of cells which were not from the nervous system. This discovery, and the studies which it made possible, opened the way to a new era in poliovirus research, the most dramatic aspect of which was the possibility for development of poliovirus vaccines. For this work Enders, Robbins, and Weller were awarded the Nobel Prize in 1954. From the Enders-Robbins-Weller technique, Dr. Jonas Salk was able to produce the first polio vaccine in 1953.

Enders began studies with another disease, measles. In 1954 he reported success in growing the virus in tissue culture and followed this by a model series of investigations that resulted in a measles vaccine in 1962. Turning his concern to cancer-related viruses in later years, he made important contributions to this field, particularly to studies of fusion of cells from different species as a means of altering cell susceptibility to viruses.

His significant contributions to many areas of virology brought him honors from all over the world, including the Presidential Medal of Freedom in 1963, but Enders continued to devote himself to his laboratory and his students. Because of the breadth and incisiveness of his thought, many of his contributions were conceptual and definitive, representing major steps opening up whole new areas for further experimentation and extension of knowledge. Enders wrote close to 200 published papers between 1929 and 1970. In 1939 he co-authored *Immunity, Principles and Application in Medicine and Public Health*. But, while achieving wide recognition and public acclaim, Enders remained a "virologists' virologist." Towards the end of his life, he sought to apply his knowledge of immunology to the fight against AIDS, especially in trying to halt the progress of the disease during its incubation period in the human body. He died September 8, 1985, of heart failure, while at his home in Waterford, Connecticut.

Further Reading

A tribute to Enders can be found in the foreword to *Perspectives in Virology VI* (1968), which was dedicated to him. The foreword was written by Frederick C. Robbins, one of Enders's colleagues, with whom he shared the Nobel Prize. Theodore L. Sourkes, *Nobel Prize Winners in Medicine and Physiology, 1901-1965* (1953; rev. ed. 1967), includes a biography of Enders and a description of his work. A biography is also in the Nobel Foundation, *Physiology or Medicine: Nobel Lectures, Including Presentation Speeches and Laureates' Biogra-*

phies (3 vols., 1964-1967). Information on his work is in any review of the literature of medical virology and in virology textbooks. □

Julius Winfield Erving

Julius Erving (born 1950), known as Dr. J., was one of the great superstars of professional basketball during the 1970s and 1980s. He was inducted into the Basketball Hall of Fame in 1993 and went on to work for NBC as a studio analyst for their basketball coverage.

Julius Erving (Dr. J) began his career playing for the fledgling American Basketball Association, a league started to compete with the long-established National Basketball Association. He played for several years for the New York Nets, being named most valuable player for the 1973-74 and 1974-75 seasons. After the merger of the two leagues in 1976, Erving was traded to the Philadelphia Seventy-Sixers, where he continued a phenomenal career, playing in several all-star games, setting a slew of records, and altering the way the game was played forever by drawing attention away from the center-focused game. At the time of his retirement from the game, he was basketball's third-highest scorer.

Displayed Great Talent at a Young Age

Julius Erving was the middle child born to Julius and Callie Mae Erving (Lindsay). His father deserted the family when Julius was three, and his mother was left to raise three children on her own, working as a house cleaner. The family lived in a housing project in Hempstead, Long Island, among other poor families. Julius was a quiet, well behaved child, and at times his family was concerned that he was perhaps too withdrawn. In school, however, he was a bright student who liked to recite poetry. He was first attracted to basketball at about the age of nine, and began spending his free time at the public courts in Campbell Park. When he was ten, Irving joined the local Salvation Army team, leading it to a 27-3 season. The next year, his team was 31-1 and went on to win the Inter-County Basketball Association tournament.

Erving attending Roosevelt High School in Roosevelt, Long Island, a town not far from Hempstead, to which the family had moved when Julius was 13. Erving maintained his passion for basketball and was named to the All-County and All-Long Island teams. After graduation Erving was offered several basketball scholarships by some of the best colleges in the country. He chose the University of Massachusetts at Amherst, where his basketball mentor's friend was the coach. In his first year at U-Mass, Erving led the freshman team to an undefeated season, on the way breaking the school's freshman records for scoring and rebounding. In his next year, Erving again had a stellar season, averaging 26 points and 20 rebounds per game, leading the country in rebounds. In the summer following his sophomore year, the National Collegiate Athletic Association (NCAA) named Erving to a team of college all-stars to tour Europe and the old Soviet Union. Afterwards, Erv-

Julius Erving (center)

ing's teammates voted him the tour's most valuable player. In his junior year, Erving averaged 27 points and 19 rebounds per game.

Joined ABA

After completing his junior season, Erving decided to turn professional. This was a controversial decision in that the NCAA liked to see its players complete their degrees before turning pro. But there was a new basketball league forming, the ABA, to challenge the status of the NBA, and they were making Erving some lucrative offers. The year was 1971, and sports salaries were just beginning to skyrocket. Erving signed with an agent and took a four-year contract to play with the Virginia Squires for the sum of $500,000. He stayed with the Squires for two seasons. In his first, he was sixth in the ABA in scoring (27.3 points per game) and third in rebounding (15.7). The Squires went to the playoffs that year, and Erving was first in playoff scoring, with 33 points on average per game. In his next year with the Squires, Erving led the ABA with 31.9 points.

After the close of the 1972-73 season, Erving surprised many fans and hired a new agent to find a more lucrative contract for him. After considering a series of offers, Erving decided on a $1.8 million deal, with a $250,000 signing bonus, with the Atlanta Hawks of the NBA. By leaving the ABA for the NBA, however, Erving set himself up for legal troubles. The NBA, as the established professional basketball league in the country, had rules about college drafts, and because the Milwaukee Bucks had earned the right to first draft picks that year, they sued to stop the deal. Erving's old agents and his old team, the Virginia Squires also went to court. It was a complicated, highly publicized case that was finally sent to arbitration to be settled before the 1973-74 season. The arbitrators arranged a settlement that sent Erving from the Squires to the New York Nets, of the ABA, in exchange for the Nets' highest scorer and a cash payment of $750,000. The Nets also had to pay the Atlanta Hawks a settlement fee of $400,000, and then were free to sign Erving to an eight-year contract that would pay him $2.8 million.

One of the Greatest Athletes Ever

In Erving's first season with the Nets (1973-74), the young superstar won his second straight league scoring championship, averaging 27.4 points per game, and led the team to the championship against the Utah Stars. In the final series, Erving led both teams in scoring with 27.9 points per game, scoring 47 points in the last game, which brought the Nets the championship four games to one. In the next season, the Nets floundered, playing erratically. In the first round of the play-offs that year against the St. Louis Spirits, Erving had two good games but his performance wasn't enough to keep the team afloat, and the reigning champs were defeated in the first round.

By the 1975-76 season it was pretty clear that the ABA would merge with the NBA after the season. The leaders of the ABA had attracted star talent, like Erving and others, and had many teams playing on par with the older, established league. Basketball was also becoming big business and showed signs that it would continue to grow. Although the Nets again played sporadically that year, they made it to the championship against the Denver Nuggets. It was a hard fought series coming down to an exciting final game in New York; it showcased Erving to be one of the greatest athletes of modern times, and is considered one of the best games in basketball history. At one point The Nets trailed by 20 points, but managed to come back and win the game, largely as a result of Erving's play. *Sports Illustrated* called Erving's performance "the greatest individual performance by a basketball player at any level anywhere." For the championship series, Erving averaged 37.7 points, 14.2 rebounds and six assists per game. In his ABA career, Erving scored 11,662 points in total, a per-game average of 29.

Demanded Higher Salary

As anticipated, the next year the ABA and NBA merged. Erving was offered a contract to continue playing for the Nets, but he felt the money was insufficient for a player of his caliber, so he held out for a better offer. Erving was one of the first superstar athletes outside of baseball—which had seen skyrocketing salaries and athlete hold-outs for years—to demand increasingly large sums of money. Ultimately, he signed with the Philadelphia 76ers, already a playoff team with substantial talent, including Darrel Dawkins, Caldwell Jones, Doug Collins and George Mc-Ginnis.

The 76ers led their division through most of the season, and Erving scored thirty points during the all-star game and was named MVP. In the ABA, he had been in many ways, a superstar alone and unchallenged. The Sixers, however, were loaded with big names and big egos, and consequently exhibited little team work. They made it to the championship but lost to the Portland Trailblazers after winning the first two games of the series. They had a similar season the following year with the Sixers making it into the playoffs but being eliminated early.

In the 1978-79 season, the management of the Philadelphia 76ers realized that they had a flawed strategy of hiring a team of expensive superstars and thinking that would automatically lead to championships. They traded all their big names except Erving and named him captain, deciding to build a team around their most talented, most team-oriented player. However, that first season of rebuilding did not go well, and in the next season, 1979-80, the Sixers had their best regular season record in over a decade but were eliminated in the playoffs, losing to the Los Angeles Lakers with their soon-to-be-named rookie of the year, Magic Johnson.

Inducted into Basketball Hall of Fame

The following season, 1980-81, Erving was named MVP; the first time that award had gone to a non-center in 17 years. Erving's play had revolutionized basketball, taking offense out to the perimeter instead of just on the boards. They made it to the playoffs again, but this year they came up against their old rivals, the Boston Celtics, with their second-year superstar Larry Bird, and lost a heartbreaking series after being up three games to one. In 1981-82, the Sixers were again left without a championship. That year they made it past the Celtics, but lost to a rampaging Los Angeles Lakers in the finals.

For 1982-83, Philadelphia, by now quite tired of losing to the Celtics and Lakers, signed Moses Malone, hoping to beef up their offense to go against Jabar and Johnson on the Lakers and Bird and McHale on the Celtics. That year they played phenomenally well and made it to the championships, where, once again, they faced their perennial foes from the west, the Lakers. With Malone, however, the Sixers had an added dimension and they took the series in four games straight. It was Erving's first and last NBA championship. The Sixers' prominence steadily diminished over the next couple of years, and in 1987, Julius Erving retired from basketball, after becoming the third player, after Wilt Chamberlain and Kareem Abdul-Jabbar, to score 30,000 career points.

After retiring from basketball, Erving became a successful businessman, buying a Coca Cola bottling business. In 1993 he was inducted into the Basketball Hall of Fame and was hired by NBC as a studio analyst for their basketball coverage. In 1994 *Sports Illustrated* named him to its "40 for the Ages" list, a listing of the forty greatest athletes of all time.

Further Reading

Wilker, Josh, *Julius Erving: Basketball Great,* Chelsea House, 1995.

Porter, David L., *Biographical Dictionary of American Sports,* Greenwood Press, 1995. □

Medgar Evers

Medgar Evers (1925-1963), field secretary for the National Association for the Advancement of Colored People (NAACP), was one of the first martyrs of the civil rights movement. His death prompted President John Kennedy to ask Congress for a comprehensive civil-rights bill, which President Lyndon Johnson signed into law the following year.

The Mississippi in which Medgar Evers lived was a place of blatant discrimination where blacks dared not even speak of civil rights, much less actively campaign for them. Evers, a thoughtful and committed member of the National Association for the Advancement of Colored People (NAACP), wanted to change his native state. He paid for his convictions with his life, becoming the first major civil rights leader to be assassinated in the 1960s. He was shot in the back on June 12, 1963, after returning late from a meeting. He was 37 years old.

Evers was featured on a nine-man death list in the deep South as early as 1955. He and his family endured numerous threats and other violent acts, making them well aware of the danger surrounding Evers because of his activism. Still he persisted in his efforts to integrate public facilities, schools, and restaurants. He organized voter registration drives and demonstrations. He spoke eloquently about the plight of his people and pleaded with the all-white government of Mississippi for some sort of progress in race relations. To those people who opposed such things, he was thought to be a very dangerous man. "We both knew he was going to die," Myrlie Evers said of her husband in *Esquire.* "Medgar didn't want to be a martyr. But if he had to die to get us that far, he was willing to do it."

In some ways, the death of Medgar Evers was a milestone in the hard-fought integration war that rocked America in the 1950s and 1960s. While the assassination of such a prominent black figure foreshadowed the violence to come, it also spurred other civil rights leaders—themselves targets of white supremacists—to new fervor. They, in turn, were able to infuse their followers—both black and white—with a new and expanded sense of purpose, one that replaced apprehension with anger. *Esquire* contributor Maryanne Vollers wrote: "People who lived through those days will tell you that something shifted in their hearts after Medgar Evers died, something that put them beyond fear. . . . At that point a new motto was born: After Medgar, no more fear."

A Course in Racism

Evers was born in 1925 in Decatur, Mississippi. He was the third of four children of a small farm owner who also worked at a nearby sawmill. Young Medgar grew up fast in Mississippi. His social standing was impressed upon him every day. In *The Martyrs: Sixteen Who Gave Their Lives for Racial Justice,* Jack Mendelsohn quoted Evers at length about his childhood. "I was born in Decatur here in Mississippi, and when we were walking to school in the first grade white kids in their schoolbuses would throw things at us and yell filthy things," the civil rights leader recollected. "This was a mild start. If you're a kid in Mississippi this is the elementary course.

"I graduated pretty quickly. When I was eleven or twelve a close friend of the family got lynched. I guess he was about forty years old, married, and we used to play with his kids. I remember the Saturday night a bunch of white men beat him to death at the Decatur fairgrounds because he sassed back a white woman. They just left him dead on the ground. Everyone in town knew it but never [said] a word in public. I went down and saw his bloody clothes. They left those clothes on a fence for about a year. Every Negro in town was supposed to get the message from those clothes and I can see those clothes now in my mind's eye. . . . But nothing was said in public. No sermons in church. No news. No protest. It was as though this man just dissolved except for the bloody clothes. . . . Just before I went into the Army I began wondering how long I could stand it. I used to watch the Saturday night sport of white men trying to run down a Negro with their car, or white gangs coming through town to beat up a Negro."

Evers was determined not to cave in under such pressure. He walked twelve miles *each way* to earn his high school diploma, and then he joined the Army during the Second World War. Perhaps it was during the years of fighting in both France and Germany for his and other countries' freedom that convinced Evers to fight on his own shores for the freedom of blacks. After serving honorably in the war he was discharged in 1946.

Evers returned to Decatur where he was reunited with his brother Charlie, who had also fought in the war. The young men decided they wanted to vote in the next election. They registered to vote without incident, but as the election drew near, whites in the area began to warn and threaten Evers's father. When election day came, the Evers brothers found their polling place blocked by an armed crowd of white Mississippians, estimated by Evers to be 200 strong. "All we wanted to be was ordinary citizens," he declared in *Martyrs*. "We fought during the war for America and Mississippi was included. Now after the Germans and the Japanese hadn't killed us, it looked as though the white Mississippians would." Evers and his brother did not vote that day.

What they did instead was join the NAACP and become active in its ranks. Evers was already busy with NAACP projects when he was a student at Alcorn A & M College in Lorman, Mississippi. He entered college in 1948, majored in business administration, and graduated in 1952. During his senior year he married a fellow student, Myrlie Beasley. After graduation the young couple moved near Evers's hometown and were able to live comfortably on his earnings as an insurance salesman.

Mandated Change for Mississippi

Still the scars of racism kept accumulating. Evers was astounded by the living conditions of the rural blacks he visited on behalf of his insurance company. Then in 1954 he witnessed yet another attempted lynching. "[My father] was on his deathbed in the hospital in Union [Mississippi]," Evers related in *Martyrs*. "The Negro ward was in the basement and it was terribly stuffy. My Daddy was dying slowly, in the basement of a hospital and at one point I just had to walk outside so I wouldn't burst. On that very night a Negro had fought with a white man in Union and a white mob had shot the Negro in the leg. The police brought the Negro to the hospital but the mob was outside the hospital, armed with pistols and rifles, yelling for the Negro. I walked out into the middle of it. I just stood there and everything was too much for me. . . . It seemed that this would never change. It was that way for my Daddy, it was that way for me, and it looked as though it would be that way for my children. I was so mad I just stood there trembling and tears rolled down my cheeks."

Evers quit the insurance business and went to work for the NAACP full-time as a chapter organizer. He applied to the University of Mississippi law school but was denied admission and did not press his case. Within two years he was named state field secretary of the NAACP. Still in his early thirties, he was one of the most vocal and recognizable NAACP members in his state. In his dealings with whites and blacks alike, Evers spoke constantly of the need to overcome hatred, to promote understanding and equality between the races. It was not a message that everyone in Mississippi wanted to hear.

The Evers family—Medgar, Myrlie and their children—moved to the state capital of Jackson, where Evers worked closely with black church leaders and other civil rights activists. Telephone threats were a constant source of anxi-

ety in the home, and at one point Evers taught his children to fall on the floor whenever they heard a strange noise outside. "We lived with death as a constant companion 24 hours a day," Myrlie Evers remembered in *Ebony* magazine. "Medgar knew what he was doing, and he knew what the risks were. He just decided that he had to do what he had to do. But I knew at some point in time that he would be taken from me."

Evers must have also had a sense that his life would be cut short when what had begun as threats turned increasingly to violence. A few weeks prior to his death, someone threw a firebomb at his home. Afraid that snipers were waiting for her outside, Mrs. Evers put the fire out with the garden hose. The incident did not deter Evers from his rounds of voter registration nor from his strident plea for a biracial committee to address social concerns in Jackson. His days were filled with meetings, economic boycotts, marches, prayer vigils, and picket lines—and with bailing out demonstrators arrested by the all-white police force. It was not uncommon for Evers to work twenty hours a day.

Some weeks before his death, Evers delivered a radio address about the NAACP and its aims in Mississippi. "The NAACP believes that Jackson *can* change if it *wills* to do so," he stated, as quoted in *Martyrs*. "If there should be resistance, how much better to have turbulence to effect improvement, rather than turbulence to maintain a stand-pat policy. We believe that there are white Mississippians who want to go forward on the race question. Their religion tells them there is something wrong with the old system. Their sense of justice and fair play sends them the same message. But whether Jackson and the State choose to change or not, the years of change are upon us. In the racial picture, things will never be as they once were."

Two Fallen Leaders—One Theme

On June 12, 1963, U.S. president John F. Kennedy—who would be assassinated only a few short months later—echoed this sentiment in an address to the nation. Kennedy called the white resistance to civil rights for blacks "a moral crisis" and pledged his support to federal action on integration.

That same night, Evers returned home just after midnight from a series of NAACP functions. As he left his car with a handful of t-shirts that read "Jim Crow Must Go," he was shot in the back. His wife and children, who had been waiting up for him, found him bleeding to death on the doorstep. "I opened the door, and there was Medgar at the steps, face down in blood," Myrlie Evers remembered in *People* magazine. "The children ran out and were shouting, 'Daddy, get up!'"

Evers died fifty minutes later at the hospital. On the day of his funeral in Jackson, even the use of beatings and other strong-arm police tactics could not quell the anger among the thousands of black mourners. The NAACP posthumously awarded its 1963 Spingarn medal to Medgar Evers. It was a fitting tribute to a man who had given so much to the organization and had given his life for its cause.

Rewards were offered by the governor of Mississippi and several all-white newspapers for information about

Evers's murderer, but few came forward with information. However, an FBI investigation uncovered a suspect, Byron de la Beckwith, an outspoken opponent of integration and a founding member of Mississippi's White Citizens Council. A gun found 150 feet from the site of the shooting had Beckwith's fingerprint on it. Several witnesses placed Beckwith in Evers's neighborhood that night. On the other hand, Beckwith denied shooting Evers and claimed that his gun had been stolen days before the incident. He too produced witnesses—one of them a policeman—who swore before the court that Beckwith was some 60 miles from Evers's home on the night he was killed.

Beckwith was tried twice in Mississippi for Evers's murder, once in 1964 and again the following year. Both trials ended in hung juries. Sam Baily, an Evers associate, commented in *Esquire* that during those years "a white man got more time for killing a rabbit out of season than for killing a Negro in Mississippi."

After the second trial, Myrlie Evers took her children and moved to California, where she earned a degree from Pomona College and was eventually named to the Los Angeles Commission of Public Works. However, her conviction that justice was never served in her husband's case kept Mrs. Evers involved in the search for new evidence. As recently as 1991, Byron de la Beckwith was arrested a third time on charges of murdering Medgar Evers. Beckwith was extradited to Mississippi to await trial again, still maintaining his innocence and still committed to the platform of white supremacy.

The Evers Legacy

Perhaps the most encouraging aspect of Medgar Evers's story lies in the attitudes of his two sons and one daughter.

Though they experienced firsthand the destructive ways of bigotry and hatred, Evers's children appear to be very well-adjusted individuals. "My children turned out to be wonderfully strong and loving adults," Myrlie Evers concluded *Ebony*. "It has taken time to heal the wounds [from their father's assassination] and I'm not really sure all the wounds are healed. We still hurt, but we can talk about it now and cry about it openly with each other, and the bitterness and anger have gone."

At the same time, Mrs. Evers asserted in *People* that she hopes for Beckwith's conviction on the murder charges. (He was, indeed, convicted after the third trial.) "People have said, 'Let it go, it's been a long time. Why bring up all the pain and anger again?'" she explained. "But I *can't* let it go. It's not finished for me, my children or . . . grandchildren. I walked side by side with Medgar in everything he did. This [new] trial is going the last mile of the way."

Further Reading

Altman, Susan, *Extraordinary Black Americans from Colonial to Contemporary Times,* Children's Press, 1989.

Branch, Taylor, *Parting the Waters: America in the King Years, 1954-63,* Simon and Schuster, 1988.

Mendelsohn, Jack, *The Martyrs: Sixteen Who Gave Their Lives for Racial Justice,* Harper, 1966.

Ebony, June 1988.

Esquire, July 1991.

Essence, February 1986.

Newsweek, July 23, 1990.

People, February 11, 1991. □

F

James Farmer

African American civil rights activist James Farmer (1920-1999) helped organize the 1960s "freedom rides" which led to the desegregation of interstate buses and bus terminals. He also played a major role in the activities of the Congress of Racial Equality (CORE).

James Farmer along with a group of University of Chicago students founded the Congress of Racial Equality (CORE) in Chicago in 1942. The purpose of this interracial group was to work for an end to racial segregation using nonviolent tactics similar to those developed by Mahatma Gandhi. Farmer was the first leader of CORE but became inactive after several years. In the 1960s when the civil rights movement was gaining momentum Farmer was re-elected as the director of CORE. He also was one of the group of civil rights leaders who planned the March on Washington in 1963.

Farmer was born in Marshall, Texas, in 1920. His father held a doctorate in theology from Boston University and his mother a teaching certificate from Bethune-Cookman Institute. Farmer entered Wiley College in Texas at 14 years of age with the idea of becoming a doctor. However, after he received a Bachelor of Science degree in chemistry he decided that he would enter the ministry. When his father joined the faculty at Howard University in Washington, D.C., Farmer entered the School of Religion there. He graduated in 1941 but refused to work in a segregated church. He accepted a job with a pacifist group based in New York called the Fellowship of Reconciliation (FOR) and was assigned to work in Chicago. From his Chicago base he visited other areas in the midwest speaking about pacifism and racial equality.

As a consequence of this work and his study and observation of the Gandhi movement he addressed several proposals to FOR leaders suggesting the formation of a committee dedicated to racial equality. It was first called the Committee of Racial Equality and, finally, the Congress of Racial Equality. Farmer served as national chairman of CORE from 1942 to 1944 and again in 1950. He was elected national director in 1961 and served in that position until 1966. Even during the years that Farmer was not leading CORE he remained interested in the organization's work. During the period from about 1945 to 1959 Farmer worked as a labor union organizer. For the next two years, 1960-1961, he worked as a program director for the National Association for the Advancement of Colored People (NAACP).

Farmer was working for the NAACP when he was called back to CORE to lead the 1961 "freedom ride." Several Supreme Court rulings led to CORE's decision to sponsor freedom rides. In 1946 the Supreme Court had ruled that racially segregated seating on interstate buses was unconstitutional, and in 1960 it declared that segregation in terminals used by interstate passengers was also unconstitutional. Yet the southern states continued to force blacks to sit in the back of the bus and to use segregated facilities. The 13 CORE freedom riders decided to travel by bus from Washington, D.C., to New Orleans with white members sitting in the back and black riders in the front. All of the riders were instructed to refuse to move when they were asked. They also decided that at the bus terminals the white riders would use the "for colored" facilities and the black the "for white."

The riders left from Washington, D.C., and made their historic trip without violence until they arrived in Alabama. In that state the freedom riders were attacked and beaten.

Finally, the bus was burned by hostile whites. Youths who were members of the Student Non-Violent Coordinating Committee (SNCC) volunteered to act as replacements or reinforcements for the original 13 CORE riders. Although hundreds of riders spent weeks in Alabama prisons, new recruits continued to come forward. The conditions in the jails were almost primitive and the guards usually hostile. Although many riders continued to be attacked in other southern states, the idea of freedom rides caught on. CORE received nationwide attention, and James Farmer became well-known as a civil rights leader. The freedom ride, along with sit-ins at lunch counters and the Montgomery bus boycott led by Martin Luther King, Jr., captured the imagination of the nation and exposed to the world through photographs, newspaper accounts, and motion pictures the brutal retaliation of many southern whites against the actions of the demonstrators. Concerned whites and blacks decided that it was time for racial discrimination and segregation to come to an end.

Farmer began to meet regularly with a group of black leaders that came to be known as the "big six" of civil rights. The group included Farmer; King, leader of the Southern Christian Leadership Conference; Dorothy Height of the National Council of Negro Women; John Lewis (or sometimes James Forman) from SNCC; Roy Wilkins of the NAACP; and Whitney Young of the National Urban League. This group of leaders met regularly and sometimes invited other civil rights leaders to attend. When A. Philip Randolph, a labor leader, asked to make a presentation before the group, he proposed that the group revise his idea of a massive march on Washington, D.C., a plan that he origi-

nally had formulated in 1941. The purpose of the march was to dramatize the need for jobs, freedom, and civil rights legislation. The group agreed to support the march. When it took place in Washington, D.C., on August 28, 1963, over 250,000 blacks and whites participated. However, Farmer was in jail and could not attend.

Farmer continued to lead CORE, which grew quickly during the early 1960s. Numerous sit-ins and boycotts occurred and thousands of people, many of them students, were involved. When Farmer resigned as the leader of CORE in 1966 he continued to be active in a number of areas. He taught at several universities and in 1968 he ran unsuccessfully against Shirley Chisholm for the New York 12th district seat in the House of Representatives. In 1969 President Nixon appointed him assistant secretary for administration of the Department of Health, Education and Welfare. In that position, he initiated affirmative action and hiring practices at the HEW. Unhappy with the Nixon administration, Farmer resigned the following year to resume teaching.

Over the years Farmer taught and lectured at numerous institutions, and in the mid 1980s began teaching at Mary Washington College in Fredericksburg, Virginia, eventually joining their staff as a history professor. In 1996 he had over 250 students on his roster, more than any other history teacher at the liberal arts college. He remains a vital and active presence, despite a battle with diabetes that has left him blind in one eye, and without the use of his left leg. For his efforts, Farmer was awarded the Presidential Medal of Freedom in 1998 by President Clinton.

James Farmer died of congestive heart failure at Mary Washington Hospital in Fredericksburg, Virginia on July 9, 1999.

Further Reading

Farmer wrote numerous articles, as well as two books entitled *Freedom, When?* (1965) and *Lay Bare the Heart; An Autobiography of the Civil Rights Movement* (1985). August Meier wrote *CORE; A Study in the Civil Rights Movement, 1942-1968* (1973), which includes important information about Farmer's role in the organization. □

Philo T. Farnsworth

Philo T. Farnsworth (1906–1971) is known as the father of television by proving, as a young man, that pictures could be televised electronically.

On the statue erected in his honor in the U. S. Capitol Statuary Hall, Philo T. Farnsworth is called the Father of Television . He was the first person to propose that pictures could be televised electronically, which he did when he was 14 years old. By the time he was 21, Farnsworth had proved his ideas by televising the world's first electronically-produced image. From the day he sketched out for his high school chemistry teacher his ideas for harnessing electricity to transmit images, until his death in 1971, Farnsworth amassed a portfolio of over 100 television-related patents, some of which are still in use today.

Farnsworth was born in Indian Creek, Utah, on August 19, 1906. The first of five children born to Serena Bastian and Lewis Edwin Farnsworth, he was named after his grandfather, Philo Taylor Farnsworth I, the leader of the Mormon pioneers who settled that area of southwestern Utah. Although there was no electricity where he lived, Farnsworth learned as much as he could about it from his father and from technical and radio magazines. Lewis Farnsworth was a farmer and regaled his son with technical discussions about the telephone, gramophone, locomotives, and anything else the younger Farnsworth was curious about. When the family moved to a farm in Idaho with its own power plant, he poked and probed and mastered the lighting system and was soon put in charge of maintaining it. It had never run so smoothly. Farnsworth was adept at inventing gadgets even before he went to high school, and he won a national invention contest when he was 13 years old.

Dreaming of Television

In 1920, he read that some inventors were attempting to transmit visual images by mechanical means. For the next two years, he worked on an electronic alternative that he was convinced would be faster and better; he came up with the basic design for an apparatus in 1922. Farnsworth discussed his ideas and showed sketches of the apparatus to his high school chemistry teacher Justin Tolman. Little did they know that this discussion would later be critical in settling a patent dispute between Farnsworth and his competitor at the Radio Corporation of America (RCA), Vladimir Zworykin.

Farnsworth took physics courses by correspondence from the University of Utah and later enrolled at Brigham Young University. He was largely self-taught but so impressed two of his chemistry professors at BYU with his ideas about television that they gave him the run of the chemistry and glass labs to start work on his theories.

In 1924, Farnsworth's father died and he was left with the responsibility of supporting the family. After a short time in the navy, he moved to Salt Lake City to work as a canvasser for the Community Chest. There Farnsworth made friends with George Everson, the businessman who was organizing the fund-raising effort, and his associate Leslie Gorrell. Farnsworth told Everson and Gorrell about his ideas for a television, and they invested $6,000 in his venture. With additional backing from a group of bankers in San Francisco, Farnsworth was given a research lab and a year to prove his concepts.

Building the First Television System

Farnsworth was married to his college sweetheart Elma Pem Gardner on May 27, 1926, and the next day they left for California, where Farnsworth would set up his lab in San Francisco. With assistance from his wife, Elma, better known as Pem, and her brother Cliff, Farnsworth designed and built all the components—from the vacuum transmitter tubes to the image scanner and the receiver—that made up his first television system. The key invention was his Image Dissector camera, which scanned relatively slowly in one direction and relatively quickly in the opposite direction, making possible much greater scanning speeds than had been achieved earlier. All television receivers use this basic system of scanning.

On September 7, 1927, three weeks before the deadline, Farnsworth gathered his friends and engineering colleagues in a room adjoining the lab and amazed them with the first two-dimensional image ever transmitted by television—the image of his wife and assistant, Pem. His backers continued their support for a year and in September 1928, the first television system was unveiled to the world. In 1929, some of the bankers who invested in the research formed a company called Television Laboratories Inc., of which Farnsworth was named vice president and director of research.

The Challenge of the Marketplace

At the same time, RCA began aggressively competing with Farnsworth for control of the emerging television market and challenged the patent on his invention. With the testimony of Farnsworth's high school teacher, Justin Tolman, it was determined that Farnsworth had indeed documented his ideas one year before RCA's Vladimir Zworykin. This was but the first of many challenges from RCA, but in the end the corporate giant was forced to work out a cross-licensing arrangement with Farnsworth.

The victor in dozens of legal challenges by RCA, Farnsworth eventually licensed his television patents to the growing industry and let others refine and develop his basic inventions. His patents were first licensed in Germany and Great Britain, and only later did the Federal Communications Commission allocate broadcast channels in the United States. During his early years in San Francisco, Farnsworth did other important work as well. He made the first cold cathode-ray tube, the first simple electron microscope, and a means for using radio waves to sense direction—an innovation now known as radar. He received more than 300 patents worldwide during his career.

Farnsworth eventually set up his own company, which boomed during World War II with government contracts to develop electronic surveillance and other equipment. The Farnsworth Radio and Television Corp. took a downturn after the war and was sold to the International Telephone and Telegraph Company (ITT) in 1949. Farnsworth remained with the company for some time as a research consultant. Late in his life he turned his attention to the field of atomic energy. Farnsworth died of emphysema on March 11, 1971, in Holladay, a suburb of Salt Lake City.

For his pioneering work, Farnsworth received the First Gold Medal awarded by the National Television Broadcasters Association in 1944. During his lifetime he also was presented with honorary doctorates in science from Indiana Technical College (1951) and Brigham Young University (1968). Posthumously, the inventor was remembered with a twenty-cent stamp with his likeness, issued in 1983, and his induction into the National Inventors Hall of Fame in 1984.

The Philo T. Farnsworth Memorial Museum was dedicated in his honor in Rigby, Idaho, in 1988.

Further Reading

Dedication of the Statue of Philo T. Farnsworth, Proceedings in the U.S. Capital Rotunda, U.S. Government Printing Office, 1990.

The Story of Television: The Life of Philo T. Farnsworth by George Everson. Norton, 1949.

Distant Vision: Romance and Discovery on an Invisible Frontier by Elma Farnsworth. Pemberly-Kent, 1990.

BYU Today, "Philo T. Farnsworth: The Father of Television" by Dennis May (May 1989), pp. 33–36. ☐

David Glasgow Farragut

The American naval officer David Glasgow Farragut (1801-1870) was the hero of two of the most important Union naval victories in the Civil War. He became the first admiral in the U.S. Navy.

James (later David) G. Farragut was born on July 5, 1801, near Knoxville, Tenn., the son of George Farragut, a U.S. Army and Navy officer. After his mother's death in 1808, James was informally adopted by Commander David Porter, who had the boy appointed a midshipman 2 years later. Farragut changed his first name from James to David while sailing with Porter on the *Essex* during the War of 1812. Farragut brought a prize ship into Valparaiso, Chile, in 1813. The following year the British captured the *Essex.*

Farragut served in the Mediterranean (1815-1820) and temporarily commanded the brig *Spark.* After passing the midshipman's exam in 1821, he hunted pirates in the Caribbean (1822-1824) with Porter and for a short time commanded the schooner *Ferret.* On Sept. 2, 1824, he married Susan C. Marchant and in 1825 became a lieutenant.

From the 1820s to 1861 Farragut frequently served ashore at the Norfolk, Va., naval yard. In 1833 his ship was stationed off Charleston, S.C., during the Nullification Crisis. Promoted to commander in 1841, Farragut commanded the sloop *Decatur* on the Brazil station the next year. His first wife had died in 1840, and 3 years later he married Virginia D. Loyall, with whom he had one son. Farragut commanded the sloop *Saratoga* on blockade duty during the Mexican War. From 1854 to 1858 he supervised the construction of the naval yard at Mare Island, Calif. When Virginia seceded from the Union in 1861, he switched his permanent residence from Virginia to New York and offered his services to the North, but he remained under suspicion for months.

In January 1862 the Department of the Navy, convinced of his loyalty, made Farragut commander of the West Gulf Blockading Squadron. On April 24, after a 6-day bombardment, he ran past the forts below New Orleans with 17 ships and captured the South's largest port the next day. He continued up the Mississippi past the Vicksburg batteries on June 28 but could not capture the town. He passed the batteries again on July 14 in an unsuccessful effort to sink

the *Arkansas.* Two days later he became the first rear admiral in the U.S. Navy.

In March 1863 Farragut led two ships past the batteries at Port Hudson on the Mississippi, but the fort surrendered in July only after a siege—several days after the Vicksburg victory. His next objective was the port of Mobile. On Aug. 5, 1864, under heavy fire, he sailed 18 ships between the Confederate forts at the heavily mined mouth of Mobile Bay. He captured the ironclad *Tennessee* following a fierce struggle inside the harbor and then received the surrender of the forts, thus sealing off the second-largest Confederate port on the Gulf of Mexico. That fall Farragut was relieved of command because of ill health. In December he received the new rank of vice-admiral. He became the first admiral of the U.S. Navy in 1866.

Farragut commanded the European squadron on a goodwill tour in 1867-1868. He died while visiting the Portsmouth, N.H., naval yard on Aug. 14, 1870.

Further Reading

The most complete biography of Farragut is Charles Lee Lewis, *David Glasgow Farragut* (2 vols., 1941-1943). Briefer volumes are Alfred Thayer Mahan, *Admiral Farragut* (1892), and John Randolph Spears, *David G. Farragut* (1905). His son, Loyall Farragut, collected source material in *The Life of David Glasgow Farragut* (1879).

Additional Sources

Lewis, Charles Lee, *David Glasgow Farragut,* New York: Arno Press, 1941-43, 1980. ☐

Louis Farrakhan

Louis Farrakhan (born 1933) is a leader of one branch of the Nation of Islam, more popularly known as the Black Muslims. Beginning in the mid-1970s he emerged as a popular and militant spokesman for Black Nationalism.

Louis Eugene Walcott was born on May 11, 1933, and grew up in the Roxbury neighborhood of Boston. After joining the Nation of Islam in the 1950s, he took the name Louis X (a standard Nation of Islam practice indicating that one's identity and culture were stolen during slavery) and later Louis Farrakhan. In high school he was an honor student, a good track athlete, and an active Episcopalian. After two years of college he embarked on a career as a professional violinist and singer who used such stage names as "Calypso Gene" and "The Charmer."

At the age of 21, in 1955, Farrakhan was taken by a friend to hear Elijah Muhammad, the leader of the Nation of Islam. Muhammad was the second head of the movement, having attained his position following the mysterious disappearance of founder W.D. Fard in 1934, and had overseen its growth to tens or hundreds of thousands of members with an extensive network of farms, restaurants, stores, schools, and other businesses and institutions. Muhammad's message excoriated "white devils" and promised that the day would soon arrive when God would restore African Americans, who were regarded as the original humans, to their rightful position as leaders of the world. Muhammad also imposed strict standards of behavior on his followers, who were forbidden from smoking, drinking, fighting, eating pork, and other behaviors regarded as destructive and were commanded to say prayers, attend religious services regularly, improve their education, and provide extensive service to the movement. Farrakhan joined the movement soon after hearing its leader speak.

The newcomer's ability and dedication were quickly appreciated by Muhammad, who appointed him minister of the Boston mosque. After the death of Malcolm X in 1965 he was appointed leader of the important Harlem Temple No. 7 and official spokesperson for Elijah Muhammad. He was also given the symbolically important task of introducing Muhammad at rallies on Savior's Day, a major Nation of Islam holiday celebrating Fard's birthday.

Elijah Muhammad died in 1975 and was succeeded by his son Wallace Muhammad, who proved much quieter and more moderate than his father. At Wallace Muhammad's invitation Farrakhan moved to Chicago to work in the movement's headquarters. Soon Wallace Muhammad began to pursue a program of moderation for the movement, abandoning its antiwhite rhetoric (and even admitting whites to membership) and building bridges to the larger world from the Islamic community. That program resulted in a movement that today functions as a relatively conventional expression of Islam.

Farrakhan became a major voice of the "purist" faction composed of members who rejected the move toward moderation. He resigned from the movement in 1978 and organized a new Nation of Islam that closely resembled Elijah

Muhammad's original movement, with dress and behavior codes and Muslim institutions and businesses. The racial theology and bitterly antiwhite rhetoric of Elijah Muhammad once again became standard. The reconstituted movement grew quietly but steadily as Farrakhan opened mosques in American cities and reached out to the wider African American community through publications and a radio show.

Farrakhan's movement, which in 1983 was estimated to have between five and ten thousand members, remained relatively obscure until March 1984, when controversy suddenly erupted over his association with presidential candidate Jesse Jackson. Farrakhan, who had earlier counseled his devoted followers to avoid political involvements, had thrown his movement behind Jackson, providing, in addition to rhetorical support before African American audiences, bodyguards for the candidate. Farrakhan had registered to vote for the first time and urged his followers to do the same. Jackson had returned the favor by appearing as the featured speaker at the Muslim Savior's Day rally in February 1984.

In March, however, Farrakhan condemned Milton Coleman, an African American reporter for *Washington Post,* as a traitor after Coleman disclosed that Jackson had, in a conversation with campaign aides, referred to Jews as "Hymies" and to New York City as "Hymietown." In a speech, Farrakhan said of Coleman, "One day soon we will punish you with death," although he later denied that he was threatening Coleman's life. In the ensuing controversy it became known that Farrakhan had acclaimed Hitler as "a very great man" and had pronounced Judaism a "gutter religion." He also described the creation of Israel as an "outlaw act." Jackson never repudiated Farrakhan's support, but the Muslim's profile was lowered throughout the rest of the campaign.

Controversy about Farrakhan deepened when it became known that during the 1980s he had visited Libya and received a $5-million interest-free loan from dictator Muammar Gaddafi to help build Muslim institutions and businesses. Farrakhan explained that he sought to raise hundreds of millions of dollars for African American self-improvement programs from all of the groups, including Arabs, that had been involved in the slave trade and the destruction of African culture.

After his time of greatest publicity during the presidential campaign of 1984, Farrakhan continued his extensive public speaking schedule and continued to wield influence among African Americans far beyond the membership of his own movement. He and his wife, Betsy, had nine children and lived in a mainly white upscale neighborhood on the far South Side of Chicago.

In 1993, on his 60th birthday, Farrakhan performed a violin concert on Chicago's South Side in an attempt to better his image. The "concert" was held at a Temple, in hopes that tensions between Farrakhan and the Jewish community could be mended. Besides the "Clean n Fresh" product line, Farrakhan opened a $5 million restaurant in March 1995. The Salaam Restaurant and Bakery was built with funds collected from followers and the sale of the *Final Call,* an Islamic newspaper.

Farrakhan has always had a loyal following. This fact was most evident on October 16, 1995 in Washington D.C. Farrakhan had called upon at least one million African American men to converge on the nation's capital to reinvigorate their community. The "Million Man March" was to create a solidarity amongst the African American community. Many feel that the march was also designed to help bridge a gap between whites and African Americans. Farrakhan had support from the likes of Maya Angelou, Jesse Jackson, Stevie Wonder and a host of other notable personalities. The march surprised many, not only because of the sheer force of attendance, but because Farrakhan was able to not only promote, but deliver a non-violent protest in Washington D.C.

Farrakhan was hospitalized in April of 1999 and underwent surgery to treat prostate cancer.

Further Reading

Farrakhan has given few interviews and has not been the subject of a major biographical study. One helpful article is Clarence Page's "Deciphering Farrakhan," in *Chicago* magazine (August 1984). The Nation of Islam's newspaper, *The Final Call,* provides a general exposition of Farrakhan's outlook. Other articles pertaining to Farrakhan include "No Innocent Abroad" by Jack E. White, *Time* (February 26, 1996) and "Million Man March" by Eric Pooley, *Time* (October 16, 1995). □

William Faulkner

William Faulkner (1897-1962), a major American 20th-century novelist, chronicled the decline and decay of the aristocratic South with an imaginative power and psychological depth that transcend mere regionalism.

William Faulkner was born on Sept. 25, 1897, in New Albany, Miss. He grew up in Oxford, Miss., which appears in his fiction as "Jefferson" in "Yoknapatawpha County." William was the oldest of four brothers. Both parents came from wealthy families reduced to genteel poverty by the Civil War. A great-grandfather, Col. William Falkner (as the family spelled its name), had authored *The White Rose of Memphis,* a popular success of the 1880s. William's father owned a hardware store and livery stable in Oxford and later became business manager of the state university. William attended public school only fitfully after the fifth grade; he never graduated from high school.

In 1918, after the U.S. Army rejected him for being underweight and too short (5 feet 5 inches), Faulkner enlisted in the Canadian Air Force. During his brief service in World War I, he suffered a leg injury in a plane accident. In 1918 he was demobilized and made an honorary second lieutenant.

In 1919 Faulkner enrolled at the University of Mississippi as a special student but left the next year for New York City. After several odd jobs in New York and Mississippi, he became postmaster at the Mississippi University Station; he was fired in 1924. In 1925 he and a friend made a walking tour of Europe, returning home in 1926.

During the years 1926-1930 Faulkner published a series of distinguished novels, none commercially successful. But in 1931 the success of *Sanctuary,* written expressly to make money, freed him of financial worries. He went to Hollywood for a year as a scenarist and an adviser.

It was not until after World War II that Faulkner received critical acclaim. French critics recognized his power first; André Malraux wrote an appreciative preface to *Sanctuary,* and Jean Paul Sartre wrote a long critical essay on Faulkner. The turning point for Faulkner's reputation came in 1946, when Malcolm Cowley published the influential *The Portable Faulkner* (at this time all of Faulkner's books were out of print!).

The groundswell of praise for Faulkner's work culminated in a 1949 Nobel Prize for literature. His 1955 lecture tour of Japan is recorded in *Faulkner at Nagano* (1956). In 1957-1958 he was writer-in-residence at the University of Virginia; his dialogues with students make up *Faulkner in the University* (1959). *William Faulkner: Essays, Speeches and Public Letters* (1965) and *The Faulkner-Cowley File* (1966) offer further insights into the man.

Faulkner had married Estelle Oldham in 1929, and they lived together in Oxford until his death on July 6, 1962. He was a quiet, dapper, courteous man, mustachioed and sharp-eyed. He steadfastly refused the role of celebrity: he permitted no prying into his private life and rarely granted interviews.

Poetry and Short Stories

During the early 1920s Faulkner wrote poetry and fiction. In the volume of verse *The Marble Faun* (1922), a printer's error allegedly introduced the "u" into the author's name, which he decided to retain. The money for another book of poems, *The Green Bough* (1933), was supplied by a lawyer friend, Philip Stone, on whom the lawyer in Faulkner's later fiction is modeled. Faulkner's poetry shows the poet's taste for language but lacks stylistic discipline.

Faulkner is considered a fine practitioner of the short-story form, and some of his stories, such as "A Rose for Emily," are widely anthologized. His collections—*These Thirteen* (1931), *Doctor Martino and Other Stories* (1934), *Go Down, Moses and Other Stories* (1942), and *Knight's Gambit* (1949)—deal with themes similar to those in his novels and include many of the same characters.

Early Novels

Soldiers' Pay (1926) and *Mosquitoes* (1927) precede *Sartoris* (1927), Faulkner's first important work, in which he begins his Yoknapatawpha saga. This saga, Faulkner's imaginative recreation of the tragedy of the American South, is a Balzacian provincial cycle in which each novel interrelates, clarifies, and redefines the characters. The central figure is Bayard Sartoris, returned from the war, who drives and drinks violently to compensate for his sense of alienation. He seems determined to find some extraordinary form of self-destruction. He becomes an experimental aviator and dies in a crash, leaving his pregnant wife to sustain the family name. The novel introduces families that reappear in many of Faulkner's novels and stories: the Sartoris and Compson families, representing the agrarian, aristocratic Old South; and the Snopes clan, representing the ruthless, mercantile New South.

"The Sound and the Fury"

The book generally regarded as Faulkner's masterpiece, *The Sound and the Fury* (1929), is a radical departure from conventional novelistic form. It uses a stream-of-consciousness method, rendering a different type of mentality in each of its four sections. The title, taken from Macbeth's utterance of cosmic despair in Shakespeare's play, is a clue to the profound pessimism of the novel, which records the decay and degeneracy of the Compson family and, by implication, of the aristocratic South. It is difficult to read, and Faulkner's "Appendix," written much later at the publisher's request, hardly clarifies it.

Each section takes place in a single day; three sections are set in 1928 and one in 1910. The difficulties begin with the fact that the 1910 section is placed second in the book, and the other three are not sequential in their 1928 three-day span. Further, the opening section is rendered in the stream of consciousness of an idiot, who cannot distinguish past from present.

Unquestionably the most difficult for Faulkner to write, the Benjy section (of April 7, 1928) is also the most difficult to read. It has been likened to a prose poem, with the succeeding three sections being simply variations on its theme of futility. Because the mentally impaired Benjy lives in a state of timelessness, his report is purely sensuous, and the reader must figure out his own chronology. Faulkner gives two aids: the device of signaling time shifts by alternating the typeface between bold and italic, and the variance of the African American attending Benjy (Roskus and Dilsey ca. 1898; Versh, T.P., and Frony ca. 1910; Luster ca. 1928).

Out of Benjy's garbled report come a number of facts and motifs. He is 33 years old, in the constant care of an African American youth named Luster. Benjy is tormented by the absence of his sister, Candace, though she has been out of the household for 18 years; each time he hears golfers on the neighboring course call "Caddy!" (coincidentally her nickname), he is painfully reminded of her. The golf course, formerly part of the Compson estate, was sold so that Benjy's older brother, Quentin, could attend Harvard, where he committed suicide in 1910. Mrs. Compson is a self-pitying woman; Mr. Compson was a drunkard; Uncle Maury was a womanizer; Candace was sexually promiscuous and, in turn, her daughter, confusingly called Quentin (after her dead uncle), is also promiscuous. Benjy has been castrated at his brother Jason's order.

Ironically, the most sensitive and intelligent Compson, Quentin (whose day in the novel is June 1, 1910), shares Benjy's obsession about their sister. Candace and the past dominate Quentin's section, which is set in Boston on the day he commits suicide. His musings add more facts in the novel's mosaic. The head of the family, Mr. Compson, is wise but cynical and despairing. Quentin has falsely confessed incest with Candace to his father; the father has not believed him. Quentin had fought one of Candace's lovers over her "honor." He is oppressed by knowing that the pregnant Candace is to be married off to a northern banker; the impending marriage is symbolic to Quentin of his irremediable and intolerable severance from Candace and is the reason for his suicidal state. Quentin's ludicrously methodical preparations for his suicide culminate when the last thing he does before leaving to kill himself is brush his teeth.

Jason (his day in the novel is April 6, 1928) is one of the great comic villains of literature. He has an irrational, jealous loathing of Candace. Now head of the family, he complains bitterly of his responsibilities as guardian of Candace's daughter, Quentin, while systematically stealing the money Candace sends for her care. Jason is cast in the Snopes mold—materialistic, greedy, and cunning. What makes him humorous is his self-pity. He sees himself as victim—of Candace, who he feels has cost him a desired job; of his niece, whose promiscuity seems a personal affront; of Benjy, whose condition causes embarrassment; of Mrs. Compson, whom he constantly bullies and whose inefficiency has burdened him; of the Jews, whom he blames for his stock market losses; of the servants, whose employment necessitates his own work at a menial job. Jason's lack of soul is evident in all his habits. He leaves no mark on anything and lives totally in the present—the perfect Philistine of the New South.

The novel's final section, the only one told in the third person, gives the point of view of the sensible old black servant, Dilsey (her day is April 8, 1928). As with other Faulkner African Americans, her presence is chiefly functional: her good sense and solidity point up the decadence of the whites. In this section Jason meets with an ironic, overwhelming defeat. The novel's chief social implication is that the South is doomed.

Novels of the 1930s

As I Lay Dying (1930) is a farcical burlesque epic, again using the multiple stream-of-consciousness method to tell the grotesque, humorous story of a family of poor whites intent on fulfilling the mother's deathbed request for burial. Sanctuary (1931), taken seriously by most critics, was discounted by Faulkner as a "potboiler." It is the lurid tale of Popeye, a sexually mutilated bootlegger, who has degenerate sexual acts performed for his gratification. One of his victims is a college girl whose lie in Popeye's behalf at the trial of another bootlegger results in the latter's conviction of Popeye's crime. In an ironic ending, Popeye is hanged for a crime of which he is innocent.

The story in Light in August (1932) takes place in a single day. It is overly complicated by a subplot. Beginning with a pregnant girl searching for her lover, this plot is subordinated to the story of Joe Christmas (same initials as Jesus Christ), whose uncertain racial identity perplexes him. Though structurally unsound, Light in August generates enormous power and probably ranks second among Faulkner's books.

Late Novels

Faulkner's creativity ebbed after 1935. Though occasionally interesting and fitfully brilliant, his work tended to be increasingly repetitious, perverse, and mannered to the point of self-parody.

Pylon (1935), one of Faulkner's weakest novels, is the story of a flying circus team. Absalom, Absalom! (1936) is an extremely complex novel; the title comes from the biblical cry of David ("My son, my son!"). This novel tells of a poor white from the Virginia hills who marries an aristocractic Mississippi woman, inadvertently launching a three-generation family cycle of violence, degeneracy, and mental retardation.

Two minor novels, The Unvanquished (1938) and The Wild Palms (1939), were followed by an uneven but intriguing satire of the Snopes clan, The Hamlet (1940). Of this novel's four parts, the first and the last manifest Faulkner's greatest faults: they are talky and oblique and seem out of focus. The middle sections, however, are Faulkner at his best.

Intruder in the Dust (1948) takes a liberal view of southern race relations. Lucas Beauchamp, an eccentric old African American, is saved from a false murder charge through the efforts of fair-minded whites. A Fable (1954) is a very poor parable of Christ and Judas. The Town (1957), The Mansion (1959), and The Reivers (1962), a trilogy that is part of the Yoknapatawpha saga, are generally regarded as minor works.

Further Reading

Faulkner's thoughts on literature and many other subjects can be found in James B. Meriwether and Michael Millgate, eds., Lion in the Garden: Interviews with William Faulkner, 1926-1962 (1968). Faulkner is discussed in several memoirs: John Faulkner, My Brother Bill: An Affectionate Reminiscence (1963), and Murry C. Falkner, The Falkners of Mississippi: A Memoir (1967). A biography of Faulkner is in the introduction of Edmond L. Volpe, A Reader's Guide to William Faulkner (1964).

Some of the best critical work on Faulkner is in Frederick J. Hoffman and Olga W. Vickery, eds., William Faulkner: Three Decades of Criticism (1960). Although Joseph Blotner's biography, in progress, should be the definitive work, useful studies of Faulkner's life and work include Irving Malin, William Faulkner: An Interpretation (1957); William Van O'Connor, William Faulkner (1959); Hyatt Howe Waggoner, William Faulkner: From Jefferson to the World (1959); Michael Millgate, The Achievement of William Faulkner (1966); and H. Edward Richardson, William Faulkner: Journey to Self-Discovery (1969). See also Robert Penn Warren, ed., Faulkner: A Collection of Critical Essays (1966), and Richard P. Adams, Faulkner: Myth and Motion (1968). □

Richard Phillips Feynman

The theoretical work of the American physicist Richard Phillips Feynman (1918-1988) opened up the doors to research in quantum electrodynamics. He shared the 1965 Nobel Prize in Physics.

Richard Feynman was born on May 11, 1918, in Far Rockaway, a suburb of New York City. He lived there until 1935, when he left to attend the Massachusetts Institute of Technology. After receiving a bachelor's degree in physics in 1939, he went to Princeton University, where he received a Ph.D. in 1942. While at Princeton, Feynman worked on the Manhattan Project, which eventually led him to Los Alamos, New Mexico, in 1943 to work on the atomic bomb. In 1946 he went to Cornell University, where he remained as an associate professor of theoretical physics until 1951. He spent half of that year in Brazil lecturing at the University of Rio and then became a Tolman professor of physics at the California Institute of Technology, where he stayed for more than 30 years. He had three wives and two children, Carl and Michelle.

Solves Problems in the Theory of Quantum Electrodynamics

Feynman's primary contribution to physics was in the field of quantum electrodynamics, which is the study of the interactions of electromagnetic radiation with atoms and with fundamental particles, such as electrons. Because the equations that compose it are applicable to atomic physics, chemistry, and electromagnetism, quantum electrodynamics is one of the most useful tools in understanding physical phenomena.

The field initially grew out of work done by P. Dirac, W. Heisenberg, W. Pauli, and E. Fermi in the late 1920s. The original theory was constructed by integrating quantum mechanics into classical electrodynamics. It provided a reason-

able explanation of the dual wave-particle nature of light by explaining how it was possible for light to behave like a wave under certain conditions and like a particle (a "photon") on other occasions. Dirac in particular introduced a theory that described the behavior of an electron in accordance with both relativity and quantum mechanics. His theory brought together almost everything that was known about particle physics in the 1920s. However, when the principles behind electromagnetic interactions were brought into Dirac's equation, numerous mathematical problems arose: meaningless or infinite answers were obtained when the theory was applied to certain experimental data.

Feynman found a way to bypass, though not solve, these problems. Be redefining the existing value of the charge and the mass of the electron (a process known as "renormalization"), he managed to make the "divergent integrals" irrelevant—these were the terms in the theory which had previously led to meaningless answers. Thus, while some divergent terms still exist in quantum electrodynamics, they no longer enter the calculations of measurable quantities from theory.

The significance of Feynman's contribution is enormous. He gave the theory of quantum electrodynamics a true physical meaning as well as an experimental use. The renormalized values for the electron's charge and mass provide finite, accurate means of measuring electron properties such as magnetic moment. This theory has also made a detailed description of the fine structure of the hydrogen atom possible. It also presents a precise picture of the collisions of electrons, positrons (anti-electrons), and photons in matter.

Feynman was awarded the Nobel Prize for his work in quantum electrodynamics in 1965, together with fellow American Julian Schwinger and Shinichiro Tomonaga of Japan, both of whom had separately developed similar theories, but using different mathematical methods. Feynman's theory was especially distinct from the other two in its use of graphic models to describe the intermediate states that a changing electrodynamic system passes through. These models are known as "Feynman diagrams" and are widely used in the analysis of problems involving pair production, Compton scattering, and many other quantum-electrodynamic problems.

Feynman was fond of using visual techniques to solve problems. In addition to his Feynman diagrams, he developed a method of analyzing MASER (microwave amplification by stimulated emission of radiation) devices that relies heavily on creating accurate pictorial representations of the interactions involved. A MASER device is one that uses the natural oscillations of molecules to generate or amplify signals in the microwave region of the electromagnetic spectrum; they are used in radios and amplifiers, among other things. Feynman's method for analyzing these devices greatly simplified and shortened the solutions, as well as brought out the important features of the device much more rapidly.

Feynman also worked on the theory of liquid helium, supporting the work of the Russian physicist L. D. Landau. Landau had shown that below a certain temperature the properties of liquid helium were similar to those of a mixture of two fluids; this is known as the two-fluid model. Feynman showed that a roton, which is a quantity of rotational motion that can be found in liquid helium, is the quantum mechanical equivalent of a rapidly spinning ring whose diameter is almost equal to the distance between the helium atoms in the liquid. This discovery gave Landau's theory a foundation in atomic theory.

Contributes to Knowledge of Quarks

Richard Feynman did work in many other areas of physics, including important work on the theory of Beta-decay, a process whereby the nucleus of a radioactive atom emits an electron, thereby transforming into a different atom with a different atomic number. His interest in the weak nuclear force—which is the force that makes the process of radioactive decay possible—led Feynman and American physicist Murray Gell-Mann to the supposition that the emission of beta-particles from radioactive nuclei acts as the chief agitator in the decay process. As James Gleick explained in *Genius,* Feynman also contributed to a "theory of partons, hypothetical hard particles inside the atom's nucleus, that helped produce the modern understanding of quarks." Quarks are the most elementary subatomic particles.

Feynman wrote many theoretical physics books which are in use in universities around the country, as well as a series entitled Feynman's Lectures in Physics, which he put together based on several terms of physics lectures he gave at the California Institute of Technology in 1965. The lectures presented a completely revolutionary approach to teaching university physics, providing a valuable resource to all physics majors. He also dabbled in many areas outside of physics, including drumming and drawing.

Feynman received the Albert Einstein Award in 1954, and he was warded the Niels Bohr International Gold Medal in 1973. He was a member of the National Academy of Science and a foreign member of the Royal Society in London.

Explains Why the Shuttle Exploded

In January 1986, the space shuttle *Challenger* exploded above Cape Kennedy, Florida. Feynman was named to the 12-member special (Rogers) commission that investigated the accident. When public hearings began in February, the discussion quickly turned toward the effect of cold temperatures on O-rings. These rubber rings seal the joints of the solid rocket boosters on either side of the large external tank that holds the liquid oxygen and hydrogen fuel for the shuttle. Using a glass of ice water, Feynman demonstrated how slowly the O-ring regained its original shape when it was cold. Because of the O-ring's slow reaction time, hot gases had escaped, eroded the ring, and burned a hole in the side of the right solid rocket booster, ultimately causing the explosion of the space craft.

In October 1979, Feynman was diagnosed with Myxoid liposarcoma, a rare cancer that affects the soft tissues of the body. The tumor from the cancer weighed six pounds and was located in the back of his abdomen, where it destroyed his left kidney. Feynman was diagnosed with another cancerous abdominal tumor in October 1987 and died of complications on February 19, 1988.

Further Reading

Feynman wrote two volumes of autobiographical sketches. *Surely You're Joking, Mr. Feynman''* (1985) is a collection of anecdotes that gives the reader an excellent sense of Feynman's personality. This was followed by *What Do You Care What Other People Think? Further Adventures of a Curious Character* (1988). A short biography of him and a slightly more detailed description of the work that led him to the Nobel Prize can be found in *Nobel Prizes 1965,* published by the Nobel Foundation. The physicist Freeman Dyson's autobiography, *Disturbing the Universe* (1979), tells about Feynman's method of work. An explanation of elementary particle and quantum physics, including Feynman diagrams, can be found in Douglas C. Gianocoli's *Physics* (1980). In *Genius: The Life and Science of Richard Feynman,* James Gleick describes both the nature of the problems with which Feynman dealt and also the ways in which Feynman's solutions differed form those of other physicists. David L. and Judith R. Goodstein describe one of his solutions in *Feynman's Lost Lecture: The Motion of Planets Around the Sun*(1996).

Additional Sources

Gribbin, John and Mary Gribbin, *Richard Feynman: A Life in Science* (1997).

Jagdish Mehra, *The Beat of a Different Drum: The Life and Science of Richard Feynman.* Oxford University Press, 1994. □

Millard Fillmore

The major contribution of Millard Fillmore (1800-1874), thirteenth president of the United States, was his signing of the Compromise of 1850.

Millard Fillmore was born in Cayuga County, N.Y., the son of a poor farmer. Although he held several legal clerkships, he was largely self-taught in the law. He entered politics in association with Thurlow Weed and William H. Seward, helping to organize the Anti-Masonic party as a major third party in the North. As one of the party's leaders in the New York Assembly, Fillmore sponsored reforms, including abolishing debtor imprisonment and a bankruptcy bill. As a member of the U.S. House of Representatives in the 1830s and 1840s, he led his party into the newly formed Whig party. He was elected comptroller of New York State in 1846.

In 1848 Fillmore was elected vice president of the United States under Zachary Taylor. This proved an unpleasant experience, as he was excluded from all patronage and policy-making decisions. He was unable to prevent Taylor's opposition to Henry Clay's proposals for ending the sectional crisis over the extension of slavery into territories acquired by the Mexican War; but before Taylor could veto Clay's compromise bill, he died. Fillmore, now president, quickly accepted the five bills which made up the Compromise of 1850. This was the high point of his administration and demonstrated his attempt to find a middle ground on the slavery question. However, he was attacked by antislavery groups, especially for his vigorous enforcement of the Fugitive Slave Law, which was part of the compromise. Fillmore believed that slavery was evil but, as long as it existed, had to be protected.

Fillmore's policies all aimed at turning the country away from the slavery question. His most important recommendation was that the U.S. government build a transcontinental railroad. His foreign policy, formulated with Secretary of State Daniel Webster, had similar goals. In marked contrast to the aggressive policy followed by the United States during the rest of the 1840s and 1850s (when Democratic administrations made every effort to acquire additional territory), Fillmore sought to encourage trade through peaceful relations. One of his major undertakings was to send Commodore Matthew Perry to open Japan to American commerce.

In 1852 Fillmore was repudiated by the Whigs. After he ran unsuccessfully for president in 1856 as the Know-Nothing party's candidate, he returned to Buffalo to devote himself to local civic projects. He died on March 8, 1874.

Further Reading

The definitive biography of Fillmore is Robert J. Rayback's objective *Millard Fillmore* (1959). For background on Fillmore's New York career see the books by Glyndon G. Van Deusen on the leaders of the Whig party in the Empire State: *Thurlow Weed: Wizard of the Lobby* (1947), *Horace Greeley: Nineteenth-Century Crusader* (1953), and *William Henry Seward* (1967). □

Francis Scott Key Fitzgerald

The American author Francis Scott Key Fitzgerald (1896-1940), a legendary figure of the 1920s, was a scrupulous artist, a graceful stylist, and an exceptional craftsman. His tragic life was an ironic analog to his romantic art.

On Sept. 24, 1896, F. Scott Fitzgerald was born in St. Paul, Minn. His family was Irish Catholic, his mother's side wealthy. The family lived for some years in Buffalo and Syracuse; but in 1908, when Scott's father lost his job, they returned to St. Paul. For the most part, Scott was privately educated; he attended Newman School in Hackensack, N.J., from 1911 to 1913.

Fitzgerald enrolled at Princeton University in 1913 and struck up enduring friendships with Edmund Wilson and John Peale Bishop. Because of ill health and low grades, he left college in 1915. He returned to Princeton in 1916 but left a year later without a degree and joined the Army with a second lieutenant's commission. Stationed in Alabama in 1918, he met Zelda Sayre, then 18 years old; he would marry her a few years later. After his Army discharge he took an advertising job briefly. Back home in St. Paul, he finished his first novel, *This Side of Paradise,* which was accepted by Scribner's in 1919, and that same year he had remarkable success placing nine short stories in leading commercial journals.

First Publications

Upon publication of *This Side of Paradise* (1920), Fitzgerald married Sayre in New York City. Of this period he later recalled riding up Fifth Avenue in a cab—young, rich, famous, and in love (he might easily have added handsome)—suddenly bursting into tears because he knew he would never be so happy again. He was right. Despite great earnings and fame, he and Zelda lived luxuriously, dissolutely, and tragically.

A daughter was born in 1921 after the couple had spent some time in Europe. When Fitzgerald's second novel, *The Beautiful and the Damned* (1922), and a collection of short stories, *Tales of the Jazz Age* (1922), sold very well, they rented a house on Long Island and ran into debt because of their extravagance. Fitzgerald attempted to recoup by writing a play, *The Vegetable* (1923), but it flopped quickly. The Fitzgeralds went to Europe for over 2 years. The high points of this sojourn were publication of *The Great Gatsby* (1925) and the beginning of Scott's friendship with Ernest Hemingway. In 1927 Scott went to Hollywood on his first movie assignment. Afterward the Fitzgeralds again went abroad several times.

Zelda's first major nervous breakdown, in 1930, and treatment in a Swiss clinic became the basis for Fitzgerald's next novel, *Tender Is the Night* (1934). Zelda spent the rest of her life in and out of sanitariums, and Fitzgerald's own life ran a parallel disastrous course.

Analysis of the Novels

This Side of Paradise (1920), an autobiographical novel, tells of the youth and early manhood of a Princeton undergraduate. In the climactic action his loyalties shift from football to literature, with a concomitant growth in his character. This patchy work struck a nerve in the reading public, chiefly for its new type of heroine—the "flapper," a young woman in revolt against the double standard, who smokes, drinks, dances, and is considered to be somewhat promiscuous.

The Beautiful and the Damned (1922) deals with a dissolute couple, Anthony Patch, grandson of a millionaire, and his debutante wife. They live indolently, extravagantly, and quarrelsomely on the expectations of Tony's inheritance, but the grandfather discovers Tony's alcoholism and profligacy and disinherits him; however, after the grandfather dies, the will is broken. Ironically, the inheritance reinforces Tony's spiritual disintegration. As with most of Fitzgerald's novels, the autobiographical elements are fairly obvious.

The Great Gatsby (1925) is an American classic, generally regarded as Fitzgerald's finest work. It extends and synthesizes the themes that pervade all of his fiction: the callous indifference of wealth, the hollowness of the American success myth, and the sleaziness of the contemporary scene. It is the story of Jay Gatz, a successful, vaguely disreputable man, who has a background of poverty and has pretentiously altered his name to "Gatsby." A naively vulgar parvenu, he nonetheless emerges as morally superior to the slightly covert snobs who free-load at his parties and the reckless rich whom he so hopelessly emulates. Gatsby dies quixotically attempting to reclaim his former love, Daisy.

With T. S. Eliot's poem *The Waste Land* and Ernest Hemingway's *The Sun Also Rises*, *The Great Gatsby* is a major contribution to the creative record of the barren spirituality of the 20th century. Ironically, in *Gatsby* an ash heap dominates the landscape between Long Island and Manhattan; Gatsby's memorabilia include rigorous self-improvement schedules and Benjamin Franklin homilies, but he rises to success as a bootlegger; Gatsby, whose notion of elegance is his pink suit, silk shirts, cream-colored car, and large house with swimming pool, has a similarly shallow knowledge of people and never sees Daisy's superficiality; finally, the green light on his dock, a multisymbol of lush vegetation (for the Pilgrims) or riches (for contemporary Americans), is ultimately a deceit—a forlorn, romantic image ending the novel.

Fitzgerald's characters are memorable despite his spare, ideographic method of delineation: Gatsby, whose pet term of address is "Old Sport," is seen only as "a pink suit"; Daisy's husband is identified by the wad of muscle beneath his suit jacket; Daisy has "a voice like money." Nowhere is Fitzgerald's contrast with contemporary author Thomas Wolfe better illustrated: Wolfe believed in "putting in," and Fitzgerald in "taking out," in extreme selectivity and economy in his art.

In its original form *Tender Is the Night* (1934; later restructured by Malcolm Cowley) is structurally imperfect.

Set in Europe, chiefly on the Riviera, the first half is told by a 19-year-old starlet who has a crush on the hero, Dick Diver, a young American psychiatrist. The second half is seen through the eyes of Dick and of Nicole, the wealthy American schizophrenic whom he marries, cures, and is destroyed by. Dick ultimately returns to America and becomes a small-town practitioner and an alcoholic. The theme is parasitism—the health of one person gained at the expense of another—and the facts bear an unmistakable resemblance to Scott and Zelda's marriage.

The Last Tycoon (1941), published posthumously after Edmund Wilson put it together from Fitzgerald's unfinished manuscript, is the story of a movie producer. Though Wilson calls it Fitzgerald's most mature work, it has received minimal critical attention.

Short Stories

Some of Fitzgerald's best work is in the short-story form. The titles of his collections are extraordinarily representative of the spirit of the times. *Flappers and Philosophers* (1921) contains "The Off-Shore Pirate" and "The Ice Palace." *Tales of the Jazz Age* (1922) includes "May Day" and "The Diamond as Big as the Ritz," two exquisite stories. The best-known pieces in *All the Sad Young Men* (1926) are "Winter Dreams," a quintessential instance of Fitzgerald's romantic vision, and "The Rich Boy." Fitzgerald's final collection, *Taps at Reveille* (1935), includes "Babylon Revisited," perhaps his most widely anthologized story.

Last Years

Fitzgerald earned over $400,000 between 1919 and 1934, but he and Zelda lived so expensively that they barely managed to cover their bills. When *Tender Is the Night* failed to excite interest, financial problems became acute; by 1937 Fitzgerald owed $40,000 despite continued earnings from magazine stories. Zelda had been permanently returned to the sanitarium in 1934; and the years 1935-1937 saw Fitzgerald's own descent—increasing alcoholism and physical illness—which he described with poignant candor in articles appearing in *Esquire* in the mid-1930s.

In 1937 Fitzgerald signed a movie contract at a weekly salary of $1,000. His liaison with gossip columnist Sheilah Graham during the last 3 years of his life is described in her *Beloved Infidel* (1958). But the heartbreak and dissolution took their toll, and after two heart attacks Fitzgerald died on Dec. 21, 1940. Zelda Fitzgerald died in a fire in 1947 at Highland Sanitarium, Asheville, N.C., leaving a novel, *Save Me the Waltz* (1932, American edition).

Further Reading

Fitzgerald's *The Crack-up,* edited by Edmund Wilson (1945), is a revealing but fragmentary autobiographical collection of essays and letters. The standard work on Fitzgerald is Andrew Turnbull, *Scott Fitzgerald* (1962), a full and reliable biography, though not sufficiently critical. An exciting, sometimes inaccurate biography is Arthur Mizener, *The Far Side of Paradise* (1951). See also Alfred Kazin, ed., *F. Scott Fitzgerald: The Man and His Work* (1951); Sheilah Graham, *Beloved Infidel: The Education of a Woman* (1958); James E. Miller, Jr., *F. Scott Fitzgerald: His Art and His Technique* (1964); Robert F. Sklar,

F. Scott Fitzgerald: The Last Laocoön (1967), a study of Fitzgerald as an intellectual; and Nancy Milford, *Zelda: A Biography* (1970), a brilliant study of Fitzgerald's wife and their marriage. For literary background see Alfred Kazin, *On Native Grounds: An Interpretation of Modern American Prose Literature* (1942).

Tate, Mary Jo, *F. Scott Fitzgerald A to Z: The Essential Reference to His Life and Work,* Facts on File, 1997. ☐

Paul Flory

Paul Flory (1910-1985), founder of the science of polymers, was a researcher in macronuclear chemistry and was awarded the Nobel Prize in 1974.

Paul Flory is widely recognized as the founder of the science of polymers. The Nobel Prize in chemistry he received in 1974 was awarded not for any single specific discovery, but, more generally, "for his fundamental achievements, both theoretical and experimental, in the physical chemistry of macromolecules." That statement accurately reflects the wide-ranging character of Flory's career. He worked in both industrial and academic institutions and was interested equally in the theory of macromolecules and in the practical applications of that theory.

Paul John Flory was born in Sterling, Illinois, on June 19, 1910. His parents were Ezra Flory, a clergyman and educator, and Martha (Brumbaugh) Flory, a former school teacher. Ezra and Martha's ancestors were German, but they had resided in the United States for six generations. Both the Flory and the Brumbaugh families had always been farmers, and Paul's parents were the first in their line ever to have attended college.

After graduation from Elgin High School, Flory enrolled at his mother's alma mater, Manchester College, in North Manchester, Indiana. The college was small, with an enrollment of only 600. He earned his bachelor's degree in only three years, at least partly because the college "hadn't much more than three years to offer at the time," as he was quoted as having said by Richard J. Seltzer in *Chemical and Engineering News.* An important influence on Flory at Manchester was chemistry professor Carl W. Holl. Holl apparently convinced Flory to pursue a graduate program in chemistry. In June of 1931, therefore, Flory entered Ohio State University and, in spite of an inadequate background in mathematics and chemistry, earned his master's degree in organic chemistry in less than three months. He then began work immediately on a doctorate, but switched to the field of physical chemistry. He completed his research on the photochemistry of nitric oxide and was granted his Ph.D. in 1934.

Chance Assignment Leads to Polymers

Flory's doctoral advisor, Herrick L. Johnston, tried to convince him to stay on at Ohio State after graduation. Instead, however, he accepted a job at the chemical giant, Du Pont, as a research chemist. There he was assigned to a research team headed by Wallace H. Carothers, who was later to invent the process for making nylon and neoprene.

Flory's opportunity to study polymers was ironic in that, prior to this job, he knew next to nothing about the subject. Having almost *any* job during the depths of the Great Depression was fortunate, and Flory was the envy of many classmates at Ohio State for having received the Du Pont offer.

Flory's work on the Carothers team placed him at the leading edge of chemical research. Chemists had only recently begun to unravel the structure of macromolecules, very large molecules with hundreds or thousands of atoms, and then to understand their relationship to polymers, molecules that have chemically combined to become a single, larger molecule. The study of polymers was even more difficult than that of macromolecules because, while the latter are very large in size, they have definite chemical compositions that are always the same for any one substance. Polymers, on the other hand, have variable size and composition. For example, polyethylene, a common polymer, can consist of anywhere from a few hundred to many thousands of the same basic unit (monomer), arranged always in a straight chain or with cross links between chains.

With his background in both organic and physical chemistry, Flory was the logical person to be assigned the responsibility of learning more about the physical structure of polymer molecules. That task was made more difficult by the variability of size and shape from one polymer molecule to another—even among those of the same substance. Flory's solution to this problem was to make use of statistical mechanics to average out the properties of different molecules. That technique had already been applied to polymers by the Swiss chemical physicist Werner Kuhn and two Austrian scientists, Herman Mark and Eugene Guth. But Flory really developed the method to its highest point in his research at Du Pont.

During his four years at Du Pont, Flory made a number of advances in the understanding of polymer structure and reactions. He made the rather surprising discovery, for example, that the rate at which polymers react chemically is not affected by the size of the molecules of which they are made. In 1937, he discovered that a growing polymeric chain is able to terminate its own growth and start a new chain by reacting with other molecules that are present in the reaction, such as those of the solvent. While working at Du Pont, Flory met and, on March 7, 1936, married Emily Catherine Tabor. The Florys had two daughters, Susan and Melinda, and a son, Paul John, Jr. Flory's work at Du Pont came to an unexpected halt when, during one of his periodic bouts of depression, Carothers committed suicide in 1937. Although deeply affected by the tragedy, Flory stayed on for another year before resigning to accept a job as research associate with the Basic Science Research Laboratory at the University of Cincinnati. His most important achievement there was the development of a theory that explains the process of gelation, which involves crosslinking in polymers to form a gel-like substance.

Wartime Need Prompts New Discoveries

Flory's stay at the University of Cincinnati was relatively brief. Shortly after World War II began, he accepted an offer from the Esso (now Exxon) Laboratories of the Standard Oil Development Company to do research on rubber. It was apparent to many American chemists and government officials that the spread of war to the Pacific would imperil, if not totally cut off, the United States' supply of natural rubber. A massive crash program was initiated, therefore, to develop synthetic substitutes for natural rubber. Flory's approach was to learn enough information about the nature of rubber molecules to be able to predict in advance which synthetic products were likely to be good candidates as synthetic substitutes ("elastomers"). One result of this research was the discovery of a method by which the structure of polymers can be studied. Flory found that when polymers are immersed in a solvent, they tend to expand in such a way that, at some point, their molecular structure is relatively easy to observe.

In 1943, Flory was offered an opportunity to become the leader of a small team doing basic research on rubber at the Goodyear Tire and Rubber Company in Akron, Ohio. He accepted that offer and remained at Goodyear until 1948. One of his discoveries there was that irregularities in the molecular structure of rubber can significantly affect the tensile strength of the material.

In 1948, Flory was invited by Peter Debye, the chair of Cornell University's department of chemistry, to give the prestigious George Fisher Baker Lectures in Chemistry. Cornell and Flory were obviously well pleased with each other as a result of this experience, and when Debye offered him a regular appointment in the chemistry department beginning in the fall of 1948, Flory accepted—according to Maurice

Morton in *Rubber Chemistry and Technology*—"without hesitation." The Baker Lectures he presented were compiled and published by Cornell University Press in 1953 as *Principles of Polymer Chemistry*. Flory continued his studies of polymers at Cornell and made two useful discoveries. One was that for each polymer solution there is some temperature at which the molecular structure of the polymer is most easily studied. Flory called that temperature the theta point, although it is now more widely known as the Flory temperature. Flory also refined a method developed earlier by the German chemist Hermann Staudinger to discover the configuration of polymer molecules using viscosity. Finally, in 1956, he published one of the first papers ever written on the subject of liquid crystals, a material ubiquitous in today's world, but one that was not to be developed in practice until more than a decade after Flory's paper was published.

In 1957, Flory became executive director of research at the Mellon Institute of Industrial Research in Pittsburgh. His charge at Mellon was to create and develop a program of basic research, a focus that had been absent from that institution, where applied research and development had always been of primary importance. The job was a demanding one involving the supervision of more than a hundred fellowships. Eventually, Flory realized that he disliked administrative work and was making little progress in refocusing Mellon on basic research. Thus, when offered the opportunity in 1961, he resigned from Mellon to accept a post at the department of chemistry at Stanford University. Five years later, he was appointed Stanford's first J. G. Jackson-C. J. Wood Professor of Chemistry. When he retired from Stanford in 1975, he was named J. G. Jackson-C. J. Wood Professor Emeritus. In 1974, a year before his official retirement, Flory won three of the highest awards given for chemistry—the National Medal of Science, the American Chemical Society's Priestley Medal, and the Nobel Prize in chemistry. These awards capped a career in which, as Seltzer pointed out, Flory had "won almost every major award in science and chemistry."

Flory's influence on the chemical profession extended far beyond his own research work. He was widely respected as an outstanding teacher who thoroughly enjoyed working with his graduate students. A number of his students later went on to take important positions in academic institutions and industrial organizations around the nation. His influence was also felt as a result of his two books, *Principles of Polymer Chemistry,* published in 1953, and *Statistical Mechanics of Chain Molecules,* published in 1969. Leo Mandelkern, a professor of chemistry at Florida State University, is quoted by Seltzer as referring to the former work as "the bible" in its field, while the latter has been translated into both Russian and Japanese.

Supports Human Rights as Nobel Prize Winner

Flory was also active in the political arena, especially after his retirement in 1975. He and his wife decided to use the prestige of the Nobel Prize to work in support of human rights, especially in the former Soviet Union and throughout Eastern Europe. He served on the Committee on Human

Rights of the National Academy of Sciences from 1979 to 1984 and was a delegate to the 1980 Scientific Forum in Hamburg, at which the topic of human rights was discussed. As quoted by Seltzer, Morris Pripstein, chair of Scientists for Sakharov, Orlov, and Scharansky, described Flory as "very passionate on human rights. . . . You could always count on him." At one point, Flory offered himself to the Soviet government as a hostage if it would allow Soviet scientist Andrei Sakharov's wife, Yelena Bonner, to come to the West for medical treatment. The Soviets declined the offer, but eventually did allow Bonner to receive the necessary treatment in Italy and the United States.

Flory led an active life with a special interest in swimming and golf. In the words of Ken A. Dill, professor of chemistry at the University of California, San Francisco, as quoted by Seltzer, Flory was "a warm and compassionate human being. He had a sense of life, a sense of humor, and a playful spirit. He was interested in, and cared deeply about, those around him. He did everything with a passion; he didn't do anything half way." Flory died on September 8, 1985, while working at his weekend home in Big Sur, California. According to Seltzer, at Flory's memorial service in Stanford, James Economy, chair of the American Chemical Society's division of polymer chemistry, expressed the view that Flory was "fortunate to depart from us while still at his peak, not having to suffer the vicissitudes of old age, and leaving us with a sharply etched memory of one of the major scientific contributors of the twentieth century."

Further Reading

Morton, Maurice, "Paul John Flory, 1910–1985, part I: The Physical Chemistry of Polymer Synthesis," in *Rubber Chemistry and Technology,* May-June, 1987, pp. G47-G57.

Seltzer, Richard J., "Paul Flory: A Giant Who Excelled in Many Roles," in *Chemical and Engineering News,* December 23, 1985, pp. 27–30. □

Malcolm Forbes

Millionaire Malcolm Forbes (1919-1990) was the publisher of *Forbes* magazine from 1957 to 1990.

The entire world knew how old Malcolm Forbes was when he died in 1990; extensive press coverage of his lavish 70th (and last) birthday party thrown in Morocco in September of 1989 insured that everyone who had not been invited would know what they had missed. Characterized as a man who loved the spotlight, who shamelessly enjoyed the privileges his money afforded him, and who was always in pursuit of adventure, Forbes was a balloonist, a motorcyclist, and a sailor who took many trips on his huge yacht, the "Highlander." He collected anything precious and beautiful, most famously, Faberge eggs. His son Robert was quoted in the Chicago Tribune as emphasizing Forbes's playful nature in a eulogy: "He was so many things to so many of us. Boss, bon vivant, raconteur, balloonist, columnist, happiest millionaire, leader of the pack . . . source, mentor, friend, super this, mega that, father, grandfather, father-in-law, uncle, cousin and sparkling, naughty boy."

Also ex-husband, as his wife of 39 years, Roberta Remsen Laidlaw, had divorced him in 1985. As Malcolm, Jr., explained in *Forbes*, his parents still loved each other but could no longer live together. Forbes was often seen in the company of movie star Elizabeth Taylor, and the two answered speculation about an impending marriage by saying that they were merely good friends.

Inherited Wealth

A savvy businessman by all accounts, Forbes inherited his wealth from his father, B.C. (Bertie) Forbes, who established him at the Fairfield Times newspaper as owner and publisher only days after his graduation from Princeton. As he was fond of saying, he was loaded with "sheer ability, spelled i-n-h-e-r-i-t-a-n-c-e," as quoted in *Forbes*. He went on to publish the Lancaster Tribune in 1942, and four years later, after a stint in the Army on the European front of World War II, he joined the staff at *Forbes* magazine. He was first an associate publisher, then publisher, editor, editor-in-chief, vice-president, and, finally, president. As a politician, Forbes was less than successful; he said that he was "nosed out by a landslide" in a New Jersey race for governor in 1957.

Lavish Lifestyle

Forbes was loath to put a real figure to his income and holdings, though he published practically everybody else's value. Early in 1990, the *New York Post* estimated Forbes's holdings by toting up his collections, houses, and publications, but as *Time* magazine reported it, the estimates were generous; "Malcolm is a billionaire, but only if you swallow an estimate of $65 million for his flagship magazine's annual profits." *People* magazine lists eight houses, a palace in Tangier, Morocco, a chateau in Normandy and the island of Lauthala in Fiji as his dwellings. His famous birthday party was held in Tangier, and aroused the disgust of many outsiders who found the display gratuitously expensive. Forbes added some fuel to the flames by suggesting that the party be tax-deductible, as it was for business purposes. His company, Forbes Inc., actually did pay for the party, just as it would pay for any publicity campaign. Forbes's flamboyant consumerism served the firm well, and his enthusiastic spending habits earned him the nickname "the happiest millionaire." Although not as obviously a philanthropist, Forbes gave millions of dollars each year to charities, and had been at a charity bridge tournament the day he died. "Malcolm Forbes was a giant of American business," said then President George Bush, as quoted in *Forbes.* "His success in publishing reflected the tremendous vitality of our nation and served to inform and inspire a generation of successful business leaders. He was greatly admired and will be greatly missed." Former president Ronald Reagan offered a similar tribute: "Malcolm was truly a dear friend and we will miss him sorely. We hold our memories of him close to our hearts and are thankful to have known him."

Gerald Ford

Gerald Ford (born 1913) served as Republican leader in the House of Representatives before being selected by President Nixon to replace Spiro Agnew as vice president in 1973. A year later he replaced Nixon himself, who resigned due to the Watergate crisis. In the 1976 presidential election Ford lost to Jimmy Carter.

Gerald Ford was born Leslie Lynch King, Jr., in Omaha, Nebraska, on July 14, 1913. Shortly afterward, his mother divorced and moved to Grand Rapids, Michigan. After she remarried, he was adopted by and legally renamed for his stepfather, becoming Gerald Rudolph Ford, Jr.

Ford's personality and career were clearly shaped by his family and community. Though not wealthy, the family was by Ford's later account "secure, orderly, and happy." His early years were rather ideal: handsome and popular, Gerald worked hard and graduated in the top five percent of his high school class. He also excelled in football, winning a full athletic scholarship to the University of Michigan, where he played center and, in his final year, was selected to participate in the Shrine College All-Star game. His football experiences, Ford later contended, helped instill in him a sense of fair play and obedience to rules.

Ford had a good formal education. After graduation from the University of Michigan, where he developed a strong interest in economics, he was admitted to Yale Law School. Here he graduated in the top quarter percent of the class (1941), which included such future luminaries as Potter Stewart and Cyrus Vance. Immediately after graduation, Ford joined with his college friend Philip Buchen in a law partnership in Grand Rapids; in early 1942 he enlisted in the Navy, serving throughout World War II and receiving his discharge as a lieutenant commander in February 1946.

Early Political Career

Ford was now ideally positioned to begin the political career which had always interested him. His stepfather was the Republican county chairman in 1944, which was certainly an advantage for Ford. A staunch admirer of Grand Rapids' conservative-but-internationalist senator Arthur Vandenberg, young Ford re-established himself in law practice and took on the Fifth District's isolationist congressman, Bartel Jonkman, in the 1948 primary for a seat in the House of Representatives. He won with 62 percent of the primary vote and repeated that generous margin of victory against his Democratic foe in the general election.

From the outset of his House career Gerald Ford displayed the qualities—and enjoyed the kind of help from others—which led to his rise to power in the lower house. His loyal adherence to the party line and cultivation of good will in his personal relations was soon rewarded with a seat on the prestigious Appropriations Committee. When Dwight Eisenhower gained the White House in 1952, Ford again found himself in an advantageous position since he had been one of 18 Republican congressmen who had initially written Eisenhower to urge him to seek the nomination.

Rise to House Leadership

During the 1950s Ford epitomized the so-called "Eisenhower wing" of the GOP ("Grand Old Party") in both his active support for internationalism in foreign policy (coupled with a nationalistic and patriotic tone) and his basic conservatism on domestic issues. He also developed close associations with other young GOP congressmen such as Robert Griffin of Michigan and Melvin Laird of Wisconsin who were rising to positions of influence in the House. Meanwhile, he continued to build his reputation as a solid party man with expertise on defense matters.

In 1963 he reaped the first tangible rewards of his party regularity, hard work, and good fellowship as he was elevated to the chairmanship of the House Republican Conference. Two years later, at the outset of the 89th Congress, a revolt led by his young, image-conscious party colleagues (prominent among them Griffin, Laird, Charles Goodell of New York, and Donald Rumsfeld of Illinois) propelled Ford into the post of minority leader.

Minority Leader

In a sense, Ford was fortunate to be in the minority party throughout his tenure as floor leader, for those years (1965-1973)—dominated by the Vietnam War and Watergate—presented nearly insurmountable obstacles to constructive policymaking. He tried to maintain a "positive" image for the GOP, initially supporting President Johnson's policies in Vietnam while attempting to pose responsible alternatives to Great Society measures. Gradually he broke from Johnson's Vietnam policy, calling for more aggressive pursuit of victory there.

During the Nixon years, Ford gained increasing visibility as symbol and spokesman for GOP policies. His party loyalty as minority leader made him a valuable asset to the Nixon administration. He was instrumental in securing passage of revenue-sharing, helped push the ill-fated Family Assistance (welfare reform) Plan, and took a pragmatic, essentially unsympathetic stance on civil rights issues— especially school bussing. He made perhaps his greatest public impact in these years when in 1970—seemingly in retaliation for the Senate's rejection of two conservative Southerners nominated by Nixon for seats on the Supreme Court—he called for the impeachment of the liberal Justice William O. Douglas, claiming Douglas was guilty of corruption and inappropriate behavior. The impeachment effort was unsuccessful, and when the ailing Douglas eventually retired from the Court in 1975 Ford issued a laudatory public statement.

Ford also enhanced his reputation as a "hawk" on defense matters during these years. He was one of the few members of Congress who was kept informed by Nixon of the bombings of Cambodia before the controversial invasion of that country in the spring of 1970. Even after the Watergate scandal broke in 1973, Ford remained doggedly loyal long after many of his party colleagues had begun to distance themselves from President Nixon.

Ford retained his personal popularity with all elements of the GOP even while involving himself deeply in these controversial areas. His reputation for non-ideological practicality ("a Congressman's Congressman," he was sometimes labeled), coupled with personal qualities of openness, geniality, and candor, made him the most popular (and uncontroversial) of all possible choices for nomination by Nixon to the vice presidency in late 1973, under the terms of the 25th Amendment, to succeed the disgraced Spiro T. Agnew.

Loyal Vice President

The appropriate congressional committees conducted thorough hearings on even the well-liked Ford, but discovered no evidence linking him to Watergate. He was confirmed by votes of 92 to three in the Senate and 387 to 35 in the House, becoming the nation's first unelected vice president on December 6, 1973. At his swearing-in, Ford charmed a public sorely in need of discovering a lovable politician, stating with humility, "I am a Ford, not a Lincoln." He promised "to uphold the Constitution, to do what is right . . ., and . . . to do the very best that I can do for America."

Nixon and Ford were never personally close, but the latter proved to be a perfect choice for the job. His characteristic loyalty determined his course: during the eight-plus months he served as vice president, Ford made approximately 500 public appearances in 40 states, traveling over 100,000 miles to defend the president. He was faithful to Nixon to the end; even in early August of 1974, after the House Judiciary Committee had voted a first article of impeachment against the president, Ford continued to defend Nixon and condemned the committee action as "partisan."

Always a realist, however, Ford allowed aides to lay the groundwork for his possible transition to the White House. When Nixon resigned on August 9, 1974, the unelected vice president was prepared to become the nation's first unelected president.

The White House Years

Once in the White House, Ford displayed a more consistently conservative ideology than ever before. While holding generally to the policies of the Nixon administration, he proved more unshakably committed than his predecessor to both a conservative, free market economic approach and strongly nationalistic defense and foreign policies. In attempting to translate his objectives into policy, however, President Ford was frequently blocked by a Democratic Congress intent on flexing its muscles in the wake of Watergate and Nixon's fall. The result was a running battle of vetoes and attempted overrides throughout the brief Ford presidency.

Ford made two quick tactical errors, whatever the merits of the two decisions. On September 8, 1974 he granted a full pardon to Richard Nixon, in advance, for any crimes he may have committed while in office, and a week later he announced a limited amnesty program for Vietnam-era deserters and draft evaders which angered the nationalistic right even while, in stark contrast to the pardon of Nixon, it seemed to many others not to go far enough in attempting to heal the wounds of the Vietnam War.

Gerald Ford governed the nation in a difficult period. Though president for only 895 days (the fifth shortest tenure in American history), he faced tremendous problems. After the furor surrounding the pardon subsided, the most important issues faced by Ford were inflation and unemployment, the continuing energy crisis, and the repercussions—both actual and psychological—from the final "loss" of South Vietnam in April 1975. Ford consistently championed legislative proposals to effect economic recovery by reducing taxes, spending, and the federal role in the national economy, but he got little from Congress except a temporary tax reduction. Federal spending continued to rise despite his call for a lowered spending ceiling. By late 1976 inflation, at least, had been checked somewhat; on the other hand, unemployment remained a major problem, and the 1976 election occurred in the midst of a recession. In energy matters, congressional Democrats consistently opposed Ford's proposals to tax imported oil and to deregulate domestic oil and natural gas. Eventually Congress approved only a very gradual decontrol measure.

Ford believed he was particularly hampered by Congress in foreign affairs. Having passed the War Powers Resolution in late 1973, the legislative branch first investigated, and then tried to impose restrictions on, the actions of the Central Intelligence Agency (CIA). In the area of war powers, Ford clearly bested his congressional adversaries. In the *Mayaquez* incident of May 1975 (involving the seizure of a U.S.-registered ship of that name by Cambodia), Ford retaliated with aerial attacks and a 175-marine assault without engaging the formal mechanisms required by the 1973 resolution. Although the actual success of this commando operation was debatable (39 crew members and the ship rescued, at a total cost of 41 other American lives), American honor had been vindicated and Ford's approval ratings rose sharply. Having succeeded in defying its provisions, Ford continued to speak out against the War Powers Resolution as unconstitutional even after he left the White House.

Ford basically continued Nixon's foreign policies, and Secretary of State Henry Kissinger was a dominant force in his administration as he had been under Nixon. Under increasing pressure from the nationalist right, Ford stopped using the word "detente," but he continued Nixon's efforts to negotiate a second SALT (Strategic Arms Limitation Treaty), and in 1975 he signed the Helsinki Accords, which recognized political arrangements in Eastern Europe which had been disputed for more than a generation.

The 1976 Election

Ford had originally stated he would not be a candidate on the national ticket in 1976, but he changed his mind. He faced a stiff challenge for the nomination, however; former Governor Ronald Reagan of California, champion of the Republican right, battled him through the 1976 primary season before succumbing narrowly at the convention. Running against Democrat Jimmy Carter of Georgia in November, Ford could not quite close the large gap by which he had trailed initially. He fell just short of victory. He received over 39 million popular votes to Carter's 40.8 million, winning 240 electoral votes to his opponent's 297. At the age of

63 he left public office—at the exact time he had earlier decided that he would retire.

Gerald Ford prospered as much after leaving the White House as any president had ever done. Moving their primary residence to near Palm Springs, California, he and his popular wife Betty (the former Elizabeth Warren, whom he married in 1948) also maintained homes in Vail, Colorado, and Los Angeles. Besides serving as a consultant to various businesses, by the mid-1980s Ford was on the boards of directors of several major companies, including Shearson/American Express, Beneficial Corporation of New Jersey, and Twentieth Century-Fox Film Corporation. Estimated to be earning $1 million per year, Ford shared a number of investments with millionaire Leonard Firestone and busied himself with numerous speaking engagements. Some criticized him for trading on his prestige for self-interest, but Ford remained clear of charges of wrongdoing and saw no reason to apologize for his success. Long a spokesman for free enterprise and individual initiative, it is somehow fitting that he became a millionaire in his post-presidential years.

In December, 1996 *Business Week* said that the former President had amassed a fortune of close to $300 million over the past two decades, largely from buying and selling U.S. banks and thrifts. Still, his fiscal success didn't diminish his concern over Congress's decision to cut off funds for all living former Presidents as of 1998. In July 1996 Ford paid a visit to several Congressmen, in the hope of urging a Congressional change of heart. Unfortunately for Presidents Carter, Reagan, and Ford, it appears that the Congressional decision is firm, especially in this era of scrutinizing every item in the Federal budget.

In 1997 Ford participated in "The Presidents' Summit on America's Future," along with former presidents Bush and Carter, and President Clinton, as well as General Colin Powell, and former first ladies Nancy Reagan and Lady Bird Johnson. The purpose of the gathering was to discuss volunteerism and community service, and marked the first occasion when living former presidents convened on a domestic policy.

Further Reading

Richard Reeves's *A Ford Not a Lincoln* (1975) and Jerald F. ter Horst's *Gerald Ford and the Future of the Presidency* (1974) provide interesting coverage of his pre-presidential years; the former is more critical than the latter. Ford's autobiography, *A Time to Heal* (1979), is the best source available on his early life, while Robert Hartmann's *Palace Politics: An Inside Account of the Ford Years* (1980) and Ron Nessen's *It Sure Looks Different from the Inside* (1978) give interesting glimpses of Ford as president. The most systematic treatment of Ford's presidency is in A. James Reichley, *Conservatives in an Age of Change: The Nixon and Ford Administrations* (1981). Also see Robert Hartman's *Palace Politics: An Inside Account of the Ford Years* (1990). □

Henry Ford

After founding the Ford Motor Company, the American industrialist Henry Ford (1863-1947) developed a system of mass production based on the assembly line and the

conveyor belt which produced a low-priced car within reach of middle-class Americans.

The oldest of six children, Henry Ford was born on July 30, 1863, on a prosperous farm near Dearborn, Mich. He attended school until the age of 15, meanwhile developing a dislike of farm life and a fascination for machinery. In 1879 Ford left for Detroit. He became an apprentice in a machine shop and then moved to the Detroit Drydock Company. During his apprenticeship he received $2.50 a week, but room and board cost $3.50 so he labored nights repairing clocks and watches. He later worked for Westinghouse, locating and repairing road engines.

His father wanted Henry to be a farmer and offered him 40 acres of timberland, provided he give up machinery. Henry accepted the proposition, then built a first-class machinist's workshop on the property. His father was disappointed, but Henry did use the 2 years on the farm to win a bride, Clara Bryant.

Ford's First Car

Ford began to spend more and more time in Detroit working for the Edison Illuminating Company, which later became the Detroit Edison Company. By 1891 he had left the farm permanently. Four years later he became chief engineer; he met Thomas A. Edison, who eventually became one of his closest friends.

Ford devoted his spare time to building an automobile with an internal combustion engine. His first car, finished in 1896, followed the attempts, some successful, of many other innovators. His was a small car driven by a two-

cylinder, four-cycle motor and by far the lightest (500 pounds) of the early American vehicles. The car was mounted on bicycle wheels and had no reverse gear.

In 1899 the Detroit Edison Company forced Ford to choose between automobiles and his job. Ford chose cars and that year formed the Detroit Automobile Company, which collapsed after he disagreed with his financial backers. His next venture was the unsuccessful Henry Ford Automobile Company. Ford did gain some status through the building of racing cars, which culminated in the "999," driven by the famous Barney Oldfield.

Ford Motor Company

By this time Ford had conceived the idea of a low-priced car for the masses, but this notion flew in the face of popular thought, which considered cars as only for the rich. After the "999" victories Alex Y. Malcomson, a Detroit coal dealer, offered to aid Ford in a new company. The result was the Ford Motor Company, founded in 1903, its small, $28,000 capitalization supplied mostly by Malcomson. However, exchanges of stock were made to obtain a small plant, motors, and transmissions. Ford's stock was in return for his services. Much of the firm's success can be credited to Ford's assistants—James S. Couzens, C. H. Wills, and John and Horace Dodge.

By 1903 over 1,500 firms had attempted to enter the fledgling automobile industry, but only a few, such as Ransom Olds, had become firmly established. Ford began production of a Model A, which imitated the Oldsmobile, and followed with other models, to the letter S. The public responded, and the company flourished. By 1907 profits exceeded $1,100,000, and the net worth of the company stood at $1,038,822.

Ford also defeated the Selden patent, which had been granted on a "road engine" in 1895. Rather than challenge the patent's validity, manufacturers secured a license to produce engines. When Ford was denied such a license, he fought back; after 8 years of litigation, the courts decided the patent was valid but not infringed. The case gave the Ford Company valuable publicity, with Ford cast as the underdog, but by the time the issue was settled, the situations had been reversed.

New Principles

In 1909 Ford made the momentous decision to manufacture only one type of car—the Model T, or the "Tin Lizzie." By now he firmly controlled the company, having bought out Malcomson. The Model T was durable, easy to operate, and economical; it sold for $850 and came in one color—black. Within 4 years Ford was producing over 40,000 cars per year.

During this rapid expansion Ford adhered to two principles: cutting costs by increasing efficiency and paying high wages to his employees. In production methods Ford believed the work should be brought by conveyor belt to the worker at waist-high level. This assembly-line technique required 7 years to perfect. In 1914 he startled the industrial world by raising the minimum wage to $5 a day, almost double the company's average wage. In addition, the "Tin

Lizzie'' had dropped in price to $600; it later went down to $360.

World War I

Ford was now an internationally known figure, but his public activities were less successful than his industrial ones. In 1915 his peace ship, the *Oskar II,* sailed to Europe to seek an end to World War I. His suit against the *Chicago Tribune* for calling him an anarchist received unfortunate publicity. In 1918 his race for the U.S. Senate as a Democrat met a narrow defeat. Ford's saddest mistake was his approval of an anti-Semitic campaign waged by the Ford-owned newspaper, the *Dearborn Independent.*

When the United States entered World War I, Ford's output of military equipment and his promise to rebate all profits on war production (he never did) silenced critics. By the end of the conflict his giant River Rouge plant, the world's largest industrial facility, was nearing completion. Ford gained total control of the company by buying the outstanding stock.

In the early 1920s the company continued its rapid growth, at one point producing 60 percent of the total United States output. But clouds stirred on the horizon. Ford was an inflexible man and continued to rely on the Model T, even as public tastes shifted. By the middle of the decade Ford had lost his dominant position to the General Motors Company. He finally saw his error and in 1927 stopped production of the Model T. However, since the new Model A was not produced for 18 months, there was a good deal of unemployment among Ford workers. The new car still did not permanently overtake the GM competition, Chevrolet; and Ford remained second.

Final Years

Ford's last years were frustrating. He never accepted the changes brought about by the Depression and the 1930s New Deal. He fell under the spell of Harry Bennett, a notorious figure with underworld connections, who, as head of Ford's security department, influenced every phase of company operations and created friction between Ford and his son Edsel. For various reasons Ford alone in his industry refused to cooperate with the National Recovery Administration. He did not like labor unions, refused to recognize the United Automobile Workers, and brutally repressed their attempts to organize the workers of his company.

Ford engaged in some philanthropic activity, such as the Henry Ford Hospital in Detroit. The original purpose of the Ford Foundation, established in 1936 and now one of the world's largest foundations, was to avoid estate taxes. Ford's greatest philanthropic accomplishment was the Ford Museum and Greenfield Village in Dearborn, Michigan.

A stroke in 1938 slowed Ford, but he did not trust Edsel and so continued to exercise control of his company. During World War II Ford at first made pacifist statements but did retool and contribute greatly to the war effort. Ford's grandson Henry Ford II took over the company after the war. Henry Ford died on April 7, 1947.

Further Reading

Ford's own books, written in collaboration with Samuel Crowther, provide useful information: *My Life and Work* (1922), *Today and Tomorrow* (1926), and *Moving Forward* (1930). The writings on Ford are voluminous. The most authoritative on the man and the company are by Allan Nevins and Frank E. Hill, *Ford: The Times, the Man, the Company* (1954), *Ford: Expansion and Challenge, 1915-1933* (1957), and *Ford: Decline and Rebirth, 1933-1962* (1963). The best short studies are Keith Theodore Sward, *The Legend of Henry Ford* (1948), and Roger Burlingame, *Henry Ford: A Great Life in Brief* (1955). More recent works are Booton Herndon, *Ford: An Unconventional Biography of the Men and Their Times* (1969), and John B. Rae, *Henry Ford* (1969). Of the books by men who worked with Ford, Charles E. Sorensen, *My Forty Years with Ford* (1956), is worth reading. See also William Adams Simonds, *Henry Ford: His Life, His Work, His Genius* (1943), and William C. Richards, *The Last Billionaire: Henry Ford* (1948). □

John Sean O'Feeney Ford

John Sean O'Feeney Ford (ca. 1895-1973) was an American film director who, with other pioneers in the movie industry, transformed a rudimentary entertainment medium into a highly personalized and expressive art form.

John Sean O'Feeney Ford was born around February 1, 1895, the youngest child of Irish immigrant parents. Ford graduated from high school in 1913 and attended the University of Maine. He entered the film industry in 1914 as a property man, directed his first film, *Tornado,* in 1917, and continued to produce silent films at the rate of five to ten each year. He established his reputation as a leading silent-film maker with *The Iron Horse* (1924), one of the first epic westerns, and *Four Sons* (1928), his initial attempt at a personal cinematic statement. Both films are now part of the silent-screen museum repertory.

But Ford was to make his great contribution as a director of talking motion pictures and in 1935 produced *The Informer,* often described as the first creative sound film. Dealing with a tragic incident in the Irish Rebellion of 1922, Ford and his scriptwriter transformed a melodramatic novel into a compassionate, intensely dramatic, visually expressive film. It received the Academy Award and the New York Film Critics Award for best direction. That same year Ford directed *Steamboat 'Round the Bend* and *The Whole Town's Talking,* which though neglected at the time are now considered on a par with *The Informer.*

With *Stagecoach* (1939) Ford established the American western as mythic archetype. His sculptured landscapes and pictorial compositions immediately impressed critics and audiences. With this film Ford formally renounced the realistic montage film theories of D.W. Griffith and the Russian director Sergei Eisenstein to develop a film esthetic that substituted camera movement and precise framing of spatial relationships for dramatic cutting and visual contrast. Ford utilized auditory effects to increase a scene's psychological tension.

In 1940 Ford began work on the film version of John Steinbeck's Depression novel, *The Grapes of Wrath*. Ignoring Steinbeck's propagandistic intentions and philosophizing, Ford concentrated on the human elements in the story and unified the episodic structure of the novel with a controlled use of visual symbolism. The film remains remarkable in several respects, most notably in Ford's ability to achieve an appropriately harsh and naturalistic style without sacrificing his poetic sensibility. This success brought the director his second Oscar and New York Film Critics Award. The following year Ford's most romantic film, *How Green Was My Valley*, a lyrical and nostalgic evocation of life in a Welsh mining town, earned him his third series of awards.

In addition to his work for the American Office of Strategic Services during World War II, Ford produced two excellent naval documentaries in 1945, a sex hygiene film for soldiers, and a commercial war movie, *They Were Expendable* (1945). After the war Ford released his second great western, *My Darling Clementine* (1946), which combined epic realism with poetic luminosity to create the most beautiful western to date. This was Ford's finest film. Only slightly less successful were *Fort Apache* (1948) and *She Wore a Yellow Ribbon* (1949). His best film of the early 1950s was *The Quiet Man* (1952), a delightfully energetic comedy about exotic domestic rituals in a small Irish province, for which he received his fourth Oscar. *The Searchers* (1957) was an intense, psychological western about a group of pioneers seeking a young girl captured by the Indians. Ford next turned to the conflicts of ward politics in the Irish section of Boston in *The Last Hurrah* (1958).

With the exception of *Sergeant Rutledge* (1961) and *The Man Who Shot Liberty Valance* (1963), Ford's films of the 1960s were not on the same level as his earlier work. *Cheyenne Autumn* (1964), treating the tragedy of the American Indian, lacked his characteristic personal involvement and visual freshness. *Young Cassidy*, a biography of writer Sean O'Casey, was abandoned by the ailing Ford and completed by a lesser British director. Partially deaf and afflicted with poor vision (he wore a patch over one eye), Ford lived with his wife in Los Angeles during the early 1970s and died in 1973.

Over the years Ford evolved a concise cinematic vocabulary, consisting of subtle camera movement, graduated long shots, and unobtrusive editing. Notable for their realistic detail, pictorial beauty, and dynamic action sequences, his films have exerted a pronounced influence on the work of other directors. Winner of numerous awards and international citations, Ford is unique among American directors in having won the admiration of the middlebrow, establishment critics for his early social dramas (*The Informer, The Grapes of Wrath*) and the respect of the intellectual European and avant-garde critics for the more stylized films (*My Darling Clementine, The Searchers*) of his later years. As film historian Andrew Sarris recorded, "Ford developed his craft in the twenties, achieved dramatic force in the thirties, epic sweep in the forties, and symbolic evocation in the fifties."

Further Reading

The outstanding critical and biographical studies of Ford are in French. The only full-length work in English is Peter Bogdanovich, *John Ford* (1968). Of particular interest are sections in Roger Manvell, *Film* (1946); George Bluestone, *Novels into Film* (1957); and Andrew Sarris, *The American Cinema, 1929-1968* (1968). Jean Mitry's *Cahiers du cinema* interview with the director can be found in Andrew Sarris, ed., *Interviews with Film Directors* (1968). □

James Forman

James Forman (born 1928), a writer, journalist, political philosopher, human rights activist, and revolutionary socialist, was a leader of the Student Non-violent Coordinating Committee (SNCC) during most of its active period.

James Forman was born in Chicago, Illinois, on October 4, 1928. He spent his early life on a farm in Marshall County, Mississippi. Upon graduating from Englewood High School in Chicago, he attended junior college for a semester. He then joined the U.S. Air Force as a personnel classification specialist. Having completed a four-year tour-of-duty, he enrolled at the University of Southern California; however, his studies were interrupted when a false arrest charge kept him from taking his final examinations. This also gave a new meaning to the racism he had observed in the armed services and elsewhere.

Returning from Chicago, Forman excelled in the intellectually-charged environment of Roosevelt University. There he served as president of the student body and chief delegate to the 1956 National Student Association. In the fall of 1957 he began graduate studies at Boston University in African affairs, yet could not reconcile himself to studying Africa when children in Little Rock, Arkansas, were trying to integrate a school. He left Boston and went to the South as a reporter for the *Chicago Defender*. During this period he also wrote a novel about the ideal interracial civil rights group whose philosophy of non-violence would produce massive social change.

Forman returned to Chicago to teach, and became involved with the Emergency Relief Committee, a group affiliated with the Congress of Racial Equality (CORE) and dedicated to providing food and clothing to black sharecroppers evicted from their homes for registering to vote in Fayette County, Tennessee. In 1960 he formally joined the civil rights movement by going to Monroe, North Carolina, to assist Robert F. Williams, head of the local chapter of the National Association for the Advancement of Colored People (NAACP). In his confrontation with local white people, Williams had been censured by the NAACP for his call of armed self-defense. Though still teaching in Chicago, Forman maintained his ties with the southern student activists and from them heard about a newly formed group called SNCC (Student Non-violent Coordinating Committee), which was structured much like the organization his novel suggested. After some debate, Forman left teaching and went to SNCC's national headquarters in Atlanta. Within a week he was appointed executive secretary, in 1961.

Forman's greatest contribution to SNCC in eight years of involvement was his ability to provide the administrative skills and political sophistication the organization needed. He hired an efficient staff, brought professionalism to the research and fund-raising activities as well as discipline and direction to SNCC's various factions. He realized the need for specialized skills and made office-work, research, and fund-raising all part of SNCC's revolutionary activities.

As executive secretary of SNCC, Forman was involved in every major civil rights controversy in the nation. He coordinated the famous "Freedom Rides" and advocated the use of white civil rights workers in white communities. He started the Albany Movement, which paved the way for Martin Luther King's campaign there. He criticized the 1963 March on Washington as a "sell-out" by black leaders to the Kennedy administration and the liberal-labor vote. In 1964 Forman and Fannie Lou Hamer opposed the compromise worked out by the Democratic Party and the Mississippi Freedom Democratic Party at the Democratic National Convention. In addition, he questioned the capitalistic orientation of mainstream black leaders and castigated them for not understanding the correlations among capitalism, racism, and imperialism. Forman also noted that most civil rights groups were not effective or enduring because they were "leader-centered" rather than being "group or people-centered." Some of those other civil rights leaders saw Forman as something of a hothead. As James Farmer noted in his autobiography, *Lay Bare the Heart*, "Forman was volatile and uncompromising, an angry young man. His head had been clubbed many times on the front lines in

Dixie. He was impatient with Urban League and NAACP types; he was nervous and perhaps a trifle battle-fatigued."

As director of the International Affairs Commission of SNCC, Forman and ten other staff members went to Africa in 1964 as guests of the government of Guinea. This trip began to alter his views, and he developed a global analysis of racism. His understanding was shaped by reading the works of Frantz Fanon, Che Guevara, Kwame Nkhrumah, Fidel Castro, and Malcolm X. In 1967 he delivered a paper in Zambia entitled: "The Invisible Struggle Against Racism, Colonialism and Apartheid." His internationalist orientation lead him to accept an appointment in the Black Panther Party (BPP) as minister of foreign affairs and director of political education in 1968. (Early in 1967 SNCC and the BPP had coordinated a number of ventures and activities.)

This alliance soon ended, and Forman even left SNCC in 1969 when he was essentially deposed by H. Rap Brown, then chairman of the committee. Before Forman left, he delivered one of the most provocative challenges to come out of the 1960s. In a speech given in April of 1969 at the Black Economic Development Conference, Forman called for "a revolutionary black vanguard" to seize the government and redirect its resources. In addition, in his now famous "Black Manifesto" he demanded that "white Christian Churches and Jewish Synagogues, which are part and parcel of the system of capitalism," pay half-a-billion dollars to blacks for reparations for slavery and racial exploitation. He wanted the money to create new black institutions. Specifically, he demanded a Southern Land Bank, four major publishing and printing enterprises, four television networks, a Black Labor Strike and Defense Fund Training Center, and a new black university. Interesting enough, some funds did come in; however, most were given to the traditional black churches and organizations.

In some ways, "The Black Manifesto" was Forman's greatest moment. He had linked contemporary wealth with historic exploitation; thus, he presented the ultimate challenge to American society. In the early 1970s Forman spent most of his time writing his mammoth work on black revolutionaries. In 1977 he enrolled as a graduate student at Cornell University. He received a Masters of Professional Studies (M.P.S.) in African and Afro-American history in 1980.

In 1983 Forman served a one-year term as legislative assistant to the president of the Metropolitan Washington Central Labor Council (AFL-CIO). He was chairman of the Unemployed and Poverty Council (UPAC), a civil and human rights group in Washington, D.C. As one of the major leaders of the civil rights era, James Forman continued to represent a dimension of black activism which sought to develop a revolutionary organization in America. He also received a Ph.D. in 1985 from the Union of Experimental Colleges and Universities in cooperation with the Institute of Policy Studies. In April 1990, Forman was honored by the National Conference of Black Mayors, who awarded him their Fannie Lou Hamer Freedom Award.

Further Reading

Forman was a prolific writer. He was most noted for: *1967: High Tide of Black Resistance* (1967); *Sammy Younge, Jr.: The First Black College Student to Die in the Black Liberation Movement* (1968); *Liberation: Viendra d'une Chose Noir* (1968); "The Black Manifesto" (1969); *The Political Thought of James Forman* (1970); *The Making of Black Revolutionaries* (1972, 1985); and *Self-Detention: An Examination of the Question and its Applications to the African-American People* (1980, 1984). He also wrote for newspapers, journals, and magazines. Books in which Forman is discussed in detail include *Black Awakening in Capitalist America: An Analytical History* by Robert L. Allen (1969); *In Struggle: SNCC and the Black Awakening of the 1960s* by Claybourne Carson (1981); *Power on the Left: American Radical Movements Since 1946* by Lawrence Lader (1979); and *The River of No Return: The Autobiography of a Black Militant and the Life and Death of SNCC* by Cleveland Sellers and Robert Terrell (1973). A Web site containing information on SNCC's formation in the 1960s, and an article entitled *SNCC: Basis of Black Power* can be found at http://jefferson.village.virginia.edu/sixties/HTML_docs/Primary/manifestos/SNCC_bla. ☐

Timothy Thomas Fortune

Timothy Thomas Fortune (1856–1928) was one of the most prominent black journalists involved in the flourishing black press of the post–Civil War era.

Though not as well known today as many of his contemporaries, T. Thomas Fortune was the foremost African American journalist of the late nineteenth and early twentieth centuries. Using his editorial position at a series of black newspapers in New York City, Fortune established himself as a leading spokesman and defender of the rights of African Americans in both the South and the North.

Besides using his journalistic pulpit to demand equal economic opportunity for blacks and equal protection under the law, Fortune founded the Afro-American League, an equal rights organization that preceded the Niagara Movement and the National Association for the Advancement of Colored People (NAACP), to extend this battle into the political arena. But his great hopes for the league never materialized, and he gradually began to abandon his militant position in favor of educator/activist Booker T. Washington's compromising, accommodationist stance. Fortune's later years, wracked by alcohol abuse, depression, and poverty, precipitated a decline in his once-prominent reputation as well.

Fortune was born a slave in Marianna, Florida, in 1856. Early in his boyhood he was exposed to the three factors that later dominated his life—journalism, white racism, and politics. After slavery was abolished in 1863, his father, Emanuel Fortune, went on to become a member of the 1868 Florida constitutional convention and the state's House of Representatives. Southern whites, resentful of black political participation, intimidated blacks through acts of violence; Jackson County, the Fortunes' hometown, witnessed some of the worst examples. Continued threats from the Ku Klux Klan forced the elder Fortune to move to Jacksonville, where he remained active in Florida politics until the 1890s.

Young Fortune became a page in the state Senate, observing firsthand some of the more sordid aspects of post–Civil War Reconstruction era politics, in particular white politicians who took advantage of black voters. He also preferred to spend his time hanging around the offices of various local newspapers rather than in school. As a result, when he left Florida in 1876 at the age of 19, his formal education consisted of only a few months spent in schools sponsored by the Freedmen's Bureau, but his informal education had trained him to be a printer's apprentice.

Fortune entered the preparatory department of Howard University in Washington, D.C. Lack of money limited his stay to one year, and he spent part of his time there working in the printshop of the *People's Advocate,* an early black newspaper. While in Washington he married his Florida sweetheart, Carrie Smiley. For the next two years he taught school and read voraciously on his own in literature, history, government, and law. Largely self-taught, he developed a distinctive writing and eloquent speaking style that few of his contemporaries could match.

Back in Florida, Fortune seethed under the South's racial intolerance, which seemed to increase after Reconstruction, the period of postwar transition during which the southern states were reintegrated into the Union. Leaving for good in 1881, he moved to New York City, working as a printer at the *New York Sun.* Soon he caught the attention of *Sun* editor Charles A. Dana, who promoted him to the editorial staff. But within the year Fortune left to follow in the footsteps of earlier black writers like John B. Russwurm and Frederick Douglass who had established their own newspapers to voice the black cause. Securing financial backing, he became editor and co-owner first of the weekly *New York Globe,* and then of the *New York Freeman,* which in 1887 was renamed the *New York Age.* It soon became the country's leading black newspaper.

Part of the reason for the papers' success was their high literary quality and Fortune's meticulous editing. More important, however, were their distinctive editorials written by his talented pen. Fortune's unabashed and indignant denunciations of American racism, as well as his reasoned arguments in favor of equal treatment and equality for blacks, made him the most influential black journalist in the United States.

Early on he summed up his viewpoint in an essay entitled "The Editor's Mission." Blacks must have a voice in deciding their own destiny, Fortune wrote, and not trust whites to define their "place." Since most of the northern and southern white press was opposed to equal rights, blacks needed their own newspapers to counter this influence. "The mark of color," he said, made the African American "a social pariah, to be robbed, beaten, and lynched," and one who "has got his own salvation to work out, of equality before the laws, with almost the entire population of the country arrayed against him." Leading this struggle was the special mission of the black editor.

Typical of his editorials was Fortune's scathing critique of the U.S. Supreme Court's 1883 decision, which declared the Civil Rights Act of 1875 unconstitutional. (The Civil Rights Act had guaranteed equal justice to all, regardless of race.) The ruling left blacks feeling as if they had been "baptized in ice water," he wrote. "We are declared to be created equal, and entitled to certain rights," but given the Court's interpretation "there is no law to protect us in the enjoyment of them. We are aliens in our own land."

The Militant Editor

Increasingly bitter over governmental failure to protect its black citizens, Fortune began to urge blacks not only to defend themselves with physical force, but also "to assert their manhood and citizenship" by striking back against white outrages. "We do not counsel violence," he wrote in a *Globe* editorial, "we counsel manly retaliation." Frequent similar remarks began to alarm both whites and cautious blacks, giving Fortune a growing reputation as a dangerous agitator.

Continuing his outspoken crusade against segregation and for equal rights, Fortune campaigned against racially separate schools in New York City. Occasionally he was arrested for protesting against racial discrimination in public accommodations. Typical of his denunciation of any form of racial distinction was his attack on antimiscegenation laws, which prohibited sexual relations between a man and a woman of different races, and his defense of the rights of persons of different racial backgrounds to marry. He also began popularizing the term "Afro-American" in contrast to the more popular use at the time of "colored" and "Negro."

The publication of *Black and White: Land, Labor and Politics in the South* in 1884 was the crowning effort of this radical phase of Fortune's career. Divided into two parts, the book first bitterly and eloquently rebuked American racism. Speaking firsthand, Fortune described the prejudices of white society, particularly in the current South where blacks "are more absolutely under the control of the southern whites; they are more systematically robbed of their labor; they are more poorly housed, clothed and fed, than under the slave regime."

In the book's second half, Fortune applied the theories of American economist Henry George and German political philosopher Karl Marx to southern society, portraying blacks as akin to peasant and laboring classes throughout the world. He predicted that the region's future battles would not be racial or political, but labor-based. Calling for organization and union between northern and southern laborers, black and white, he concluded that "the condition of the black and white laborer is the same, and . . . consequently their cause is common."

Redemption Through Politics

Though his primary roles remained those of editor and journalist, Fortune increasingly regarded political activity as indispensable to achieving his goal of equal rights for all. Black Americans would have to use their political rights to protect themselves and determine their own destiny. But his disillusionment with the existing political parties and skepticism of white politicians made this a tortuous path to chart or follow.

Unlike most African Americans of his era, Fortune held no special affinity for the Republican Party. While most black leaders and black newspapers felt a special allegiance to the party of Abraham Lincoln, Fortune denounced the Compromise of 1877, whereby the Republicans ended Reconstruction and sacrificed the constitutional rights of southern blacks to retain the presidency.

His 1885 pamphlet, *The Negro in Politics,* openly challenged Frederick Douglass's dictum that "the Republican Party is the ship, all else the open sea." Instead, Fortune decreed "Race first, then party!" Declaring that the Republicans had deserted their black supporters, he actively campaigned for Grover Cleveland, the Democratic presidential candidate, in 1888. But after Cleveland's defeat, he acknowledged that the southern-dominated Democratic party was hopelessly racist and grudgingly became a nominal Republican.

Afro-American League

Besides attempting to mobilize black Americans through the press and political action, Fortune proposed the creation of an Afro-American League. As set forth in an 1887 editorial, he envisioned a national all-black coalition of state and local chapters to assert equal rights and protest discrimination, disenfranchisement, lynching, and mob law.

In December of 1889, more than one hundred delegates from 23 states met in Chicago to organize the league. Their goal was attaining full citizenship and equality. Speaking as temporary chairman, Fortune declared, "We shall no longer accept in silence a condition which degrades manhood and makes a mockery of our citizenship."

Instead of the controversial Fortune, delegates elected a more conciliatory figure as league president: Joseph C. Price, president of Livingstone College. Fortune became the secretary. Despite his strenuous efforts to organize local chapters and raise funds, the league faltered. At its second convention in 1891, delegates came from only seven states. Hopes for a significant legal victory in a railroad discrimination case to publicize the organization and its mission were thwarted. Lack of funds and mass support caused the league to fold in 1893.

Five years later the idea was resurrected as the National Afro-American Council. Fortune now had doubts about such an organization and initially refused to accept its presidency. But he remained close to the group and became president in 1902. Like its predecessor, the council made few achievements. Fortune, discouraged over the seeming apathy of the black masses, resigned the presidency in 1904.

The Perils of Independent Thinking

After the death of Frederick Douglass in 1895, Fortune became the best known militant black spokesman in the North. But his crusading attitude and political independence exacted a toll. Most small newspapers of his era, white or black, depended upon political advertising and patronage as their main source of income. Black newspapers generally supported the Republican Party. When Fortune proudly trumpeted his independent political leanings, he effectively closed the door on Republican monetary support or advertising.

As a result, Fortune's papers faced recurring financial crises. Compelled to seek outside work, he frequently freelanced for his old paper, the *Sun,* and many other publications. Gradually he became dependent upon small sums from Booker T. Washington, the more pragmatic and conciliatory educator and black leader.

Alliance With Washington

Washington and Fortune seemingly made strange bedfellows. Apparent opposites—the former a soft-spoken accommodationist and the latter a militant agitator—in actuality, they were very good friends who corresponded almost daily throughout the 1890s. Their relationship was based on mutual affection, mutual self-interest, similar backgrounds, and the same ultimate goals for people of color. Born as slaves in the same year and growing up in the Reconstruction South, both men felt a deep obligation to their native region and a duty to improve the condition of southern blacks.

Like Washington, Fortune emphasized the importance of education and believed that practical vocational training was the immediate educational need for blacks as they emerged from slavery. He, too, counseled success through thrift, hard work, and the acquisition of land, believing that education and economic progress were necessary before blacks could attain full citizenship rights.

Although the two leaders played different roles and presented contrasting public images, their alliance was mutually useful. Fortune was editor of the leading black newspaper, and Washington needed the *Age* to present and defend his ideas and methods. Fortune also helped edit Washington's speeches and was the ghostwriter for books and articles appearing under his name, including *A New Negro for a New Century* and *The Negro in Business.*

Similarly, as Washington's reputation and influence grew, particularly in Republican circles, he could be a powerful friend. For years he secretly subsidized the *Age,* helping to keep it solvent. Fortune hoped for Washington's intercession with President Theodore Roosevelt for a permanent political appointment, but all he received was a temporary mission to the Philippines in 1903.

Fortune's dependency on Washington continued to grow. He bought an expensive house, Maple Hill, in Red Bank, New Jersey, in 1901. Its mortgage payments, added to the financial woes of the *Age,* compounded his monetary problems. As attacks mounted on Washington for his accommodationist methods, Fortune felt compelled to defend his friend. But Washington's more militant black critics, notably W. E. B. Du Bois and the leaders of the 1905 Niagara Movement, simply denounced Fortune as an untrustworthy, former "Afro-American agitator."

A new generation of black leaders was appearing, and Fortune's influence was beginning to wane. He broke with Washington and joined members of the Niagara Group in criticizing President Roosevelt's discharge of black troops following a riot in Brownsville, Texas, in 1906.

Declining Years

Needing Washington's support though ideologically drawn to his detractors, Fortune faced a crossroads: his life began to disintegrate. Disillusioned and discouraged after his long efforts on behalf of black America, he separated from his wife, increased his heavy drinking, and suffered what his contemporaries described as a nervous breakdown. Washington took control of the *Age* in 1907 by becoming one of the principal stockholders. Later that year Fortune sold his interest in the paper to Fred R. Moore, who became the new editor. This effectively ended Fortune's influence as a black leader.

Now a confirmed alcoholic, Fortune spent the next several years as a virtual derelict, unable to find steady employment. Desperate, he wrote a plaintive letter to Washington's secretary in 1913 asking: "What am I to do? The Negro papers are not able to pay for extra work and the daily papers do not care for Negro productions of any kind. Under such circumstances I face the future with $5 in hand and 57 years as handicap."

From time to time he found work as an editorial writer and correspondent for the *Age* and the *Amsterdam News.* He edited the *Washington Sun* for a few months before it folded. Slowly he recovered. In 1919 he joined the staff of the *Norfolk Journal and Guide,* continuing to write commentaries and editorials for the rest of his life. He became editor of *Negro World,* black nationalist leader Marcus Garvey's publication, in 1923, remaining there until his death in 1928.

In "The Quick and the Dead," an article published soon after Washington's death, Fortune attempted to evaluate his own role as a black leader. He praised his early crusading efforts for civil rights as editor and then organizer of the Afro-American League, attributing his failure to apathy and lack of support in the black community.

Many critics agree that it was all but impossible for anyone to achieve the ambitious goals Fortune had set given the climate of the times in which he lived. And when he abandoned his militant ideology to promote Washington's more accommodationist methods, Fortune destroyed his own credibility as a leader—and his personal integrity as well. This was something he could not live with, and it seemed to destroy him. As Emma Lou Thornbrough wrote in her biography *T. Thomas Fortune: Militant Journalist,* "Unable to bend as Washington had, he was broken."

Further Reading

Fortune, T. Thomas, *Black and White: Land, Labor and Politics in the South,* Arno Press, 1968.

Franklin, John Hope and August Meier, editors, *Black Leaders of the 20th Century,* University of Illinois Press, 1981.

Franklin, John Hope, *From Slavery to Freedom: A History of Negro Americans,* Alfred A. Knopf, 1947.

Thornbrough, Emma Lou, *T. Thomas Fortune: Militant Journalist,* University of Chicago Press, 1972. □

Bob Fosse

Legendary director/choreographer Bob Fosse (1927–1987) is known for hits such as *Sweet Charity*, with its trademark jazzy number, "Hey Big Spender," and *Cabaret*.

Bob Fosse began his unusual career as a dancer in the late 1940s, touring with companies of *Call Me Mister* and *Make Mine Manhattan*. After playing the lead in a summer-stock production of *Pal Joey*, then choreographing a showcase called *Talent 52*, Fosse was given a screen test by M-G-M and went on to appear in the film *Kiss Me Kate* (1953). This appearance, in a highly original dance number, led to Fosse's first job as a choreographer, the Jerome Robbins-directed Broadway hit *The Pajama Game* (1954). Soon after, he met the talented dancer Gwen Verdon, and the two proceeded to collaborate on several hit shows, including *Damn Yankees* (1955, film 1958), *New Girl in Town* (1957), and *Redhead* (1959). (Fosse and Verdon married soon after.) He was also frequently sought out as the "doctor" on shows in trouble, especially *How to Succeed in Business Without Really Trying* and *Little Me* (both 1962).

Choreography Showcased Unique Style

Fosse's best collaboration with Verdon, *Sweet Charity* (1966, film 1969), demonstrated their perfect compatibility as a creative team and also flaunted his trademark style as a choreographer. Strongly influenced by choreographer Jack Cole, Fosse staged dance numbers that were highly stylized, using staccato movements and erotic suggestion. The

"Steam Heat" number from *The Pajama Game* and "Hey Big Spender" from *Sweet Charity* were trademark Fosse numbers—jazzy, machinelike motion and cocky, angular, even grotesque poses. He favored style over substance (his patented knee slides and spread-finger hands), and minimalistic costuming (all black, accentuated by hats and gloves). A perfectionist, Fosse liked detail in his choreography and would position his dancers down to the angles of their feet or their little fingers. As his career progressed, Fosse became increasingly fascinated with expressing sexuality and decadence through dance.

Had Hit with *Cabaret*

Fosse's peak year was 1973. In addition to his *Cabaret* Oscar, he nabbed Tonys for his direction and choreography of the Broadway musical *Pippin*, the eerily magical and sexually decadent story of the son of King Charlemagne on a journey of self-discovery. Like *Cabaret* , *Pippin* featured exaggerated, grotesque makeup and costuming and erotic dance numbers. Fosse's experiment—to place the story and music at the service of choreography—paid off when *Pippin* (helped by a television advertising campaign) became Fosse's longest-running Broadway show. That same year he won an Emmy for directing and choreographing Minnelli's television special *Liza with a Z*, which garnered high ratings and featured groundbreaking production numbers. In 1973 Fosse seemed to be everywhere.

Heart Attack Led to Autobiographical Film

In *Lenny* (1974), an exploration of the life of controversial comic Lenny Bruce, Fosse experimented with a mock-documentary filmmaking style. He identified with Bruce's attempt to liberate inhibited audiences with shocking and challenging material. Fosse suffered a heart attack while editing *Lenny* and rehearsing the successful Broadway musical *Chicago* (1975), which starred Verdon as notorious murderess Roxie Hart. *Chicago* was a cynical, stylized homage to 1920s-era burlesque and vaudeville. In the fascinating but disturbing film *All That Jazz* (1979), he used the heart attack (including a filmed bypass operation) to kill off the main character, an obsessive, womanizing, workaholic director clearly based on Fosse. His other 1970s stage musical was the innovative *Dancin'* (1978), which featured three acts constructed purely of dance numbers, eliminating story, song, and characters.

Fosse's work in the 1980s received mixed responses. His film *Star 80* (1983) explored the violent, obsessive relationship between Playboy-model-turned-actress Dorothy Stratten and Paul Snider, the husband who brutally murdered her in 1980. Audiences and critics did not respond to the tough, gruesome subject matter. Nor did they appear to enjoy the jazz ballet *Big Deal* (1986), Fosse's last Broadway show. A revival of *Sweet Charity* in 1986 was more successful, but just as the touring company was about to be launched, Fosse died of a heart attack on 23 September 1987.

Further Reading

Martin Gottfried, *All His Jazz: The Life and Death of Bob Fosse* (New York: Bantam Books, 1990).

Kevin Boyd Grubb, *Razzle Dazzle: The Life and Work of Bob Fosse* (New York: St. Martin's Press, 1989). ☐

Felix Frankfurter

Felix Frankfurter (1882-1965), an associate justice of the U.S. Supreme Court, demonstrated a strong sense for civil liberties.

Felix Frankfurter was born in Vienna, Austria, on Nov. 15, 1882. At the age of 12 he and his six brothers and sisters were taken to the United States. Life on the East Side of New York City served as the background for Frankfurter's social interests.

Following graduation from the College of the City of New York in 1902, Frankfurter entered Harvard Law School. He became editor of the *Harvard Law Review* and earned his degree in 1906 with honors. Henry Stimson, the U.S. attorney for the Southern District of New York, appointed Frankfurter an assistant in 1906. When President William Howard Taft named Stimson secretary of war in 1911, Stimson took Frankfurter along as law officer of the Bureau of Insular Affairs.

Frankfurter returned to Harvard Law School as a professor in 1914. Eventually he was named the first Byrne professor of administrative law. His Harvard years were broken by government service during World War I. As a special assistant to the secretary of war, and later in the same capacity to the secretary of labor, he helped formulate policy. Again at Harvard, Frankfurter became involved in numerous cases of national prominence: the Scopes trial (1925), the silk strike in New Jersey, and the attempt to suppress the *American Mercury* in Boston. He fought for the release of Nicola Sacco and Bartolomeo Vanzetti in 1927 and helped found the American Civil Liberties Union. During Franklin D. Roosevelt's presidency Frankfurter worked on the Security Exchange Act of 1934 and helped formulate the Utility Holding Company Act.

Frankfurter was made a Supreme Court justice in 1939. From the beginning his opinions were challenged as extremely liberal. However, he took a resolute position on the Constitution and its place in American society. He understood that this document could survive only so long as the Court guarded its prerogatives.

Decisions in the civil rights area found Frankfurter strongly for the individual. His opinion on the movie *The Miracle* was typical. When the highest court in New York State ruled the film sacrilegious, Frankfurter saw this as an invasion of private rights. He was also strongly opposed to congressional committees and their investigating procedures.

Frankfurter had married Marion A. Denman after World War I. The marriage produced no children, and during World War II the Frankfurters adopted three English refugee children.

Further Reading

An excellent biography is Helen S. Thomas, *Felix Frankfurter, Scholar on the Bench* (1960). See also Wallace Mendelson, ed., *Felix Frankfurter: A Tribute* (1964), and Liva Baker, *Felix Frankfurter* (1969). Special studies are Patricia A. Edgeworth, *Mr. Justice Frankfurter and the Administration of Criminal Justice* (1955), which describes an area of law not usually associated with Frankfurter and offers a new view of him, and Clyde Edward Jacobs, *Justice Frankfurter and Civil Liberties* (1961). ☐

Benjamin Franklin

Benjamin Franklin (1706-1790) was a leader of America's Revolutionary generation. His character and thought were shaped by a blending of Puritan heritage, Enlightenment philosophy, and the New World environment.

Benjamin Franklin was born in Boston into a pious Puritan household. His forebears had come to New England in 1683 to avoid the zealous Anglicanism of England's Restoration era. Franklin's father was a candlemaker and skillful mechanic, but, his son said, his "great Excellence lay in a sound Understanding, and solid Judgment." Benjamin praised his mother as "a discreet and virtuous Woman" who raised a family of 13 children. In honoring his parents and in his affection for New England ways, Franklin demonstrated the permanence of his Puritan heritage.

His Philosophy

Rejecting the Calvinist theology of his father, Franklin opened himself to the more secular world view of Sir Isaac Newton and John Locke. He read the deist philosophers, virtually memorized the English paper *Spectator,* and otherwise gave allegiance to the Enlightenment. Like his favorite author, Joseph Addison, Franklin sought to add the good sense and tolerance of the new philosophy to his Puritan earnestness. Thus, by the time he left home at the age of 17, his character and attitude toward life had already achieved a basic orientation.

The circumstances of his flight from home also reveal essential qualities. Denied a formal education by his family's poverty, Franklin became an apprentice to his brother James, printer of a Boston newspaper. While learning the technical part of the business, Franklin read every word that came into the shop and was soon writing clever pieces signed "Silence Dogood," satirizing the Boston establishment. When the authorities imprisoned James for his criticisms, Benjamin continued the paper himself. Having thus learned to resist oppression, he refused to suffer his brother's petty tyrannies and in 1723 ran away to Philadelphia.

Successful Businessman

Penniless and without friends in the new city, Franklin soon demonstrated his enterprise and skill as a printer and gained employment. In 1724 he went to England, where he quickly became a master printer, sowed wild oats, and lived among the aspiring writers of London. He returned to Philadelphia and soon had his own press, publishing a newspa-

per (*Pennsylvania Gazette*), *Poor Richard's Almanack,* and a good share of the public printing of the province. He became clerk of the Pennsylvania Assembly and postmaster of Philadelphia, at the same time operating a bookshop and entering partnerships with printers from Nova Scotia to the West Indies. He was so successful that at the age of 42 he retired. He received a comfortable income from his business for 20 more years.

Franklin philosophized about his success and applied his understanding to civic enterprises. The philosophy appears in the adages of "Poor Richard" and in the scheme for moral virtue Franklin explained later in his famous *Autobiography.* He extolled hard work, thriftiness, and honesty as the poor man's means for escaping the prison of want and explained how any man could develop an exemplary character with practice and perseverance. Though sayings like "Sloth maketh all things difficult, but Industry all easy" do not amount to a profound philosophy of life (as Franklin knew perfectly well), they do suggest useful first steps for self-improvement. The huge circulation of both the sayings of "Poor Richard" (under the title "The Way to Wealth") and the *Autobiography,* plus their distorted use by miserly and small-minded apostles of thrift, led later to scathing assaults on Franklin by Nathaniel Hawthorne, Mark Twain, and D. H. Lawrence—but they in fact criticize a caricature, not the whole Franklin.

Civic Leader

Franklin became involved in civic improvement in 1727 by organizing the Junto, a club of aspiring tradesmen like himself, that met each week. In the unformed society of Philadelphia it seemed obvious to these men that their success in business and improvement of the city's life required the same thing: plans and institutions to deal with needs cooperatively. Thus, Franklin led the Junto in sponsoring civic improvements: a library, a fire company, a learned society, a college, an insurance company, and a hospital. He also made effective proposals for a militia; for paving, cleaning, and lighting the streets; and for a night watch. His simple but influential social belief that men of goodwill, organizing and acting together, could deal effectively with civic concerns remained with him throughout his life.

Work in Science

Franklin next turned to science. He had already invented the Pennsylvania fireplace (soon called the Franklin stove). His attention fastened primarily on electricity. He read the new treatises on the subject and acquired ingenious equipment. In his famous kite experiment, proving that lightning is a form of electricity, he linked laboratory experiments with static electricity to the great universal force and made a previously mysterious and terrifying natural phenomenon understandable. Franklin's letters concerning his discoveries and theories about electricity to the Royal Society in London brought him fame. The invention of the lightning rod, which soon appeared on buildings all over the world, added to his stature. His scientific ingenuity, earning him election to the Royal Society in 1756, also found outlet in the theory of heat, charting the Gulf Stream, ship design, meteorology, and the invention of bifocal lenses and a harmonica. He insisted that the scientific approach, by making clear what was unknown as well as what was known, would "help to make a vain man humble" and, by directing the experiments and insights of others to areas of ignorance and mystery, would greatly expand human knowledge. Franklin the scientist, then, seemed to epitomize the 18th-century faith in the capacity of men to understand themselves and the world in which they lived.

Political Career

Competing with science for Franklin's attention was his growing involvement in politics. His election in 1751 to the Pennsylvania Assembly began nearly 40 years as a public official. He used his influence at first mainly to further the cause of his various civic enterprises. But he also became a leader in the long-dominant Quaker party, opposing the Proprietary party, which sought to preserve the power of the Penn family in affairs of Pennsylvania. Franklin devised legislative strategy and wrote powerful resolves on behalf of the Assembly, denying Proprietary exemption from taxation and otherwise defending the right of the elected representatives of the people to regulate their own affairs.

Colonial Rights within the Empire

At first Franklin had not the slightest thought about America's separation from Great Britain. He had grown up with allegiance to Britain and had a deep appreciation of the culture of the country of William Shakespeare, John Milton, Joseph Addison, and Alexander Pope. In 1751 he celebrated the rapid increase of colonial population as a great "accession of power to the British Empire," a big and happy family wherein the prosperity of the parent and the growth of the children were mutually beneficial.

Franklin expressed his patriotism by proposing a Plan of Union within the empire at Albany in 1754, and a year later in giving extensive service to Gen. Edward Braddock's expedition to recapture Ft. Duquesne from the French. To defend the empire during the French and Indian War (1754-1763), Franklin persuaded the Quaker Assembly to pass the first militia law in Pennsylvania, appropriate money for defense, and appoint commissioners (including himself) to carry on full-scale war. As the war progressed, he worked with British commanders to win a North American empire for Britain. For 3 decades or more Franklin allied himself in thought and deed with such men as William Pitt, who conceived of Britain as a vital, freedom-extending realm as dear (and useful) to its subjects in Boston and Philadelphia as to those in London or Bristol.

Even in this patriotism of empire, however, the seeds of disaffection appeared. The Albany plan, Franklin noted, dividing power between the king and the colonial assemblies, was disapproved by the Crown "as having placed too much weight in the democratic part of the constitution, and [by] every assembly as having allowed too much to [Royal] Prerogative." Franklin also thought it incredibly selfish for the proprietor of Pennsylvania to try to avoid taxation of his vast lands. He sided, he declared in 1756, with "the people

of this province . . . generally of the middling sort." Thus, when he went to England in 1757 as agent of the Assembly, he was alarmed to hear the president of the Privy Council declare: "You Americans have wrong ideas of the nature of your constitution; you contend the King's instructions to his governors are not laws. . . . But those instructions . . . are . . . the Law of the Land; for the King is the Legislator of the Colonies." Though Franklin worked within the empire to resist this presumption, it was clear from the start that if it continued to dominate, Franklin's empire loyalty would wither and die.

Franklin lived in England from 1757 to 1762, seeking aid in restraining Proprietary power in Pennsylvania, meanwhile enjoying English social and intellectual life. He attended meetings of the Royal Society, heard great orchestras play the works of George Frederick Handel, made grand tours of the Continent, and was awarded honorary doctorate degrees by St. Andrews (1759) and Oxford (1762).

Back in America for nearly 2 years (1762-1764), Franklin traveled through the Colonies as deputy postmaster general for North America. In 20 years Franklin vastly improved postal service and at the same time made his position lucrative. He also continued his aid to poorer members of his family, especially his sister, and to the family of his wife, the former Deborah Read, whom he had married in 1730. They had two children, Frankie, who died at 4, and Sally, who married Richard Bache. Deborah Franklin also reared her husband's illegitimate son, William, often his father's close companion, who was appointed governor of New Jersey and was later to be notable as a loyalist during the Revolution. Franklin considered Deborah, who died in 1774, a good wife, mother, and helpmate, though she did not share his intellectual interests or even much of his social life.

Politics occupied most of Franklin's busy months at home. He opposed the bloody revenges frontiersmen visited on innocent Native Americans in the wake of Chief Pontiac's Conspiracy, and he campaigned to further restrict the proprietor's power. On this and other issues Franklin lost his seat in the Assembly (after 13 consecutive victories) in an especially scurrilous campaign. His Quaker party retained enough power, however, to return him to England as agent, commissioned especially to petition that Pennsylvania be taken over as a royal colony—a petition Franklin set aside when the perils of royal government loomed ever larger.

More Radical Position

Franklin played a central role in the great crises that led to the Declaration of Independence in 1776. He first advised obedience to the Stamp Act. But learning of the violent protest against it in America, he stiffened his own opposition, notably in a dramatic appearance before Parliament in 1766, when he outlined, plainly and bluntly, American insistence on substantial self-government. Encouraged by repeal of the act, Franklin again expressed his faith in the grand prospects for America within the empire and worked with Pitt, Lord Camden, and other Englishmen who wanted to liberalize both government at home and relations with the Colonies.

Yet Franklin mounted a strong propaganda assault on the Townshend Duties of 1767. In fact, Franklin's position was increasingly untenable. He was in countless official, personal, and sentimental ways committed to the British Empire, but he was more committed to the life-style he knew in America and which he now began to record in his *Autobiography*. The ideal solution, of course, was to find fulfillment for the life-style under the British flag. He only slowly realized that, at least under the policies of George III and Lord North, the two were incompatible.

Franklin's personal fame, as well as his appointment as agent for Georgia (1768) and for Massachusetts (1770), made him the foremost American spokesman in Britain for 10 crucial years, from 1765 to 1775. Protesting the Tea Act in 1773, he wrote two of his most skillful and famous political satires, *An Edict by the King of Prussia* and *Rules by Which a Great Empire May Be Reduced to a Small One*. These were merely the best of hundreds displaying Franklin's clever pen in aid of his chosen causes.

In 1774-1775 Franklin's agency in England came to an unhappy end. His friends in Massachusetts, against his instructions, published letters of Governor Thomas Hutchinson that Franklin had obtained in confidence. Exposed as an apparently dishonest schemer, Franklin was chastised before the Privy Council in 1774 and simultaneously deprived of his postmaster general's office. Then, in danger of being imprisoned as a traitor, Franklin continued to work with Pitt and others for conciliation, but the Boston Tea Party, the Coercive Acts, and the buildup of British troops in America doomed such efforts. When Franklin left England in March 1775, he was sure that "the extream corruption . . . in this old rotten State" would ensure "more Mischief than Benefit from a closer Union" between England and the Colonies.

The Revolutionary

In the next 18 months in America, Franklin reveled in the "glorious public virtue" of his compatriots. He served on the Pennsylvania Committee of Safety and in the Continental Congress, submitted articles of confederation for the united colonies, and helped draft a new constitution for Pennsylvania. He even went to Montreal to entice Canada to join the new union. He helped draft the Declaration of Independence and was among those who readily subscribed his name to it—at the age of 70 he had become a fervent revolutionist.

Franklin's skill was most in demand, though, as a diplomat to secure desperately needed aid for the new nation. In October 1776, appointed commissioner to France, he embarked with his two grandchildren. In France he began the most amazing personal success story in the history of diplomacy. His journey to Paris was a triumphal procession, and in the capital the literary and scientific community greeted him as a living embodiment of all the virtues the *philosophes* extolled.

Franklin played the role of the simple Quaker, exalted by his plainness amid the gaudy pomp of the court of Louis XVI. In a dramatic encounter at the French Academy, Franklin and the aged Voltaire embraced amid cheers. French intellectuals lionized Franklin, who, still a minister of an unrecognized country, established residence in the suburb of Auteuil, where he created friendships that became part of the legend of Franklin among the ladies of Paris. As usual, Franklin wrote witty letters, printed bagatelles, told stories, and otherwise displayed his brilliant personality.

Diplomatic Tasks in France

Franklin's diplomatic tasks proved more difficult. Though France was anxious that England be humbled, it could not afford openly to aid the American rebels unless success seemed probable. For a year (1777) Franklin worked behind the scenes to hasten war supplies across the Atlantic, block British diplomacy, and ingratiate himself with the French foreign minister and others who might help the United States. He also worked with the other American commissioners, Silas Deane and Arthur Lee, as those two strange compatriots quarreled with increasing bitterness. In December 1777 news of the American victory at Saratoga persuaded Louis XVI and his ministers to enter into an alliance with the United States, finally signed by Franklin and the other commissioners. Lee and Deane soon returned, quarreling, to America, leaving Franklin behind as the first American minister to the court of Versailles.

For 7 years Franklin was the premier American representative in Europe, conducting normal diplomacy and acting as purchasing agent, recruiting officer, loan negotiator, admiralty court, and intelligence chief. Nearly 80, Franklin carried his immense and varied burden effectively and in a way that retained French goodwill. He helped get French armies and navies on their way to North America, continued his efforts to supply American armies, outfitted John Paul Jones and numerous American privateers, and secured virtually all the outside aid that came to the American rebels.

Peace Commissioner

When, after Yorktown (1781), peace with independence became possible, Franklin made the first contact with British emissaries. During the summer of 1782 as the other peace commissioners, John Adams and John Jay, made their way to Paris, Franklin set terms close to those finally agreed to: independence, guaranteed fishing rights, evacuation of all British forces, and a western boundary on the Mississippi. Though Franklin insisted on working closely with French negotiators, he never subordinated American to French interests as his critics have claimed. In fact, the subtle Franklin, the intrepid Adams, and the resourceful Jay made an ideal team, winning for the United States a peace treaty of genuine national independence in 1783.

Viewing America's place in the world as his mission to France drew to a close, Franklin combined realism with idealism. "Our firm connection with France," he noted, "gives us weight with England, and respect throughout Europe." Thus balancing between the great nations, Franklin thought "a few years of peace will improve, will restore and increase our strength; but our future safety will depend on our union and our virtue." He stated many times there was "no such thing as a good war or a bad peace." Not the least isolationist or aggressive, he thought the peaceful needs of the United States required it to trade and cooperate honorably with nations all over the world.

Franklin left France in 1785 and landed in Philadelphia to the cheers of his countrymen. Honored as a living sage, he accepted election for 3 years as president of the Supreme Executive Council of Pennsylvania, became president of the Pennsylvania Society for Promoting the Abolition of Slavery, and resumed his activity in the American Philosophical Society, the University of Pennsylvania, and other civic projects. Though suffering from a physical disorder, he also maintained his large correspondence, wrote essays, and finished the last half of his *Autobiography*.

Framing of a New Government

Franklin's most notable service, however, was his attendance at the daily sessions of the Constitutional Convention during the summer of 1787. Too infirm to speak much in debate and less creative in political philosophy than some of his younger colleagues, he bolstered the confidence of the convention and, through good humor and suggestions for compromise, helped prevent its disruption in animosity. He gave decisive support to the "Great Compromise" over representation and dozens of times calmed volatile tempers and frayed nerves. At the convention's close, he asked each member, who like himself might not entirely approve of the Constitution, to "doubt a little of his own infallibility" and sign the document to give it a chance as the best frame of government human ingenuity could at that time produce. His last public service was to urge ratification of the Constitution and to approve the inauguration of the new government under his longtime friend George Washington. Franklin died peacefully on April 17, 1790.

Further Reading

Franklin's writings are in Albert H. Smyth, ed., *The Writings of Benjamin Franklin* (10 vols., 1905-1907), and Leonard Labaree and others, eds., *The Papers of Benjamin Franklin* (11 vols. to date, 1959-1968) and *The Autobiography of Benjamin Franklin* (1964). The best biography is Carl Van Doren, *Benjamin Franklin* (1938). For special studies see Carl and Jessica Bridenbaugh, *Rebels and Gentlemen: Philadelphia in the Age of Franklin* (1942); Verner W. Crane, *Benjamin Franklin and a Rising People* (1954), on Franklin's politics; Gerald Stourzh, *Benjamin Franklin and American Foreign Policy* (1954); I. Bernard Cohen, *Franklin and Newton* (1956), on Franklin's scientific work; Alfred O. Aldridge, *Franklin and His French Contemporaries* (1957); Ralph L. Ketcham, *Benjamin Franklin* (1965), for Franklin's thought; and Claude A. Lopez, *Franklin and the Ladies of Paris* (1966). ☐

John Charles Frémont

John Charles Frémont (1813-1890) was an American explorer, politician, and soldier. Through his explorations in the West he stimulated the American desire to own that region. He was the first presidential candidate of the Republican party.

orn on Jan. 31, 1813, in Savannah, Ga., John C. Frémont was the illegitimate son of a French émigré, John Charles Frémon (*sic*), and Mrs. Anne Whiting Pryor. He was raised in Charleston, S. C. Frémont proved precocious, especially in mathematics and the natural sciences, as well as handsome. He attended Charleston College (1829-1831) but was expelled for irregular attendance.

Through the influence of Joel R. Poinsett, Frémont obtained a post as teacher of mathematics on the sloop *Natchez* and visited South American waters in 1833. In 1836 he helped survey a railroad route between Charleston and Cincinnati, and in 1836-1837 he worked on a survey of Cherokee lands in Georgia.

His Explorations

In 1838, through the influence of Poinsett, Frémont obtained a commission as second lieutenant in the Corps of Topographical Engineers of the U.S. Army. Assigned to the expedition of J. N. Nicollet which explored in Minnesota and the Dakotas, he gained knowledge of natural science and topographical engineering, as well as experience on the frontier. Also through Nicollet, he met the powerful senator from Missouri Thomas Hart Benton—and fell in love with Benton's daughter Jessie.

Benton secured an appointment for Frémont to explore the Des Moines River, which was accomplished in 1841. That fall he married Jessie Benton, gaining her father as protector. In 1842 Frémont was sent to explore the Wind River chain of the Rockies and to make a scientific exploration of the Oregon Trail. Employing Kit Carson as guide, he followed the trail through South Pass. His report was filled with tales of adventure and contained an excellent map. Frémont was on his way to becoming a popular hero with a reputation as the "Great Pathfinder," but, in reality, he had been following the trails of mountain men.

In 1843 Frémont headed an expedition that explored South Pass, the Columbia River, and the Oregon country, returning by way of Sutter's Fort in Mexican California. His report was printed just as James K. Polk became president, a time when expansionist feeling was high; the 10,000 copies of this report increased Frémont's heroic stature.

Mexican War

In 1845 Polk sent Frémont and soldiers (with Kit Carson as guide) to California. Expelled from California by its governor, Frémont wintered in Oregon. Polk's orders arrived in May. Frémont then marched to Sutter's Fort and there on June 14, 1846, assumed command of the American settlers' Bear Flag Revolt. Aided by commodores J. D. Sloat and Robert F. Stockton, his forces were victorious, and he received the surrender of California at Cahuenga on Jan. 13, 1847.

Immediately Frémont became embroiled in a fight for the governorship of California with Gen. Stephen W. Kearny, who had marched overland from Missouri. Frémont was arrested, taken to Washington, D.C., and tried for mutiny, insubordination, and conduct prejudicial to good order. Found guilty, he was ordered dismissed from the Army. Polk remitted the penalty, but Frémont, in anger, resigned.

Political Career

Frémont moved to California, on the way conducting a private survey for a railroad route. In California he acquired land in the Sierra foothills, the Mariposa estate, and grew wealthy from mining. He bought real estate in San Francisco and lived lavishly, winning election as U.S. senator from California. He drew the short term and served only from Sept. 9, 1850, to March 4, 1851. Afterward he visited Paris and London, where he raised funds for ambitious schemes on the Mariposa. In 1853-1854 he conducted another private expedition surveying a railroad route, along the 37th-38th parallels.

In 1856 the newly formed Republican party named Frémont its first presidential candidate because of his strong stand on free soil in Kansas and his attitude against enforcement of the Fugitive Slave Law. His campaign suffered from a shortage of funds, and he lost, but he was at the peak of his career.

Subsequent Career

Frémont's overspeculation at the Mariposa led to his loss of this property. Then in 1861, at the outbreak of the Civil War, he performed disastrously as a major general at St. Louis and in western Virginia. In 1864 Radical Republicans approached Frémont about running for president in opposition to Abraham Lincoln; Frémont first accepted, then declined ungraciously.

After the war he was involved in promoting the Kansas and Pacific and the Memphis and Little Rock railroads. Both lines went bankrupt in 1870, leaving Frémont almost penniless. In 1878 his claim that the Republican party owed him a debt netted him appointment as governor of Arizona. He held the position until 1881, when angry protests from that territory led to his removal.

Frémont's old age was filled with frustrating schemes to recoup his fortune—while he was supported by his wife's authorship. In 1890 he was pensioned at $6,000 per year as a major general; he died 3 months later (July 13, 1890) in New York.

Further Reading

Only one volume of Frémont's autobiographical *Memoirs of My Life* (1887) was published. Jesse Benton Frémont wrote several works that give information about her husband's career, the best of which are *Souvenirs of My Time* (1887) and *Far-West Sketches* (1890). Good biographies include Frederick S. Dellenbaugh, *Frémont and '49* (1914), which has excellent sketches of his expeditions; Cardinal Goodwin's critical *John Charles Frémont: An Explanation of His Career* (1930); and Allan Nevins's laudatory *Frémont: The West's Greatest Adventurer* (2 vols., 1928) and his more balanced, one volume edition, *Frémont: Pathmaker of the West* (1939). □

Milton Friedman

Milton Friedman (born 1912) was the founder and leading proponent of "monetarism," an economic doctrine which considers the supply of money (and changes therein) to be the primary determinant of nominal income and prices in the economy.

Milton Friedman, a native of Brooklyn, New York, was born July 31, 1912. After earning an undergraduate degree from Rutgers University in 1932 and a master's degree from the University of Chicago the following year, Friedman became a research economist with the National Bureau of Economic Research in New York and later with the U.S. Treasury Tax Research Division. He earned a doctorate in economics from Columbia University in 1946 and after brief spells at Wisconsin and Minnesota universities returned to the University of Chicago to begin a long and distinguished career of teaching and research. After retiring in 1979 Friedman continued an active schedule of research and publishing at the Hoover Institute of Stanford University.

According to the monetarist view which Friedman developed and popularized, the private economy is basically stable unless disturbed by rapid money supply fluctuations or other government actions. Friedman advocated a "constant monetary rule" whereby the nation's money supply would grow by a fixed percentage each year, thereby avoiding overexpansion and inflation.

Blamed the "Fed" for Depression

Friedman's positions consistently put him at odds with the Federal Reserve System (often called the "Fed"), the central bank legislated by Congress in 1913 to create and control the nation's money supply. In his monumental *A Monetary History of the United States, 1867-1960* (with Anna J. Schwartz, 1963) Friedman provided a startling analysis of the Great Depression (1929-1933), arguing that the Fed deserved considerable blame for allowing a dramatic fall in the money supply during this period. The traditional Keynesian view is that the Fed played an insignificant role and was powerless to stem the economic slide.

Although Friedman resisted offers to take government jobs himself, his ideas achieved considerable success in altering government policies. This was reflected, for example, in the historic setting of monetary growth targets by the Federal Reserve Board in 1979, a practice which Friedman had long advocated.

Friedman was also a staunch defender of the free enterprise system and a proponent of individual responsibility and action. In *Capitalism and Freedom* (1962) he outlined his concept of the proper role of government in a free society. These views were popularized through a regular *Newsweek* column starting in 1966 and through books such as *There Is No Such Thing As A Free Lunch*. His ideas were brought vividly home to the American public through an award-winning ten-part television series in 1980 entitled *Free to Choose* (co-authored with his wife, Rose Friedman).

Prolific Writer

As a scholar Friedman was prolific. Among his other well-known books are *Essays in Positive Economics* (1953), which included famous papers on the methodology of economics; *Studies in the Quantity Theory of Money* (1956), which revitalized the classic quantity theory of money as a foundation for monetarism; *A Theory of the Consumption Function* (1957), which provided a novel explanation for consumption decisions based on lifetime rather than current income; and *Monetary Trends in the United States and the United Kingdom* (co-authored with Anna J. Schwartz, 1982).

Friedman's articles in professional journals consistently challenged orthodox views and presented new ways of understanding economic data and events. In "The Role of Monetary Policy" in *American Economic Review* (1968) Friedman invented the now famous "long run natural rate of unemployment." This article provided strong arguments for refuting the simple Phillips Curve hypothesis that less unemployment could be achieved at the cost of higher inflation. The Phillips Curve analysis had been used by policy-makers to justify expansionary fiscal spending. Friedman's analysis, however, showed that attempts to lower the rate of unemployment below the "natural" level would cause only temporary reductions in unemployment and in the long run produce higher inflation along with higher unemployment.

In subsequent writings Friedman elaborated his views on these issues (*A Theoretical Framework for Monetary Analysis*, 1971, and "Nobel Lecture: Inflation and Unemployment," in *Journal of Political Economy*, 1977). Friedman's explanation for "stagflation," the existence of stagnant demand and high unemployment simultaneous with inflation, proved to be more convincing than orthodox Key-

nesian theories and provided tremendous impetus for defections from the Keynesian camp.

Nobel Prize Winner

Friedman's achievements were recognized early in his career. In 1951 he was awarded the John Bates Clark Medal of the American Economic Association, and in 1962 he was awarded the Paul Snowden Russell Distinguished Service Chair at the University of Chicago. In 1976 Friedman won his greatest honor, the Nobel Prize in Economics. Throughout his career Friedman earned numerous other awards and honorary doctorates from colleges and universities throughout the world.

In addition to his prolific writing, Friedman found time to be president of the American Economic Association (1967), vice-president of the Western Economic Association (1982-1983), and president of the Mont Pelerin Society (1970-1972). He was on the board of editors of the *American Economic Review* (1951-1953) and of *Econometrica* (1957-1969) and a member of the advisory board of the *Journal of Money, Credit, and Banking* (1968 into the mid-1980s).

In 1992 a reviewer breathlessly summarized the accomplishments of Friedman's book *Money Mischief: Episodes in Monetary History*, suggesting the economist has the rare ability to communicate his message to the non-academic. "Friedman compares inflation to alcoholism; blames the rise of Chinese communism, in large part, on an inadequately controlled money supply; defines and describes $MV = PT$ in four brief paragraphs; tells how three Scottish chemists ruined William Jennings Bryan's political career through their pioneering work with gold; and relates many other anecdotes befitting the book's subtitle, *Episodes in Monetary History*."

Held Strong Views

When Friedman would speak on, for instance, the woes of the U.S. education system, his free-market and anti-union views were readily apparent. "Why is it that our educational system is turning out youngsters who cannot read, write, or figure? The answer—simple but nonetheless correct—is that our current school system is a monopoly that is being run primarily by the teachers' unions: the National Education Association and the American Federation of Teachers. They are among the strongest trade unions in the country and among the most powerful lobbying groups.

"The people who run the unions aren't bad people; they're good people—just like all the rest of us. But their interests and the interests of a good school system are not the same."

Friedman was equally outspoken on the legalization of drugs. When an interviewer asked what good would come of it, the economist said, "I see America with half the number of prisons, half the number of prisoners, then thousand fewer homicides a year, inner cities in which there's a chance for these poor people to live without being afraid for their lives, citizens who might be respectable who are now addicts not being subject to becoming criminals in order to get their drug, being able to get drugs for which they're sure of the quality. You know, the same thing happened under prohibition of alcohol as is happening now (with drugs)."

Milton Friedman will be remembered as one of the most gifted economists of the 20th century. His iconoclasm often made him a controversial figure, yet unfolding events showed him to be ahead of his time, such as in resisting the spread of federal government power and in being a "watch-dog" of the monetary authority. He excelled as an orator and debater. His popular writings in *Newsweek* and elsewhere provided succinct and novel solutions for economic ills which would allow the free market to work, such as the "negative income tax," an all-volunteer army, and floating exchange rates. While economists continue to debate the relevance of "monetarism" for policy decisions, there is little question that Friedman left the profession with and valuable new insights on economic behavior.

Further Reading

Additional information on Friedman can be found in L. Silk, *The Economists* (1976); Karl Brunner (editor), *Milton Friedman in Our Time* (1979); R. Sobel (author of four articles for this publication; see contributor list), *The Worldly Economists* (1980); Jr. Shackleton and G. Locksley (editors), *Twelve Contemporary Economists* (1981); and Mark Blaug, *Great Economists Since Keynes* (1985).

The opposing, in large part, Keynesian economics was developed by John Maynard Keynes in *The General Theory of Employment, Interest, and Money* (1936). See also Hirsch, Abraham, *Milton Friedman: Economics in Theory and Practice,* Harvester Wheatsheaf, 1990. □

Robert Lee Frost

Robert Lee Frost (1874-1963) was an intentionally American and traditionalist poet in an age of internationalized and experimental art. He used New England idioms, characters, and settings, recalling the roots of American culture, to get at universal experience.

Robert Frost was born in San Francisco on March 26, 1874. His father came from prerevolutionary Maine and New Hampshire stock but hated New England because the Civil War it had supported had robbed his own father of employment in the cotton mill economy. When Frost's father graduated from Harvard in 1872, he left New England. He paused in Lewistown, Pa., to teach and married another teacher, Isabelle Moodie, a Scotswoman. They moved to San Francisco, where the elder Frost became an editor and politician. Their first child was named for the Southern hero Gen. Robert E. Lee.

When Frost's father died in 1884, his will stipulated burial in New England. His wife and two children, Robert and Jeanie, went east for the funeral. Lacking funds to return to California, they settled in Salem, Mass., where Mrs. Frost taught school.

Transplanted New Englander

Robert had been a city boy, a proud Californian, and no student. Transplanted, he grew sensitive to New England's

speechways, taciturn characters, and customs. He also became a serious student and graduated from Lawrence High School as valedictorian and class poet in 1892. He enrolled at Dartmouth College but soon left. He had become engaged to Elinor White, classmate and fellow valedictorian, who was completing her college education. Frost moved from job to job, working in mills, at newspaper reporting, and at teaching, all the while writing poetry. In 1894 he sold his first poem, "My Butterfly," to the *New York Independent.* Overjoyed, he had two copies of a booklet of lyrics privately printed, one for his fiancée and one for himself. He delivered Elinor's copy in person but did not find her response adequate. Thinking he had lost her, he tore up his copy and wandered south as far as the Dismal Swamp (from Virginia to North Carolina), even contemplating suicide.

In 1895, however, Frost married Elinor and tried to make a career of teaching. He helped his mother run a small private school in Lawrence, Mass., where his first son was born. He spent 2 years at Harvard (1897-1899), but again undergraduate study proved uncongenial. With a newborn daughter as well as a son, he tried chicken farming at Methuen, Mass., and in 1900, when his nervousness was diagnosed as a forewarning of tuberculosis, he moved his poultry business to Derry, N.H. There his first son soon died. In 1906 Frost was stricken with pneumonia and almost died, and a year later his fourth daughter died. This grief and suffering, as well as lesser frustrations in personal life and business, turned Frost more and more to poetry. Once again he tried teaching, in Derry and then in Plymouth, N.H.

Creation of the Poet

In 1912, almost 40 and with only a few poems published, Frost sold his farm and used an annuity from his grandfather to go to England and gamble everything on poetry. The family settled on a farm in Buckinghamshire, and Frost began to write. Ezra Pound, the expatriate American poet, helped him get published in periodicals, but Frost resented Pound's excessive management.

Frost published *A Boy's Will* (1913), and it was well received. Though it contains some 19th-century diction, the words and rhythms are generally colloquial and subtly simple. Written in conventional rhymed stanzas and blank verse, the poems begin in delight and end in wisdom, as Frost later said poems should. They move through various subjective moods toward modest revelations. Such poems as "Into My Own," "Mowing," and "A Tuft of Flowers" convey an inclination toward nature, solitude, and meditation, toward the beauty of fact, and toward a New England individualism that acknowledges a need for love and community.

North of Boston (1914), also published in England, is more objective, made up mainly of blank verse monologues and dramatic narratives. "The Death of the Hired Man," soberly suspenseful and compassionate, with lyric moments of waiting, has more to do with the mutual understanding in a marriage than with death. "Mending Wall" is a bantering satire contrasting a tradition-bound farmer and his neighbor, a straight-faced tease. In "After Apple-picking" the picker asks quizzically whether he should settle for being plain tired or inflate his state by identifying it with the drowsiness of autumn. "Home Burial" and "A Servant of Servants" dramatize respectively a hysteria bred of loneliness and death, and the precarious sanity of a rural drudge.

North of Boston compounded the success of *A Boy's Will,* and the two volumes announced the two modes of Frost's best poetry, the lyric and the narrative. Although immediately established as a nature poet, he did not idealize nature. He addressed not only its loveliness but also the isolation, harshness, and anxiety its New England intimates had to endure. The reticence of his poetry, however, is not simply that of a taciturn New Englander; it restrains tremendous psychic and sexual forces, a violent and suicidal bent, and deep emotional needs that occasionally flashed out in his poetry and personal life.

Frost's place in literary tradition had also begun to clarify. His work led back to aspects of Thomas Hardy, Emily Dickinson, and Ralph Waldo Emerson, and Yankees Oliver Wendell Holmes, James Russell Lowell, and John Greenleaf Whittier, and to characteristics of William Wordsworth, English 18th-century meditators on landscape, John Donne, and the Latin idylls and eclogues of Theocritus and Virgil. But Frost's irony and ambiguity, his concreteness and colloquial tone, his skepticism and honesty bespoke the modern.

A Public Figure

When the Frosts returned to America in 1915, *North of Boston* was a best seller. Sudden acclaim embarrassed Frost, who had always avoided crowds. He withdrew to a small farm in Franconia, N.H., but financial need soon compelled him to respond to demands for readings and lectures. In 1915 and 1916 he was respectively Phi Beta Kappa poet at Tufts College and at Harvard. He conquered his shyness, developing an epigrammatic, folksy platform manner that made him one of the most popular performers in America and abroad. His tall muscular body and rugged face with its pale watchful eyes became a familiar sight; as the hair whitened, the face grew craggy, and the body thickened, those eyes remained the same.

From Frost's talks, his few published essays, and his poems, the outline of a poetic theory emerged. He strove for the sound of sense, for the colloquial, for a tension between the natural rhythm of speech and the basic iambic meter of English verse. He felt that the emotion that began a poem should generate a form through likenesses and contraries and lead to a clarification of experience. This was the way to spontaneity and surprise.

Mountain Interval (1916) brought together lyrics and narratives. The five dramatic lyrics of "The Hill Wife" look at a marriage dying on a solitary farm. On the other hand, "Meeting and Passing" uses a few vivid images to infuse a courtship walk with the promise of joy. The hilarious slide in "Brown's Descent" and the youthful tree-swinging of "Birches" (although its exuberance is restrained from hyperbole by "matter of fact") are countered by the deadly accident of "Out, Out—."

In 1917 Frost became one of the first poets-in-residence on an American campus. He taught at Amherst from 1917 to 1920, in 1918 receiving a master of arts, the first of many academic honors. The following year he moved his farm base to South Saftsbury, Vt. In 1920 he cofounded the Bread Loaf School of English of Middlebury College, serving there each summer as lecturer and consultant. From 1921 to 1923 he was poet-in-residence at the University of Michigan.

Frost's *Selected Poems* and a new volume, *New Hampshire,* appeared in 1923. For the latter, in 1924 Frost received the first of four Pulitzer Prizes. Though the title poem does not present Frost at his best, the volume also contains such lovely lyrics as "Fire and Ice," "Nothing Gold Can Stay," and "To Earthward." In "For Once, Then Something" Frost slyly joshes critics who ask for deep, deep insights; and in the dramatic narrative "The Witch of Coös" he turns a rustic comedy into a grotesque story of adultery and murder. "Two Look at Two" dramatizes a hushed encounter between human lovers and animal lovers.

Frost returned to Amherst for 2 years in 1923 and to the University of Michigan in 1925 and then settled at Amherst in 1926.

West Running Brook (1928) continued Frost's tonal variations and mingling of lyrics and narratives. The lyric "Tree at My Window" appeared along with "Acquainted with the Night," a narrative of a despairing nightwalker in a city where time is "neither right nor wrong." The title poem, recalling John Donne, is a little drama of married lovers and their thoughts upon a stream that goes "by contraries," a stream that itself contains a contrary, a wave thrown back against the current by a rock, a "backward motion toward the source" that emblems the lovers' own tendency.

Frost visited England and Paris in 1928 and published his *Collected Poems* in 1930. In 1934 he suffered another excruciating loss in the death of his daughter Marjorie. He returned to Harvard in 1936 and in the same year published *A Further Range.*

This volume contains considerable social comment, but in the context of a worldwide depression some of it seemed oversimplified and untimely. "Two Tramps at Mud Time," however, puts men's need, and therefore right, to work in dramatically personal terms. "The Drumlin Woodchuck" recommends a distrustful defensiveness in order to survive for love; and "Departmental," another fable, satirizes bureaucracy through the antics of ants. "Build Soil—A Political Pastoral" recalls Virgil's First Eclogue. Frost's character Depression Tityrus declares, "I'd let things take their course And then I'd take the credit." Among the shorter pieces, several speak of inadequacy, disillusion, or malevolence—"Desert Places," "Neither Out Far Nor In Deep," "Provide, Provide," and "Design."

Later Work and Personal Tragedy

Honors, forebodings, and tragedies continued to crowd in on Frost. Because of his weak lungs, his doctor ordered him south in 1936, and thereafter he spent his winters in Florida. Frost served on the Harvard faculty during 1936-1937 and received an honorary doctorate. After his wife died of a heart attack in 1938, Frost resigned from the Amherst faculty and sold his house. That same year he was elected to the Board of Overseers of Harvard College. In 1939 his second *Collected Poems* appeared, and he began a 3-year stay at Harvard. In 1940 his only surviving son committed suicide.

A Witness Tree (1942) included the lyric "Happiness Makes Up in Height for What It Lacks in Length" and "Come In," in which the speaker prefers the guiding light of stars to the romantic dark of the woods and the song of an unseen bird. *Steeple Bush* (1947) contained the beautiful elegy of decay "Directive." The monologist visits an abandoned village where he used to live and, through allusions to the Holy Grail, converts the visit into a journey back toward a source, a stream beside which he administers communion to himself: "Drink and be whole again against confusion."

In 1945 Frost essayed something new in *A Masque of Reason,* a verse drama, too chatty for the stage. A modernization of the biblical story of Job, it is theistic and sets forth good-humoredly the Puritanic conviction that man, with his finite mind, must remain separate from God. *A Masque of Mercy* (1947), a companion verse drama based on the story of Jonah, has a heretical or individualistic air about it but still comes out essentially orthodox, suggesting that man with his limited knowledge must try to act justly and mercifully, for action is his salvation if it complies with God's will. "Nothing can make injustice just but mercy."

Frost's *Complete Poems* appeared in 1949, and in 1950 the U.S. Senate felicitated him on his seventy-fifth birthday. In 1957 he returned to England to receive doctoral degrees from Oxford and Cambridge. On his eighty-fifth birthday the Senate again felicitated him. In 1961, at the inaugura-

tion of John F. Kennedy, Frost recited "The Gift Outright," the first time a poet had honored a presidential inauguration. A final volume, *In the Clearing,* appeared in 1962.

On Jan. 29, 1963, Frost died in Boston of complications following an operation. He was buried in the family plot in Old Bennington, Vt. His "lover's quarrel with the world" was over.

Further Reading

Lawrence R. Thompson has completed the first two volumes of an official Frost biography, *Robert Frost,* vol. 1: *The Early Years, 1874-1915* (1966), and vol. 2: *Years of Triumph* (1970). A biography that sees Frost as a loving family man rather than self-involved and independent can be found in Jay Parini, *Robert Frost: A Life* (1999) . A useful critical biography is Philip L. Gerber, *Robert Frost* (1967). Margaret Bartlett Anderson provides an informal view in *Robert Frost and John Bartlett: The Record of a Friendship* (1963). An interesting biography by a friend is Louis Mertins, *Robert Frost: Life and Talks-Walking* (1965). An account of Frost's trip to the Soviet Union is Franklin D. Reeve, *Robert Frost in Russia* (1964).

Two sound introductions are Lawrence R. Thompson, *Fire and Ice: The Art and Thought of Robert Frost* (1942), and Sidney Cox, *A Swinger of Birches* (1957). The poet Amy Lowell includes a discussion of Frost in *Tendencies in Modern American Poetry* (1917). Reuben A. Brower concentrates on poetic criticism in *The Poetry of Robert Frost* (1963). More specialized studies are John F. Lynen, *The Pastoral Art of Robert Frost* (1960); James M. Cox, ed., *Robert Frost: A Collection of Critical Essays* (1962), which contains varied critical assessments of Frost; and James R. Squires, *The Major Themes of Robert Frost* (1963). □

Richard Buckminster Fuller

Richard Buckminster Fuller (1895-1983), American architect and engineer, was in a broad sense a product designer who understood architecture as well as the engineering sciences in relation to mass production and in association with the idea of total environment.

R. Buckminster Fuller was best known for his work on the Dymaxion House, Dymaxion Bathroom, and Dymaxion Car and as the inventor of the geodesic dome—as a means of attaining maximum space related to environment with minimal use of raw materials. "My philosophy," he wrote in *No More Secondhand Gods,* "requires of me that I convert not only my own experiences but whatever I can learn of other men's experiences into statements of evolutionary trending and concomitantly defined problem challenges and responses. My philosophy further requires that I at least attempt to solve the problems by inanimate invention." He also described himself as an "explorer in comprehensive anticipation design."

Fuller was born July 12, 1895, in Milton, Massachusetts, and attended Milton Academy. Even at an early age he was a nonconformist, and in 1913 he rejected formal education at Harvard, the college that had nurtured four generations of Fullers. During World War I he was commissioned in the U.S. Navy, where he had an opportunity to indulge

his creative imagination; he designed a seaplane rescue mast and boom.

Dymaxion Concept

In peacetime Fuller's energies were channeled into the Stockade Building System, which failed because of ignorant contractors, inflexible building codes, and financial opposition. This failure, as well as the death of his daughter of rheumatic fever, forced him into an intense period of work, resulting in 1927 in the Dymaxion House. (The word Dymaxion is a compounding of the words "dynamism" and "maximum.") Circular in plan to prevent heat loss and with a tiny heating unit and air-conditioning unit, the house, 50 feet in diameter, weighed 6,000 pounds. It would have cost approximately $6,500 and could have been assembled from a 250-cubic-foot package transported anywhere. The cost of development would have been about $100 million.

In 1933 Fuller followed this with the three-wheel, front-wheel-drive Dymaxion Car. It was built like an airplane body, was air-conditioned, and could have traveled at 120 miles per hour.

Phelps Dodge Corporation developed the copper Dymaxion Bathroom in 1936. (Aluminum, plastics, and such materials were not readily available or reasonably priced in the mid-1930s.) The quart of water necessary for a 10-minute bath would, in addition, provide an invigorating massage. The bathroom would have been free of sewage pipes, and waste material would have been stored for pickup and processing.

Following World War II, Beech Aircraft Company at Wichita, Kansas, wanted to convert their aircraft production plant into an assembly line for a Dymaxion House, which became known as the Wichita House of 1945-1946. Labor unions supported the project in order to retain full employment, but financial backers and the industry decided against it. In this failure America lost a chance, in 1945, to work toward solving housing and allied problems that came to plague the cities by the 1970s.

Geodesic Domes

Undaunted, Fuller began developing his ideas on geodesic domes, using the tetrahedron (of four triangular sides), economic in material and weight and thus of maximum efficiency, as a basic component. After numerous experimental prototypes, industry began to understand the advantages of such structures. In 1953 the Ford Company built a geodesic dome in Dearborn, Michigan, 93 feet in diameter; the Marine Corps built numerous smaller ones; and in 1958-1959 the Union Tank Car Company of Baton Rouge, Louisiana, constructed a dome 384 feet in diameter. Fuller's proposal for a hemispherical dome two miles in diameter to cover a portion of Manhattan Island, New York, to enclose a controlled environment was not acted on. But perhaps the best opportunity for a gigantic temporary structure of this kind was lost when the president of the 1964 World's Fair vetoed a proposed dome which would have covered 646 acres.

The United States Pavilion at Montreal's Expo 1967 was a three-quarter globe designed by Fuller, 200 feet high and 250 feet in diameter. Although the structure and its contents drew some sharp criticism, they represented "Creative America." Fuller's later experiments were geared toward an understanding of the world's resources and their efficient utilization.

Fuller's Influence

Fuller functioned primarily as a catalyst. He was important to the 20th century not only because of his own inventiveness but also for his influence upon the new generation. The pioneers of the modern movement, such as Ludwig Mies van der Rohe, have less influence than Fuller, who was the forerunner of concepts of the efficient utilization of materials and, with the Bauhaus, of mass production.

Fuller's philosophy of design contributed to the faith many contemporary architects have placed in the computer-age concept of "megastructure"—the idea of incorporating a city into a single giant structural complex, encompassing all functions of the urban environment, into which individual cells of habitation can be "plugged" or onto which they can be "clipped."

Although megastructure is impractical, with regard to structural feasibility and cost in the third quarter of the 20th century, when new structural techniques evolve and when the populace and its leadership understand the need for comprehensive planning then megastructure could be one possible solution to population growth and the habitation of man on a grand scale. Still, some critics argue that such an environment would be inhuman as well as impractical.

British critic Kenneth Clark considers ideas such as megastructure "the most disreputable of all forms of public utterance," which "threatens to impair our humanity."

Fuller was elected to the American Academy and Institute of Arts and Letters and held more than 2,000 patents. From 1959 until his death, due to a heart attack, on July 1, 1983, Fuller was a research professor in design science and a professor emeritus at Southern Illinois University, as well as a popular lecturer. During his life, Fuller wrote 25 books.

Further Reading

Fuller's ideas are presented in his *Nine Chains to the Moon* (1938); *No More Secondhand Gods, and Other Writings* (1963); and *Ideas and Integrities: A Spontaneous Autobiographical Disclosure* (1963). Fuller's contemporary influence is examined in James T. Badlwin, *Buckyworks: Buckminster Fuller's Ideas Today,* John Wiley & Sons, Inc., 1996. A biography is Robert Snyder, *R. Buckminster Fuller: An Autobiographical Monologue/Scenario,* St. Martin's Press, 1980. The Fuller Research Foundation published *Dymaxion Index: Bibliography and Published Items Regarding Dymaxion and Buckminster Fuller, 1927-1953* (rev. ed. 1953). Other works that discuss Fuller's influence include Reyner Banham, *The New Brutalism; Ethic or Aesthetic?* (1966), and Royston Landau, *New Directions in British Architecture* (1968). □

Robert Fulton

Robert Fulton (1765-1815), American inventor, civil engineer, and artist, established the first regular and commercially successful steamboat operation.

Robert Fulton was born November 14, 1765, in Lancaster County, Pa. His father worked at farming, among other jobs, and died when Robert was a small boy. By the age of 10 Robert showed promise as an artist and was employed by local gunsmiths to make designs for their work. At 17 he went to Philadelphia, the cultural center of the Atlantic seaboard, and spent 4 years making portraits and doing miniatures. Financially successful, he was able to buy a farm near the city for his mother.

In 1786 Fulton went to London to study painting with Benjamin West, who had been a family friend and was by this time one of the leading American painters living in England. England was already in the midst of its industrial revolution, and Fulton was fascinated by the new engineering enterprises—canals, mines, bridges, roads, and factories. His interest became professional, and after about 1793 he gave up painting as a vocation, pursuing it only for his own amusement.

As early as 1794 Fulton considered using steam power to drive a boat. Seven years earlier John Fitch had successfully demonstrated his steamboat on the Delaware River at Philadelphia, but in the interim no one had been able to make both a mechanical and commercial success of the idea. Though the British government had banned the export of steam engines, Fulton wrote to the firm of Boulton and Watt about the possibility of buying a ready–made engine to be applied to boat propulsion.

Most of Fulton's energy during these years was devoted to more conventional problems of civil and mechanical engineering. He patented in England a "double-incline plane" for hauling canal boats over difficult terrain and machines to saw marble, to spin flax, and to twist hemp for rope. He built a mechanical dredge to speed the construction of canals and in 1796 published his illustrated pamphlet, *A Treatise on the Improvement of Canal Navigation.*

For the next 10 years Fulton devoted himself to the development of underwater warfare through the invention and improvement of a submarine and explosive torpedoes. It is thought that he believed that if warfare were made sufficiently destructive and horrible it would be abandoned—a fallacy often invoked by inventors of military devices. He tried to interest the French government in his experiments, and he obtained the promise of prizes for any British ships he might destroy with his devices. In 1801 he proceeded with his submarine, the *Nautilus,* against various ships but was unsuccessful. By 1804 his failure to win French money for destroying British ships led him to offer to destroy French ships for the British government. Once again he failed in combat, although he was able to blow up one ship during an experiment.

In 1802 Fulton had met Robert R. Livingston, formerly a partner in another steamboat venture but recently appointed U.S. minister to the French government. Despite the failure of Fulton's earlier ventures, Livingston agreed to support Fulton's old idea of building a steamboat. In 1803 an engine was ordered (disassembled and with many duplicate parts) from Boulton and Watt, to be delivered in New

York City. But it was 1806 before permission to export the engine was obtained, the parts were assembled, and Fulton was able to sail for America.

The engine was put together in New York and set aboard a locally built vessel. One of the problems was to determine the proper proportions for a steamboat. Fulton was convinced that science dictated a very long and narrow hull, though experience later proved him wrong. Although Livingston had been an advocate of a kind of jet propulsion for steamboats (that is, a jet of water forced out the back of the boat under high pressure), the two now settled on paddle wheels as the best method. On Aug. 17, 1807, the *Clermont* (as it was later named) began its first successful voyage up the Hudson River to Albany, N.Y. Under way it averaged 5 miles per hour.

After the voyage of the *Clermont,* steamboats appeared up and down the Atlantic Coast, and Fulton himself introduced the first steamboat on the western waters. Before his death on February 24, 1815 he had erected a large boat works in New Jersey and directed the building of one ferryboat, a torpedo boat, and 17 regular steamboats.

Fulton's success, where at least a dozen other American inventors had failed, had many causes. In Livingston he had a rich and politically powerful patron who was able to obtain a lucrative monopoly on the steam navigation of the state's waters. Fulton also began his work with a first-class engine, purchased from Boulton and Watt, the world's leading engine builders. Previous inventors, including John Fitch, had had to build their own engines. Also, Fulton was able to employ mechanics and experimenters who had, over the past 2 decades, gained considerable experience with steam engines. It was Fulton's luck and genius to be able to combine these elements into a commercially successful steamboat venture.

Further Reading

The first, and still useful, biography of Fulton is Cadwallader D. Colden, *The Life of Robert Fulton* (1817). The best biography is H. W. Dickinson, *Robert Fulton, Engineer and Artist: His Life and Works* (1913). Also useful is George Dangerfield, *Chancellor Robert R. Livingston of New York, 1746-1813* (1960). For the prehistory of steamboats see James Thomas Flexner, *Steamboats Come True: American Inventors in Action* (1944). □

G

George Gallup

George Gallup (1901-1984) was a pioneer in the field of public opinion polling. He developed methods for perfecting the selection of sample populations, interviewing techniques, and formulation of questions. He also was a teacher and a proponent of educational reform.

George Horace Gallup was born on November 18, 1901, in the small town of Jefferson, Iowa. He was the son of George Henry Gallup, a farmer as well as a real estate dealer in agricultural land, and of Nettie Davenport. All of his higher education took place at the University of Iowa where he received a B.A. in 1923, an M.A. in 1925, and a Ph.D. in 1928. On December 27, 1925, he married Ophelia Smith Miller. They had two sons, Alec Miller and George Horace, Jr., who carried on their father's polling organization, and a daughter, Julia Gallup Laughlin.

From Teaching to Polling

Gallup's career as a teacher began after he received a bachelor's degree and stayed to teach journalism and psychology from 1923 to 1929 at his alma mater, the University of Iowa. He then moved to Drake University at Des Moines, Iowa, where he served as head of the Department of Journalism until 1931. In that year he moved to Northwestern University, Evanston, Illinois, as professor of journalism and advertising. The next year he moved to New York City to join the advertising agency of Young and Rubicam as director of research and then as vice-president from 1937 to 1947. From 1933 to 1937 he was also professor of journalism at Columbia University, but he had to give up this position shortly after he formed his own polling company, the American Institute of Public Opinion (Gallup Poll), in 1935, where he concentrated on attitude research. He was

also the founder (1939) and president of the Audience Research Institute. Other positions were: chief executive officer and chairman of the board of Gallup Organization, Inc., and president of Public Opinion Surveys, Inc., and of Gallup International Research Institutes, Inc., which had 35 affiliates doing research in over 70 foreign countries.

Apart from these business positions Gallup was active in professional and public service groups. He was president of the International Association of Public Opinion Institutes, 1947-1984, and of the National Municipal League, 1953-1956, and chair of the All-America Cities Award Committee, a jury which selects All-America cities on the basis of intelligent and effective citizen activity. He founded Quill and Scroll, an international honor society for high school journalists, and served as chair of its board of trustees. Gallup continued in nearly all of these offices until his death of heart failure on July 27, 1984, in Tschingel, Switzerland.

A Pioneer in Polling

By 1944 George Gallup was widely recognized as one of the major pioneers in public opinion polling and had participated in the creation of methods to achieve a high degree of accuracy in discovering the public's opinions on a wide variety of issues. He first developed his research techniques to test audience reaction to advertising and features sections of both newspapers and magazines and then sharpened his survey methods to include radio audiences.

Gallup had firm beliefs in the validity of polling. In fact, he believed that polls made a positive contribution to the democratic process. He wrote that public opinion polls provided political leaders with an accurate gauge of public opinion, proved that the common people do make good decisions, focused attention on major issues of the day, uncovered many "areas of ignorance," helped administra-

343

tors of government departments to make wiser decisions, made it more difficult for political bosses to pick presidential candidates "in smoke-filled rooms," revealed that the people are not motivated in their voting solely by self-interest, and helped define the "mandate" of the people in national elections.

During the 1930s and 1940s he improved the methods of pre-election surveys so as to gain accuracy. The results of polls taken in 392 elections in the United States and several foreign countries by his American Institute of Public Opinion achieved a mean average error of only 3.9 percent. Such a high degree of accuracy resulted from his methods of choosing population samples that are highly representative of the nation, of interviewing people rather than mailing out questionnaires, and of polling right up to election day in order to discover any changes in opinion over time.

In later life Gallup came to recognize that pre-election surveys had very little influence on politicians, many of whom expressed some contempt for them. He therefore dismissed the claim that polls were dangerous to a free political process because of their undue influence on politicians. Majority opinion, as made known by opinion polls, is "not necessarily a controlling factor in the legislation that emerges from Congress." In his view, "well-organized minorities can and do thwart the will of the majority." To safeguard the interests of the majority he recommended greater use of the initiative and referendum, both on a state and national scale. He firmly believed, however, that a carefully prepared opinion survey could be as accurate as a referendum and would be a lot cheaper.

Always an Educator

George Gallup was best known as an entrepreneur in the business of discovering what people think about issues. But he was also an educator, and this experience, plus his study of the attitudes of millions of people, led him to formulate a philosophy of education which he described in *The Miracle Ahead* (1964). The collective views of people, he affirmed, are usually sound and logical; the people are not led by their emotions as elitists claim. However, their thinking about issues does not go deep enough. Humans have been slow to recognize the great power of the brain and make too little use of it. Thus far humanity has made real progress in enhancing its comfort and well-being, but in human relations we are no more advanced than the ancient Greeks. To achieve greater and more rapid progress, a new education system must be created to enhance our mental powers. The present system does not encourage in students a conception of education as a lifelong process. It does not provide mastery of the major fields of knowledge or essential communication skills nor the creative talents needed to find new and better solutions to the student's and society's problems. Training the mind involves the teaching of perception or awareness, concentration, organization of data, objectivity, problem solving, decision making, and creativity. Gallup was particularly affirmative toward the case history method of teaching, which offers "perhaps the best method that mankind has yet found to transmit wisdom as opposed to knowledge."

Awards and Publications

Gallup was widely honored for his creative work and enjoyed a long list of awards: distinguished achievement award, Syracuse University, 1950; honor award, University of Missouri, 1958; elected to Hall of Fame in Distribution, 1962; Distinguished Citizen Award, National Municipal League, 1962; Advertising Gold Medal, *Printers' Ink,* 1964; Parlin Award, American Marketing Association, 1965; Christopher Columbus International Prize, 1968; distinguished achievement award from New Jersey chapter of American Marketing Association, 1975; National Association of Secondary School Principals award, 1975; elected to Advertising Hall of Fame, 1977, and to Market Research Hall of Fame, 1978. He received honorary LL.D. degrees from Northwestern University, Drake University, Boston University, Chattanooga University, and the University of Iowa; an honorary D.Sc. from Tufts University; an honorary L.H.D. from Colgate University; and an honorary D.C.L. from Rider College.

His most important publications were: *The Pulse of Democracy: The Public Opinion Poll and How It Works* (1940, reprinted 1968); *A Guidebook to Public Opinion Polls* (1944); *Secrets of Long Life* (1960); *The Miracle Ahead* (1964); *A Survey of the Public's Attitudes Toward the Public Schools* (1969); *Attitudes of Young Americans* (1971); *The Gallup Poll: Public Opinion, 1935-1971* (1972); *Sophisticated Poll Watcher's Guide* (1976); and *The Gallup Poll: 1972-77* (1978). He was editor of *The Gallup Poll: Public Opinion* (1979–1983).

Further Reading

Gallup's books are the best sources for his opinions and philosophy. Books on opinion surveys and his role are Albert H.
Cantril, editor, *Polling on the Issues* (1980) and A. H. Cantril
and Charles W. Roll, *Polls: Their Use and Misuse in Politics*
(1972). The following articles provide reviews of his books
and some information on his career: *TIME* (May 3, 1948);
Newsweek (August 20, 1956); *New Republic* (December 16,
1972; April 8, 1978); *Psychology Today* (June 1973); and
American Historical Review (October 1973). The best obituary, with pertinent data on his career, was in the *New York
Times* (July 28 and 29, 1984). □

James Abram Garfield

**James Abram Garfield (1831-1881) was an American Civil
War general before becoming the twentieth president of
the United States. He was assassinated after 6 months in
office.**

James A. Garfield was born in the log cabin of American
myth on Nov. 19, 1831, near Cleveland, Ohio. Although
his family dated back to the Massachusetts Bay Colony,
his immediate ancestors had not prospered, and Garfield's
upbringing was plagued by dire poverty. His father died
when James was 2 years old, and he was early put out to
labor to help keep the family intact.

Garfield matriculated at the Western Reserve Eclectic
Institute, later called Hiram College. He graduated from
Williams College and, before he was 30, became a lay
preacher for the Disciples of Christ. He taught school briefly
and returned to Hiram as a professor and head of the college, but he did not enjoy the life. "You and I know," he
wrote a friend, "that teaching is not the work in which a
man can live and grow." Still, Garfield remained bookish
throughout his life, and while by no means brilliant or
original, he emerges as truly distinctive in his occasional
writings, letters, and diary. These reveal a perspicacious
mind, shrewd insight into his contemporaries' personalities,
and a rare comprehension among politicos of the day of the
vast changes through which the United States was going.

War and Politics

In 1859 Garfield was elected to the Ohio Senate and
became a leading Union supporter in the Civil War. He
accepted a commission as colonel and, typically, set about
studying military strategy and organization. His readings
must have been well selected because his rise in rank was
rapid even for the Civil War era. An active role in the Battle
of Middle Creek on Jan. 10, 1862, made him a brigadier
general, and, in April, he fought during the bloody second
day at Shiloh. After that he left the lines to become chief of
staff through the Chickamauga campaign, organizing a division of military information and being promoted to major
general.

Garfield's military career reflected the dexterity with
which he would later escape political crises unscathed, for
although he was closely associated with several disasters
that ruined associates, he himself escaped blame. Indeed, in
December 1863 Garfield was elected to the House of Rep-

resentatives in recognition of his military service and, until
his death, was never again out of Federal office. His Ohio
district was safe for Republicans, so Garfield could concentrate on the affairs of office, and he was the leader of his
party in the House during the presidency of Rutherford B.
Hayes.

Garfield was capable of neatly straddling a volatile
issue. He was never so strong on the high-tariff issue as were
most of his Republican colleagues and, as late as his presidential campaign of 1880, he remained publicly equivocal
on the issue of Federal patronage. The Federal jobs at the
disposal of the party in power were the life-blood of politics
during the "gilded age." One wing of the Republican
party—the "stalwarts"—called for no dalliance on the
question, claiming the jobs as the just due of those who
worked to put the party in power. Another wing of reformers, the "doctrinaires," felt that the quality of government would be improved if Federal jobs were assigned on
the basis of merit. Garfield attempted to placate both sides.

On the money question Garfield was firm, standing
unalterably for "hard" currency when many of his former
constituents called for inflation. But he was less steadfast on
the Southern question, alternating between "waving the
bloody shirt"—exploiting Northern bitterness toward the
South over the war—and supporting a more compromising
attitude.

Monetary Scandal

Scandal nearly wrecked Garfield's career when he was
accused of accepting money in return for supporting a con-

gressional subsidy of the transcontinental railroad's construction company. But he managed to sidestep and survive the accusation, and he also weathered the revelation that he had accepted a legal fee from a company involved in government-contracted improvement of Washington streets. These lapses in ethics were more the result of carelessness than personal corruption, and Garfield in his last years was extremely careful to avoid any possible conflicts of interest. On the whole, he had a good record in the graft-sullied political world of the day, and reformers who could not support James G. Blaine were willing to accept Garfield.

In 1880 Garfield was elected to the U.S. Senate from Ohio, but before he took his seat, he agreed to manage John Sherman's campaign to win the Republican presidential nomination. The chief Republican candidates that year were former U.S. president Ulysses S. Grant and Senator James G. Blaine. Sherman's hopes were based on an anticipated deadlock between the two front-runners, which would force the convention to turn to him as a compromise candidate. The convention did, indeed, deadlock and settle on a third person, but that person was Garfield rather than Sherman. Toward the end of his life Sherman became convinced that his manager had actively betrayed him, but close examination of the records by several historians indicates that this was not so. Garfield knew before the convention that certain parties were working for him as a compromise candidate, but he neither encouraged nor effectively discouraged the talk. He certainly had presidential ambitions, but like a good party regular, he recognized Sherman's seniority among Ohio politicians and was willing to wait his turn. When the opportunity beckoned in 1880, he was more than ready.

Election to the Presidency

The immediate problem was the party's "stalwarts." Garfield had selected one of their number, Chester A. Arthur, as his vice-presidential candidate, but the leader of the "stalwarts." New York politician Roscoe Conkling, refused to work to get the important New York vote without specific promises from Garfield on patronage. Conkling believed that he received such promises and did help elect Garfield, but soon after the election, the two fell out. Garfield named Conkling's archenemy, James G. Blaine, to be his secretary of state and increasingly relied on Blaine's counsel. In a battle over the appointment of the collector of customs for the Port of New York (one of the richest plums in the Federal patronage), Conkling resigned his Senate seat and asked the New York Legislature, in effect, to rebuke the President by reelecting him. What might have happened under normal circumstances is impossible to tell, for on July 2, 1881, Garfield was shot in the back in a Washington railroad station by a deranged man named Charles Guiteau, who claimed he had killed the President in order to put Chester A. Arthur into office.

Garfield did not die immediately. But doctors could not locate one of the bullets, and infection eventually sapped his strength. Conkling was not reelected in the shocked aftermath of the shooting, and a civil service reform bill aimed at Conkling-style politics eventually passed Congress. But

Garfield never left his bed; he died at Alberon, N.J., on Sept. 19, 1881.

A well-featured, heavily bearded man whose piercing eyes are the most striking feature of his photographs, Garfield was a significant figure in the development of congressional power during the 1860s and 1870s. His premature death precludes knowledge of how his perceptions of the changes America was undergoing might have impacted the successfulness of his presidency.

Further Reading

A primary source of information on Garfield is Theodore Clarke Smith, *The Life and Letters of James Garfield* (2 vols., 1925). An excellent biography is Robert Granville Caldwell, *James A. Garfield: Party Chieftain* (1931). Earlier works on Garfield tend to be absurdly laudatory, virtually ignoring problems connected with Garfield's military career and financial dealings. Garfield is discussed in Kenneth W. Wheeler, ed., *For the Union: Ohio Leaders in the Civil War* (1968). The best political survey of the age is H. Wayne Morgan, *From Hayes to McKinley: National Party Politics, 1877-1896* (1969). For the election of 1880 see Arthur M. Schlesinger, Jr., ed., *History of American Presidential Elections* (4 vols., 1971). ☐

William Lloyd Garrison

William Lloyd Garrison (1805-1879), American editor, reformer, and antislavery crusader, became the symbol of the age of aggressive abolitionism.

William Lloyd Garrison was born on Dec. 10, 1805, in Newburyport, Mass. His father deserted the family in 1808, and the three children were raised in near poverty by their mother, a hardworking, deeply religious woman. Young Garrison lived for a time in the home of a kindly Baptist deacon, where he received the bare rudiments of an education. He was later apprenticed to a shoemaker, a cabinetmaker, and finally to the printer and editor of the *Newburyport Herald*.

Editor and Printer

Garrison borrowed money in 1826 to buy part of the *Newburyport Free Press*; it soon failed. He worked as a printer in Boston and in 1827 helped edit a temperance paper, the *National Philanthropist*. Seeing life as an uncompromising moral crusade against sin, and believing it possible to perfect a Christian society by reforming men and institutions, Garrison fitted easily into the evangelical currents of his time. In 1828 a meeting with Benjamin Lundy, the Quaker antislavery editor of the *Genius of Emancipation*, called his attention to that cause. Since 1828 was a presidential election year, Garrison accepted editorship of a pro-Jackson newspaper in Vermont, in which he also supported pacifism, temperance, and the emancipation of slaves. After the election, Garrison accepted a position with Lundy on the *Genius* in Baltimore.

Garrison's Brand of Abolitionism

The antislavery movement at this time was decentralized and divided. Some people believed slavery should be

him as a symbol of unbridled Northern antislavery radicalism; Georgia, in fact, offered $5,000 for his arrest and conviction. Garrison, for his part, continued to pour invective not only on slaveholders but on those who failed to attack the system as violently as he; Northerners who equivocated were guilty of "moral lapses," Southerners were "Satanic man stealers." His bitter attacks on the colonizationists, summarized in *Thoughts on Colonization* (1832), and his running battle with the New England clergy (whose churches he called "cages of unclean birds") for their refusal to condemn slavery unconditionally probably lost more adherents for the antislavery cause than they gained. Garrison introduced discussions into his paper of "other topics . . . intimately connected with the great doctrine of inalienable human rights," among them women's rights, capital punishment, antisabbatarianism, and temperance (he also opposed theaters and tobacco). Thus by the late 1830s abolition was but one portion (albeit the most important) of Garrison's plan for the "universal emancipation" of all men from all forms of sin and injustice.

Organizing the Movement

Recognizing the need for organization, Garrison was instrumental in forming the New England Antislavery Society (later the Massachusetts Antislavery Society) in 1832 and served as its secretary and salaried agent. He visited England in 1833, returning to help found the national American Antislavery Society. In September 1834 he married Helen Benson of Connecticut, who bore him seven children, five of whom survived. When his friend George Thompson, the British abolitionist, visited Boston in 1835, feeling ran so high that a "respectable broadcloth mob," as Garrison called it, failing to find Thompson, seized and manhandled Garrison. Garrison's refusal to consider political action as a way of abolishing slavery (he felt it would delay it) and his desire to join the antislavery movement to other reforms gradually alienated many supporters. In 1840 his stand seriously divided the American Antislavery Society and led to formation of the rival American and Foreign Antislavery Society.

In 1844 Garrison adopted the slogan "No union with slaveholders," arguing that since the Constitution was a proslavery document, the Union it held together should be dissolved by the separation of free from slave states. Yet, despite his reputation, Garrison was a pacifist and did not believe in violence. He thought Harriet Beecher Stowe's *Uncle Tom's Cabin* important chiefly as a novel of "Christian non-resistance," and though he respected John Brown's aim, he did not approve of his method. He wanted, he wrote, "nothing more than the peaceful abolition of slavery, by an appeal to the reason and conscience of the slaveholder."

Civil War

Garrison supported the Civil War for he believed it an act of providence to destroy slavery, and his son served as an officer in a Massachusetts African American regiment. Critical at first of President Abraham Lincoln for making preservation of the union rather than abolition of slavery his

abolished gradually, some immediately; some believed slaves should be only partly free until educated and capable of being absorbed into society, others that they ought to be freed but settled in colonies outside the United States. There were those who saw slavery as a moral and religious issue; others considered abolition a problem to be decided by legal and political means. Garrison, like Lundy, at first favored gradual emancipation and colonization. But soon Garrison opposed both means as slow and impractical, asking in his first editorial in the *Genius* for "immediate and complete emancipation" of slaves.

Garrison's militancy got the paper and himself into trouble. Successfully sued for libel, he spent 44 days in jail, emerging in June 1830 with plans for an abolitionist paper of his own. Encouraged by Boston friends, he and a partner published the first number of the *Liberator* on Jan. 1, 1831, bearing the motto, "Our country is the world—our countrymen are mankind," adapted from Thomas Paine. Attacking the "timidity, injustice, and absurdity" of gradualists and colonizationists, Garrison declared himself for "the immediate enfranchisement of our slave population." Promising to be "as harsh as truth, and as uncompromising as justice," he warned his readers, "I am in earnest—I will not equivocate—I will not excuse—I will not retreat a single inch—*and I will be heard.*"

The *Liberator,* which never had a circulation of over 3,000 and annually lost money, soon gained Garrison a national abolitionist reputation. Southerners assumed a connection between his aggressive journalism and Nat Turner's 1831 slave rebellion in Virginia and tended to see chief aim, Garrison praised the President's Emancipation Proclamation and supported his reelection in 1864—as Wendell Phillips and some other abolitionists did not. Garrison favored dissolution of the American Antislavery Society in 1865, believing its work done, but he lost to Phillips, who wished to continue it. Garrison wrote his last editorial on Dec. 29, 1865, "the object for which the *Liberator* was commenced—the extermination of chattel slavery—having been gloriously consummated," and retired to Roxbury, Mass., writing occasionally for the press. He died on May 24, 1879.

Despite his reputation, Garrison's influence was restricted to New England (where it was not unchallenged), and his brand of immediatism was never the majority view. When the main thrust of abolition after 1840 turned political, pointing toward the Free Soil and Republican parties, Garrison remained outside, and in terms of practical accomplishment, others did more than he. Yet it was Garrison who became the general symbol of abolitionism. He was influential in relating it to issues of free speech, free press, and the rights of assembly and petition and to the powerful religious evangelism of the times. In his harsh and tactless way, he forced popular awareness of the gap between what the Declaration of Independence and the Constitution said and what the nation did, constantly challenging the country to put its ideals into practice.

Further Reading

The biography written by Garrison's sons, Wendell Phillips Garrison and Francis Jackson Garrison, *William Lloyd Garrison* (4 vols., 1885-1889), though not wholly trustworthy, is essential. Oliver Johnson, *William Lloyd Garrison and His Times,* with an introduction by John Greenleaf Whittier (1880), is unduly admiring. Ralph Korngold's study of Wendell Phillips and Garrison, *Two Friends of Man* (1950), is excellent. Russel B. Nye, *William Lloyd Garrison and the Humanitarian Reformers* (1955), is a useful short biography. Walter M. Merrill, *Against Wind and Tide* (1963), and John L. Thomas, *The Liberator: William Lloyd Garrison* (1963), are good recent studies. George M. Fredrickson, ed., *William Lloyd Garrison* (1968), is a three-part work comprising a selection of Garrison's writings, articles expressing opinions of him by his contemporaries, and articles by modern writers appraising his work. Henry Mayer's *All on Fire: William Lloyd Garrison and the Aboliting of Slavery* (1998) focuses specifically on Garrison as an abolitionist. □

William Henry Gates III

Microsoft cofounder and chief executive officer William (Bill) H. Gates III (born 1955) became the wealthiest man in America and one of the most influential personalities on the ever-evolving information superhighway and computer industry.

William (Bill) Henry Gates III became the most famous businessman in recent history. His supreme accomplishment was to design and develop innovative software for the personal computer, making PC's universally popular machines. In user friendly language, communicating with computers is a matter of

"translating" a person's native language into the codes that a computer understands. The easier this translation is to make, the easier it is to work with the computer and the more accessible and widely used the computer becomes. Gates' gift for software design, as well as his skills in business, made Microsoft, the company he cofounded with a high school friend in Richmond, Washington, a multi billion-dollar empire.

Love of Computer Technology

Gates was born on October 28, 1955 in Seattle, Washington. He was the second child and only son of William Henry Gates Jr., a prominent Seattle attorney, and Mary Maxwell, a former school teacher. Gates had two siblings. His sister, Kristi, one year his senior, became his tax accountant. Libby, nine years his junior, lived in Seattle raising her two children. Although Gates' parents had a law career in mind for their son, he developed an early interest in computer science and began studying computers in the seventh grade at Seattle's Lakeside School. Lakeside was a private school chosen by Gates' parents in the hopes that it would be more challenging for their son's intellectual drive and insatiable curiosity. At Lakeside Gates became acquainted with Paul Allen, a classmate with similar interests in technology who would eventually become his business partner.

Gates' early experiences with computers included debugging (eliminating errors from) programs for the Computer Center Corporation's PDP-10, helping to computerize electric power grids for the Bonneville Power Administration, and founding with Allen a firm called Traf-O-Data while still in high school. Their small company earned them $20 thousand in fees for analyzing local traffic patterns.

While working with the Computer Center's PDP-10, Gates was responsible for what was probably the first computer virus, a program that copies itself into other programs and ruins data. Discovering that the machine was connected to a national network of computers called Cybernet, Gates invaded the network and installed a program on the main computer that sent itself to the rest of the network's computers and crashed. When Gates was found out, he was severely reprimanded and he kept away from computers for his entire junior year at Lakeside. Without the lure of computers, Gates made plans in 1970 for college and law school. But by 1971 he was back helping Allen write a class scheduling program for their school's computer.

The Article That Started It All

Gates entered Harvard University in 1973 and pursued his studies for the next year and a half. However, his life was to change in January of 1975 when Popular Mechanics carried a cover story on a $350 microcomputer, the Altair, made by a firm called MITS in New Mexico. When Allen excitedly showed him the story, Gates knew where he wanted to be: at the forefront of computer software design.

Gates and Allen first wrote a BASIC interpreter for the Altair computer. BASIC was a simple, interactive computer language designed in the 1960s. "Interpreter" describes a program that executes a source program by reading it one line at a time, performing operations one line at a time, and performing operations immediately. MITS, which encouraged and helped Gates and Allen, finally challenged them to bring their software in for a demonstration. Because they did not own an Altair (nor had they seen the 8080 microprocessing chip that was at the heart of the machine), Gates had to write and test his BASIC interpreter on a simulator program which acted like the 8080. Nonetheless, their BASIC ran the first time it was tested at MITS.

Gates dropped out of Harvard in 1975, ending his academic life and beginning his career in earnest as a software designer and entrepreneur. At this time, Gates and Allen cofounded Microsoft. They wrote programs for the early Apple and Commodore machines and expanded BASIC to run on microcomputers other than the Altair. One of Gates' most significant opportunities arrived in 1980 when he was approached by IBM to help with their personal computer project, code name Project Chess. Eventually asked to design the operating system for the new machine, Gates developed the Microsoft Disk Operating System, or MS-DOS. Not only did he sell IBM on the new operating system, but he also convinced the computer giant to shed the veil of secrecy surrounding the specifications of its PC so that others could write software for the machine. The result was the proliferation of licenses for MS-DOS as software developers quickly moved to become compatible with IBM. Over two million copies of MS-DOS were sold by 1984. Because IMB's PC architecture was opened up by Gates, MS-DOS and its related applications can run on almost any IBM-compatible PC. By the early 1990s, Microsoft had sold more than 100 million copies of MS-DOS, making the operating system the all-time leader in software sales. For his achievements in science and technology, Gates received the Howard Vollum Award in 1984 by Reed College in Portland, Oregon.

In 1987 Gates entered the world of computer-driven multimedia when he began promoting CD-ROM technology. CD-ROM is an optical storage medium easily connected to a PC, and a CD-ROM disc has an incredibly larger capacity that can store encyclopedias, feature films, and complex interactive games. Gates hoped to expand his business by combining PCS with the information reservoirs provided by CD-ROM and was soon marketing a number of multimedia products.

Gates' competitive drive and fierce desire to win has made him a powerful force in business but has also consumed much of his personal life. In the six years between 1978 and 1984 he took a total of only two weeks vacation. In 1985 a popular magazine included him on their list of most eligible bachelors. His status did not change until New Year's day 1994 when he married Melinda French, a Microsoft manager, on the Hawaiian island of Lanai. The ceremony was held on the island's Challenge golf course and Gates kept it private by buying out the unused rooms at the local hotel and by hiring all of the helicopters in the area to keep photographers from using them. His fortune at the time of his marriage was estimated at close to seven billion dollars. By 1997 his worth was estimated at approximately $37 billion, earning him the "richest man in America" title.

In *Hard Drive,* James Wallace and Jim Erickson quote Gates as saying, "I can do anything if I put my mind to it." His ambition has made him the head of a robust, innovative software firm and the richest man in America.

The Future for Microsoft

Gates emits the same competitiveness, drive, ambition, and need to win that was present 21 years ago when he dropped out of Harvard to start Microsoft. But some of the players have changed. Allen left Microsoft to become one of the country's most successful hi-tech venture-capital investors and owner of the Portland Trail Blazers basketball team. However, he returned to serve on Microsoft's board. Gates considers Steve Ballmer, a former Harvard classmate, his best friend and closest advisor. He hired Ballmer away from Proctor & Gamble in 1980 with the lure of a $50 thousand a year salary and a share of the business. In an interview with *Newsweek,* Gates is quoted as saying, "I think it's a phenomenal business partnership.... And within the company, everyone has understood that we work very closely together and have a very common view of where we want to go." Gates shared his vision for the future of Microsoft with *Information Outlook.* Gates said, "We're in four businesses today, and in ten years we'll be in the same four businesses; desktop operating systems, productivity applications, server software, and interactive content business." He believes that speech recognition, natural language understanding, automatic learning, flat screen displays, and optic fiber will have the greatest technological impacts on the industry over the next 15 years.

Many of Gates' detractors criticize him not just for his success, but because they feel he tries to unfairly and maybe even illegally leverage his company's dominance of the desktop operating systems. Once Microsoft integrates its Internet browser, Explorer, and its Microsoft Network into its Windows Operating Systems, it will have the ultimate—Active Desktop—due out with Windows 97. Critics feel it will put all other entries at a disadvantage. "If improving a product based on customer input is willful maintenance of trying to stay in business and not have Netscape turn their browser into the most popular operating system, then I think that is what we are supposed to do," was Gates' response to his critics as quoted by *Time*.

Gates and his wife had their first child, Jennifer, in April of 1996. Although many describe Gates as cold, relentless, and impersonal, his friends find him more reflective since his marriage and the birth of his daughter. Further, he recognizes his overall contribution. While he appears a little less exhausting and more civil, friends say he still pushes hard and keeps score.

Gates expects to run Microsoft for at least the next ten years at which time he plans to retire and focus on giving his money away. His philanthropic endeavors have been guided by his interests. He has directed those efforts primarily toward educational sources such as schools and libraries.

Further Reading

Since 1981 business magazine articles have described aspects of Gates' career. *Gates: How Microsoft's Mogul Reinvented an Industry—and Made Himself the Richest Man in America* by Stephen Manes and Paul Andrews (1994) is an authoritative and detailed biography. *Big Blues, The Unmaking of IBM* by Paul Carroll (1993) favorably compares Gates' entrepreneurial approach to business to IBM's management by committee approach. "E-Mail From Bill" by John Seabrook, *New Yorker* magazine (January 10, 1994) provides insight to Gates' goals and personality. *Architects of the Future, Microsoft Corporation 1993 Annual Report* contains product descriptions and marketshare analysis along with income statements and a discussion of litigation and federal agencies' inquiries. *PC Week* provides updates on the latest Microsoft products.

For books about Bill Gates see: *Encyclopedia of Computer Science,* Van Nostrand Reinhold, 1993 p 519. Gates, Bill with Nathan Myhevrold and Peter Rinearson, *The Road Ahead.* Ichbiah, David and Susan L. Knepper, *The Making of Microsoft,* Prima, 1991. Manes, Stephen and Paul Andrews, *Gates,* Doubleday, 1993. Slater, Robert, *Portraits in Silicon,* MIT Press, 1987. Wallace, James and Jim Erickson, *Hard Drive,* Wiley, 1992.

For periodical articles about Bill Gates see: *The Future of Microsoft.* Economist, V327, May 22, 1993, pp. 25-27. *Information Outlook,* May 1997. *National Review,* January 27, 1997. *New York Times,* January 3, 1994. *New Yorker,* January 10, 1994, pp. 48-61. *Newsweek,* June 23, 1997. *PC Magazine,* March 25, 1997. *Time,* January 13, 1997. □

Theodor Geisel

Theodor Geisel (1904–1991), better known as Dr. Seuss, wrote the popular children's book *The Cat in the Hat* among others.

Theodor Geisel, better known to millions of children as Dr. Seuss, brought a whimsical touch and a colorful imagination to the world of children's books. Before Geisel, juvenile books were largely pastel, predictable, and dominated by a didactic tone. Though Dr. Seuss books sometimes included morals, they sounded less like behavioral guidelines and more like, "listen to your feelings" and "take care of the environment," universal ideas that would win over the hearts of youngsters from around the world; Geisel's 47 books were translated into 20 languages and have sold more than 200 million copies. Of the ten bestselling hardcover children's books of all time, four were written by Geisel: *The Cat in the Hat, Green Eggs and Ham, One Fish, Two Fish, Red Fish, Blue Fish,* and *Hop on Pop.*

Wrote for Adults as well as Children

Geisel's last two books spent several months on the bestseller lists and include themes that appeal to adults as well as children. "Finally I can say that I write not for kids but for *people*," he commented in the *Los Angeles Times*. Many of his readers were surprised to learn that Geisel had no children of his own, though he had stepchildren from his second marriage to Audrey Stone Dimond; he once said, "You make 'em, I amuse 'em," as quoted in the *Chicago Tribune*. According to the *Los Angeles Times*, the author also remarked, "I don't think spending your days surrounded by kids is necessary to write the kind of books I write. . . . Once a writer starts talking down to kids, he's lost. Kids can pick up on that kind of thing."

Practiced Drawing at the Zoo

When he was a child, Geisel practiced sketching at the local zoo, where his father was superintendent. He went on to graduate from Dartmouth College in 1925 and subsequently studied at the Lincoln College of Oxford University. After dropping out of Oxford, he traveled throughout Europe, mingling with emigres in Paris, including writer Ernest Hemingway. Eventually returning to New York, he spent 15 years in advertising before joining the army and making two Oscar-winning documentaries, *Hitler Lives* and *Design for Death*.

Geisel began writing the verses of his first book, *And to Think That I Saw It on Mulberry Street,* in 1936 during a rough sea passage. Published a year later, the book won much acclaim, largely because of its unique drawings. All of Geisel's books, in fact, feature crazy-looking creatures that are sometimes based on real animals, but usually consist of such bizarre combinations of objects as a centipede and a horse and a camel with a feather duster on its head. Unlike many puppeteers and cartoonists who have capitalized on their creations by selling their most familiar images to big-time toymakers, though, Dr. Seuss concentrated his efforts on creating captivating books.

"Basically an Educator"

Admired among fellow authors and editors for his honesty and hard work, the Pulitzer Prize-winning author, according to Ruth MacDonald in the *Chicago Tribune,* "perfected the art of telling great stories with a vocabulary as small as sometimes 52 or 53 words." "[Geisel] was not only a master of word and rhyme and an original and eccentric artist," declared Gerald Harrison, president of Random House's merchandise division, in *Publisher's Weekly,* "but down deep, I think he was basically an educator. He helped teach kids that reading was a joy and not a chore. . . . For those of us who worked with him, he taught us to strive for excellence in all the books we published."

Further Reading

See *Chicago Tribune,* 9/26/91; *Entertainment Weekly,* 10/11/91; *Los Angeles Times,* 9/26/91; *People,* 10/7/91; *Publishers Weekly,* 10/25/91; and the *Times* (London) 9/27/91. □

Murray Gell-Mann

The American physicist Murray Gell-Mann (born 1929) coined the definition "quarks" to describe the triplets of particles that form the cores of atoms. The Nobel Prize winner for physics in 1969, he helped to develop the Stanford model, which describes the behavior of subatomic particles and their forces.

Murray Gell-Mann was born on September 15, 1929, in New York City of Austrian immigrant parents. A precocious child, he attended a special school for gifted children, where he took a physics course. "It was the dullest course I've ever taken," he told *Omni* magazine in 1985, "and the only course I've ever done badly in!"

Early Academic Career

Gell-Mann graduated from school at the age of 15 and entered Yale University, where he sailed through a bachelor's degree to earn his diploma in 1948. Next came graduate study at the Massachusetts Institute of Technology (MIT), where he claims to have found out, for the very first time, what true scientific research can achieve. Totally committed to his work, he completed his doctorate in 1951, and proceeded to the Princeton Institute for Advanced Studies, where he had been awarded a research grant.

Gell-Mann's first academic appointment was in 1952 with the Institute for Nuclear Studies at the University of Chicago, where he started the work on elementary particles that was to bring him the Nobel Prize in physics in 1969. In 1955 he moved to the California Institute of Technology (CalTech). A member of the National Academy of Sciences and the American Academy of Arts and Sciences, Gell-Mann was the recipient of the Dannie Heineman Prize of the American Physical Society in 1959 and of numerous special lectureships and honors.

Order out of Chaos

Gell-Mann was one of the young physicists of the 1950s who tried to bring order into the chaotic field of elementary particles. In 1953 he proposed the invariant quality of "strangeness" to explain the behavior of some of the elementary particles. This quality, he noted, was conserved in strong and electromagnetic interactions but not in weak interactions. Strangeness proved useful in ordering the particles to form a classification chart somewhat analogous to the periodic table of elements. The chart not only listed families of particles, but by means of it Gell-Mann was able to predict the existence of a hitherto unknown particle, omega-minus, which was detected in 1964.

Physicists began using the term "strange particles" to describe a group of particles, inclusive for K-mesons and hyperons, that exhibited several peculiarities. To explain the anomalously long lifetimes of these particles, Gell-Mann advanced the theory of "associated production": the strong forces responsible for strange particles could act to create them only in batches of more than one at a time. Using his strangeness formulations, Gell-Mann also gave descriptions in detail of numerous decay events of strange particles, as well as prophesying the existence of the neutral xi particle.

In his continuing search for a more general elementary particle theory, Gell-Mann introduced a hypothetical particle, the quark, which is viewed as the fundamental stable constituent of the other particles and therefore is possibly the ultimate building block in the physical universe. Although quarks were not known to exist in the early 1960s when he began to work on particle physics, by the mid-1990s six types, forming three pairs, had been positively identified, and Gell-Mann does not rule out the possibility that there may be many more waiting for discovery.

During the Cold War years, Gell-Mann's work on particle physics was useful to the U.S. defense industries and the military. Notable among his assignments was his antisubmarine work for the Rand Corporation, and his service as a consultant to the Institute for Defense Analysis, especially with regard to the detection of nuclear test detonations.

His formal place of employment, however, was the University of Chicago, where he remained until 1955. The following year he took a professorship at CalTech.

A settled home on the coveted west coast notwithstanding, Gell-Mann left California in 1993 to work at the Santa Fe Institute—an institution he co-founded in 1984—to focus on complex adaptive systems, an interdisciplinary field.

Gell-Mann has written and co-authored many papers. His longer works include: *The Discovery of Subatomic Particles*, (1983) and *The Quark and the Jaguar*.

A Man of Many Interests

A man of wide interests, Gell-Mann speaks 13 languages fluently, is an accomplished ornithologist, and is very knowledgeable about the archeology of the Southwestern United States. A passionate conservationist, he helped to establish a nonprofit organization called the World Resources Institute.

Further Reading

Information on Murray Gell-Man can be found in *Omni* (May, 1985) and *The Scientific Life* (1962), contains an interesting interview with Gell-Mann. For background information on elementary particle physics see David Park, *Contemporary Physics* (1964). □

Richard Andrew Gephardt

United States Congressman Richard Andrew Gephardt (born 1941) has served in the U.S. House of Representatives since 1977 and was a candidate for the Democratic nomination for president in 1988. His protectionist campaign theme failed to win him the nomination. In 1989 he became Democratic majority leader in the House.

Richard A. Gephardt, first elected to Congress in 1976 from Missouri's Third Congressional District, epitomized the new breed of Democratic politicians which emerged in the 1970s and 1980s. These politicians, often labeled Atari Democrats, sought to wed the traditional party concern for social issues with new technology and fiscal conservatism. Gephardt's record reflects this new political pragmatism, which borrows from both liberal and conservative beliefs. The south St. Louis congressman endorsed constitutional amendments to ban abortion and school bussing; he supported tuition credits for parents of children in private schools, and school prayer; and he opposed gun control legislation. Yet he also supported a freeze on nuclear weapons and led the opposition to the MX missile. He also worked to stop military aid to the Nicaraguan Contras during the 1980s.

Richard Andrew Gephardt was born in St. Louis, Missouri, on January 31, 1941, to Louis Andrew and Loreen (Cassell) Gephardt, both the grandchildren of German immigrants. After completing high school in St. Louis, Gephardt enrolled at Northwestern University in Evanston, Illinois, majoring in speech and drama. He received a B.S. degree in 1962. He obtained a J.D. degree from the law school at the University of Michigan in 1965. One year later, in August 1966, Gephardt married Jane Ann Byrnes, formerly of Nebraska, whom he had met when both were undergraduates at Northwestern.

Early Political Career

Returning to south St. Louis where he was raised, Gephardt became active in ward politics and in 1971 was elected to the St. Louis board of aldermen. Five years later Gephardt ran for the Third District congressional seat vacated by retiring Congresswoman Leonor Sullivan. The middle-class, predominately white district, composed of Roman Catholic ethnic neighborhoods in south St. Louis, suburbs in St. Louis County, and a section of primarily rural Jefferson County, mirrored his centrist political philosophy. The 35-year-old Gephardt easily defeated his opponent, State Senator Donald Gralicke, in the Democratic primary

and took 64 percent of the vote in the general election against his Republican opponent, Joseph Badaracco.

After his arrival in Washington in 1977, Representative Gephardt quickly rose to prominence. Fellow Missouri Congressman Richard Bolling, then chairman of the House Rules Committee, arranged his assignment on the House Ways and Means Committee, a rare honor for a freshman legislator. Two years later Gephardt won a seat on the House Budget Committee. Through service on the Budget Committee Gephardt established his reputation as a fiscal conservative. In 1982 he and New Jersey Senator Bill Bradley sponsored the Fair Tax Act, popularly known as the Bradley-Gephardt Bill, which eventually became the Tax Reform Act of 1986. By 1984 Gephardt had joined the "inner circle" of House Democratic leadership with his selection as chairman of their caucus, the fourth-highest post behind speaker, majority leader, and majority whip.

Gephardt also organized attempts to reestablish the centrist position in the national Democratic Party following presidential party nominee Walter Mondale's overwhelming defeat by President Ronald Reagan in the 1984 càmpaign. In 1985 he announced the creation of the Democratic Leadership Council, composed of younger Democrats from the South and West including Georgia Senator Sam Nunn and Governors Bruce Babbitt of Arizona and Charles S. Robb of Virginia.

The Gephardt Amendment

Gephardt's best-known initiative was the Gephardt amendment, which directed the federal government to identify those nations with large trade surpluses with the United States and take action against any country that has achieved its advantage by unfair practices. The amendment called for negotiation, but if that failed, the president would be required to impose tariffs and take other punitive action that would reduce the trading partner's surplus by 10 percent per year. The Gephardt amendment proved particularly popular among blue collar workers threatened by the loss of employment in the automobile and steel industries and among Americans dissatisfied with the rapid rise of Japanese economic power. The amendment passed in the House by a four-vote margin and was added to the Omnibus Trade Bill of 1987. The Senate, however, rejected the controversial proposal aided by President Ronald Reagan's threat to veto the measure if it reached his desk.

Ran For the Presidential Nomination

Riding on the popularity of his amendment and his prestige as chair of the Democratic Leadership Council, Gephardt on February 23, 1987, became the first Democrat to declare his candidacy for the 1988 presidential nomination. In a 30-minute speech in St. Louis he established his campaign theme when he declared before the audience, "The next president must be as tough in negotiating the terms of trade as this president has been in negotiating with the Russians." When reminded that Democratic presidential nominee Walter Mondale came under sharp attack in the 1984 campaign for taking a protectionist stance, Gephardt replied, "The facts have changed. Mondale was talking about an issue that was about to happen. Now it has happened."

Gephardt plunged energetically into the race, particularly in the crucial Iowa caucus campaign. After months of dogged determination and some good fortune following the political demise of former Colorado Senator Gary Hart, Gephardt won the caucus contest on February 8, 1988. He then emerged as the frontrunner until his defeat by Massachusetts Governor Michael Dukakis in the New Hampshire primary one week later. Undaunted, Gephardt continued his campaign, winning the South Dakota primary on February 23 and hoping for a breakthrough on "Super Tuesday," the March 8 primary held simultaneously in 20 states. He won only in Missouri, his home state. Hoping to capitalize on the disaffection of blue collar automobile workers because of Japanese competition, the faltering and nearly broke Gephardt campaign focused all of its remaining energy on the March 23 Michigan primary. Rev. Jesse Jackson, however, staged a stunning upset, winning 53 percent of the vote; Dukakis got 29 percent, and Gephardt only 13 percent. Two days later Gephardt withdrew from the race.

Became House Majority Leader

Easily reelected to his congressional seat in 1988, Gephardt, who had campaigned in Iowa, New Hampshire, and Michigan as the populist outsider, quickly resumed his rapid ascent in the House Democratic leadership hierarchy. In 1989 he succeeded Congressman Thomas Foley to become House majority leader. In that role Gephardt continued to garner public attention with his spirited attacks on the

Bush administration. In March 1990, for example, Gephardt criticized what he termed President Bush's failure to capitalize on the political changes sweeping across Eastern Europe. Unveiling a Democratic alternative on Eastern Europe, Gephardt, in a speech before the Center for National Policy, outlined a broad initiative to support the reforms of Soviet President Mikhail S. Gorbachev through increased aid to emerging Eastern Bloc democracies and through a proposal to send U.S. food aid to the Soviet Union. Moreover, Gephardt continued to espouse the theme of economic nationalism, which was the center of his unsuccessful presidential campaign. However, he began to link trade policy with incentives to improve American education and the quality of American manufactured products.

Gephardt did not make another bid for the presidency in 1992. He often bumped heads with President Clinton. He opposed Clinton's North American Free Trade Agreement (NAFTA) because he believed it exported U.S. jobs overseas. In 1994 when Republicans became House majority, Gephardt was elected minority leader. According to the *New York Times,* Gephardt said he hoped to develop ''a strategy to represent the workers, the middle-income families, the poor families of this country.'' That year he announced a middle-class tax cut and, later, a plan to simplify tax rates. Both announcements came days before Clinton was to reveal his own plans for similar ideas. These actions were a source of friction between Clinton and Gephardt.

Further Reading

No book-length biographies currently exist on Richard Gephardt. However, brief discussions of his life and political accomplishments can be found in H. Rinie, ''The Gephardt File: Rebel Without A Cause,'' *U.S. News and World Report* (February 8, 1988); Elizabeth Drew, *Election Journal: Political Events of 1987-1988* (1989); and the *New York Times Biographical Service,* Vol. 18 (February 1987). See also Morton Kondracke, ''Man for All Seasons,'' *The New Republic* (July 3, 1989) and the *Los Angeles Times* (March 8, 1990). For Gephardt's vision for the Democratic Party, see David Corn, ''Beyond 'Too Far,''' *The Nation* (April 10, 1995). Information about the Gephardt/Clinton clash over NAFTA is in Amy Borrus, ''The Latest Trade War: Democrat vs. Democrat,'' *Business Week* (March 10, 1997) ☐

Geronimo

The career of Apache warrior Geronimo (1829-1909) was symbolic of the struggle for a Native American way of life in conflict with that of the advancing American frontiersmen.

Geronimo was born in No-doyohn Canyon in Arizona in June 1829. As he grew to manhood, he was apparently indolent, for he was called Goyakla, ''He Who Yawns.'' In 1858 his mother, wife, and three children were killed by Mexican bounty hunters, seeking scalps. ''I could not call back my loved ones, I could not bring back the dead Apaches, but I could rejoice in . . . revenge,'' he later declared. During the next 15 years he rose steadily as a war leader among the Apaches. Apache

agent John Clum, who arrested Geronimo in 1877, described him as ''erect as a mountain pine, while every outline of his symmetrical form indicated strength and endurance. His abundant ebony locks draped his ample shoulders, his stern features, his keen piercing eye, and his proud and graceful posture combined to create in him the model of an Apache war-chief.''

Forced onto the reservation at San Carlos in Arizona, Geronimo was a minor leader in the 1881 Apache outbreak. Gen. George Crook pursued the Apaches and forced them to return. In 1885 they fled San Carlos again, angry at being cheated on their rations and unhappy with rules which forbade many of their tribal customs; Geronimo led the renegades. Pursued by American and Mexican troops, the Apaches nevertheless conducted numerous raids on both sides of the international boundary. In 1886 they met to discuss surrender terms but reneged and escaped again.

For 4 months these 39 renegades were pursued by 5,000 American soldiers, an equal number of Mexican troops, plus many bounty hunters, but they never were forced into battle. In September, Geronimo agreed to surrender to Gen. Nelson A. Miles on the condition that after 2 years' imprisonment he would be returned to Arizona. President Grover Cleveland ignored these terms, however. Geronimo and his followers were imprisoned at Ft. Pickens, Fla. In 1894, moved to Ft. Sill in Oklahoma, they were interred as prisoners of war, although allowed to prosper as farmers.

Geronimo later toured with a ''Wild West'' show, was an ''attraction'' at the Omaha and Buffalo expositions, and was exhibited at the St. Louis World's Fair (1904). He died at Ft. Sill in 1909, still a prisoner of war.

Further Reading

Geronimo's reminiscences, *Geronimo's Story of His Life,* were recorded and edited by S. M. Barrett in 1906. The best account of Geronimo's career by one of his contemporaries is John G. Bourke, *On the Border with Crook* (1891). More recent and comprehensive is O. B. Faulk, *The Geronimo Campaign* (1969). □

Elbridge Gerry

Elbridge Gerry (1744-1814), American patriot and statesman, signed the Declaration of Independence and was vice president under James Madison.

Elbridge Gerry was one of 12 children born to Thomas and Elizabeth Gerry. Little is known of his youth, from his birth on July 17, 1744, in Marblehead, Mass., to his 1758 entrance to Harvard College. Upon graduation in 1762, he entered his father's prosperous mercantile firm. He joined a Marblehead social group that became increasingly political as Massachusetts felt the impact of Britain's imperial policy. In 1765 Gerry argued publicly that Americans might in conscience evade the new Stamp Act duties. In 1770 he served on the local Committee of Inspection to enforce the boycott of the Townshend Act, and 2 years later he aided Sam Adams in setting up committees of correspondence. With John and Sam Adams, Gerry made up the patriot triumvirate in the Bay Colony.

Prelude to Revolution

Gerry early became militantly anti-British. He opposed British efforts to place judges out of reach of public control, to send Anglican bishops to America, and to enlarge the royal civil and military establishment in the Colonies. He was equally hostile to popular democracy: when Marblehead mobs in 1774 destroyed a local hospital he had helped establish, he denounced the "savage mobility" and withdrew from politics.

Gerry returned to public life when the Coercive Acts (1774) closed the port of Boston, and Marblehead became the port of entry for donations from other Colonies. He organized the relief effort and sought to prevent profiteering. He resumed his place on the local committee of correspondence and became one of the leading figures in the Provincial Congress. Active with John Hancock in collecting military stores, Gerry was almost captured by the British troops en route to Concord on April 18, 1775.

With the Revolutionary War under way, Gerry labored in the Second Continental Congress to prepare his colleagues for separation from Britain. He urged state taxes adequate to maintain a stable currency and preserve public credit and worked to create an effective military establishment, although he preferred a citizen militia in peacetime. He considered the new national government under the Articles of Confederation "the finishing stroke of our Independence."

An Antifederalist

In 1780 Gerry left Congress in a huff over what he considered an affront to his state and did not resume his seat until 1783. In the interim he tended to his personal fortune. He bought a large confiscated Tory estate in Cambridge and retired from active business. In 1786 he married Ann Thompson, daughter of a New York merchant.

At the Constitutional Convention (1787) Gerry favored congressional payment of the national debt and assumption of state debts. He expressed fears of excessive democracy and opposed popular election of Congress. But, equally fearful of aristocracy, he demanded annual elections, an enumeration of the powers of the national government, and, especially, a Bill of Rights. He refused to sign the Constitution and spoke vigorously against ratification in Massachusetts on the ground that without a safeguard such as a Bill of Rights, Federal government would eventually subvert republicanism. What Gerry sought was a workable balance between governmental power and popular liberty.

National Politics

Despite his objections, Gerry accepted a seat in the Federal Congress in 1789, where he endorsed Alexander Hamilton's funding scheme, demanded full justice for the public creditors, and bought shares in the Bank of the United States. He returned to private life from 1793 until 1797, when President John Adams appointed him to a three-member delegation to France. Gerry was as shocked as his colleagues by the French government's demand for a bribe as a precondition for treaty negotiations. But, convinced that hostility between the two republics must be avoided, Gerry remained after his colleagues departed. Publication of the "XYZ" papers at home, while he was still attempting to negotiate with Talleyrand, damaged Gerry's reputation. However, Adams defended his conduct as opening the door to the later and more successful mission which produced the Franco-American Convention of 1800.

Governor and U.S. Vice President

Elected governor of Massachusetts in 1810, Gerry followed a moderate policy toward Federalist officeholders but later turned more partisan. In addition to large-scale replacement of Federalist by Republican officials, Gerry approved a bill in 1812 to redistrict the state so as to give Republicans disproportionate representation in the legislature. (The new shape of Essex County, roughly similar to a salamander, was caricatured by opponents with Gerry's profile at its head, thus coining the word "gerrymander.") In the 1812 election Gerry lost the governorship. He was made vice president under James Madison and held this post until his death on Nov. 23, 1814.

Further Reading

An early biography is by Gerry's son-in-law, James T. Austin, *The Life of Elbridge Gerry,* 2 vols. (1828-1829). It has been superseded by a modern scholarly biography by George A. Billias (see below). Two collections of source materials provide valuable information on Gerry's congressional career and the "XYZ" affair: Russell W. Knight, ed., *Elbridge Gerry's Letterbook: Paris, 1797-1798* (1966), and C. Harvey Gardiner, ed., *A Study in Dissent: The Warren-Gerry Correspondence, 1776-1792* (1968). Gerry's role in the "XYZ" affair is treated fully in Alexander De Conde, *The Quasi-War: The Politics and Diplomacy of the Undeclared War with France, 1797-1801* (1966). His activities in the Constitutional Convention are traced in Max Farrand, ed., *Records of the Federal Convention*, 4 vols. (1911-1937). A perceptive account of Gerry's career is Samuel E. Morison's essay, "Elbridge Gerry, Gentleman Democrat" (1929), which was republished in Morison's *By Land and by Sea* (1953).

Additional Sources

Billias, George Athan, *Elbridge Gerry, founding father and republican statesman,* New York: McGraw-Hill, 1976. □

George Gershwin

American composer George Gershwin (1898-1937) was eminently successful in popular music, as well as in the classical field with several concert works and an opera that have become standards in the contemporary repertory.

George Gershwin played a prominent role in one of the most colorful eras of American popular music: the so-called age of Tin Pan Alley—roughly 1890-1930—when popular music became big business. In Tin Pan Alley (28th Street between Broadway and Fifth Avenue in New York City) numerous music publishing houses poured forth popular songs each year. The musical theater and the private parlor rang with the sounds of ragtime, romantic ballads, and comedy songs. Talented composers such as Gershwin, Irving Berlin, and Jerome Kern, among dozens of lesser figures, fed this lucrative music-making machine and flourished.

George Gershwin was born in Brooklyn in New York City on Sept. 26, 1898, the son of Rose and Morris Gershovitz, immigrants from Russia. After settling in New York's Lower East Side, his father changed the family name to Gershvin; when George entered the professional world of music, he altered the name to Gershwin.

When George was 12, the moderately well-off family purchased a piano; he soon showed a marked inclination for improvising melodies and was given piano lessons. Later he studied the theory of music and harmony. Though Gershwin was not interested in formal education and never finished high school, he continued to study music. Even after his success in musical comedy, he studied with composer Henry Cowell and with music theorist Joseph Schillinger.

Music Business

When Gershwin was 15, he went to work for a large publisher of popular music as a try-out pianist (or "song plugger"). He began writing his own songs about this time (mostly with lyricist Irving Caesar), none of which his employer was interested in publishing. Finally, in 1916, his first song appeared: "When You Want 'Em You Can't Get 'Em."

Gershwin also began to get a few songs set into current musical shows, a common practice of the day. By 1918 he had shown enough promise to be hired by Harms, Inc., as a songwriter at a weekly salary. Gershwin scored his first big success in 1919 with the song "Swanee" (words by Irving Caesar), introduced by Al Jolson in *Sinbad*. In the same year he composed his first complete score, for the successful musical *La, La, Lucille.*

Musicals of the 1920s

During the 1920s Gershwin established himself as one of the musical theater's most talented and successful composers. He wrote five scores for successive editions of George White's Scandals (1920-1924) and began a series of shows with his brother, Ira, as lyricist, which included *Lady Be Good* (1924), *Primrose* (1924), *Tell Me More* (1925), *Tip Toes* (1925), *Oh Kay* (1926), *Funny Face* (1927), *Rosalie* (1928), *Treasure Girl* (1928), *Show Girl* (1929), and *Strike Up the Band* (1929).

Concert Works

In 1924 the prominent bandleader Paul Whiteman asked Gershwin to write an original "jazz" work for a concert. The result, *Rhapsody in Blue* for piano and jazz band, was Gershwin's debut in the concert hall as pianist and composer, his first attempt at writing an extended piece, and the first time jazz rhythms and blues-oriented melodies were used successfully within a classical framework.

Reviewing the premiere, Olin Downes wrote that the "composition shows extraordinary talent, just as it also shows a young composer with aims that go far beyond those of his ilk. . . ." These aims were demonstrated again in the Piano Concerto in F (1925), commissioned by Walter Damrosch for his New York Symphony; *Three Preludes* for piano (1926); and *An American in Paris* (1928), premiered by Damrosch and the New York Philharmonic. After *Rhapsody in Blue,* Gershwin himself scored all his orchestral works.

In the 1930s Gershwin composed four more musicals with Ira: *Girl Crazy* (1930); *Let 'Em Eat Cake* (1933); and *Pardon My English* (1933). He also wrote film scores, including *Damsel in Distress* and *Shall We Dance.* He spent 2 years on his last major work, the opera *Porgy and Bess* (1935), based on a novel by DuBose Heyward about a ghetto in Charleston, S. C. The composer died of a brain tumor in Beverly Hills, Calif., on July 11, 1937. To commemorate the 100th year of his birth, the Pulitzer Prize Board awarded Gershwin with a posthumous citation on April 14, 1998.

Gershwin's best songs have proved to be some of the most durable of his era, and his classical works give his career a dimension shared by none of his Tin Pan Alley companions. His fondness for African American music is responsible in part for the rhythmic vitality and blues-tinged lyricism of all his works. His best scores, especially those utilizing Ira Gershwin's trenchant and sympathetic verses, are as fresh, vigorous, and unconventional as any written for the American musical theater. Moreover, Gershwin's music has a peculiar American stamp recognized the world over.

Further Reading

David Ewen, *George Gershwin: His Journey to Greatness* (rev. ed. 1970), is the most detailed and accurate of the biographies. Isaac Goldberg, *George Gershwin: A Study in American Music* (1931; new enlarged ed. by Edith Garson, 1958), the earliest biography, was written with Gershwin's cooperation and is of special interest. See also Edward Jablonski and Lawrence D. Stewart, *The Gershwin Years* (1958). □

Jean Paul Getty

Jean Paul Getty (1892-1976) was a billionaire independent oil producer who founded and controlled the Getty Oil Company and over 200 affiliated companies.

Jean Paul Getty was born on December 15, 1892, in Minneapolis, Minnesota. His father, George Franklin Getty, was a lawyer, but in 1904 he moved his wife, Sarah Risher Getty, and his son to the Oklahoma territory to begin a successful career as an independent oilman. Two years later the family moved to Los Angeles, California, where young Getty attended private school before graduating from Polytechnic High School in 1909. After a European tour he attended the University of Southern California and the University of California at Berkeley; he spent his summers working on his father's oil rigs as a "roustabout." In 1912 Getty enrolled in Oxford University in England, from which he received a degree in economics and political science in 1914.

In 1914 Getty arrived in Tulsa, Oklahoma, determined to strike it rich as a wildcat oil producer. Although he operated independently of his father's Minnehoma Oil Company, his father's loans and financial backing enabled him to begin buying and selling oil leases in the red-bed area of Oklahoma. Getty saw himself as a modern oil man, relying on geological data and not simply on the instinct of the experienced veterans, but he also thrived on the excitement, gamble, risks, and high stakes of the oil business. Getty's own first successful well came in in 1916, and by the fall of that year he had made his first million dollars as a wildcatter and lease broker.

For the next two years Getty "retired" to the life of a wealthy playboy in Los Angeles, but he returned to the oil business in 1919. During the 1920s he and his father continued to be enormously successful both in drilling their own wells and in buying and selling oil leases, and Getty became more active in California than in Oklahoma. He amassed a personal fortune of over three million dollars and acquired a third interest in what was to become the Getty Oil Company.

After his father's death in 1930 Paul Getty became the president of the George Getty Oil Company (successor to Minnehoma Oil), but his mother inherited the controlling interest, as his father had been upset with his son's profligate personal life. During the 1930s Getty followed several paths to both short-term and long-term success. His wells continued to produce, and profits poured in. He also bought a controlling interest in the Pacific Western Oil Corporation, one of the ten largest oil companies in California. After a series of agreements with his mother he obtained the controlling interest in the George Getty Oil Company, and he began real estate dealings, including the purchase of the Hotel Pierre in New York City.

The Getty Oil Company

Getty's ambition was to build up an independent, self-contained oil business involving refining, transporting, and selling oil as well as exploration and drilling. To that end he began in the 1930s to gain control of the Tidewater Oil Company. Getty pursued that goal in a series of complicated maneuvers, which involved tilting with the giant Standard Oil of New Jersey, until in the 1950s he had control of Tidewater, Skelly Oil, and the Mission Corporation. In 1967 these companies merged into the Getty Oil Company, the foundation of Getty's fortune. Getty had a majority or controlling interest in Getty Oil and its nearly 200 affiliated and subsidiary firms, and he remained its president until his death in 1976.

At the outbreak of World War II, Getty, a yachtsman, volunteered for service in the Navy, but his offer was rejected. At the request of Naval officers, however, he took over personal management of Spartan Aircraft, a Skelly and Getty subsidiary. The corporation manufactured trainers and airplane parts, and it later converted to the profitable production of mobile homes.

After the war Getty took a lucrative gamble on oil rights in the Middle East. In 1949 he secured the oil rights in Saudi Arabia's half of the Neutral Zone, a barren tract between Saudi Arabia and Kuwait. He made major concessions to

King Saud, which shocked the large oil companies, but after three years and a $30 million investment, Getty found the huge oil deposits which helped make him a billionaire.

In his business career, Getty continued to invest and reinvest; his fortune consisted not of cash, but stocks, corporate assets, and real estate. A loner, he saw himself as a solitary knight in fierce battle with the giant "Seven Sisters" oil firms, and that competitive urge fueled his desire to build a larger and larger fortune.

A "Public" Personal Life

In 1957 *Fortune* magazine published a list of the richest men in America. Getty's name headed the list, and the resultant publicity turned the reclusive Getty into an object of public fascination and legend. Getty complained about the fame, the requests for money, and the assumption that he would pick up every restaurant check, but he also furthered his own legends: he wrote articles on such topics as "How To Be Rich" and pretended to poverty by wearing rumpled suits and threadbare sweaters. The public was fascinated by Getty's wealth and extravagance and also by his reputed stinginess. After 1959 he stopped living out of hotel rooms and established his home and offices at Sutton Place, a 16th-century, 700-acre manor outside London. The huge estate, with its gardens, pools, trout stream, and priceless furnishings, was also a near garrison, with elaborate security arrangements. Giant Alsatian dogs had the run of the estate, and there were also two caged lions, Nero and Teresa. Numerous stories circulated about Getty's penny-pitching; the most famous incident was the installation of a pay telephone on the Sutton Place grounds. Getty offered various explanations, but the public preferred to see the phone booth as a symbol of his stinginess.

The public also seemed to like to read into Getty's life the lesson that money does not buy happiness. Getty was married five times: to Jeannette Dumont (1923), Allene Ashby (1925), Adolphine Helmle (1928), Ann Rork (1932), and Louisa Lynch (1939); each marriage ended in divorce. He had five sons, two of whom predeceased him, and his relationship with each of them was difficult. His grandson, J. Paul Getty III, was kidnapped in Italy in 1973. Although he was returned for a ransom, part of his ear had been cut off. Getty was a celebrity, and public interest, fueled by envy and admiration, focused on Getty's tragedies as well as his billions.

Besides oil, Getty's major interest was art. He began serious collecting in the 1930s—European paintings, furniture, Greek and Roman sculptures, 18th-century tapestries, silver, and fine Persian carpets, including the 16th-century Ardabil carpet from Tabriz. He housed his collection at Sutton Place and at his ranch house at Malibu, California, one wing of which he opened as the J. Paul Getty Museum in 1954. In 1969 construction began on a new Getty Museum, also on his Malibu property. The huge building is a replica of an ancient Roman villa found near the ruins of Pompeii, and the extensive Getty collection was moved there after his death.

Jean Paul Getty died at Sutton Place on June 6, 1976; he is buried on his Malibu estate.

Further Reading

Getty wrote two autobiographies, *My Life and Fortunes* (1963) and *As I See It* (1976). He wrote about his art collection in *The Joys of Collecting* (1965) and published such advice books as *How To Be Rich* (1965) and *How To Be A Successful Executive* (1971). A biography written with Getty's cooperation is Ralph Hewins, *The Richest American: J. Paul Getty* (1960); the *New York Times* obituary of June 6, 1976, also provides useful information. In *The Seven Sisters: The Great Oil Companies and the World They Shaped* (1975) Anthony Sampson discusses Getty's role as an independent oil producer. Two biographies in 1986 added little new information: *The House of Getty* by Russell Miller and *The Great Getty: The Life and Loves of J. Paul Getty—Richest Man in the World* by Robert Lenzner. □

Dizzy Gillespie

Fifty years after helping found a new style of progressive jazz that came to be known as bebop, Dizzy Gillespie's (1917-1993) music is still a major contributing factor to the development of modern jazz.

As a trumpet virtuoso Gillespie stands firmly as a major influence in the development of the jazz trumpet. His band was a virtual training ground for younger musicians. In 1990 he led and wrote the arrangements for a group that included bassist John Lee, guitarist Ed Cherry, drummer Ignacio Berroa, conga drummer Paul Hawkins, and saxophonist Ron Holloway. More than 40 years earlier Gillespie was the first bandleader to use a conga player. Employing Latin rhythms and forging an Afro-Cuban style of polyrhythmic music was one of Gillespie's many contributions to the development of modern jazz.

Before Gillespie there was New Orleans musician Buddy Bolden—the earliest known jazz cornetist—who was followed by King Oliver, Louis Armstrong, and Roy Eldridge. In his memoir, *To Be or Not to Bop*, Gillespie described the influence of Armstrong and Eldridge on his trumpet playing: "Roy Eldridge was a French-style trumpet player. Eldridge was in a direct line from Louis Armstrong, and he was the voice of that era, the thirties. I hardly ever listened to Louis, but was always aware of where Roy's inspiration came from. So I was looking at Louis Armstrong, you see, because they are one and the same. My inspiration came through Roy Eldridge, from Louis Armstrong and King Oliver and Buddy Bolden. That's the way it happened."

Gillespie played with bands in Philadelphia from 1935 to 1937 before moving to New York. In Philadelphia, where his family had moved from Cheraw, South Carolina, Gillespie learned Eldridge's trumpet solos from fellow trumpeter Charlie Shavers. It was then that Gillespie earned his nickname for his erratic and mischievous behavior. When Gillespie was in the Frankie Fairfax band in Philadelphia he carried his new trumpet in a paper bag; that inspired fellow musicians like Bill Doggett to call him "Dizzy." While Gillespie himself acknowledged the paper bag incident, but he said the nickname didn't stick until later.

Gillespie's basic style of solo trumpet playing at that time involved "running them changes"—improvising on chord changes in a song and introducing new chord changes based on the song's melody. He had taught himself piano and used the instrument to experiment with new melodies and chord changes. When he went to New York in 1937 he did not have a specific job, but was introduced to other musicians by Shavers. Gillespie joined in jam sessions, sometimes after hours at clubs in Harlem like Monroe's Uptown House and Dicky Wells's. He would also sit in with bands; while jamming one night with Chick Webb's band at the Savoy Ballroom, Gillespie met Mario Bauza, a Cuban trumpeter who introduced him to Latin rhythms.

Already a Musical Force at 19

Within a year Gillespie was hired by the Teddy Hill Orchestra for a European tour when the regular trumpet player didn't want to go. Hill probably liked Gillespie's style, which was similar at that time to Roy Eldridge's; Eldridge had left Hill's band to join Fletcher Henderson. By 1937—when he was only 19—Gillespie had already made a name for himself among New York musicians, who couldn't help but notice his radically fresh take on solo trumpet playing: he utilized the upper register of notes above high C, played with great speed, and used new rhythms and chord changes. Gillespie made his first recordings with the Teddy Hill Orchestra just prior to leaving for Europe on "The Cotton Club Show."

Gillespie joined the Cab CallowayOrchestra in 1939 and stayed until 1941. Gillespie wrote in his memoir, "It was the best job that you could possibly have, high class." Calloway played the Cotton Club and toured extensively. During this period Gillespie continued to play all-night jam sessions at Minton's and Monroe's Uptown House to develop his musical knowledge and style. In 1939 the most in-demand trumpet players for recording dates in New York were Eldridge, Shavers, and Buck Clayton. Gillespie was fourth on the list, but somehow managed to land a recording date with Lionel Hampton, which resulted in the famed "Hot Mallets" session. In this session Gillespie became the first musician to record in the modern jazz style with a small group. Lionel Hampton said of the session, as quoted in Gillespie's book, "[Gillespie] came out with a new style, came out with a bebop style. He came out with a different style than we'd ever heard before. A lot of people don't know that was the creation of bebop, the beginning of bebop." Of course, it wasn't called bebop just yet.

Gillespie left Calloway in 1941 following a misunderstanding. During a performance someone from the vicinity of the trumpet section was having fun aiming spitballs at the bandleader, who was singing in front of the band at the time. Naturally Calloway assumed Gillespie was responsible. By most accounts, however, Gillespie was completely innocent and had been set up. Words led to action; Gillespie pulled a knife on Calloway and actually cut him a few times. While the two later reconciled and remained friends, Gillespie was forced to leave the band. This well-known incident illustrates the flip side of Gillespie's jovial personality; he often found himself in situations where he might need to defend himself, and was fully prepared to do so.

Inspired by Charlie Parker

Gillespie joined the Earl "Fatha" Hines band in 1942, about the same time Charlie Parker did. Although Parker became famous as an alto saxophonist, he was playing tenor sax at that time. Gillespie first met Parker in Kansas City in 1940 when he was on tour with Cab Calloway. The two of them jammed together at the Booker T. Washington Hotel for several hours. Gillespie ventured in *To Be or Not to Bebop,* "I guess Charlie Parker and I had a meeting of the minds, because both of us inspired each other." They spent a lot of time together during their stint with the Hines band.

By the time he joined Hines, Gillespie had composed "A Night in Tunisia," one of his most famous songs. He was also writing arrangements for other bandleaders, including Hill, Calloway, Jimmy Dorsey, and Woody Herman. He wrote bebop arrangements, as most bandleaders at that time were interested in having one or two bebop numbers in their repertoires. Several musicians have commented that even if Gillespie had not been able to play the trumpet, he could have made a name for himself on the basis of his original compositions and arrangements. Other jazz standards credited in whole or in part to Gillespie include "Groovin' High," "Manteca," "Woody 'n You," "Con Alma," and "Salt Peanuts."

Bebop Born on 52nd Street

A large part of the Earl Hines band departed in 1943 to form a new group headed by Billy Eckstine. Former Hines members who joined Eckstine included Sarah Vaughan, Gillespie, Parker, and others. The band also featured saxophonists Gene Ammons and Dexter Gordon. Gillespie became musical director for Eckstine, whose backers got him a job on 52nd Street. Gillespie stayed with Eckstine for about seven months, touring and playing on 52nd Street. "The Street," as it was described by critic Pete Migdol in Gillespie's memoir, "was the hippest block with regard to its short distance and that amount of music. . . . This was the top talent street, and it was, of course, discoverer of a lot of the new people for that era."

After leaving Eckstine, Gillespie substituted in the Duke EllingtonOrchestra for about four weeks, then formed his own group to play at the newly opened Onyx Club on 52nd Street. Gillespie had been playing bebop whenever he could since 1940, the year he married Lorraine Willis. Now he was able to play it full time. 52nd Street became the proving ground for a new jazz style that had previously been played primarily at late night jam sessions.

"The opening of the Onyx Club represented the birth of the bebop era," Gillespie recalled in his book. "In our long sojourn on 52nd Street we spread our message to a much wider audience." His first quintet at the Onyx Club in 1944 included Oscar Pettiford on bass, Max Roach on drums, George Wallington on piano, and Don Byas on tenor sax. Gillespie had tried to get Parker to join, but he had temporarily returned to Kansas City.

Quintet Revolutionized Jazz

Also in 1944 Gillespie received the New Star Award from *Esquire* magazine, the first of many awards he would receive in his career. Describing the new style his quintet played, Gillespie wrote, "We'd take the chord structures of various standard and pop tunes and create new chords, melodies, and songs from them." For example, Tadd Dameron's composition "Hothouse" was based on "What Is This Thing Called Love," and Parker's "Ornithology" came out of "How High The Moon." Gillespie also noted, "Our music had developed more into a type of music for listeners." There would be little dancing to bebop. Rhythm and phrasing, however, were also important to the new jazz style. "The most important thing about our music was, of course, the style, how you got from one note to another, how it was played. . . . We had a special way of phrasing. Not only did we change harmonic structure, but we also changed rhythmic structure."

Gillespie's quintet also played other clubs, including the Downbeat and the Three Deuces, where the group included Charlie Parker—by then on alto sax—and Bud Powell on piano. Gillespie also played for two months in Hollywood with Parker, vibraphonist Milt Jackson, bassist Ray Brown, pianist Al Haig, and drummer Stan Levy. This was the West Coast debut of bebop and it was very well received. In fact, it was around this time that the term "bebop" came into use. Gillespie recalled, "People, when they'd wanna ask for one of those numbers and didn't know the name, would ask for bebop. And the press picked it up and started calling it bebop. The first time the term bebop appeared in print was while we played at the Onyx Club."

1953 Triumph in Toronto

Gillespie's quintet and the presentation of modern jazz in that format reached its apex in 1953—with a concert at Massey Hall in Toronto that featured Gillespie, Parker, Powell, Roach, and legendary jazz bassist Charles Mingus. As Roach recalled in Gillespie's memoir, "The five people that Dizzy had originally thought about in the group at the Onyx didn't really materialize until we did Jazz at Massey Hall, that album, in 1953." Billed by jazz critics as "the greatest jazz concert ever," it was recorded by Mingus—a last-minute substitute for Pettiford—and later released on Debut Records.

From the big bands and orchestras that he first organized in the late 1940s, to the small combos of the early 1950s that served as incubators for young musicians like saxophone giant John Coltrane, Gillespie's influence consistently defined modern jazz. Though the enterprise was short-lived, Gillespie had his own record label, Dee Gee Records, from 1951-53. He appeared at the historic first Newport Jazz Festival in 1954. And he later played the role of unofficial ambassador of jazz, beginning with a 1956 world tour sponsored by the U.S. State Department. These are just a few of the many accomplishments highlighting the career of this remarkably accomplished titan of contemporary American music.

In 1989, the year he became 72 years of age, Dizzy Gillespie received a Lifetime Achievement Award at the National Association of Recording Arts and Sciences' Grammy Award ceremonies. The honor—one of many bestowed on the trumpet virtuoso—recognized nearly 50 years of pioneering jazz performances. That same year he received the National Medal of Arts from President George Bush "for his trail-blazing work as a musician who helped elevate jazz to an art form of the first rank, and for sharing his gift with listeners around the world."

Not letting age slow him down, in 1989 Gillespie gave 300 performances in 27 countries, appeared in 100 U.S. cities in 31 states and the District of Columbia, headlined three television specials, performed with two symphonies, and recorded four albums. He was also crowned a traditional chief in Nigeria, received the Commandre d'Ordre des Artes et Lettres—France's most prestigious cultural award—was named regent professor by the University of California, and received his fourteenth honorary doctoral degree, this one from the Berklee College of Music. The next year, at the Kennedy Center for the Performing Arts ceremonies celebrating the centennial of American jazz, Gillespie received the American Society of Composers, Authors, and Publishers' Duke Award for 50 years of achievement as a composer, performer, and bandleader.

Although his health was failing due to pancreatic cancer, Gillespie continued to play the music that he loved late in his life. His last public appearance was in Seattle in February of 1992. Gillespie passed away quietly in his sleep on October 6, 1993 at the age of 75.

Further Reading

Feather, Leonard, *The Encyclopedia of Jazz in the Sixties,* Horizon, 1966.

Feather, Leonard, *The Encyclopedia of Jazz in the Seventies,* Horizon, 1976.

Horricks, Raymond, *Dizzy Gillespie and the Bebop Revolution,* Hippocrene, 1984.

Koster, Piet, and Chris Sellers, *Dizzy Gillespie, Volume 1: 1937-1953,* Micrography, 1986.

McRae, Barry, *Dizzy Gillespie,* Universe Books, 1988.

New Grove Dictionary of Jazz, Macmillan, 1988.

Detroit Free Press, January 7, 1993; January 8, 1993.

Down Beat, December 1985; January 1986; September 1989; August 1990.

Entertainment Weekly, January 22, 1993.

IAJRC Journal, Winter 1991.

Maclean's, March 20, 1989.

New Yorker, September 17, 1990.

New York Times, January 7, 1993; January 13, 1993; January 17, 1993.

Time, January 18, 1993.

Times (London), January 8, 1993.

Washington Post, January 7, 1993; January 10, 1993. □

Newt Gingrich

Hailed as *Time*'s "Man of the Year" in 1995 and touted by some historians as this century's most influential Speaker, U. S. Representative Newt Gingrich (born 1943) held on to his Speaker's post by a narrow margin of only three votes in 1997. "For better or worse, he has changed the language and substance of American politics perhaps like no other politician in recent history," said Time magazine's editor James Gaines. The man who felled the former Speaker of the House Jim Wright on ethics violations was himself charged and fined for his own violation of House ethics in 1996. His "Contract with America" fell short of its promises and his conservative stance has taken on a liberal hue. After Republicans faired worse than expected in the 1998 elections, Gingrich announced that he would step down as Speaker of the House and clear the way for new leadership.

Bomb Thrower or Visionary?

"Our view is that Newt Gingrich is a bomb thrower, " *Time* reported. A fire-breathing Republican Congressman from Georgia, he is more interested in right-wing grandstanding than in fostering bi-partisanship. . . . Another view is that Newt Gingrich is a visionary. An impassioned reformer . . . ;fbwho;rb innovative thinking and respect for deeply felt American values to the House." In any case, Congress has not been quite the same since Gingrich was first elected to represent Georgia's Sixth Congressional District in 1978.

Born in Harrisburg, Pennsylvania to 19-year-old mechanic, Newton C. McPherson, and 16-year-old, Kathleen Daugherty, Newt's life had a rough start. His parents split within days of their marriage. His mother remarried Robert B. Gingrich, a career soldier, three years later. Gingrich maintained his ties to the McPherson family. Even as a political figure, he wore a McPherson tartan tie.

As the stepson of an Army officer, Newt Gingrich moved from town to town attending five schools in eight years both here and abroad. Gingrich recalls how his experience formed his political approach to Howard Fineman in *Newsweek*. "Politics and war are remarkably similar systems," said Gingrich. "You grow up an Army brat named Newton, and you learn about combat."

In 1960, the Gingrich family moved from Fort Benning, Georgia. Not long after, Gingrich pursued his political career in Columbus. In fact, within a few months in Georgia, he ran a successful campaign for his friend's election to class president. At Emory University in Atlanta, Gingrich established a Young Republicans club.

Fired Up Republicans in Washington

From the time he landed in Washington in 1978, he gained a national reputation for his combative style and his leadership of a collection of young, aggressive, conservative House Republicans. "For his first five years in office," the New York Times said, "Mr. Gingrich, along with a band of young conservative Republicans turned their junior status to advantage and waged guerrilla warfare against democratic

House leadership and even their own party's leaders. Under Mr. Gingrich's tutelage, about a dozen of the insurgents formed a group known as the Conservative Opportunity Society (COS) Republicans. Mr. Gingrich maintains, have become so accustomed to their minority status that they need to be prodded to challenge the status quo."

The tenets of Gingrich's philosophy were echoed by the COS—the antithesis of the "liberal welfare state," a state that he regularly criticizes. In 1984, "he turned preliminary sessions of he Republican national convention into a battleground until the Conservative Opportunity Society was inserted into the platform," the *Atlantic* said.

Gingrich was also well-known for his special taste for colleagues roasted on the moral spit of an ethics committee investigation. In 1979, during his first term, he called for the expulsion of Representative Charles Diggs, a Democrat from Michigan, who had been convicted of embezzlement. In 1983, he called for the expulsion of two representatives who allegedly had sexual relations with teenagers working as pages in the House. And later, of course, Gingrich spearheaded the movement to oust Jim Wright.

Grabbed Public Attention

In the early 1980's, Gingrich launched a new weapon, taking advantage of a rule allowing House members to read items into the record after Congressional sessions. He gave frequent speeches criticizing Democrats for their position on a wide range of issues, from communism to school prayer to Central America—speeches given before an empty House chamber, but broadcast nationwide on the cable network C-SPAN. This tactic was also used by Gingrich's followers—a group of conservative Republicans elected mostly in the 1980s and labeled the party's "young Turks," in contrast to the GOP's less aggressive old guard.

In the spring of 1984, an angry Thomas P. "Tip" O'Neill, then Speaker of the House, ordered the cable TV cameras to periodically pan the chamber to show that Gingrich was speaking to an empty House. O'Neill called Gingrich's tactics "the lowest thing I have seen in my 32 years in the House." The confrontation resulted in a rare House rebuke to the Speaker and wide coverage for Gingrich— something he valued highly. *Newsweek* defined what it called Gingrich's Newtonian law: conflict equals exposure equals power. "If you are in the newspaper everyday and on the TV often enough then you must be important."

Gingrich wrote in the Conservative Digest: "The Democratic Party is now controlled by a coalition of liberal activists, corrupt big city machines, labor union bosses and House incumbents who use gerrymandering, rigged election rules and a million dollars from taxpayers per election cycle to buy invulnerability. When Republicans have the courage to point out just how unrepresentative, and even weird, liberal values are, we gain votes. . . . Fear and corruption now stalk the House of Representatives in a way we've never witnessed before in our history."

Proved Wright Wrong

Gingrich's battle against Jim Wright began in 1987; a one-man crusade which few in Washington took seriously.

Before Gingrich was through, however, more than 70 House Republicans signed his letter asking the House's ethics committee to investigate Wright. The accusations were related to Wright's links to a Texas developer, to his favors to savings and loan operators, and the way in which he published and sold a book of his speeches and writings *Reflections of a Public Man.* Wright received unusually large royalties and sold the book to political contributors—an arrangement seemingly designed to circumvent ceilings on donations.

Gingrich was ruthless on the offensive. His dramatic contentions won him necessary Congressional allies and his rhetorical skills made him eminently quotable, thus a media darling. "I'm so deeply frightened by the nature of the corrupt left-wing machine in the House that it would have been worse to do nothing," he was quoted as saying in the *New York Times.* "Jim Wright has reached a point psychologically, in his ego, where there are no boundaries left." Following the investigation, the ethics committee said it had reason to believe Wright had violated House rules 69 times. Less than two months later, on June 6, 1989, Wright resigned as Speaker.

In March 1989, in the midst of his war with Wright, Gingrich's Republican colleagues elected him to the post of Minority Whip by a narrow 87-85 margin. The vote signaled "a wake-up call to incumbent GOP leaders from younger members who want a more aggressive, active party," said the *Congressional Quarterly Weekly Report.* "Gingrich's promotion from backbench bomb thrower to Minority Whip was an expression of seething impatience among House Republicans with their seemingly minority status."

Gingrich's supporters pointed to his energy, communication skills, and commitment to capturing a majority of House seats. "A year ago, no one would have predicted that this enfant terrible of the Republican Party could mount a credible bid for the leadership—let alone snag its No. 2 slot," the *Weekly Review* said, "But Republicans became particularly frustrated with their decade-old minority status in the House when the Reagan era came to an end: Even the eight year reign of a president as popular as Reagan couldn't deliver them from their plight. Gingrich's call for radical change fell on responsive ears."

Gingrich's high-profile role put his personal moral standards in the spotlight. His opponents resurrected the contradictions between Gingrich's ethics-and-traditional-values stand and his messy divorce from his first wife, who was cancer stricken. Democrats *Newsweek* said, also point out "his management of a political action committee that raised $200,000—and gave $900 to candidates." After Gingrich took on Wright, the Democratic Congressional Campaign Committee publicized a 1977 deal in which Gingrich received $13,000 from a group of friends to write a novel. He wasn't in Congress at the time, although he had run twice unsuccessfully for the seat which he eventually won in 1978. Democrats say the arrangement allowed Gingrich's backers to support him financially and get a tax shelter in the bargain. Gingrich said he did research in Europe and wrote three chapters, but the book was rejected by publishers.

In addition to these charges, two days before Gingrich was elected Minority Whip, the *Washington Post* reported that he had persuaded 21 supporters to contribute $105,000 to promote *Window of Opportunity: A Blueprint for the Future,* which he co-authored in 1984 with his second wife, Marianne, and science fiction writer David Drake. The book sold only 12,000 hardcover copies; the investors reaped tax benefits and Gingrich and his wife made about $30,000. Gingrich acknowledged that this book deal was "as weird as Wright's," but was on the up and up because "we wrote a real book for a real (publisher) that was sold in real bookstores." The book deal remained a question mark in Gingrich's past that did not stall his political career in the 1990s.

In October of 1990, Gingrich gained headlines again when he opposed—and led 105 fellow Republicans in voting down—a proposed budget package. His defiance and disregard for the presidential endorsement angered Senate Minority Leader Robert Dole, who was quoted in *Newsweek:* "You pay a price for leadership. If you don't want to pay the penalty, maybe you ought to find another line of work." Dole felt Gingrich, fearful of his personal popularity, fought the budget in ignorance of the bi-partisan agreements that had been the fruit of hard work.

Reached Career-Long Dream

In November 1990, despite his growing reputation on the national level, Gingrich had a scare in his home district at the election. He won by a narrow margin of 983 votes of the nearly 156,000 cast in Georgia's Sixth District. The root of Gingrich's trouble at home was his blockage of federal mediation in the 1989 strike at Eastern Airlines. The Atlanta airport is of great importance to the surrounding communities, and 6,000 employees of Eastern lived in his district. Obviously shaken, Gingrich told his constituents that he had received their warning in the close re-election, and would more closely carry out their mandate in his coming term in office.

Gingrich spent the next four years pursuing his goal of achieving a Republican Majority in Congress. He reached his dream in 1994. On September 27, 1994, Gingrich and his associates presented his brainchild—the "Contract with America," a 100-day House Republican plan to revolutionize Congress, spending, and federal government operations. With Gingrich's consistent campaign support for Republican candidates all over the country, they received the partisan majority in the November elections.

As a result, Newt Gingrich took over as Speaker of the House in January of 1995. During his first year, he faced the challenge of living up to the promises detailed in the "Contract" and also once again confronted ethics charges but did not receive any convictions. He published two books in 1995—the nonfiction *To Renew America* and the fiction novel *1945.*

A Tenuous Second Term

Unlike his first election to the House as Speaker in 1995, Newt Gingrich won his second term by a narrow margin of three votes. Not only was the Speaker under investigation by the ethics committee for allegedly violating House standards by knowingly abusing the tax code in raising tax-deductible funds for a college course he taught, he was also criticized for his book deal with HarperCollins. Gingrich was originally offered a $4.5 million advance for two books, due to very strong criticism, he declined the offer and settled for royalties instead.

While exonerated from 74 of the 75 ethics charges levied against him, the one that he was charged with, admitted to, and levied a $300,000 fine for was enough to tarnish the rising star enough to put his second term as Speaker on shaky ground. Gingrich's greatest challenge was now coming from within his own Party.

Gingrich came under intense fire from within the Republican Party. Many claimed that he had damaged the Party beyond repair and the best thing for him to do was to step down. The problem with that scenario was that the Republican Party had no successor that they felt strongly enough about to force a "coup" although there had been much talk of it. Unlike 1995 and 1996 when the Republican majority was united, they became a house divided. "The way some Republicans tell it," according to an account in the *Economist* "their troubles are wrought by Newt Gingrich. Two years ago Mr. Gingrich was celebrated (among those with short memories) as the most powerful Speaker of this century; now a fellow House Republican describes him as 'road kill on the highway of American politics.'" Gingrich has been described as a man with no agenda, who cannot decide if he is conservative or liberal. The lackluster start of the 105th Congress, when compared to the 104th, clearly defined the state of affairs within the Republican majority-held House and the Party itself.

Proving that he had not entirely lost his political foothold, Gingrich was re-elected to Congress in 1998. However, he decided to step down as Speaker of the House. That decision was followed by his total resignation from Congress. After his departure, Gingrich became a political consultant. In October 1999 he agreed to join the Fox News Channel as a contributor to cover the 2000 election.

Gingrich filed for divorce from his second wife in mid-1999, which was finalized on April 6, 2000. He acknowledged a seven-year relationship with Callista Bisek, a clerk from the House Agriculture Committee. On August 18, 2000 Gingrich and Bisek were married.

Further Reading

Anderson, Alfred F., *Challenging Newt Gingrich Chapter by Chapter* (1996).

Wilson, John K., *Newt Gingrich: Captial Crimes and Misdemeanors* (1996).

Warner, Judith, *Newt Gingrich: Speaker to America* (1995).

Gingrich, Newt, *Newt Gingrich's Renewing American Civilization* (audio cassette, 1997). □

Allen Ginsberg

The American poet Allen Ginsberg (1926-1997) was one of the most celebrated figures in contemporary American literature. He was a leading member of the "Beat Movement" and helped lead the revolt against "academic poetry" and the cultural and political establishment of the mid-20th century.

Allen Ginsberg was born on June 3, 1926, in Newark, New Jersey, to Russian-Jewish parents. He had an emotionally troubled childhood that was later reflected in his poetry. His mother, Naomi, suffered from various mental illnesses, and was periodically institutionalized during his adolescence. Contributing to Ginsberg's growing confusion during these years was his growing awareness of his homosexuality, which he concealed from both his peers and his parents until he was in his twenties.

Ginsberg enrolled at Columbia University with the intention of becoming a lawyer. At Columbia, he fell in with a crowd that included writers Jack Kerouac and William Burroughs, as well as Lucien Carr and Neal Cassaday. Around the time he was a student at Columbia, Ginsberg got into some trouble with the police. His apartment was used as a base for a robbery, and in order to avoid being charged as an accomplice, he pleaded insanity. He ended up spending several months in a mental hospital.

After graduating with a bachelor of arts from Columbia in 1948, Ginsberg worked as a market researcher in New York and then migrated to San Francisco, where he became a principal figure in the "Beat Generation" literary movement. The Beat movement was an American social and literary movement originated in the 1950s where artists, derisively called "beatniks," expressed their alienation from conventional society by adopting a style of seedy dress, detached manners, and a "hip" vocabulary. Generally indifferent to social problems, they advocated sensory awareness that might be induced by drugs, jazz, sex, or the disciplines of Zen Buddhism. Ginsberg's *Howl and Other Poems* (1956), along with Kerouac's *On the Road* ultimately became the "Beat" movement's twin scriptures.

Howl's raw, graphic language dealt with human discontent and despair, moral and social ills, Ginsberg's homosexuality, and his mother's communist beliefs. Many traditional critics were astonished. While some commentators shared the attitude of Walter Sutton, who considered *Howl* "a tirade revealing an animus directed outward against those who do not share the poet's social and sexual orientation," others echoed the opinion of Paul Zweig, who argued that the poem "almost singlehandedly dislocated the traditional poetry of the 1950s." The publisher, poet Lawrence Ferlinghetti, became a defendant in an obscenity trial, but was later acquitted after testimony led Judge Clayton W. Horn to rule that *Howl* was not obscene. Still, leading literary and popular journals typically complained that *Howl* was vulgar and undisciplined. Another critic complained that "Ginsberg made it seem like anybody could write poetry."

Nevertheless, Ginsberg's triumphant synthesis of sociology and mysticism, Blake and Walt Whitman, and the Bible and Marxism, had found an audience. Declaiming his poems in coffeehouses, jazz clubs, and colleges, Ginsberg (with a thick, untrimmed beard and his balding head heavily fringed with hair) reinforced his dual image: a saint to the underground minority, a freak to the mainstream majority.

Ginsberg's next volume *Kaddish and Other Poems 1958-1960* (1961), delved further into his past. Based on the "Kaddish," a traditional Hebrew prayer for the dead, it poignantly expressed the anger, love, and confusion felt towards his mother while rendering the social and historical milieu which informed his mother's troubled life. Some critics considered this piece to be his most important work. John Tytell explained "*Kaddish* testified for Ginsberg's capacity for involvement with another human in torment, for the acceptance of another's weirdness."

Ginsberg had visions while reading the poetry of William Blake. These visions led him to experiment with drugs, and he took LSD under the guidance of the late Timothy Leary in the 1960s. He said that some of his best poetry was written under the influence of drugs: the second part of *Howl* with peyote, *Kaddish* with amphetamines, and *Wales - A Visitation* with LSD. However, after a trip to India in 1962, where he was introduced to yoga and meditation, he, generally, changed his mind about drugs. He believed that yoga and meditation were far superior to raising one's consciousness, but still believed that psychedilcs could prove helpful in writing poetry.

Ginsberg was a visible political activist in the 1960s and 1970s. He coined the term and advocated "flower power," a strategy in which antiwar demonstrators promoted positive values like peace and love to dramatize their opposition to the death and destruction caused by the Vietnam War. He protested at the 1968 Democratic Convention in Chicago and later testified on behalf of the "Chicago Seven" who were prosecuted on conspiracy charges. Ginsberg was later jailed after demonstrating against President Richard Nixon at the 1972 Republican Convention in Miami. He was also a staunch advocate for gay rights. When asked to describe his social and political views, he simply responded "Absolute defiance." These experiences, as well as his conversion to Buddhism, his concerns about aging, and the anguish over the deaths of close friends Kerouac and Cassaday, heavily influenced Ginsberg's work.

Ginsberg was a survivor, as he outlived enemies like J. Edgar Hoover who thought he was a threat to the establishment. He remained durable, and was an icon of American counterculture for four decades. It could be said that if one generation outgrew him, a new one rose to show their interest. In the 1990s, he was a favorite on MTV, and collaborated with the band *Sonic Youth* and singer Bono of *U2*.

In later years, Ginsberg's health began to fail. He suffered from cirrhosis of the liver, bouts of hepatitis, diabetes, and Bell's palsy, which left his face partially paralyzed. As he continued his relentless self-promotion and an exhausting schedule, Ginsberg accomplished what few writers attain: his acclaim and celebrity were at their height at his death. He had always said he wanted to die peacefully, and on April 5, 1997, at the age of 70, just days after being diagnosed with terminal liver cancer, he died, surrounded by "close friends and lovers" in his New York apartment. Ferlinghetti stated, "He went the way he wanted to go." Longtime friend and former California lawmaker Tom Hayden told CNN, "Allen was like a prophet of the 1960s." His most recent works before his death were *Selected Poems, 1947-1955* and a rock cd *The Ballad of the Skeletons*. *Death & Fame: Poems 1993–1997*, (1999), edited by Bob Rosenthal, Peter Hale, and Bill Morgan, chronologically arranges Ginsberg's poems from this period, 21 of which were completed in the month prior to his death.

There are also excellent pieces in his other collections: *Empty Mirror* (1962); *Reality Sandwiches* (1963); *The Yage Letters* (1964), written with William Burroughs; *The Marihuana Papers* (1966); *TV Baby Poem* (1968); *Planet News 1961-1967* (1969); *Ankor Wat* (1969); and *Indian Journals* (1970).

Further Reading

Serious attention to Ginsberg's work is lacking, but Jane Kramer, *Allen Ginsberg in America* (1969), is a sympathetic, excellent biography. Obituaries which extensively detailed Ginberg's life and his writings appeared in the April 6, 1997 editions of the *New York Times* and the *Los Angeles Times*. □

Rudolph William Giuliani

Former U.S. Attorney Rudolph Giuliani became the 107th mayor of New York City in 1994 on the Republican ticket. He was the first non-Democrat to become mayor in 24 years.

In January 1994, Rudolph William Giuliani became New York City's first Republican mayor since John Lindsey was elected in 1965. Giuliani's tough-on crime platform perhaps clinched the victory for the former U.S. attorney for the state of New York. In the years since his election, this tough stance seems to have paid off; in 1995, Giuliani announced that the murder rate in New York City had dropped by nearly one-fifth, the biggest annual decline in decades. However, he remains a controversial political figure, and on at least one occasion he has committed a widely-criticized breach of diplomacy—when he ejected Yasser Arafat Leader of the Palestine Liberation Organization (PLO) and winner of the Nobel Peace Prize, from a New York concert.

Started in Courts

Giuliani was born into a second-generation immigrant Italian family in Brooklyn, New York, on May 28, 1944. He was the only child of Harold and Helen Giuliani. As a child, the young Giuliani sometimes worked in his parent's bar and grill. The elder Giuliani was determined that his son attend college and rise above the family business. Rudolph Giuliani was educated in Catholic schools and then attended the all-male, Roman Catholic Manhattan College.

There he seriously considered entering the priesthood, but eventually decided on law. He graduated from New York University's law school in 1968, and went on to have an impressive career in government, working first as a law clerk for a federal judge, and then as an assistant United States attorney for the Southern District of New York. Giuliani took on sensational corruption cases, and his reputation as a dogged prosecutor grew.

In 1975 Giuliani went to Washington, D.C. to work in President Gerald Ford's administration, under Judge Harold Tyler, deputy attorney general in the Justice department. Giuliani originally a liberal Democrat, had recently defected to the Republican party. When President Jimmy Carter took office in 1977, Giuliani followed Tyler to work for his law firm. Giuliani moved back to Washington under President Ronald Reagan, as associate attorney general in the Justice department. There, Giuliani took considerable flak for refusing asylum to Haitian refugees, deeming that the Duvalier regime was merely economically—not politically—oppressive to its people.

Became U.S. Attorney in New York

In 1983 Giuliani returned to New York for good, this time as U.S. attorney for the Southern District. In that position, Giuliani enjoyed some high-profile successes. He infiltrated some of the most powerful Mafia crime families and indicted a New York parking violations bureau official as part of a bribery ring. In the spring of 1986, uncovered the New York insider trading scandal, handing down indictments against several Wall Street investors. Among those arrested was Ivan Boesky, who turned himself in before Giuliani could indict him. In exchange for a lesser charge, Boesky agreed to pay $100 million and to secretly tape record conversations with other insider traders.

However, Giuliani has often been criticized for his grandstanding style. One of the lost legendary examples during his years as U.S. attorney was the arrest of three men involved in the insider trading scandal—Richard B. Wigton, a Kidder, Peabody executive; Timothy L. Tabor, a former employee of Kidder, Peabody; and Robert M. Freeman of Goldman, Sachs. Two of the men had been handcuffed at work and paraded in front of their colleagues, to the media's delight. The charges against all three were later dropped.

Mayoral Hopes

Giuliani eventually left the U.S. attorney's office, but still remained one of the most prominent and controversial figures in New York politics, going before the polls in 1989 in his first hotly contested mayoral race against David Dinkins. In that election, the main issue was racial strife, which was threatening to tear the city apart. Giuliani's conservative political stance was less appealing to voters than that of Dinkins, a liberal Democrat.

But in one of the most racially charged events to occur in New York City, Mayor Dinkins stumbled badly. In 1992, in the mostly Jewish section of Crown Heights in Brooklyn, a car in a Hasidic motorcade hit a young black child. After, a mob of angry blacks descended on a Jewish scholar visiting from Australia, stabbing him to death. Riots followed, in which 80 Jews and 50 policemen were injured. A jury later acquitted the man charged with the killing, following which Dinkins issued a lukewarm statement "expressing faith in he jury system . . . roundly denounced as insensitive to Jewish concerns," wrote Todd S. Purdum in the *New York Times Magazine*. Dinkins's Crown Heights blunder opened the door for Giuliani to the Jewish vote.

Still, Giuliani's tough-guy approach has been difficult for New Yorkers to embrace. In the fall of 1992, Giuliani made an appearance at a rally for the Policemen's Benevolent Association (PBA), a gathering of "raucous, beer-drinking, overwhelming white police officers"outside City Hall, wrote Purdum in the same article. Crowd members bore racially offensive signs critical of Dinkins, among the now legendary, "Dump the washroom attendant!" The demeanor of the crowd, which later moved in droves to block traffic on the Brooklyn Bridge, reflected badly on Giuliani. But what tainted him the most was his address to the PBA, in which he used expletives that Dinkins had originally used to respond to an officer's charge that the mayor did not support the police.

The rally was a major political fiasco for Giuliani. According to writer Purdam, he probably gained no votes from it—the police officers either were already supporters or lived outside of the city. And it damaged the reputation he was trying to build—that of a peacemaker. The speech he made after his loss in the 1989 election also damaged him. He announced that Dinkins had won, and in response, his election aides started booing. Giuliani began screaming, "Shut-up!" repeatedly. Later he said he feared that the crowd was out of hand, and their remarks would seem racially motivated.

Prior to the 1993 elections, many New Yorkers were horrified by a Giuliani plan to put 90-day limits on stays at homeless shelters. He remarked that he thought offering, unlimited access was actually "very cruel." "It sounds generous and compassionate," Giuliani was quoted as saying in a *New York* magazine article, "but it isn't. There's an understanding of human psychology that's missing. The less you expect of people, the less you get. The more you expect, the more you get." Giuliani also alienated liberal voters by his statement that he would bar controversial Muslim leader Louis Farrakhan from speaking at Yankee stadium, depriving him of his First Amendment rights.

Many political analysts say that Giuliani's attitudes seem to be a throwback to earlier times, that they distort and oversimplify the growing complexity of urban problems. Wrote Catherine S. Manegold in the *New York Times* after the election, "Throughout this year's campaign, Mr. Giuliani spoke tirelessly about the need to 'clean up' a city that he sees in moral and physical decline. To his supporters, he came across as a tough-edged iconoclast bent on bringing order out of urban chaos, a crusading Batman to New York City's gritty Gotham."

Yet other pundits call Giuliani a candidate for the future, and one who transcends political lines. "With his emphasis on individual responsibility, Giuliani is much closer in political philosophy to the New Democrat Bill Clinton claims to be than to David Dinkins is," said Fred Siegel, a professor of humanities, quoted in a *New York* magazine article.

To save Giuliani from his gaffes, he hired campaign mastermind David Garth, who was on the winning side in five of the last seven New York mayoral contests.Garth also went to bat for Vice-President Al Gore during the 1988 presidential primary, and handed a victory to Arlen Specter in a 1992 Republican senatorial race in which he was trailing. Garth helped solidify Giuliani's image as a "fusion candidate" just as Garth had done for John Lindsey's election in 1965, assembling minority candidates and representatives of minority districts to run on the same ticket.

With Garth maneuvering what a *New York Times Magazine* article dubbed "the race race," Giuliani was also able to capitalize on his anti-crime reputation. Dinkins maintained that crime decreased during hid term and according to John Taylor in a *New York* magazine piece, they had. Murders fell from 2,262 in 1990 to 2,055 in 1992, Taylor wrote. But to New Yorkers, the prevailing perception was that crime was on the rise. "One reason is the increasing brutality and capriciousness committed," wrote Taylor. "Entire families are executed in drug wars. Teenagers kill each other over sneakers. Robbers casually shoot victims even if they have surrendered wallets. The proliferation of carjackings means people are no longer safe even in their automobiles." One of Giuliani's campaign promises, along with creating jobs through tax cuts, and reducing administration in schools in order to increase money spent on teachers and students, was to crack down on such crimes, and he had the resume to back it up.

Still, many New Yorkers expressed dissatisfaction with both candidates. *Time* magazine ran a short article entitled "The Politics of Disgust," in which Janice C. Simpson claimed that "The only movement [in the polls] is the rising disapproval rating for both [candidates]. Neither candidate is getting across a message that he can be an urban Mr. Fixit. Dinkins comes off as a courtly but unimaginative bureaucrat with a taste for fussy clothes and fancy ceremonies. Giuliani has a reputation as a humorless autocrat with an abrasive management style that involves shooting first and asking questions later." An editorial in the *New York Times* began its editorial for David Dinkins with an expression of voter sentiment just before the election: "Something must be badly wrong with a system that can't produce candidates better than David Dinkins and Rudolph Giuliani. The real issues are being oversimplified. It doesn't really matter who wins."

Time writer Janice Simpson predicted that in a race "with no candidate who stands out as a clear vote for competence," that voting would break down along racial lines. That happened in the 1989 election, and also in the 1993 election. According to Felicia R. Lee in the *New York Times,* Simpson was correct. More than 90 percent of blacks voted for Dinkins, and so did most Hispanic voters. But very three out of four white votes went to Giuliani.

Lee wrote that New York City's black population was deeply disappointed by the election results, which indeed turned out to be a race based on race. "None interviewed said that Mr. Dinkins was a great mayor, but they said he tried to delve into the social factors behind problems like crime during a time of dwindling resources. Most said that despite his flaws, Mr. Dinkins would have won re-election had he been white. "Beyond that," Lee continued, "their concern was that Mayor-elect Rudolph W. Giuliani has surrounded himself with mostly white males with little understanding of issues of concerns to blacks, poor people, or other special interests."

Mayor Giuliani

According to Alison Mitchell writing in the *New York Times,* Giuliani addressed those concerns in his victory speech. Standing at the lectern with David Dinkins, the mayor-elect said it was time for the city to join as one, "whether you voted for me, for David Dinkins or you decided not to vote or you voted for any of the other candidates, we are all New Yorkers."

Tough on Crime

In the years since he was elected, Giuliani has maintained his emphasis on crime-fighting, using a range of methods—Comstat, a computerized analysis of crime statistics and police accountability, low tolerance for misdemeanor crimes especially gun and drug possession, targeting high-crime areas, holding local commanders responsible for results in their precincts, and implementing corporate management techniques in the police force.

In an article printed in *American City and County* Janet Ward said that it wasn't easy to shock New Yorkers—especially with good news. However, at a New Year's Eve (1996) press conference in Time Square, Mayor Giuliani and Police Commissioner Safir did just that. "When the ball comes down in Times Square tonight," said Giuliani "it will be coming down in one of the safest cities in America." Ward went on to say that it had been a long time since "one of the safest cities" and "New York" were used in the same sentence, but the facts support the claim. The city had realized double-digit decline in crimes for the past three years. New York had 48,016 or 15.7 percent fewer crimes in 1996. Overall, Giuliani said, "the city has seen 163,428 fewer felonies since 1993, a drop of almost 40 percent. Additionally, 1996 saw the city's lowest number of crime complaints in 27 years. The big crime, murder, dropped 16 percent in 1996 and has fallen nearly half since 1993."

Giuliani called the decline "a very significant success," and proof that New York is becoming safer. "People outside of New York City are very often almost shocked by the notion that it is not the most dangerous city in America," Giuliani was quoted as saying in *The Daily Telegraph.* "That's a reputation that the city, despite all of the statistical information to the contrary, can't quite shake." However, the drop in crime has not been attributed to any one factor. Some have suggested that it may be due to a demographic shift—a decline the population of teenage males, the group that is statistically most likely to commit crime. Another is that the crack epidemic, which hit the city in the mid-1980s, began to ease up in the early 1990s. But the New York City police commissioner says that police effectiveness has more to do with it than the media and other observers are willing to give them credit for.

Giuliani has also continued to harass the Mafia. In September of 1995, he appointed a monitor to inspect the books of the five-day Feast of Saint Gennaro, the annual carnival of New York's Little Italy. Few New Yorkers were surprised when the Grand Jury investigating the case announced that the Mafia skimmed the profits of the street vendors at the festival. However, only the most cynical were not surprised when it was revealed that the dollar bills which the devout pinned to the statue of Saint Gennero—intended for the Catholic church and its charities—also ended up in the pockets of the Mob.

Giuliani has sometimes committed mistakes in international diplomacy. In October 1995, Giuliani ejected Yasser Arafat, leader of the Palestine Liberation Organization (PLO) and winner of the Nobel Peace Prize, from a concert at New York's Lincoln Center, which was part of the UN's 50th anniversary celebrations. Despite intense criticism from the White House, the State Department, the UN, and even some Jewish groups, Giuliani defended his decision, claiming that Arafat had "never been held to account for the murders [for which] he was implicated." Just a few days earlier, when Cuba's President, Fidel Castro, was in New York, Giuliani had refused to invite him to a gala dinner. "It's my party and I'll invite who I want," he was quoted as saying in *The Daily Telegraph.*

After New York senator Daniel Patrick Moynihan announced that he would not seek re-election to Congress in 2000, Giuliani's name was mentioned as a possible successor. During the campaign Giuliani announced that he had been diagnosed with an early stage of prostate cancer and that he was seeking a separation agreement from his wife. In May 2000, Giuliani decided to drop out of the Senate race.

John Herschel Glenn, Jr.

John Herschel Glenn, Jr. (born 1921) was a military test pilot, astronaut, businessman, and U.S. senator from Ohio. In 1984 he unsuccessfully sought the Democratic nomination for president.

John Glenn was born in Cambridge, Ohio, on July 18, 1921, to John Herschel Glenn, Sr., a plumbing contractor, and Clara Sproat Glenn. His parents had two other children who died in infancy, and they later adopted his sister Jean. He was reared nearby in the small town of New Concord and graduated from high school in 1939. Glenn credits his parents for instilling his deep rooted Presbyterian faith and its accompanying philosophy that everyone is given certain talents and has a duty to use them to the fullest. He enrolled at Muskingum College, a Presbyterian school in New Concord, to study chemical engineering, but left there to enlist for naval aviation training following America's entry into World War II. He married his high school sweetheart, Anna Margaret (Annie) Castor, in April 1943. They had two children, John David and Carolyn Ann.

Commissioned in the Marine Corps Reserve in March 1943, Glenn was assigned to squadron VMO-155 and ordered to the Pacific. The squadron, equipped with F4U Corsairs, was based on Majuro in the Marshall Islands and flew a variety of bombing and strafing missions against Japanese garrisons on other islands in the area. Glenn flew 59 combat missions while stationed there. After returning to the United States, he served principally as a flight instructor and was promoted to captain in July 1945. He remained on active duty after the war and was brought into the regular Marine Corps in 1946.

In the Korean conflict Glenn flew jets in ground support missions for the Marines and in air-to-air combat in the Air Force's new F-86 fighters as an exchange pilot, completing a total of 90 missions between February and September 1953. He gained a reputation for taking the battle to the enemy at such close range that often he would come back with a seemingly unflyable aircraft. Once, he returned in a plane with more than 200 holes in it, and it was immediately nicknamed "Glenn's flying doily."

Test Pilot to Astronaut

He was promoted to major in February 1953 and after his return from Korea worked tirelessly to make up for his lack of a college degree (awarded 1962) by self-study in engineering subjects and attending service schools. He was assigned to the Navy's Patuxent River test pilot school and later to the Bureau of Aeronautics. Glenn developed a project in which an F8U Crusader jet fighter would try to break the non-stop transcontinental speed record, refueling

in mid-air three times. He received permission to make the attempt himself and on July 16, 1957, flew from Los Angeles to New York in 3 hours, 23 minutes. For this feat a fifth Distinguished Flying Cross was added to the many medals he had earned in wartime.

Spurred by the successful Russian Sputnik satellite, the U.S. government in 1958 began Project Mercury, a top-priority plan to place a man in orbit around the earth. Glenn went through a selection process of strenuous and exacting physical and psychological testing and was named one of the seven Mercury astronauts in April 1959. Promoted to lieutenant colonel the same month, Glenn was the senior astronaut in rank and age. Motivated by a deep religious faith and a tenacious devotion to duty, he reflected an earnest confidence that helped win the space program widespread public support.

Glenn was backup pilot for both the suborbital flights of Alan Shepard and Virgil "Gus" Grissom in 1961. He was chosen for the first orbital mission, "Friendship 7," circling the earth three times on February 20, 1962. It was a technological triumph, but part way through the nearly five-hour flight a data sensor indicated that his space capsule's protective heatshield had become dislocated. On these early missions no repairs could be made in space, and if the heatshield actually had slipped, Glenn would have perished without a trace in the fireball of re-entry into the atmosphere. The next week a relieved nation celebrated his safe return with parades in New York and Washington, D.C., as well as New Concord; not since Charles Lindbergh had the public so acclaimed a peacetime hero. Glenn responded on behalf of all the astronauts with a simple and moving speech before a joint meeting of Congress.

President John F. Kennedy admired the astronauts and their deeds and became Glenn's personal friend. He advised Glenn to finish his Marine career and seek public office, but after Kennedy's death Glenn's political future became more difficult. Moreover, in February 1964 Glenn suffered a severe inner-ear injury in a fall in the bathroom of his Columbus, Ohio, apartment. When he was taken to a military hospital in San Antonio for treatment speculation circulated that his problem was a delayed result of his space flight, but these rumors were dispelled when initial reports of the accident were clarified. His lengthy convalescence forced postponement of his retirement from the Marines and made him abandon as well his declared plans to run in the Democratic primary for U.S. senator from Ohio. By late 1964 he had recovered and was even able to fly jet fighters once again. Glenn asked that the Marine Corps not consider him for higher rank as he still intended to retire. President Lyndon Johnson set aside his request, however, and promoted him to full colonel at a White House ceremony in October 1964. Glenn then retired in January 1965.

Businessman to Politician

Glenn became an executive of Royal Crown Cola International from 1965 to 1969, when he resigned to try again for the Senate. Although his political organization was inexperienced, he was narrowly defeated in the Democratic primary of 1970 by Howard Metzenbaum, who was himself defeated by Robert A. Taft, Jr., in the general election. Between 1970 and 1974 Glenn became a partial owner of motels near Orlando, Florida. Along with other investments, they made him a wealthy man.

In 1974 Glenn made his third try for the Senate, again opposing Metzenbaum in the primary. This time Glenn's campaigning and organization were much improved. Glenn defeated Metzenbaum and went on to win the general election by one million votes. (Metzenbaum later won election as Ohio's second senator.) In the Senate Glenn was a member of the Foreign Relations and Governmental Affairs committees. He was respected as a hard-working senator, at his best when dealing with technical issues. His voting record tended to be conservative on national defense and foreign affairs, but more liberal on domestic social issues. He was the principal author of the Nuclear Nonproliferation Act of 1978, which sought to limit the spread of nuclear weapons. In 1980 he was re-elected by a margin of 1.6 million votes—the largest in Ohio history—in the face of a nationwide Republican trend.

In April 1983 Glenn announced his intention to seek the Democratic presidential nomination. He had been called "a Democratic Eisenhower," and many expected him to have the best chance to defeat the acknowledged front-runner, former Vice President Walter Mondale, in the primaries. Unlike Ike, however, Glenn somehow could not convey his charming and warm private personality to voters nationwide. His political organization suffered from frequent changes in key personnel and was inept in the timing of campaign events. Almost everywhere Glenn was enthusiastically received, but often disappointed his audiences with long, overly detailed speeches. His campaign steadily lost momentum as Mondale, a seasoned politician, racked up many endorsements among the diverse groups that comprise the national Democratic Party. Glenn's best showing was a second-place finish in Alabama, and he withdrew in March 1984, leaving the race to Senator Gary Hart, who had captured much of the vote of the "baby-boom" generation; the Reverend Jesse Jackson, who was forging a coalition among minorities; and Mondale, ultimately selected as the party's nominee.

After again winning his seat both in the 1986 and 1992 elections, Senator Glenn remained a strong voice in the Congress for a permanent research station in space, and supported increased funding for education, scientific research and space exploration. He announced in 1997 that he would not seek another term in the senate, but retire to pursue other interests. He was then assigned to the Senate Campaign Finance Reform Committee as vice-chair. He also approached NASA with the proposition that he be sent into space again so that they could study the effects of exposure to weightlessness on older Americans. Glenn, still in good physical shape, got his wish and re-entered the space program. On October 29, 1998, Glenn became the oldest person to go into space, 36 years after his first historic flight. After an nine day flight aboard the shuttle Discovery, Glenn returned to earth to undergo testing to discover the effects of spaceflight on the elderly.

John Glenn spent most of his adult life serving the nation. The ending of his 1962 address before Congress shows why he won the admiration of millions with his modesty and quiet patriotism: "We are all proud to have been privileged to be part of this effort, to represent our country as we have. As our knowledge of the universe in which we live increases, may God grant us the wisdom and guidance to use it wisely."

Further Reading

Most information about Glenn is found in periodicals; the only biography yet published was written before his entry into politics. *John H. Glenn: Astronaut,* by Lt. Col. Philip N. Pierce, USMC, and Karl Schuon (1962), covers his early life, his Marine career, and his orbital flight. Anyone wishing to find out more about Glenn's Marine career is advised to consult the History and Museums Division, Headquarters, U.S. Marine Corps, Washington, DC 20380. *We Seven* by The Astronauts (M. Scott Carpenter, et al., 1962) includes writings by Glenn on his flight, as well as detailed descriptions of his training. Among official government publications is the National Aeronautics and Space Administration's *This New Ocean: A History of Project Mercury* (1966) by Lloyd S. Swenson, Jr., et al. A best-selling, rather irreverent look at Project Mercury is *The Right Stuff* by Tom Wolfe (1979). A motion picture based on Wolfe's book appeared in 1983, but affected Glenn's candidacy little. Of value for those interested in Glenn's political career is the 1983 pamphlet *John Glenn,* published by Political Profiles, Inc., of Washington, DC, which includes a biographical sketch written by Jon Margolis. *Letters to John Glenn John Glenn: Astronaut* (1962) by Philip Pierce and Karl Schuon, Van Riper's *Glenn: The Astronaut Who Would Be President* (1983) examines Glenn's political years. Also a visit to Senator Glenn's website on the Internet at http://little.nhlink.net/john-glenn/jglenn.htm yields much information on his current activities □

Robert Hutchings Goddard

The American pioneer in rocketry Robert Hutchings Goddard (1882-1945) was one of the founders of the science of astronautics.

Robert Goddard was born on October 5, 1882, in Worcester, Mass., the son of Nahum Danford Goddard, a businessman, and Fannie Hoyt Goddard. From his earliest youth Goddard suffered from pulmonary tuberculosis. Although he remained out of school for long periods, he kept up with his academic studies, and he read voluminously in *Cassell's Popular Educator* and science fiction.

In 1904 Goddard enrolled at Worcester Polytechnic Institute and received his degree in physics in 1908. He then entered the graduate school of Clark University, where he was granted a master's degree in 1910 and received his doctorate a year later.

Early Investigations in Rocketry

Goddard went to the Palmer Physical Laboratory of Princeton University as a research fellow in 1912. He proposed a research project he described as "the positive result of force on a material dielectric carrying a displacement

current." In the course of his experimentation he developed a vacuum-tube oscillator that he subsequently patented in 1915, well before that of Lee De Forest.

While Goddard's days in the laboratory were given over to his research in radio, his nights were free to work upon the fundamentals of rocketry. Approaching the problem theoretically, he was able by 1913 to prove that a rocket of 200 pounds' initial mass could achieve escape velocity for a 1-pound mass if the propellant was of gun cotton at 50 percent efficiency or greater. He began patenting many of the rocket concepts that ultimately gave him a total of more than 200 patents in this particular field of technology. They were to cover many of the fundamentals in areas such as propellants, guidance and control, and structure. For example, his patent granted on July 7, 1914, clearly identifies the concept of multistaging of rockets, without which the landing of men on the moon or sending probes to Mars and Venus would not be possible.

When his health permitted, Goddard returned to teaching and research at Clark University. By this time he was wholly devoted to rocketry. He built a vacuum chamber in which he fired small, solid-propellant rockets to study the effects of different types of nozzles in such an environment. Having exhausted his own funds and not wishing to draw further on the resources of the university, he applied to the Smithsonian for a grant of $5,000, which he was awarded in 1917. With these funds he began the study of rocketry in earnest.

During World War I the U.S. Army Signal Corps provided $20,000 to the Smithsonian Institution for research in

applied rocketry by Goddard. He moved to the Mt. Wilson Observatory in California and set up a workshop in which to experiment with solid-propellant rockets as weapons. There, with two assistants, Henry C. Parker and Clarence N. Hickman, he set to work on two projects.

Parker worked on a rocket with a single charge that could be launched from an open tube. This was the forebear of the World War II bazooka. Meanwhile, Hickman devoted his energies to one of Goddard's pet but more complex problems—a rocket propelled by the injection of successive solid charges into its motor. Parker's rocket proved to be successful, but Hickman's was simply unworkable. However, both rockets were demonstrated for military officials, but despite the success and the obvious enthusiasm of the military, the armistice 4 days after the demonstration canceled all Army interest in Goddard and his rockets. It was not revived for 26 years.

Liquid-propellant Rockets

In 1919 the Smithsonian Institution published Goddard's monograph "A Method of Reaching Extreme Altitudes," which he had submitted earlier to that organization with a request for research funds. The newspapers, seeing a casual reference to the moon and the prospect of hitting it with a rocket loaded with flash powder, pushed Goddard into the headlines. Being a reticent man as well as a dedicated physicist, he recoiled from the unwanted publicity and resisted further attempts by publications to present the subject.

During the decades of the 1920s and 1930s Goddard's research was supported by erratic and unpredictable funding from Clark University, the U.S. Navy, the Smithsonian Institution, and the Carnegie Foundation. From static testing of small solid-propellant rockets Goddard graduated to liquid-propellant motors. His long experimentation with solid-propellant rockets had by the early 1920s convinced him that the efficiency of such motors was simply too low ever to be of use in space travel. Indeed, by the early 1920s he had daringly mentioned liquid hydrogen (not then obtainable) and liquid oxygen, that is, nuclear and ionic propulsion for rockets.

Goddard's first liquid-propellant rocket was launched in 1926 from a farm near Auburn, Mass. Present on the occasion as photographer was the young Mrs. Esther Goddard, whom Goddard had married in 1924. The rocket reached an altitude of 41 feet and a range of 184 feet and traveled the distance in only 2 1/2 seconds. It was not a statistically impressive performance, but neither was that at Kitty Hawk, N. C., on December 17, 1903.

Work in New Mexico

Needing more room and a milder outdoor climate for his experiments, Goddard moved to New Mexico, near Roswell, in 1930. His Mescalero Ranch was only 100 miles from the White Sands Missile Range. There, in a well-equipped machine shop, Goddard and a small team of assistants began work on the design and fabrication of liquid-propellant rockets that were the direct forebears of the Saturn 5 and Titan 3C space boosters of the 1960s.

The first launching in New Mexico took place in 1930. In 1932 a rocket with a gyroscopic stabilizer was flown. In that same year Goddard returned to Clark University because of the economic depression. During the succeeding 2 years at Clark he continued his research as well as he could and received several patents that grew out of his work in New Mexico.

After Goddard returned to the ranch, the rockets grew larger and flew higher. On March 31, 1935, a 15-foot-tall model reached an altitude of 7,500 feet under gyroscopic control. Goddard's research continued here until 1942. During these years he turned his attention to a high-speed turbopump for delivering the propellants to the combustion chamber of the motor. It was a component that had long held up his development of a really efficient rocket.

Return East

On May 28, 1940, Goddard met with officers of the U.S. Army Air Corps and Navy in Washington, D.C., to brief them on his rockets and their potential as weapons. In 1941 he finally received a small contract from the Army Air Corps and Navy to develop a liquid-propellant jet-assist-takeoff rocket for aircraft. In July 1942 he left Roswell to continue his research at the Navy Engineering Experimental Station at Annapolis, Md. There his experiments met with technical success, but an attempt to demonstrate the motor on an actual aircraft ended in failure and the loss of the plane. As rockets of all types, especially the V-1 and V-2, began making the headlines, Goddard received offers of jobs from many companies; he accepted the invitation from Curtiss-Wright, where he worked until his death on Aug. 10, 1945.

Further Reading

The Papers of Robert H. Goddard was edited by Esther C. Goddard and G. Edward Pendray (3 vols., 1970). The only full-length biography of Goddard is Milton Lehman, *This High Man: The Life of Robert H. Goddard* (1963). Anne Perkins Dewey, *Robert Goddard, Space Pioneer* (1962), is a biography for younger readers. For general reading on rocketry during the period in which Goddard figured prominently see Willy Ley, *Rockets Missiles, and Men in Space* (1952; rev. ed. 1968); Beryl Williams and Samuel Epstein, *The Rocket Pioneers on the Road to Space* (1955); and Wernher von Braun and Frederick I. Ordway III, *History of Rocketry and Space Travel* (1966). Useful books on astronautics in general include Frederick I. Ordway, James P. Gardner, and Mitchell R. Sharpe, *Basic Astronautics: An Introduction to Space Science, Engineering, and Medicine* (1962), and Mitchell R. Sharpe, *Living in Space: The Astronaut and His Environment* (1969). □

Barry Goldwater

Barry Goldwater (1909–1998) was elected as a Republican to the U.S. Senate five times between 1952 and 1980, leaving temporarily to run unsuccessfully for president in 1964. His outspoken conservatism gained him the label "Mr. Conservative" in American politics. He was considered the most important American conservative between Senator Robert Taft's death in 1953 and Ronald Reagan's election as governor of California in 1966.

arry Morris Goldwater was born in Phoenix, Arizona, on January 1, 1909, the first child of Baron and Josephine Williams Goldwater. His Polish-born grandfather and great-uncle had migrated to the Arizona territory from the California Gold Rush fields. They discovered that there were easier ways to make a fortune—such as operating a bordello and bar. They also founded a small general store, J. Goldwater & Bro., in La Paz in 1867. Soon the brothers opened stores throughout Arizona with the Phoenix branch, established in 1872, becoming the flagship of the family operation. This store was headed by Barry Goldwater's father, Baron. Barry was an indifferent student at Phoenix's Union High school, where he showed early leadership abilities when his classmates elected him as president of the Freshman class. His principal suggested that he might be happier elsewhere, so young Barry was sent by his family to finish his last four years at Staunton Military Academy in Virginia. There he won the medal as best all-around cadet and began his lifelong interest in the military. Although he hoped to attend the U.S. Military Academy at West Point, his ill father insisted he enroll at the University of Arizona. He completed only one year, dropping out to join the family department store business when his father died in 1929.

Successful Businessman

Goldwater showed good aptitude for the retail business, rising from a junior clerkship to the presidency of the firm by 1937. He was an innovative manager, setting up the first employees' health-hospitalization plan of any Phoenix mercantile firm, forming a flying club for his employees, introducing a number of novel product lines, and creating a national reputation for the store by taking out advertisements in the *New Yorker*. In addition to being the most prestigious store in Phoenix, the Goldwater enterprise shared the city's booster spirit, cooperating in civic initiatives to improve the city and attract new residents.

He was the first Phoenix businessman to hire African Americans as sales clerks, thereby breaking the "color barrier" in the city's hiring practices. It was during this time as well that Goldwater overworked himself into two nervous breakdowns and began to have trouble with alcohol, two issues that his later political opponents wee always quick to recall.

In September 1934 Goldwater culminated a brief courtship by marrying Margaret (Peggy) Johnson, daughter of a successful Indiana businessman whose firm later became part of Borg-Warner. The couple had four children, Joanne (1936), Barry Jr. (1938), Michael (1940), and Peggy (1944).

Goldwater eagerly interrupted his business career to take part in World War II. Though his age seemingly disqualified him from the air combat assignment he coveted, Goldwater parlayed his decade-old reserve commission into an assignment in the Army Air Force. He served first as an instructor in the gunnery command. Then, for most of the war, he used the flying skills he had learned in the late 1920s to pilot supply runs in the India-Burma theater and across the Atlantic as well. When the war ended he accepted the task of organizing the Arizona Air National Guard, eventually achieving the rank of brigadier general in the Air Force Reserve.

By the late 1940s Goldwater was a locally prominent figure, winning acclaim as Phoenix's "Man of the Year" in 1949. He had joined in a citizens' reform effort resulting in a revised city charter that gave extensive powers to a city manager and called for at-large election of the city council. When suitable council candidates failed to emerge in 1949 Goldwater ran for a council seat himself, leading the city-wide ticket in the nonpartisan election.

"Mr. Conservative"

Goldwater soon outgrew local politics. Frustrated with the policies of the New and Fair Deals, in 1950 he devoted his energies to managing the successful gubernatorial campaign of Howard Pyle. Sensing an opportunity for the Republican party to become truly competitive in the state for the first time, he decided to challenge Democratic Senate Majority Leader Ernest McFarland in the 1952 election. Campaigning as a staunchly conservative critic of "Trumanism," excessive federal spending, the "no win" U.S. strategy in the Korean War, and what he saw as a weak and futile foreign policy toward the Soviet Union, Goldwater eked out a narrow victory. He squeaked by on the coattails of Republican presidential candidate Eisenhower by over 35,000 votes and began his long and distinguished national political career.

Goldwater's entry into the Senate was at a critical time for conservatives. The twenty years that had passed since Republicans held power had seen the New Deal Domestic Reforms, World War II and the rise of the Cold War. The American political landscape was very different from when Herbert Hoover promised a "chicken in every pot". Many questioned if conservatism with its emphasis on state's rights and limited central government was even relevant in the new atmosphere Initially a supporter of the Robert A. Taft over Eisenhower for the 1952 Republican nomination, Goldwater maintained independence from Eisenhower's programs and was one of his most outspoken critics. Notably he criticized foreign aid spending and supported Senator Joseph McCarthy's campaign against "Communism-in-government" even after McCarthy clearly lost favor with Eisenhower. In December 1954 the Arizonan was one of only 22 senators (all Republicans) who took McCarthy's side in the vote to censure the Wisconsin senator. Though he agreed with Eisenhower on most domestic issues, Goldwater often took more extreme positions than the president—especially in his condemnation of labor unions, his opposition to federal action in civil rights matters, and his advocacy of a strongly nationalist foreign policy. At one point castigating the Eisenhower policies as a "dime-store New Deal," he opposed Eisenhower's use of federal troops in the Little Rock integration crisis and criticized the administration for producing balanced budgets in only three of its eight years.

Goldwater gained in influence during the 1950s. Through his effective leadership of the Republican Senatorial Campaign Committee he won affection and respect from his party colleagues. After his solid re-election victory (with 56 percent of the vote) in 1958 Goldwater began to receive considerable media attention as the leader of the conservative movement. He enhanced this image through a thrice-weekly syndicated newspaper column and by publishing in 1960 an extended statement of his political creed, *The Conscience of the Conservative* (which eventually sold 3.5 million copies). He was viewed, despite often contradictory and inconsistent casual remarks, as a straight-from-the-gut conservative whose appeal stemmed from the fact that his own profound confusion somehow reflected his supporter's anxiety. Wisely foregoing a political battle with Republican liberals in 1960, he settled for exercising behind-the-scenes influence on the platform while supporting Richard Nixon for the presidential nomination. His loyalty to the party ticket won him Nixon's support for the future.

Presidential Candidate

Goldwater later contended that he was not eager for the 1964 nomination against the popular Kennedy, but he came increasingly to be regarded as his party's likely nominee. Friendly rivals from their years together in the Senate, he and Kennedy even discussed the type of campaigns they might wage against each other. Kennedy's assassination and the accession of Texas-born Lyndon B. Johnson to the presidency further reduced Goldwater's enthusiasm for the nomination; as Johnson's appeal in the South and West threatened to keep Goldwater from capitalizing on his own natural strengths in those areas. By the end of 1963, however, he succumbed to pressures from the informal "Draft Goldwater" group that had been in existence since 1961; he announced his candidacy on January 3, 1964.

Goldwater chose to enter only selected primaries, while building support in states where delegates were selected by other means. After a damaging loss in the New Hampshire primary at the start of the campaign, he won important victories in Illinois and Nebraska; then, in early June he defeated his only real competition for the nomination—New York Governor Nelson Rockefeller—in the crucial California primary. Goldwater's nomination was then inevitable. He won on the first ballot at the convention in San Francisco, but events revealed the depth of division in the party: Rockefeller was booed by the predominantly conservative delegates, while nominee Goldwater was pilloried by his liberal foes (and the press) for a statement in his acceptance speech: "I would remind you that extremism in the defense of liberty is no vice. And let me remind you that moderation in the pursuit of justice is no virtue."

While Goldwater added to his own problems by making some gratuitous and inappropriate statements in the campaign, he never had a chance to defeat Johnson. Public perception of Goldwater as an extremist was fed by events at the GOP convention and by his well-known opposition to federal civil rights laws (he did not oppose integration, but thought that states properly had jurisdiction in such matters). The result was a Johnson landslide: Goldwater received only 38.8 percent of the vote and carried only five states in the deep South and Arizona. Goldwater's appeal to persons who wanted a return to a prewar American way of life was swept aside in view of Johnson's progressive Great Society.

Elder Statesman

Goldwater was never again considered a viable presidential candidate, but his stature in the party and as a spokesman for the conservative cause was firmly established. Back in private life (he had given up the chance to run for re-election in 1964), he announced that Nixon was his choice for the presidency in 1968 and then set about putting his own career back on track. In 1968, as Nixon narrowly won the presidency, Goldwater was elected once again to the Senate (with 57 percent of the vote).

His White House ambitions put aside, Goldwater reestablished himself as a forceful presence in the Senate. He strongly backed the American military involvement in Vietnam and, as a prominent member of the Armed Services Committee, he gave strong support to the Nixon administration's aggressive defense policies. He was more critical on domestic issues, where he again thought Nixon too inclined to temporize; in particular, he felt the wage-price guidelines of the early 1970s were a "disaster."

Never one to waver in a political cause, Goldwater remained loyal to Nixon, suspending judgment while the Watergate crisis unfolded in 1973 and early 1974. He did not finally break from Nixon until the revelation, on August 5, 1974, that the president had indeed acted to obstruct justice in the Watergate case. Because of his stature and unquestioned integrity, Goldwater's defection was a symbolic final blow to Nixon, who resigned from the presidency four days later.

Goldwater won his most convincing re-election victory in 1974, being returned to the Senate by a 58 percent vote. He was impatient with what he regarded as President Ford's vacillations on policy—as he had been with Nixon—but again he was a loyal (if outspoken) follower, supporting the president over Ronald Reagan for the 1976 Republican nomination. Ford's defeat placed in the White House a president for whom Goldwater developed genuine contempt, Jimmy Carter. He opposed Carter on nearly every major issue, including defense cutbacks, diplomatic recognition for the People's Republic of China, and the Panama Canal treaties. In 1980 he was an early, enthusiastic backer of his fellow conservative, Ronald Reagan, for the Republican nomination. Reagan's easy victory over Carter was accomplished on a platform echoing many of Goldwater's earlier positions. Goldwater himself was again re-elected in 1980, though with a narrower margin of victory than every before. His age (71) and frequent hospitalizations apparently played a part in making the result so close, a fact suggesting that his fifth term in the Senate would be his last.

Although he regained his seat in 1988, Goldwater nevertheless was never again a power in the conservative movement. His libertarian streak made him uncomfortable with his own party's New Right social agenda. The strong desire of this New Right to use coercive power of the state to influence morality were at odds with what Goldwater believed were matters of personal choice. In 1979 Goldwater published his political memoir, *With No Apologies;* he wrote it early, he said, because he believed "the Republic is in danger" and "time is short." With Reagan's re-election in 1984, Goldwater's fears for the future abated somewhat. Yet he remained curiously unconnected to the upsurge of political conservatism reflected in Reagan's successes. Fiercely independent and seemingly out of step with the majority throughout his political career, he somehow seemed apart even from the "New Conservatives" dominating his party in the 1980s.

Nearing the end of 30 years in the Senate, Goldwater seemed to take special pleasure in the license afforded an elder statesman, daring to speak out against spokesmen for the Moral Majority whom he thought too self-serving as well as against his more traditional moderate-to-left targets.

After his retirement in 1987, Goldwater returned to Phoenix where he was still considered an asset to any political campaign. During the 1996 presidential campaign, Goldwater's opinions and endorsements were continually sought. He eventually supported the candidacy of Senate majority leader Robert Dole, he was highly vocal in his praise of the possibility of former Joint Chiefs of Staff Colin Powell as president. One of Goldwater's major interests as Chairman of the Armed Services Committee was the passage of the Goldwater-Nichols Military Reform Act, which authorized the chairman of the Joint Chief's of Staff's ability to order other branches of the military to cooperate with one another. This act cut through bitter interservice rivalry that often crippled military operations, and enabled theater commanders to simply order different services under their command to work together without first going up the chain of command in Washington.

In 1996 Goldwater suffered a stroke that left damage on the frontal lobe of his brain. Alzheimer's disease began to set in in 1997. On May 29, 1998, Goldwater died of natural causes at the age of 89 in his home in Paradise Valley, Arizona.

Though he suffered one of the worst electoral defeats in history when he sought the presidency, Barry Goldwater will certainly be considered one of the leading political figures of his era as he was responsible for ushering the conservative wing of the Republican party and relegating the moderates to a secondary position, thereby changing the face of American politics for decades.

Further Reading

The best account of Goldwater's life and career is his autobiography, *With No Apologies: The Personal and Political Memoirs of United States Senator Barry Goldwater* (1979). In the 1960s, when he was considered a presidential possibility, two biographies appeared; the more valuable is Jack Bell, *Mr. Conservative: Barry Goldwater* (1962); *Barry Goldwater: Freedom Is His Flight Plan* (1962), written by his long-time political aide Stephen Shadegg, is naturally very favorable in its view. Goldwater's 1964 presidential campaign is treated in John H. Kessel, *The Goldwater Coalition: Republican Strategies in 1964* (1968); Richard Rovere, *The Goldwater Caper* (1965); F. Clifton White, *Suite 3505: The Story of the Draft Goldwater Movement* (1967); and Theodore H. White, *The Making of the President 1964* (1965). In addition, Goldwater wrote a number of books expressing his political credo, including *The Conscience of a Conservative* (1960), *Why Not Victory? A Fresh Look at American Foreign Policy* (1962), *The Conscience of a Majority* (1970), and *The Coming Breakpoint* (1976). Finally, a number of studies of the Republican Party in recent times give considerable attention to his political impact, including Michael W. Miles, *The Odyssey of the American Right* (1980) and David W. Reinhard, *The Republican Right Since 1945* (1983). A lively interview in *Jet* describes Goldwater's ongoing independence July 24, 1995. □

Samuel Gompers

The American labor leader Samuel Gompers (1850-1924) was the most significant single figure in the history of the American labor movement. He founded and was the first president of the American Federation of Labor.

Few great social movements have been so influenced by one man as was the American labor movement by Samuel Gompers. He virtually stamped his personality and viewpoint on the American Federation of Labor (AFL). This heritage included both Gompers's social conservatism and his truculent firmness on behalf of the organized skilled workers of the country. His is a unique success story, of an utterly penniless immigrant who became the confidant of presidents and industrialists.

Gompers was born on January 27, 1850, in east London, England. His family was Dutch-Jewish in origin and had lived in England for only a few years. The family was extremely poor, but at the age of 6 Gompers was sent to a Jewish free school, where he received the rudiments of an education virtually unknown to his class. The education

was brief, however, and Gompers was apprenticed first to a shoemaker and then in his father's cigar-making trade. In 1863, when Gompers was 13, the family moved to the tenement slums of the Lower East Side of New York City. The family soon numbered 11 members, and Gompers again went to work as a cigar-maker.

Cigar-makers' Union

Naturally gregarious and energetic, Gompers joined numerous organizations in the bustling immigrant world of New York City. But from the start nothing was so important to him as the small Cigar-makers' Local Union No. 15, which he joined with his father in 1864. Gompers immediately rose to leadership of the group. At the age of 16 he regularly represented his fellow workers in altercations with their employers, and he discussed politics and economics with articulate workingmen many years his senior.

This was a time of technological flux in cigar-making, as in practically every branch of American industry. Machines were being introduced which eliminated many highly skilled workers. The cigar-makers were distinguished, however, by the intelligence with which they studied their problems. The nature of the work—the quietness of the process, for example—permitted and even encouraged discussion of economic questions, and this environment provided Gompers with an excellent social schooling. The most significant influence upon his life was a formerly prominent Scandinavian socialist, Ferdinand Laurel, who had become disillusioned with Marxism and taught Gompers that workingmen ought to avoid both politics and utopian dreaming in favor of winning immediate "bread and butter" gains in their wages, hours, and conditions.

In fact, Gompers had many contacts with socialists, though, from his earliest days, he had little time for their ideals. Basing his own unionism on a "pure and simple" materialistic approach, he built the Cigar-makers' International Union into a viable trade association despite technology and unsuccessful strikes.

American Federation of Labor

With Adolph Strasser, the head of the German-speaking branch of the Cigar-makers' Union (Gompers led the English-speaking branch), and several other trade union leaders, Gompers helped to set up in 1881 a loose federation of trade unions which, in 1886, became the AFL. Founded during the heyday of the Knights of Labor, the AFL differed from the older organization in nearly every respect. The Knights emphasized the solidarity of labor regardless of craft and admitted unskilled as well as skilled workers to membership. The AFL, with Gompers as its president, was a federation of autonomous craft unions which admitted only members of specific crafts (carpenters, cigar-makers, and so on) and made no provision for the unskilled. The Knights looked forward to a society in which the wage system would be abolished and cooperation would govern the economy, whereas the AFL unions were interested only in improving the day-to-day material life of their members. The socialists' attempt to capture the AFL in 1894 did succeed in unseating Gompers for a year, but he was firmly back in power by 1895 and, if anything, more bitterly hostile to socialism in the unions than ever.

"Socialism holds nothing but unhappiness for the human race," Gompers said in 1918. "Socialism is the fad of fanatics . . . and it has no place in the hearts of those who would secure the fight for freedom and preserve democracy." Throughout his career he inveighed against the flourishing Socialist party and the numerous attempts to form revolutionary unions. Although many forces account for the failure of socialist thought among American unions, Gompers's influence at the head of the movement for 40 years cannot be discounted.

Devotion to Unionism

However, if Gompers was hostile to the socialists, he was as devoted to the cause of unionism as any other American labor leader before or since. He was the first national union leader to recognize and encourage the strike as labor's most effective weapon. Further, when issued an injunction in 1906 not to boycott the antilabor Buck Stove and Range Company, he defied the courts (albeit gingerly) and was sentenced to a year in prison for contempt (a conviction later reversed on appeal). Gompers spent only one night in jail (a rare distinction among labor leaders of his day) and, characteristically, was contemptuous of, rather than sympathetic with, those with whom he shared his cell. But his devotion to unionism and the rhetoric with which he denounced avaricious industrialists matched anything of his time.

National Prominence

Although the leader of a socially disreputable movement, Gompers had good relations with several presidents and became something of an adviser to president Woodrow Wilson. In 1901 he was one of the founders of the National Civic Federation (an alliance of businessmen willing to tolerate unions and conservative union leaders), and Wilson found it politically expedient and worthwhile to have the support of the AFL during World War I. Gompers supported the war vigorously, attempting to halt AFL strikes for the duration and denouncing socialists and pacifists. He served as president of the International Commission on Labor Legislation at the Versailles Peace Conference and on various other advisory committees.

During the 1920s, though in failing health, Gompers served as a spokesman for the Mexican revolutionary government in Washington and considered himself instrumental in securing American recognition of the new regime. He was received with high honors by President Plutarco Elias Calles in 1924, but, realizing that the end was near, Gompers returned early to the United States and died in San Antonio, Texas, on December 13. Characteristically, his last words were: "Nurse, this is the end. God bless our American institutions. May they grow better day by day." What had begun as expedient for Gompers—acceptance of the capitalist system and working within it—had become his gospel. Indeed, he was one of the makers of the modern institutions of which he spoke in that he won for capitalism the loyalty of labor and for labor a part in industrial decision making.

Gompers the Man

Among friends, Gompers was gregarious and convivial. He enjoyed eating and drinking, sometimes excessively (he was a vociferous enemy of prohibition), and at home he was the classic 19th-century paterfamilias with a retiring, worshipful wife and a large brood of deferential children.

Gompers first made his reputation as an orator and always delivered a speech well. He spoke widely in the cause of the AFL, rose to great heights of eloquence on occasion, and thanks to an agile mind and sharp tongue was rarely bested in debate. He mixed with equal ease among awkward workmen and in the polished society of Washington's highest circles. He had been a militant anticlerical in his youth and never attended a church or synagogue except to speak on labor's behalf. Although of Jewish heritage and education, he did not think of himself as a Jew or, for that matter, as a member of any religion. None of his books was distinguished except his autobiography, *Seventy Years of Life and Labor* (1925).

Further Reading

Gompers's autobiography, *Seventy Years of Life and Labor* (2 vols., 1925; rev. ed. in 1 vol., 1943), is indispensable. The most comprehensive and authoritative biography is Bernard Mandel, *Samuel Gompers* (1963). Also valuable are Philip Taft, *The A. F. of L. in the Time of Gompers* (1957), and Marc Karson, *American Labor Unions and Politics, 1900-1918* (1958). The best among the brief surveys of American labor are Foster Rhea Dulles, *Labor in America* (1949; 3d ed. 1966); Henry Pelling, *American Labor* (1960); and Thomas R. Brooks, *Toil and Trouble: A History of American Labor* (1964). □

Benny Goodman

Benny Goodman (1909-1986) was a great jazz clarinetist and leader of one of the most popular big bands of the Swing Era (1935-1945).

Benjamin David Goodman was born in Chicago, Illinois, on May 30, 1909, of a large, poor Jewish family. (A brother, Harry, was later a bassist in Benny's band.) Benny studied music at Hull House and at the age of 10 was already a proficient clarinetist. At age 12, appearing on stage in a talent contest, he did an imitation of the prevailing clarinet favorite, Ted Lewis; so impressed was popular bandleader Ben Pollack that five years later he sent for Goodman to join the band at the Venice ballroom in Los Angeles. After a three-year stint with Pollack, Goodman left in 1929 to free-lance in New York City in pit bands and on radio and recordings. In 1934 he led his first band on an NBC radio series called "Let's Dance" (which became the title of Goodman's theme song). The band also played at Billy Rose's Music Hall and at the Roosevelt Hotel and made a handful of records for the Columbia and Victor labels.

In 1935, armed with a repertory developed by some great African American arrangers (Benny Carter, Edgar Sampson, Horace Henderson, and ex-bandleader and Swing Era genius Fletcher Henderson), the band embarked on a most significant road trip. Not especially successful in most of its cross-country engagements, the band arrived at the Palomar Ballroom in Los Angeles in a discouraged mood. The evening of August 21, 1935, began inauspiciously, the audience lukewarm to the band's mostly restrained dance music. In desperation Goodman called for the band to launch into a couple of "flagwavers" (up-tempo crowd-pleasers)—"Sometimes I'm Happy" and "King Porter Stomp"—and the crowd reaction was ultimately to send shock waves through the entire pop music world. Hundreds of people stopped dancing and massed around the bandstand, responding enthusiastically and knowledgably to arrangements and solos that they recognized from the just recently released records. (Apparently Goodman had been too conservative both early in his tour and earlier that night and had underestimated his audience.)

The Palomar engagement turned out to be not only a personal triumph for the band but for swing music in general, serving notice to the music business that "sweet" dance music would have to move over and make room for the upstart (and more jazz-based) sound. Goodman's popularity soared: the band topped almost all the magazine and theater polls, their record sales were astronomical, they were given a weekly cigarette-sponsored radio show, and they were featured in two big-budget movies, "Hollywood Hotel" and "The Big Broadcast of 1937." But an even greater triumph awaited. Impresario John Hammond rented that bastion of classical music, Carnegie Hall, for a concert that was to win respectability for the music. The night of January 16, 1938, is now legendary; responding to the electric expectancy of the overflow audience, the band outdid itself, improving on recorded favorites like "King Porter Stomp," "Bugle Call Rag," "Down South Camp Meeting," and "Don't Be That Way." It capped off the evening with a lengthy, classic version of "Sing, Sing, Sing" which featured some brilliant solo work by trumpeter Harry James, pianist Jess Stacy, and Benny himself.

Two of the finest musicians ever to work with Goodman were pianist Teddy Wilson and vibraphonist-drummer Lionel Hampton. Both were with the band from the mid-1930s and both were present at Carnegie Hall, but they were used only in trio and quartet contexts because of the unwritten rule forbidding racially integrated bands. Goodman has the distinction of being the first white leader (Artie Shaw and Charlie Barnet followed suit) to challenge segregation in the music business, and as the restrictions eased he hired other African American greats such as guitarist Charlie Christian, trumpeter Cootie Williams, bassist Slam Stewart, and tenor saxophonist Wardell Gray.

Goodman's band had a greater personnel turnover than most bands, and an endless array of top-notch musicians moved through the band, among them trumpeters Bunny Berigan, Harry James, and Ziggy Elman; trombonist Lou McGarity; tenor saxophonists Bud Freeman, Georgie Auld, Zoot Sims, and Stan Getz; pianists Mel Powell and Joe Bushkin; vibists Red Norvo and Terry Gibbs; and drummers Dave Tough and Louis Bellson. Most defected to other bands and a few to start their own bands (Krupa, James, and Hampton). Overwhelmingly, musicians found Goodman an uncongenial employer: he was reputed to be stern and tight-fisted. A taciturn, scholarly-looking man, Goodman was unflattering referred to in music circles as "The Ray" because of his habit of glaring at any player guilty of a "clam" or "clinker" (a wrong note), even in rehearsal. A virtuoso clarinetist equally at home performing Mozart (which he did in concerts and on records), Goodman was less than patient with technical imperfection.

After World War II the clarinet, which, along with the tenor saxophone, had been the Swing Era's glamour instrument, was relegated to a minor role in bebop's scheme of things. Even the peerless Buddy DeFranco, the definitive bebop clarinetist, was unluckily marginal in an alto saxophone-and-trumpet-dominated idiom. Goodman struggled for a while to reconcile himself to the new music, but in 1950 he decided to disband, and from that time forward his public appearances were rare and were chiefly with small groups (usually sextets or septets) and almost exclusively for television specials or recordings or European tours. In 1950 he toured Europe with a septet that included two other jazz greats, trumpeter Roy Eldridge and tenor saxophonist Zoot Sims. His most celebrated tour, however, was part of the first-ever cultural exchange with the Soviet Union. In 1962, at the behest of the State Department, he went to Russia with a septet that included Sims and alto saxophonist Phil Woods. The trip was a smashing success and contributed greatly to the popularization of American jazz in Eastern Europe.

After his marriage in 1941, Goodman's home was New York City; his wife Alice (John Hammond's sister) died in 1978; they had two daughters, and she had three by a previous marriage. Goodman maintained his habit of spot-performing and in 1985 made a surprise and, by all accounts, spectacular appearance at the Kool Jazz Festival in New York. He died the following year of an apparent heart attack.

With his withdrawal from the limelight, most observers felt that he became a deeper, less flashy player than he was in the glory years when he was fronting the country's most popular swing band. His ultimate contribution to jazz, however, is still being debated: much post-1940s jazz criticism retrospectively judged him to have been overrated relative to the era's other great clarinetist-leader, Artie Shaw, and to the great early Black players of the instrument (Jimmy Noone, Johnny Dodds, Edmond Hall, and Lester Young, a tenor saxophonist who "doubled" on clarinet) and the great white traditionalist Pee Wee Russell. Esthetic evaluations are problematical at best and tend to fluctuate from era to era, but Goodman's technical mastery, burnished tone, highly individual (and influential) solo style, and undeniable *swing* certainly earned him a permanent place in the jazz pantheon.

Further Reading

There is no serious biography of Goodman. There was a promotional autobiography, written with the help of Irving Kolodin, in 1939 called *The Kingdom of Swing*. A film biography produced in 1955 titled "The Benny Goodman Story" is more Hollywood than Goodman. Probably the best source is a biography-discography by D. Russell O'Connor and Warren W. Hicks, *Benny Goodman—On the Record* (1969). □

Charles Goodyear

Charles Goodyear (1800-1860), American inventor, experimented with, perfected, and promoted the use of vulcanized rubber. He was instrumental in establishing the rubber industry in the United States.

Charles Goodyear was born on Dec. 29, 1800, in New Haven, Conn. He attended the local public schools. His father was an inventor, manufacturer, and merchant of hardware, especially of farm tools. When Charles was 17, his father sent him to Philadelphia to learn the business, and at 21 he returned to become his father's partner. He married at the age of 24 and 2 years later opened a store in Philadelphia. In 1830 a lifetime of financial distress began for the Goodyears when both father and son went bankrupt.

On a trip to New York City that year, Goodyear visited a store that sold goods made of india rubber, a product only recently manufactured in America. Inspired by the possibilities of the material, he determined to improve its usefulness. His first experiments were carried out in jail, where he had been sent for failure to pay his debts.

In 1837 Goodyear settled his family on the charity of friends near New Haven and went to New York to continue

his work. He received a patent for an improved type of rubber and was able to find a modest amount of financial backing. After moving to Massachusetts, he met Nathaniel M. Hayward, an inventor, whose patent on a process for mixing sulfur with rubber he bought. Goodyear intended to combine the new patented process with his old one, which involved coating rubber with an acid and metal.

During an argument one day in his shop, Goodyear accidentally dropped a piece of the sulfur-impregnated rubber on a hot stove. Instead of melting, it merely charred slightly. Realizing the importance of this (two major drawbacks to using rubber were that it melted at high temperatures and tended to harden at low temperatures), he began experiments to discover the proper proportions and method of baking the new type of rubber, which he called "vulcanized." His critical patent was issued on June 15, 1844, after he had borrowed $50,000 for experiments, little of which was ever repaid. He claimed to have found more than 500 uses for rubber and received patents in all countries except England, where Thomas Hancock had invented vulcanization in 1843. When Goodyear died in 1860, he left his wife and six children $200,000 in debt.

Further Reading

Biographies of Goodyear include Ralph Frank Wolf, *India Rubber Man: The Story of Charles Goodyear* (1939), and Adolph C. Regli, *Rubber's Goodyear: The Story of a Man's Perseverance* (1941). A shorter study is in John C. Patterson, *America's Greatest Inventors* (1943). □

Berry Gordy, Jr.

Berry Gordy, Jr. (born 1929), founded Motown, the fledgling record company of 1959 that grew into the most successful African American enterprise in the United States and was responsible for a new sound that transformed popular music.

Berry Gordy, Jr., was born in 1929 and reared in Detroit. He was not the first businessman in the family; both parents were self-employed, his father as a plastering contractor, his mother as an insurance agent. Gordy dropped out of Northeastern High School in his junior year to pursue a career as a Featherweight boxer. Between 1948 and 1951 he fought 15 Golden Gloves matches, 12 of which he won, but his fighting career was clipped short when he was drafted to serve in the Korean War.

Upon his discharge from the Army in 1953, Berry Gordy returned to Detroit and used his service pay to open the Three-D Record Mart. His love for the jazz of Stan Kenton, Charlie Parker, and Thelonius Monk influenced his inventory more than his customers' requests for "things like Fats Domino," and his business soon failed.

Gordy worked for his father for a short period and then as a chrome trimmer on the assembly line at the Ford Motor Company. The monotony was formidable, and Gordy's way of overcoming it was to write songs in his head, some of which were recorded by local singers. Decca Records

bought several of his compositions, including "Reet Petite" and "Lonely Teardrops" (both recorded by Jackie Wilson), and when Gordy compared his royalty checks to what Decca made from the modest hits, he realized that writing the hits wasn't enough. He needed to own them.

At the suggestion of a friend, teenage singer William "Smokey" Robinson, Gordy borrowed $700 from his father and formed his own company to manufacture and market records. Motown Records was headquartered in a row house on Detroit's West Grand Boulevard, where Gordy slept on the second floor and made records on the first. In time the company expanded, with nine buildings on the same street housing its branches: Jobete, music publishers; Hitsville USA, a recording studio; musical accompanists; International Talent Management Inc; the Motown Artist's Development Department (the embodiment of Gordy's personal interest in his performers, where they were taught to eat, dress, and act like polished professionals); and the Motown Record Corporation, an umbrella for several labels of Motown, including Gordy, Tamla, VIP, and Soul (the last being reserved for the hit song-writing machine of Brian Holland, Lamont Dozier, and Eddie Holland).

In 1960 Motown released "Shop Around," written by Smokey Robinson and performed by him and the Miracles. The song sold more than a million copies, and with that gold record, Berry Gordy's company launched the most successful and influential era in the history of popular music.

The Motown Sound was a musical genre that combined classic African American gospel singing with the new rock-and-roll sound that was being shaped by Elvis Presley and the Beatles. In a sense, this reflected the old "R & B" (for rhythm and blues), but it defined a new generation.

Motown produced over 110 number one hit songs and countless top-ten records, including "Please Mr. Postman," "Reach Out, I'll Be There," "My Girl," "Stop! In the Name of Love," "For Once in My Life," "How Sweet It Is To Be Loved by You," "Heard It Through the Grapevine," "My Guy," "Dancing in the Streets," "Your Precious Love," "Where Did Our Love Go," "Baby Love," "I Hear a Symphony," "I Want You Back," and "I'll Be There." Equally impressive is a list of artists that Gordy brought into the spotlight: Diana Ross and the Supremes, the Jackson Five, Stevie Wonder, Smokey Robinson and the Miracles, the Four Tops, the Temptations, Gladys Knight and the Pips, Tammi Terrell and Marvin Gaye, the Marvelettes, Mary Wells, and Martha Reeves and the Vandellas.

By the mid 1970s, some of the Motown artists had begun to resist Gordy's tight control. Defectors began to break up Gordy's "family" of stars. The first to leave was Gladys Knight and the Pips, and in 1975 the Jackson Five announced that they would be moving to Epic Records when their Motown contract expired.

Although Gordy kept Stevie Wonder at Motown by promising him $13 million over seven years in the famous "Wonderdeal" of 1975, Gordy's public statements usually expressed disappointment that his superstars came to value money over loyalty. This sentiment was heard often from Gordy when, in 1981, Diana Ross announced her move to RCA Records.

Ross's move was particularly surprising and bitter for Gordy in view of the fact that in 1972 he moved his headquarters to Los Angeles to begin a career in film, not only for himself, but so he could turn Diana Ross into a movie star. His first production was the 1972 Paramount release "Lady Sings the Blues," the story of Billie Holiday starring Ross. The picture was nominated for five Academy Awards and grossed more than $8.5 million. In 1975 Gordy directed Ross in "Mahogany," the story of a African American fashion model's rise to fame. Although the film did well at the box office, it was not nearly the critical success of "Lady."

Other Gordy films were "The Bingo Long Traveling All Stars and Motor Kings" (1976), "Almost Summer" (1978), "The Wiz" (1978) starring Michael Jackson and Diana Ross, and "The Last Dragon" (1985).

In June 1988 Gordy sold his company to MCA, Inc. He retained control of Jobete, the music publishing operation, and Motown's film division, but sold the record label to the entertainment conglomerate for $61 million. He told the newspaper *Daily Variety* that he wanted to "ensure the perpetuation of Motown and its heritage."

Esther Edwards, Berry Gordy's sister, was also interested in preserving Motown's heritage. The brick house at 2648 West Grand Boulevard, once modestly and unknowingly named "Hitsville USA," is now the site of the Motown Museum, thanks to the pack-rat tendency of Edwards. She saved hundreds of boxes of memorabilia, including original music scores, posters, and photographs, and until 1988 most of the mementos were stuck to the walls with thumbtacks. In an effort to have the collection professionally preserved, Michael Jackson, whose ties to Berry were still strong in 1990, donated the proceeds of the Detroit stop of his "Bad" tour—$125,000—to the Motown Museum.

Berry Gordy married Thelma Coleman in 1953. They had two sons, Berry IV and Terry, and one daughter, Hazel, who married Jermaine Jackson in 1973. Gordy's second marriage was to Raynoma Liles in 1959; they had one son, Kerry. Gordy also had a son with Margaret Norton in 1964 whom they named Kennedy, after John F. Kennedy, and who changed his name to Rockwell and recorded for Motown in 1984. In the Los Angeles area Gordy lived in a Bel Air estate and highly valued his privacy, rarely dealing with the press. In late 1994 a plan was announced to make a tribute album to Gordy. Even though Gordy was often times hailed as an entrepreneur, he was first and foremost a songwriter. Singers who have signed on to sing some of Gordy's songs on the tribute album include Diana Ross, the Four Tops, the Temptations and Smokey Robinson.

Further Reading

Numerous books recount the rise of Motown as a major contributor to popular music, all of which feature Berry Gordy as the man who started it all. Two books which tell the story particularly well, with outstanding photographs, are *Motown: Hot Wax, City Cool and Solid Gold* (1986) by J. Randy Taraborrelli and *The Motown Story* (1985) by Don Waller. Two more worthy accounts of Gordy and his empire are *Motown: This History* (1988) by Sharon Davis and *Where Did Our Love Go? The Rise and Fall of the Motown Sound* (1985) by Nelson George, with a foreword by Quincy Jones. Two of Gordy's family members have written telling tales of the man: *Berry, Me and Motown* (1990) by Raynoma Gordy Singleton, Gordy's second wife; and *Movin' Up: Pop Gordy Tells His Story* (1979) by Berry Gordy Senior. Gordy was interviewed by the popular media numerous times over the years, especially in 1983 during the celebration of Motown's 25th anniversary. *Newsweek* (May 23, 1983) featured an interview and well-told background story. □

Albert Gore, Jr.

U.S. representative, senator, and 45th vice president of the United States, Albert Gore, Jr. (born 1948), was the son of a long-time Democratic congressman from Tennessee.

Albert Gore, Jr., was born in Washington, D.C., on March 31, 1948. His father, Albert Gore, Sr., was serving as a Democratic member of the U.S. House of Representatives from Tennessee. The senior Gore was to serve in the House and the Senate for nearly three decades. His mother was Pauline (LaFon) Gore. She had the distinction of being one of the first women to graduate from the law school at Vanderbilt University.

Since his father's occupation kept the family mainly in the nation's capital, young Gore grew up in Washington, D.C. He attended St. Alban's Episcopal School for Boys, where he was an honor student and captain of the football team. Gore went to Harvard University. In 1969 he received a B.A. degree, with honors, in government. He was interested in becoming a writer, rather than entering his father's "business" as a politician. After graduation he enlisted in the army, although he opposed the United States' intervention in the Vietnam War.

While stationed in Vietnam, Gore served as an army reporter. He sent some of his stories to a newspaper in Nashville, Tennessee, which published them. After Gore left the military service in 1971, the Nashville *Tennessean* hired him as an investigative reporter and, later, as an editorial writer. In addition to his journalism career, Gore was a home builder, a land developer, and a livestock and tobacco farmer.

Interested in religion and philosophy, Gore enrolled in the Graduate School of Religion at Vanderbilt University during the 1971-1972 academic year. In 1974 he entered Vanderbilt's law school but left to enter elective office two years later.

In 1976 Gore decided to run for a seat in the U.S. House of Representatives. Having a famous name, running in the district that sent his father to the Congress for many terms, he won the primary election against eight other candidates and went on to win in the general election. He ran successfully in the three following elections. Gore claimed some early attention in 1980 when he was assigned to the House Intelligence Committee studying nuclear arms. Gore researched and eventually published a comprehensive manifesto on arms restructuring for future security, which was published in the February 1982 issue of *Congressional Quarterly*. In 1984 Gore campaigned for a seat in the U.S. Senate that had just become vacant. He won that office with a large margin of votes.

While in Congress Gore was interested in several issues. He focused attention on health-related matters and on cleaning up the environment. He worked for nuclear arms control and disarmament, as well as other strategic defense issues. He stressed the potential of new technologies, such as biotechnology and computer development.

The race for the 1988 presidential election attracted Gore. He was only 39 years old at the time. He ran on traditional domestic Democratic views and was tough on foreign policy issues. He failed, however, to develop a national theme for his campaign and was criticized for changing positions and issues. He was successful in gaining public support in the primaries during the early spring and won more votes than any other candidate in southern states. However, he obtained only small percentages of votes in other states and withdrew from the presidential nomination campaigns in mid-April. Two years later he won election to a second term in the U.S. Senate. He chose not to seek the presidency in 1992, citing family concerns (young Albert had been hit by an automobile and was seriously injured). It was during this time that Gore wrote the book *Earth in the Balance: Ecology and the Human Spirit,* which expressed his concern, ideas, and recommendations on conservation and the global environment. In the book he wrote about his own personal and political experiences and legislative actions on the environmental issue. One of Gore's statements in the book that sums up his philosophy regarding the environment and human interaction is, "We must make the rescue of the environment the central organizing principle for civilization."

Events took a surprising turn in the summer of 1992. Bill Clinton selected Gore as his vice-presidential nominee. The choice startled many people because it ended a long-standing pattern of a candidate choosing a vice presidential nominee to "balance the ticket." Both men were of the same age, region, and reputation and moderate in political outlook. Clinton's idea was to project a new generation of leadership as a campaign theme. Gore did balance Clinton's strength by bringing to the ticket his experience in foreign and defense policy, expertise in environmental and new technology matters, and an image as an unwavering family man.

The highlight for many who followed the campaigns of 1992 was a series of debates, one of which involved Gore and his opponents, Republican Dan Quayle and Independent James Stockdale. The proceedings were marked by moments of high comedy—Quayle and Gore arguing over the wording of *Earth in the Balance*; Stockdale admitting his hearing aid was off—and clear party positioning. Qualye attacked Gore's record of environmental concern, claiming Gore was placing endangered species over people's jobs. Gore countered that a well-run environmental program would create jobs while preserving nature. Stockdale pointed out that such bickering was exactly why Congress was engulfed in gridlock.

Clinton and Gore won the election in 1992. Gore was inaugurated as the 45th vice president on January 20, 1993. At the age of 44 years, he became one of the youngest people to hold the position. Clinton and Gore were re-elected in 1996, running against Republicans Bob Dole and Jack Kemp.

During his time as vice-president, Gore continued to stress environmental concerns. In 1997 the White House launched an effort to start producing a report card on the health of the nation's ecosystems. This project was carried out by an environmental think tank and initiated by Gore.

Also in 1997, Gore's crystal clear reputation was somewhat tarnished when he was accused of—and admitted to—making fund-raising telephone calls from the White House during the 1996 presidential campaign. Gore held a press conference on March 3, 1997, to defend his actions, saying there was nothing illegal about what he had done, although he admitted it may not have been a wise choice. Gore was also criticized for toasting Li Peng, initiator of the Tiananmen Square Massacre, during a trip to China. In September 1997, Buddhist nuns testified before the Senate panel investigating the abuses of campaign fund-raising. The nuns admitted that donors were illegally reimbursed by their temple after a fund-raiser attended by Gore, and that they had destroyed and/or altered records to avoid embarrassing their temple. Some believe these incidents have further damaged Gore's reputation.

Gore announced his candidacy for the 2000 presidential election on June 16, 1999. The Democratic Party formally nominated him as their candidate on August 16, 2000. He and Texas governor George W. Bush faced off in one of the closest presidential contests in American history. Each man was poised to take the White House; it all hinged on Florida's 25 electoral votes. Confusing ballots and other voting irregularities led to demands for a hand re-count in several Florida counties. Florida's secretary of state certified Bush's 537-vote lead over Gore, but the state supreme court favored a recount. On December 13, 2000, Gore conceded the election after the U.S. Supreme Court ruled in a 5-4 decision that recounting Florida votes would be unconstitutional.

Gore is a devoted family man. He married his college sweetheart, Mary Elizabeth "Tipper" Aitcheson, on May 19, 1970. Tipper was born on August 19, 1948, in Washington, D.C. She held a B.A. degree from Boston University and a master of arts in psychology from George Peabody College. She was an active mother and politician's spouse, as well as working to forward her own issues. She gained attention through her efforts to influence the record industry to rate and label obscene and violent lyrics. She was co-founder of the Parents Music Resource Center, which monitors musical and video presentations that glorify casual sex and violence. The Gores had four children: Karenna (born August 6, 1973), Kristin (born June 5, 1977), Sarah (born January 7, 1979), and Albert III (born October 19, 1982).

Further Reading

Albert Gore, Jr., wrote *Earth in the Balance: Ecology and the Human Spirit* (1992). Gore also wrote a book with Bill Clinton outlining their 1992 campaign issues and policies, *Putting People First* (1992). The book includes a brief biography of Gore's public service. His political career can be followed in issues of *The Almanac of American Politics* by Michael Barone and Grant Ujifusa, which appeared during the years Gore was in Congress. His activity as Congressman and vice president can be followed in the *Congressional Quarterly's Weekly Reports.* Gore is listed in *Who's Who in America* (1996) and *Who's Who in the World* (1996). Peter Goldman and Tom Mathews, *Quest for the Presidency: The 1988 Campaign,* is one of many books recording the politics of that year. For information on his bid for the presidential nomination in 2000, see *National Journal* (March 29, 1997; May 31, 1997), *Time* (April 28, 1997), and *Chicago Defender* (April 5, 1997). For a report on Gore's encounter in China, see *New Republic* (April 14, 1997). *Science* (May 9, 1997) discusses some of Gore's environmental efforts. □

William Crawford Gorgas

William Crawford Gorgas (1854-1920), surgeon general of the U.S. Army, conquered yellow fever in the Panama Canal Zone, thus making the building of the canal possible.

William C. Gorgas was born October 3, 1854, near Mobile, Ala., the son of Josiah Gorgas, later a Confederate general and vice-chancellor of the University of the South at Sewanee, Tenn. Young Gorgas's early education was irregular because of the Civil War, but in 1875 he took a bachelor of arts degree from the University of the South.

Desiring a military career, Gorgas exhausted every possible means of getting an appointment to West Point, then decided to enter the Army by way of a medical degree. After graduating from the Bellevue Medical College in New York City and serving an internship at the Bellevue Hospital, he was appointed to the Medical Corps of the U.S. Army in

June 1880. Then followed tours of duty at various Texas posts, in North Dakota, and nearly 10 years at Ft. Barrancas, Fla., a notorious yellow fever area to which Gorgas was assigned because he had previously had the disease and was therefore immune. In 1883 he married Marie Cook Doughty.

After the occupation of Havana, Cuba, by American troops in 1898, Gorgas took charge of a yellow fever camp at Siboney. Later that year he became chief sanitary officer of Havana. Acting on information furnished by the Yellow Fever Commission of U.S. Army physician Walter Reed that a particular strain of mosquito was the carrier of yellow fever, Gorgas deprived the mosquito of breeding places, quickly destroying the carrier and ridding the city of yellow fever. This work brought him an international reputation.

In 1904, when work commenced on the Panama Canal, Gorgas went to the Canal Zone to take charge of sanitation. Although it was known that yellow fever had been largely responsible for the French failure to build the canal, Gorgas encountered continuing opposition to his antimosquito measures from an economy-minded administration. He persevered, however, and, with the support of President Theodore Roosevelt, finally succeeded in making the cities of Panama and Colón models of sanitation.

As a result of his work in the Canal Zone, Gorgas came to be generally regarded as the world's foremost sanitary expert. A number of foreign governments and international commissions sought his aid, and his book *Sanitation in Panama* (1915) quickly became a classic in the public health field. In 1914 he was appointed surgeon general of the

Army, and he served in that capacity until his retirement 4 years later. He died in London on July 3, 1920, and is buried in the Arlington National Cemetery.

Further Reading

Marie D. Gorgas and Burton J. Hendrick, *William Crawford Gorgas: His Life and Work* (1924), is an intimate biography from material furnished by Gorgas's wife. See also John M. Gibson, *Physician to the World: The Life of General William C. Gorgas* (1950). □

Stephen Jay Gould

The American paleontologist Stephen Jay Gould (born 1941) was awarded the Schuchert Award for 1975 by the Paleontological Society for his work in evolutionary theory. He is also the author of several books popularizing current scientific issues.

Stephen Jay Gould was born on September 10, 1941, in New York City, the son of Leonard and Eleanor (Rosenberg) Gould. His father was a court reporter and amateur naturalist. Leonard Gould was a self taught man and a Marxist who took his son to the American Museum of Natural History when the boy was five years old. It was here that the young Gould saw his first dinosaur, a Tyrannosaurus Rex, and decided that he was going to devote his life to the study of geologic periods. Gould's his mother was an artist. After a summer at the University of Colorado, Gould received his education at Antioch College in Yellow Springs, Ohio, graduating with an A.B. in 1963. He then moved on to graduate school in evolutionary biology and paleontology at Columbia University, where he remained for two years. He married Deborah Lee, an artist, on October 3, 1965, then left to take a job in 1966 at Antioch College as professor of geology. The following year he moved on to Harvard to take an assistant professorship, and in that same year he finished his doctoral work, completing his degree program from Columbia. In 1971 he was promoted to associate professor, and in 1973 to full professor of geology. He also became curator of invertebrate paleontology at Harvard's Museum of Comparative Zoology. At Harvard he expanded his study of land snails to the West Indies and other parts of the world.

Gould was one of the founders of the punctuated equilibrium school of evolution. The gradualism promoted by Charles Darwin and propounded in the neo-Darwinian synthesis of the 1930s stressed gradual modification of organic structures over long periods of geologic time. Gould argued that evolution proceeds quite rapidly at crucial points, with speciation occurring almost instantaneously. This could be due to quite sudden genetic mutations—his favorite example is the panda's "thumb," a modification of the wrist bone allowing the panda to strip leaves from bamboo shoots. Such a transformation must have occurred all at once, he reasoned, or it would not have been preserved by natural selection, having no useful function in a rudimentary stage. This process would account for the lack of transitional forms throughout the fossil record, a problem Darwin lamented but expected to be resolved by future paleontologists.

In addition to his work as a serious professional paleontologist, Gould spent much time trying to make science accessible to lay readers as well as scholars As a popular writer and amateur historian of science, Gould concentrated upon the cultural "embeddedness" of science, seeing it as a creative human endeavor neither abstracted from society nor objectively pursuing un-interpreted data. Such embeddedness means that the science of a particular period shares the assumptions and prejudices of that period. This is as characteristic of modern science as it was of the science of antiquity—Arthur Jensen, who argued for the genetic inferiority of Blacks, for instance, is probably not more, and possibly much less, objective than Aristotle. Both tend to biologize human nature and intelligence. In his book *The Mismeasure of Man,* for which he won the National Book Critics Circle Award for Essays and Criticism in 1982, Gould features an explanation of the misuse of intelligence testing to assign value to human beings and to promote cultural prejudice. Although he concedes that human intelligence has a specific location in the brain and that it can be measured by a standard number score, he argues that any efforts to label groups as possessing inherently inferior or superior intelligence based upon these measurements represent a misuse of scientific data and a violation of the scientific process.

In 1981 Gould served as an expert witness at a trial in Little Rock, Arkansas that challenged a state law mandating the teaching of creation science in tandem with evolution.

Gould's testimony argued that the theories of creationism are belied by all available scientific evidence and therefore do not deserve scientific status. Due to this testimony, Creationism was recognized as a religion and not a science. During that same year, Gould was awarded a prose fellows award from the MacArthur Foundation.

In July of 1982 Gould was diagnosed with mesothelioma, a particularly deadly form of cancer. He recovered from his illness and the treatment, but found that he had to continue his work with a new sense of urgency. He further explored the misuse of standardized testing to label social groups rather than study the effects of social factors on intelligence.

Both of Gould's careers gave evidence of a firm commitment to the liberatory elements in science. He borrows legitimately upon his earned prestige in biology to argue against one of its central paradigms—biological determinism—and he uses his literary skills to popularize the debate, exposing the dangers inherent in all biologizations of human abilities. Gould received critical recognition for his work in both areas. In 1975 he was given the Schuchert Award by the Paleontological Society for his original work in evolutionary theory. For his book *The Panda's Thumb,* he received two awards: the Notable Book citation from the American Library Association in 1980 and the American Book Award in Science for 1981. Likewise, he received two awards for his other major work, *The Mismeasure of Man:* the National Book Critics Circle Award for general nonfiction in 1981 and the American Book Award nomination in science for 1982. Gould was also a National Science Foundation grantee. He is a member of several scientific societies—American Association for the Advancement of Science, American Society of Naturalists, Paleontological Society, Society for the Study of Evolution, Society of Systematic Zoology, and Sigma Xi. As the author of more than 200 evolutionary essays collect in eight volumes Gould is a publishing phenomenon, with topics ranging from evolution, to his successful battle with cancer, Edgar Allan Poe, shells, and why there are no .400 hitters in baseball to name a few. Eminently readable, Gould explains complex ideas in simple understandable language that bridges the gap between scholars and lay persons alike. It is this that gives his work durability and credibility.

Gould resides in Cambridge, Massachusetts, with his wife and two children, Jesse and Ethan. He is an accomplished baritone with an undying love for Gilbert and Sullivan operettas, sang in the Boston Cecilia Society. In *The Flaming's Smile* he wrote "I could not dent the richness in a hundred lifetimes, but I simply must have a look at a few more of those pretty pebbles."

Further Reading

There is little biographical information on Stephen Jay Gould, though *Contemporary Authors, New Revision Series,* vol. 10, provides a brief but intelligent sketch.

All of his popular works are worth reading. These are, chronologically: *Even Since Darwin* (1977); *Ontogeny and Phylogeny* (1977); *The Panda's Thumb* (1980); contributor, Ernst Mayr, editor, *The Evolutionary Synthesis* (1980); *A View of Life*

(1981); *The Mismeasure of Man* (1981); and *Hen's Teeth and Horse's Toes* (1983). □

William Franklin Graham, Jr.

The American evangelist and charismatic preacher Billy Graham (born 1918) became a leading spokesman for Fundamentalism when he initiated a series of tours of the United States and Europe that led to large-scale evangelism.

William Franklin Graham, Jr. was born November 7, 1918, on a dairy farm near Charlotte, North Carolina, which his paternal grandfather Crook Graham bought after serving in the Confederate army. Young Billy would read from his collection of history books. He also practiced baseball when finished with his chores, because and his ambition was to become a professional baseball player. It was changed into a commitment to an evangelical career by a religious conversion experience when he was 16. Graham was ordained a Southern Baptist minister in 1939. He was educated in conservative Christian colleges: Bob Jones University in Greenville, South Carolina, the Florida Bible Institute (now called Trinity College) near Tampa, and Wheaton College in Illinois, where he received a bachelor of arts degree in anthropology in 1943. On August 13 of that year he married Ruth McCue Bell, a fellow student and daughter of a medical missionary. Their first daughter, Virginia, was born two years later, followed by Anne in 1948, Ruth in 1950, and sons William in 1952 and Nelson in 1958. For many years the Graham family made its home in Montreat, North Carolina.

After a period as minister of the First Baptist Church in Western Springs, Illinois, Graham became a traveling "tent evangelist," the calling which in a few years brought him to national prominence.

Graham was first vice president of Youth for Christ International from 1945 to 1948. He served as president of Northwestern College in Minneapolis from 1947 to 1952. He met singer George Beverly Shea and song leader Cliff Barrows and the three formed a lasting partnership. The three began offering revival meetings in small churches and started developing a following. In 1949, Graham, Shea, and Barrows had a meeting in Los Angeles and rather than the usual crowd of 3,000 or so, more than 10,000 turned out to hear the backwoods preacher and his team. He was the founder and president of the Billy Graham Evangelistic Association and editor in chief of *Decision* magazine. The organization is run by a board of directors that pays Graham an annual salary equivalent to that of a community pastor. The first year it amounted to $15,000. Today, the institute has a cash flow of more than $50 million a year. His radio program, *Hour of Decision,* began in 1950, and he wrote a daily newspaper column. Graham's published writings include *Calling Youth to Christ* (1947), *Revival in Our Times* (1950), *America's Hour of Decision* (1951), *Korean Diary* (1953), *My Answer* (1960), and *World Aflame* (1965).

Graham turns over all the royalties from his books and all his speaking fees.

Graham launched his worldwide ministry with his first overseas tour in 1954 to Great Britain. Crowds of more than two million people attended his rallies. He even met with Queen Elizabeth II. At a 16-week rally in New York City three years later, more than two million packed Madison Square Gardens to hear the young preacher. Graham has preached the Gospel to more people in live audiences than anyone else in history totaling more than 210 million people in more than 185 countries and territories. Since his crusades began his work has propelled him to more than 400 rallies in nearly every corner of the world. He conducts an average of six crusades a year in the United States and abroad. In the mid-1950s Graham took his crusade to India, Hong Kong, Japan, Korea, and the Philippines. He has also been to Rio de Janeiro, Nairobi, Seoul, Poland, Romania, and Slovakia, filling jam-packed churches and meeting with government and religious leaders wherever he travels.

Graham's Message

Graham's message has remained the same and is based on traditional Biblical study. It is simply this: "Choose Christ as I did. Mankind is sinful, but through Christ those sins are forgiven and people can live in peace." In other words, this is a message of love and hope. Graham has been friends with many world figures, especially the presidents starting with Harry Truman who sought advice from Graham and Richard Nixon was a frequent golf partner. On April 9, 1996, together with President William Clinton, he led

12,000 mourners in Oklahoma City to grieve for victims of the Federal Building bombing. Graham has been the chaplain at many Inaugural Ceremonies; in fact his eighth Inauguration invocation in January 1997 was inspired by our Founding Fathers, noting that "technology and social engineering had yet to solve the ancient problems of human greed and selfishness." Graham has maintained an untouchable integrity, unlike Jimmy Swaggart and Jim Bakker who were involved in sex and money scandals that ruined their careers.

Prodigal Son to Take Over

Graham has decided that when he retires or dies his son Franklin will take over his $88 million-a-year ministry. The younger Graham, who continually rebelled against his father as a teenager and was expelled from college, was a "heck-raiser" as a boy, has long since gone straight. He now runs two world relief organizations and has done some preaching. It has been said that Franklin does not have the presence of his father and will not be able to replicate the senior Graham's impact on American Protestantism. Graham, in his seventies, shows no sign of slowing down regardless of his advancing illness, Parkinson's disease. It will eventually take away his ability to feed himself or even button his clothes. He walks with difficulty now and can write only his name, but he still has enough energy to work on his memoirs. Ruth, Graham's wife, "never slows down." Her presence and vitality have helped ease the frustration brought on by his illness. Together, Ruth and Billy have three daughters, two sons, 19 grandchildren and eight great grandchildren. Graham states that "I don't see anybody in Scripture retiring from preaching," and along with Pope John Paul II, who also has Parkinson's Disease, keeps chugging along.

The Cove

One of Graham's dreams was to build a training center to serve as a retreat for religious evangelists. It is located in Asheville, North Carolina. Each year, dozens of seminars are taught, featuring biblically grounded speakers. Cove seminars help those attend to Grow in God's Word, gain a deeper understanding of God, take time for personal renewal, and acquire tools for stronger Christian walk.

Graham Archives

The Archives of the Billy Graham Center are located at Wheaton College in Wheaton, Illinois. They contain many collections with documents relating to African Christianity. Most of these contain the work of North American missionaries or evangelists in Africa, though there is a substantial amount of material documenting the activities and beliefs of African churches, leaders, and quasi-ecclesiastical organizations. Most of the records are twentieth-century and about 75 percent are concerned with east or central Africa.

Graham has received numerous awards from various institutions and organizations, including honorary doctorates from Baylor University, the Citadel, and William Jewell College. He received the Barnard Baruch Award in 1955; Humane Order of African Redemption, 1960; gold award of the George Washington Carver Memorial Institute, 1963; Horatio Alger Award, 1965; Franciscans International Award, 1972; Man of the South Award, 1974; Liberty Bell Award, 1975; Templeton Prize for Progress in Religion, 1982; and the William Booth Award of the Salvation Army, 1989.

Graham's crusades have taken him to all the major cities of the United States and Europe and to such far-off areas as North Africa, India, and Australia. Although basically a fundamentalist in his theology, individualistic in his religious and ethical approach, and traditional in his appeal, he always sought and obtained a broad base of ecumenical support for his evangelistic campaigns. Graham brought evangelism to a new level of sophistication in organization, techniques, support, and prestige. Graham once stated that "It seems to me that the whole world, regardless of culture and religious tradition, is searching for something spiritual." The most important thing that counts (for Graham) is what happens in the hearts of men." Graham is the most respectable symbol of American evangelicalism.

Further Reading

The official biography of Graham is John C. Pollock, *Billy Graham: The Authorized Biography* (1966). Other helpful biographical studies include William G. McLoughlin, *Billy Graham: Revivalist in a Secular Age* (1960), Curtis Mitchell, *Billy Graham: The Making of a Crusader* (1966), *The Reader's Companion to American History* (1997), *Gospel Communications Network (GCN), Time Daily* (Nov. 95), and *People* (1997). □

Ulysses Simpson Grant

Ulysses Simpson Grant (1822-1885), having led the Northern armies to victory in the Civil War, was elected eighteenth president of the United States.

As a general in the Civil War, Ulysses S. Grant possessed the right qualities for prosecuting offensive warfare against the brilliant tactics of his Southern adversary Robert E. Lee. Bold and indefatigable, Grant believed in destroying enemy armies rather than merely occupying enemy territory. His strategic genius and tenacity overcame the Confederates' advantage of fighting a defensive war on their own territory. However, Grant lacked the political experience and subtlety to cope with the nation's postwar problems, and his presidency was marred by scandals and an economic depression.

Ulysses S. Grant was born on April 27, 1822, in a cabin at Point Pleasant, Ohio. He attended district schools and worked at his father's tannery and farm. In 1839 Grant's father secured an appointment to West Point for his unenthusiastic son. Grant excelled as a horseman but was an indifferent student. When he graduated in 1843, he accepted an infantry commission. Although not in sympathy with American objectives in the war with Mexico in 1846, he fought courageously under Zachary Taylor and Winfield Scott, emerging from the conflict as a captain.

In subsequent years Capt. "Sam" Grant served at a variety of bleak army posts. Lonely for his wife and son (he had married Julia Dent in 1848), the taciturn, unhappy captain began drinking. Warned by his commanding officer, Grant resigned from the Army in July 1854. He borrowed money for transportation to St. Louis, Mo., where he joined his family and tried a series of occupations without much success: farmer, realtor, candidate for county engineer, and customshouse clerk. He was working as a store clerk at the beginning of the Civil War in 1861.

Rise to Fame

This was a war Grant did believe in, and he offered his services. The governor of Illinois appointed him colonel of the 21st Illinois Volunteers in June 1861. Grant took his regiment to Missouri, where, to his surprise, he was promoted to brigadier general.

Grant persuaded his superiors to authorize an attack on Ft. Henry on the Tennessee River and Ft. Donelson on the Cumberland in order to gain Union control of these two important rivers. Preceded by gunboats, Grant's 17,000 troops marched out of Cairo, Ill., on Feb. 2, 1862. After Ft. Henry surrendered, the soldiers took Ft. Donelson. Here Confederate general Simon B. Buckner, one of Grant's West Point classmates (and the man who, much earlier, had loaned the impecunious captain the money to rejoin his family), requested an armistice. Grant's reply became famous: "No terms except an unconditional and immediate surrender can be accepted. I propose to move immediately upon your works." Buckner surrendered. One of the first important Northern victories of the war, the capture of Ft. Donelson won Grant promotion to major general.

Grant next concentrated 38,000 men at Pittsburgh Landing (Shiloh) on the Tennessee River, preparing for an offensive. He unwisely neglected to prepare for a possible Confederate counteroffensive. At dawn on April 6, 1862, the Confederate attack surprised the sleeping Union soldiers. Grant did his best to prevent a rout, and at the end of the day Union lines still held, but the Confederates were in command of most of the field. The next day the Union Army counterattacked with 25,000 fresh troops, who had arrived during the night, and drove the Southerners into full retreat. The North had triumphed in one of the bloodiest battles of the war, but Grant was criticized for his carelessness. Urged to replace Grant, President Abraham Lincoln refused, saying, "I can't spare this man—he fights."

Grant set out to recoup his reputation and secure Union control of the Mississippi River by taking the rebel stronghold at Vicksburg, Miss. Several attempts were frustrated; in the North criticism of Grant was growing and there were reports that he had begun drinking heavily. But in April 1863 Grant embarked on a bold scheme to take Vicksburg. While he marched his 20,000 men past the fortress on the opposite (west) bank, an ironclad fleet sailed by the batteries. The flotilla rendezvoused with Grant below the fort and transported the troops across the river. In one of the most brilliant gambles of the war, Grant cut himself off from his base in the midst of enemy territory with numerically inferior forces. The gamble paid off. Grant drove one Confederate Army from the city of Jackson, then turned and defeated a second force at Champion's Hill, forcing the rebels to withdraw to Vicksburg on May 20. Union troops laid siege to Vicksburg, and on July 4 the garrison surrendered. Ten days later the last Confederate outpost on the Mississippi fell. Thus, the Confederacy was cut in two. Coming at the same time as the Northern victory at Gettysburg, this was the turning point of the war.

Grant was given command of the Western Department, and in the fall of 1863 he took command of the Union Army pinned down at Chattanooga after its defeat in the Battle of Chickamauga. In a series of battles on November 23, 24, and 25, the rejuvenated Northern troops dislodged the besieging Confederates, the most spirited infantry charge of the war climaxing the encounter. It was a great victory; Congress created the rank of lieutenant general for Grant, who was placed in command of all the armies of the Union.

Architect of Victory

Grant was at the summit of his career. A reticent man, unimpressive in physical appearance, he gave few clues to the reasons for his success. He rarely communicated his thinking; he was the epitome of the strong, silent type. But Grant had deep resources of character, a quietly forceful personality that won the respect and confidence of subordinates, and a decisiveness and bulldog tenacity that served him well in planning and carrying out military operations.

In the spring of 1864 the Union armies launched a coordinated offensive designed to bring the war to an end. However, Lee brilliantly staved off Grant's stronger Army of

the Potomac in a series of battles in Virginia. Union forces suffered fearful losses, especially at Cold Harbor, while war weariness and criticism of Grant as a "butcher" mounted in the North.

Lee moved into entrenchments at Petersburg, Va., and Grant settled down there for a long siege. Meanwhile, Gen. William T. Sherman captured Atlanta and began his march through Georgia, South Carolina, and North Carolina, cutting what remained of the Confederacy into pieces. In the spring of 1865 Lee fell back to Appomattox, where on April 9 he met Grant in the courthouse to receive the generous terms of surrender.

Postwar Political Career

After Lincoln's death Grant was the North's foremost war hero. Both sides in the Reconstruction controversy, between President Andrew Johnson and congressional Republicans, jockeyed for his support. A tour of the South in 1865 convinced Grant that the "mass of thinking men" there accepted defeat and were willing to return to the Union without rancor. But the increasing defiance of former Confederates in 1866, their persecution of those who were freed (200,000 African Americans had fought for the Union, and Grant believed they had contributed heavily to Northern victory), and harassment of Unionist officials and occupation troops gradually pushed Grant toward support of the punitive Reconstruction policy of the Republicans. He accepted the Republican presidential nomination in 1868, won the election, and took office on March 4, 1869.

Grant was, to put it mildly, an undistinguished president. His personal loyalty to subordinates, especially old army comrades, prevented him from taking action against associates implicated in dishonest dealings. Government departments were riddled with corruption, and Grant did little to correct this. Turmoil and violence in the South created the necessity for constant Federal intervention, which inevitably alienated large segments of opinion, North and South. In 1872 a sizable number of Republicans bolted the party, formed the Liberal Republican party, and combined with the Democrats to nominate Horace Greeley for the presidency on a platform of civil service reform and home rule in the South. Grant won reelection, but as more scandals came to light during his second term and his Southern policy proved increasingly unpopular, his reputation plunged. The economic panic of 1873 ushered in a major depression; in 1874 the Democrats won control of the House of Representatives for the first time in 16 years.

Yet Grant's two terms were not devoid of positive achievements. In foreign policy the steady hand of Secretary of State Hamilton Fish kept the United States out of a potential war with Spain. The greenback dollar moved toward stabilization, and the war debt was funded on a sound basis. Still, on balance, Grant's presidency was an unhappy aftermath to his military success. Nevertheless, in 1877 he was still a hero, and on a trip abroad after his presidency he was feted in European capitals.

In 1880 Grant again allowed himself to be a candidate for the Republican presidential nomination but fell barely short of success in the convention. Retiring to private life, he made ill-advised investments that led to bankruptcy in 1884. While slowly dying of cancer of the throat, he set to work on his military memoirs to provide an income for his wife and relatives after his death. Through months of terrible pain his courage and determination sustained him as he wrote in longhand the story of his army career. The reticent, uncommunicative general revealed a genius for this kind of writing, and his two-volume *Personal Memoirs* is one of the great classics of military literature. The memoirs earned $450,000 for his heirs, but the hero of Appomattox died on July 23, 1885, at Mount McGregor before he knew of his literary triumph.

Further Reading

The *Personal Memoirs of U.S. Grant* (2 vols., 1885-1886; rep. 1962) is a starting point for a view of Grant's generalship. Another biographical source is Geoffrey Perret, *Ulysses S. Grant* (1997). Important primary sources are the accounts by Grant's military aide, Adam Badeau, *Military History of Ulysses S. Grant: From April, 1861 to April, 1865* (3 vols., 1868-1881) and *Grant in Peace: From Appomattox to Mount McGregor* (1887). The best one-volume study of Grant's military leadership is J. F. C. Fuller, *The Generalship of Ulysses S. Grant* (1958). Lloyd Lewis, *Captain Sam Grant* (1950), carries Grant's career to the outbreak of the Civil War. Bruce Catton's *Grant Moves South* (1960) and *Grant Takes Command* (1969) provide the best account of Grant's military career. Still the fullest study of Grant's presidency is William B. Hesseltine, *Ulysses S. Grant, Politician* (1935). □

Andrew M. Greeley

An American Catholic priest, Andrew M. Greeley (born 1928) wrote sociological studies of American religion and of ethnicity, popular presentations of the Catholic faith, and a number of novels.

Andrew M. Greeley was born in Oak Park, Illinois, February 5, 1928. From an early age he determined to become a priest, attending a seminary high school and college. He received an A.B. from St. Mary of the Lake Seminary in Chicago in 1950, an S.T.B. in 1952, and an S.T.L. in 1954, when he was ordained. From 1954 to 1964 he served as an assistant pastor at Christ the King parish in Chicago, during which time he studied sociology at the University of Chicago, receiving a Ph.D. in 1962. His dissertation dealt with the influence of religion on the career plans of 1961 college graduates.

Combined Sociology and Faith

Sociology, an interest in Catholic education, and a ministry to Catholic youth dominated Greeley's early career and writings. From 1961 to 1968 he was a program director at the National Opinion Research Center in Chicago, and in 1973 he became the director of the Center for the Study of American Pluralism. He taught sociology at the University of Chicago from 1963 to 1972, and beginning in 1978 he taught intermittently at the University of Arizona.

Greeley's first writings included such titles as *The Church and the Suburbs* (1959) and *Religion and Career*

(1963), works in which he put empirical sociology to use. At the same time, he was drawing on his ministerial work with young Catholics in books such as *Strangers in the House* (1961), which described the problems of Catholic teenagers. In the late 1960s he did several studies of Catholic education, concluding that the religious impact of parochial schooling seemed negligible. He was also intent on explaining the Christian faith to lay people, producing readable books such as *The Jesus Myth* (1971) and *The Moses Myth* (1971). In 1972 he published the results of a two-year study of American priests, reporting widespread dissatisfaction. Although this work had been underwritten by the American Catholic bishops, they repudiated its findings, leading Greeley to comment: "Honesty compels me to say that I believe the present leadership in the church to be morally, intellectually, and religiously bankrupt." A significant aspect of Greeley's profile after 1972 was alienation from the American Catholic bishops.

Joining his interest in sociology to a strong sense of his Irish-Catholic heritage, Greeley ventured into the area of ethnicity in 1974, studying the impact of ethnic background and lamenting the assimilation of Irish-Catholics to American Protestant models. In his assessments of American Catholic faith after the Second Vatican Council (1962-1965), he focused on the 1968 encyclical of Pope Paul IV that reaffirmed the ban on artificial birth control. In Greeley's view, this encyclical greatly lowered the credibility of church leaders in the eyes of American Catholics and accounted for a significant drop in church attendance. Another reason for the drop was Vatican II's shift from a God of law to a God of love, who might be presumed to look more to the heart than such externals as attendance at Sunday Mass.

Became a Popular Novelist

Greeley had always written for newspapers and magazines, as well as giving radio and television interviews, but he advanced the popular thrust of his work in 1979 with reports on the elections of Popes John Paul I and John Paul II, for which he traveled to Rome. In 1981 he launched what proved to be a hugely successful career as a novelist with *The Cardinal Sins*, a potboiler depicting the sordid, all-too-human inside of clerical and upper-class Chicago Catholic culture. After that beginning he poured forth a stream of best-sellers (*Thy Brother's Wife* [1982], *Ascent into Hell* [1984], *Virgin and Martyr* [1985], *The Final Planet* [1987], and *Angel Fire* [1988]). From the handsome royalties these novels earned, Greeley endowed a chair at the University of Chicago Divinity School in memory of his parents.

Few literary critics spoke well of Greeley's novels, but obviously they struck a chord in the lay population. Readers of newspapers, secular and Catholic, were familiar with Greeley's syndicated columns and occasional pieces, which were remarkable for their cantankerous ability to spotlight troubling issues (for example, homosexuality among the Catholic clergy). Greeley had a great gift for clear prose and a courageous desire to speak frankly about the actual experience of faith, both personal and social. He continued to draw on data of the National Opinion Research Institute to illuminate religious, ethnic, educational, and other trends in American culture. His own theological positions were moderate to slightly conservative, but he championed a reworking of the Church's attitudes toward sexuality and made a strong case for the importance of the religious imagination (so as to express theology through stories). Steadily he urged the Church to attend to the findings of empirical social science, so as to make its ministry more realistic and credible. His feuds with the late Cardinal Cody, and with many other personages with whom he disagreed, enlivened church life in Chicago and intrigued readers of his columns.

Living independently, and wealthy because of his royalties, Andrew Greeley went his own way, making a unique contribution to American church life. His books number over 100, and he was one of the most quoted American Catholic priests, appearing in *TV Guide* and on numerous talk shows. In fact, few American Catholics have had a greater popular impact. Slowly, serious students of current American Catholic culture are beginning to account Greeley an influence worthy of scholarly investigation.

Further Reading

So prolific is author Andrew Greeley that the best policy would be to sample the several different genres in which he wrote: sociological studies of American religion, popular presentations of Catholic faith, studies of ethnicity, and novels. A good specimen of the first genre might be *Communal Catholics* (1976), *Religion: A Secular Theory* (1982), or *The Catholic Myth* (1990). Among his popular presentations of Catholic faith, *The Jesus Myth* (1971) remains a high point. His works on ethnicity are illumined by his 1974 book

Ethnicity. His novels have improved from the 1981 *The Cardinal Sins*, so the more recent works are more impressive. As an example of the critical attention that Greeley is beginning to receive, see Ingrid Shaefer, editor *Andrew Greeley's World* (1989). □

Alan Greenspan

Appointed chairman of the nation's central bank just two months before the stock market crash of 1987, American economist Alan Greenspan (born 1926) acted quickly to avert a general financial collapse.

Alan Greenspan was born in New York City on March 6, 1926, to Herman H. and Rose G. Greenspan. His bachelor's (1948), master's (1950), and Ph.D. (1977) degrees in economics were all earned at New York University. For three decades, 1954-1974 and 1977-1987, he was chairman and president of an economic consulting firm in New York City, Townsend-Greenspan & Co., Inc. His distinguished record during this time is reflected by his elections as chairman of the Conference of Business Economists, president of the National Association of Business Economists, and director of the National Economists Club.

His career in the private sector was interrupted by calls to public service, first as chairman of President Ford's Council of Economic Advisors (1974-1977), then as chairman of President Reagan's Commission on Social Security Reform (1981-1983), as well as several other presidential boards and commissions. These included President Reagan's Economic Policy Advisory Board, and a consultant to the Congressional Budget Office.

Career With the Federal Reserve System

Greenspan assumed his most important public position on August 11, 1987, replacing Paul A. Volcker as chairman of the Board of Governors of the Federal Reserve System (the Fed). The Fed seeks to control the creation of money and to influence key interest rates, thereby controlling fluctuations in prices of financial market assets, such as stocks and bonds. Perhaps most important among the Fed's responsibilities is to provide temporary loans (through the so-called "discount window") to banks and other financial institutions in times of need. This "lender of last resort" function was the primary reason the Fed was created by Congress in 1913, since individual bank failure had often spread to other banks, leading to a general financial market collapse.

Less than two months after assuming office, Greenspan was faced with such a financial market crisis. After peaking at 2,722 in August of 1987, the Dow Jones industrial average (an index of 30 major industrial stock prices) floated downward by 17 percent over the next month and a half. Suddenly, on "Black Monday," October 19, the market collapsed by more than 500 points as terrified sellers dumped millions of shares. Falling stock prices automatically triggered millions of additional sale orders owing to computerized program trading. Buyers that had previously bought stocks "on margin"—borrowing some portion of the purchase price using the stock as collateral—were then

subject to margin calls and forced to provide additional collateral when these stock prices fell. Many of these stock holders were thus also forced to sell.

What consequently resulted was the largest one-day drop in stock prices in U.S. history, with over 20 percent of the New York Stock Exchange wealth evaporating overnight. The securities firms (brokerage firms and dealer-brokers) that as middlemen provide for orderly trading in stocks on the New York Exchange were hard-pressed to find operating capital as Black Monday wore on, particularly when major domestic and foreign banks withdrew their loans as the alarm spread. The financial system neared collapse from a lack of ready cash (a "liquidity" crisis). Many other financial institutions would have faced insolvency had the market continued to drop the following day.

Acting quickly, Greenspan met with top Fed officials and mapped a strategy for easing the cash crunch, using the Fed's virtually unlimited reserves to bolster the troubled financial institutions. Before the market opened on Tuesday, October 20, Greenspan announced the Fed's "readiness to serve as a source of liquidity to support the economic and financial systems." With the full force and power of the Fed backing these institutions, fear of a general collapse receded and the Dow-Jones industrial average rebounded with a rally of over 100 points on that day.

Incidentally, the bull market of the "Roaring Twenties" had collapsed on October 29, 1929, with again the Fed, acting through the New York Regional Federal Reserve Bank, providing needed short-term liquidity to stop the financial panic from spreading to other sectors of the economy. In contrast to 1987, however, the Crash of 1929 foretold and contributed to a long-term economy-wide collapse. This was partially due to infighting over monetary policy at the Fed, which allowed the money supply to fall by a third over the period from 1929-1933 and which contributed to banking panics that led more than a fifth of the nation's banks to suspend operation.

Yet Greenspan's worries were far from over. On the inflation front, he found cause for considerable alarm. The federal budget deficit had swollen to $221 billion by 1986 and was exerting a powerful inflationary effect on the macroeconomy. While the deficit stabilized at around $150 billion for the remainder of the decade, the collapse of many federally-insured savings and loan institutions was obligating the government to pay out many hundreds of billions of dollars more in the future. The overall effect was to raise interest rates, thereby supplanting spending for capital investment in the private sector. Thus future supply productivity might be hampered at the very time demand was increasing.

Reappointed Despite Differences

Having weathered the financial market panic of 1987, Greenspan sought to send a clear signal that the fight against inflation was now his top priority. This meant slowing the growth of financial reserves that add to the money supply, which, when spent, put upward pressure on prices. Thus the Fed is faced with the dubious task of fighting unemployment (by expanding reserves) and simultaneously fighting inflation. His four-year term as chairman expired in 1991. However, President Bush announced that he would reappoint Greenspan to another term, although the recession caused tension between them.

In 1996, Clinton also reappointed him, despite different financial policies. Greenspan has been criticized for raising interest rates at the first sign of inflation even when the economy has been slow and unemployment high, whereas Clinton believed in strong economic growth, even if it meant a small rise in inflation. Since interest rate hikes mean fewer businesses take out loans to expand, and therefore fewer jobs, the 1996 reappointment surprised many. On April 6, 1997 Greenspan accepted a nomination from Clinton for another four-year term, beginning June 2000. In an effort to stimulate a flagging economy during the first year of the Bush administration, Greenspan lowered interest rates several times.

He had also served previously as a member of *Time* magazine's Board of Economists and senior advisor to the Brookings Institution Panel on Economic Activity. In addition, Greenspan served as corporate director to numerous banks and manufacturing companies, including J. P. Morgan (the nation's fourth-largest commercial bank) and Alcoa (the nation's largest aluminum company). His honorary degrees were numerous, including those from Wake Forest, Colgate, Hofstra, and Pace, and he was the joint recipient with Arthur Burns (a Fed chairman in the 1970s) and William Simon (a former treasury secretary) of the Thomas Jefferson Award for the Greatest Public Service Performed by an appointed official, presented by the American Institute for Public Service (1976).

Further Reading

General discussion of the Fed's operating procedures are outlined in U.S. Board of Governors, *The Federal Reserve System: Purposes and Functions*. For an inside look at the workings of the Fed, see William Greider, *Secrets of the Temple: How the Federal Reserve Runs the Country* (1987). Greenspan's views on inflation are given in *Weapons Against Inflation* (1979). As Greenspan is always making new decisions regarding interest rates, there are numerous articles to be found in periodicals such as *Business Week* and *Money*. For a good comprehensive work on his career, see Robert Sherrill "The Inflation of Alan Greenspan", *The Nation* (March 11, 1996). For a brief look at the differences in the philosophies of Greenspan and Clinton, see Owen Ullmann "Clinton and Greenspan: Is an Explosion Coming?", *Business Week* (June 6, 1994).

Fascinating discussions of the Crash of 1987 are found in "Terrible Tuesday: How the Stock Market Almost Disintegrated a Day After the Crash," *Wall Street Journal* (November 20, 1987) and Frederic S. Mishkin, *Money, Banking, and Financial Markets* (1989). The most famous monetary scholars of the Great Depression are Milton Friedman and Anna J. Schwartz, *A Monetary History of the United States, 1867-1960* (1963), but for a more readable classic account, see John Kenneth Galbraith, *The Great Crash, 1929* (1955). □

Dick Gregory

A renowned comedian, Dick Gregory (born 1932) used his wit and humor to advance his deep interest in civil rights and world peace.

Dick Gregory was born Richard Claxton Gregory on October 12, 1932, into poverty and deprivation in St. Louis, Missouri. In some ways his humble beginnings fueled the topical racial comedy which catapulted him into fame in the 1960s. He attended Southern Illinois University in Carbondale from 1951 to 1956. In 1953 he received the school's Outstanding Athlete Award.

By 1958 Gregory was making his debut in show business by appearing at the Esquire and Roberts show clubs in Chicago and at the Club Apex in nearby Robbins, Illinois. His regular appearances on television included the Jack Paar and Mike Douglas shows which made him one of the best known African Americans. The radicalization which transformed many Americans during the 1960s led Gregory to see things in a global perspective. Many of his public appearances started to combine comedy with political commentary. He became an outspoken opponent of American involvement in Vietnam and of racial as well as ethnic discrimination in America and elsewhere.

In the United States Gregory was one of the first modern spokespersons to suggest that the Census Bureau undercounts minorities, particularly in large cities. In 1966, through a series of fund-raisers, he shipped 10,000 pounds of navy beans to Marks, Mississippi, to feed hungry people. In addition, he advocated large families as a way to both counter and protest racism.

Internationally, Gregory was a major leader of the antiwar movement. He traveled to France to protest French involvement in Indo-China and to Northern Ireland to advise Irish Republican Army (IRA) political protesters on techniques for fasting. In his campaign against hunger he traveled to Ethiopia more than ten times. In 1968 the Peace and Freedom Party nominated him as its presidential candidate in recognition of his efforts to make the world a better place.

In 1981 Gregory—who formerly weighed 350 pounds, smoked four packs of cigarettes and drank a fifth of Scotch a day—put his dietary knowledge to the test. In the planning stages for more than six years, he conducted "the longest medically supervised scientific fast in the history of the planet." During this "Dick Gregory's Zero Nutrition Fasting Experiment" he lived on a gallon of water and prayer for 70 days at Dillard University's Flint-Goodridge Hospital. Upon its completion, he demonstrated his good health by walking and jogging the 100 miles between New Orleans and Baton Rouge, Louisiana. From this experiment he created his "4-X Fasting Formula," which included a "Life-Centric Monitor" and an emphasis on colonetics. The fast also indicated that the body can prolong the time it can go without food.

Gregory announced a vow of celibacy in 1981. As the father of ten children and a former performer of a risqué night club act, this news was somewhat surprising. It was a part of a philosophy of life which sought to switch from the animal to the divine nature of man.

In his concern for health and nutrition, he came to believe that agricultural resources exist to assure each man, woman, and child a chemically safe, nutritionally sound, and physiologically efficient diet. Multi-level distribution rights to his nutrition formula—Dick Gregory's Slim-safe Bahamian Diet—were sold for a reported $100 million when the special formulation became commercially available in August of 1984. Articles in *People* and *USA Today* made the diet a favorite among the general public. Gregory lamented the lack of health food stores in Black communities and sought to promote an awareness of the importance of natural foods and the dangers of the traditional soul food diet. He believes because their diets and lifestyles tend to include higher than average amounts of salt, sugar, cholesterol, alcohol and drugs that Blacks have a shorter life expectancy.

A large percentage of the profits from the sales of products developed by the Dick Gregory Health Enterprise in Chicago was earmarked for the poor and for Black civil rights groups such as the National Association for the Advancement of Colored People (NAACP), the Southern Christian Leadership Conference (SCLC), the United Negro College Fund, and the Rosa Parks Foundation. In addition, Gregory acquired a major interest in the Frankie Jennings Cosmetics Company to fulfill his dream of marketing products such as vitamins, shampoo, juices, and cookies. Howard and Xavier universities were researching and testing sites for his products. Another campaign was to inform the public about the ills of alcohol, caffeine, and drug consumption.

Dick Gregory is a deeply spiritual man but was not limited to any traditional religion or formulized dogma. Instead, he advocates the attainment of oneness with a "Godself," which he believed was the most complete state of being. He advocates a holistic approach to life through diet, fitness, and spiritual awareness.

Even at 64 Gregory was still doing his one-man stand up comedy show, *Dick Gregory, LIVE!* As late as 1996 he was opening in Chicago. In March of 1997 he was the fifth annual Dr. Martin Luther King, Jr., Guestship speaker at Elmhurst College. He credited much of his success to the support and trust of his wife Lillian (Lil), whom he married in 1959.

Further Reading

There is no published biography of Dick Gregory. He has, however, written extensively of himself and his beliefs in *Nigger: An Autobiography* (1964). Two magazine articles of interest are "My Answer to Genocide," *Ebony* (October 1981) and a discussion of his 4-X Formula in *Black Enterprise* (May 1985). Gregory has published the following books: *From the Back of the Bus* (1962); *What's Happening* (1965); *The Shadow That Scares Me* (1968); *Write Me In* (1968); *No More Lies* (1971); *Dick Gregory's Political Primer* (1972); *Dick Gregory's Natural Diet . . . Nature* (1973); *Up From Nigger* (1976); and *Dick Gregory's Bible Tales* (1978).

Additional Sources

Newsmakers 1990, issue 3.

Chicago Tribune, "Comedian-activist set to speak at college," 2/16/97; "Long Comedy Club Absence Hasn't Dulled Dick Gregory," 08/24/96.

Village Voice, 1/16/96, Vol. 41 Issue 3, p64.

Amsterdam News, 11/23/96, Vol. 87 Issue 47, p30. □

David Wark Griffith

David Wark Griffith (1875-1948), American filmmaker, was a pioneer director-producer who invented much of the basic technical grammar of modern cinema.

On Jan. 22, 1875, D.W. Griffith was born at Crestwood, Oldham County, Ky., the descendant of a distinguished (but impoverished) Southern family. Scantily educated but convinced of his "aristocracy," he became an actor at 18 in Louisville. For 10 years he was a supporting player in provincial companies, using the stage name Lawrence Griffith to protect his family's honor but his real name for the plays and poetry he was trying to publish. In 1906 he secretly married actress Linda Arvidson Johnson, who viewed his literary and directorial aspirations unsympathetically and, after 5 years, left him.

Early Films

In 1907 Griffith sold a poem to *Frank Leslie's Weekly* and a play, *A Fool and a Girl,* to actor James K. Hackett. The play promptly failed, and Griffith was driven to try the then unsavory movie business. E. S. Porter, whose *Great Train Robbery* was the first "story" film, gave him the lead in a primitive one-reeler called *Rescued from an Eagle's Nest* and unwittingly started Griffith toward greatness.

In 1908 Griffith sold several stories to the Biograph Company and also acted in them. Within a few months he had a chance to direct. The success of his first effort, *The Adventures of Dollie,* led to regular employment, a series of rapidly improving contracts, and pride enough in his work to use his real name.

During 5 years with Biograph, Griffith made hundreds of short pictures and gradually won consent to increase their length beyond one reel, thus enabling him to expand narrative content. With the help of his famed cameraman, G. W. "Billy" Bitzer, he made revolutionary technical innovations in film making. He also started the cinema careers of Mary Pickford, Mack Sennett, the Gish sisters, Lionel Barrymore, and many others.

Griffith Classics

In 1913 Griffith formed an independent company. Within 2 years he completed his epic masterpiece *The Birth of a Nation* (1915), often considered the most important film ever made. Dealing with the Civil War and its aftermath in the South, it was, for its day, incredibly long (12 reels) and expensive ($100,000). However, it grossed $18 million within a few years of release and established once and for all the astonishing power and potentiality of cinema as a serious art form. The film also aroused storms of controversy because of its treatment of African Americans and Ku Klux Klansmen.

Determined to clear himself of charges of prejudice, Griffith next made one of the most enormous, complex, and ambitious pictures in history. *Intolerance* (1916) attempted to interweave four parallel stories—modern, biblical, 16th-century French, and Babylonian—into a monumental sermon on the evils of inhumanity. His financial backers were

Griffith had led the new medium of film into unexplored areas of spectacle, realism, intimacy, and social content. His contributions to the technique of film art include the invention of the close-up, the long shot, the fadeout, night shots, high and low photographic angles, crosscutting, backlighting, the moving camera, and many other devices that are now taken for granted. Despite his genius, he was, except for 39 weeks on radio, unemployed and unemployable for the last 17 years of his life. A second marriage ended in divorce in 1947, and a year later, at age 73, he died, alone and almost forgotten, in a shabby sidestreet Hollywood hotel.

Further Reading

The literature on Griffith and his achievements is extensive. Useful introductory works are Iris Barry, *D. W. Griffith, American Film Master* (1940); a popular biography by Homer Croy, *Star Maker: The Story of D. W. Griffith* (1959); and Lillian Gish, *Lillian Gish: The Movies, Mr. Griffith and Me* (1969).

Additional Sources

Schickel, Richard, *D.W. Griffith: an American life,* New York: Limelight Editions, 1996.

Williams, Martin T., *Griffith, first artist of the movies,* New York: Oxford University Press, 1980. □

John Grisham

Popular novelist John Grisham (born 1955) is the author of several thrillers that have been made into blockbuster films. His works, which center around the legal profession, include *A Time to Kill, The Firm, The Client,* and *The Pelican Brief.*

It is no understatement that John Grisham, author of the legal thrillers *A Time to Kill, The Firm, The Pelican Brief,* and *The Client,* has achieved the status of what *Entertainment Weekly* called "a genuine pop-culture demigod." His have shared unprecedented weeks—and months—on best-seller lists, have numbered more than 60 million in print across the world, and have been translated into 31 languages. Dubbed "grab-it-at-the-airport" novels, they have also made their author a multimillionaire; Grisham's income for the 1992-93 fiscal year alone was $25 million. Along with author Scott Turow, also a former practicing attorney, Grisham has been credited with mastering a genre: the fast-paced, plot-driven legal thriller that thrusts an unwitting, sympathetic hero or heroine in the middle of a corrupt conspiracy and provides them with the means to extricate themselves. Despite his seemingly untouchable success, Grisham still wants each novel he writes to improve upon the last. "[Right now] I could crank out anything, and it would sell," he told the same source. "But I want the next to be better than the first five. That keeps me awake at night."

Drawn to Courtroom Drama

Born in Arkansas in 1955, Grisham spent much of his childhood traveling with his family throughout the South, settling for short periods in places where his father, a con-

appalled; audiences found it chaotic and exhausting; but for all its faults, *Intolerance* established techniques and conventions which permanently affected film making. Individual fragments of this huge, disjointed picture became the basis for entire schools of cinematic development. The overpowering Babylonian sequences with immense crowds and sumptuous spectacle provided Cecil B. DeMille and others with the substance of their whole careers.

Formation of United Artists

In 1917 Griffith made a propaganda film for the British government, *Hearts of the World,* which served mainly to display the director's ultimately fatal tendency toward melodrama and sentimentality.

Returning to the United States, Griffith joined Mary Pickford, Douglas Fairbanks, and Charlie Chaplin in forming United Artists, through which he released such famous pictures as *Broken Blossoms* (1919), *Way Down East* (1920), and *Orphans of the Storm* (1921); their varying success temporarily relieved his steadily mounting financial difficulties.

After his important film *Isn't Life Wonderful* (1924), Griffith was increasingly out of tune with popular taste and with the growing film industry. He was obliged to work as an employee in the new Hollywood studio system. After 1927 the transition to "talkies" posed further problems, and although he managed one more independent production in 1930 (*Abraham Lincoln*), his career was finished by 1931. He received one small directing assignment, for which he was not paid, in 1936.

struction worker, managed to find work. When Grisham was 12, he moved with his parents and four siblings to Southaven, Mississippi. "We didn't have a lot of money," he remembered in *People*, "but we didn't know it. We were well fed and loved and scrubbed." Though not a stellar student in high school, he excelled in sports—baseball, in particular—and was captivated by the novels of John Steinbeck. Grisham later attended Mississippi State University, where he received his B.S. degree in accounting and decided on a career as a tax attorney. His first course on tax law at the University of Mississippi dampened his interest, however, and he switched to criminal-defense law instead, discovering that he was drawn to courtroom drama and had the ability to think well under pressure.

After graduating from law school and passing the bar exam in 1981, Grisham married Renee Jones, a childhood friend from Southaven, and the couple returned to their home town where Grisham became a litigator. In recalling his first murder trial, he told *People*, "I defended a guy who shot another guy in self-defense, but I had to explain why he shot him in the head six times at three-inch range. It was a pretty gruesome case, but I won." When he shifted his focus to more lucrative civil cases, his practice began to thrive, and he is credited with one of the largest damage settlements in De Soto County, which he won on behalf of a child who sustained extensive burns when a water heater exploded. In 1983 Grisham was elected to the Mississippi state legislature, where he served as a Democrat for seven years, hoping to increase spending for education. However, he resigned from his position before the end of his second

term, because, as he told the same source, "I realized it was impossible to make changes."

Inspired by Real-Life Trial

The incident that inspired Grisham's first novel, *A Time to Kill*, occurred years before it was actually written, when he was still practicing law in Southaven in 1984. One day he went to the local courthouse to observe a trial and heard a ten-year-old girl testify against a man who had raped her, leaving her for dead. "I never felt such emotion and human drama in my life," Grisham remembered in *People*. "I became obsessed wondering what it would be like if the girl's father killed that rapist and was put on trial. I had to write it down." Despite the 70 hours a week he was putting in at his own firm, he was able to complete *A Time to Kill* by waking up at 5:00 each morning to write, a schedule that he adhered to for three years. Then, in 1987, after the manuscript had been rejected by several publishers, New York agent Jay Garon offered to represent Grisham. Garon made a deal with Wynwood Press for $15,000, and two years later, 5,000 copies of *A Time to Kill* were published, one thousand of which Grisham bought himself. Although Grisham was initially reluctant to allow *A Time to Kill* to be made into a movie, he relented when he was allowed to hand pick filmmaker Joel Schumacher, with whom Grisham had worked on the 1994 film version of *The Client*, to direct the film. *A Time to Kill* was released in 1996.

The Firm was also rejected by numerous publishers and might have suffered a similar fate as *A Time to Kill* if a bootleg copy of the manuscript hadn't started a bidding war in Hollywood. Early in 1990 Renee Grisham called her husband out of church to inform him that Paramount had offered him $600,000 for the movie rights to his book, and Grisham soon signed a contract with Doubleday, one of the publishers who had rejected *A Time to Kill* two years earlier. *The Firm* is the story of Harvard Law School graduate Mitchell McDeere, who signs on with a prestigious Memphis law firm offering him an irresistible package: an excellent salary and such perks as a new BMW car, a low-interest mortgage, and membership in a posh country club. Yet just as Mitchell and his wife, Abby, are settling into their new upscale lifestyle, two of the firm's lawyers die mysteriously, and FBI investigators start pressuring the young lawyer for inside information. When he learns that the Mafia has set up the firm to launder money, Mitch faces the decision of whether to cooperate with the FBI and risk his life, or be implicated with the other firm members and spend time in prison. For Grisham, completing *The Firm* signalled a turning point: he decided to close his law practice and write full time.

Best-Seller for 47 Weeks

People magazine called *The Firm* a "thriller of the first order, powered to pulse-racing perfection by the realism of its malevolent barristers," and *Library Journal* noted that Grisham "set a daringly high standard, one that his readers will hope he can reach again and again." A *New York Times* best-seller for 47 weeks—and the longest-running paperback on *Publishers Weekly* best-seller list—*The Firm* was made into a the 1992 film directed by Sidney Pollack, starring Tom Cruise, Gene Hackman, Jeanne Tripplehorn, and Holly Hunter, among others.

Grisham's next effort to be adapted for the big screen 1993's *The Pelican Brief,* featuring Julia Roberts and Denzel Washington. Although Grisham usually disassociates himself from the movie versions of his novels, he was apparently pleased with this one, which he and wife Renee first watched with President and Mrs. Clinton at the White House. Not only was it rated PG-13, meaning that his children could see it, but it was, as he told *Entertainment Weekly,* "a wonderful adaptation of the novel. [Director] Alan Pakula's vision was very similar to mine."

In this story, Darby Shaw, a Tulane University law student, prepares a legal brief that becomes a crucial puzzle piece in an FBI investigation of a suspected conspiracy behind the murders of two Supreme Court justices. Like Mitch in *The Firm,* Darby spends much of her time narrowly escaping the evil forces around her, though here Grisham targets other bureaucratic agencies—the CIA and White House, in addition to the FBI—as demoralized and corrupt. This novel, however, did not fare as well with reviewers: *Time* claimed that it "is as close to its predecessor as you can get without running *The Firm* through the office copier"; *Publishers Weekly* complained that the "hairbreadth escapes . . . are too many and too frequent, and the menace wears thin, partly because the characters lack the humanity of those in Grisham's earlier novels." Nevertheless Grisham remained stoic about the criticism, telling Michelle Bearden of *Publishers Weekly:* "It's the American way. As a rookie, people were really pulling for me with *The Firm,* but the second time around, those same people were secretly wishing I would fail so they could rip me to shreds."

Ordinary People, Heroic Deeds

Grisham has gotten into the habit of beginning his next novel the morning after he has sent a completed manuscript to agent Garon in New York. In shaping a story he adheres to what he considers three basic principles: an opening that grips readers and makes them want to continue reading, a middle that sustains the narrative tension, and an ending that brings the action to an edge-of-your-seat climax. As in *The Firm* and *The Pelican Brief,* his protagonists are often ordinary people who find themselves caught in the middle of a conspiracy and must perform heroic feats to save their own and others' lives. "And always, there's something dark, shadowy and sinister lurking in the background," the author told Bearden. While he seems to have hit on a surefire formula for his novels, Grisham credits Renee, who offers him particular advice on his women characters, for her role as an editor and a critic. His manuscripts must meet with her approval before publishers even see them. "She makes those [editors] in New York look like children," he was quoted as saying in *Publishers Weekly.*

In reflecting on what appears to be a trend—popular books being written by attorneys-turned-writers—Grisham confided to Bearden that "most lawyers I know would rather be doing something else." Yet he admits, according to *People,* that much of the fiction churned out by these professionals is "dreadful," and that to be a "master" of the

genre—a category in which he places only himself and authors Scott Turow and Steve Martini—a writer must be able to convey the legal aspects of a story without overwhelming or alienating the reader. *Publishers Weekly* commended Grisham on this very point in its review of *The Firm:* "[The author] lucidly describes law procedures at the highest levels, smoothly meshing them with the criminal events of the narrative." Still Grisham acknowledges that in some respects, his writing process still needs fine-tuning. In particular, he wishes that he had dedicated more time to *The Pelican Brief* and *The Client,* which he wrote in three months and six months, respectively. He has also endeavored to address past criticism that his novels contain shallow characters by slowing down the narrative pace in his most recent books and adding more depth and dimension to the personalities he creates.

Developed Characters in *The Client*

The Client, which is not a true mystery because the crime, motive, and criminal are all revealed within the first chapter of the book, reflects Grisham's growing interest in character development. Mark Sway, a streetwise 11-year-old who has grown up too fast due to an absent father and little money, becomes the unwitting witness to a suicide; yet before he kills himself, lawyer Jerome Clifford tells Mark where the body of a U.S. senator has been buried and who the killer is. Once word spreads to the Mafia and FBI that Mark has this information, his life is in danger, and he retains the legal services of Reggie Love, a middle-aged female attorney whose life has been even more difficult than his own. Grisham not only put their relationship at the emotional center of *The Client* but also invented more complex and well-rounded minor characters than in past books, and his efforts did not go unnoticed among reviewers: *Publishers Weekly* commended his creation of "two singular protagonists sure to elicit readers' empathy," and *People* found the character of Reggie Love to be "a truly memorable heroine . . . well worth a return visit."

With his novel *The Chamber,* Grisham put in more time—it took more than nine months to write—*and* wrote it out longhand, which he had not done since he had penned his first effort, *A Time to Kill. The Chamber* features Sam Cayhall, an aging former Ku Klux Klan member who has been convicted of bombing the office of a Jewish civil rights lawyer and killing the man's two young sons. In trying to prevent Cayhall's execution after he has received the death penalty, a shrewd lawyer named Adam—who turns out to be Cayhall's grandson—not only faces bureaucratic agencies that seem as debased as the criminal himself but, finally, he confronts his own conscience. *Time* applauded Grisham for his struggle to show the complexities of capital punishment as an ethical issue: "[The Chamber] is a work produced by painful writhing over a terrible paradox; vengeance may be justified, but killing is a shameful, demeaning response to evil." Grisham was also pleased with the outcome of this novel and particularly proud of its characters. "It's much more about the people," he told *Entertainment Weekly.* "It will appeal to different kinds of readers. I have no doubts about it."

Returned to the Courtroom

For Grisham, the 1980s meant hard work and, at times, going without. While *A Time to Kill* has since joined the ranks of his other novels in best-sellerdom, it was not very long ago that he couldn't give copies away for free. "We'd give them as Christmas gifts," his friend and fellow state legislator Bobby Moak recalled in *Entertainment Weekly*. "A truckload got wet and mildewed, so we just took 'em to the dump. It was hell gettin' rid of those dadgum things." That was a far cry from Grisham's success in the 1990s. He was paid a $3.75 million advance for the *The Chamber,* and his 1995 book, *The Rainmaker,* shot to the top of the best-seller lists. In *The Rainmaker,* a poor young lawyer fights a corrupt insurance company. *Entertainment Weekly* commented, "*The Rainmaker* seems very tapped into America's current skepticism about lawyers and the legal system."

Continuing his focus on the legal system and current topics, Grisham in 1996 released *The Runaway Jury.* The story centers around a trial in which a woman, Celeste Wood, is suing a cigarette company for the death of her husband, Jacob. There is much intrigue and inside dealings with the jury, especially the secretive juror Nicholas Easter. Christopher Lehmann-Haupt in the *New York Times* commented, "The story's suspense builds like that of a lengthening cigarette ash that refuses to drop off," and praised the plot as "entertainingly unpredictable."

In addition to his writing career, in 1995 Grisham announced he was returning to the courtroom. He had not practiced law for seven years, but agreed to represent the estate of an employee of the Illinois Central Railroad who was killed on the job. He had accepted the case in 1991. *USA Today* reported that Grisham "came across as a nice guy: well-prepared, deferential, sincere-sounding and self-effacing."

Continuing to craft best-selling novels, Grisham saw the publication of *The Partner* in 1997. In this story, a lawyer steals $90 million from his firm and its wealthiest client, fakes his own death, and flees to Brazil. Grisham's legal thriller of 1998, *The Street Lawyer,* delves into the world of the homeless from the perspective of an overworked, affluent young lawyer. "For lawyers, the main dream of escape is to get out of the profession," Grisham told the *New York Times.* "They dream about a big settlement, a home run, so that they can use the money to do something else." Grisham himself has taken the money and run, all the way to Hollywood, which routinely turns his novels into movies. His latest work, *The Testament* (1999), abandons the courtroom in favor of the Brazilian jungle, proving that Grisham can pen an adventure tale as well as a legal thriller.

In the wake of his success, Grisham continues to rely on friends and family to help him stay grounded. He and Renee have used part of their windfall to build a Victorian-style home on 20 acres of land in Oxford, Mississippi, and he spends as much time as he can with his children—attending his daughter Shea's soccer matches and coaching his son Ty in Little League. Grisham, who never loses sight of the fact that his success may be transient, remains positive about those blessings in his life that cannot be measured by book sales. "Ten years from now I plan to be sitting here, looking out over my land," he told *People*. "I hope I'll be writing books, but if not, I'll be on my pond fishing with my kids. I feel like the luckiest guy I know."

Additional Sources

Entertainment Weekly, April 1, 1994; May 5, 1995.

Library Journal, January 1991.

New York Times, May 23, 1996, p. B5; March 31, 1997, p. C11.

Newsweek, February 15, 1999.

People, April 8, 1991; March 16, 1992; March 15, 1993.

Publishers Weekly, January 11, 1991; January 20, 1992; February 1, 1993; February 22, 1993.

Time, March 9, 1992; June 20, 1994. □

Andrew S. Grove

For 30 years, American businessman Andrew S. Grove (born 1936) has served in a variety of high-level posts at Intel Corp., considered one of the most powerful microprocessor manufacturers in the world.

From humble beginnings in Hungary, Grove went on to become chief executive officer (CEO) and chairperson of one the most powerful microprocessor manufacturing companies in the world, Intel Corp. He is highly regarded both as a physicist in the field of semiconductors as well as an expert in management. With Intel, he has helped to usher in an information revolution unmatched by anything since the invention of the printing press. As noted by Walter Isaacson in *Time*": *Time* chooses as its 1997 Man of the Year Andrew Steven Grove, chairman and CEO of Intel, the person most responsible for the amazing growth in the power and innovative potential of microchips."

Early Life

Andrew Steven Grove was born András Gróf in Budapest, Hungary, on September 2, 1936. His father, George, was a dairyman, and his mother, Maria, worked as a bookkeeping clerk. The family was of Jewish descent and World War II proved to be a difficult time; Grove would see nothing but trouble until he departed from Europe. At the age of four, a wave of scarlet fever swept through Hungary. Grove was not spared, and over the course of the illness, his hearing was seriously damaged. The following year, his father was removed to a Nazi work camp. Grove and his mother changed their names and moved in with Christian acquaintances, who hid them during the Nazi pogroms of 1944. After the war, his father miraculously reappeared, though weakened by typhus and pneumonia. Grove, hoping to attend college in a few years, dabbled in journalism and took voice lessons, dreaming of perhaps becoming an opera singer. Political circumstances again intervened, however, in 1956, when Soviet tanks arrived in Budapest to put down the Hungarian Revolution. His father's occupation, as a private business owner, made Grove a potential dissident in the eyes of the communists. So, rather than face the possibility of prison, Grove and a friend fled to Austria.

From there, Grove made his way to the United States, where he moved in with an uncle who had immigrated to New York in the early 1930s. He enrolled in the City College of New York (CCNY), studying chemical engineering and waiting tables to pay his tuition. In the summer of 1957, he met a woman named Eva, who became his wife the following year. Grove graduated from CCNY in 1960, after which he and Eva relocated to California, where he entered the Ph.D. program at the University of California, Berkeley. There, as at CCNY, he performed spectacularly. Upon his graduation in 1963, he went to work for Fairchild Semiconductor, a small company which had recently been created by a few of the more forward-thinking engineers on the West Coast. He also began teaching at Berkeley, a side career he has continued to the present day.

At Fairchild, along with the head of the research department, Gordon Moore, and two other colleagues, Bruce Deal and Edward Snow, Grove helped create the first marketable silicon-based integrated circuit. This was a major step for the computer industry, which, until then, used transistors as switching elements in their products. To be sure, transistors were far better than their predecessors, vacuum tubes. Vacuum tubes were bulky, and they generated a tremendous amount of heat and consumed an equally large amount of electricity. The transistor was considerably smaller, and required no heating element. The drawback was that they had to be used individually. In order to move forward, the industry required that more than one transistor occupy a single unit. The solution to this dilemma came as early as 1959, but it would take several years, and the particular combination of talents that existed at Fairchild,

under the leadership of general manager Bob Noyce, to create a reliable, mass-produced integrated circuit. That accomplishment stood poised to revolutionize the industry, and thereafter, the world.

Grove Moves to Intel

None of this made much of an impact on the top executives of Fairchild—they displayed the same lack of vision that kills so many high-technology companies even today. So, in 1968, frustrated with the state of affairs, Noyce secured the support of Arthur Rock, a prominent high-tech investor, and with Gordon Moore's help, started a company called Intel (short for Integrated Electronics). With these three men, the company looked unsinkable. Their decision to employ Grove as director of operations was, however, in the words of Tim Jackson's history of Intel, "so bizarre that it mystified most of the people who were watching the new business take shape." Up to that point, Grove had virtually no manufacturing experience at all, plus he was decidedly unusual. Jackson continued, "Grove spoke English with an accent that was almost incomprehensible. Over his head, he wore an awkward hearing-aid device that looked like a product of Eastern European engineering." Furthermore, he had a severe temper, and an equally severe manner of maintaining discipline and control. None-the-less, Noyce and Moore admired his intelligence and drive, and they believed he was the right man. Grove tacitly agreed, leaving Fairchild almost immediately.

The doubts held by onlookers concerning his abilities were quickly put to rest. Grove guided the development of manufacturing processes first for the company's computer memory products, then for its first general-purpose microprocessor (the component that serves as the "brain" of modern desktop computers), outstripping all competitors and even the company which had licensed their technology to provide the "second-source" so important to computer companies at that time. The early years of the company were particularly hectic, as the demands of the high-tech sector tended to change dramatically and unpredictably. Thus, despite the concentrated talent at their disposal, Intel found itself constantly changing gears, and struggling to keep up with the latest developments. Grove's force of will aided the company greatly during this period, but an insight of Moore's was necessary for long-term stability. Moore's Law, as the insight came to be known, was that chip power would continue to double roughly every 18 months for the foreseeable future. Thus, Intel was able to chart its course ahead of the fact rather than leaping after changes in demand.

Moore's Law did not, however, eliminate all difficulties. The first major crisis began in the mid-1970s, when Japanese companies, who could manufacture memory chips at much lower costs, began dumping large quantities of cut-rate chips on American markets, seriously reducing demand for Intel's products. This was a major blow for the company, whose business relied at that time primarily on the sale of memory. They responded by shifting their emphasis to microprocessors, but many rival American companies collapsed under the pressure. In 1981, the chip market took another nosedive, and once again, many companies were caught unprepared. Grove, rather than laying off employees, ordered them to work 25 percent overtime for free. The strategy succeeded, and Intel survived.

Grove's hard work and demanding management style, while criticized by many, brought ever-increasing profits for Intel, and in 1979, he was made president of the company. Four years later, he published his second book, *High Output Management,* which was subsequently translated into 11 languages (his first volume, *Physics and Technology of Semiconductor Devices,* was published in 1967 during his tenure at Fairchild). His third book, *One-on-One with Andy Grove,* was published in 1987. He also wrote a regular management column which appeared in several newspapers, as well as occasional pieces for the *Wall Street Journal, Fortune,* and the *New York Times.* He became the CEO of Intel in 1987. The decade of the 1980s brought him recognition outside of the company as well. He received honorary doctorates from the City College of New York and from Worcester Polytechnic Institute in 1985 and 1989, respectively. Furthermore, he was honored in 1987 with the Engineering Leadership Recognition Award.

The Half-Billion Dollar Mistake

Intel's biggest stumbling block came abruptly in 1994, with the release of the company's Pentium processor. The chip was flawed slightly, performing math calculations incorrectly. The error was small, and would not have affected the vast majority of users—only people running math-intensive programs like those required for nuclear research or astrophysics. Grove decided that there would therefore be no reason to order a recall. Those who called in to ask about the problem were simply told not to worry. Intel's customers didn't see the matter the same way, and in short order, the flaw was suddenly the topic of technology columns in newspapers around the world. After much deliberation, Grove backed off his position, and Intel began replacing the faulty chips. The crisis cost the company half a billion dollars, but in the end the decision to switch courses wound up bolstering their image. Intel was stronger than ever.

As noted by Isaacson in *Time,* Intel controls 90% of the microprocessor market. They also face little in the way of competition, although the combined efforts of IBM, Apple, and Motorola are beginning to have some effect. Grove, certainly not one to rest on his laurels, has made the 1990s a productive decade for himself as well. His fourth book, *Only the Paranoid Survive: How to Exploit the Crisis Points that Challenge Every Company and Career,* was published in 1996, and several more awards have been forthcoming as well. In 1993, he received a Medal of Achievement from the American Engineering Association, and, in March of 1994 he was elected a Fellow of the Academy of Arts and Sciences. The following year, he was awarded the Heinz Family Foundation Award for Technology and the Economy. Finally, *Time* magazine named him their Man of the Year in 1997.

The challenges in Intel's future are many. The increasing popularity of sub-$1000 computers could prove damag-

ing to the company's flagship product, the high-end Pentium II. Also, Intel has had to cope with increasing scrutiny from the U.S. Federal government, which has grown uneasy with the monopolistic characteristics of Intel and its chief ally, Microsoft. Grove's level of participation in these issues is definitely declining, however. In 1996, he was diagnosed with prostate cancer, and although treatment was successful he began actively grooming a successor, Craig Barrett. In March of 1998, Grove stepped down as CEO, though he remains chairperson. Outside the corporate world, he teaches a class in the business school at Stanford University. A modest man, Grove commented in the *Wall Street Journal,* "One position says you ought to put some effort into making sure that people know what you do. The opposite is, look, you'll never get 100 percent credit, so just do your stuff. Advertising your achievements will probably make you look like a jerk anyway. I lean toward the second view."

Further Reading

Grove, Andrew S., *High Output Management,* Vintage, 1995.

Grove, Andrew S., *One-On-One With Andy Grove: How to Manage Your Boss, Yourself, and Your Co-Workers,* Penguin, 1989.

Grove, Andrew S., *Only the Paranoid Survive: How to Exploit the Crisis Points That Challenge Every Company and Career,* Currency Doubleday, 1996.

Grove, Andrew S., *Physics and Technology of Semiconductor Devices,* Wiley, 1967.

Jackson, Tim, *Inside Intel,* Dutton, 1997.

Business Week, April 13, 1998.

Fortune, April 27, 1998; May 11, 1998.

Time, December, 1997, p. 46

U.S. News and World Report, April 6, 1998.

Intel Corp., "Executive Bio—Andrew S. Grove," http://www.intel.com/pressroom/kits/bios/grove.htm (March 31, 1998). □

Woodrow Wilson Guthrie

Writer and performer of folk songs, Woodrow Wilson Guthrie (1912-1967) composed "This Land Is Your Land," an unofficial national anthem.

Guthrie was born July 14, 1912, in Okemah, Oklahoma. He had little formal education, for which he compensated to a degree with intensive reading. Guthrie led one of the most tragic lives of any notable American. His father was a failure in both politics and business and died on skid row. His mother killed his only sister in an insane rage before dying of Huntington's chorea, which she passed on to Guthrie. In later years Guthrie lost his own infant daughter in a fire. Virtually orphaned at the age of 14 when his family broke up, Guthrie developed an itinerant way of life that he never entirely abandoned until his final hospitalization.

In the course of his travels Guthrie learned to perform folk songs, first those of others but later increasingly his

own. In 1937 he obtained through a cousin the first of many, usually short-lived, radio jobs, singing and playing on a Los Angeles station. He also acquired permanent ties to the Communist Party. In 1940 he arrived in New York and was discovered by Alan Lomax, assistant director of the Archive of Folk Songs of the Library of Congress. Lomax recorded many of Guthrie's songs for the library and promoted his career in other ways, such as by inducing Victor Records to produce a two album, 12 record set of Guthrie's "Dust Bowl Ballads." Though they did not sell, the ballads were to have lasting influence.

In 1941 Guthrie joined the Almanac Singers, a left-wing folk music group that included Pete Seeger, ultimately, with Guthrie, its best known member. On February 14, 1942, the Almanacs achieved their greatest exposure by performing on a program called "This Is War" that was aired by all four networks. But newspaper stories about the group's Communist affiliations prevented the Almanacs from achieving commercial success, and they dissolved within a year. Most of the members of the Almanacs were ardently anti-Nazi and went into the military. Guthrie too supported the war. "This Machine Kills Fascists" was inscribed on his guitar. But he hoped to accomplish his goal at a distance, trying vainly to be exempted from the draft. To avoid induction he served in the merchant marine. That was

a dangerous strategy: two of the three ships he served on were lost. In addition, he was drafted anyway. Upon his discharge from the army in 1946 he joined People's Songs, another radical music association. It too failed because of the Communist connection, which gave even more offense during the Cold War than earlier.

Pete Seeger organized a folk-singing group called The Weavers in 1948, and for several years it produced one hit record after another. Though Guthrie was not a Weaver, their success helped his music. His "So Long, It's Been Good to Know You" became one of their most popular numbers. But The Weavers were soon blacklisted, and the vogue for popularized folk music disappeared with them. By this time Guthrie was visibly failing, and in 1952 Huntington's chorea, a gradual but invariably fatal disease of the nervous system, was diagnosed. He died of it on October 3, 1967 in New York City.

Though a poor musician and erratic performer, Guthrie wrote an estimated 1,000 songs which have earned him a secure place in musical history. When he was discovered, folk music had few fans except radicals and a handful of admirers and musicologists. Guthrie and The Weavers were responsible for its brief popularity in the late 1940s and early 1950s and influenced the greater following it developed ten years later. Though folk music became less popular, it continued to exist, and Guthrie's legacy is very much a part of it.

Guthrie's legend is harder to assess. He was famous among leftists in the 1940s, and by the 1960s, though hospitalized and unable to speak, he had become a mythic figure. Bob Dylan, before he himself became famous as the leading composer of political songs, made a pilgrimage to Guthrie's bedside. Guthrie's reputation was based on his authentic folk origins and hobo inclinations, his remarkable talents as a writer and composer, and a romantic appreciation of his politics. This last was especially misplaced. Guthrie's political instincts were populist, nourished by the indigenous American socialism that flourished briefly in Oklahoma before and during World War I. He was influenced too by the Industrial Workers of the World, the fabled Wobblies, some of whom he met in his travels. But he early became associated with the Communist Party and, though never subject to party discipline (or any other kind), faithfully followed the Communist line during its worst phases from the 1930s through the Korean War.

Further Reading

An honest though politically unsophisticated biography is Joe Klein, *Woody Guthrie: A Life* (1980). Guthrie's own memoir, *Bound for Glory* (1943), bears only a poetic relation to the truth and ends before he had gained any reputation. His miscellaneous writings, all edited by other people, include *Born To Win* (1965), *Seeds of Man* (1976), and *The Woody Guthrie Songbook* (1976). □

Alexander M. Haig, Jr.

Alexander M. Haig, Jr. (born 1924), American military leader and diplomat, served as secretary of state and as adviser to two Republican presidents.

According to a *TIME* special story on Alexander Haig in 1984, "Few American public figures have had such tempestuous careers. Alexander M. Haig, Jr. has spent much of his life in war zones—bureaucratic and geopolitical, as well as the kind for which he prepared in the U.S. Military Academy at West Point: Viet Nam, where he served as a battalion and brigade commander; as the indispensable aide-de-camp to National Security Adviser Henry Kissinger; as White House Chief of Staff during the climax of Watergate; and, after Richard Nixon's presidency fell, as Supreme Allied Commander in Europe. . . . But it was during his tenure as Ronald Reagan's Secretary of State that Haig found himself most embattled."

Haig was born in Bala-Cynwyd, Pennsylvania, a comfortable suburb of Philadelphia, on December 2, 1924, the elder of two sons of Alexander Meigs and Regina Anne Haig. He attended St. Matthias parochial school in Bala-Cynwyd and St. Joseph's preparatory school in Philadelphia, graduating from Lower Merion High School in 1942. Haig's father, an assistant city solicitor of Philadelphia, died when Haig was ten. Using savings from various afterschool jobs, Haig was able to enroll in Notre Dame in 1942.

After two years of reasonably serious study at Notre Dame, Haig obtained an appointment to West Point in 1944, thus realizing his childhood ambition of a military career. That career was to be far more spectacular than Haig's academic performance would suggest: he graduated in 1947 as the 217th ranked cadet in a class of 310. The 22-year old second lieutenant went first to the general com-

bined arms course at Fort Riley, Kansas, and then to the Armored School at Fort Knox, Kentucky. Thereafter, he was assigned to the First Cavalry Division, then performed occupation duty and lackadaisical training in Japan. He married Patricia Antoinette Fox, the daughter of General Alonzo Fox, once his commanding officer, in May 1950. They had three children.

Haig early attracted the attention of highranking superiors, serving as administrative assistant to the chief of staff of the Far East Command and, during the early months of the Korean War, as aide to the X Corps commander. Promoted to captain in late 1950, he saw combat on several occasions and took part in the Inchon landings.

A bout with hepatitis resulted in Haig's reassignment to an armored unit at Fort Knox. After completing the advanced course there he served on the faculty of West Point and pursued graduate work in business administration at Columbia University. Thereafter, his career gained momentum. He served as S-3 (operations) of an armored battalion in West Germany, earned promotion to major in 1957, and spent 1958-1959 as a staff officer at USAEUR (United States Army in Europe). Haig then spent a year (1959-1960) at the Naval War College, took an M.A. in international relations from Georgetown University in 1961, and was promoted to lieutenant colonel in 1962.

Haig's staff service from 1962 to 1964 in the office of "DCSOPS," the deputy chief of staff for military operations, was a pivotal point in his career. When Cyrus R. Vance was named deputy secretary of defense in 1964, he took along this polished Pennsylvanian as his deputy special assistant. While dealing with a wide range of policy issues relating to such diverse areas as Berlin, the intervention in the Dominican Republic, and Cuba, Haig handled interagency politics and diplomatic crises with tact and impressive efficiency. **399**

This performance led to, first, a year at the Army War College, time as a battalion commander in Vietnam (and the Distinguished Service Cross during an engagement near An Loc), and brigade command.

Following promotion to colonel and another stint at West Point, Haig returned to Washington in 1969 as chief military assistant to National Security Adviser Henry Kissinger. His fortunes rose with the aggressive Kissinger, who swiftly became President Nixon's principal adviser on international security issues. Haig proved an invaluable "chief of staff" to Kissinger and soon began to deal directly with the White House. Preferring to work in anonymity, he served, as one journalist noted, "as gatekeeper to the summit." Promoted to brigadier general and then rapidly to major general, Haig was centrally involved with arrangements for Nixon's visit to China and the Vietnam peace initiative.

Haig moved into the spotlight and controversy when President Nixon promoted him over some 240 more senior officers to be a four-star general and the Army's vice-chief of staff. Nixon's action to push Haig into the military's front rank was consonant with the effort to get the "President's men" into positions of authority in various federal agencies. However, he was soon to return to the White House, serving as special assistant to the president in 1973-1974. In the months after the Watergate break-in, Haig, once termed "the ultimate professional," played a vital role for a beleaguered President Nixon. It is not coincidental that Haig was instrumental in the negotiations leading to Nixon's resignation in August 1974 and to Gerald Ford's accession to the presidency. Soon afterwards, Haig was named commander-in-chief, United States European Command, and supreme allied commander. He spent the next five years at the North Atlantic Treaty Organization (NATO), retiring in 1979 to become head of United Technologies Corporation. It appeared that a remarkable career in military administration had closed.

Alexander Haig's industrial sojourn ended with the election of his admirer Ronald Reagan as president in 1980. Against the advice of some intimates, Reagan chose Haig—whose impeccable military record, staunch anti-Communism, and links to the Republican establishment were great assets—to be his secretary of state. A sequence of stormy confirmation hearings occurred in January 1981, setting the tone for Haig's 18-month tenure as secretary of state. Critics charged that he was unqualified intellectually and emotionally for the position of chief proponent of United States foreign policy interests.

During his brief time at the helm, Haig battled with impressive vigor, if little apparent success, with his colleagues in the Reagan administration *and* for a tough stance toward the Soviet Union and its Third World clients. Obsessed with "turf" issues, Haig will be remembered for his controversial raising of the issue of executive authority in the aftermath of the attempted assassination of President Reagan. He devoted so much time to defending the prerogatives of the secretary of state against all comers (though, principally, the national security adviser) that the agenda of unfinished business at State began to alarm even the presi-

dent. Haig's pugnacity and dogmatic views on policy toward the Soviet Union and public stumbles on such matters as Afghanistan, Poland, Lebanon, the Falklands crisis, and Nicaragua eventually eroded Reagan's confidence in him.

On his side, Haig described Reagan's close advisers as "foreign policy amateurs" who cared only about the domestic political effects of global issues. His resignation as secretary of state, which finally came on June 25, 1982, ended what had become an impossible situation. Alexander Haig returned to private office bloodied but (as his memoirs, *Caveat: Realism, Reagan, and Foreign Policy*, published in 1984, make clear) unbowed by the experience. He returned to politics long enough to try to secure the Republican nomination for president in 1988 but dropped out early when it became apparent he did not have the support to win the nomination. He remained active as a speaker on foreign policy issues, but his focus shifted from politics to private business. He was hired by the international consulting firm of Worldwide Associates, Inc. and became chairman and president of that organization.

Haig is a key player in plans to build a controversial, multi-billion dollar natural gas pipeline from Central Asia across Iran into Turkey. He is co-chairman of US-CIS Ventures Inc., the Washington, D.C.-based company that is overseeing the pipeline project. Haig believes the area of Turkmenistan has tremendous, untapped oil reserves, and that by enabling the people of Turkmenistan to utilize them, he is helping them become more independent of Russia.

Haig is also a member of the Board of Directors of America Online, Inc., Interneuron Pharmaceuticals Inc., and MGM Grand Inc., and is on the American Board of Trustees of the A.F. Burns Fellowship. Haig's most current endeavor involves Sky Station International, a start-up company based in Chantilly, Virginia, that plans to offer inexpensive phone service and high-speed Internet access to consumers worldwide. Haig's son Alex acts as president of the company, which plans to float 250 inexpensive platforms suspended by Hindenburg-like airships, rather than launch satellites as its competitors have planned. This would result in a project costing only $800 millon dollars, compared to the billions of dollars a satellite project would require. Haig and his son hope to have the system deployed within the decade.

Further Reading

For additional information on Haig see his memoirs, *Caveat: Realism, Reagan, and Foreign Policy* (1984); and *Inner Circles: How America Changed the World: A Memoir* (1992); He is prominently mentioned in the two volumes of Henry Kissinger's memoirs: *The White House Years* (1979) and *Years of Upheaval* (1982). Haig is listed in *Who's Who in America* (1996); and *Who's Who in the World* (1996). Also see *Business Week* (June 3, 1996); *New York Times* (June 5, 1997); *Washington Post* (January 20, 1995). □

David Halberstam

American journalist and author David Halberstam (born 1934) was awarded the Pulitzer Prize in 1964 for his international reporting of the Vietnam War.

David Halberstam is a versatile author who has published more than 16 books on diverse subjects such as civil rights, the world economy, the auto industry, and the war in Vietnam. He also writes about sports topics, such as basketball, baseball, and amateur rowing. Halberstam's best-selling books are characterized by voluminous research and an anecdotal, novelistic narrative style. His work has been reproduced for television and has been used as reference material and as text in the classroom.

David Halberstam was born April 10, 1934, to Charles A. and Blanche (Levy) Halberstam. His father was a surgeon and his mother worked as a teacher. The family moved around frequently when Halberstam was a child, following Charles Halberstam's military career. David Halberstam spent his youth in such cities as El Paso, Texas, Rochester, Minnesota, and Winsted, Connecticut. After his father's return from service in Europe during World War II, the family again relocated, this time to Westchester County in New York. Halberstam attended Roosevelt High School in Yonkers, New York, participating in track and writing for the school newspaper. He graduated in 1951 and was accepted at Harvard University as an undergraduate.

Halberstam did not have the best grades as a student at Harvard, but he did achieve the prestigious assignment of managing editor of the *Harvard Crimson,* the school's daily newspaper. The paper was published on a demanding deadline six days a week for an intellectual readership; it was a good beginning for the student journalist. When he graduated from college in 1955, Halberstam admitted he wanted to improve his interviewing skills. He told Brian Lamb, the host of C-Span's *Booknotes,* "I had to learn how to go out and interview ordinary people." He did that working at the West Point, Mississippi, *Daily Times Leader.* His modest beginning at the smallest daily in Mississippi taught Halberstam how to "deal with ordinary people, to listen to them, to see the value in people who didn't agree with the same things I agreed and how they worked, what their lives were," he recounted to Lamb.

Within a year Halberstam moved to the *Nashville Tennessean* where he continued to hone his skills by modeling himself upon the best reporters. He covered civil rights issues and was enthralled by a sense of violence. Halberstam told *People Weekly* writer Christopher P. Andersen, "Trucks would try and run us off the road, we'd be threatened with guns." In general he felt his experience in Tennessee was worth it "because it validated all the reasons anybody becomes a reporter in the first place."

Halberstam left the *Nashville Tennessean* in 1960 as a confident reporter. He accepted a position with the *New York Times.* In his first months with the well-known paper he covered Washington and within his first year there he was transferred to cover the war in the Congo. By 1962, Halberstam was in Vietnam.

Foreign Correspondent

Initially, Halberstam supported the United States' involvement in Vietnam. As told to *People Weekly* writer Andersen, "We were there to help another country against encroachment from within, and I did not dissent. I believed in the cause that was at stake and in the men who were fighting it." But when the Vietnam policy became more controversial, when Washington ignored assessments reported by their advisers, Halberstam started to question and criticize. Journalist William Prochnau covered the Vietnam War for *The Seattle Times.* He met Halberstam in Vietnam and described him to Lamb of *Booknotes* as "a brilliant brat" who was working for "the dominant and most prestigious newspaper in the world." Prochnau further explained to Lamb, "He was twenty-eight years old. He was a man of great passions, great angers. He felt the government was deluding itself as much as deluding the American people. It drove him to fits." Halberstam's courage enabled him to report both sides of the Vietnam experience. He was awarded the Pulitzer Prize for international reporting in 1964.

Author

About this time Halberstam began his career as a nonfiction author. He published *The Making of a Quagmire: America and Vietnam During the Kennedy Era* in 1965. This is his first nonfiction attempt to analyze American involvement in Vietnam. In 1967, Halberstam left the *New York Times.* He pursued a position as contributing editor of *Harper's* magazine. Then he published *The Unfinished Od-*

yssey of Robert Kennedy in 1969. By the time he published *Ho* in 1971, Halberstam knew the Vietnam war was lost. He returned to the subject that was an essential part of his life for several years and published *The Best and the Brightest* in 1972. Halberstam asked how the gifted leaders assembled by the Kennedy and Johnson administrations could have allowed such a tragic involvement in Vietnam. The book was his first best-seller.

The Powers That Be

In 1974, Halberstam had been a journalist for 20 years. The Watergate scandal was widely reported and Halberstam perceived, "that in both Vietnam and Watergate the principal antagonists were not the president and the Congress, or the president and the opposition party but the president and the media." Sharing his opinion with *BOMC Today* he added, "How that had happened seemed to me a rich question in its possibilities." Halberstam's speculation grew into another best seller, *The Powers That Be,* published in 1979. The book concentrates on four news reporting giants: CBS, *Time,* the *Washington Post,* and the *Los Angeles Times.* Halberstam contends that the media helped shape opinion and recent politics. He pointed out to *People Weekly* writer Andersen, why he chose those four reporting companies. "CBS was, and probably still is, the best network. *Time* is the most important opinion-shaping magazine. The *Washington Post* uncovered Watergate. And the *Los Angeles Times* invented Richard Nixon."

The Amateurs

Halberstam is a talented writer who can work on more than one project at a time. While conducting research for a major work in progress he will take a break and direct his strong investigative reporting skills to another passion: sports. Halberstam has been described as the ultimate fan. In 1981 he published *The Breaks of the Game,* a book about professional basketball and followed that in 1985 with a book about non-professional rowing called *The Amateurs.* Halberstam received his inspiration for the book while watching a pre-Olympic event on television. Amazed by the hype surrounding the athletes, Halberstam wondered if amateur athletics meant only money, endorsements, or fame. He set out to find athletes that were involved in sports for the love of the sport and not on a quest for fame or fortune. He found what he wanted in a group of amateur rowers. Sculling is an obscure sport and the success of the book surprised and pleased Halberstam who confided to Lamb on *Booknotes,* "I have a small book that I did about four young men rowing for an Olympic medal that I really love." He said *The Amateurs* "is my inner, secret favorite."

The Reckoning

While delivering *The Breaks of the Game* and *The Amateurs,* Halberstam researched and wrote *The Reckoning.* Published in 1986, *The Reckoning* was "by far the hardest book I have ever done," Halberstam told *BOMC Today.* "I wanted to do a comparative study of an American and a Japanese auto company." The book also includes the economic and cultural differences between the two coun-

tries. True to his style, Halberstam interviewed everyone in the auto industry. "I came to like the auto men of Detroit. I found these men interesting, reflective and generous with their time." He spent eight months in Tokyo, a country that, in his opinion, is receptive to receiving information but is reluctant to disclose it. "The burden was not one of language but of culture. At first I found the Nissan officials unreceptive and only superficially cooperative to what I was doing."

The Summer of '49

In 1989 Halberstam took a look at the last radio era in baseball and published *The Summer of '49.* The book chronicles the 1949 pennant race between the Boston Red Sox and the New York Yankees in a time before television and before the super-star contracts. "When you hear a game on the radio and you form a mythic vision of a DiMaggio or a Williams," Halberstam recalled to Lamb on *Booknotes,* "They live larger because you create the myth for them in the fantasy of your mind."

The Next Century

Working with material he researched for *The Reckoning* Halberstam delivered an essay in 1991 called *The Next Century.* This essay is about Americans' complacent attitude toward declining education and economic productivity. Critics consider the title a misnomer because, the essay concentrates on America since Vietnam and makes no predictions for the coming century.

Social Historian: *The Fifties*

Having told the story of America under pressure, Halberstam moved to a time when America was rich and everything seemed to work. *The Fifties,* published in 1993 includes sections on politics, civil rights, and the McCarthy period. Also covered is the impact television made on society. "There was an innocence about television," Halberstam explained to Lamb on *Booknotes.* "It really changed everything." As television developed, the pace of life suddenly sped up. There were commercials and politicians and the ideals of someone's vision of the American family coming into peoples homes. Of the time frame, *Wall Street Journal* writer Dorothy Rabinowitz recalls, "We are speaking here of a decade whose creative ferment, and level of art and culture, has never since been equaled."

Halberstam discussed with Lamb on *Booknotes* the phenomenon that "When people talk about America in the '50s . . . they talk about it as an innocent time. . . . Yet the '50s were not that innocent." The *Wall Street Journal* writer Rabinowitz contends, "This is the era now routinely described as the age of conformity, the time of hula hoops and tail fins, and sterile obedience."

October 1964: Baseball History

Moving ahead to the 1960s Halberstam returned to baseball in *October 1964,* published in 1994. Here he covers the World Series competition between the St. Louis Cardinals and the New York Yankees. The story relates the rise of the St. Louis team and the decline of the Yankee dynasty. Some historians concur that the history of baseball offers insight into labor law, race relations, urban history, and the development of a leisure industry. *October 1964,* among other books, is required reading for a history class at the University of South Florida.

The Children

While the 1960s was a decade of rich sports anecdotes it is also the decade of real social revolutions. His book titled *The Children,* published in 1998, chronicles the lives of some of the kids who challenged social order. Halberstam was a witness to the first sit-in in his early years as journalist for the *Nashville Tennessean* and regularly covered the civil rights movement for the paper. Speaking to Lamb on *Booknotes,* Halberstam said, "The first sit-ins started there, and it was a very interesting group of young black kids." Halberstam was close to the kids in age and earned their trust. He tracked their lives and tells of their experiences then and now. In a *Booklist* review, Mary Carroll noted, "*The Children* is both a survey of five central years of the civil rights movement (1960-65) and a sterling example of the genre with which Halberstam is most closely identified: collective biography."

In 1999, as the NBA (National Basketball Association) started a new season without superstar Michael Jordan, Halberstam returned to his interest in sports with the release of *Playing for Keeps: Michael Jordan and the World He Made.* The book, following Jordan's retirement from professional basketball, offers both nostalgia and an evaluation of Jordan's exemplary career.

Halberstam's typically long books are always well-researched and maintain a narrative flair that holds a reader's interest. His book topics develop from within himself. Halberstam said to *BOMC Today,* "My books have always been the result of my own curiosity: the questions I answer for other people are the questions I seek to answer for myself."

Additional Sources

Contemporary Authors, New Revision Series, Volume 45, Gale, 1995.

Lamb, Brian, *Booknotes,* Times Books, 1997.

Booklist, January 1, 1998.

National Review, February 22, 1999.

People Weekly, November 4, 1985.

Wall Street Journal, November 24, 1997.

"Booknotes Transcript," *C-Span,* July 11, 1993, http://www.booknotes.org/transcripts/10198.htm (April 1998).

Halberstam, David, "David Halberstam Talks about *The Reckoning,*" *BOMC Today,* 1987, http://www.bomc.com/ows-bin/owa/rr_authorsintheirownwords_sub?intid=12&uid= (April 1998). □

Alex Haley

Alex Haley (1921-1992) is the celebrated author of *Roots: The Saga of an American Family* (1976). By April 1977 almost two million hardcover copies of the book had been

sold and 130 million people had seen all or part of the eight-episode television series. *Roots* is thus considered by many critics a classic in African American literature and culture.

Haley, who was born in Ithaca, New York, and raised in the small town of Henning, Tennessee, became interested in his ancestry while listening to colorful stories told by his family. One story in particular, about an African ancestor who refused to be called by his slave name "Toby" and declared instead that his name was "Kintay," impressed Haley deeply. Young Haley was so fascinated by this account that he later spent twelve years researching and documenting the life of "Kunta Kinte," the character in his famous *Roots.* School records indicate that Haley was not an exceptional student. At the age of eighteen he joined the U.S. Coast Guard and began a twenty-year career in the service. He practiced his writing, at first only to alleviate boredom on the ship, and soon found himself composing love letters for his shipmates to send home to their wives and girlfriends. He wrote serious pieces as well and submitted them to various magazines.

Upon retiring from the Coast Guard, Haley decided to become a full-time writer and journalist. His first book, *The Autobiography of Malcolm X* (1965), which he cowrote with Malcolm X, was widely acclaimed upon its publication. The work sold over five million copies and launched Haley's writing career. Malcolm X was at first reluctant to work with Haley. He later told the writer: "I don't completely trust anyone . . . you I trust about twenty-five percent." Critics praised Haley for sensitively handling Malcolm X's volatile life, and the book quickly became required reading in many schools. Two weeks after *The Autobiography of Malcolm X* was completed, Haley began work on his next project, *Roots.* The tale chronicles the life of Kunta Kinte, a proud African who is kidnapped from his village in West Africa, forced to endure the middle passage—the brutal shipment of Africans to be sold in the Americas—on the slave ship *Lord Ligonier,* and made a slave on the Waller plantation in the United States. To authenticate Kunta's life and that of Kunta's grandson, Chicken George, Haley visited archives, libraries, and research repositories on three continents. He even reenacted Kunta's experience on the *Lord Ligonier.* "[Haley] somehow scourged up some money and flew to Liberia where he booked passage on the first U. S. bound ship," an *Ebony* interviewer related. "Once at sea, he spent the night lying on a board in the hold of the ship, stripped to his underwear to get a rough idea of what his African ancestor might have experienced."

Although critics generally lauded *Roots,* they seemed unsure whether to treat the work as a novel or as a historical account. While the narrative is based on factual events, the dialogue, thoughts, and emotions of the characters are fictionalized. Haley himself described the book as "faction," a mixture of fact and fiction. Most critics concurred and evaluated *Roots* as a blend of history and entertainment. Despite the fictional characterizations, Willie Lee Rose suggested in the *New York Review of Books* that Kunta Kinte's parents Omoro and Binte "could possibly become the African proto-parents of millions of Americans who are going to admire their dignity and grace." *Newsweek* applauded Haley's decision to fictionalize: "Instead of writing a scholarly monograph of little social impact, Haley has written a blockbuster in the best sense—a book that is bold in concept and ardent in execution, one that will reach millions of people and alter the way we see ourselves."

Some voiced concern, however—especially at the time of the television series—that racial tension in America would be aggravated by *Roots.* While *Time* did report several incidents of racial violence following the telecast, it commented that "most observers thought that in the long term, *Roots* would improve race relations, particularly because of the televised version's profound impact on whites. . . . A broad consensus seemed to be emerging that *Roots* would spur black identity, and hence black pride, and eventually pay important dividends." Some black leaders viewed *Roots* "as the most important civil rights event since the 1965 march on Selma," according to *Time.* Vernon Jordan, executive director of the National Urban League, called it "the single most spectacular educational experience in race relations in America." Speaking of the appeal of *Roots* among blacks, Haley added: "The blacks who are buying books are not buying them to go out and fight someone, but because they want to know who they are. . . . [The] book has touched a strong, subliminal chord."

For months after the publication of *Roots* in October 1976, Haley signed at least five hundred copies of the book daily, spoke to an average of six thousand people a day, and traveled round trip coast-to-coast at least once a week. Scarcely two years later, *Roots* had already won 271

awards, and its television adaptation had been nominated for a recordbreaking thirty-seven Emmys. Over eight million copies of the book were in print, and the text was translated into twenty-six languages. In addition to fame and fortune, *Roots* also brought Haley controversy. In 1977 two published authors, Margaret Walker and Harold Courlander, alleged separately that Haley plagiarized their work in *Roots.* Charges brought by Walker were later dropped, but Haley admitted that he unknowingly lifted three paragraphs from Courlander's *The African* (1968). A settlement was reached whereby Haley paid Courlander $500,000. The same year other accusations also arose. Mark Ottaway in *The Sunday Times* questioned Haley's research methods and the credibility of his informants, accusing Haley of "bending" data to fit his objectives. Gary B. and Elizabeth Shown Mills also challenged some of Haley's assertions. Writing in 1981 in *The Virginia Magazine of History and Biography,* they cited evidence that there was indeed a slave named Toby living on the Waller plantation. He was there, however, at least five years before the arrival of the *Lord Ligonier,* supposedly with Kunta on board.

Haley's supporters maintain that Haley never claimed *Roots* as fact or history. And even in the presence of controversy, the public image of *Roots* appears not to have suffered. It is still widely read in schools, and many college and university history and literature programs consider it an essential part of their curriculum. According to Haley himself, *Roots* is important not for its names and dates but as a reflection of human nature: "*Roots* is all of our stories. . . . It's just a matter of filling in the blanks . . . ; when you start talking about family, about lineage and ancestry, you are talking about every person on earth." Indeed, Haley's admirers contend, *Roots* remains a great book because it is the universal story of humankind's own search for its identity.

Additional Sources

The Black Press U.S.A., Iowa State University Press, 1990.

Contemporary Literary Criticism, Gale, Volume 8, 1978, Volume 12, 1980.

Dictionary of Literary Biography, Volume 38: *Afro-American Writers After 1955: Dramatists and Prose Writers,* Gale, 1985.

Black Collegian, September/October, 1985.

Christianity Today, May 6, 1977.

Ebony, April, 1977.

Forbes, February 15, 1977. □

Alexander Hamilton

The first U.S. secretary of the Treasury, Alexander Hamilton (1755-1804) was instrumental in developing the nation's first political party, the Federalists.

Alexander Hamilton's birth date is disputed, but he probably was born on Jan. 11, 1755, on the island of Nevis in the British West Indies. He was the illegitimate son of James Hamilton, a Scotsman, and Rachel Fawcett Lavien, daughter of a French Huguenot physician.

Hamilton's education was brief. He began working sometime between the ages of 11 and 13 as a clerk in a trading firm in St. Croix. In 1772 he left—perhaps encouraged and financed by his employers—to attend school in the American colonies. After a few months at an academy in New Jersey, he enrolled in King's College, New York City. Precocious enough to master most subjects without formal instruction and eager to win success and fame early in life, he left college in 1776 without graduating.

American Revolution

The outbreak of the American Revolution offered Hamilton the opportunity he craved. In March 1776 he became captain of a company of artillery and, a year later, a lieutenant colonel in the Continental Army and aide-de-camp to commanding general George Washington. Hamilton's ability was apparent, and he became one of Washington's most trusted advisers. Although he played no role in major military decisions, Hamilton's position was one of great responsibility. He drafted many of Washington's letters to high-ranking Army officers, the Continental Congress, and the states. He also was sent on important military missions and drafted major reports on the reorganization and reform of the Army. Despite the demands of his position, he found time for reading and reflection and expressed his ideas on economic policy and governmental debility in newspaper articles and in letters to influential public figures.

In February 1781, in a display of pique at a minor reprimand by Gen. Washington, Hamilton resigned his position. Earlier, on Dec. 14, 1780, he had married the daugh-

ter of Philip Schuyler, a member of one of New York's most distinguished families. In July 1781 Hamilton's persistent search for active military service was rewarded when Washington gave him command of a battalion of light infantry in the Marquis de Lafayette's corps. After the Battle of Yorktown, Hamilton returned to New York. In 1782, following a hasty apprenticeship, he was admitted to the bar.

During the Revolution, Hamilton's ideas on government, society, and economic matured. These were conditioned by his foreign birth, which obviated a strong attachment to a particular state or locality, and by his presence at Washington's headquarters, where he could see the war as a whole. Like the general himself, Hamilton was deeply disturbed that the conduct of the war was impeded by the weakness of Congress and by state and local jealousies. It was this experience rather than any theoretical commitment to a particular form of government that structured Hamilton's later advocacy of a strong central government.

Confederation Era

From the end of the Revolution to the inauguration of the first government under the Constitution, Hamilton tirelessly opposed what he described as the "dangerous prejudices in the particular states opposed to those measures which alone can give stability and prosperity to the Union." Though his extensive law practice won him recognition as one of New York's most distinguished attorneys, public affairs were his major concern.

Attending the Continental Congress as a New York delegate from November 1782 through July 1783, he unsuccessfully labored, along with James Madison and other nationalists, to invest the Confederation with powers equal to the needs of postrevolutionary America. Convinced that the pervasive commitment to states' rights obviated reform of the Articles of Confederation, Hamilton began to advocate a stronger and more efficient central government. As one of the 12 delegates to the Annapolis Convention of 1786, he drafted its resolution calling for a Constitutional Convention "to devise such further provisions as shall appear . . . necessary to render the Constitution of the Federal Government adequate to the exigencies of the Union. . . ." Similarly, as a member of the New York Legislature in 1787, he was the eloquent spokesman for continental interests as opposed to state and local ones.

Ratification of the Constitution

Hamilton was one of the New York delegates to the Constitutional Convention, which sat in Philadelphia from May to September 1787. Although he served on several important committees, his performance was disappointing, particularly when measured against his previous (and subsequent) accomplishments. His most important speech called for a government close to the English model, one so high-toned that it was unacceptable to most of the delegates.

Hamilton's contribution to the ratification of the Constitution was far more important. In October 1787 he determined to write a series of essays on behalf of the proposed Constitution. First published in New York City newspapers under the pseudonym "Publius" and collectively designated *The Federalist,* these essays were designed to persuade the people of New York to ratify the Constitution. Though *The Federalist* was written in collaboration with John Jay and James Madison, Hamilton wrote 51 of the 85 essays. First published in book form in 1788, the *Federalist* essays have been republished in many editions and languages. They constitute one of America's most original and important contributions to political philosophy and remain today the authoritative contemporary exposition of the meaning of the cryptic clauses of the U.S. Constitution. At the New York ratifying convention in 1788, Hamilton led in defending the proposed Constitution, which, owing measurably to Hamilton's labors, New York ratified.

Secretary of the Treasury

On Sept. 11, 1789, some 6 months after the new government was inaugurated, Hamilton was commissioned the nation's first secretary of the Treasury. This was the most important of the executive departments because the new government's most pressing problem was to devise ways of paying the national debt—domestic and foreign—incurred during the Revolution.

Hamilton's program, his single most brilliant achievement, also created the most bitter controversy of the first decade of American national history. It was spelled out between January 1790 and December 1791 in three major reports on the American economy: "Report on the Public Credit"; "Report on a National Bank"; and "Report on Manufactures."

In the first report Hamilton recommended payment of both the principal and interest of the public debt at par and the assumption of state debts incurred during the American Revolution. The assumption bill was defeated initially, but Hamilton rescued it by an alleged bargain with Thomas Jefferson and Madison for the locale of the national capital. Both the funding and assumption measures became law in 1791 substantially as Hamilton had proposed them.

Hamilton's "Report on a National Bank" was designed to facilitate the establishment of public credit and to enhance the powers of the new national government. Although some members of Congress doubted this body's power to charter such a great quasi-public institution, the majority accepted Hamilton's argument and passed legislation establishing the First Bank of the United States. Before signing the measure, President Washington requested his principal Cabinet officers, Jefferson and Hamilton, to submit opinions on its constitutionality. Arguing that Congress had exceeded its powers, Jefferson submitted a classic defense of a strict construction of the Constitution; affirming the Bank's constitutionality, Hamilton submitted the best argument in American political literature for a broad interpretation of the Constitution.

The "Report on Manufactures," his only major report which Congress rejected, was perhaps Hamilton's most important state paper. The culmination of his economic program, it is the clearest statement of his economic philosophy. The protection and encouragement of infant industries, he argued, would produce a better balance between agriculture

and manufacturing, promote national self-sufficiency, and enhance the nation's wealth and power.

Hamilton also submitted other significant reports which Congress accepted, including a plan for an excise on spirits and a report on the establishment of a Mint. Hamilton's economic program was not original (it drew heavily, for example, upon British practice), but it was an innovative and creative application of European precedent and American experience to the practical needs of the new country.

First Political Party

Hamilton's importance during this period was not confined to his work as finance minister. As the virtual "prime minister" of Washington's administration, he was consulted on a wide range of problems, foreign and domestic. He deserves to be ranked, moreover, as the leader of the country's first political party, the Federalist party. Hamilton himself, like most of his contemporaries, railed against parties and "factions," but when the debate over his fiscal policies revealed a deep political division among the members of Congress, Hamilton boldly assumed leadership of the proadministration group, the Federalists, just as Jefferson provided leadership for the Democratic Republicans.

Prominent Lawyer and Army General

Because of the pressing financial demands of his growing family, Hamilton retired from office in January 1795. Resuming his law practice, he soon became the most distinguished member of the New York City bar. His major preoccupation remained public affairs, however, and he continued as President Washington's adviser. The latter's famous "Farewell Address" (1796), for example, was largely based on Hamilton's draft. Nor could Hamilton remain aloof from politics. In the election of 1796 he attempted to persuade the Federalist electors to cast a unanimous vote for John Adam's running mate, Thomas Pinckney.

The high regard in which most of the country's leading Federalists held Hamilton was matched by the dislike and distrust with which many others—notably the Republicans—viewed him. He was ambitious, arrogant, and opinionated. He was also indiscreet. For example, to refute a baseless charge by James Reynolds and others that as secretary of the Treasury he was guilty of corruption, he needlessly published a defense which included a confession of adultery with Mrs. Reynolds. Such an admission undoubtedly diminished the possibility of political preferment.

During the presidency of John Adams, however, Hamilton continued to wield considerable national influence, for members of Adams's Cabinet often sought and followed his advice. In 1798 they cooperated with George Washington to secure Hamilton's appointment—over Adams's strong opposition—as inspector general and second in command of the newly augmented U.S. Army, which was preparing for a possible war against France. Since Washington declined active command, organizing and recruiting the "Provisional Army" fell to Hamilton. His military career abruptly came to an end in 1800 after John Adams, in the face of the opposition of his Cabinet and other Federalist leaders (Hamilton among them), sent a peace mission to France that negotiated a settlement of the major issues.

Retirement and the Fatal Duel

Hamilton's role in the presidential campaign of 1800 not only was a disservice to his otherwise distinguished career but also seriously wounded the Federalist party. Convinced of John Adam's ineptitude, Hamilton rashly published a long Philippic which characterized the President as a man possessed by "vanity without bounds, and a jealousy capable of discoloring every object," with a "disgusting egotism" and an "ungovernable discretion of . . . temper." Instead of discrediting Adams, the pamphlet promoted election of the Republican candidates, Jefferson and Aaron Burr. When the Jefferson-Burr tie went for decision to the House of Representatives, however, Hamilton regained his balance. Convinced that Jefferson would not undermine executive authority, Hamilton also believed that Burr was "the most unfit and dangerous man of the community." He accordingly used his considerable influence to persuade congressional leaders to select Jefferson.

Although his interest in national policies and politics was unabated, Hamilton's role in national affairs after 1801 diminished. He remained a prominent figure in the Federalist party, however, and published his opinions on public affairs in the *New York Evening Post*. He was still an ardent nationalist and in 1804 severely condemned the rumored plot of New England and New York Federalists to dismember the Union by forming a Northern confederacy. Believing Aaron Burr to be a party to this scheme, Hamilton actively opposed the Vice President's bid for the New York governorship. He was successful, and Burr, now out of favor with the Jefferson administration and discredited in his own state, charged that Hamilton's remarks had impugned his honor. Burr challenged Hamilton to a duel. Although Hamilton was reluctant, he believed that his "ability to be in future useful" demanded his acceptance. After putting his personal affairs in order, he met Burr at dawn on July 11, 1804, on the New Jersey side of the Hudson River. The two exchanged shots, and Hamilton fell, mortally wounded. Tradition has it that he deliberately misdirected his fire, leaving himself an open target for Burr's bullet. Hamilton was carried back to New York City, where he died the next afternoon.

Further Reading

Henry Cabot Lodge, ed., *The Works of Alexander Hamilton* (2d ed., 12 vols., 1903), will be replaced by Harold C. Syrett and Jacob E. Cooke, eds., *Papers,* 15 volumes of which have been published (1961-1969). Hamilton's definitive biography is Broadus Mitchell's meticulous *Alexander Hamilton* (2 vols., 1957-1962). John C. Miller, *Alexander Hamilton* (1959), is an excellent one-volume life. Useful biographies are David Loth, *Alexander Hamilton: Portrait of a Prodigy* (1939), and Nathan Schachner, *Alexander Hamilton* (1946). Also recommended are Claude G. Bowers, *Jefferson and Hamilton: The Struggle for Democracy in America* (1925), and Richard B. Morris, *Alexander Hamilton and the Founding of the Nation* (1957). □

Armand Hammer

Armand Hammer (1898-1990) was a physician turned entrepreneur and art collector whose natural talent for business made him a billionaire. His early, helpful relations with the Soviet Union made him an international figure.

Armand Hammer was born in New York City in 1898, one of three sons of Julius and Rose Robinson Hammer. Julius Hammer was the son of a Russian emigrant who worked his way through the Columbia University medical school, developed a successful medical practice, and then diversified into the wholesale drug business and retail drug stores. Armand Hammer also attended Columbia University, receiving his B.S. in 1919 and then entering the College of Physicians and Surgeons. While at the university Hammer worked with his two brothers to save and expand his father's pharmaceutical business. After World War I Hammer talked his family into buying up medical supplies after prices had plummeted. When the prices rose, the family earned a fortune; Hammer himself earned one million dollars. Hammer still found time to complete his medical degree in 1921, graduating among the top ten students in his class.

Impatient to begin medical practice and hearing of epidemics and famines in the Soviet Union, Hammer purchased a surplus army field hospital and set off to help. Upon arriving in Moscow in 1921 he concluded that the major problem was lack of food, and, using his natural business talent, he arranged a trade of Russian furs and caviar for a shipload of American wheat. He was invited to meet Lenin, who encouraged him to abandon medicine and, instead, to help the Soviet Union build up its economy. Lenin offered Hammer a concession to operate an asbestos mine in Siberia, which he was able to make profitable after several years. Hammer was also able to obtain sales concessions for several American firms, including Ford Motor Company, United States Rubber, Allis-Chalmers, and Underwood Typewriter. In 1925 the Soviet Union decided to handle its own foreign trade and offered Hammer a manufacturing concession in compensation for his agency, Allied American Corporation, which by then included 38 American businesses. Hammer asked for the right to manufacture pencils, at that time imported and expensive. He organized the A. Hammer Pencil Company, lured away the production manufacturer of a German company, started to operate in six months, and made a profit of $1 million at the end of the first year.

As the Soviet experiment with capitalism came to a close in 1926, the government asked Hammer to sell back his asbestos and later his pencil concessions. With the help and advice of his brother Victor, who had taken a degree in art history at Princeton University, Hammer used his profits to purchase Czarist works of art, which were disdained by the Soviets. Armand and his brother organized the Hammer Galleries in New York City and brought the works back with them in 1930 to sell here. As a result of that experience Hammer developed a passion for collecting and in 1936 wrote a book titled *The Quest for the Romanoff Treasure.* Hammer was forced by the Great Depression to adopt the

radical technique of selling through department stores in order to move his merchandise. He used this same technique to dispose of a large portion of the William Randolph Hearst collection in 1940. He continued as president of the gallery into the 1980s.

Hammer also speculated successfully in Soviet promissory notes. Back in America, he cornered the market in Soviet oak barrel staves needed by the American liquor industry, reviving after the repeal of prohibition. He also saw opportunities in manufacturing the contents of the barrels. In 1940, noting a surplus of potatoes at the same time that there was a shortage of whiskey, he earned a multi-million dollar profit by turning the tubers into commercial alcohol and blended whiskey. He acquired 11 distillers and formed the J. W. Dant Distilling Company, making annual profits of $3 million before selling out to established distilleries in 1954.

Hammer married three times: Baroness Olga von Root in 1927 while he was in Europe; Angela Zevely in 1943, by whom he had a son, Julian; and Frances Barrett in 1956, with whom he retired to California. But retirement soon bored Hammer, and he began looking for new ventures. In 1957 he obtained control of the Mutual Broadcasting Company and turned it over for a profit. A year earlier he had agreed to finance two wildcat oil wells for tiny Occidental Petroleum Company, and when both were successful he increased his holdings and was soon named president and chairman of the board. The net worth of the company increased from $175,000 in 1957 to $300 million in 1967. Under Hammer's leadership Occidental diversified into

chemicals, coal, and fertilizers, and in 1973 he returned to his Soviet connection, signing a multi-billion dollar, 25-year chemical fertilizer agreement under which a fertilizer plant would be built in the Soviet Union from which Occidental would receive supplies for sale abroad.

Art collecting was Hammer's principal hobby starting in the 1920s, but his approach was always to share his collection with as many people as possible, based on his conviction that art is an important force for understanding among people of all cultures. In 1965 he donated a multi-million dollar collection of works by Dutch, Flemish, German, and Italian masters of the 15th through 17th centuries to the University of California at Los Angeles and other works to the Los Angeles County Museum of Art. In 1971 he added more paintings to the County Museum and gave a large group of old masters to the National Gallery of Art in Washington, D.C. In 1972 he donated a painting by Goya worth $1 million to the Hermitage Museum in Leningrad, which had none. Hammer also owned three important collections, including more than 100 works by such masters as Rembrandt, Renoir, and Rubens, which traveled for exhibition throughout the world.

Hammer's concern for understanding among peoples led him in 1962 to donate the former Campobello Island estate of President Franklin Roosevelt, whom Hammer served as an adviser during World War II, as an international peace park. He also sponsored international conferences to bring experts together to discuss solutions to problems of human rights and world peace. In 1982 he founded the Armand Hammer United World College of the American West in Montezuma, New Mexico, the only U.S. campus of a movement dedicated to enhancing world peace and understanding through education.

Another of Hammer's concerns was the effort to find a cure for cancer. He was a board member of the Eleanor Roosevelt Cancer Foundation starting in 1960. He endowed the Armand Hammer Center for Cancer Biology at the Salk Institute in La Jolla, California, in 1969 and sponsored the annual Armand Hammer Cancer Conference there. In 1982 he established the Hammer Prize for cancer research, a 10-year, $1 million program to reward the scientists who do the most each year to advance cancer research. Hammer also pledged a $1 million prize for a cure for cancer, and he served three terms as the chairman of the panel which advises the U.S. president on the status of cancer research in the United States.

In his 80s Hammer still put in 16-hour days, seven days a week. (He once remarked that he would be willing to pay Occidental Petroleum for the privilege of letting him work.) In 1986 he sponsored medical aid for the Russians injured in the Chernobyl nuclear catastrophe. Along with his humanitarian work, Hammer also left himself open to severe criticism regarding his use of funds from Occidental stockholders. It is said he used company funds for many personal amenities and to buy works of art. He earned a reputation as a ''teflon tycoon,'' to whom charges of improprieties did not stick, though in 1976 he pleaded guilty to making illegal contributions to the Nixon 1976 presidential campaign and was fined. Hammer spent much of the 1980s trying to remove the blot on his good name, and in 1989 George Bush granted him a presidential pardon. However, some people continued to speculate about Hammer's ethics and he received his share of criticism.

Hammer made his last public appearance on November 25, 1990, at the grand opening of The Armand Hammer Museum of Art and Culture Center in Los Angeles, located just behind the Occidental Petroleum headquarters. (The museum has since come under the direction of the University of California-Los Angeles.) He died only two weeks later at the age of 92. He had suffered from chronic anemia, bronchitis, prostate enlargement, kidney ailments, an irregular heartbeat, and, most fatally, bone marrow cancer.

Further Reading

Additional information may be found in Bob Considine, *The Remarkable Life of Dr. Armand Hammer* (1975); the autobiography *Hammer* (1987); and Steve Weinberg, *Armand Hammer: The Untold Story* (1989).

Additional Sources

Art News (June 1997).

Christie Brown, "The Master Cynic," *Forbes 400* (October 17, 1994; November 18, 1996).

Edward J. Epstein, "The Last Days of Armand Hammer," *New Yorker* (September 23, 1996). □

Oscar Clendenning Hammerstein, II

Oscar Clendenning Hammerstein II (1895-1960) was perhaps the most influential lyricist and librettist of the American theater. Major musicals for which he wrote the lyrics include *Showboat*, *South Pacific*, *The King and I*, and *The Sound of Music*.

Oscar Clendenning Hammerstein II was born into a great theatrical family on July 12, 1895, in New York City. His grandfather, Oscar I, was an opera impressario and showman. His father, William, was the manager of Hammerstein's Victoria, one of the most famous vaudeville theaters of its day. His uncle, Arthur, was a well known producer. All were famous in their own right, but all would be eclipsed by the success of Oscar II, the third generation theater Hammerstein. Oscar, or "Ockie" (his lifelong nickname), dabbled in theatrical activities as a youth, but when it came time for a career choice his father pushed him away from the theater. Oscar went to Columbia University in preparation for a career in law. It was at Columbia, however, that Oscar's career in theater actually began when, at age 19, he joined the Columbia University Players as a performer in the 1915 Varsity review *On Your Way*. He participated heavily in the Varsity shows for several years, first as a performer and later as a writer. It was at Columbia that Oscar first met the young man who would later collaborate with him and with Lorenz Hart, another Columbia alumnus: Richard Rodgers.

After Oscar's first year of law school, he convinced his uncle, Arthur, to hire him as an assistant stage manager on one of his upcoming shows. By 1919 he was promoted to production stage manager for all of Arthur's shows. In his position as production stage manager Oscar was able to do some writing and re-writing on scripts in development. Eventually he was writing musical comedies of his own. His first success as a librettist came in 1922 with *Wildflower*, written with Otto Harbach. A more major success in 1924, *Rose Marie*, written with Harbach, Rudolph Friml, and Herbert P. Stohart, led to his collaboration with composer Jerome Kern. Kern and Hammerstein had both been concerned with the "integrated musical," a musical in which the book, lyrics, and score all grow from a central idea and all contribute to the story line. They adapted Edna Ferber's sprawling novel about life on a Mississippi River boat into the landmark 1925 musical *Showboat*, with Kern composing the score and Hammerstein writing the book and lyrics. *Showboat* firmly established Oscar's success and reputation as a writer and lyricist.

In 1929 Oscar divorced his wife of 12 years, Myra Finn, and married Dorothy Blanchard Jacobson. The next decade turned out to be a happy one for Oscar personally, but unhappy professionally. He spent much of his time in Hollywood, working on contract to various studios. He discovered that he did not work well under the rigorous time demands of the movie industry, having achieved his greatest success with *Showboat's* one year writing period. In 1942 he returned to New York with Dorothy and began leisurely work on an adaptation of Bizet's *Carmen*. Oscar adapted the lyrics and story to create the Americanized, all-Black *Carmen Jones*. The opera received great acclaim.

When he had finished the libretto for *Carmen Jones*, Oscar was contacted by an old Columbia acquaintance, Richard Rodgers, whose partnership with Lorenz Hart had recently dissolved. Rodgers had read Lynn Riggs' *Green Grow the Lilacs* and wanted to collaborate with Hammerstein on a musical adaptation for the Theatre Guild. Hammerstein had also read the play, and the two began work on the musical, tentatively titled *Away We Go*. Rodgers and Hammerstein worked toward the concept of the integrated musical, with Hammerstein writing most of the lyrics before Rodgers wrote the score, the reverse of the normal process. Robert Mamoulian was signed on as director, Agnes deMille as choreographer, and Terry Helburn as producer for the Theatre Guild.

When the musical, retitled *Oklahoma*, opened on Broadway on March 31, 1943, it was an enormous success, both critically and popularly. *Oklahoma* ran for 2,243 performances in its initial Broadway engagement, and in 1944 it received a special Pulitzer Prize. The team of Rodgers and Hammerstein was a success. They produced their own work and promising works by other artists and at one time had five of the highest grossing shows running at the same time on Broadway. They followed up their success with collaborations on *Carousel* (1945), *Allegro* (1947), *South Pacific* (1949), *The King and I* (1951), *Me and Juliet* (1953), *Pipe Dream* (1955), *Flower Drum Song* (1958), and *The Sound of Music* (1960), for which Howard Lindsay and Russell

Crouse wrote the book, Rodgers composed the score, and Hammerstein wrote the lyrics. *South Pacific* won the Pulitzer Prize in 1950. *South Pacific, The King and I,* and *The Sound of Music* all won Tony awards for best musical. Most of the Rodgers and Hammerstein musicals have been adapted for the screen, with the greatest success going to *Oklahoma* and *The Sound of Music.*

Hammerstein's talents as a lyricist and librettist are undeniable. Countless productions of Hammerstein musicals on Broadway, on tour, and in professional, amateur, and academic theaters around the world testify to the remarkable quality of his work. Hammerstein's influence on the next generation of lyricists and librettists was also direct and observable. Most notable was his influence on Stephen Sondheim, lyricist for such shows as *West Side Story, Sweeny Todd,* and *Sunday in the Park with George.* Sondheim was a close friend of the Hammerstein family from childhood and attributed his success in theater directly to Hammerstein's influence and guidance.

Oscar Clendenning Hammerstein II died in his home in Doylestown, Pennsylvania, on August 23, 1960, a victim of stomach cancer. He left behind three children, William and Alice by Myra Finn and James by Dorothy Blanchard Jacobson. On September 1, 1960, at 9 p.m., the lights were extinguished on Broadway in memory of Oscar Hammerstein II, the "man who owned Broadway."

Further Reading

Getting To Know Him (1977) by Hugh Fordin is the first authorized biography of Hammerstein. Fordin was given exclusive use of Hammerstein's archives and the right to tape the personal recollections of family and colleagues. Hammerstein's contribution to musical history is traced in David Ewen, *All the Years of American Popular Music* (1977) and Frederick Nolan, *The Sound of Their Music: The Story of Rodgers and Hammerstein* (1978). Stanley Green's *The Rodgers and Hammerstein Story* (1963) treats the careers of these two men separately and their actual 18 years collaboration.

Additional Sources

Citron, Stephen, *The wordsmiths: Oscar Hammerstein 2nd and Alan Jay Lerner,* New York: Oxford University Press, 1995.

Fordin, Hugh, *Getting to know him: a biography of Oscar Hammerstein II,* New York: Da Capo Press, 1995. □

John Hancock

John Hancock (1737-1793) signed the Declaration of Independence and was a leader of the movement toward revolution in the American colonies. Later prominent in the Continental Congress, he was elected Massachusetts governor for nine terms.

Born at Braintree, Mass., on Jan. 23, 1737, John Hancock was reared in the piety and penury of a Congregational minister's household. He was 7 when his father died and he became a ward of his uncle, a prominent Boston merchant. Hancock graduated from Harvard in 1754, served for a time in his uncle's office as a clerk, and went to London in 1760 as the firm's representative. In

England he witnessed the pageantry unfurled for the new king, George III, but he was not enthralled by life in the imperial capital and returned to his Boston mansion. In 1763 Hancock became a partner in his uncle's prosperous importing and provisioning business.

When his uncle died in 1764, Hancock inherited property worth almost £70,000. As a merchant prince, he naturally resisted Britain's attempt to restrict colonial trading via the Stamp Act, which was later repealed. But Hancock's mercantile ventures soon led to evasive tactics that were, in fact, smuggling.

Pushed to prominence by more militant men, Hancock was elected to the Massachusetts General Court in 1766. The British seizure of one of his smuggling vessels, the *Liberty,* became a cause célèbre and made him a popular hero. He received more votes than Samuel Adams in the next General Court election. Meanwhile, he was threatened by the Crown with fines of nearly £100,000 for the *Liberty* affair. Though the fines were never collected, neither was Hancock's ship returned.

Growing Anti-British Sentiment

British military and revenue policies after 1768 were exploited by Samuel Adams and other anti-British agitators. The Boston Massacre of 1770 increased colonial animosity and established a tension that was nurtured by the militant patriots. Hancock, for a time, wavered. However, when the tide of public opinion became clear, he announced that he was totally committed to the patriot cause, even if it cost him his life and his fortune. This took some courage.

In the rush of later events, as the Boston Tea Party of 1773 brought on more coercive laws and, finally, the Boston Port Bill of 1774, Hancock's reputation mounted. By 1775 his name was synonymous with American radicalism. How much of this was thoughtful leadership on his part and how far he had been pushed by Adams is uncertain. Hancock and Adams were, after all, the only two Americans denied amnesty when British general Thomas Gage belatedly decided to try for peaceful relations.

Continental Congress

Hancock was elected president of the Continental Congress in May 1775. He longed for command of the army around Boston and was undoubtedly disappointed when George Washington was selected. He voted for, and was the first delegate to sign, the Declaration of Independence. Then Hancock resigned as president in October 1777, pleading ill health.

Meanwhile, Hancock had married Dorothy Quincy in August 1775. Though he stayed on as part of the congressional delegation, he still longed for military glory. However, his one opportunity—in the Rhode Island campaign of 1778—was undistinguished.

Hancock was embarrassed in 1777, when Harvard College sought to regain its account books and funds. Hancock had been named treasurer of the college in 1773, and he now refused to give accounts or release funds in his care. He was forced to surrender £16,000 in 1777. In 1785 Hancock admitted that he still owed his alma mater £1,054—a sum eventually paid by his heirs.

Like most public men, Hancock had enemies. Though his detractors insisted that Hancock was a shallow man who lacked conviction and was merely an opportunist, they could not prevent his election as the first governor of Massachusetts, in 1780. He was reelected repeatedly, until an impending financial crisis coincided with his voluntary retirement in 1785. Though he claimed that his retirement was based on illness, Hancock's enemies asserted that he had seen the coming storm, which was caused in part by his ineptitude in fiscal matters. After Shays' Rebellion (1786), Hancock was reelected governor.

In 1788, elected president of the Massachusetts State Convention to ratify the new Federal Constitution, Hancock was approached by Federalists who recommended a set of amendments, hinting that—if he presented them, and if Washington declined the presidency—Hancock himself might be in line for the nation's first office. Perhaps the story is unfair, but more than one witness attested to its truth. Hancock did offer the amendments, and Massachusetts ratified the Constitution. Perhaps Hancock waited for a call that never came.

Thereafter, Hancock remained as Massachusetts governor, his popularity unchallenged. He died in office on Oct. 8, 1793.

Further Reading

The best biography of Hancock is Herbert S. Allan, *John Hancock: Patriot in Purple* (1948). William T. Baxter, *The House of Hancock: Business in Boston, 1724-1775* (1945), is a specialized study. For general background John Richard Alden, *A History of the American Revolution* (1969), is recommended. Hancock's own preserved papers are few. □

Handsome Lake

Seneca prophet Handsome Lake (ca. 1735-1815) played a major role in the revival of his own and other Iroquois League tribes.

Handsome Lake, a great leader and prophet, played a major role in the revival of the Senecas and other tribes of the Iroquois League. He preached a message that combined traditional Iroquois religious beliefs with specific white values. This message was eventually published as the Code of Handsome Lake.

Handsome Lake was born around 1735 in the Seneca village of Conewaugus, located on the Genesee River near Avon, New York. Very little is known of his parents. He was born into the Wolf clan and was named Hadawa'ko ["Shaking Snow"], but was eventually raised by the Turtle clan people. He was a half-brother to Cornplanter and an uncle of Red Jacket. Born during a time when the Seneca nation was at its peak of prosperity, Handsome Lake witnessed the gradual deterioration of his society.

Multiple factors led to the erosion of morale and the material welfare of the Iroquois. In the period after the American Revolution, the Iroquois lost most of their land and were forced to live on reservations. The reservations provided poor living conditions, and, within a relatively short period of time, many Iroquois began to suffer alcohol abuse, fighting, instability of the family unit, and accusations of witchcraft. This dismal situation was due, in part, to the basic incompatibility of the Iroquois social structure and reservation existence. The traditional religious rituals alone were inadequate to lessen the harshness of this situation. As a result, the Iroquois began searching for new solutions to their difficulties.

Brings a Message of Gaiwiio ("Good Word")

In 1799, after a period of illness due to many years of excessive alcoholic indulgence, Handsome Lake had the first of a series of visions. In his first vision, he was warned by three spiritual messengers about the dangers associated with alcohol; he was also told that witches were creating chaos within his tribe and that the persons guilty of witchcraft must repent and confess. Handsome Lake was directed to reveal these warnings to the people. His nephew Blacksnake and half-brother Cornplanter were with him during this time and believed in the power of his visions and their revelations. Shortly after Handsome Lake's first vision, he ceased drinking alcohol. When he regained his health, he began bringing a message of Gaiwiio (the "Good Word") to his people. He preached against drunkenness and other evil practices. His message outlined a moral code that was eventually referred to as the Code of Handsome Lake. The Code outlawed drunkenness, witchcraft, sexual promiscuity, wife beating, quarreling, and gambling. Hand-

Further Reading

Dockstader, Frederick J., *Great North American Indians,* New York, VanNostrand Reinhold Co., 1977; 102-103.

Leitch, Barbara A., *Chronology of the American Indian,* St. Clair Shores, Michigan, Scholarly Press, 1975; 138.

Waldman, Carl, *Who Was Who in Native American History,* Facts On File, Maple-Vail Book Mfg. Group, 1990; 144.

Wallace, Anthony F. C., "Origins of the Longhouse Religion," in *Handbook of North American Indians,* edited by William C. Sturtevant, Smithsonian Institution, 1978; 445-448. □

William Christopher Handy

The African American songwriter William Christopher Handy (1873-1958), known as the father of the blues, was the first person to notate and publish blues songs. He wrote over 60 blues, spirituals, and popular tunes.

On Nov. 16, 1873, W. C. Handy was born in Florence, Ala., the son of two Methodist ministers. He studied at Kentucky Musical College, to the dismay of his father, who regarded secular music as a branch of the devil's activities. At an early age he left home to tour with a minstrel show. As a bandleader for Mahara's Minstrels for much of the period between 1896 and 1903, he first made contract with early blues and jazz. He moved to Memphis, Tenn., and led a band that featured his attempts to incorporate blues tunes and jazz motifs into written arrangements.

In 1909 Handy wrote his first song, "Mr. Crump," for a political campaign. He changed the title to "Memphis

some Lake presented his message along with a threat that fire would destroy the world if this Code was not obeyed.

Handsome Lake soon became obsessed with witch hunting and demanded confessions from those whom he suspected of witchcraft; some of those who refused to confess were killed. His witch hunting nearly became a catalyst for war with another tribe when he accused a prominent young man from that tribe of being a witch and demanded his punishment. Gradually, the sentiment of the people turned against Handsome Lake for what they considered an overzealous pursuit of witches. As a result of this change in attitude, he stopped his accusatory methods and briefly assumed a less prominent leadership role. Handsome Lake once again became popular during the War of 1812 and attracted many new followers.

The rise of Handsome Lake's religion was more successful than most religions during that time, apparently because his code combined traditional Iroquois religion with white Christian values. It stressed survival without the sacrifice of the Iroquois identity, and recognized the realistic need to make adjustments in order to survive in their changing world. *The Code of Handsome Lake,* published around 1850, played a significant role in the preservation of the Iroquois cultural heritage and was popular throughout the Iroquois nations in Canada and in the United States. Handsome Lake, referred to as Sedwa'gowa'ne, "Our Great Teacher," died on August 10, 1815, at the Onondaga Reservation. His religious beliefs were carried on by Blacksnake and other disciples, and his teachings remain a compelling force among the Iroquois.

Blues'' when he published it in 1912. His most famous number, ''St. Louis Blues,'' appeared in 1914, followed by ''Yellow Dog Blues'' (1914), ''Beale Street Blues'' (1916), ''Careless (or ''Loveless'') Love'' (1921), and many others.

Handy is a somewhat enigmatic figure; in his lifetime he was bitterly accused by some musicians of plagiarism. It seems probable that he was less the original composer he claimed to be, more a sensitive collector of traditional material. Even if this is the case, his services as a folklorist should not be minimized; probably no one else has preserved such a wealth of blues material. As a performing musician, Handy was a competent instrumentalist in the European tradition, with no apparent ability as a jazz soloist.

Handy formed his own music publishing business in 1913. This, plus the royalties from his songs, brought him considerable wealth. But in the 1930s his sight began to fail, and by 1943 he was totally blind. In his later years he worked unceasingly for his W. C. Handy Foundation for the Blind and other charitable organizations.

His first wife, Elizabeth Price, with whom he had six children, died in 1937. In 1954, at the age of 80, he married again. He was honored by having a theater and a park in Memphis, and a library in Philadelphia, named after him during his lifetime. He died in 1958; in 1959 the W. C. Handy 6-cent postage stamp was issued.

Further Reading

Handy edited *Blues: An Anthology* (1926; reprinted in 1950 as *A Treasury of the Blues*), which contains a comprehensive selection of blues by him and others and includes biographical material on Handy. Handy's *Father of the Blues* (1941) is autobiographical, revealing Handy as likeable, generous, and at times naively conservative. See also Marshall Stern, *The Story of Jazz* (1958), and Gunther Schuller, *Early Jazz: Its Roots and Musical Development* (1968). ☐

Warren Gamaliel Harding

The twenty-ninth president of the United States, Warren Gamaliel Harding (1865-1923), highly popular during his lifetime, was later regarded as one of the worst presidents in the country's history.

Warren G. Harding was born on Nov. 2, 1865, on a farm near Blooming Grove, Ohio. He attended local schools and graduated from Ohio Central College in 1882. His father moved the family to Marion that same year. After unsatisfactory attempts to teach, study law, and sell insurance, young Harding got a job on a local newspaper. In 1884 he purchased the struggling *Marion Star* with two partners (whom he later bought out). The growth of Marion and his own business skill and editorial abilities brought prosperity to the *Star* and to Harding. On July 8, 1891, he married Florence DeWolfe, a widow with one child; they had no children of their own.

Election to Office

Active in local Republican politics, Harding was elected in 1899 to the Ohio Senate, where he served two terms and

became Republican floor leader. In 1903 he was elected lieutenant governor but retired in 1905. Although a born harmonizer who remained personally on good terms with all elements in the faction-ridden Ohio Republican party, he belonged to the Old Guard wing of the party. He ran unsuccessfully for governor in 1910. But in the Republican comeback in 1914 Harding was elected to the U.S. Senate. As a senator, Harding strongly supported business, pushing for high tariffs, favoring the return of the railroads to private hands, and denouncing radicals. He was a ''strong reservationist'' on the League of Nations, and he followed Ohio public opinion by voting for the prohibition amendment.

In 1919 Harding announced his candidacy for the Republican presidential nomination; he won the nomination on the tenth ballot. Legend has pictured Harding as a puppet in the hands of his wife or his campaign manager. But Harding was no one's puppet: he was an ambitious and calculating politician. Nor was he the handpicked nominee of a group of Old Guard senators. The convention was unbossed, and Harding, with his reputation as a loyal party man, his amiable personality, and his avoidance of controversial stands, was the second choice of the majority of the rank-and-file delegates. When the two front-runners deadlocked, the convention had swung to the handsome Ohioan.

In the election Harding successfully straddled the explosive League of Nations issue. By capitalizing on the public's yearning for a return to ''normalcy'' after World War I, Harding won by the largest popular majority yet recorded.

The President

Despite the country's postwar position as a creditor nation, Harding gave his blessing to protective farm tariffs. Devoted to governmental economy, he supported establishment of the Bureau of the Budget, sharply cut government expenditures despite depressed economic conditions, and vetoed the World War I veterans' bonus passed by Congress. He backed Secretary of the Treasury Andrew Mellon's program for repealing the excess-profits tax and lowering the income tax on the wealthy; he gave Secretary of Commerce Herbert Hoover a free hand in his efforts to promote business cooperation and efficiency; he favored turning over government-owned plants to private enterprise; he packed regulatory commissions and the Supreme Court with conservative appointees; and he strongly favored immigration restriction.

Harding wished to remain neutral in labor disputes and worked behind the scenes for conciliation, but when his hand was forced, he took management's side. Thus, after his attempted mediation in the 1922 railroad shopmen's strike failed, he approved a sweeping injunction against the strikers—this won him the bitter enmity of organized labor.

But Harding was not the archreactionary of later myth. He supported the Sheppard-Towner Act (1921), extending federal aid to the states to reduce infant mortality. He unsuccessfully proposed establishing a department of public welfare to coordinate and expand Federal programs in education, public health, child welfare, and recreation. He was instrumental in ending the 12-hour day in the steel industry. He promoted increased federal spending on highways. He commuted the sentences of most of the wartime political prisoners, including Socialist leader Eugene V. Debs. While balking at government subsidies or price-fixing to assist farmers hard hit by postwar falling prices, he approved legislation for extending credit to farmers, for stricter federal supervision of the meat industry, for regulating speculation on the grain exchanges, and for exempting farm marketing cooperatives from the antitrust laws.

Foreign Policy

In foreign policy Harding was largely guided by his prointernationalist secretary of state, Charles Evans Hughes. Although Harding regarded the 1920 election as a popular mandate against American membership in the League of Nations, his administration cooperated with the nonpolitical activities of the League, and in 1923 he came out in favor of American membership on the World Court. Adamant in demanding full repayment of Allied war debts, he was flexible in arranging terms.

Efforts were made to restore good relations with Mexico and Cuba and to terminate military intervention in Haiti and the Dominican Republic. Colombia was indemnified for the loss of Panama. The Harding administration's most important diplomatic achievement was the Washington Conference. Meeting in November 1921, the conferees formulated a series of treaties, which secured Senate ratification, fixing ratios of warships for the United States, Britain, Japan, France, and Italy, guaranteeing the territorial status quo in the Pacific, and reaffirming the independence and territorial integrity of China and the open-door principle of commercial equality.

Scandals in the Administration

By 1923 Harding was increasingly disturbed by the rumors of corruption involving high administration officials and hangers-on. But he failed to act decisively, partly because he believed the attacks were politically motivated, partly because of a misplaced loyalty to old friends. Perhaps his worst mistake was in appointing his senatorial crony Albert B. Fall as secretary of the interior. Fall persuaded Harding to transfer naval oil reserves from the Navy Department to the Department of the Interior. Then, after Fall had corruptly leased the reserves at Elk Hills, Calif., and Teapot Dome, Wyo., to oilmen, he induced Harding to defend these transactions when questions were raised in the Senate.

Although the Republicans had suffered sharp losses in the 1922 congressional elections, Harding personally remained tremendously popular. However, his health was affected by overwork and anxiety over his wife's health and the multiplying evidences of corruption in his administration. He suffered a heart attack followed by bronchopneumonia while on his cross-country tour in the summer of 1923. He died on Aug. 2, 1923, probably from a cerebral hemorrhage. The posthumous exposure of the scandals in Harding's administration—including Fall's conviction for bribery, the attorney general's forced resignation and narrow escape from jail, and prison sentences for the head of two government bureaus—and the charges that Harding had fathered an illegitimate daughter and that he drank excessively all led to his decline in public esteem.

Yet Harding was not the affable, weak, and even stupid figure of popular legend. He was a hardworking, conscientious, well-intentioned, politically skillful chief executive who was not without courage or the capacity for growth. Most contemporaries praised his success in leading the country through the painful transition from the difficulties of the postwar years, and his administration did lay foundations for later prosperity. But he showed indecisiveness and lack of leadership when faced with conflict; his mind was untrained and undisciplined; and most important, the values of small-town America which he embodied were inadequate for dealing with the problems of the postwar world.

Further Reading

There is no satisfactory biography of Harding. Francis Russell, *The Shadow of Blooming Grove: Warren G. Harding in His Times* (1968), emphasizes the scandalous aspects of Harding's private and public life. Andrew Sinclair, *The Available Man: The Life behind the Masks of Warren Gamaliel Harding* (1965), contains shrewd insights but is superficial in its research. Robert K. Murray, *The Harding Era* (1969), is a well-researched but not wholly convincing attempt to rehabilitate Harding's presidential reputation. See also William Allen White, *Masks in a Pageant* (1928), and Samuel Hopkins Adams, *Incredible Era: The Life and Times of Warren G. Harding* (1939). On the election of 1920 see Arthur M. Schlesinger, Jr., ed., *History of American Presidential Elections,* vol. 3 (1971). □

Keith Haring

Although invariably, and undeniably, tied to New York graffiti art of the 1980s, Keith Haring's (1958-1990) work represents a much more complex combination of primitive impulses, automatic writing, popular culture, and so-called "high" and "low" art.

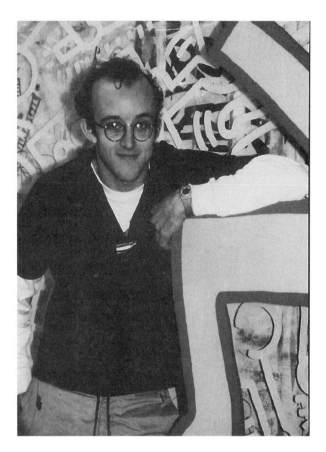

Born on May 4, 1958, Keith Haring was raised in a traditional middle-class family in Kutztown, Pennsylvania. He would later remember fondly the creative drawing sessions he and his father, an amateur artist, would have together. Haring's early influences were not unlike those of many American children growing up in the 1960s— the cartoons of Walt Disney, Dr. Seuss, Charles Schulz, and the Looney Tunes characters he would watch Saturday morning television's "The Bugs Bunny Show," television sitcoms such as "I Dream of Jeannie" and "The Monkees," and the observe powerful images in *Life* and *Look* magazines. These influences reflect the dominant role, emphasized by the Pop artists of the period, that mass media and popular culture had on American life.

After graduating high school in 1976, Haring attended the Ivy School of Professional Art in Pittsburgh, Pennsylvania. Feeling stifled by the constraints of a commercial art education, he left school after only two semesters. The catalyst for this decision was the chance reading of Robert Henri's *The Art Spirit* (1923), which inspired him to concentrate on his own art.

While working in a maintenance job for the Pittsburgh Center for the Arts (then the Pittsburgh Arts and Crafts Center), Haring explored on his own the art of Jean Dubuffet, Jackson Pollock, and Mark Tobey. His most critical influences at this time were a retrospective of the work of Pierre Alechinsky in 1977 and a lecture by the site sculptor, Christo, in 1978. Alechinsky's work, connected to the international Expressionist group CoBrA, gave Haring the confidence to create larger paintings of calligraphic and automatic writing inspired images. Christo introduced him to the possibilities of involving the public with his art. Pittsburgh was also the host of Haring's first important one-man exhibition, at the Center for the Arts in 1978.

Haring's quest for a more vibrant artistic atmosphere, however, led him that same year to New York's School of Visual Arts where he studied semiotics with Bill Beckley and explored the possibilities of video and performance art. He was profoundly influenced at this time by the writings of William Burroughs, which inspired him to experiment with the cross-referencing and interconnection of images.

The social scene in New York's East Village was of immense importance to Keith Haring and his work. He became a prominent figure in the thriving underground art world, curating informal exhibitions at Club 57 and the Mudd Club. His active involvement with the gay lifestyle was reflected in his art, which often portrayed phallic images or explicit sexual encounters.

Inspired by his interest in language and by artist Jenny Holzer, Haring began to experiment with a more public art in the summer of 1980, pasting collages of fake *New York Post* headlines on lampposts or newsstands. His interest in automatic writing and semiotics, however, led him to explore the world of graffiti artists such as SAMO (Jean-Michel Basquiat) and Fab Five Fred (Fred Brathwaite). It was here, in the subways and on the streets of New York, that Haring created his own graffiti and developed his future vocabulary of primitive cartoon-like forms. Cryptic and yet accessible, Haring's chalk-drawn "radiant babies" and "barking dogs" became familiar features on the matt black surfaces used to cover the old advertisements in the subways. Striving to make his art even more accessible, Haring passed out buttons illustrated with his drawings and collaborated on a book of his graffiti (*Art in Transit: Subway Drawings,* 1984) with photographer Tseng Kwong Chi.

Leaving school before the fall semester of 1980, Haring embarked upon a wide distribution of his semiotic forms. He began to disassociate himself from the graffiti scene, painting instead on tarpaulins and other objects, and had a one-man show at Shafrazi Gallery in 1982. His meteoric rise to world prominence after this show was truly remarkable. By the end of 1984 he had gained international recognition, exhibiting in Brazil, Spain, Japan, Italy, and England. Attempting to reach a larger public, he immersed himself in popular American culture, forming friendships with Andy Warhol and with such pop entertainers as Madonna and Grace Jones (whom he would body-paint). He became politically active, designing a Free South Africa poster (1985) and painting a section of the Berlin Wall in 1986. His interest in working with children inspired the enormous project *Citykids Speak on Liberty,* which involved 1,000 kids collaborating on a project for the Statue of Liberty centennial.

Ever increasing concern for making his art accessible led to commercial ventures such as the design for Swatch watches (1985); the Absolut Vodka advertisement (1986); and ultimately his Pop Shop (opened 1986) in which he sold T-shirts, posters, and other saleable items. It was these endeavors, as well as the graffiti images, that caused some critics and members of the art world to bemoan Haring's contribution, placing him instead among popular cultural figures. Haring maintained, however, that his intention was to make his art more accessible. Ideologically, he placed himself with Andy Warhol, the conceptual artists, and the earth artists—attempting to reach a broader public.

On February 16, 1990, at age 31, Keith Haring's life was cut short due to an AIDS-related illness. His work remains the most salient example of the diminishing line between consumerism, popular culture, and fine art in the 1980s. Despite their controversial nature, Haring's images reflect the 20th-century tradition of using primitive impulses to communicate the angst of modern times.

Further Reading

Keith Haring: The Authorized Biography by John Gruen (1991) includes interviews with the artist and those closest to him and is an invaluable source for understanding the art and life of Haring. The early work is illustrated in *Art in Transit: The Subway Drawings* (1984) and *Keith Haring* (Shafrazi Gallery, 1982). An enlightening interview by David Sheff appeared in *Rolling Stone* (August 10, 1989). Elizabeth Aubert directed an insightful video entitled *Drawing the Line: A Portrait of Keith Haring* (Biografilm, 1989). Later an attempt was made to place Haring within a broader art historical context in *Keith Haring*, edited by Germano Celant (1992). □

Joel Chandler Harris

American writer Joel Chandler Harris (1848-1908) used folklore, fiction, dialect, and other devices of local color to picture both black and white Georgians under slavery and Reconstruction.

Joel Chandler Harris was born in Eatonton, Ga., the illegitimate son of Mary Harris. Scantily educated, at 13 Harris became an apprentice printer on a little newspaper edited and published by Joseph Addison Turner, a highly literate planter, lawyer, and writer, and learned about writing under Turner's tutelage. Harris then worked on newspapers in several Southern cities. While in Savannah he met and married Esther LaRose; they had nine children. In 1876 Harris began a 24-year association with the *Atlanta Constitution*.

Harris's work as a columnist led to his creation of Uncle Remus, the black singer of songs and teller of stories. The tales, collected in *Uncle Remus: His Songs and Sayings* (1880), are based upon folklore and are told by the venerable family servant to a little boy on a Georgia plantation. The book's favorable reviews and large sales led to magazine publication of stories later collected in *Nights with*

Uncle Remus (1883), *Uncle Remus and His Friends* (1892), *Told by Uncle Remus* (1905), and others.

Remus, the old storyteller, is wise, perceptive, imaginative, poetic, and gifted with a sly sense of humor. The stories can be read for the larger picture they give of the exploited blacks who invented them. Their hero, Brer Rabbit, as Harris observed, is "the weakest and most harmless of all animals," but he is "victorious in contests with the bear, the wolf, and the fox." Thus "it is not virtue that triumphs, but helplessness; it is not malice, but mischievousness." However, since Uncle Remus's casual revelations often picture idyllically the lives of slaves and kindly whites on an antebellum plantation, these tales cultivated sympathy for Harris's people and his South. Critics believe that Harris's conscious aim was to end sectional antagonism.

In other fictional works Harris enlarged his portrayal of Southerners to include aristocrats, members of the middle class, mountaineers, and poor white farmers. Genre stories appeared in *Mingo and Other Sketches* (1884), *Free Joe* (1887), and other collections. There were two novels: *Sister Jane, Her Friends and Acquaintances* (1896) and *Gabriel Tolliver: A Story of Reconstruction* (1902). Harris died on July 3, 1908, in Atlanta.

Further Reading

Harris's *On the Plantation: A Story of a Georgia Boy's Adventures during the War* (1892), gives an autobiographical account of an important period in his life. Julia C. Harris contributed valuable intimate details in *Life and Letters of Joel Chandler Harris* (1918) and *Joel Chandler Harris as Editor and Essayist*

(1931). Probably the best biographical and critical account is Paul M. Cousins, *Joel Chandler Harris* (1968). A useful specialized study is Stella B. Brookes, *Joel Chandler Harris, Folklorist* (1950).

Additional Sources

Bickley, R. Bruce, *Joel Chandler Harris,* Athens: University of Georgia Press, 1987. □

Benjamin Harrison

U.S. president Benjamin Harrison (1833-1901), though possibly the dullest personality ever to inhabit the White House, was nevertheless a competent enough president during one of the most eventful administrations of the late 19th century.

Benjamin Harrison was born in North Bend, Ohio, on Aug. 20, 1833. The Harrisons had been among the most illustrious families of colonial Virginia, and Benjamin was the namesake of a Revolutionary soldier and signer of the Declaration of Independence. His grandfather, William Henry Harrison, who had transported the family to Ohio, was elected president as "Old Tippecanoe" in 1840.

Harrison graduated from Miami University in Oxford, Ohio, in 1852. He Married Caroline Scott of Oxford the following year. He read law for 2 years in Cincinnati, then moved to Indianapolis, Ind., where he established a prosperous practice.

Republican Politics

Harrison became a Republican immediately. He was known as a good political orator, although today his speeches seem to combine only triteness and pedantry with 19th-century bombast. His political career advanced slowly but steadily until the Civil War: he was city attorney of Indianapolis in 1857, secretary of the Republican State Central Committee in 1858, and reporter of the Indiana supreme Court in 1860. The last position proved profitable, as Harrison drew large royalties for many years from his compilation of Indiana laws.

Unlike many political contemporaries, Harrison sat out the first campaign of the Civil War. In 1862, however, he organized the Union's 70th Indiana Infantry and was commissioned as its colonel. A typical volunteer officer, he knew nothing of war making and was fortunate in being assigned to guard the newly captured Louisville and Nashville Railroad.

Harrison was not popular with his troops; apparently he was something of a martinet, and the personal coldness of which many contemporaries would later complain was already manifest. The dullness of guard duty also may have affected the unhappy command, but that was relieved in 1864, when Harrison and his men joined Gen. William T. Sherman. Harrison stayed at the front only briefly, as he was quickly requested to return to Indiana in order to head off a Democratic political threat in the fall elections. He rejoined Sherman, but only after Sherman's famous, devastating march through Georgia was complete; Harrison was brevetted as brigadier general, more for political than military services.

Postwar Career and Character

After the war Harrison built his legal practice into one of the most successful in Indiana. Still, he never neglected Republican politics. He supported the victorious radical faction of the party and during the 1870s became a spokesman for the equally dominant fiscal conservatives. He was unsuccessful as candidate for governor of Indiana in 1876 but continued to serve the party. In 1877 he again donned military uniform briefly to command troops during the national railroad strike. He was a solidly conservative Republican.

Harrison's career improved sharply in 1880. He was elected to the U.S. Senate and played an important role in winning the Republican presidential nomination for James A. Garfield. Harrison was himself a "dark horse" candidate for the nomination in 1884, but, realizing that it was the charismatic James G. Blaine's year, he refused to allow his name before the convention. It was this combination of stern party regularity and fortuitous personal decisions— rather than any particular brilliance—that accounted for Harrison's rise.

Harrison's years in the Senate were undistinguished. He played on Civil War emotionalism and appealed to anti-British sentiment but made no significant contributions to the great issues of the day. Rather, he turned his considerable legal talents to constructing interminable constitutional briefs for petty and partisan purposes. But his services paid off when he was nominated to run for president in 1888.

Harrison as President

In the presidential campaign Harrison lost the popular vote but won in the Electoral College. More than any previous Republican president, he committed his party to certain high financial and "big business" interests when, through his postmaster general, he systematized the solicitation of party funds. His administration sat during the "Billion Dollar Congress" elected in 1890, the first Congress ever to expend more than $1 billion. That famous Congress also passed a high tariff law containing reciprocity provisions (which Harrison largely wrote) that facilitated American economic expansion abroad, the landmark Sherman Antitrust Act, and the ill-fated Sherman Silver Purchase Act. Harrison's term also saw the Republican party finally abandon its commitment to defend the civil rights of Southern African Americans when Congress failed to pass a law designed to protect them.

Harrison kept in touch with his Congress on the various questions although, in the fashion of the time, he took a minimal part in the public debates. The accomplishments of the "Billion Dollar Congress," however, bear his mark: the carelessly drawn acts, intended as much to obfuscate as clarify, showed the lack of interest or inability to comprehend long-term effects which characterized Harrison's career.

Harrison was ultimately no more popular with his own party than with the Democrats. Short and portly with a stony, uncomely countenance, he seemed incapable of a warm personal relationship, let alone of the glad-handing conviviality which late-19th-century American politics frequently required. Still, he was the incumbent in 1892 and secured his party's renomination—only to lose the election to Grover Cleveland.

Actually, Harrison was to be just as happy about his defeat. Cleveland's second term was a disaster, marked by agricultural and industrial unrest with which Harrison could hardly have better coped. And Harrison was personally more suited for private life. His first wife had died in the White House, leaving him with two children. He married Mary Dimmick, by whom he had another child. He returned to his legal practice in Indiana, represented Venezuela in a celebrated boundary dispute with Great Britain, and wrote several books, including *Views of an Ex-President* (1901) and *This Country of Ours* (1897), a popular textbook for several years. He died of pneumonia on March 13, 1901.

Further Reading

Harry J. Sievers, *Benjamin Harrison* (3 vols., 1952-1968; vol. 1, 2d ed. 1960), is scarcely inspiring but includes an exhaustively detailed source book. John A. Garraty, *The New Commonwealth: 1877-1890* (1968), provides an antidote to Sievers's uncritical admiration. The presidential election of 1888 is covered in Arthur M. Schlesinger, Jr., ed., *History of American Presidential Elections* (4 vols., 1971). H. Wayne Morgan, *From Hayes to McKinley: National Party Politics, 1877-1896* (1969), is the best recent survey of late-19th-century politics. □

William Henry Harrison

William Henry Harrison (1773-1841), the ninth president of the United States, was an early administrator of the American territorial system. He gained fame as an Indian fighter and military hero before becoming president.

W illiam Henry Harrison was born in Charles City County, Va., on Feb. 9, 1773, into one of the state's leading families. His father, Benjamin Harrison, was a signer of the Declaration of Independence and governor of Virginia during the Revolution. William Henry studied at Hampden-Sidney College and at the University of Pennsylvania before receiving a commission in the U.S. Army in 1792.

Harrison served in the Ohio Territory and was aide-de-camp to Gen. Anthony Wayne at the Battle of Fallen Timbers (1794), which temporarily destroyed Indian power in the Northwest Territory. He married an Ohio girl, Anna Tuthill Symmes, in 1795. Three years later he left the Army, having attained the rank of captain. He soon was appointed secretary of the Northwest Territory and elected representative to the U.S. Congress. In Congress, Harrison's Land Act of 1800 was a major contribution to the development of America's territorial policy. Under its terms the Federal government provided cheap land and extended each settler 5 years' credit to pay for his property.

President John Adams appointed the experienced Harrison as governor of the Indiana Territory in 1801, when it was carved out of the Northwest Territory. During his 12 years in that post, Harrison's main accomplishments were the establishment of a legal system, the settlement of land disputes, and the management of Indian affairs. Harrison gained a national reputation through his victory over an Indian confederation organized by Tecumseh and his brother, the "Prophet," at the Battle of Tippecanoe. This was one of the last efforts at resistance by Indians east of the Mississippi River.

When the War of 1812 started, Harrison received a major general's commission in the U.S. Army and, after Gen. William Hull surrendered at Detroit, took command of the Northwest forces. Although failing to achieve his primary military objectives—the recapture of Detroit and the conquest of Canada—Harrison was victorious at the battle on Canada's Thames River. After the war Harrison was one of the commissioners who negotiated the Spring Wells Treaty in 1815, which completed the Federal takeover of Indian lands in the Northwest.

Political Career

Upon his return to Ohio, Harrison was elected to the U.S. House of Representatives (1816-1819). In 1825 he was elected to the U.S. Senate, where he served until 1828.

In 1828 Whig president John Quincy Adams appointed Harrison ambassador to Colombia. Having little knowledge of diplomacy, Harrison promptly tangled with Colombia's ruler, Simón Bolívar, who accused Harrison of complicity in an uprising. Incoming president Andrew Jackson, a Democrat, recalled him.

With the Whig party in temporary eclipse, Harrison returned to Ohio and went into political retirement until 1834. But the celebration that year of the twentieth anniversary of the Battle of the Thames returned him to prominence. A movement to make Harrison president gained strength in the Middle Atlantic states, where he had the backing of the leaders of the Antimasonic party, which by 1836 had largely combined with the Whigs. Since the Whig party was without a candidate for the 1836 contest and was composed of a number of discordant elements, several sectional candidates emerged to challenge the Democratic nominee, Martin Van Buren. They hoped collectively to throw the election into the House of Representatives, where one of the Whigs would emerge victorious. This strategy failed, but Harrison had proved the strongest contender.

The President

Soon after Van Buren's inauguration the movement for Harrison picked up new steam. Aided by a decline in Van Buren's popularity as a consequence of the Panic of 1837, Harrison received the Whig party's nomination at its 1839 convention with John Tyler, of Harrison's native county in Virginia, as his running mate.

The Whigs used a purposely vague program to carry Harrison to victory. Harrison refused to take a stand during the course of the campaign. He was portrayed as a simple, hardworking western farmer who lived in a log cabin and loved farm work, as contrasted to Van Buren, who was described as an eastern aristocrat living in luxury. Although the campaign rhetoric may have influenced the election, the dire economic condition of the country led to a general desire for changes, which worked in Harrison's favor.

Between his election and inauguration, Harrison was beset by numerous party quarrels over patronage. On April 4, 1841, one month after he took office, amid signs that his party was breaking up, Harrison died of pneumonia. The nation was stunned, having witnessed the first death of a president in office.

Further Reading

Dorothy Burne Goebel, *William Henry Harrison: A Political Biography* (1926), is a warm and interesting account of the life of the frontier hero, but quite outdated. Beverley W. Bond, Jr., *The Civilization of the Old Northwest, 1788-1812* (1934), is a good account of Harrison's early career and the difficulties encountered by territorial officials. Other studies include Freeman Cleaves, *Old Tippecanoe: William Henry Harrison and His Time* (1939), and James A. Green, *William Henry Harrison: His Life and Times* (1941). For the election of 1840 see Robert G. Gunderson, *The Log-Cabin Campaign* (1957), and Arthur M. Schlesinger, Jr., ed., *History of American Presidential Elections* (4 vols., 1971). □

Francis Brett Harte

Francis Brett Harte (1837-1902), known as Bret Harte, an American poet and fiction writer who specialized in local color and regional stories, set the fashion in fiction for a number of writers in the era following the Civil War.

Bret Harte, born in Albany, New York, had a somewhat sketchy education in the East before he followed his widowed and recently remarried mother and her family to the Pacific Coast in 1854. There he taught school for a year, visited the Mother Lode mining country, and worked briefly for an express company.

Early Career

Harte got his professional start between 1857 and 1860, when he was a journalist in Union, Calif. He moved to San Francisco, worked in government offices, and contributed writings to the *Golden Era* and the *Californian* which brought him prominence in literary circles. A collection of poems, *The Lost Galleon,* and a volume of parodies, *Condensed Novels,* appeared in 1867. The next year Harte became editor of a new West Coast magazine, *Overland Monthly,* and began to write a series of local sketches.

When stories set in the mining country, such as "The Luck of Roaring Camp" and "The Outcasts of Poker Flat," were read and reprinted in the East and elsewhere, Harte skyrocketed to fame. His renown increased when his comic ballad "Plain Language from Truthful James"—relating how Ah Sin, a Chinese gambler, outwitted two confidence men—became nationally famous.

By the time Harte's first collection of western local-color stories appeared in book form in 1870, eastern publishers were competing for Harte's services. In 1871 he signed a contract with the *Atlantic Monthly* at a record figure for an American writer—$10,000 for 12 monthly contributions. He left California, never to return, and journeyed eastward, receiving a triumphant welcome everywhere.

Harte as Stylist

It seemed to his contemporaries that Harte had written the first authentic fiction about gold rush California on the basis of intimate knowledge. Actually he had arrived in the West several years too late, and was in the mining camps too briefly, to know them intimately. He did what most authors who achieve immediate success do—combined old elements with new ones in a way that initially seemed to be quite novel.

For one thing, Harte used the techniques of the fiction writer most popular in America during the 1860s, Charles Dickens —despite the deft parody of Dickens included in *Condensed Novels.* Harte repeatedly borrowed some of the very elements he had burlesqued—the linking of settings with moods and actions, and the creation of memorable characters by assigning them unusual names and grotesquely incongruous characteristics.

Harte also owed a debt to the most popular American writers of the day: the native humorists. He himself claimed that the unique qualities of the American short story derived from the native comic story, and in describing this genre he might well have been analyzing his own narratives: "condensed, yet suggestive . . . delightfully extravagant—or a miracle of understatement. It voiced not only the dialect, but the habits of thought of a people or locality . . . often irreverent; it was devoid of all moral responsibility."

Like antebellum humorists, Harte stressed regional characters and mores. Like postbellum humorists, he used a style marked by fanciful figures of speech, unusual word combinations, and eccentrically shaped sentences. Not surprisingly, despite his frequent pathos, Harte was classified often as a humorist.

New Ingredient

When Harte appeared on the scene, American popular fiction was largely preachy and sentimental, showing noble characters doing noble deeds. The new ingredient in Harte's typical tale was another kind of character: his rough miners, prostitutes, dance hall girls, gamblers, and badmen proved that beneath their rugged exteriors beat hearts of gold. Many of these characters became stereo-types in western fiction, particularly in cowboy stories; so did others, such as the schoolmarm imported from the East and the aristocratic colonel from the South.

These qualities appeared in early tales and in later collections: *Mrs. Skagg's Husbands* (1873), *Tales of the Argonauts* (1875), *An Heiress of Red Dog and Other Sketches* (1878), and *Colonel Starbottle's Client, and Some Other People* (1892); and in novels: *M'Liss* (1873), *Gabriel Conroy* (1876), and *Jeff Briggs's Love Story* (1880).

As time passed, it became clear that Harte was repeating himself and that his powers—except in an occasional story—were waning. Two plays, one written in collaboration with Mark Twain, were failures. Domestic difficulties and personal problems were factors that prompted Harte to accept United States consulships in Germany and in Scotland. He went to London in 1885 and stayed there for the last 17 years of his life. His considerable reputation deteriorated steadily, and scholars eventually agreed that his chief importance derived from the fact that he set a fashion in fiction writing that would be adopted by many American writers, some of them great.

Further Reading

Geoffry B. Harte edited *The Writings of Bret Harte* (19 vols., 1896-1907) and *Letters of Bret Harte* (1926). Two good biographies are George Rippey Stewart, *Bret Harte: Argonaut and Exile* (1931), and Richard O'Connor, *Bret Harte* (1966). Margaret Duckett, *Mark Twain and Bret Harte* (1964), treats their relationship and its deterioration and reflects favorably on Harte.

Additional Sources

Stewart, George Rippey, *Bret Harte, Argonaut and exile: being an account of the life of the celebrated American humorist . . .* , New York: AMS Press, 1979, 1931. □

Nathaniel Hawthorne

The work of American fiction writer Nathaniel Hawthorne (1804-1864) was based on the history of his Puritan ancestors and the New England of his own day but, in its "power of blackness," has universal significance.

Nathaniel Hawthorne was born in Salem, Mass., on July 4, 1804, into the sixth generation of his Salem family. His ancestors included Puritan magnates, judges, and seamen. Two aspects of his heritage were especially to affect his imagination. The Hathornes (Nathaniel added the "w" to the name) had been involved in religious persecution with their first American forebear, William, and John Hathorne was one of the three judges at the 17th-century Salem witchcraft trials. Further, the family had over the generations gradually declined from its early prominence and prosperity into relative obscurity and indigence. Thus the Pyncheons and the Maules of Hawthorne's Salem novel *The House of the Seven Gables* represent the two different faces of his ancestors, and his feelings about his birthplace were mixed. With deep and unbreakable ties to Salem, he nevertheless found its physical and cultural environment as chilly as its prevalent east wind.

Early Life and Education

Nathaniel's father, a sea captain, died in 1808, leaving his wife and three children dependent on relatives. Nathaniel, the only son, spent his early years in Salem and in Maine. A leg injury immobilized the boy for a considerable period, during which he developed an exceptional taste for reading and contemplation. His childhood was calm, a little isolated but far from unhappy, especially since as a handsome and attractive only son he was idolized by his mother and his two sisters.

With the aid of his prosperous maternal uncles, the Mannings, Hawthorne attended Bowdoin College from 1821 to 1825, when he graduated. Among his classmates

were poet Henry Wadsworth Longfellow; Franklin Pierce, the future president of the United States, who was to be at his friend's deathbed; and Horatio Bridge, who was to subsidize the publication of Hawthorne's *Twice-Told Tales* in 1837. At Bowdoin, Hawthorne read widely and received solid instruction in English composition and the classics, particularly in Latin. His persistent refusal to engage in public speaking prevented his achieving any marked academic distinction, but he made a creditable record. On one occasion he was fined 50 cents for gambling at cards, but his conduct was not otherwise singled out for official disapproval. Though small and isolated, the Bowdoin of the 1820s was an unusually good college, and Hawthorne undoubtedly profited by his formal education, as well as making steadfast friends. Such men as Longfellow, Pierce, and Bridge remained devoted to him throughout life, and each would render him timely assistance.

Years as a Recluse

Hawthorne's life was not externally exciting or remarkable, but it presents an interesting symbolic pattern. As John Keats said of Shakespeare, he led a life of allegory and his works are the comments on it. Returning from Bowdoin, Hawthorne spent from 1825 to 1837 in his mother's Salem household. Later he looked back upon these years as a period of dreamlike isolation and solitude, spent in a haunted chamber, where he sat enchanted while other men moved on. The "solitary years" were, however, his literary apprenticeship, during which he learned to write tales and sketches that are still unrivaled and unique.

Recent biographers have shown that this period of Hawthorne's life was less lonely than he remembered it to be. In literal truth, he did have social engagements, played cards, and went to the theater and the Lyceum; his sister Elizabeth remarked that "if there was any gathering of people in the town he always went out; he liked a crowd." Nevertheless, he consistently remembered these 12 years as a strange, dark dream, though his view of their consequences varied.

"In this dismal chamber Fame was won," Hawthorne wrote, perhaps a little ironically, in 1836. To his fiancée, Sophia Peabody, he later confided, "If ever I should have a biographer, he ought to make great mention of this chamber in my memoirs, because so much of my lonely youth was wasted here, and here my mind and character were formed." On the whole, he felt that his isolation had been beneficial: " . . . if I had sooner made my escape into the world, I should have grown hard and rough, and been covered with earthly dust, and my heart would have become callous by rude encounters with the multitude"—an observation that he made more than once.

Writing the Short Stories

Most of Hawthorne's early stories were published anonymously in magazines and giftbooks. In his own words, he was "for a good many years, the obscurest man of letters in America." In 1837 the publication of *Twice-Told Tales* somewhat lifted this spell of darkness. In the preface to the 1851 edition he spoke of "the apparently opposite peculiarities" of these stories. Despite the circumstances under which they were written, "they are not the talk of a secluded man with his own mind and heart . . . but his attempts, and very imperfectly successful ones, to open an intercourse with the world." The *Twice-Told Tales* he supplemented with two later collections, *Mosses from an Old Manse* (1846) and *The Snow-Image* (1851), along with *Grandfather's Chair* (1841), a history for children of New England through the Revolution; the *Journal of an African Cruiser* (1845), edited from the observations of his friend Horatio Bridge while he was purser on an American frigate; and the second edition of the *Tales* (1842).

Hawthorne's short stories came slowly but steadily into critical favor, and the best of them have become American classics. It may well be claimed for them as a whole that they are the outstanding achievement in their genre to be found in the English language during the 19th century. Lucid, graceful, and well composed, they combine an old-fashioned neoclassic purity of diction with a latent and hard complexity of meaning. They are broadly allegorical but infused with imaginative passion. The combination has produced very different opinions of their value, which Hawthorne himself acutely foresaw, remarking that his touches "have often an effect of tameness," and that his work, "if you would see anything in it, requires to be read in the clear, brown, twilight atmosphere in which it was written; if opened in the sunshine, it is apt to look exceedingly like a volume of blank pages" (1851 Preface, *Twice-Told Tales*).

Hawthorne is a master of balance and suggestion who inveterately understates: the texture of his tales, as of his novels, is so delicate that some readers cannot see it at all. But many, too, will testify as Herman Melville did to his "power of blackness." Of Hawthorne's story "Young Goodman Brown," Melville wrote, "You would of course suppose that it was a simple little tale. . . . Whereas it is as deep as Dante: nor can you finish it, without addressing the author in his own words: 'It is yours to penetrate, in every bosom, the deep mystery of sin.'"

Out in the World

By his own account it was Hawthorne's love of his Salem neighbor Sophia Peabody that brought him from his "haunted chamber" out into the world. His books were far from profitable enough to support a prospective wife and family, so in 1838 he went to work in the Boston Custom House and then spent part of 1841 in the famous Brook Farm community in hopes of finding a pleasant and economical haven for Sophia and himself. It is curious that the seclusive Hawthorne was always interested in experiments in community living: in Brook Farm, in the New England Shaker settlements, and later in Greenwich Hospital in London. He was to record his mingled feelings of sympathy and skepticism about Brook Farm in *The Blithedale Romance* (1852).

At any rate, Hawthorne and Sophia, whom he married in 1842, resorted not to Brook Farm but to the Old Manse in Concord, where they spent several years of idyllic happiness in as much solitude as they could achieve. Concord, however, contained Ralph Waldo Emerson, Henry David Thoreau, and Ellery Channing, and Hawthorne was in frequent contact with these important thinkers, though his was not a nature for transcendental affirmations.

Writing the Novels

Facing the world once more, Hawthorne obtained in 1846 the position of surveyor in the Salem Custom House, from which as a Democrat he was expelled after the Whig victory in the 1848 presidential election. He did not leave without a fight and considerable bitterness, and he took revenge in the "Custom-House" introduction to *The Scarlet Letter* (1850) and in *The House of the Seven Gables* (1851), in which he portrayed his chief Whig enemy as the harsh and hypocritical Judge Pyncheon. His dismissal, however, turned out to be a blessing, since it gave him leisure in which to write his greatest and crucial success, *The Scarlet Letter*. Except for his early *Fanshawe* (1828), which he suppressed shortly after publication, *The Scarlet Letter* was his first novel, or, as he preferred to say, "romance"; thus his literary career divided into two distinct parts, since he now almost wholly abandoned the shorter tale.

The period 1850-1853 was Hawthorne's most prolific. Doubtless stimulated by the enthusiastic reception accorded *The Scarlet Letter,* he went on with *The House of the Seven Gables* and *The Blithedale Romance,* along with *A Wonder Book* (1852) and *Tanglewood Tales* (1853), exquisitely fanciful stories for children from Greek mythology. During 1850 the Hawthornes lived at the Red House in Lenox in the Berkshire Hills, and Hawthorne formed a memorable friendship with novelist Herman Melville,

whose Arrowhead Farm was some miles away on the outskirts of Pittsfield. The association was more important to Melville than to Hawthorne, since Melville was 15 years younger and much the more impressionable of the two men. It left its mark in Melville's celebrated review of *Mosses from an Old Manse,* in the dedication of his *Moby-Dick,* and in some wonderful letters. Hawthorne's share in their correspondence has not survived, but he clearly aided Melville with insight and sympathy.

Years Abroad

In 1852 Franklin Pierce was elected to the presidency of the United States, and Hawthorne, who was induced to write his campaign biography, was appointed to the important overseas post of American consul at Liverpool, in which he served form 1853 to 1857 with considerable efficiency. These English years resulted in *Our Old Home* (1863), a volume drawn from the since-published "English Note-Books." It was to give considerable offense to the English public. Hawthorne felt a very deep affinity for "our old home," but as with his other "old home," Salem, his feelings were mingled, and he did not hesitate to express them.

In 1857 the Hawthornes left England for Italy, where they spent their time primarily in Rome and Florence. They returned to England, where Hawthorne finished his last and longest complete novel, the "Roman romance" *The Marble Faun* (1860). They finally returned to the United States, after an absence of seven years, and took up residence in their first permanent home, The Wayside, at Concord, which Hawthorne had bought from Bronson Alcott.

Last Years

Hawthorne was to live only four more years. Although he had always been an exceptionally vigorous man, his health inexplicably declined; and since he refused to submit to any thorough medical examination, his malady remains mysterious. During these last years in Concord he struggled with no less than four romances, *The Ancestral Footstep, Dr. Grimshawe's Secret, Septimius Felton,* and *The Dolliver Romance,* but completed none of them. Ironically, they are obsessively concerned with the theme of "earthly immortality" and the "elixir of life," which he had earlier touched upon in stories like "Dr. Heidegger's Experiment" (*Twice-Told Tales*).

Hawthorne died on May 19, 1864. He had set off for the New Hampshire hills with Franklin Pierce. He had always been fond of such expeditions and hoped to benefit from this one. But he died the second night out in Plymouth, N.H., presumably in his sleep. The circumstances of his end were somehow representative of the man, at once settled and at the same time restless when too long in one place. He once said that New England was enough to fill his heart, yet he sought the broader experience of Europe. Modest in expectations, he had yet desired to live fully.

Hawthorne's Literary Background

The case of Hawthorne is complex, in his life and in his writings. A born writer, like Edgar Allan Poe he suffered the difficulties of the writer in early-19th-century America: an unsympathetic environment, the materialism of a physically expanding nation, the lack of an artistic tradition. His Puritan heritage was both a support and a drawback. Its tradition of soul-searching encouraged profundity, and its penchant for seeking God's Providence in natural events provided Hawthorne with a way of seeing and interpreting. It was a highly literate tradition as well. It was, however, notoriously unfriendly to art—fiction as make-believe was mere vanity, and as imitation of God's creatures and creations it was idolatry. A natural artist, Hawthorne was always to worry about the morality of imitating and analyzing human nature in his art of fiction.

With his Puritanism, Hawthorne also inherited the Augustan culture of the early 18th century—a common case in New England, but especially powerful in his. Thus came the purity of his prose style, and its coolness and balance, in a sense retrogressive in his own time. Yet he was also responsive to the influence of his near contemporaries, the English romantics. He read widely and was vitally influenced by all the chief romantic poets, William Wordsworth, Samuel Taylor Coleridge, Lord Byron, Percy Bysshe Shelley, and John Keats. Hawthorne drew especially upon Coleridge's critical principles for his own theory of the prose romance. Like the romantics, he too desired to live fully and make the best use of his sensibilities, but his impulses were tempered by Augustan moderation and Puritan self-distrust.

A serious and conscientious craftsman, Hawthorne yet was not committed (as was Henry James) to the craft of fiction, not being minded to sacrifice either himself or those who depended upon him to its demands. He held a rather too pessimistic view of his own talent, and his deep Puritan skepticism of the value of merely human effort was also a deterrent to complete dedication to fiction; the volume of his writing is substantial but not great.

Power of Darkness

Hawthorne's belief in Providence could be discouraging, but it was also a source of strength. Along with Melville, he was one of the great "no-sayers" of 19th-century America. He accepted, imaginatively if not literally, the doctrine of the Fall of Man, and thus the radical imperfection of man. In his work there is as much light as darkness, but the dark is perhaps the more dramatic hue. In imaginative literature evil can be an esthetic element with the dark as a contrast to light; and Hawthorne used contrast so effectively that Henry James believed his "darkness" to be mere fanciful playing, with evil and pain used simply as counters in his fictional game. Melville, however, perceived more deeply that Hawthorne might be fascinated with the problem of evil as an element of his design, yet at the same time treat it with the utmost seriousness ("Hawthorne and his Mosses").

Tragedy is traditionally the most complex literary form, while it is also an imaginative testing ground, in which the human spirit is broadened and deepened by its struggle with the utmost imaginable adversity. In *The Scarlet Letter,* for example, the protagonists Hester and Dimmesdale are opposed not only by Puritan society but by something in themselves, and by a mysterious and invisible principle of reality still more powerful.

Allegorical Structures and Themes

Hawthorne's fictional structures are basically allegorical confrontations of good and evil, and his characters can usually be classified as types. He writes, however, not to prove points or teach moral lessons, which are themselves his fictional materials rather than his conclusions. *The House of the Seven Gables,* for instance, has a message, "the truth, namely, that the wrongdoing of one generation lives into the successive ones, and, divesting itself of every temporary advantage, becomes a pure and uncontrollable mischief." But Hawthorne reflects that when romances do teach anything, "it is usually through a far more subtle process than the ostensible one.... A high truth, indeed, fairly, finely, and skillfully wrought out, brightening at every step, and crowning the final development of a work of fiction, may add an artistic glory, but is never any truer, and seldom any more evident, at the last page than at the first" (Preface, *The House of the Seven Gables*).

Isolation or "alienation" is Hawthorne's principal theme and problem, and loss of contact with reality is the ultimate penalty he envisions. Characteristically, this results from a separation of the "head," or intellect, and the "heart," a term that includes the emotions, the passions, and the unconscious. The heart is the custodian of man's deepest potentialities for good and evil, and it is man's vital connection with reality. Too much "head" leads always to a fatal intellectual pride, which distorts and finally destroys the wholeness of the real world. This, for Hawthorne, is the worst sin or calamity that man is heir to.

Further Reading

Randall Stewart, *Nathaniel Hawthorne* (1948), is the standard biography. Newton Arvin, *Hawthorne* (1929), contains criticism and psychological analysis. Mark Van Doren, *Nathaniel Hawthorne* (1949), presents a balanced interpretation of Hawthorne's life and principal works. Older works include Henry James, Jr., *Hawthorne* (1879).

Notable treatments of Hawthorne's art in its historical and national contexts appear in Yvor Winters, *Maule's Curse: Seven Studies in the History of American Obscurantism* (1938); F. O. Matthiessen, *American Renaissance: Art and Expression in the Age of Emerson and Whitman* (1941); Charles Feidelson, Jr., *Symbolism and American Literature* (1953); and Richard Chase, *The American Novel and Its Tradition* (1957), which is illuminating on the tradition of "romance" in America.

More specialized interpretations of Hawthorne's fiction are Richard Harter Fogle, *Hawthorne's Fiction: The Light and the Dark* (1952, rev. ed. 1964) and *Hawthorne's Imagery* (1969); Hyatt H. Waggoner, *Hawthorne: A Critical Study* (1955, rev. ed. 1963); and Roy R. Male, *Hawthorne's Tragic Vision* (1957). □

John Hay

John Hay (1838-1905) was important for shaping America's open-door policy toward the Far East. He set guidelines for much of America's diplomacy in the 20th century, involving the United States in maintaining China's territorial integrity.

Rapid change characterized the United States during the years of John Hay's public service. Retarded briefly by the Civil War, dynamic forces of urbanization and industrialization began to transform both the landscape and the mood of America. Though the railroad tie and the sweatshop were as foreign to the aristocratic world of John Hay as the reaper and the grain elevator, they combined to support a new economic system that knew few boundaries, wrenching America out of its quiet isolation and into the highly competitive arena of international politics, where Hay's contribution would be made.

Hay was born on Oct. 8, 1838, in Salem, Ind. He attended Brown University (1855-1858), where he reluctantly prepared for a career in law. In 1859 he entered a Springfield, Ill., law firm, next door to the office of Abraham Lincoln. When Lincoln was elected U.S. president, Hay became his assistant private secretary. After Lincoln's death, Hay took minor diplomatic posts in Paris, Vienna, and Madrid. Socially successful, he had no serious influence on foreign policy. In 1870 he returned to the United States. Between 1870 and 1896 he moved in and out of Republican politics, journalism, and business, surrounding himself with a patrician set of friends, including Boston aristocrats, intel-

lectuals, and prominent politicians. His widely acclaimed poems and novels were overshadowed in 1890 by his *Abraham Lincoln: A History,* a ten volume work completed with John Nicolay.

Hay became close to presidential candidate William McKinley during his 1896 campaign. As president, McKinley appointed Hay ambassador to Great Britain, where Hay smoothed out issues concerning the Spanish-American War and subsequent annexations. He returned to become McKinley's secretary of state in 1898.

Secretary of State

As secretary of state, Hay was concerned with policy in four major areas: conducting peace negotiations after the Spanish-American War, setting policy toward the Far East, improving the United States position in Latin America, and settling the dispute with Great Britain over the Alaskan boundary.

Whereas McKinley had shaped the Spanish-American War settlement (and, later, President Theodore Roosevelt was the force behind policies in Latin America), Hay exerted considerable influence in making American policy toward the Far East and in the Canadian boundary dispute. Regarding England, Hay was considered a good friend to Britain by both the English and the Americans. Though committed to United States interests, he sought solutions in the Canadian dispute that would not endanger Anglo-American understanding.

Regarding the Far East, America watched the establishment of spheres of influence in China by European powers, Russia, and Japan with apprehension, fearing that United States trade rights might be limited by new political arrangements. In 1899 Hay asked the six governments directly involved to approve a formula guaranteeing that in their spheres of influence the rights and privileges of other nations would be respected and discriminatory port dues and railroad rates would not be levied and that Chinese officials would continue to collect tariffs. Although the six nations responded coolly, Hay announced that the open-door principle had been accepted, and the American press described the policy as a tremendous success. When an antiforeign uprising broke out in China in 1900, Hay sent a second set of notes, urging the open-door policy for all of the Chinese Empire and maintenance of the territorial integrity of China. Traditional protection of American economic interests thus was tied to the overly ambitious task of preserving the territory of China; under the guise of America's historic mission to support the cause of freedom, this would lead the United States to ever stronger commitments in the Far East.

When the assassination of McKinley made Roosevelt president, Hay increasingly gave way to presidential leadership in foreign policy. Following Roosevelt's lead concerning the building of an Isthmian canal, Hay obtained British consent to a United States canal under the Hay-Pauncefote treaties of 1900 and 1901. Though he supported Roosevelt's policy toward the new Panamanian Republic and the acquisition of the Canal Zone in 1903, Hay did little to actually shape Latin American policy.

The 1903 Alaskan-Canadian boundary dispute with Great Britain was settled amiably by commissioners, as Hay had suggested. Soon after, serious illness forced Hay to assume a virtually inactive role as secretary of state. He retained the office until his death on July 1, 1905, in Newbury, N. H.

Further Reading

Hay's correspondence is gathered in William R. Thayer, *The Life and Letters of John Hay* (2 vols., 1915). Tyler Dennett's biography, *John Hay: From Poetry to Politics* (1933), treats Hay's career colorfully and sympathetically. Scholars have generally focused their attention on Hay's role as secretary of state. An able assessment by Foster R. Dulles is in Norman A. Graebner, ed., *An Uncertain Tradition: American Secretaries of State in the Twentieth Century* (1961), and a general description of the diplomacy of the period is in Thomas McCormick, *A Fair Field and No Favor* (1967). For contrasting interpretations of the origins of the open-door policy see George F. Kennan, *American Diplomacy, 1900-1950* (1951), and William A. Williams, *The Tragedy of American Diplomacy* (1959; rev. ed. 1962). ☐

Rutherford Birchard Hayes

Rutherford Birchard Hayes (1822-1893), nineteenth president of the United States, supervised the Republican party's unsuccessful attempt to build a Southern wing based on old white "Whig" elements.

Rutherford B. Hayes was born Oct. 4, 1822, in Delaware, Ohio. His family, recently moved from New England, was well-to-do. Born 2 months after his father's death, Hayes was dominated by his neurotic mother and sister and patronized by his wealthy uncle Sardis Birchard.

Birchard was a critical influence in Hayes's life and helped pay for his education. Graduating from Kenyon College with highest honors in 1842, Hayes went to Harvard Law School in 1843. In 1845 he moved to Lower Sandusky (now Fremont), Ohio, to practice law under his uncle's sponsorship. Easygoing and pliable, Hayes was inclined to accept the conservative ideals surrounding him, and he adopted his uncle's Whig politics and distaste for abolitionists. The tall, handsome Hayes was a congenial and ready conversationalist, and he enjoyed considerable popularity in the town. Nevertheless, in 1849 he moved to Cincinnati, then the most important city in the West.

The young lawyer's personability and good showing in a celebrated homicide case soon won Hayes some reputation and political notice. Like most Northern Whigs during the late 1850s, Hayes had turned to the Republican party. However, he was not excessively interested in political questions; during the momentous election of 1860 he wrote, "I cannot get up much interest in the contest." He preferred the casual society of the "best people," travel, and occasional lectures on temperance.

War Years

Hayes's life of genteel idleness ended with the Civil War. He accepted a commission as major of the 23d Ohio Infantry. Now, for the first time in his life, he truly reveled in an all-masculine world, and he later looked back on the war as "the best years of our lives." He was brave to the point of recklessness and was wounded four times, once seriously. He rose to the rank of major general. What was more significant, his war record catapulted him into prominence in Ohio politics. While he was still in the military, he was nominated by the Republicans to serve in Congress and was elected without campaigning. He went to Washington for two terms, beginning in 1864.

In 1867 Hayes was elected governor of Ohio. He compiled a "moderate" record on all issues and retired to what he regarded as a permanent private life in 1871. However, in 1875, Republican leaders prevailed on him to stand again for governor, with the possibility of the presidential nomination the next year clearly understood. Successful, he entered his third term.

Disputed Election

Hayes entered the Republican nominating convention of 1876 as a minor candidate. The favorite, James G. Blaine, faced a number of opponents. In addition, the Republicans were sensitive to charges of political corruption, as the administration of Ulysses S. Grant had been blackened by scandal and Blaine had been implicated in a stock manipulation deal. Blaine's rivals withdrew one by one in favor of the deliberately "passive" Hayes.

The election, which pitted Republican Hayes against Democrat Samuel J. Tilden, proved more difficult. Owing to questions of the legitimacy of vote casting and counting in several states, the whole election was questioned and the country plunged into debate. Finally, a congressional commission was established to decide the election. By a curious twist the commission was composed of eight Republicans and only seven Democrats. However, the dispute was settled, and Hayes took office in March 1877 without further serious incident because the Republicans had made informal agreements with Southern Democrats to work toward establishment of a new political alliance between men of means in both the North and the South. Hayes's party thus hoped to drive a wedge between the two wings of its opposition.

Hayes was more than happy with the plan. He was naturally a "Whig" and had been uncomfortable with Grant's "bloody shirt" politics. He did not personally regard deals with the Southern Democrats as abandoning the Republican commitment to Southern blacks; rather, he hoped to win paternalistic protection for them by encouraging the growth of the Republican party among whites.

As president, Hayes withdrew the last Federal troops from the South and, as a symbol of the end of this phase of the Reconstruction, decorated Confederate graves on Memorial Day, 1877. "My task was to wipe out the color line, to abolish sectionalism; to end the war and bring peace," Hayes remembered, but by 1878 he had to state, "I am reluctantly forced to admit that the experiment was a failure."

Though Hayes was as meticulous with detail as ever and dispensed his presidential duties ably, he abhorred active leadership. He pledged to serve only one term, and the Republicans were happy to retire him. Hayes spent his final years in prosperous retirement in Lower Sandusky, distracting himself with active participation in the Grand Army of the Republic and other veterans' organizations. He died on Jan. 17, 1893.

Further Reading

Hamilton J. Eckenrode, *Rutherford B. Hayes: Statesman of Reunion* (1930), is highly favorable to Hayes but suffers from a blatantly racist approach to the questions of Reconstruction that loomed so large in Hayes's career. Harry Barnard, *Rutherford B. Hayes and His America* (1954), is a model of thorough historical research and possesses shrewd insights. T. Harry Williams, *Hayes of the Twenty-third* (1965), is a fascinating account of Hayes's war years. C. Vann Woodward, *Reunion and Reaction* (1951; rev. ed. 1956), is the indispensable insight into the ending of Reconstruction, and H. Wayne Morgan, *From Hayes to McKinley* (1969), is the best recent overall account of the period. For the election of 1876 see Arthur M. Schlesinger, Jr., ed., *History of American Presidential Elections,* vol. 2 (1971). □

William Randolph Hearst

William Randolph Hearst (1863-1951) was the American publisher, editor, and proprietor—for almost half a century—of the most extensive journalistic empire ever assembled by one man.

On April 29, 1863, William Randolph Hearst was born in San Francisco. He received the best education that his coarse-grained, multimillionaire father and his refined, schoolteacher mother (more than 20 years her husband's junior) could buy: private tutors, private schools, grand tours of Europe, and Harvard College. Hearst inherited his father's ambition and energy, but neither his father's fortune nor need to make his own way in the world. George Hearst had amassed millions in mining properties, which he left, not to his son but to his wife—who compensated for his crass unfaithfulness by wantonly spoiling their only offspring.

Young Hearst's journalistic career began in 1887, two years after he was expelled from Harvard. "I want the San Francisco Examiner," he wrote his father, who owned the newspaper and granted the request. The *Daily Examiner* became young Hearst's laboratory, where he indulged a talent for making fake news and faking real news in such a way as to create maximum public shock. From the outset he obtained top talent by paying top prices. Ambrose Bierce, at the peak of his fame, became Hearst's first star performer.

Building a Journalistic Empire

But to get an all-star cast and an audience of millions, Hearst had to move his headquarters to New York City in 1895, four years after his father's death. By this time his mother had liquidated $7,500,000 of her husband's mining properties and turned over the proceeds to her son, who immediately purchased the decrepit *New York Morning Journal*. Within a year Hearst ran up the circulation from

77,000 to over a million by spending enough money to beat the aging Joseph Pulitzer's *World* at its own sensationalist game. Sometimes Hearst hired away the *World*'s more aggressive executives and reporters; sometimes he outbid all competitors in the open market, as when he got Richard Harding Davis to report and Frederick Remington to illustrate the ongoing Spanish-American War.

The *Journal* had got its start by raiding the *World* of its talents and its readers. Next, to Arthur Brisbane's portentous front-page column entitled "Today," and to black-and-white daily comic strips and colored Sunday supplements, Hearst added frenetic reporting of sports, crime, sex, scandal, and human-interest stories. "A Hearst newspaper is like a screaming woman running down the street with her throat cut," said Hearst writer Arthur James Pegler. Hearst's slam-bang showmanship attracted new readers and nonreaders, but on no one did the *Journal* cast so potent a spell as on its master of ceremonies.

During the last five years of the 19th century Hearst set his pattern for the first half of the 20th. The *Journal* supported the Democratic party, yet Hearst opposed the free-silver campaign of Democratic presidential candidate William Jennings Bryan in 1896. In 1898 Hearst backed the Spanish-American War, which Bryan and the Democrats opposed. Further, Hearst's wealth cut him off from the troubled masses to whom his newspapers appealed. He could not grasp the rudimentary problems raised by the issues of free silver and the war with Spain. Thus, for five years Hearst stood in the mainstream of the history of his time and did not even get his feet wet.

Entering Politics

Having shaken up San Francisco with the *Examiner* and New York with the *Journal,* Hearst established the *Chicago American* in 1900, the *Chicago Examiner* in 1902, and the *Boston American* and the *Los Angeles Examiner* in 1904. These acquisitions marked more than an extension of Hearst's journalistic empire, they reflected his sweeping decision to seek the U.S. presidency. However, he had chosen the wrong path to the wrong goal at the wrong time. To begin with, journalism and politics rarely mix; each is a full-time occupation. Furthermore, Hearst never even qualified as a great journalist. At most he was a showman whose very flair for a certain type of metropolitan journalism did him more harm than good in national politics. Finally, he had little preparation and less aptitude to win success in either field in the rough-and-tumble atmosphere of 20th-century America. The contrasts between his towering presence and his close-set eyes, his courtly manner, and his high-pitched voice did not present the typical image of a successful politician.

In 1902 and 1904 Hearst won election to the House of Representatives as a New York Tammany Democrat. But his journalistic activities and his $2 million presidential campaign left him little time to speak, vote, or answer roll calls in Congress. His absenteeism disgusted his colleagues and dismayed his constituents. Nevertheless, he found time to run as an independent candidate for mayor of New York in 1905 and, in 1906, as Democratic candidate for governor. His loss in both elections ended Hearst's political career.

The 45 years of anticlimax that followed gave ample scope to those defects of character, inheritance, and environment which a perverse fate had bequeathed Hearst. In 1903, the day before his fortieth birthday, he married 21-year-old Millicent Willson, a show girl with whom he had been smitten for several years, giving up Tessie Powers, a waitress he had supported since his Harvard days. The Hearsts had five boys, but in 1917 Hearst fell in love with another show girl, 20-year-old Marion Davies of the Ziegfeld Follies. He maintained a liaison with her that ended only at his death. He spent millions on her career as a movie actress, backing such sentimental slush as *When Knighthood Was in Flower* and *Little Old New York,* while ignoring her real talents as a comedienne.

When Hearst's mother died in 1919, he came into his patrimony and took up permanent residence on his father's 168,000-acre San Simeon Ranch in southern California. There he spent $37 million on a private castle. He put $50 million into New York City real estate and another $50 million into his art collection—the largest ever assembled by a single individual.

Hearst Publications

During the 1920s one American in every four read a Hearst newspaper. Hearst owned 20 daily and 11 Sunday papers in 13 cities, the King Features syndication service, the International News Service, the *American Weekly* (a syndicated Sunday supplement), International News Reel, and six magazines, including *Cosmopolitan, Good House-keeping,* and *Harper's Bazaar.*

Yet, for all his getting and spending, Hearst had few powers to lay waste and none to hoard. Originally a progressive Democrat, he had no truck with the Republican expansionists—Theodore Roosevelt, Henry Cabot Lodge, Elihu Root—who supported the Spanish-American War, which Hearst claimed he had made but which actually had made his *Journal.* Hearst then fought every reform Democratic leader from Bryan to Franklin Roosevelt; he opposed American participation in both world wars.

In 1927 the Hearst newspapers printed unchecked, forged documents charging that the Mexican government had paid several U.S. senators more than $1 million to support a Central American plot to wage war against the United States. (Ironically, this fiasco led President Calvin Coolidge to appoint Dwight Morrow as ambassador to Mexico, thereby launching a new era in U.S.-Latin American relations.) From this scandal the Hearst press suffered not at all. Nothing was lost save honor, and that had gone long since.

In the next 10 years, however, Hearst's funds and the empire suddenly ran out. In 1937 the two corporations that controlled the empire found themselves $126 million in debt. Hearst had to turn them over to a seven-member conservation committee, which managed to stave off bankruptcy only at the expense of much of Hearst's private fortune and all of his public powers as a newspaper lord. He died on August 14, 1951.

Some of Hearst's biographers have stressed his split personality—as if that differentiated him from the rest of mankind. The word "nihilist" provides a more precise clue. Not that Hearst's nihilism incorporated any of the revolutionary passion that impelled the Bolshevik Lenin or the destructive passion that impelled the Nazi Hitler. Hearst's nihilism had no more substance than Hearst himself possessed. In fact, no notable of his time left so faint an imprint on its sands.

Further Reading

Edmund D. Coblentz, ed., *William Randolph Hearst: A Portrait in His Own Words* (1952), is a compilation of Hearst's public and private documents. Judicious interpretations of Hearst's life are Oliver Carlson and Ernest Sutherland Bates, *Hearst: Lord of San Simeon* (1936); John William Tebbel's sympathetic *The Life and Good Times of William Randolph Hearst* (1952); and William A. Swanberg, *Citizen Hearst* (1961). Ferdinand Lundberg, *Imperial Hearst: A Social Biography* (1936), is a scathing attack. See also John K. Winkler, *William Randolph Hearst: A New Appraisal* (1955). For an examination of Hearst's early career and political aspirations, see Ben Procter's *William Randolph Hearst: The Early Years, 1863–1910* (1998). □

Joseph Heller

Joseph Heller (1923-1999) is a popular and respected writer whose first and best-known novel, *Catch-22* (1961), is considered a classic of the post-World War II era. Presenting human existence as absurd and fragmented, this irreverent, witty novel satirizes capitalism and the military bureaucracy.

Heller's tragicomic vision of modern life, found in all of his novels, focuses on the erosion of humanistic values and highlights the ways in which language obscures and confuses reality. In addition, Heller's use of anachronism reflects the disordered nature of contemporary existence. His protagonists are antiheroes who search for meaning in their lives and struggle to avoid being overwhelmed by such institutions as the military, big business, government, and religion. *Catch-22* is most often interpreted as an antiwar protest novel that foreshadowed the widespread resistance to the Vietnam War that erupted in the late 1960s. While Heller's later novels have received mixed reviews, *Catch-22* continues to be highly regarded as a trenchant satire of the big business of modern warfare.

Heller was born in Brooklyn, New York, to first generation Russian-Jewish immigrants. His father, a bakery-truck driver, died after a bungled operation when Heller was only five years old. Many critics believe that Heller developed the sardonic, wisecracking humor that has marked his writing style while growing up in the Coney Island section of Brooklyn. After graduating from high school in 1941, he worked briefly in an insurance office, an experience he later drew upon for the novel *Something Happened* (1974). In 1942, Heller enlisted in the Army Air Corps. Two years later he was sent to Corsica, where he flew sixty combat missions as a wing bombardier, earning an Air Medal and a Presidential Unit Citation. It is generally agreed that Heller's war years in the Mediterranean theater had only a minimal impact on his conception of *Catch-22*. Discharged from the military in 1945, Heller married Shirley Held and began his college education. He obtained a B.A. in English from New York University, an M.A. from Columbia University, and attended Oxford University as a Fulbright Scholar for a year before becoming an English instructor at Pennsylvania State University. Two years later Heller began working as an advertising copywriter, securing positions at such magazines as *Time, Look,* and *McCall's* from 1952 to 1961. The office settings of these companies also yielded material for *Something Happened.* During this time Heller was also writing short stories and scripts for film and television as well as working on *Catch-22.* Although his stories easily found publication, Heller considered them insubstantial and derivative of Ernest Hemingway's works. After the phenomenal success of *Catch-22,* Heller quit his job at *McCall's* and concentrated exclusively on writing fiction and plays. In December of 1981, he contracted Guillain-Barre syndrome, a rare type of polyneuritis that afflicts the peripheral nervous system. Heller chronicled his medical problems and difficult recovery in *No Laughing Matter* (1986) with Speed Vogel, a friend who helped him during his illness.

Catch-22 concerns a World War II bombardier named Yossarian who believes his foolish, ambitious, mean-spirited commanding officers are more dangerous than the enemy. In order to avoid flying more missions, Yossarian retreats to a hospital with a mysterious liver complaint, sabotages his plane, and tries to get himself declared insane.

Variously defined throughout the novel, "Catch-22" refers to the ways in which bureaucracies control the people who work for them. The term first appears when Yossarian asks to be declared insane. In this instance, Catch-22 demands that anyone who is insane must be excused from flying missions. The "catch" is that one must ask to be excused; anyone who does so is showing "rational fear in the face of clear and present danger," is therefore sane, and must continue to fly. In its final, most ominous form, Catch-22 declares "they have the right to do anything we can't stop them from doing." Although most critics identify Yossarian as a coward and an antihero, they also sympathize with his urgent need to protect himself from this brutal universal law. Some critics have questioned the moral status of Yossarian's actions, noting in particular that he seems to be motivated merely by self-preservation, and that the enemy he refuses to fight is led by Adolf Hitler. Others, however, contend that while *Catch-22* is ostensibly a war novel, World War II and the Air Force base where most of the novel's action takes place function primarily as a microcosm that demonstrates the disintegration of language and human value in a bureaucratic state.

Heller embodies his satire of capitalism in the character of Milo Minderbinder, whose obsessive pursuit of profits causes many deaths and much suffering among his fellow soldiers. Originally a mess hall officer, Milo organizes a powerful black market syndicate capable of cornering the Egyptian cotton market and bombing the American base on Pianosa for the Germans. On the surface Milo's adventures form a straightforward, optimistic success story that some commentators have likened to the Horatio Alger tales popular at the turn of the twentieth century. The narrative line that follows Yossarian, on the other hand, is characterized by his confused, frustrated, and frightened psychological state. The juxtaposition of these two narrative threads provides a disjointed, almost schizophrenic structure that reasserts the absurd logic depicted in *Catch-22.*

Structurally, *Catch-22* is episodic and repetitive. The majority of the narrative is composed of a series of cyclical flashbacks of increasing detail and ominousness. The most important recurring incident is the death of a serviceman named Snowden that occurs before the opening of the story but is referred to and recounted periodically throughout the novel. In the penultimate chapter, Yossarian relives the full horror and comprehends the significance of this senseless death as it reflects the human condition and his own situation. This narrative method led many critics, particularly early reviewers, to condemn Heller's novel as formless. Norman Mailer's oft-repeated jibe: "One could take out a hundred pages anywhere from the middle of *Catch-22,* and not even the author could be certain they were gone" has been refuted by Heller himself, and has inspired other critics to carefully trace the chronology of ever-darkening events that provide the loose structure of this novel.

Heller poignantly and consistently satirizes language, particularly the system of euphemisms and oxymorons that passes for official speech in the United States Armed Forces. In the world of *Catch-22* metaphorical language has a dangerously literal power. The death of Doc Daneeka is an example: when the plane that Doc is falsely reported to be on crashes and no one sees him parachute to safety, he is presumed dead and his living presence is insufficient to convince anyone that he is really alive. Similarly, when Yossarian rips up his girlfriend's address in rage, she disappears, never to be seen again. Marcus K. Billson III summarized this technique: "The world of [*Catch-22*]projects the horrific, yet all too real, power of language to divest itself from any necessity of reference, to function as an independent, totally autonomous medium with its own perfect system and logic. That such a language pretends to mirror anything but itself is a commonplace delusion Heller satirizes throughout the novel. Yet, civilization is informed by this very pretense, and Heller shows how man is tragically and comically tricked and manipulated by such an absurdity."

Heller's second novel, *Something Happened,* centers on Bob Slocum, a middle-aged businessman who has a large, successful company but who feels emotionally empty. Narrating in a monotone, Slocum attempts to find the source of his malaise and his belief that modern American bourgeois life has lost meaning, by probing into his past and exploring his relationships with his wife, children, and co-workers. Although critics consider Slocum a generally dislikable character, he ultimately achieves sympathy because he has so thoroughly assimilated the values of his business that he has lost his own identity. Many commentators have viewed Slocum as an Everyman, a moral cipher who exemplifies the age's declining spirit. While initial reviews of *Something Happened* were mixed, more recent criticism has often deemed this novel superior to and more sophisticated than *Catch-22,* particularly citing Heller's shift from exaggeration to suggestion. In his critical biography *Joseph Heller,* Robert Merrill described *Something Happened* as "the most convincing study we have of what it is like to participate in the struggle that is postwar America."

Good as Gold (1979) marks Heller's first fictional use of his Jewish heritage and childhood experiences in Coney Island. The protagonist of this novel, Bruce Gold, is an unfulfilled college professor who is writing a book about "the Jewish experience," but he also harbors political ambitions. Offered a high government position after giving a positive review of a book written by the president, Gold accepts, leaves his wife and children, and finds himself immersed in a farcical bureaucracy in which officials speak in a confusing, contradictory language. In this novel, Heller harshly satirizes former Secretary of State Henry Kissinger, a Jew who has essentially forsaken his Jewishness. As a result, the author draws an analogy between the themes of political powerlust and corruption with Jewish identity. Similarly, Gold's motives for entering politics are strictly self-aggrandizing, as he seeks financial, sexual, and social rewards. When his older brother dies, however, Gold realizes the importance of his Jewish heritage and family, and decides to leave Washington. Throughout the novel, Heller alternates the narrative between scenes of Gold's large, garrulous Jewish family and the mostly gentile milieu of Washington, employing realism to depict the former and parody to portray the latter.

Heller's next novel, *God Knows* (1984), is a retelling of the biblical story of King David, the psalmist of the Old Testament. A memoir in the form of a monologue by David, the text abounds with anachronistic speech, combining the Bible's lyricism with a Jewish-American dialect reminiscent of the comic routines of such humorists as Lenny Bruce, Mel Brooks, and Woody Allen. In an attempt to determine the origin of his despondency near the end of his life, David ruminates on the widespread loss of faith and sense of community, the uses of art, and the seeming absence of God. In *Picture This* (1988), Heller utilizes Rembrandt's painting "Aristotle Contemplating the Bust of Homer" to draw parallels between ancient Greece, seventeenth-century Holland, and contemporary America. Moving backward and forward among these eras, this novel meditates on art, money, injustice, the folly of war, and the failures of democracy. Critics questioned whether *Picture This* should be considered a novel, a work of history, or a political tract.

Heller's first play, *We Bombed in New Haven* (1967), concerns a group of actors who believe they are portraying an Air Force squadron in an unspecified modern war. The action alternates between scenes where the players act out their parts in the "script" and scenes where they converse among themselves out of "character," expressing dissatisfaction with their roles. This distancing technique, which recalls the work of Bertolt Brecht and Luigi Pirandello, alerts the audience to the play's artificiality. As in *Catch-22,* this drama exposes what Heller perceives as the illogic and moral bankruptcy of the United States military. Many critics have also interpreted *We Bombed in New Haven* as a protest against America's participation in the Vietnam War. Heller has also adapted *Catch-22* for the stage, but critics generally consider this work inferior to the novel.

While Heller's place in twentieth-century letters is assured with *Catch-22,* he is also highly regarded for his other works, which present a comic vision of modern society with serious moral implications. A major theme throughout his writing is the conflict that occurs when individuals interact with such powerful institutions as corporations, the military, and the federal government. Heller's novels have displayed increasing pessimism over the inability of individuals to reverse society's slide toward corruption and degeneration. He renders the chaos and absurdity of contemporary existence through disjointed chronology, anachronistic and oxymoronic language, and repetition of events. In all his work, Heller emphasizes that it is necessary to identify and take responsibility for our social and personal evils and to make beneficial changes in our behavior.

Joseph Heller died of heart failure in East Hampton, New York on December 12, 1999.

Further Reading

A Dangerous Crossing, Southern Illinois University Press, 1973.

Aichinger, Peter, *The American Soldier in Fiction, 1880-1963,* Iowa State University Press, 1975.

American Novels of the Second World War, Mouton, 1969.

Authors in the News, Volume 1, Gale, 1976.

Bergonzi, Bernard, *The Situation of the Novel,* University of Pittsburgh Press, 1970.

Bier, Jesse, *The Rise and Fall of American Humor,* Holt, 1968.

Bruccoli, Matthew J. and C. E. Frazer Clark, Jr., editors, *Pages: The World of Books, Writers, and Writing,* Gale, 1976. □

Jesse Helms

Jesse Helms (born 1921), conservative Senator from North Carolina, is well liked by the religious right for his position on abortion rights, school prayer, and school busing.

Born in Monroe, North Carolina, Jesse Helms studied at Wingate Junior College and Wake Forest University before serving in the navy during World War II. He became active in politics while working as a journalist in Raleigh, North Carolina, and served as an adviser to Willis Smith during his campaign for the U.S. Senate in 1950. After Smith's victory in what is regarded as the most virulently racist election in North Carolina history, Helms worked in Washington as an administrative assistant for Smith (1951-1953) and then briefly for Sen. Alton Lennon (1953). Returning to North Carolina in 1953, he worked as a television commentator and as a lobbyist for the banking industry before his election to the Senate as a Republican in 1972. He has been reelected by close margins in 1978, 1984, and 1990. In 1972 and 1984, presidential election years, he ran behind the Republican presidential nominee.

Ideological Purity

Helms has developed a reputation as an ideological purist. His record in the Senate has been consistently anti-United Nations, anti-Communist, anti-government spending, anti-welfare, anti-arms control, anti-foreign aid, and pro-military. His only major political about-face was his 1985 switch from an anti-Israeli position to one that is pro-Israel—one said to have been prompted in part by the narrowness of his 1984 victory over an opponent who received substantial contributions from pro-Israel individuals and groups outside North Carolina.

Support from the Religious Right

Helms is known for his derisive treatment of those he opposes—from Martin Luther King to the Soviet Union to homosexuals—and he has an old-time southern politician's visceral appeal for conservative, mostly rural, white North Carolinians. Said to have an Old Testament sense of good and evil, he has had close ties to the religious right throughout his career, and during his campaigns he has made frequent appearances on the shows of the televangelists Jim Bakker and Pat Robertson. Leaders of Jerry Falwell's Moral Majority have spoken on his behalf at political rallies.

Pushing Conservative Causes

Helms has not often been successful in getting his own legislation passed. In 1982 he failed to implement measures that would have stripped the Supreme Court of jurisdiction over cases involving abortion, school prayer, and school busing. He has cast dozens of votes to outlaw or restrict abortion, to eliminate busing for school integration, and to do away with food stamps. In 1989—after he became enraged over the inclusion of homoerotic photographs by Robert Mapplethorpe and Andres Serrano's photograph of a crucifix in a glass of urine in exhibits funded by the National Endowment for the Arts (NEA)—he tried unsuccessfully to convince the Senate to pass a bill that banned the funding of "obscene" art by the NEA or any other federal agency.

Blocking Nominations

Helms has also used his position on the committee to block or hold up nominations regardless of which party controlled the White House. He opposed Republican Gerald Ford's nominations of Nelson Rockefeller for vice president and Donald Rumsfeld for secretary of defense. Many of Democrat Jimmy Carter's nominees faced the same treatment, as did Caspar Weinberger, whom Republican Ronald Reagan nominated for secretary of defense. In 1981 Helms stalled Senate approval of several Reagan appointees as undersecretaries of state, including Lawrence Eagleburger, Chester Crocker, Robert Hormats, and Thomas Enders. In 1985 Helms held up the confirmation of Thomas Pickering as ambassador to Israel at a time of crucial discussions over possible exchanges of western hostages in Beirut for Arabs in Israeli prisons.

Right-Wing Ties

The animosity between Helms and Pickering stemmed from Pickering's service as ambassador to El Salvador, where he was actively trying to work with the Duarte government while Helms had close ties to Duarte's ultraright-wing opponent, Roberto D'Aubuisson. Helms has been closely tied to various right-wing governments, including the regime of Augusto Pinochet in Chile. Beginning in 1986 Helms served as chairman of the editorial advisory board of the International Freedom Foundation, a front organization for the South African Defense Fund, which set up and funded the foundation to conduct political warfare against opponents of apartheid in the United States. Other prominent conservative Republicans connected to the foundation included representatives Dan Burton and Robert Dornan of California and African American political activist Alan Keyes. In 1988 Helms led the fight to pass legislation that required the United States to maintain two embassies in Israel, one in Tel Aviv, the secular capital, and one in Jerusalem, in the contested West Bank region.

The Foreign Relations Committee

Throughout the 1980s Helms was consistently a thorn in the sides of Democratic and Republican administrations as he tried to promote his own ultraconservative foreign-policy agenda. But as chairman of the Senate Foreign Relations Committee he had the power to do so. His staff included former intelligence personnel who have retained ties within their agencies, and he promoted the hiring of his staffers and aides for key positions in the various national security agencies. After the GOP took control of both houses of Congress, Helms attempted to dismantle U.S. foreign policy. In March of 1995 he introduced a bill to get rid of USAID, the United States Information Agency, and the Arms Control and Disarmament Agency. The Democrats filibustered the bill, but to get even Helms shut down the Foreign Relations Committee for four months. Even though foreign aid makes up only one percent of the federal budget, Helms thinks that foreign aid is "the greatest racket of all time" and "the ripoff of the American taxpayers." Informational holds can be placed on projects to temporarily delay funding. The last time the GOP controlled the Senate, there were five holds placed in four years; Helms placed eighty-four holds in 1995. He maintained his presence in the Senate after the 1996 election, defeating former Charlotte mayor Harvey Gantt with a 52.6% share of the vote.

In March 1996 the Helms-Burton Act was signed into law, sponsored by Helms and Republican Representative Dan Burton of Indiana. The law was designed to pressure Cuba to adopt democratic reforms and was approved a month after Cuban warplanes shot down two civilian aircraft, killing four Cuban-Americans on board. It was bitterly criticized by Canada and the European Union.

On April 18, 1997, Clinton approved a plan to reorganize the State Department, a decision that responded to a long-standing demand by Helms. The plan aimed to consolidate the Arms Control and Disarmament Agency and the U.S. Information Agency into the State Department by 1999. Helms remained feisty, as in the fall of 1997, he refused to hold a hearing on President Clinton's nomination of moderate Republican William Weld to be ambassador to Mexico, noting that the former Massachusetts governor was soft on drugs. Although he began to face mounting criticism, "Senator No" wasn't budging. Helms won the battle, as Weld asked the White House to withdraw his nomination in mid-September.

His next battle appears to be federal arts funding, as Helms is among politicians who want to eliminate the National Endowment for the Arts. He stated in a speech to his colleagues, "It is self-evident that many of the beneficiaries of NEA grants are contemptuous of traditional moral standards."

Further Reading

Furgurson, Ernest B., *Hard Right: The Rise of Jesse Helms*, Norton, 1986.

Mother Jones, May 1995.

New Republic, November 12, 1990.

New York Times, April 18, 1997.

New York Times Magazine, October 28, 1990. □

Ernest Miller Hemingway

Ernest Miller Hemingway (1898-1961), American Nobel Prize-winning author, was one of the most celebrated and influential literary stylists of the 20th century.

Ernest Hemingway was a legend in his own life-time—in a sense, a legend of his own making. He worked hard at being a composite of all the manly attributes he

distinguished himself as a scholar and athlete—he ran away from home twice. However, his first real chance for escape came in 1917, when the United States entered World War I. He volunteered for active service in the infantry but was rejected because of eye trouble.

After spending several months as a reporter for the *Kansas City Star,* Hemingway enlisted in the Red Cross medical service, driving an ambulance on the Italian front. He was badly wounded in the knee at Fossalta di Piave; yet, still under heavy mortar fire, he carried a wounded man on his back a considerable distance to the aid station. After having over 200 shell fragments removed from his legs and body, Hemingway next enlisted in the Italian infantry, served on the Austrian front until the armistice, and was decorated for bravery by the Italian government.

Learning His Trade

Shortly after the war Hemingway worked as a foreign correspondent in the Near East for the *Toronto Star.* When he returned to Michigan, he had already decided to commit himself to fiction writing. His excellent journalism and the publication in magazines of several experimental short stories had impressed the well-known author Sherwood Anderson, who, when Hemingway decided to return to Europe, gave him letters of introduction to expatriates Gertrude Stein and Ezra Pound. Hemingway and his bride, Hadley Richardson, journeyed to Paris, where he served his literary apprenticeship under these two prominent authors. Despite the abject poverty in which he and his wife lived, these were the happiest years of Hemingway's life, as well as the most artistically fruitful.

In 1923 Hemingway published his first book, *Three Stories and Ten Poems.* The poems are insignificant, but the stories give strong indication of his emerging genius. "Out of Season" already contains the psychological tension and moral ambivalence characteristic of his mature work. With *In Our Time* (1925) Hemingway's years of apprenticeship ended. In this collection of stories, he drew on his experiences while summering in Michigan to depict the initiation into the world of pain and violence of young Nick Adams, a prototype for later Hemingway heroes. The atrocities he had witnessed as a journalist in the Near East became the brief vignettes about intense suffering that formed interchapters for the collection. One story, "Indian Camp," which sets the tone for the entire volume, has Nick accompanying his father, Dr. Adams, on a call during which the physician performs a caesarean operation with no anesthetic. They discover afterward that the squaw's husband, unable to bear his wife's screams, has killed himself by nearly severing his head with a razor. The story is written in Hemingway's characteristically terse, economic prose. "The End of Something" and "The Three Day Blow" deal with Nick's disturbed reaction to the end of a love affair. "The Big Two-hearted River" describes a young man just returned from war and his desperate attempt to prevent mental breakdown.

gave to his fictional heroes—a hard drinker, big-game hunter, fearless soldier, amateur boxer, and bullfight *aficionado.* Because the man and his fiction often seemed indistinguishable, critics have had difficulty judging his work objectively. His protagonists—virile and laconic— have been extravagantly praised and vehemently denounced. In his obsession with violence and death, the Hemingway creation has been rivaled only by the Byronic myth of the 19th century. Despite sensational publicity and personal invective, Hemingway now ranks among America's great writers. His critical stature rests solidly upon a small body of exceptional writing, distinguished for its stylistic purity, emotional veracity, moral integrity, and dramatic intensity of vision.

Ernest Hemingway was born in Oak Park, Ill., on July 21, 1898. His father was a country physician, who taught his son hunting and fishing; his mother was a religiously puritanical woman, active in church affairs, who led her boy to play the cello and sing in the choir. Hemingway's early years were spent largely in combating the repressive feminine influence of his mother and nurturing the masculine influence of his father. He spent the summers with his family in the woods of northern Michigan, where he often accompanied his father on professional calls. The discovery of his father's apparent cowardice, later depicted in the short story "The Doctor and the Doctor's Wife," and his suicide several years later left the boy with an emotional scar.

Despite the intense pleasure Hemingway derived from outdoor life, and his popularity in high school—where he

Major Novels

Hemingway returned to the United States in 1926 with the manuscripts of two novels and several short stories. *The Torrents of Spring* (1926), a parody of Sherwood Anderson, was written very quickly, largely for the purpose of breaking his contract with Boni and Liveright, who was also Anderson's publisher. That May, Scribner's issued Hemingway's second novel, *The Sun Also Rises*. This novel, the major statement of the "lost generation," describes a group of expatriate Americans and Englishmen, all of whom have suffered physically and emotionally during the war; their aimless existence vividly expresses the spiritual bankruptcy and moral atrophy of an entire generation. Hemingway's second volume of short stories, *Men without Women* (1927), contains "The Killers," about a man who refuses to run from gangsters determined to kill him; "The Light of the World," dealing with Nick Adams's premature introduction to the sickening world of prostitution and homosexuality; and "The Undefeated," concerning an aging bullfighter whose courage and dedication constitute a moral victory in the face of physical defeat and death.

In December 1929 *A Farewell to Arms* was published. This novel tells the story of a tragically terminated love affair between an American soldier and an English nurse, starkly silhouetted against the bleakness of war and a collapsing world order. It contains a philosophical expression of the Hemingway code of stoical endurance in a violent age: "The world breaks everyone," reflects the protagonist, "and afterward many are strong in the broken places. But those that it will not break it kills. It kills the very good and the very gentle and the very brave impartially. If you are none of those you can be sure that it will kill you too, but there will be no special hurry."

Hemingway revealed his passionate interest in bullfighting in *Death in the Afternoon* (1932), a humorous and inventive nonfiction study. In 1933 Scribner's published his final collection of short stories, *Winner Take Nothing*. This volume, containing his most bitter and disillusioned writing, deals almost exclusively with emotional breakdown, impotence, and homosexuality.

Hemingway's African safari in 1934 provided the material for another nonfiction work, *The Green Hills of Africa* (1935), as well as two of his finest short stories, "The Short Happy Life of Francis Macomber" and "The Snows of Kilimanjaro." Both stories concern attainment of self-realization and moral integrity through contact with fear and death.

Hemingway wrote *To Have and Have Not* (1937) in response to the 1930s depression. The novel, inadequately conceived and poorly executed, deals with a Florida smuggler whose illegal activities and frequent brutalities mask his sense of ethics and strength of character. Mortally wounded by the gangsters with whom he has been dealing, the individualistic hero comes to the startling realization that "One man alone ain't got no—chance."

The chief political catalyst in Hemingway's life was the Spanish Civil War. In 1936 he had returned to Spain as a newspaper reporter and participated in raising funds for the Spanish Republic until the war's end in 1939. In 1937 he collaborated on the documentary film *The Spanish Earth*. Hemingway's only writing during this period was a play, *The Fifth Column* (1936; produced in New York in 1940), a sincere but dramatically ineffective attempt to portray the conditions prevailing during the siege of Madrid.

Seventeen months after that war ended, Hemingway completed *For Whom the Bell Tolls* (1940). His most ambitious novel, it describes an American professor's involvement with a loyalist guerrilla band and his brief, idyllic love affair with a Spanish girl. A vivid, intelligently conceived narrative, it is written in less lyrical and more dramatic prose than his earlier work. Hemingway deliberately avoided having the book used as propaganda, despite its strained attempt at an affirmative resolution, by carefully balancing fascist atrocities with a heartless massacre by a peasant mob.

World War II

Following the critical and popular success of *For Whom the Bell Tolls*, Hemingway lapsed into a literary silence that lasted a full decade and was largely the result of his strenuous, frequently reckless, activities during World War II. In 1942 as a *Collier's* correspondent with the 3d Army, he witnessed some of the bloodiest battles in Europe. Although he served in no official capacity, he commanded a personal battalion of over 200 troops and was granted the respect and privileges normally accorded a general. At this time he received the affectionate appellation of "Papa" from his admirers, both military and literary.

In 1944 while in London, Hemingway met and soon married Mary Welsh, a *Time* reporter. His three previous marriages—to Hadley Richardson, mother of one son; to Pauline Pfeiffer, mother of his second and third sons; and to Martha Gelhorn—had all ended in divorce. Following the war, Hemingway and his wife purchased a home, Finca Vigia, near Havana, Cuba. Hemingway's only literary work was some anecdotal articles for *Esquire;* the remainder of his time was spent fishing, hunting, battling critics, and providing copy for gossip columnists. In 1950 he ended his literary silence with *Across the River and into the Trees,* a narrative, flawed by maudlin self-pity, about a retired Army colonel dying of a heart condition in Venice and his dreamy love affair with a pubescent girl.

Last Works

Hemingway's remarkable gift for recovery once again asserted itself in 1952 with the appearance of a novella about an extraordinary battle between a tired old Cuban fisherman and a giant marlin. *The Old Man and the Sea,* immediately hailed a masterpiece, was awarded the Pulitzer Prize in 1953. Although lacking the emotional tensions of his longer works, this novella possesses a generosity of spirit and reverence for life which make it an appropriate conclusion for Hemingway's career. In 1954 Hemingway won the Nobel Prize for literature.

Hemingway's rapidly deteriorating physical condition and an increasingly severe psychological disturbance drastically curtailed his literary capabilities in the last years of his life. A nostalgic journey to Africa planned by the author and his wife in 1954 ended in their plane crash over the Belgian Congo. Hemingway suffered severe burns and internal injuries from which he never fully recovered. Additional strain occurred when the revolutionary Cuban government of Fidel Castro forced the Hemingways to leave Finca Vigía. After only a few months in their new home in Ketchum, Idaho, Hemingway was admitted to the Mayo Clinic to be treated for hypertension and emotional depression and was later treated by electroshock therapy. Scornful of an illness which humiliated him physically and impaired his writing, he killed himself with a shotgun on July 2, 1961.

Shortly after Hemingway's death, literary critic Malcolm Cowley and scholar Carlos Baker were entrusted with the task of going through the writer's remaining manuscripts to decide what material might be publishable. The first posthumous work, *A Moveable Feast* (1964), is an elegiac reminiscence of Hemingway's early years in Paris, containing some fine writing as well as brilliant vignettes of his famous contemporaries. A year later the *Atlantic Monthly* published a few insignificant short stories and two long, rambling poems. In 1967 William White edited a collection of Hemingway's best journalism under the title *By-Line Ernest Hemingway*.

Further Reading

The authorized biography of Hemingway is Carlos Baker, *Ernest Hemingway: A Life Story* (1969). A controversial portrait is A. E. Hotchner, *Papa Hemingway: A Personal Memoir* (1966). Among the major full-length critical studies are Carlos Baker, *Ernest Hemingway: The Writer as Artist* (1952; 3d rev. ed. 1963), a textual study with emphasis on structure and symbolism; Philip Young, *Ernest Hemingway* (1952; rev. ed. 1966); Earl Rovit, *Ernest Hemingway* (1963); Richard B. Hovey, *Hemingway: The Inward Terrain* (1968); and Leo Gurko's more general *Ernest Hemingway and the Pursuit of Heroism* (1968).

The most valuable early critical essays on Hemingway are Edmund Wilson, "Hemingway: Gauge of Morale," in *Wound and the Bow* (1941); Robert Penn Warren, "Ernest Hemingway," in *Selected Essays* (1958); and Malcolm Cowley, "Nightmare and Ritual in Hemingway," reprinted in Robert Percy Weeks, ed., *Hemingway: A Collection of Critical Essays* (1962). The two major critical collections are John K. McCaffery, ed., *Ernest Hemingway: The Man and His Work* (1950), and Carlos Baker, ed., *Hemingway and His Critics: An International Anthology* (1961). See also the relevant sections in Joseph Warren Beach, *American Fiction, 1920-1940* (1941); Edwin Berry Burgum, *The Novel and the World's Dilemma* (1947); Wilbur M. Frohock, *The Novel of Violence in America, 1920-1950* (1950; 2d rev. ed. 1958); Frederick J. Hoffman, *The Modern Novel in America, 1900-1950* (1951); and Ray B. West, *The Short Story in America, 1900-1950* (1952). □

Jimi Hendrix

Jimi Hendrix (1942-1970) is perhaps the most innovative electric guitarist of all time, combining blues, hard rock, modern jazz, and soul into his own unmistakable sound.

In the few years between his emergence as a solo artist and his death from a barbiturate overdose at the height of his fame, Jimi Hendrix wrought a slew of radical changes on pop music. Arguably the most innovative electric guitarist of all time, he combined the raw passion of the blues, the sonic aggression of hard rock, the aural adventure of psychedelia and modern jazz, and the symphonic lyricism of progressive soul, melding these disparate inclinations into a style that, even when heard in fragments, remains unmistakably his own.

Had his instrumental prowess been his only contribution, Hendrix would remain a towering figure in modern music. But he was also a supremely gifted songwriter, as the myriad cover versions of his songs by such diverse artists as Eric Clapton, the Pretenders, Frank Zappa, Rickie Lee Jones, Living Colour, The Cure, jazz composer Gil Evans, and many others attest. When funk pioneer George Clinton was asked by a *Rolling Stone* interviewer how Hendrix had influenced Clinton's band Funkadelic, he responded, "He was it. He took noise to church."

At the time of his death, Hendrix was working desperately on an ambitious project that seemed designed to bridge a dazzling array of musical territories. Though he never completed that record, he did lay the groundwork for a range of bold stylistic hybrids, and he continues to influence those who hear his work. "Hendrix left an indelible, fiercely individual mark on popular music," wrote David Fricke in *Rolling Stone,* "accelerating rock's already dynamic rate of change in the late 1960s with his revolutionary synthesis of guitar violence, improvisational nerve, spacey melodic reveries and a confessional intensity born of the blues." Indeed, as one of the late musician's friends told the authors of the biography *Electric Gypsy*, Hendrix revealed, "I sacrifice part of my soul every time I play."

Raised by His Father

The man who would achieve fame as Jimi Hendrix was born Johnny Allen Hendrix in Seattle, Washington, in 1942. His father, Al—a gifted jazz dancer who worked at a number of jobs including landscape gardening—bore much of the responsibility of raising the boy and his brother, Leon, as did their grandmother and various family friends. This was due to the unreliability of Al's wife, Lucille, who drank excessively and would disappear for extended periods. Al Hendrix won custody of his sons and exercised as much discipline as he could, but the boys—young Johnny especially—worshipped their absentee mother; numerous biographers have hypothesized that in later years the guitarist looked to her as his muse. Al later changed his older son's name to James Marshall Hendrix.

Jimmy Hendrix wanted a guitar early on; before acquiring his first real instrument, he plucked a number of surrogates, including a broom and a one-stringed ukelele. Al at last procured a guitar for him, and the precocious 12-year-old restrung it upside down—as a left-hander, he was forced to turn the instrument in the opposite direction from how it is usually played, which left the low strings on the bottom unless he rearranged them—proceeding to teach himself blues songs from records by greats like B. B. King and Muddy Waters. The guitar rarely left his side and even lay beside him as he slept. By his mid-teens, Hendrix was playing blues and R&B with his band the Rocking Kings. He played behind his back, between his legs, and over his head—as had many blues guitarists before him. Thus he endeared himself to audiences, if not to all musicians.

It was therefore a shock to his father and friends when Hendrix joined the armed forces at age 17 and left his guitar behind. He volunteered for the 101st Airborne Division as a paratrooper and was soon jumping out of airplanes (he would later use his instrument to evoke the otherworldly sounds and sensations of freefall). Eventually he sent for his guitar and became the object of much derision and abuse from his peers, who considered Hendrix's extravagant devotion to the instrument freakish.

Performed on the "Chitlin Circuit"

An exception was a young private named Billy Cox. Himself an aspiring bassist with a taste for jazz as well as R&B, Cox overheard guitar music coming from inside a club on the camp that sounded, as he told *Electric Gypsy* authors Harry Shapiro and Caesar Glebbeek, "somewhere between [German classical composer Ludwig von] Beethoven and [blues icon] John Lee Hooker." He immediately suggested that he and Hendrix form a band; soon their quintet was entertaining troops all over the region. Eventually, though, Hendrix tired of army discipline and managed—with the

help of a well-timed and overdramatized injury—to obtain a discharge. Cox got out two months later.

After a few unproductive months, the two musicians headed for Nashville, Tennessee, which was just gaining a national reputation for its recording scene. Their new band, the King Kasuals—a revamped version of their service combo—landed a regular gig at the El Morocco club. Hendrix rapidly established himself as one of the hottest guitarists in town. At the time, however, he had no confidence in his singing and was content to back R&B artists, among them Curtis Mayfield, whose soulful guitar playing combined rhythm and lead and strongly influenced Hendrix's later balladry.

Over the next few years, Hendrix logged time in several R&B road shows—on what came to be known, somewhat disparagingly, as the "Chitlin Circuit"—though he didn't last long with any one act; his wild hair and compelling stage presence often stole the thunder from bandleaders who expected their musicians to play their assigned parts and stay in the background. From the seminal rocker Little Richard, Hendrix lifted much of what would become his signature look as an artist. Richard admired the guitarist's playing but viewed his taste for the limelight as a threat. The Isley Brothers gave Hendrix a bit more freedom; he was allowed to stretch out onstage and contributed a fiery solo to their 1964 single "Testify." The Isley Brothers hit showcases the passion and budding virtuosity that would soon make Hendrix a sensation.

Hendrix then played with saxophonist King Curtis and later with friend Curtis Knight (cowriting and recording some sides with the latter that would be exploited after he achieved fame). In 1965 he signed—for a one-dollar advance—a record contract with Knight's manager and PPX Productions head Ed Chalpin, the first of many costly and ill-advised legal entanglements that characterized Hendrix's career. It was around this time that he formed his own group, Jimmy James & the Blue Flames (which included a future member of the psychedelic rock group Spirit), moved to New York, and played endless low-paying gigs at the Cafe Wha? in Greenwich Village. His increasingly daring guitar work would make itself known, however.

Gave "Experience" New Meaning

Linda Keith, then girlfriend of Rolling Stones guitarist Keith Richards, was sufficiently impressed by Hendrix to recommend him to Chas Chandler, bassist for British rock sensations the Animals and an aspiring manager. Chandler was stunned by Hendrix and urged him to come to London. The road-weary Hendrix was justifiably skeptical, but Chandler turned out to be the real thing. Soon the guitarist was en route to the United Kingdom.

Chandler suggested changing the spelling of Hendrix's first name to Jimi, though the oft-cited assertion that he made this suggestion on the flight to London may be untrue. In any event, they touched down in September of 1966 and immediately put a band together with two British musicians, guitarist Noel Redding—who came to Chandler's office hoping to audition for the Animals but would, instead, be handed a bass for the first time—and jazz-influenced drummer John "Mitch" Mitchell, who won a coin toss to beat out his only competitor.

Mitchell's exuberant, round-the-kit playing combined the frenetic psychedelic blues attack of his most famous British peers with a post-bop virtuosity that recalled Elvin Jones, one-time skinsman for visionary jazz saxophonist John Coltrane. Many critics would later suggest that the Hendrix-Mitchell chemistry paralleled that between the two jazz players. Thus was born the Jimi Hendrix Experience. "Together, they complemented the rhythmic idiosyncrasies of Hendrix's songs and playing style with their own turbulent blend of hardy soul dynamics and breathtaking acid-jazz breakaways," wrote *Rolling Stone*'s Fricke. "The sound was fluid enough for open-ended jamming yet free of excess instrumental baggage, tight and heavy in the hard-rock clutches."

Meanwhile, Hendrix had found his voice not only as a songwriter but as a singer. Both his vocalizing and lyrics were profoundly influenced by folk-rock trailblazer Bob Dylan, whose unpretty plainsong voice and personal, surrealistic writing inspired Hendrix to cover his work—witness the rocking hit version of "All Along the Watchtower"—and to emulate it.

The Experience coalesced in a whirlwind couple of weeks, playing its debut gig in Paris opening for French pop star Johnny Hallyday at the Paris Olympia. Having signed with Track Records, they commenced recording their debut album the following month and by December had released their first single, a cover version of the folk-rock standard "Hey Joe." Hendrix's relaxed take on this often frantically rendered song added menace to the violent imagery of the lyrics and lent the title character's flight from justice considerable heft with concise, emotional bursts of lead guitar.

"Hey Joe" became a hit, and Hendrix proceeded to terrify London's biggest rock stars with his electrifying stage show. "It's the most psychedelic experience I ever had, going to see Hendrix play," guitarist Pete Townshend of The Who told Charles Shaar Murray, author of *Crosstown Traffic*. "When he started to play, something changed: colours changed, everything changed." Townshend—who claims never to have been a heavy user of psychedelic substances—recalled "flames and water dripping out of the ends of his hands." Eric Clapton, guitar "God" of rock until Hendrix's arrival, invited the young American onstage to play with his group Cream; soon "God" slunk offstage and was found in his dressing room with his head in his hands. Cream later wrote their psychedelic riff-rock smash "Sunshine of Your Love" in tribute to the American firebrand; he eventually adopted it into his live set without knowing he'd inspired it.

Unlike Townshend, Hendrix had a special fondness for hallucinogens like LSD and was also an enthusiastic marijuana smoker. In addition, scores of women flocked to him, and his "Wild Man of Borneo" reputation made him seem—to those who didn't know him—like some kind of omnivorous Yank tornado. Yet he is almost universally remembered as a shy, diffident person, occasionally explosive but largely gentle and naive; he was in no way prepared for the stormy sea of fame or the cynical manipulations of the music business. As Shapiro and Glebbeek pointed out in *Electric Gypsy*, he was dashed between the extremes of sporadic hero worship and institutional racism. "Feted as the greatest rock guitarist in the world, acclaimed as a Dionysian superstud and refused service at the tattiest redneck lunch counters—Jimi Hendrix was treated as superhuman and subhuman, but rarely just human," the authors attest. Even so, he seemed to care little about issues of color and was especially frustrated by the suggestion that he played "white music" or "black music."

Stirred Up a "Purple Haze"

The Experience's debut album, *Are You Experienced?*—released in the United States on the Reprise label—was a watershed in popular music, only kept from the top chart position by one of the few albums that arguably exceeds it in importance: the Beatles' *Sgt. Pepper's Lonely Hearts Club Band*. Hendrix produced a psychedelic rock anthem in the disoriented "Purple Haze," elegiac soul with the ballad "The Wind Cries Mary," R&B brimstone with "Fire," and proto-jazz rock with "Third Stone from the Sun." The U.K. version of the record included the signature Hendrix blues "Red House," released the following year in the United States on a singles collection. *Are You Experienced?* was an epochal debut, full of innovative studio effects and Hendrix's advanced use of feedback and tremolo. Then, in 1967, the band took the landmark Monterey Pop Festival by storm; Hendrix's ceremonial burning of his guitar—a highly theatrical routine that he somehow invested with the solemnity of a ritual sacrifice—left audiences stunned and appropriately worshipful.

Hendrix returned to the United States a hero. Crowds swarmed to watch this "wild man" play with his teeth, play behind his head, make relatively explicit love to—and, with any luck, torch—his Fender Stratocaster, and otherwise update the blues showman tradition with revolutionary fervor. What sometimes got lost in this impressive performance, to Hendrix's eternal dismay, was the music.

In the meantime, Chas Chandler made the best of the Experience's disastrous, abortive tour with wholesome TV popsters the Monkees by starting a rumor that the ultraconservative Daughters of the American Revolution had forced out the group. When Hendrix wasn't playing concerts or engaging in marathon studio sessions, he could invariably be found jamming at local clubs with anyone and everyone.

The Jimi Hendrix Experience's follow-up album, *Axis: Bold as Love,* demonstrated Hendrix's balladry and general songcraft to even greater effect, particularly on "Little Wing," which has been covered numerous times. Yet Hendrix was deeply dissatisfied by the way his albums had been cut and mixed and by a number of other factors. The trio format limited him—Redding played the bass parts Hendrix wrote but added little spice to the band dynamic—and he quickly tired of the theatrics audiences had come to expect. When he neglected to play the flashy guitar hero, crowds often grew restless, filling him with frustration and even contempt.

Hendrix longed to expand his musical range and to this end began work on the one album over which he exercised complete control, the sprawling double-length *Electric Ladyland.* Featuring a vast crew of guest players, the epic blues "Voodoo Child," and the plaintive mini-symphony "Burning of the Midnight Lamp"—as well as the hit single "Crosstown Traffic"—it was the most far-reaching achievement of his brief recording career. "You don't care what people say so much," he told *Down Beat,* "you just go on and do what you want to do." Increasingly, this would not be as easy as Hendrix made it sound.

It was at this point that the unscrupulous Ed Chalpin sued Hendrix's management over his 1966 contract with the guitarist, disrupting his affairs for several years. Meanwhile, the enormous recording costs Hendrix had amassed making *Electric Ladyland* induced Chandler and comanager Mike Jeffreys to build a custom studio—Electric Ladyland Studios—that would be rented out when the guitarist wasn't using it. But this, too, cost a fortune, necessitating endless touring that resulted in extreme road fatigue. The Experience broke up, and Hendrix began working with bassist Cox again, also recruiting drummer Buddy Miles for a soul-rock trio he called Band of Gypsys.

Revamped the National Anthem

In 1969 Hendrix appeared at the famed Woodstock festival in New York state, where his performance of the "Star-Spangled Banner"—complete with apocalyptic guitar noise—captured the anguish of the Vietnam War era and became a legend and a vital component of every time-capsule summary of the period. As Living Colour guitarist and Black Rock Coalition founder Vernon Reid told *Crosstown Traffic* author Murray, "At that moment, he became one of the greats, like Coltrane or [bop saxophone luminary Charlie] Parker or [woodwind innovator Eric] Dolphy. He plugged into something deep, something beyond good or bad playing. It was just 'there it is.'"

Various interested parties hoped to team Hendrix with trumpeter-bandleader-composer Miles Davis, one of the preeminent creative forces in post-bop jazz; though this never materialized, Hendrix did play with a number of musicians in Davis's circle and showed a marked interest in elements of what would come to be called "fusion," an amalgam of jazz and rock. He also declared, in a late interview quoted by Murray, that he wanted a "big band" and expressed the desire for "other musicians to play my stuff," saying, "I want to be a good writer."

The Band of Gypsys recorded a live album and, of legal necessity, handed it over to Chalpin; it is the only document of their short-lived band dynamic, one that tantalizingly demonstrates how a different rhythm section affected Hendrix's guitar work. Cox and Miles—who, as black sidemen, symbolized to Hendrix's more literal-minded political advisors a welcome concession to the black militancy of the day—did something Redding and Mitchell hadn't: they grooved. Much of the funk-rock and funk-metal that followed owes a huge debt to this corner of Hendrix's creativity. The scorching "Machine Gun" has been hailed by critics as a masterpiece.

But the trio was short-lived; soon Miles was out, Mitchell returned, and Hendrix recorded a number of tracks for what was to be perhaps the fullest realization of the sound he heard in his head: another double album, this one titled *First Rays of the New Rising Sun.* All available evidence suggests it would have melded soul, jazz, psychedelia, hard rock, and a few styles as yet unimagined. Tragically, after a slew of dispirited performances and perpetual self-medication, Jimi Hendrix died of a sleeping-pill overdose on September 18, 1970, before he could complete the ambitious work. He was buried in Seattle.

The Hendrix estate was mired in litigation for many years; Al Hendrix at last found an aggressive lawyer and in 1994—after a protracted struggle—looked to regain control of much of his son's music. In the years after the guitarist's death, hundreds of "new Hendrix albums" appeared, featuring everything from studio outtakes to pre-Experience club performances to rambling interviews. Consumers have gotten the shortest end of the stick, with a sizeable group of what rock industry consensus regards as the ultimate bottom-feeders profiting from these paltry and often grotesquely misrepresented scraps. Such exploitation, however, has scarcely tarnished Jimi Hendrix's shining legacy.

Bits and pieces of what would have been First Rays appeared on three of many posthumous releases—*The Cry of Love,* the soundtrack to the meandering hippie film *Rainbow Bridge,* and 1995's *Voodoo Soup,* of which *Vibe*'s Joseph V. Tirella commented, "The title is silly but apt, since this album is a delicious soup of sorts, a bouillabaisse of musical flavors." Of all his posthumous recordings, *Voodoo Soup* garnered the best general reviews. *Entertainment Weekly* queried, "Another Hendrix hodgepodge? Yes . . . The catch is that this one . . . is as fluid and cohesive as a preconceived record, without a bad song in the bunch."

In less than four years, Hendrix had established himself as one of the most important figures in pop music history. His influence extends to virtually every corner of contemporary music, from funk to heavy metal to fusion to the "harmolodic" school of New York free jazz to alternative rock. Well into the 1990s, Hendrix's presence on the rock scene practically makes a myth of his physical absence: MCA Records released remastered versions of his classic albums on CD as well as a compilation of his blues pieces and his complete Woodstock set.

In 1992 Hendrix was inducted into the Rock and Roll Hall of Fame. The following year he received the Grammy Awards Lifetime Achievement Award. And notable rock, rap, and blues artists contributed cover versions of his songs to the high-profile 1993 tribute album *Stone Free.* That same year Hendrix archivist Bill Nitopi published *Cherokee Mist: The Lost Writings,* an ensemble of various forms of personal memorabilia including Hendrix's unpublished writings such as letters to family and friends, "never-before-seen" photographs, and notes on unrecorded music. The book title was meant to pay homage to Hendrix's Native American heritage.

Hendrix mania even extended into mid-1990s cyberculture when the Jimi Hendrix Foundation created an Internet web site (http://www.wavenet.com/~jhendrix) for aficionados. Named after the classic Hendrix tune "Room Full of Mirrors," the web site was characterized in

Newsweek as "part shrine, part fanzine . . . [with] high-culture and low-culture perspectives on Hendrix." Considering the amount of unreleased Hendrix music—of varied quality and in the hands of those with varied integrity—he will likely remain as prolific posthumously as any new artist. Meanwhile, his groundbreaking, heartfelt body of work will certainly continue to inspire musicians and listeners with every new rising sun.

Further Reading

Murray, Charles Shaar, *Crosstown Traffic: Jimi Hendrix and the Rock 'N' Roll Revolution,* St. Martin's, 1989.

Rees, Dafydd, and Luke Crampton, *Rock Movers & Shakers,* Billboard, 1991.

Shapiro, Harry, and Caesar Glebbeek, *Jimi Hendrix: Electric Gypsy,* St. Martin's, 1991.

Billboard, December 14, 1968, p. 10; September 26, 1970, p. 3.

Down Beat, February 1994, pp. 38-39.

Entertainment Weekly, April 21, 1995, p. 54.

Jet, January 31, 1994, p. 61.

Musician, February 1993, p. 44.

Newsweek, January 16, 1995, p. 64; August 7, 1995, p. 10.

Q, July 1994, pp. 46-49.

Rolling Stone, September 20, 1990, pp. 75-78; February 6, 1992, pp. 40-48, 94.

Vibe, May 1994; August 1995. ☐

Joseph Henry

Joseph Henry (1797-1878), American physicist and electrical experimenter, was primarily important for his role in the institutional development of science in America.

Joseph Henry was born December 17, 1797, in Albany, N. Y. He attended the common school until the age of 14, when he was apprenticed to a jeweler. He later studied at the Albany Academy and in 1826 became professor of mathematics there. He immediately began researching a comparatively new field—the relation of electric currents to magnetism. The important result of this work was Henry's discovery of induced currents. In 1832 he was appointed professor of natural philosophy (chemistry and physics) in the College of New Jersey at Princeton.

In 1846 Henry became the first secretary and director of the Smithsonian Institution in Washington, D.C., a position he held for the rest of his life. Under his direction the institution encouraged and supported original research. Although a large portion of the income settled on the institution by Congress was for the support of the museum, art gallery, laboratory, and library, Henry took every opportunity to divest the institution of such burdens.

As the Smithsonian's director, Henry acted as one of the major coordinators of government science. Among the projects he originated was the system of receiving simultaneous weather reports by telegraph and basing weather predictions on them. From these beginnings came the U.S. Weather Bureau. During the Civil War he served on the Navy's permanent commission to evaluate inventions and on the Lighthouse Board.

Henry was elected to the American Philosophical Society in 1835. He helped organize the American Association for the Advancement of Science in 1847 and was an original member of the National Academy of Sciences, chartered by Congress in 1863. He became vice president of the National Academy in 1866 and was president from 1868 until his death. He was responsible for reorganizing the academy and transforming it from a society that emphasized governmental service to an honorary organization which recognized "original research."

Henry died on May 13, 1878. By concurrent resolution a memorial service was held in his honor on the evening of January 16, 1879, in the hall of the House of Representatives, and by act of Congress a bronze statue was erected at Washington in his memory.

Further Reading

The only modern biography of Henry is Thomas Coulson, *Joseph Henry: His Life and Work* (1950), a largely uncritical account that does not adequately stress Henry's institutional contributions. Detailed accounts of Henry's life and work are in James Gerald Crowther, *Famous American Men of Science* (1937); Bernard Jaffe, *Men of Science in America* (1944; rev. ed. 1958); and Bessie Zaban Jones, ed., *The Golden Age of Science,* containing a memoir by Asa Gray (1966). Henry's career and influence are discussed at length in Paul Henry Oehser, *Sons of Science: The Story of the Smithsonian Institution and Its Leaders* (1949), and Bessie Zaban Jones, *Lighthouse of the Skies: The Smithsonian Astrophysical Observatory: Background and History, 1846-1955* (1965). A Me-

morial of Joseph Henry, containing several biographical sketches and a complete bibliography, was published by order of Congress in 1880 (published also as *Smithsonian Miscellaneous Collections,* vol. 21, 1887). □

Patrick Henry

Patrick Henry (1736-1799), American orator and revolutionary, was a leader in Virginia politics for 30 years and a supremely eloquent voice during the American Revolution.

Patrick Henry was born into a family of lesser gentry in Hanover County, Va. He received a good education from his father and his uncle, an Anglican clergyman. He largely failed at attempts to become a storekeeper and a farmer, and his early marriage to Sarah Shelton made him at 35 the father of six children, whom he was always hard-pressed to support. A cursory training in law at Williamsburg about 1760, admission to the bar, and a modest beginning in a crowded profession did not at first improve his standing.

Eloquent Patriot

In 1763, defending a Louisa County parish against claims by its Anglican rector, Henry discovered the twin foundations of his public career—a deep empathy for injustice to the plain people and an eloquent voice that could overwhelm a jury. After he had scorned ecclesiastical arrogance and the British power supporting it, Henry's listeners carried him triumphantly from the courtroom. Two years later, as a member of the House of Burgesses, he made his stirring speech denouncing the Stamp Act. Henry also sponsored resolves against the Stamp Act, denying the power of Parliament to tax Virginians, which, published throughout the Colonies, marked him as an early radical leader. For 10 years Henry used his powerful voice and popular support to lead the anti-British movement in the Virginia Legislature.

During the crisis precipitated by the Boston Tea Party and the Coercive Acts, Henry was at the pinnacle of his career. He spurred the House of Burgesses to repeated defiances of the stubborn royal governor, Lord Dunmore. In August 1774 Henry, George Washington, Richard Henry Lee, and others traveled to Philadelphia as the Virginia delegation to the First Continental Congress. Henry stood with the Adamses of Massachusetts and other radicals, urging firm resistance to Britain, and union among the Colonies. "The distinctions between Virginians, Pennsylvanians, New Yorkers, and New Englanders are no more," Henry said. "I am not a Virginian, but an American." John Adams referred to Henry as the "Demosthenes of America." Back home in Virginia, Henry resumed his leadership of the radical party, "encouraging disobedience and exciting a spirit of revolt among the people," reported Lord Dunmore, who, as a result of Henry's exertions, was soon driven from the colony.

Elected to the first Virginia Revolutionary Convention, of March 1775, Henry made one of the most famous orations in American history. Attempting to gain support for measures to arm the colony of Virginia, Henry declared that Britain, by dozens of rash and oppressive measures, had proved its hostility. "We must fight!" Henry proclaimed. "An appeal to arms and to the God of Hosts is all that is left us! . . . Is life so dear, or peace so sweet, as to be purchased at the price of chains and slavery? Forbid it almighty God! I know not what course others may take; but as for me, give me liberty or give me death!" The delegates were entranced by Henry's eloquence and swept away by his fervor. Virginia rushed down the road to independence.

Henry capped his seditious activities during the spring of 1775 by leading a contingent of militia that forced reparations for gunpowder stolen by British marines from the Williamsburg arsenal. In the Second Continental Congress, of May-September 1775, Henry again spoke boldly for the radicals. In Virginia for 6 months he commanded the state's regular forces, but exhibiting no particular military talent, he resigned to resume civilian leadership. At the Virginia Convention of May-July 1776, Henry sponsored resolves calling for independence that eventuated in the Declaration of Independence by Congress on July 4, 1776. "His eloquence," wrote a young listener, "unlocked the secret springs of the human heart, robbed danger of all its terror, and broke the key-stone in the arch of royal power." Henry was elected first governor of Virginia under its constitution as an independent commonwealth.

Revolutionary Governor

In three terms as wartime governor (1776-1779), Henry worked effectively to marshal Virginia's resources to support Congress and George Washington's army. He also promoted George Rogers Clark's expedition, which drove the British from the Northwest Territory. During the years of Henry's governorship, the legislature, led by Thomas Jefferson, passed reforms transforming Virginia from a royal colony into a self-governing republic.

Henry's retirement from the governorship gave him time to attend to pressing family concerns. His first wife had died in 1775, leaving him six children, aged 4 to 20. Two years later he married Dorothea Dandridge, who was half his age and came from a prominent Tidewater family. Beginning in 1778, Henry had 11 children by his second wife, thus giving him family responsibilities that taxed his resources and provided abundant distraction from public life.

Meanwhile, Henry continued to serve in the Virginia Assembly, engaging in oratorical battles with Richard Henry Lee and sharing leadership during the breakdown in government after the British invasion of Virginia in 1780-1781. Though Henry backed some measures for strengthening the Continental Congress, his concern increasingly centered on Virginia and on efforts to expand its trade, boundaries, and power.

After the Revolution, Henry served two further terms as governor of Virginia (1784-1786). Increasingly opposed to a stronger federation, he refused to be a delegate to the Constitutional Convention of 1787. As an old revolutionary, he distrusted the ambitions of men like Virginia's James Madison and New York's Alexander Hamilton, fearing that they would sacrifice simple, republican virtues to the alleged needs of a grandiose nation.

"Peaceable Citizen" Henry

At the Virginia Convention of 1788, Henry engaged Madison and his colleagues in a dramatic debate. He called upon all his oratorical powers to parade before the delegates the tyrannies that would result under the new Constitution: Federal tax gatherers would harass men working peacefully in their own vineyards, citizens would be hauled off for trial in distant courts before unknown judges, and the president would prove to be a worse tyrant than even George III. Furthermore, in his most telling practical arguments, Henry insisted the new Federal government would favor British and Tory creditors and negotiate away American rights to use the Mississippi River. The Federalists nevertheless managed to win a narrow victory, which Henry accepted by announcing that he would be "a peaceable citizen." He had enough power in the legislature, however, to see that Virginia sent Antifederalist senators to the first Congress, and he almost succeeded in excluding Madison from a seat in the House of Representatives.

Finally, shorn of his domination of Virginia politics, Henry largely retired from public life. He resumed his lucrative law practice, earning huge fees from winning case after case before juries overwhelmed by his powerful pleas. He also extended his real estate interests, which, through skillful speculations, made him at his death one of the largest landowners in Virginia, with huge tracts in Kentucky, Georgia, and the Carolinas as well. His continuing national fame, and his switch by 1793 to support of President Washington and the Federalists, led to a series of proffered appointments: as senator, as minister to Spain and to France, as chief justice of the Supreme Court, and as secretary of state. In poor health and content to stay amid his huge progeny, Henry refused them all. Only one final cause—repeal of the Virginia Resolutions of 1798—prompted his return to politics. In 1799 Henry won election to the Assembly, causing the Jeffersonians to fear that he would carry the state back under the Federalist banner. Henry was mortally ill, however. On June 6, 1799, he died of cancer at his Red Hill plantation and was laid to rest under a plain slab containing the words "His fame his best epitaph."

Further Reading

Two early accounts of Henry, often inaccurate but filled with the drama of his life and containing extracts from the small surviving body of his earlier papers, reminiscences of his associates, and "reconstructions" of his speeches, are William Wirt, *Sketches of the Life and Character of Patrick Henry* (1817; 15th ed. 1852), and William Wirt Henry, *Patrick Henry: Life, Correspondence and Speeches* (3 vols., 1891). The standard biography of Henry is Robert D. Meade, *Patrick Henry* (2 vols., 1957-1969). A hostile view of Henry's career is given in Irving Brant, *James Madison* (6 vols., 1941-1961). □

Matthew A. Henson

Matthew A. Henson (1866-1955) always accompanied Robert Peary on his Arctic explorations. As a result, he was part of the first expedition to reach the North Pole.

Matthew A. Henson was born in Charles County, Maryland, south of Washington, D.C. on August 8, 1866. Henson was an African-American, whose parents had been born free. When he was young, he moved with his parents to Washington. Both of his parents had died by the time he was seven. He was raised by an uncle and attended a segregated school in Washington for six years. At the age of 13, he went to Baltimore and found a job as a cabin boy on a ship bound for China. He was befriended by the ship's captain, Captain Childs, and worked his way up to being an able-bodied seaman. During that period he sailed to China, Japan, the Philippines, North Africa, Spain, France, and Russia. Childs died when Henson was 17, and he left the sea to look for work on land.

In 1888 Henson was working in a clothing store in Washington when he met a young U.S. Navy lieutenant, Robert Peary, who had come in to buy a tropical helmet. Peary offered to hire him as a valet. Henson did not like the idea of becoming a personal servant, but he thought it would be worthwhile to accompany Peary to Nicaragua where he was headed to survey for a possible canal across Central America. They spent a year together in Nicaragua and then Henson worked as a messenger when Peary was stationed at League Island Navy Yard. Peary was interested in the possibilities of Arctic exploration and had made a first trip to Greenland in 1886 with the intention of being the first to cross the Greenland ice cap. He was beaten by Roald Amundsen and he then set himself the goal of being the first person to reach the North Pole.

Peary returned to northern Greenland in June 1891, and Henson accompanied him along with Peary's wife, Josephine, and other assistants, including Frederick Albert Cook. During this first trip Henson started to learn about the way of life of the Inuit who lived at the northern end of Greenland, to learn to speak their language and to learn how to use their knowledge of survival in the Arctic. Henson became very popular among the Inuit where he was credited with learning their language and adapting their customs better than any other outsider. He was nicknamed Maripaluk—"kind Matthew."

Henson returned with Peary to Greenland in June 1893, at which time he adopted a young Inuit orphan named Kudlooktoo and taught him to speak English. On this expedition Peary and Henson crossed the northern end of Greenland from their base at Etah to the northeastern corner of the island at Independence Bay in "Peary Land." Henson later wrote, "The memory of the winter and summer of 1894 and 1895 will never leave me . . . the recollections of the long race with death across the 450 miles of the ice-cap of North Greenland in 1895 . . . are still the most vivid." They returned to the United States in September 1895, and Henson vowed never to return.

But he did return—in the summers of 1896, 1897, 1898, 1900, and 1902. In July 1905 Peary and Henson went back north to Greenland again, this time with the intention of traveling over the polar ice cap to the North Pole. Starting in early 1906 they traveled by dog sled over the frozen sea, but it turned out to be an unusually warm winter and early spring, and they encountered too many stretches of open water to be able to continue. They got to within 160 miles of the Pole, the farthest north any one had reached to that time.

Peary and Henson set out again on July 6, 1908 on a ship named after the U.S. president, the *Roosevelt,* with an expedition that included 21 members. They sailed to Etah in Greenland and took on board 50 Inuit who were to help set up the supply bases on the route to the Pole. They then went to Cape Columbia at the northern end of Ellesmere Island. Peary and Henson set out from there on the morning of March 1, 1909. They were accompanied by or met up with various advance teams along the way. One of these support teams was headed by Professor Ross Marvin of Cornell University. It set up its last supply depot 230 miles from the Pole and then headed back for Cape Columbia. Marvin never made it. One of the Inuit in the party, Kudlukto, said that he had fallen into a stretch of open water and drowned. Years later Kudlukto confessed that he had shot Marvin and dumped his body in the water when he refused to let one of Kudlukto's young cousins ride on a dog sled.

On March 31 Peary and other members of the expedition were at 87°47', the farthest north any man had reached—about 150 miles from the Pole. At that point Peary told Captain Bob Bartlett, commander of the *Roosevelt,* to return to Cape Columbia. He would make the last dash to the Pole accompanied by Henson. Bartlett was bitterly disappointed, and the next morning walked alone to the north for a few miles as though he would try to make it on his own. He then turned around and headed south. It made sense for Peary to take Henson: he had much more Arctic experience and was

an acknowledged master with the dog teams. But there have always been suggestions that Peary sent Bartlett back because he did not want to share the honor of reaching the Pole with anyone else. Given the racial prejudice at the time, Henson and the four Inuit—Ootah, Seegloo, Ooqueah, and Egingwah—did not "count."

A couple of days later, on April 3, Henson was crossing a lane of moving ice, and one of the blocks of ice that he was using for support slipped and he fell into the water. Fortunately one of the Inuit was next to him and was able to pull him out immediately or he would have frozen and drowned. The normal day's procedure was for Peary to leave the night's camp early in the morning and push ahead for two hours breaking the trail ahead. The others would pack up the camp and then catch up with Peary. Then Peary (who at the age of 52 was already suffering from the leukemia that would later kill him) would ride in one of the dogsleds while Henson went ahead and broke trail. They would not see each other until the end of the day.

On April 6, 1909 Henson arrived at a spot that he, just by calculating the distance traveled, thought must be the North Pole. When Peary arrived 45 minutes later, Henson greeted him by saying, "I think I'm the first man to sit on the top of the world." Peary was furious. Peary then attached an American flag to a staff, and the whole expedition went to sleep. At 12:50 p.m. there was a break in the clouds, and Peary was able to take a reading of their location. It showed that they were 3 miles short of the Pole. After another nap, Peary took another reading and then set out with Egingwah and Seegloo to where he thought the Pole must be—without telling Henson. They then spent 30 hours in the vicinity of the Pole, and Henson officially raised the flag over what Peary's calculations told him was the North Pole. (Whether it really was the Pole or not has been a source of controversy ever since.)

Peary and Henson and the four Inuit arrived back at the spot where they had left Bartlett at midnight on April 9, an incredible speed—and reached Cape Columbia on April 23. They stayed there until July 17 when the ice had melted enough for the *Roosevelt* to steam into open water. They telegraphed news of their triumph from Labrador on September 6, 1909. But by that time, the world already thought that Frederick Cook had been the first one to reach the Pole. Peary spent the next few years defending his claims and was eventually vindicated.

By the time Henson got back to the United States he weighed 112 pounds (his normal weight was 155 pounds), and he was forced to spend several months recovering. For a while, he accompanied Peary on his lecture tours, where he would be exhibited in his Inuit clothes. In 1912 he wrote a book about his experiences (*A Negro at the North Pole*). However, the book died quickly, and Henson was forced to take a job as a porter working for $16 a week. Thanks to some politically influential friends he was later given a job as a messenger at the United States Customs house in New York at a salary of $20 a week, which was later raised to $40 a week. He retired in 1936, at which time there was an effort to have him awarded the Congressional Medal of Honor, but nothing came of it.

As racial attitudes in the United States changed, Henson began to receive more recognition. He was elected a full member of the Explorers Club in New York in 1937, the first Black member. In 1945 all of the survivors of the North Pole expedition received the Navy Medal, but Henson's was awarded in private. When he went to attend a banquet in his honor in Chicago in 1948, none of the downtown hotels would allow him to register because of his race. In 1950, however, he was introduced to President Truman and in 1954 was received by President Eisenhower in the White House. He died in New York in 1955 at the age of 88 and was buried in a private cemetery there. Years later, in 1988, when news of his achievements received more publicity, he was reburied at Arlington National Cemetery with full military honors in a plot next to Peary's.

Since Peary and Henson were both married at the time of their Arctic expeditions, it is not surprising that there was no public knowledge that both of them had liaisons with Inuit women. Dating from the 1905 expedition, they both fathered children—Peary had two sons and Henson had a boy named Anaukaq. This information came to light in 1986 when it was revealed that the small Greenland village of Moriussaq was largely made up of Henson's descendants, who had prospered as traders and hunters.

Further Reading

Henson's autobiography, *A Negro Explorer at the North Pole* was first published in 1912 (New York: 1912). It was reprinted in 1969 with a slightly different title: *A Black Explorer at the North Pole* (New York: Walker and Company). This edition was reprinted as a paperback by the University of Nebraska Press in Lincoln in 1989.

There are two biographies of Henson: Bradley Robinson, *Dark Companion* (New York: Robert M. McBride & Co., 1947) and Floyd Miller, *Ahdoolo!: The Biography of Matthew A. Henson* (New York: E.P. Dutton & Co., 1963).

The story of Henson's descendants is told in "The Henson Family" by S. Allen Counter in the 100th anniversary edition of the *National Geographic* magazine (September 1988, pp. 422-429). □

Alfred Day Hershey

Alfred Day Hershey (1908-1997) shared the Nobel Prize in medicine for his research on viruses.

By seeking to understand the reproduction of viruses, the simplest form of life, Alfred Day Hershey made important discoveries about the nature of deoxyribonucleic acid (DNA) and laid the groundwork for modern molecular genetics. Highly regarded as an experimental scientist, Hershey is perhaps best known for the 1952 "blender experiment" that he and Martha Chase conducted to demonstrate that DNA, not protein, was the genetic material of life. This discovery stimulated further research into DNA, including the discovery by James Watson and Francis Crick of the double-helix structure of DNA the following year. Hershey's work with bacteriophages, the viruses that prey on bacteria, was often carried out in loose collaboration with other scientists working with bacteriophages.

Hershey shared the Nobel Prize in Physiology or Medicine in 1969 with Max Delbrück and Salvador Edward Luria. The Nobel Committee praised the three scientists for their contributions to molecular biology. Their basic research into viruses also helped others develop vaccines against viral diseases such as polio.

Hershey was born on December 4, 1908, in Owosso, Michigan, to Robert Day Hershey and Alma Wilbur Hershey. His father worked for an auto manufacturer. Alfred attended public schools in Owosso and nearby Lansing. He received his B.S. in bacteriology from Michigan State College (now Michigan State University) in 1930 and his Ph.D. in chemistry from the same school in 1934. As a graduate student, Hershey's interest in bacteriology and the biochemistry of life was already evident. His doctoral dissertation was on the chemistry of *Brucella*, the bacteria responsible for brucellosis, also known as undulant fever. Undulant fever is transmitted to humans from cattle and causes recurrent fevers and joint pain. After receiving his Ph.D., Hershey took a position as a research assistant in the Department of Bacteriology at the Washington University School of Medicine in St. Louis. There he worked with Jacques Jacob Bronfenbrenner, one of the pioneers in bacteriophage research in the United States. During the sixteen years he spent teaching and conducting research at Washington University, from 1934 to 1950, Hershey was promoted to instructor (1936), assistant professor (1938), and associate professor (1942).

Bacteriophages—known simply as phages—had been discovered in 1915, only nineteen years before Hershey began his career. Phages are viruses that reproduce by preying on bacteria, first attacking and then dissolving them. For scientists who study bacteria, phages are a source of irritation because they can destroy bacterial cultures. But other scientists are fascinated by this tiny organism. Perhaps the smallest living thing, phages consist of little more than the protein and DNA (the molecule of heredity) found in a cellular nucleus. Remarkably efficient, however, phages reproduce by conquering bacteria and subverting them to the phage particles' own needs. This type of reproduction is known as replication. Little was known about the particulars of this process when Hershey was a young scientist.

By studying viral replication, scientists hoped to learn more about the viral diseases that attack humans, like mumps, the common cold, German measles, and polio. But the study of bacteriophages also promised findings with implications that reached far beyond disease cures into the realm of understanding life itself. If Hershey and other researchers could determine how phages replicated, they stood to learn how higher organisms—including humans—passed genetic information from generation to generation.

Exposing the Secret Life of Viruses

Hershey's study of phages soon yielded several discoveries that furthered an understanding of genetic inheritance and change. In 1945 he showed that phages were capable of spontaneous mutation. Faced with a bacterial culture known to be resistant to phage attack, most, but not all, phages would die. By mutating, some phages survived to attack the bacteria and replicate. This finding was significant because it showed that mutations did not occur gradually, as one school of scientific thought believed, but rather occurred immediately and spontaneously in viruses. It also helped explain why viral attack is so difficult to prevent. In 1946 Hershey made another discovery that changed what scientists thought about viruses. He showed that if different strains of phages infected the same bacterial cell, they could combine or exchange genetic material. This is similar to what occurs when higher forms of life sexually reproduce, of course. But it was the first time viruses were shown to combine genetic material. Hershey called this phenomenon genetic recombination.

Hershey was not the only scientist who saw the potential in working with bacteriophages. Two other influential scientists were also pursuing the same line of investigation. Max Delbrück, a physicist, had been studying phages in the United States since he fled Nazi Germany in 1937. Studying genetic recombination independently of Hershey, he reached the same results that Hershey did in the same year. Similarly, Salvador Edward Luria, a biologist and physician who immigrated to the United States from Italy in 1940, had independently confirmed Hershey's work on spontaneous mutation in 1945. Although the three men never worked side by side in the same laboratory, they were collaborators nonetheless. Through conversation and correspondence, they shared results and encouraged each other in their phage research. Indeed, these three scientists formed the core of the self-declared "phage group," a loose-knit clique of scientists who encouraged research on particular strains

of bacteriophage. By avoiding competition and duplication, the group hoped to advance phage research that much faster.

The "Blender Experiment"

In 1950 Hershey accepted a position as a staff scientist in the department of genetics (now the Genetics Research Unit) of the Carnegie Institute at Cold Spring Harbor, New York. It was at Cold Spring Harbor that Hershey conducted his most influential experiment. Hershey wished to prove conclusively that the genetic material in phages was DNA. Analysis with an electron microscope had showed that phages consist only of DNA surrounded by a protein shell. Other scientists' experiments had revealed that during replication some part of the parental phages was being transferred to their offspring. The task before Hershey was to show that it was the phage DNA that was passed on to succeeding generations and that gave the signal for replication and growth.

Although Hershey was not alone in having reached the belief that DNA was the stuff of life, many scientists were unconvinced. They doubted that DNA had the complexity needed to carry the blueprint for life and believed instead that the genetic code resided in protein, a far more elaborate molecule. Furthermore, no one had yet demonstrated the technical skill needed to design an experiment that would answer the question once and for all.

With Martha Chase, Hershey found a way to determine what role each of the phage components played in replication. In experiments done in 1951 and 1952, Hershey used radioactive phosphorus to tag the DNA and radioactive sulfur to tag the protein. (The DNA contains no sulfur and the protein contains no phosphorus.) Hershey and Chase then allowed the marked phage particles to infect a bacterial culture and to begin the process of replication. This process was interrupted when the scientists spun the culture at a high speed in a Waring blender.

In this manner, Hershey and Chase learned that the shearing action of the blender separated the phage protein from the bacterial cells. Apparently while the phage DNA entered the bacterium and forced it to start replicating phage particles, the phage protein remained outside, attached to the cell wall. The researchers surmised that the phage particle attached itself to the outside of a bacterium by its protein "tail" and literally injected its nucleic acid into the cell. DNA, and not protein, was responsible for communicating the genetic information needed to produce the next generation of phage.

Clearly DNA seemed to hold the key to heredity for all forms of life, not just viruses. Yet while the blender experiment answered one question about DNA, it also raised a host of other questions. Now scientists wanted to know more about the action of DNA. How did DNA operate? How did it replicate itself? How did it direct the production of proteins? What was its chemical structure? Until that last question was answered, scientists could only speculate about answers to the others. Hershey's achievement spurred other scientists into DNA research.

In 1953, a year after Hershey's blender experiment, the structure of DNA was determined in Cambridge, England, by James Dewey Watson and Francis Harry Compton Crick. Watson, who was only twenty-five years old when the structure was announced, had worked with Luria at the University of Indiana. For their discovery of DNA's double-helix structure, Watson and Crick received the Nobel Prize in 1962.

Career Honored with a Belated Nobel Prize

Hershey, Delbrück, and Luria also received a Nobel Prize for their contributions to molecular biology, but not until 1969. This seeming delay in recognition for their accomplishments prompted the New York Times to ask in an October 20, 1969, editorial: "Delbrück, Hershey and Luria richly deserve their awards, but why did they have to wait so long for this recognition? Every person associated with molecular biology knows that these are the grand pioneers of the field, the giants on whom others—some of whom received the Nobel Prize years ago—depended for their own great achievements." Yet other scientists observed that the blender experiment merely offered experimental proof of a theoretical belief that was already widely held. After the blender experiment, Hershey continued investigating the structure of phage DNA. Although human DNA winds double-stranded like a spiral staircase, Hershey found that some phage DNA is single-stranded and some is circular. In 1962 Hershey was named director of the Genetics Research Unit at Cold Spring Harbor. He retired in 1974 and died of cardiopulmonary failure at the age of 88 on May 22, 1997.

Hershey was "known to his colleagues as a very quiet, withdrawn sort of man who avoids crowds and noise and most hectic social activities," according to the report of the 1969 Nobel Prize in the October 17, 1969, New York Times. His hobbies were woodworking, reading, gardening, and sailing. He married Harriet Davidson, a former research assistant, on November 15, 1945. She later became an editor of the Cold Spring Harbor Symposia on Quantitative Biology. She and Hershey had one child, a son named Peter Manning. Born on August 7, 1956, Peter was twelve years old when Hershey won the Nobel Prize.

In addition to the Nobel Prize, Hershey received the Albert Lasker Award of the American Public Health Association (1958) and the Kimber Genetics Award of the National Academy of Sciences (1965) for his discoveries concerning the genetic structure and replication processes of viruses. He was elected to the National Academy of Sciences in 1958.

Further Reading

Fox, Daniel M., editor, Nobel Laureates in Medicine or Physiology: A Biographical Dictionary, Garland, 1990.

Magner, Lois N., History of the Life Sciences, Dekker, 1979.

McGraw-Hill Modern Scientists and Engineers, McGraw-Hill, 1980.

Wasson, Tyler, editor, Nobel Prize Winners, H. W. Wilson, 1987.

New York Times, October 17, 1969, p. 24; October 20, 1969, p. 46.

Science, October 24, 1969, p. 479–481.

"Three Americans Share Nobel Prize for Medicine for Work on Bacteriophage," in Chemical and Engineering News, October 27, 1969, p. 16.

Time, October 24, 1969, p. 84. □

Abraham Joshua Heschel

Abraham Joshua Heschel (1907-1972) was a Polish-born American theologian, educator, and philosopher who sought to build a modern philosophy of religion on the basis of ancient Jewish tradition. Among other posts, he held the chair of professor of Jewish ethics and mysticism at the Jewish Theological Seminary of America, New York City.

With his birth in Warsaw, Poland, in 1907, Abraham Joshua Heschel entered a family that counted back seven generations of Hasidic rabbis. His father was Rabbi Moshe Mordecai, and his ancestors helped to found the Polish Hasidic movement, a Jewish sect of mystics, in the eighteenth century. Both his father and his mother, Reisel Perlow Heschel, instilled in him a love of learning as he grew up in the orthodox ghetto of Warsaw. As a young man, he wrote poetry, and his collection of Yiddish verse was published years later (1933) in his home city.

Student and Teacher Years

Following a traditional Jewish education in Warsaw, Heschel went to Berlin, where he studied at the university and also taught the Talmud, during 1932-33, at the Hochschule fur die Wissenschaft des Judentums. He earned his PhD degree from Berlin University in 1933 and accepted a fellowship at the Hochschule, graduating the following year. Over the next three years, three published works established him as a scholar and author of note: Maimonides: Eine Biographie, concerning the medieval Jewish philosopher (1935); Die Prophetie, on Hebrew prophesy (1936); and Don Jizchak Abravalel, about the fifteenth-century Jewish statesman of Spain (1937).

In 1937, Heschel went to Frankfurt am Main to teach at the noted Judisches Lehrhaus. But war clouds were gathering in Europe, and he was deported from Nazi Germany in 1938. He returned to Warsaw for a few months of teaching at the Institute of Judaistic Studies, but the Nazi invasion of his homeland forced him to London where he founded the Institute for Jewish Learning.

The United States had not yet entered World War II when Heschel arrived in Cincinnati, Ohio, where he joined the faculty of Hebrew Union College in 1940. Five years later he took the chair of professor of Jewish ethics and mysticism at Jewish Theological Seminary of America in New York City. Heschel, who became an American citizen in 1945, married concert pianist Sylvia Straus in 1946, and they had one daughter, Hannah. He remained at the Jewish Theological Seminary until his death in New York City on December 23, 1972.

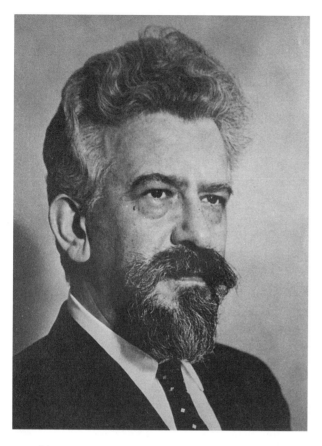

Teachings and Published Works

Abraham Heschel wished to construct a modern philosophy of religion on the basis of ancient Jewish tradition and teachings. In traditional Jewish piety, he observed an inner depth of devotion that he sought to convey to twentieth-century humans. "The Jew is never alone in the face of God," he said, "for the Torah is always with him."

Heschel's concern for the piety of the individual involved him in the civil rights demonstrations of the 1960s and early 1970s to end discrimination against blacks in America. He was one of the first religious leaders in the United States to speak out against the escalating war in Vietnam. And he risked the wrath of fellow Jews by meeting with Pope Paul VI at the Vatican in Rome to discuss Jewish feelings concerning Vatican Council II. Some Jewish leaders objected to the trip, but Heschel felt it important that Jewish approval be added, if possible, to some of the Council's decrees, such as the denial of any Jewish guilt in the crucifixion of Jesus.

In addition to his teachings, Heschel is well known for his writings. They include: his magnum opus, *Man Is Not Alone: A Philosophy of Religion* (1951), *The Sabbath: Its Meaning for Modern Man* (1951), *Man's Quest for God: Studies in Prayer and Symbolism* (1954), *God in Search of Man* (1955), *The Prophets* (1962), *Who Is Man?* (1965), and *The Insecurity of Freedom: Essays on Human Existence* (1966). These books provide insights into his existentialist philosophy of Judaism with its central concept based on a "theology of pathos," in which God is a god of pathos, "revealed in a personal and intimate relation to the world. . . . He is also moved and affected by what happens in the world and reacts accordingly." This divine pathos, in turn, evokes a human response of sympathy for God, by which "man experiences God as his own being"—Heschel's "religion of sympathy."

The element of time occupies an important place in Heschel's theology, since "Time is perpetual innovation, a synonym for continuous creation," and human existence in time is communion with God and a reaction to the continuous action of God. From this concept of time, Heschel derived his theory of human freedom as "a spiritual event." According to Heschel, the individual learns about God not by reason and intellect, but through experience, divine revelation, and sacred deeds, all of which enable the individual to form a relationship—a "leap of action" rather than of faith—with God.

In addition to his scholarly and philosophical writings, Heschel authored several works on Jewish life in eastern Europe. Chief among them is *The Earth Is the Lord's: The Inner World of the Jew in East Europe* (1950), in which he theorizes that the "golden age" of European Jewish life was in the Jewish culture of eastern Europe. In the 1960s Heschel was active in the movement to aid the Jews of the Soviet Union.

Further Reading

An excellent introduction to Heschel's thought is in *Between God and Man: An Interpretation of Judaism, from the Writings of Abraham J. Heschel,* selected, edited, and introduced by Fritz A. Rothschild (1959). For a more scholarly biography, see *Abraham Joshua Heschel: Prophetic Witness,* written by Edward K. Kaplan and Samuel H. Dresner (1998). See also: *Who's Who in America, New York Times,* Dec. 24, 1972. □

James Butler Hickok

James Butler Hickok (1837-1876), American gunfighter, scout, and spy, brought law to the untamed West. In his lifetime he became the symbolic western hero.

James Hickok was born on May 27, 1837, in Troy Grove, Ill. The Hickok family was abolitionist and evidently schooled him in the "genteel tradition." In 1855 he left home for Kansas. He filed land claims in Johnson County and apparently wanted to become a farmer.

By 1858, after serving briefly as constable, Hickok was working for the famous express company Russell, Majors and Waddell. Early in 1861 the firm stationed him at their Rock Creek, Nebr., station as assistant stock tender. There Hickok and fellow employees killed David McCanles and his two companions, who had come—unarmed—to collect the delinquent payments on the Rock Creek station land. Tried for murder, Hickok and the express company workers pleaded self-defense and were acquitted.

During the Civil War, Hickok served the Union forces creditably as wagon master, scout, and spy. Just after the war, while gambling, Hickok killed David Tutt, a former Confederate, in the prototype setting for later stories and movies—an iron-nerved shoot-out in the public square of

Hickok was about 6 feet tall, with a good physique and pale blue eyes. He often wore fancy shirts, a red vest, the latest design in trousers, and a flat, wide-brimmed hat. Many thought him handsome, and women found him attractive. In manner he reflected the genteel tradition of quiet courtesy.

During 1872 and 1873 Wild Bill drifted around Kansas and Missouri gambling. Once he wrote to a St. Louis newspaper denying he had been killed by some Texans. He next appeared in Cheyenne and stayed nearby during 1874 and 1875. Here Wild Bill probably met "Calamity Jane" Cannary. He married a widowed circus owner in Cheyenne in 1876. He also gambled considerably and was several times dubbed a vagrant and ordered out of town.

Hickok left Cheyenne for the Black Hills soon after his marriage, arriving at Deadwood, Dakota Territory, in July with "Colorado Charlie" Utter and Calamity Jane. He looked briefly for a mining claim and gambled in various saloons. On Aug. 2, 1876, while playing cards, he was shot in the back of the head; Hickok had forgotten to keep his back to the wall. His hand—two aces, two eights, and a jack—became known as the "dead man's hand."

Further Reading

Frank J. Wilstach, *Wild Bill Hickok: The Prince of Pistoleers* (1926), is interesting and fairly accurate. Well researched and factually correct is Joseph G. Rosa, *They Called Him Wild Bill: The Life and Adventures of James Butler Hickok* (1964). Another reliable work is William Elsey Connelley, *Wild Bill and His Era* (1933). A useful biography is Richard O'Connor, *Wild Bill Hickok* (1959). Kent Ladd Steckmesser, *The Western Hero in History and Legend* (1965), is a study of the folklore that created myths about the West and its rugged heroes. □

Rolando Hinojosa

Rolando Hinojosa is one of the most prolific and well-respected Hispanic novelists in the United States. Not only has he created memorable Mexican American and white characters, but he has completely populated a fictional county in the lower Rio Grande Valley of Texas through his continuing generational narrative that he calls the Klail City Death Trip Series.

The first Chicano author to receive a major international literary award, Rolando Hinojosa won the prestigious Premio Casa de las Américas for *Klail City y sus alrededores* (*Klail City*), part of a series of novels known to English-speaking readers as "The Klail City Death Trip." Hinojosa's fiction, often infused with satire or subtle humor, is widely praised for its multiple narratives that unite many characters' individual perspectives into the unique combined voice of the Chicano people. Hinojosa has also produced essays, poetry, and a detective novel titled *Partners in Crime*.

Hinojosa was born in Texas's Lower Rio Grande Valley to a family with strong Mexican and American roots: his father fought in the Mexican Revolution while his mother maintained the family north of the border. An avid reader

Springfield, Mo. Tried for murder, he was again acquitted. Shortly afterward an inflated story about Hickok was published in *Harper's Magazine,* and from this grew the legend of "Wild Bill," the western hero.

Early in 1866, as deputy U.S. marshal at Fort Riley, Kans., Wild Bill was told to establish order. Conditions were close to chaos, with growing enmity between emigrant train scouts and discontented soldiers. Hickok quieted the fort. When the ordinarily reticent and soft-spoken marshal shouted, "This has gone far enough," it usually intimidated even the most unruly. If not, his fist or pistol barrel reinforced his voice. Later he rounded up deserters, horse thieves, and illegal timber cutters. He also gambled and drank.

In late 1869 Hickok became sheriff of Hays City, Kans., where drinking, gambling, and prostitution often led to violence. In 4 months as sheriff there Hickok helped establish law and order, although in doing so he killed two men. The lawless element understandably resented Hickok, and several attempts were made on his life. Thus he developed a habit of standing or sitting with his back to a wall.

Hickok appeared briefly in a Wild West show before becoming city marshal of Abilene, Kans., in 1871. Abilene was a railhead, and many cowboys ended their trail drives with pistol shots and uninhibited drinking. Once again Hickok used weapons and threats to keep order. In October one man was killed by Hickok's bullet during a group "spree." A policeman was also killed by running into the cross fire. Citizens supported Hickok's actions, but he was discharged in December.

during childhood, Hinojosa was raised speaking Spanish until he attended junior high, where English was the primary spoken language. Like his grandmother, mother, and three of his four siblings, Hinojosa became a teacher; he has held several academic posts and has also been active in administration and consulting work. Although he prefers to write in Spanish, Hinojosa has also translated his own books and written others in English.

Hinojosa entered the literary scene with the 1973 *Estampas del valle y otras obras,* which was translated as *Sketches of the Valley and Other Works.* The four-part novel consists of loosely connected sketches, narratives, monologues, and dialogues, offering a composite picture of Chicano life in the fictitious Belken County town of Klail City, Texas. The first part of *Estampas* introduces Jehú Malacara, a nine-year-old boy who is left to live with exploitative relatives after the deaths of his parents. Hinojosa synthesizes the portrait of Jehú's life through comic and satiric sketches and narratives of incidents and characters surrounding him. The second section is a collection of pieces about a murder, presented through newspaper accounts, court documents, and testimonials from the defendant's relatives. A third segment, narrated by an omniscient storyteller, is a selection of sketches depicting people from various social groups in Klail City, while the fourth section introduces the series' other main character, Jehú's cousin Rafa Buenrostro. Also orphaned during childhood, Rafa narrates a succession of experiences and recollections of his life. Hinojosa later rewrote *Estampas del valle y otras obras* in English, publishing it as *The Valley* in 1983.

Hinojosa's aggregate portrait of the Spanish southwest continues in *Klail City y sus alredededores,* published in English as *Klail City.* Like its predecessor, *Klail City* is composed of interwoven narratives, conversations, and anecdotes illustrating the town's collective life spanning fifty years. Winner of the 1976 Premio Casa de las Américas, the book was cited for its "richness of imagery, the sensitive creation of dialogues, the collage-like structure based on a pattern of converging individual destinies, the masterful control of the temporal element and its testimonial value," according to Charles M. Tatum in *World Literature Today.* Introducing more than one hundred characters and developing further the portraits of Rafa and Jehú, *Klail City* prompts *Western American Literature* writer Lourdes Torres to praise Hinojosa for his "unusual talent for capturing the language and spirit of his subject matter."

Korean Love Songs from Klail City Death Trip and *Claros varones de Belken* are Hinojosa's third and fourth installments in the series. A novel comprised of several long poems originally written in English and published in 1978, *Korean Love Songs* presents protagonist Rafa Buenrostro's narration of his experiences as a soldier in the Korean War. In poems such as "Friendly Fire" and "Rafe," Hinojosa explores army life, grief, male friendships, discrimination, and the reality of death presented through dispassionate, often ironic descriptions of the atrocity of war. *Claros varones de Belken* (*Fair Gentlemen of Belken County*), released three years later, follows Jehú and Rafa as they narrate accounts of their experiences serving in the Korean War, attending the University of Texas at Austin, and beginning careers as high school teachers in Klail City. The book also includes the narratives of two more major characters, writer P. Galindo and local historian Esteban Echevarría, who comment on their own and others' circumstances. Writing about *Fair Gentlemen of Belken County, World Literature Today* contributor Tatum comments that Hinojosa's "creative strength and major characteristic is his ability to render this fictional reality utilizing a collective voice deeply rooted in the Hispanic tradition of the Texas-Mexico border." Also expressing a favorable opinion of the book was *Los Angeles Times Book Review* writer Alejandro Morales, who concludes that "the scores of names and multiple narrators at first pose a challenge, but quickly the imagery, language and subtle folk humor of Belken County win the reader's favor."

Hinojosa continued the "Klail City Death Trip" series with *Mi querido Rafa.* Translated as *Dear Rafe,* the novel is divided into two parts and consists of letters and interviews. The first half of the work is written in epistolary style, containing only letters from Jehú—now a successful bank officer—to his cousin Rafa. Between the novel's two parts, however, Jehú suddenly leaves his important position at the Klail City First National Bank, and in the second section Galindo interviews twenty-one community members about possible reasons for Jehú's resignation. The two major characters are depicted through dialogue going on around and about them; the reader obtains a glimpse of Rafa's personality through Jehú's letters, and Jehú's life is sketched through the opinions of the townspeople. *San Francisco Review of Books* writer Arnold Williams compares the power of Hinojosa's fictional milieu, striking even in translation, to that of twentieth-century Jewish writer Isaac Bashevis Singer, noting that "Hinojosa is such a master of English that he captures the same intimacy and idiomatic word play in his re-creations."

After writing *Rites and Witnesses,* the sixth novel in the "Klail City Death Trip" series, Hinojosa turned to a conventional form of the novel with the 1985 *Partners in Crime,* a detective thriller about the murder of a Belken County district attorney and several Mexican nationals in a local bar. Detective squads from both sides of the border are called to investigate the case; clues lead to an established and powerful cocaine smuggling ring. Jehú and Rafa reappear in the novel as minor characters who nevertheless play important parts in the mystery's development. "Those who might mourn the ending of the ['Klail City Death Trip' series] and their narrative experimentation and look askance at Hinojosa's attempting such a predictable and recipe-oriented genre as the murder mystery need not worry," concludes Williams. "He can weave a social fabric that is interesting, surprising, realistic and still entertaining."

Hinojosa told *Contemporary Authors:* "I enjoy writing, of course, but I enjoy the re-writing even more: four or five rewritings are not uncommon. Once finished, though, it's on to something else. At this date, every work done in Spanish has also been done in English with the exception of *Claros varones de Belken,* although I did work quite closely on the idiomatic expressions which I found to be at the heart of the telling of the story.

"I usually don't read reviews; articles by learned scholars, however, are something else. They've devoted much time and thought to their work, and it is only fair I read them and take them seriously. The articles come from France, Germany, Spain, and so on, as well as from the United States. I find them not only interesting but, at times, revelatory. I don't know how much I am influenced by them, but I'm sure I am, as much as I am influenced by a lifetime of reading. Scholars do keep one on one's toes, but not, obviously, at their mercy. Writing has allowed me to meet writers as diverse as Julio Cortázar, Ishmael Reed, Elena Poniatowski and George Lamming.

"My goal is to set down in fiction the history of the Lower Rio Grande Valley, and with *Becky and Her Friends*, [which came] out in 1990, I am right on schedule. The Spanish version will also be out the same year. A German scholar, Wolfgang Karrer, from Osnabrueck University has a census of my characters; they number some one thousand. That makes me an Abraham of some sort.

"Personally and professionally, my life as a professor and as a writer inseparably combines vocation with avocation. My ability in both languages is most helpful, and thanks for this goes to my parents and to the place where I was raised."

In 1993, Hinojosa released *The Useless Servants*. This is a novel of the Korean War, told in the form of the journal of Rafe Buenestro, a Mexican American soldier. This novel exposes the negative treatment Mexican Americans and African Americans received from their fellow soldiers. *Publishers Weekly* says that in this book, "Hinojosa gives us a graphic picture of the unchanging face of war—raw, gritty and inhumane."

Further Reading

Bruce-Novoa, Juan, *Chicano Authors: Inquiry by Interview,* University of Texas Press, 1980.

Contemporary Authors, Volume 131, Gale, 1991.

Dictionary of Literary Biography, Volume 82: *Chicano Writers, First Series,* Gale, 1989.

Saldívar, José David, editor, *The Rolando Hinojosa Reader: Essays Historical and Critical,* Arte Público Press, 1985.

Hispania, September, 1986.

Los Angeles Times Book Review, April 12, 1987.

Publishers Weekly, November 28, 1986.

San Francisco Review of Books, spring, 1985, fall/winter, 1985.

Western American Literature, fall, 1988.

World Literature Today, summer, 1977, summer 1986. □

Alger Hiss

A former U.S. State Department official, Alger Hiss (1904-1996) was indicted in 1948 and convicted in 1950 of having provided classified documents to an admitted Com-

munist, Whittaker Chambers. Hiss became a controversial figure and his case helped precipitate McCarthyite politics during the early Cold War years.

Alger Hiss was born on November 11, 1904, in Baltimore, Maryland, of a genteel, long-established middle class Baltimore family. An exceptional student, confident and aristocratic in demeanor, Hiss attended Johns Hopkins University on scholarship. Compiling an outstanding record in the classroom and as a student leader, he graduated in 1926, earning a scholarship to Harvard Law School. Hiss's academic achievements included appointment to the law review staff, and he developed an intellectual and political friendship with Harvard law professor Felix Frankfurter. On Frankfurter's recommendation, in 1929 Hiss was appointed a clerk to Supreme Court Justice Oliver Wendell Holmes, Jr. Later that year, on December 11, he married Priscilla Fansler Hobson, whom he had met and courted while an undergraduate. Upon completion of his clerkship, Hiss accepted an appointment in 1930 with the Boston law firm of Choate, Hall & Stewart, leaving in 1932 to accept an appointment with the New York City law firm of Cotton, Franklin, Wright & Gordon.

Having moved leftward during law school under Frankfurter's influence and then his wife's socialist leanings, Hiss was further influenced by the political and economic crisis of the Great Depression to abandon in 1933 a promising career in corporate law for a position with the Legal Division of the Agricultural Adjustment Agency (AAA), headed by Jerome Frank. Associating with an able group of predominantly radical attorneys, in July 1934 Hiss was loaned by the Agriculture Department to assist the staff of the Senate Special Committee to Investigate the Munitions Industry, the so-called Nye Committee. An able investigator, Hiss became disenchanted with the committee's isolationism and with the department following a purge of the Legal Division in a dispute over policy toward landowners.

In August 1935 Hiss accepted a position as a consultant with the Department of Justice and was assigned to the solicitor general's office headed by Stanley Reed. Hiss assisted in preparing the department's defense of the constitutionality of AAA's policy of imposing a processing tax on producers of commodities. His work helping prepare the department's response to an expected court challenge to the administration's reciprocal trade agreements policy rekindled Hiss's interest in international developments, and in September 1936 he accepted an appointment to the staff of Assistant Secretary of State for Economic Affairs Francis Sayre.

A Promising Career Cut Short

As a State Department employee, Hiss's career fortunes improved swiftly. With the outbreak of World War II, Hiss came to devote his time and talents to the task of formulating and developing the structure of a permanent postwar collective security organization, which became the United Nations. Hiss's expertise in the area of international organization resulted in his participation as a rather low-level functionary at the 1943 Dumbarton Oaks Conference as well as his selection as a member of the U.S. delegation to the Yalta Conference of February 1945. Subsequently he received an appointment to head the State Department's Office of Special Policy Planning and later to serve as executive-secretary in August 1945 of the San Francisco Conference at which the United Nations Charter was drafted and approved. Hiss remained in the State Department until February 1947, when he accepted the office of president of the Carnegie Endowment for International Peace.

Hiss's promising career was abruptly shattered by events having their origins in the highly charged confrontation between congressional conservatives and the Truman administration during the early Cold War years. In dramatic and extensively publicized testimony before the House Committee on Un-American Activities (HUAC) on August 3, 1948, Whittaker Chambers, an admitted ex-Communist and at the time senior editor of *Time* magazine, identified Hiss as a member of a Communist cell which had operated in Washington, D.C., in the mid-1930s. Denying then that Hiss's activities included espionage, Chambers claimed instead that Hiss's role, as that of the other individuals whom he concurrently identified as Communists, was to promote Communist infiltration of the federal bureaucracy in order to advance Communist policy.

Demanding the right to appear before the HUAC, Hiss denied Chambers' charges of Communist membership (and further claim to close friendship) and challenged Chambers to repeat the charges without congressional immunity so that he could bring suit for libel. Chambers did so during an August 27, 1948, interview on "Meet the Press," and Hiss sued him for libel. In his congressional testimony, Chambers

had repeated allegations he had made earlier about Hiss's pro-Communist activities, either to Assistant Secretary of State Adolf Berle in 1939 or to the FBI in 1942, 1945, and 1946. In these earlier interviews Chambers had also only accused Hiss of Communist membership and denied having any evidence which could support more serious allegations. In 1945 and 1946, moreover, the FBI had initiated an investigation of Hiss without any result. At the same time, conservatives in the Congress as early as 1946 were somehow privy to Chambers' then non-public accusations involving Hiss.

The Hiss-Chambers confrontation took a dramatic turn in November-December 1948. On December 2, 1948, Chambers turned over to the HUAC counsel 58 microfilm frames of State Department documents dated in 1938. Chambers claimed to have received the original documents from Hiss in the 1930s in his capacity as a courier for a Soviet espionage operation. Earlier, on November 17, 1948, during pre-trial hearings involving Hiss's libel suit, Chambers had produced copies of two other sets of documents, also dated in 1938, which he claimed had been given to him by Hiss: typewritten facsimiles of original State Department documents and handwritten summaries of others, in Hiss's handwriting.

Abruptly altering his earlier testimony, Chambers thereafter maintained that his relationship with Hiss involved espionage, adding that Hiss was one of the "most zealous" Communist spies operating in Washington during the 1930s. Based on this changed testimony and the documentary evidence, on December 15, 1948, a federal grand jury indicted Hiss on two counts of perjury: his denial of having given classified State Department documents to Chambers in 1938 and his denial of having met Chambers after 1937. While Hiss had only been indicted for perjury, his trial was publicly perceived as an espionage case— technically Hiss could not be indicted for espionage since the alleged activity occurred in 1938, in peacetime, and since there was no second witness to corroborate Chambers' allegations.

The Perjury Trials

Hiss's trial on the perjury charges began on May 31, 1949, in New York City and ended when the jury on July 7, 1949, was unable to reach the unanimity required for conviction (voting 8-4 for conviction). After a four-month delay, as Hiss's attorneys sought unsuccessfully to have the trial moved from New York, Hiss was retried in November 1949. In the second trial, the prosecution's strategy shifted to focus on the documents and not Chambers' credibility (Hiss's defense had capitalized effectively on the numerous changes in Chambers' testimony about his relationship with Hiss and his own activities as a Communist). This strategy succeeded, and on January 21, 1950, the jury convicted Hiss on both perjury counts. Sentenced to five years at the Lewisburg, Pennsylvania, federal penitentiary, Hiss was released in 1954, a scarred and controversial figure.

As with the Dreyfus Case of the 1890s in France, Hiss's indictment and conviction assumed major political significance during the Cold War years, a significance that transcended the specific issues brought out at the trial and had little bearing on the "espionage" importance of the documents Chambers had produced in 1948. The Hiss-Chambers confrontation had seemingly confirmed the existence of a serious internal security threat, thereby legitimizing the politics of exposure dramatically exploited by the House Committee on Un-American Activities and championed during the early 1950s by Sen. Joseph McCarthy. Because the Hiss-Chambers relationship had been uncovered by the HUAC over the opposition of the Truman administration, Hiss's conviction seemed to document the success of Communists in obtaining sensitive positions in the State Department and in shaping the by-then controversial policies of the Roosevelt and Truman administrations toward the Soviet Union at Yalta, Potsdam, and thereafter.

Throughout the trial, and extending after his release from prison, Hiss steadfastly affirmed his own innocence, claiming to have been the victim of unfair tactics and publicity. His various efforts at exoneration—whether unsuccessfully petitioning for a new trial in the 1950s or filing a *coram nobis* suit in the 1970s—proved unsuccessful. Hiss thought he may have achieved his vindication when in 1992, after the fall of the Soviet Union, Russian General Dimitri Volkogonov, who was in charge of intelligence archives, claimed there was no evidence that indicated Hiss was a spy. However, he later recanted his statement, saying he had misunderstood. Four years later, researchers found Soviet transmissions in U.S. intelligence documents that suggested an American, code-named "Ales," perhaps Hiss, had been spying on the United States during the time in question.

Hiss maintained his innocence up until his death on November 15, 1996, at the age of 92. Daniel Schorr of National Public Radio said in 1996, "We don't know to this day whether he was guilty."

Hiss's case, and the question of his innocence or guilt, continues to divide American intellectuals and activists. In a complex way, the Hiss-Chambers case at the time and currently encapsulates the division over McCarthyism and internal security policy which shaped the politics of Cold War America.

Hiss wrote two memoirs: *In the Court of Public Opinion* (1957) and *Recollections of a Life* (1988).

Further Reading

The literature on the Hiss case and on Hiss's career divides sharply along lines of his assumed innocence or guilt. See Athan Theoharis, "Unanswered Questions: Chambers, Nixon, the FBI, and the Hiss Case," in Athan Theoharis (editor), *Beyond the Hiss Case: The FBI, Congress, and the Cold War* (1982); "Alger Hiss, Perjurer," *The Detroit News* (November 20, 1996); Eric Breindel, "The Faithful Traitor," *National Review* (February 10, 1997); Evan Thomas, "An American Melodrama," *Newsweek* (November 25, 1996); William Buckley, "Alger Hiss Could Never Admit his Guilt," *Salt Lake Tribune* (December 13, 1996). Also see *The American Spectator* Online Update (November 19-25, 1996) at http://www.amspec.org/exclusives/update_archives.html. □

James R. Hoffa

Jimmy Hoffa's (1913-1975?) name will always be synonymous with the International Brotherhood of Teamsters, the largest union in the United States. Hoffa secured his place in union history with his zealous support of the Teamsters, which included conflicts with law enforcement and union leadership, dealings with organized crime leaders, criminal indictments, felony convictions, and, many speculate, his own murder.

Jimmy Hoffa is a name which will forever be associated with, and even synonymous with, the International Brotherhood of Teamsters, the largest union in the United States. From the 1930s Hoffa persevered through clashes with police, struggles with union members, fights for control of his union, known associations with organized crime, several indictments, a pair of felony convictions, banishment from union activity and even death to survive as a symbol of the Teamsters. Labor historians disagree about his relative value or disservice to the labor movement in America, but no one can question his legacy of power or his status as a legend.

Early Leadership

Hoffa's career in labor activity began as a teenager in the 1930s, when he engineered a strike on a Kroger grocery store loading dock in southwest Detroit. The strike was called the moment a huge trailer of fresh strawberries came in. Management knew it wouldn't take the food long to spoil, and a new contract was reached in an hour. Within a year, Hoffa's "Strawberry Boys" joined Teamsters Local 674, and later merged with Truck Drivers Local 299. Hoffa demonstrated his clout when he transformed the local from a 40-member unit with $400 to its name to a 5,000-member unit with $50,000 in the bank.

Organized Crime Connections

In 1941 Hoffa entered a phase of his life which would remain with him until the end and would define a large part of his reputation when he formed his first alliance with organized crime. Involved in a turf fight with the Congress of Industrialized Organizations, he asked for help from some of Detroit's east side gangsters to roust his opposition. The east side crowd was happy to oblige, and drove the CIO local out of town. Contacts between Hoffa and the mob would continue for the rest of his life. Some of the activities Hoffa engaged in with organized crime are rumors, while others are known for sure, but his connection to mob figures were never a secret, nor did he try to keep them one.

Tough Times for Unions

The union movement was unpopular in many quarters in the pre-World War II United States, and Hoffa's early experiences with the truckers' union were trying. Company goons, labor goons, and the police all were physical threats, Hoffa's car was bombed, his office was smashed, and he was once arrested 18 times in a single day. "When you went out on strike in those days, you got your head broken," he

remembered to the *Detroit News.* "The cops would beat your brains out if you even got caught talking about unions." By the time he was 28, Hoffa was vice president and chief negotiator for the union. In one major negotiation he threatened to shut down one trucking company and leave others open, a ploy which won the union an unheard-of statewide contract.

Hoffa Elected Teamsters Vice President

In 1952 Hoffa won election as international vice president of the Teamsters under president Dave Beck, who was already under investigation by federal agencies. Hoffa centralized the administration and bargaining procedures of the union in the international union office and succeeded in creating the first national freight-hauling agreement.

In 1957 Beck was summoned before the U.S. Senate's McClellan Committee, where he took the Fifth Amendment approximately two hundred times. When Beck finished his testimony, he had little credibility left as the Teamsters leader. Hoffa moved in. The election to put Hoffa in the presidency was disputed, and the government publicly emphasized Hoffa's connections with organized-crime figures. Nevertheless, Hoffa held on to the presidency and avoided jail for almost a decade.

Hoffa's entrenchment in the Teamsters went hand-in-hand with the mob's entrenchment in the Teamsters. Several organized crime figures assumed positions in the union, and a phony Teamster local was reportedly set up in Detroit as a front for drug dealing. Rumors persisted that Hoffa had murder contracts out on John Kennedy and/or Robert Ken-

nedy, and Hoffa's unconcealed satisfaction at the assassination of both brothers didn't dispel the rumors. He never hesitated to use force in the operations of his union, either: An economics professor who had a 90-day inside look at the Teamsters in the early 1960s wrote, quoted in the *Detroit News,* "As recently as 1962, I heard him order the beating of a man 3,000 miles away, and on another occasion, I heard him instruct his cadre on precisely how to ambush non-union truck drivers with gunfire . . . to frighten them, not to kill."

Criminal Activities

Hoffa faced a series of major felony trials in the 1960s. One factor which had worked in his favor at avoiding prosecution was that Attorney General Robert Kennedy and FBI director J. Edgar Hoover disliked each other too much to cooperate to prosecute him, but in 1962 he was tried for taking a million-dollar kickback for guaranteeing a company labor peace. He was acquitted, but on the last day of the trial he was accused of trying to bribe jurors. That charge brought Hoffa a conviction and an eight-year prison term in 1964, and two months later he suffered another conviction for mail fraud and misuse of a $20-million pension fund. The result was a 13-year combined sentence, which was commuted by President Richard Nixon in 1971 after Hoffa had served just under five years, during which he retained his presidency of the Teamsters.

One of the terms of Hoffa's commuted sentence was that he refrain from union activity, but he made no bones about wanting to regain the presidency of the Teamsters. He lost an appeal on the restriction before the U.S. Supreme Court in 1973, but still hoped to displace Frank Fitzsimmons, whom he had picked himself to serve as president upon his release from prison.

Mystery

That ambition reached its conclusion on the afternoon of July 30, 1975. Hoffa had apparently received an invitation to lunch at the Machus Red Fox restaurant in Southfield, Michigan. The mob had a good working relationship with Fitzsimmons at this time, and wanted to stop Hoffa from regaining control of the Teamsters. Hoffa presumably thought he was being invited to a meeting to work out an arrangement with the mob, but instead he may have been invited to his own murder. No one has ever been arrested in the Hoffa case, no body has ever been found, and no one has ever definitively solved the mystery, but this is the scenario which most parties, including the FBI, believe to be true: Anthony Provenzano, a mobster and New Jersey Teamsters boss, asked Hoffa to meet him for lunch to patch up their relationship, which had become strained while Hoffa was in prison. Anthony Giacalone had arranged the lunch, but neither he nor Provenzano showed up. Hoffa was picked up by several men in a maroon Mercury sedan, was murdered in Detroit and his body was disposed of at a mob-owned sanitation company in Hamtramck, Michigan. Hoffa was officially declared "presumed dead" in 1982.

Immortalized on Film

The Hoffa legend was immortalized in 1992 when director Danny DeVito put it on the big screen in the film *Hoffa*. The film, which admitted to taking some liberties with the truth, received mixed reviews, and some criticism was leveled at it for historical inaccuracies and an overly sympathetic, even apologetic portrayal of the title character by Jack Nicholson. In perhaps the perfect postscript to the Hoffa legend, Sean Wilentz, writing in the *New Republic*, blasted the film for having been conceived, originated, and outlined by organized crime figures.

Further Reading

Walter Sheridan, *The Fall and Rise of Jimmy Hoffa* (New York: Saturday Review Press, 1972).

Arthur A. Sloane, *Hoffa* (Cambridge: MIT Press, 1991). □

Abbie Hoffman

Writer and activist Abbie Hoffman (1936-1989) was best known for his anti-war protests as a leader of the Youth International Party in the 1960s.

Abbie Hoffman was born November 30, 1936, in Worcester, Massachusetts, and educated at Brandeis University (B.A., 1959) and the University of California, Berkeley (M.A., 1960). Like so many other activists of the 1960s, Hoffman was radicalized by participating in the civil rights movement. Among other activities, he founded a store—Liberty House—to sell products manufactured by co-operatives of poor people in Mississippi. In mid-decade he turned his attention to the war in Vietnam, which heated up just when Black Power was driving whites out of black freedom organizations. Hoffman's unique contribution, with Jerry Rubin, was to unite political activism with the emergent counter-culture. As a rule the two movements were antithetical, politics drawing young men and women into public affairs, the counter-culture attracting others to the private pleasures of rock music, drugs, indigency, and liberated sex.

Hoffman made activism glamorous, so to speak, by staging such media events as throwing money onto the floor of the New York Stock Exchange and wearing an American flag shirt on television. Hoffman's theory was that by ridiculing the symbols of authority one weakened its power as well. Deprived of legitimacy, Wall Street and Washington might wither away, or perhaps they would become so frail as to be easily overthrown. These hopes appear more unlikely in retrospect than they did at the time, when authority seemed discredited and many young people believed that the revolution was at hand.

Hoffman's Youth International Party, formed in 1968, was not so much an organization as a way of life. It enabled counter-culturists, known as hippies in their passive state, to express themselves politically without having to elect officers, pay dues, attend meetings, or perform any of the tiresome work associated with real parties. The yippies, as Hoffman's followers were called, assembled at irregular in-

tervals to hold Festivals of Life. These gatherings featured rock music, guerrilla theater, poetry reading, obscene language, and other activities meant to delight the young and aggravate the old.

Their most publicized effort took place at the Democratic National Convention of 1968. In cooperation with the National Mobilization to End the War in Vietnam some 2,500 yippies danced, sang, smoked marijuana, and advertised the virtues of their own candidate for president, a live pig named Pigasus. Poet Allen Ginsberg chanted mantras for peace. Hoffman inscribed dirty words on his forehead. All this inflamed Mayor Richard Daley of Chicago, whose police attacked the yippies with clubs and tear gas, then arrested many for having provoked uniformed officers to riot. The result was a famous trial when eight demonstration leaders—including Hoffman, Jerry Rubin, Tom Hayden of Students for a Democratic Society, and Bobby Seale of the Black Panthers—were indicted for conspiring to incite these riots. Most of the defendants abused and ridiculed Judge Julius Hoffman (no relation), destroying his composure. He had Seale bound and gagged, then declared a mistrial in Seale's case. The other seven were found guilty of various offenses, but as the trial had been a farce their convictions were not sustained.

This was the height of Hoffman's celebrity. With the war in Vietnam winding down and the turbulent 1960s giving way to quieter times Hoffman found himself at loose ends. On August 28, 1973, he was arrested for possession of a large quantity of cocaine. Claiming to have been framed, Hoffman jumped bail and went underground. The next seven years were busy and productive ones for Hoffman, whom the police could not seem to find even though he granted interviews to national magazines, served as travel editor of *Crawdaddy* magazine, and published two books and some 35 articles. In 1980 he surfaced and disclosed that he had been living for the previous four years in Thousand Islands, New York, under the name of Barry Freed. As environmental activist "Freed," minus the long hair and beard of his yippie days, he had appeared on local television and radio, been commended by the governor of New York, testified before a U.S. Senate subcommittee, and been appointed to a federal water resources commission. After serving a year in jail Hoffman returned to Thousand Islands where, as Barry Freed, he continued to campaign for the environment between engagements as a speaker on college campuses.

Hoffman's place in history will depend upon how much weight is given to his activities in the 1960s. Besides providing the young with a good deal of entertainment, Hoffman wrote extensively on behalf of social change. His *Revolution for the Hell of It* (1968) more or less seriously advocated transforming society by means of psychedelic drugs, rock bands, sexual freedom, communes, and the like. Similar themes informed many of his other books, which collectively sold over three million copies. He also figured in some of the most important events of the period. These included not only the Chicago demonstrations in 1968, but the earlier March on the Pentagon, October 21, 1967. At that event some 75,000 demonstrators gathered in Washington, many following Hoffman's lead in attempting to levitate the great military headquarters building. Whether Hoffman's efforts did anything to shorten the war is doubtful. The methods he employed, though they generated an immense volume of publicity, were short-lived, as were the theories he advocated in connection with them. Yet, whatever the lasting results, if any, of his stunts, Hoffman is likely to be remembered as one of the boldest and most imaginative spokesmen for the counter-culture in its days of glory.

Although there is some controversy concerning Hoffman's death in 1989, it seems certain that he killed himself with a lethal combination of 150 pheno-barbital pills and alcohol.

Further Reading

Among Hoffman's own books are: *Revolution for the Hell of It,* New York: Dial Press, Inc., (1968); (with Jerry Rubin and Ed Sanders), *Vote!* (1972); (with Anita Hoffman), *To America with Love: Letters from the Underground,* Stonehill Publishing, Inc., (1976); and *Square Dancing in the Ice Age* (1982). *Woodstock Nation: A Talk-Rock Album* New York: Random House (1969.) There are several biographies of Abbie Hoffman, in varying degrees of quality. Hoffman wrote his autobiography, *Soon to be a Major Motion Picture,* New York: Berkley Books, (1980), the year he surrendered to federal authorities.

Since Hoffman's death a great many books have appeared which explore the details of his life and his socio-political views and actions. There is even an Abbie Hoffman website on the Internet which contains reviews of his books and discussions of his life and political actions. There is also a copy of *Steal This Book,* New York: Private Editions, Inc., (1971), which may be down-loaded. The original volume was self-published, rock-

eted to the best seller list and sold more than one-quarter million copies at $1.95, the original volumes must all be in private hands as no copies seem to exist in libraries, and book dealers are asking $100.00 per copy if they have one.

Abbie Hoffman's place in history may be that of a political prankster; however, many current volumes are discussing him seriously as a political activist, for example, David DeLeon's *Leaders from the 1960s: A Biographical Sourcebook of American Activists,* Westport, Connecticut: Greenwood Press, (1994); Marty Jezer's *Abbie Hoffman: American Rebel,* New Brunswick, NJ: Rutgers University Press (1992); Jack Hoffman and Daniel Simon's *Run Run Run: The Lives of Abbie Hoffman,* New York: G.P. Putnam's Sons (1994); Theodore L. Becker and Anthony L. Dodson's *Live This Book: Abbie Hoffman's Philosophy for a Free and Green America,* Chicago: The Noble Press, Inc. (1991); and Jonah Ruskin's *For the Hell of It: The Life and Times of Abbie Hoffman,* University of California Press (1996). □

Oliver Wendell Holmes

Oliver Wendell Holmes (1809-1894), American physician and author, contributed to the advancement of medicine and wrote witty essays and popular poems.

Oliver Wendell Holmes was born in Cambridge, Mass., on Aug. 29, 1809, scion of a well-established New England family. Following his graduation from Harvard in 1829, he studied at the law school for a year (during which time he wrote the popular poem "Old Ironsides"). He gave up law in favor of a career in medicine.

He rounded out his training at the Harvard Medical School with 2 years of study in Paris (1833-1835), where he learned new techniques and approaches in medicine, reflected in two important early papers, "Homeopathy, and Its Kindred Delusions" (1842) and "The Contagiousness of Puerperal Fever" (1843).

Holmes took his medical degree at Harvard in 1836. From 1838 to 1840 he served as professor of anatomy at Dartmouth College. In 1840 he married Amelia Lee Jackson and returned to general practice. He was appointed Parkman professor of anatomy and physiology at Harvard Medical School in 1847 and served as dean from 1847 to 1853. Holmes remained at Harvard until 1882 and established himself as an excellent lecturer and teacher.

Holmes's deterministic belief that man was the product of his heredity and environment provided the direction for his three pioneering, psychologically oriented "medicated" (as he termed them) novels: *Elsie Venner* (1861), *The Guardian Angel* (1867), and *A Mortal Antipathy* (1885).

Holmes held very definite opinions on a wide variety of subjects. He found the perfect outlet for expressing his ideas in the pages of the *Atlantic Monthly,* to which he contributed several series of chatty essays interspersed with light poetry. These were gathered in *The Autocrat of the Breakfast-Table* (1858), *The Professor at the Breakfast-Table* (1860), *The Poet at the Breakfast-Table* (1872), and *Over the Teacups* (1891). In addition to these and his volumes of verse, he also wrote biographies of John L. Motley (1879) and Ralph Waldo Emerson (1885). Among his best-known poems are "The Deacon's Masterpiece," "The Last Leaf," "The Chambered Nautilus," "My Aunt," "The Moral Bully," and "Brother Jonathan's Lament for Sister Caroline."

As scientist, teacher, lecturer, essayist, and writer of light verse, Holmes left his mark on his age, and many honors came to him both at home and abroad. He died on Oct. 7, 1894.

Further Reading

The Writings of Oliver Wendell Holmes (13 vols., 1891-1892) is standard. *The Complete Poetical Works of Oliver Wendell Holmes* (1895) is an excellent one-volume edition. The best biography is Eleanor M. Tilton, *Amiable Autocrat: A Biography of Dr. Oliver Wendell Holmes* (1947). A sound study is Mark A. De Wolfe Howe, *Holmes of the Breakfast-Table* (1939). Clarence P. Oberndorf offers a stimulating discussion and abridgments of Holmes's "medicated" novels in *The Psychiatric Novels of Oliver Wendell Holmes* (1943; 2d ed. 1946). □

Oliver Wendell Holmes, Jr.

As a jurist and a legal writer, Oliver Wendell Holmes, Jr. (1841-1935), contributed mightily to the debate in the early 20th century concerning the role of law in a rapidly changing America.

The U.S. government is based on a document written in 1787, the Constitution, and an issue almost from the beginning of the new nation was the extent to which the demands of an ever-changing society could be encompassed within this structure. Few men played a more important role in this discourse than Oliver Wendell Holmes, Jr. Not only did he personally contribute to the debate, but he also served as a symbol to a generation of legal and political thinkers.

Oliver Wendell Holmes, Jr., was born in Boston, Mass., on March 8, 1841, into one of the city's most illustrious families. His father, Oliver Wendell Holmes, among the leading medical practitioners of his day, was also a writer and wit, famous to readers of the *Atlantic Monthly* as "the autocrat of the breakfast table." His family life brought young Oliver into contact with many of Boston's leading intellectuals, including Ralph Waldo Emerson, America's foremost essayist and lecturer during this period.

Harvard and the Civil War

Holmes entered Harvard College in 1857. There is little evidence that his college education was of great importance to him. Aside from the education he received simply by virtue of his family's ties, Holmes's greatest learning experience was his part in the Civil War. His participation in many battles resulted in three wounds, of which he was very proud. Throughout the rest of his life he marked his wounds' anniversaries in letters to various correspondents. He left the military in July 1864.

The impact of the war on Holmes had less to do with the political issues over which it had been fought than with its demonstration of the importance of commitment to a higher cause. Holmes grew up in a world where many accepted beliefs were being challenged, and his response stressed the importance of devoting oneself to a cause even if it was incomprehensible. In his speech "The Soldier's Faith," he said: "I do not know what is true. I do not know the meaning of the universe. But in the midst of doubt, in the collapse of creeds, there is one thing I do not doubt, . . . and that is that the faith is true and adorable which leads a soldier to throw away his life in obedience to a blindly accepted duty, in a cause which he little understands, in a plan of campaign of which he has no notion, under tactics of which he does not see the use."

Furthermore, the war confirmed Holmes's rejection of sentimentality and even humanitarianism. He regarded all of life as a battle, with victory going to the strongest. In this way he fully accepted the emphasis of his age on "survival of the fittest." Unlike many of his contemporaries, however, he pointed out that the strongest force in a society was its majority. When he became a judge, he used this argument to favor judicial acquiescence before majority rule.

Legal Career

After leaving the regiment Holmes attended Harvard Law School, from which he graduated in 1866. He was admitted to the Massachusetts bar the following year. After his first trip to England, he threw himself into his legal career, both as a practitioner and as a scholar. After experience in other firms, he helped found the firm of Shattuck, Holmes and Munroe, where he primarily practiced commercial law. The time that remained after practice he used for scholarly work.

Between 1870 and 1873 Holmes edited the *American Law Review*. Furthermore, 1873 saw the publication of the twelfth edition of Chancellor James Kent's classic *Commentaries on American Law*, which Holmes had brought up to date. Throughout the 1870s Holmes was also researching the questions he would consider in a set of lectures at the Lowell Institute in 1880. These, published the following year as *The Common Law*, brought him worldwide fame.

The first paragraph of *The Common Law* contains what is probably Holmes's most famous sentence: "The life of the law has not been logic: it has been experience." He goes on to argue that law is a series of responses to felt social problems, not simply a set of logical deductions from abstract theories. His book contributed to the awakening interest in the United States in "sociological jurisprudence," the interrelation between law and other social institutions.

Judicial Career

After less than a year as professor of law at Harvard Law School, Holmes became an associate justice of the Supreme Judicial Court of Massachusetts on Jan. 3, 1883. He was promoted to chief justice on Aug. 5, 1899. His reputation as a daring thinker grew during his tenure on the court, principally because of several opinions, some dissenting, in which he upheld the right of the state to engage in regulation of the economy and other social issues.

When Theodore Roosevelt became president in 1901, he was eager to appoint men to the Supreme Court who would uphold the new laws he himself wanted passed and who would confirm the changing conception of the role of government with which he was identified. Viewing Holmes as such a man, Roosevelt appointed him to the U.S. Supreme Court; Holmes took his seat on Dec. 8, 1902, at the relatively advanced age of 61. He served on the Court until Jan. 12, 1932.

Holmes's most important early opinions dealt with regulation of the national economy. He argued vigorously for wide latitude for the states in this and in other areas of social policy. His most famous opinion in the economic sphere is probably *Lochner v. New York;* he dissented when the Court struck down a New York law limiting the hours a baker could be made to work. He rejected the Court's social theorizing; for him the key question was not the correctness or incorrectness of economic theories but rather "the right of a majority to embody their opinions in law."

Holmes became even more famous after World War I because of his opinions regarding the regulation of freedom of speech. Though his reasoning was not always impeccable, he used his writing skills (probably the greatest of any Supreme Court justice in American history) to evoke a powerful sense of the importance of civil liberties. In *Schenck v. United States* (1919) he upheld the conviction of a man who had advocated draft resistance, but only after finding him a "clear and present danger" to the peace and order of society. He later dissented from other convictions of political dissidents whom he did not regard as presenting that threat.

In *Abrams v. United States* (1919) Holmes wrote his most passionate defense of free speech, arguing that only a "free trade in ideas" could guarantee the attainment of truth. He argued that "we should be eternally vigilant against attempts to check the expression of opinions that we loathe and believe to be fraught with death, unless they so immediately threaten immediate interference with the lawful and pressing purposes of the law that an immediate check is required to save the country."

Tall, erect, and handsome in his youth, Holmes had grown into an even more imposing man, with a splendid handlebar moustache and white hair. As an elderly judge, he was surrounded often by admiring younger men and was, by all accounts, a lively figure. In his old age he was increasingly admired by many of those who would lead the next political generation. He left the Court before it accepted his theories concerning its role in regulating the economy (as it did, indeed, accept them in the 1940s).

Holmes had married Fanny Dixwell on June 17, 1872. The marriage lasted until her death in 1929; they had no children. Holmes died on March 6, 1935.

Further Reading

A source for Holmes's own writings is Max Lerner, ed., *The Mind and Faith of Justice Holmes: His Speeches, Essays, Letters, and Judicial Opinions,* which also contains Lerner's important introduction to Holmes. Catherine Drinker Bowen, *Yankee from Olympus: Justice Holmes and His Family* (1944), is a popular biography that has had a great public impact. Mark DeWolfe Howe completed two volumes of the definitive scholarly biography before his death; *Justice Oliver Wendell Holmes: The Shaping Years, 1841-1870* (1957) and *The Proving Years, 1870-1882* (1963). Felix Frankfurter, *Mr. Justice Holmes and the Supreme Court* (1938; 2d ed. 1961), is a laudatory assessment of Holmes. For specific treatment of Holmes's judicial career see Samuel J. Konefsky, *The Legacy of Holmes and Brandeis: A Study in the Influence of Ideas* (1956). Recommended for general background are Eric F. Goldman, *Rendezvous with Destiny: A History of Modern American Reform* (1952; rev. ed. abr. 1956), and Arthur M. Schlesinger, Jr., *The Age of Roosevelt,* vol. 1 (1957). ☐

Benjamin Lawson Hooks

Attorney Benjamin Lawson Hooks (born 1925) was the executive director of the National Association for the Advancement of Colored People and served from 1972 to 1977 as the first African American commissioner of the Federal Communications Commission. He led the historic prayer vigil in Washington DC in 1979 against the Mott anti-busing amendment which was eventually defeated in Congress.

Benjamin Lawson Hooks, the fifth of seven children, was born in Memphis, Tennessee, in 1925 to Robert B. and Bessie Hooks. Hooks' family was relatively prosperous because, in 1907, his father and uncle established a successful photography business that was widely patronized by the Memphis African-American community. Because the society was so rigidly segregated along racial lines at that time, many establishments would not serve African Americans. Consequently, numerous African American-owned businesses were founded in the South to meet the needs of the African American populace. His grandmother, a musician who graduated from Berea College in Kentucky, was the second African American female college graduate in the nation. With such evidence of success and hard work as his personal examples, Hooks was encouraged to do well in his studies and prepare for higher education.

Following the Depression of 1929, changes occurred in the Hooks family's standard of living. With money so scarce during those years, African American clients could rarely afford the luxury of wedding pictures or family portraits, so business came to a virtual standstill. They were sad days indeed when the lights were turned out in the Hooks' home and when the bank foreclosed on the mortgage. Still, the family always had clothing and shelter, and no one ever went hungry. In the years after the Depression the family business revived and even several decades later, after his father's death, one of Hooks' brothers continued to maintain it. Perhaps because of the rigors of business life and social prominence in the African American community, Hooks' parents were careful to see that all of their children were conscientious about their appearance, attitude, and academic performance. Hooks learned discipline from his parents' teaching and example.

After completing high school, Hooks decided to remain in Memphis to study pre-law at LeMoyne College. He successfully completed that program and then headed for Italy, where he served in the army during World War II guarding Italian prisoners of war. He felt humiliated that these prisoners were allowed to eat in restaurants that were off limits to him, and that in Memphis, they would have more rights than he. The experience deepened his resolve to do something about the bigotry in the South. When he returned to the United States, he continued his studies at Howard University. From there he went to Chicago where he attended DePaul University Law School—since no law school in the South would admit him. Although he could have established a law practice in Chicago when he graduated in 1948, he chose to return to Memphis to aid in the struggle for civil rights in the South. From 1949 to 1965 he practiced law in Memphis, as one of the few African American lawyers in town. He recalled in *Jet* magazine "At that time you were insulted by law clerks, excluded from white bar associations and when I was in court, I was lucky to be called 'Ben.' Usually it was just 'boy' [But] the judges were always fair. The discrimination of those days has changed and today, the South is ahead of the North in many respects of civil rights progress."

In 1949, Hooks met a 24 year old teacher named Frances Dancy, whom he met at the Shelby County Fair. In 1952 they were married. Frances Hooks recalled in *Ebony* magazine that her husband was "good-looking, very quiet very intelligent . . . He loved to go around to churches and that type of thing, so I started going with him. He was really a good catch."

For years Hooks resisted the call to the gospel ministry. His father had little respect for organized religion, and Hooks had no urge to go against his father's wishes. However, in 1955 he began to preach, and in 1956 he was ordained a Baptist minister. He joined Reverend Martin Luther King's Southern Christian Leadership Conference. He pastored a church in Memphis and one in Detroit at the same time. Hooks, a man of many talents, was not content with his two chosen professions. His interest in business prompted him to become a bank director, the co-founder of a life insurance company, and the founder of an unsuccessful fried-chicken franchise. After several attempts to be elected to public office as a Republican candidate, his political ambitions were realized when he was appointed to serve as a criminal judge in Shelby County (Memphis) in 1965. He thus became the first African American criminal court judge in Tennessee history. The following year he was elected to the same position.

No matter how busy he was with his varied activities, Hooks always found time to take part in civil rights protests. He became a life member of the National Association for the Advancement of Colored People (NAACP) and served on the board of the Southern Christian Leadership Conference (SCLC). He was a pioneer in the NAACP-sponsored restaurant sit-ins and other boycotts that demonstrated the economic power as well as the anger of the African American community against the discrimination that was so pervasive at the time. In spite of his shyness he became a proficient orator whose combination of quick wit and homespun humor delighted audiences. He used this ability as the moderator of television shows called *Conversations in Black and White* and *Forty Percent Speak* (the percent of the African American population of Memphis) and as a panelist on the program *What Is Your Faith?*

Federal Communications Commissioner

Hooks was so often in the public eye that it is not surprising that Tennessee Senator Howard Baker submitted his name to President Richard M. Nixon for political appointment. While he was campaigning, Nixon had promised African American voters that he would see that they were treated fairly by the broadcast media. Thus, in 1972 when there was a vacancy on the seven-member board of the Federal Communications Commission (FCC), Hooks was named to fill it. Although Hooks was not the choice of the most articulate African American groups, including the Black Congressional Caucus, the great majority acquiesced gracefully to his appointment. Benjamin and Frances Hooks soon moved to Washington, D.C. Fortunately for Hooks, his wife matched him in energy, stamina and ambition. She often served as his assistant, secretary, advisor, and traveling companion, even though it meant that her own distinguished career as a teacher and guidance counselor was sacrificed. She told *Ebony* magazine, "He said he needed me to help him. Few husbands tell their wives that they need them after thirty years of marriage, so I gave it up and here I am. Right by his side."

The new position at the FCC gave Hooks a real opportunity to effectuate change in the roles of minorities in the entire broadcast industry. The FCC was responsible for granting licenses to television, radio, and cable television stations and for regulating long distance telephone, telegraph, and satellite communications systems. Hooks felt that his primary role was to bring a minority point of view to the commission. He stated that although he had been nominated by the president, he represented the interests of African Americans, the largest minority in the nation. Hooks was appalled to find that only three percent of those employed by the FCC were African American people, and they were generally in low-paying positions. He encouraged the commission to hire more African American workers at all levels. By the time that he left FCC, African Americans constituted about 11 percent of the employee population. Hooks made a concerted effort during his years as a commissioner to see that African Americans were fairly treated in news coverage and to urge public television stations to be more responsive to the needs of African American viewers by including historical and cultural programming directed toward them.

National Association for the Advancement of Colored People

After serving on the FCC for five years, Hooks was asked to be the executive director of the NAACP, the organization which had formed the vanguard of civil rights advocacy from the beginning of the 20th century. Roy Wilkins, who had held the director's position since 1955, was retiring, and the NAACP board of directors wanted an able leader to take his place. They unanimously agreed that Hooks was the man. He resigned from the commission and officially began his directorship on August 1, 1977.

When Hooks took over the organization, the NAACP was in financial straits and membership had dwindled from half a million to just over 200,000. Still the NAACP had local and regional offices throughout the country. He immediately directed his attention toward rebuilding the economic base of the association through a concentrated membership drive. He also advocated increased employment opportunities for minorities and the complete removal of United States businesses from South Africa. He told *Ebony* magazine "Black Americans are not defeated. . . .The civil rights movement is not dead. If anyone thinks we are going to stop agitating, they had better think again. If anyone thinks that we are going to stop litigating, they had better close the courts. If anyone thinks we are not going to demonstrate and protest . . . they had better roll up the sidewalks."

Hooks' tenure at the NAACP was fraught with bitter internal controversy. He was suspended by the chair of the NAACP's board, Margaret Bush Wilson, after she accused him of mismanagement. These charges were never proven. In fact he was backed by a majority of 64 member board and continued his tenure until his retirement in 1992.

Throughout his career, Hooks has been a staunch advocate for self-help among the African American community. He urges wealthy and middle class African Americans to give time and resources to those who are less fortunate. "Its time today. . .to bring it out of the closet. No longer can we provide polite, explicable reasons why Black America cannot do more for itself" he told the 1990 NAACP convention as quoted by the *Chicago Tribune*. "I am calling for a moratorium on excuses. I challenge black America today—all of us—to set aside our alibis."

After his retirement, Hooks served as Pastor of Middle Baptist Church and president of the National Civil Rights Museum, both in Memphis. He also taught at Fisk University.

Further Reading

There is no full-length biography of Hooks. However, articles and biographical sketches are included in *Ebony Success Library* (1973); *Ebony* magazine (June 1975); *Jet* (December 1972); and *Broadcasting* (April 1972). See also Minnie Finch, *The NAACP, Its Fight for Justice* (1981) and Warren D. James, *NAACP, Triumphs of a Pressure Group, 1909-1980* (1980). □

Herbert Clark Hoover

Herbert Clark Hoover (1874-1964), thirty-first president of the United States, could not halt the severest economic depression in American history because his governmental theories prevented him from taking drastic steps.

On Aug. 10, 1874, Herbert Hoover was born at West Branch, Iowa, of Quaker ancestry. His father died when he was 6 and, after his mother's death less than 3 years later, he went to live with an uncle in Oregon. In 1891 he entered Stanford University, where he specialized in geology.

After graduating, Hoover worked as a mining engineer in the western United States, Australia, and China. In 1901 he became a junior partner in a London-based mining firm and 7 years later set up on his own. During these years he amassed a fortune estimated at $4 million. On Feb. 10, 1899, he married his college sweetheart, Lou Henry; they had two sons, Herbert, Jr., and Allan.

In London when World War I broke out, Hoover was asked to head the Belgian relief program. He was so successful that in May 1917 President Woodrow Wilson called him back to head the U.S. Food Administration. After the armistice he was placed in charge of the American Relief Administration, organized to feed war-ravaged Europe. When the congressional appropriation ran out, Hoover successfully appealed for private contributions to keep the work going.

Hoover was talked of as a possible 1920 presidential candidate by admirers in both parties. Although he publicly declared himself a Republican, the party's Old Guard disliked him because he was a late convert, and its isolationist wing disapproved of his advocacy of the League of Nations. Republican president Warren G. Harding, however, appointed him secretary of commerce, a post he held through the following administration of Calvin Coolidge.

Secretary of Commerce

During the 1920s Hoover set forth the basic philosophy that would guide him throughout his career. His central

tenet was individualism, by which he meant equality of opportunity for each man to make the fullest possible use of his abilities. But he insisted that individualism be tempered by a sense of social responsibility and voluntary cooperation for the general good; he rejected old-fashioned free competition as wasteful. He believed that the government's function was to conserve natural resources, protect equality of opportunity, encourage business efficiency, promote scientific research, and build major public works.

Hoover transformed the Commerce Department into an effective instrument for implementing his philosophy. He fostered the growth of trade associations to bring improved efficiency and stability to industry, promoted American foreign trade, and expanded the Department's information and statistical services. He also set up a Division of Housing to encourage home building, built the Bureau of Standards into one of the country's leading scientific research institutions, and successfully pushed for stronger government regulation of the commercial aviation and radio industries.

Hoover's influence became increasingly important in all economic questions facing the Federal government. Believing that management and labor must cooperate for the good of all, he favored collective bargaining (though not the closed shop), worked behind the scenes to resolve labor disputes, and encouraged development of privately financed unemployment insurance. For relief to farmers he opposed government price-fixing of agricultural products, instead favoring increased Federal assistance to farm marketing cooperatives.

After Coolidge decided not to run again in 1928, Hoover was the popular choice of the party rank and file and won the Republican presidential nomination on the first ballot. In the election he defeated Democrat Alfred E. Smith by over 6 million votes, even breaking the "solid South."

Foreign Affairs

Hoover's record in foreign affairs was mixed. Immediately after his election he made a successful goodwill tour of Latin America, and throughout his term he actively worked for a good-neighbor policy south of the border. He was interested in promoting international disarmament, but the London Naval Conference of 1930 was only partly successful, and his efforts at the Geneva Disarmament Conference (which met in 1932 to secure abolition or reduction of offensive weapons) failed. His administration's worst mistake concerned the Japanese invasion and occupation of Manchuria in 1931. Secretary of State Henry Stimson was willing to impose economic sanctions against Japan, but Hoover, fearful of instigating a war, limited the American response to the ineffectual Stimson Nonrecognition Doctrine.

Domestic Policy

Domestically, Hoover expanded the national forests and parks, laid the groundwork for many of the later New Deal accomplishments in water-resource development, increased Federal highway spending, was instrumental in setting up the privately financed Research Committee on Social Trends, reorganized the Federal prison system, promoted the growth of civilian aviation, and even approved a bill which drastically limited the use of injunctions in labor disputes.

On the other hand, Hoover's opposition to government competition with business led him to veto a bill for government operation of the hydroelectric facilities at Muscle Shoals, Ala. And despite warnings from economists of its disastrous consequences for international trade and economic stability, he signed legislation which raised the average level of tariff duties from roughly 30 to about 59 percent. But what most damaged his reputation was the inadequacy of his response to the depression that followed the stock market crash of October-November 1929.

Voluntarism versus Federal Intervention

Although previous chief executives had taken the position that the business cycle would simply have to run its course, Hoover believed that the government could and should act to cushion economic shocks. When the Depression hit, he made repeated optimistic statements about the economy to bolster business confidence, had the Federal Reserve Board follow an "easy money" policy, and accelerated work on Federal projects. However, his major emphasis was on voluntary action rather than government intervention: he exhorted industry to maintain employment and wages, induced bankers to establish the National Credit Corporation to assist threatened banks, and relied upon the traditional agencies of private charity and local government to provide relief for the unemployed.

But this voluntarism was a failure. The business community lacked the discipline and sense of social responsibility for effective cooperation. Yet, despite increasing hardship in all sectors, Hoover was convinced that the country was basically sound. He held that the causes of the Depression lay outside the United States. To prevent the threatened breakdown of the German economy under the burden of reparations payments—which would have jeopardized millions of dollars of American loans—he arranged a one-year moratorium on payment both of reparations and inter-Allied war debts.

By late 1931 Hoover was driven to embrace more direct Federal intervention. He established the Reconstruction Finance Corporation to make emergency loans to financial institutions and certain corporations. He supported the Glass-Steagall Act, which liberalized the Federal Reserve System's credit requirements; and the Federal Home Loan Bank Act, to assist building and loan societies, savings banks, and insurance companies in expanding loans for residential construction. Hoover's program rested on the assumption that infusing additional credit into the economy would be enough to revive business activity. Still the economy continued its downward slide.

Nevertheless, Hoover stood firm against the massive public-works spending that Democrats and progressive Republicans increasingly demanded. He was adamantly against any direct Federal relief for the unemployed, not only for budgetary reasons, but because he was determined to preserve what he regarded as the fundamental American principles of individual and local responsibility.

Despite sharp Republican losses in the 1930 congressional elections, Hoover largely had his way. He successfully fought a proposal to strengthen the ineffective U.S. Employment Service. And the Relief and Construction Act (1932), which authorized loans of $1.5 billion to state and local agencies for self-liquidating public works and $300 million to the states for relief purposes, was watered down to meet his specifications. He suffered only two major legislative defeats: a proposed sales tax for balancing the budget and an overridden veto on the bill permitting veterans to borrow up to 50 percent of the face value of their bonus certificates.

"Bonus Army" Blunder

In his personal relations Hoover was affable and genial, a sensitive and humane idealist—qualities he was unable to project to the public. His sensitivity to criticism led to poor relations with the press, and his resistance to direct Federal relief made him appear callous to the suffering around him.

Perhaps Hoover's worst blunder was his handling of the "bonus army." An estimated 17,000 former servicemen flocked to Washington in the spring of 1932 to demand that Congress authorize the immediate payment in full of their bonus certificates. When the Senate, under Hoover's prodding, defeated the measure, most returned to their homes. An attempt by Washington police to evict those remaining resulted in the death of two veterans and two policemen.

Hoover then called out Federal troops on July 28, 1932—an action that made him even more unpopular.

New Deal Triumphs

In the 1932 campaign Hoover warned that the program of Democratic nominee Franklin D. Roosevelt threatened a "radical departure" from the American way of life. His efforts to cooperate with the president-elect came to naught, because Roosevelt and his "Brain Trust" correctly suspected that Hoover wanted to commit the new administration to a continuation of his own policies. When Hoover left office in March 1933, nearly the entire United States economy was paralyzed.

In the years that followed, Hoover remained politically active, attacking Roosevelt's New Deal policies, which he blamed for prolonging the Depression by destroying business confidence. Prior to Pearl Harbor, Hoover was a strong isolationist; after World War II he was a leading exponent of the "Fortress America" theory.

Elder Statesman

When Hoover left office, he was probably the most hated president in American history. Only the passage of time led to a fairer judgment. In 1947 President Harry S. Truman appointed him chairman of the Commission on Organization of the Executive Branch of the Government. In 1953 President Dwight Eisenhower appointed him to the same job. The work of these two Hoover commissions provided the basis for a major reorganization of the executive branch. When he died on Oct. 20, 1964, Hoover was widely respected as one of the nation's foremost elder statesmen.

Hoover did more than any previous chief executive to combat a depression, but the limitations of his political and social philosophy proved his undoing. Perhaps the most significant result of his experiment in voluntarism was that its failure prepared the public to accept the farreaching expansion of Federal authority under the New Deal.

Further Reading

Before his death Hoover completed his *Memoirs* (3 vols., 1951-1952), covering the years up to 1941. There is no adequate biography. Eugene Lyons, *Herbert Hoover: A Biography* (1964), is superficial and eulogistic. Harris Gaylord Warren, *Herbert Hoover and the Great Depression* (1959), and Albert U. Romansco, *The Poverty of Abundance: Hoover, the Nation, the Depression* (1965), are useful, but both suffer from lack of access to the Hoover papers. See also Harold Wolfe, *Herbert Hoover, Public Servant and Leader of the Loyal Opposition: A Study of his Life and Career* (1956). A discussion of foreign policy is Robert H. Ferrell, *American Diplomacy in the Great Depression: Hoover-Stimson Foreign Policy, 1929-1933* (1957). ☐

John Edgar Hoover

J. Edgar Hoover (1895-1972) was appointed assistant director of the Bureau of Investigation in 1921, and director in 1924; he was the popular (and then controversial) direc-

tor of the U.S. Federal Bureau of Investigation from 1935 until his death in 1972, at age 77.

J. Edgar Hoover was born into a Scottish Presbyterian family of civil servants in Washington, D.C. on New Year's Day, 1895; his mother called him Edgar from the day he was born. He was a leader of the student cadet corps in high school, and a champion debater. He taught Sunday school at Old First Presbyterian Church. His lifelong guiding principles were formed early: he was convinced that middle-class Protestant morality was at the core of American values, and he harbored a deep distrust of alien ideas and movements that called those values into question.

Working days and attending school at nights, Hoover earned his Bachelor of Law degree with honors from George Washington University in 1916. He excelled in mock court proceedings. In 1917 he earned a Master of Law degree and got a job with the Alien Enemy Bureau in the Department of Justice, administering the regulations governing the hundreds of thousands of German and Austro-Hungarian aliens interned or supervised by the department. In response to a series of bombings in the spring of 1919, supposedly carried out by radicals, Attorney General A. Mitchell Palmer decided to concentrate on aliens, since they could be deported summarily and wholesale, without due process, and in 1920 he put the 24-year-old Hoover in charge of the operation. Within a short period of time, Hoover had written briefs arguing that alien members of the new American Communist and Communist Labor parties were subject to deportation under the immigration laws; planned a raid on the headquarters of the Union of Russian Workers; and put

Emma Goldman, Alexander Berkman, and 247 other "radicals" on a ship for the Soviet Union. A few days later, Hoover led a nationwide operation which arrested more than four thousand alien Communists.

While civil libertarians deplored the Justice Department's tactics and treatment of prisoners, Hoover had established his reputation as an organizational genius. In 1921, he was appointed assistant director of the Bureau of Investigation. Three years later, when the bureau had become known as "the most corrupt and incompetent agency in Washington," Hoover was appointed Acting Director by a new Attorney General, Harlan Fiske Stone (later Associate Justice, then Chief Justice of the Supreme Court). Hoover took the job under the conditions that he would tolerate no political meddling and that he wanted sole control of merit promotions. Stone agreed. Almost immediately, the new director instituted new personnel policies; he fired agents he considered unqualified, abolished promotions based on seniority, introduced uniform performance appraisals, and laid out strict rules of conduct (including instructions that forbade the use of intoxicating beverages, on or off the job). He established new lines of authority (all regional officers were to report directly to Hoover) and did whatever he could to create power for his agency. At the time, for example, the Bureau had jurisdiction over little more than car-thefts. Agents were not allowed to carry firearms until 1934, and they did not have the power of arrest. Law enforcement was a state activity, not a federal one. Gradually, Hoover professionalized the organization and freed it from the taint of corruption. He was a pioneer in the areas of personnel training, the use of scientific laboratory techniques, accurate reporting, and filing large volumes of material. By 1926, state law enforcement agencies began contributing their fingerprint cards to the Bureau of Investigation. Early on, Hoover laid the foundation for a world-class crime fighting organization.

During this period, Hoover still maintained his card file of over 450,000 names of "radicals" and worked on building the bureau "his way, " but the agency slumbered through the violence of the Roaring Twenties. It took the Lindbergh kidnapping in 1932 to convince Congress that there was a need for national legislation authorizing the Federal government to act against crimes of violence on other than government reservations; companion legislation between 1932 and 1934 augmented that authority, and the FBI (so named in 1935) was in business, chasing down the likes of Machine Gun Kelly, Baby Face Nelson, Ma Barker and her sons, and John Dillinger.

Hoover was famous for his successes in public relations, legend-building and image-making his Bureau into a Hollywood extravaganza, firmly entrenched as a mainstay of popular culture through films, comic strips, books, and carefully orchestrated publicity campaigns. The FBI and its director became dear to the hearts of the American people and Hoover himself became a hero of almost mythic proportions. But during most of the 1930s, Hoover was relatively obscure, merely the head of just one of several investigatory agencies. In the art of public relations, Hoover was the beneficiary of Franklin Roosevelt's Attorney General

Homer Cummings, who between 1933 and 1937 developed a massive, multi-front public relations campaign to make law enforcement a national movement wholly dependant on public support for its success in dealing with the gangsters of the Depression era. When Cummings suffered political decline, Hoover now head of the nation's only national law enforcement agency adopted many of his methods, always looking for new public enemies to protect the nation against. In the coming years, these were to include Nazi spies, Communists, Black Panthers, the New Left, and Martin Luther King, Jr. As for law enforcement, Hoover mostly abandoned it altogether after 1936.

After World War II Hoover took from the growing tension between the United States and the Soviet Union a mandate to prepare for domestic sabotage and subversion, and to round up Communists, siding with such anti-Communists as Richard M. Nixon and Senator Joseph R. McCarthy. He pursued the investigation of Alger Hiss that discredited the domestic security policies of the Truman Administration; he uncovered the alleged atom spy conspiracy of Klaus Fuchs, Harry Gold, and Julius and Ethel Rosenberg (who were subsequently executed as traitors); and his Bureau provided the evidence for the Smith Act convictions of the top leadership of the American Communist Party (later overturned by the U.S. Supreme Court).

During the late 1950s, Hoover developed a counterintelligence program (COINTELPRO) to covertly harass the remnants of the American Communist Party. In the 1960s he extended the program to harass and disrupt the Ku Klux Klan, the black militant movement and the antiwar movements, particularly targeting the Black Panthers and the Students for a Democratic Society. Now into his 70s, Hoover extended his defense of "Americanism" with public attacks on Martin Luther King, Jr., and two attorneys general Robert Kennedy and Ramsey Clark. His tactic in all cases included illegal wiretapping and microphone surveillance.

During all these years, Hoover managed to overlook organized crime. Robert Kennedy became a thorn in Hoover's side when he demonstrated otherwise as assistant counsel on the Kefauver committee's investigations into organized crime. Hoover ignored political corruption and white collar crime. Most of his work was political, in two senses of the word. First, he target individuals, groups, and movements which offended his moral sense. Second, he collected compromising information provided by his agents on all sorts of public officials. The fact that he had such information in his personal files or was merely thought to have such information was enough to sway congressional votes in favor of FBI appropriations requests and to keep presidents from removing him from office, even long after mandatory retirement age. The perception of "such information" worked both ways, however. It was long thought that Hoover denied the existence of organized crime because certain Mafia figures had photographs and other documentation of Hoover's alleged and widely-believed homosexuality. However, nothing could be proved, as after his death, Hoover's secretary obeyed instructions that all his personal files be burned.

J. Edgar Hoover died in May, 1972, still the Director of the FBI, and became the only civil servant to be honored with a state funeral. Post-Watergate investigations of the FBI's abuses of civil liberties under Hoover and recent releases of FBI files under the Freedom of Information Act (including files his secretary missed) have destroyed Hoover's reputation. Recent scholarly works have asserted that Anthony Summers book(1993), exposing Hoover's homosexuality, was based on slender and dubious evidence. Other works have also shown the FBI's ineffectiveness in pursuing organized-crime figures had little to do with Hoover's vulnerability, but rather from his lack of accountability, his use of illegal investigative techniques, and his obsessive focus on his own political agenda. J. Edgar Hoover's methods contributed substantially to a culture of lawlessness in the FBI itself. Within a few years of his death, public opinion about Hoover had shifted to the point that his name by itself conjured up the image of a government at war with the rights and liberties of its citizens.

Further Reading

Hoover's own writings *Masters of Deceit: The Story of Communism in America and How To Fight It* (1958) and *J. Edgar Hoover on Communism* (1969) were written for him by FBI publicists. The book that purports to expose Hoover's private life, Anthony Summers' *Official and Confidential: The Secret Life of J. Edgar Hoover* (1993), was not highly regarded even by Hoover's critics. Richard Gid Powers *G-Men: Hoover's FBI in American Popular Culture* (1983); Athan G. Theoharis and John Stuart Cox *The Boss J. Edgar Hoover and the Great American Inquisition* (1988); and Ronald Kessler *The FBI: Inside the World's Most Powerful Law Enforcement Agency* (1993) are useful works, as is the older "oral biography" by Ovid Demaris *The Director: An Oral Biography of J. Edgar Hoover*. Scholars will want to see three microfilm collections of documents edited by Athan Theoharis, *The J. Edgar Hoover Official and Confidential File* (1996); *FBI Wiretaps, Bugs, and Break-Ins: The National Security Electronic Surveillance Card File and the Surreptitious Entries File* (1996); and *The Louis Nichols Official and Confidential File and the Clyde Tolson Personal File* (1996). See also Alan Theoharis *J. Edgar Hoover, Sex, and Crime: An Historical Antidote* (1995); Alan Theoharis *From the Secret Files of J. Edgar Hoover* (1993); Richard Gid Powers, *Secrecy and Power: The Life of J. Edgar Hoover* (1993); Mark North, *Act of Treason: The Role of J. Edgar Hoover in the Assassination of President Kennedy* (1992); Curt Gentry *J. Edgar Hoover: The Man and His Secrets* (1992); Nelson Blackstock, *COINTELPRO: The FBI's Secret War on Political Freedom* (1988); Ward Churchill and James Vander Wall's two books, *The COINTELPRO Papers: Documents from the FBI's Secret Wars Against Dissent in the United States* (1990); and *Agents of Repression: The FBI's Secret War Against the American Indian Movement and the Black Panther Party* (1990). □

Bob Hope

In addition to his successes on radio, in movies, on television, and in live shows, Bob Hope (born 1903) has developed a reputation for his untiring efforts to entertain and

boost the morale of American military personnel stationed all over the world and for the numerous appearances he has made in the name of various charities.

B ob Hope is perhaps the most widely known and loved stand-up comedian in America. On July 13, 1969, long before Hope reached his greatest fame, the *Milwaukee Journal* stated that Hope had "undoubtedly been the source of more news, and more newspaper feature stories than any other entertainer in modern history."

"Hopeless" Childhood

Born in Eltham, England on May 30, 1903, Leslie Townes Hope was one of seven surviving boys. By the age of four he was a skilled mimic and loved to sing and dance. In 1908 Hope's family moved from England to Cleveland, Ohio. Hope's father, Harry, was a hard-drinking stonemason whose income was irregular. For Hope, who looked and sounded British, the Americanization process was difficult. The Cleveland neighborhood in which he lived was tough, and the neighborhood kids made fun of him. They inverted his name, Leslie Hope, to create the nickname "Hopelessly." When he shortened his name to Les, they countered with another nickname, "Hopeless." Hope was a scrappy kid and to ward off the ridicule he fought easily and sometimes successfully, developing into a boxer of some skill.

As a youth Hope sold two-cent newspapers on the streets of Cleveland to supplement his family's income. On one occasion a gentleman in a long black limousine waited while Hope, who did not have change for a dime, rushed into a nearby store to get change. When he returned he received a lecture about the importance of keeping change in order to take advantage of all business opportunities. The man was oil magnate John D. Rockefeller, founder of Standard Oil Company.

As a teenager Hope once boasted that he would rather be an actor than hold an honest job, and he participated in all kinds of school and amateur training groups, specializing in dancing and in the one-liner jokes for which he ultimately became famous. He gained a great deal of experience in an act Hope formed with a comedian from Columbus, Ohio, named George Byrne. Adopting the name Lester, Hope went with Byrne to New York City in 1926. He and Byrne performed in cities and towns outside New York City, and finally appeared in a New York City vaudeville production called "Sidewalks." They were fired within a month, however, because the show was a success and did not need the short dancing act that Hope and Byrne performed.

Vaudeville Comic

Hope got his first trial as a solo act at Chicago's Stratford Theatre in 1928. For this solo appearance he changed his name to Bob because he felt that would be "chummier" and look better on a theatre marquee. In solo appearances, Hope always made his audience feel at ease and comfortable with his self-deprecating humor. He worked desperately hard and succeeded but soon left the Stratford to tour midwestern cities.

From 1920 to 1937 Hope performed in all kinds of shows in vaudeville both on and off Broadway. Vaudeville was hard work for Hope. A typical show consisted of comedians running a patter of one-liners around various kinds of variety acts ranging from dancing dogs to sword-swallowers but featuring mainly dancing. Hope is considered a master of the one-liner. In later years Hope sometimes employed up to three joke writers at a time. One standard line when he boards an airplane is, "I knew it was an old plane when I found Lindbergh's lunch on the seat." He used a line in 1970 when he met with the English Royal Family: "I've never seen so much royalty.... It looks like a chess game . . . live!" In 1932, when fifteen million Americans suffered the joblessness of the Great Depression, Hope was earning a thousand dollars a week in his particular kind of vaudeville act. But he was not satisfied. Hope was always ambitious and wanted to improve. He yearned, as he said, "to be the best," to be the outstanding comic in the business.

Hope and Crosby

Hope met actor and singer Bing Crosby in 1932. They liked each other immediately because their personalities and styles of acting fitted well, and they started performing together in song and dance routines. Hope met aspiring actress Delores Reade in 1933 and later married her. Already well established as a comedian by 1935, Hope that year joined the "Ziegfield Follies" and performed in cities outside New York; then on January 30, 1936, he opened in the "Follies" at New York City's Winter Garden Theatre, with such stars as Fanny Brice and Eve Arden. The "Ziegfield Follies" was a new vaudeville high for Hope. The

show was the musical highlight of Broadway, consisting of dazzlingly beautiful girls and costumes, witty lines between the actors and actresses, and music by such great composers as Vernon Duke and Ira Gershwin. During his years in vaudeville, Hope was on the stage with such actors as Jimmy Durante, Ethel Merman, Edgar Bergen and Charlie McCarthy, Al Jolson, and many others.

Although Hope had acted in some short motion picture comedies as early as 1934, he began his feature-length movie career in Hollywood in 1938, with the Paramount film *The Big Broadcast of 1938* starring Hope, W.C. Fields, Martha Raye, Dorothy Lamour, and Shirley Ross. This was the beginning of an active career in film entertainment for Hope, who went on to appear in fifty-two movies; six of these comprise the *Road to. . .* series featuring Hope, Crosby, and Dorothy Lamour.

Hope has always been fiercely patriotic about his adopted country. On December 7, 1941, when Japanese attack planes bombed the American naval installation in Hawaii's Pearl Harbor, thereby provoking U.S. participation in the Second World War, Hope denounced the attack. On December 16, during a radio broadcast, Hope declared his patriotism and voiced optimism about the outcome of the war: "There is no need to tell a nation to keep smiling when it's never stopped. It is that ability to laugh the makes us the great people that we are . . . Americans!"

Performed for the Troops

One of Hope's former stand-ins who had joined the armed forces knew of Hope's reputation for charitable work and in 1942 asked the comedian to make an entertainment tour of Alaskan Army bases. Hope enlisted Frances Langford, Jerry Colonna, Tony Romany, and other performers to put together a variety show for the troops stationed there. That was the beginning of a commitment on Hope's part that has never ended. Every year, especially during the Christmas season, Hope has spearheaded a drive to present shows to American men and women in the armed forces. His service to American troops added to Hope's established reputation for activity in the name of numerous charities and benefits, including political, cultural, and humanitarian causes. In fact, at the Academy Awards on February 21, 1941, Hope was given an honorary award "to pay tribute . . . to a man who has devoted his time and energy to many causes. His unselfishness in playing countless benefits has earned him a unique position in a hectic community where his untiring efforts are deeply, profoundly appreciated." Hope also won honorary Oscars in 1940, 1944, 1952, and 1965.

Hope has long been many Americans' favorite comedian, from the average radio-listener and movie-goer to the rich and powerful. He often enjoyed a close relationship with the men serving as President of the United States. Since the administration of Franklin Roosevelt, Hope has appeared many times at the White House. President Jimmy Carter, in paying tribute to the man who had entertained America for so long, commented on Hope's role as White House guest: "I've been in office 489 days.... In three weeks more I'll have stayed in the White House as many times as Bob Hope has." Hope's seventy-fifth birthday party, held in the Washington Kennedy Center to honor the United Service Organization (USO), was attended by members of Congress and many of Hope's acting friends, including John Wayne, Elizabeth Taylor, and George Burns.

Another celebration was held at the Kennedy Center in 1983 when Hope turned eighty years old, this time hosted by President Ronald Reagan and his wife, Nancy. Again Hope's friends were present to honor the occasion, including models Cheryl Tiegs and Christie Brinkley. At the celebration Hope was still what *Time* magazine called "The All-American Wisecracker," and showed no signs of slowing down.

Hope can look back upon a life that has been full to the brim. One of his writers, Larry Klein, once said: "You know, if you had your life to live over again, you wouldn't have time to do it." Hope answered: "I wouldn't want to live it over again. It's been pretty exciting up to now. The encore might not be as much fun." Behind all Hope's humor is a serious core that directs his life, as evidenced by his efforts to help others less fortunate than himself. Some of his charitable activities involve golf benefits. A twelve stroke handicapper, Hope has played the game all his life, often joining presidents, Hollywood's greats, and golf's immortals on the links. Because of the benefits the game brings to charities, Hope agreed in 1964 to have the Palm Springs Classic golf tournament renamed The Bob Hope Desert Classic, and he has hosted it ever since. Hope's serious side was also apparent in the preface to his 1963 book *I Owe Russia $1200,* in which he wrote: "Yes, the conquest of space is within our grasp, but as we reach out we seem to have diminished the inward search. No significant breakthrough has yet been made in the art of human relations. So perhaps this is the precise moment in history for each of us to look into his heart and his conscience and determine in what way we may be responsible for our present dilemma."

Celebrated the First 90 Years

In May 1993, NBC celebrated Hope's 90th birthday with the three-hour special "Bob Hope: The First Ninety Years." The show, which won an Emmy, featured tributes from every living U.S. president at that time—Richard Nixon, Gerald Ford, Jimmy Carter, Ronald Reagan, George Bush, and Bill Clinton. By then, according to *TV Guide,* Hope had made more than 500 TV shows and 70 movies. Hope concluded his 60–year contract with NBC on November 23, 1996, when his final NBC TV special, *Laughing With the Presidents* was aired.

The Guinness Book of World Records called Hope the most honored entertainer in the world. By mid-1995, he had received more than 2,000 awards and citations, including 54 honorary doctorate degrees, *The Saturday Evening Post* reported. An additional honor came in June of 1998 when Hope and his wife were bestowed with papal knighthood by the Archbishop of Los Angeles. At age 92, he released a book, video, and two compact discs commemorating the 50th anniversary of the end of the Second World War. *The Saturday Evening Post* printed this excerpt from Hope's

book: "I was there. I saw your sons and your husbands, your brothers and your sweethearts. I saw how they worked, played, fought, and lived. I saw some of them die. I saw more courage, more good humor in the face of discomfort, more love in an era of hate, and more devotion to duty than could exist under tyranny."

Further Reading

Faith, William Robert, *Bob Hope: A Life in Comedy,* Putnam, 1982.

Hope, Bob, *I Never Left Home,* Simon & Schuster, 1944.

Hope, Bob, *Have Tux, Will Travel: Bob Hope's Own Story,* Pocket Books, 1956.

Good Housekeeping, July 1982, pp. 107-130; December 1994, pp. 88 +.

New York Times, January, 1985, p. 50.

The Saturday Evening Post, May/June 1995, pp. 16 +.

Time, May 30, 1983.

TV Guide, May 21-27, 1983, pp. 14-16; May 8, 1993, p. 25

Los Angeles Times November 23, 1996, Sec: F, p: 1, col: 2. □

John Hope

African American educator, religious leader, and champion of racial equality, John Hope (1868-1936) advocated liberal education for black youth and formed the first consortium of African American colleges in America.

John Hope was born in Augusta, Georgia, on June 3, 1868. He finished the eighth grade, then worked in a restaurant. Encouraged to seek further schooling, in 1886 Hope enrolled in the Worcester Academy in Massachusetts. In 1890 he entered Brown University on a scholarship. Graduating in 1894, he was the commencement orator. That year Hope took a position at Roger Williams University in Nashville. He married Lugenia Burns in 1897; the couple had two sons.

Hope joined the faculty of Atlanta Baptist (now Morehouse) College in 1898. A master teacher, he deeply influenced the intellectual and moral growth of his students. He also had a strong impact on his peers. His writings were published in the *Occasional Papers of the American Negro Academy* and in other places. In 1906 he became the first black president of the college. As always, he stressed general culture, human dignity, and Christian principles.

Hope fought for racial equality in every way he could. In 1906 he joined W. E. B. Du Bois and others in the Niagara movement. He was the only college president (white or black) to participate in this protest meeting, which culminated in the founding of the National Association for the Advancement of Colored People (NAACP). In 1915 Hope was appointed to the NAACP advisory board.

Working to improve the living conditions of black people in Atlanta, Hope got Federal aid for slum clearance on Atlanta's West Side and secured funds for building model apartments for African Americans. During World War I, as special secretary for the YMCA in France, he devoted himself to the welfare of black soldiers there.

In 1929 Hope became president of Atlanta University, the first black institution in the South to offer graduate degrees. Under his leadership the university attained the highest regional accreditation rating a black institution could receive. Hope worked to affiliate Atlanta's six black colleges; three affiliated in 1929, and the others joined later.

Among his many honors, Hope was elected Phi Beta Kappa at Brown in 1919. He received the Harmon Award for distinguished service in education in 1929 and was awarded the doctor of laws degree by Bates College and Brown, Bucknell, Howard, and McMasters universities. He served as president of the National Association of Teachers in Colored Schools, the Georgia Commission for Work among Negro Boys, the Commission on Interracial Cooperation, and the Association for the Study of Negro Life and History. Among his other positions, he was a member of the Executive Committee of the New York Urban League and a delegate to the International Missionary Council.

Hope died on February 20, 1936. He was awarded the Spingarn Medal posthumously for his outstanding services to African Americans.

Further Reading

The only full and complete biography of Hope is Ridgely Torrence, *The Story of John Hope* (1948), which is a thoroughly researched work. Clarence A. Bacote, *The Story of Atlanta University: A Century of Service, 1865-1965* (1969), contains a chapter dealing with Hope's administration. There is a sketch of Hope in Wilhelmena S. Robinson, *Historical Negro Biographies* (1967; 2d ed. 1968). □

Edward Hopper

A pioneer in picturing the 20th-century American scene, Edward Hopper (1882-1967) was a realist whose portrayal of his native country was uncompromising, yet filled with deep emotional content.

Edward Hopper was born on July 22, 1882, in Nyack, N.Y. At 17 he entered a New York school for illustrators; then from 1900 he studied for about 6 years at the New York School of Art, mostly under Robert Henri, whose emphasis on contemporary life strongly influenced him. Between 1906 and 1910 Hopper made three long visits to Europe, spent mostly in France but also including travel to other countries. In Paris he worked on his own, painting outdoor city scenes, and drawing Parisian types. After 1910 he never went abroad again.

Back home, from about 1908 Hopper began painting aspects of the native scene that few others attempted. In contrast to most former Henri students, he was interested less in the human element than in the physical features of the American city and country. But his pictures were too honest to be popular; they were rejected regularly by academic juries and failed to sell. Until he was over 40 he supported himself by commercial art and illustration, which he loathed; but he found time in summers to paint.

In 1915 Hopper took up etching, and in the 60-odd plates produced in the next 8 years, especially between

1919 and 1923, he first expressed in a mature style what he felt about the American scene. His prints presented everyday aspects of America with utter truthfulness, fresh direct vision, and an undertone of intense feeling. They were his first works to be admitted to the big exhibitions, to win prizes, and to attract attention from critics. With this recognition he began in the early 1920s to paint more and with a new assurance, at first in oil, then in watercolor. Thenceforth the two mediums were equally important in his work.

The 1920s brought great changes in Hopper's private life. In 1924 he married the painter Josephine Verstille Nivison, who had also studied under Henri. The couple spent winters in New York, on the top floor of an old house on Washington Square where Hopper had lived since 1913. He was now able to give up commercial work, and they could spend whole summers in New England, particularly on the seacoast. In 1930 they built a house in South Truro on Cape Cod, where they lived almost half the year thenceforth, with occasional long automobile trips, including several to the Far West and Mexico. Both of them preferred a life of the utmost simplicity and frugality, devoted to painting and country living.

Hopper's subject matter can be divided into three main categories: the city, the small town, and the country. His city scenes were concerned not with the busy life of streets and crowds, but with the city itself as a physical organism, a huge complex of steel, stone, concrete, and glass. When one or two women do appear, they seem to embody the loneliness of so many city dwellers. Often his city interiors at night are seen through windows, from the standpoint of an outside spectator. Light plays an essential role: sunlight and shadow on the city's massive structures, and the varied night lights—streetlamps, store windows, lighted interiors. This interplay of lights of differing colors and intensities turns familiar scenes into pictorial dramas.

Hopper's portrayal of the American small town showed a full awareness of what to others might seem its ugly aspects: the stark New England houses and churches, the pretentious flamboyance of late-19th-century mansions, the unpainted tenements of run-down sections. But there was no overt satire; rather, a deep emotional attachment to his native environment in all its ugliness, banality, and beauty. It was his world; he accepted it, and in a basically affirmative spirit, built his art out of it. It was this combination of love and revealing truth that gave his portrait of contemporary America its depth and intensity.

In his landscapes Hopper broke with the academic idyllicism that focused on unspoiled nature and ignored the works of man. Those prominent features of the American landscape, the railroad and the automobile highway, were essential elements in his works. He liked the relation between the forms of nature and of manmade things—the straight lines of railway tracks; the sharp angles of farm buildings; the clean, functional shapes of lighthouses. Instead of impressionist softness, he liked to picture the clear air, strong sunlight, and high cool skies of the Northeast. His landscapes have a crystalline clarity and often a poignant sense of solitude and stillness.

Hopper's art owed much to his command of design. His paintings were never merely naturalistic renderings but consciously composed works of art. His design had certain marked characteristics. It was built largely on straight lines; the overall structure was usually horizontal, but the horizontals were countered by strong verticals, creating his typical angularity. His style showed no softening with the years; indeed, his later oils were even more uncompromising in their rectilinear construction and reveal interesting parallels with geometric abstraction.

After his breakthrough in the 1920s, Hopper received many honors and awards, and increasing admiration from both traditionalists and the avant-garde. He died in his Washington Square studio on May 15, 1967.

Further Reading

Lloyd Goodrich, *Edward Hopper* (1971), is a fully illustrated biographical and critical study. *Saõ Paulo 9* (1967), the catalog of the Biennial Exhibition held in Saõ Paulo, Brazil, that featured Hopper, contains essays on him by William C. Seitz and Goodrich. □

Vladimir Horowitz

American pianist Vladimir Horowitz (ca. 1904-1989) was among the last performers in the 19th-century grand-virtuoso tradition. While his phenomenal technique sometimes overwhelmed the music, the power and energy of his playing were unsurpassed.

During his lifetime, Vladimir Horowitz was recognized as the greatest piano virtuoso of the 20th century. Michael Walsh noted in an 1986 report "At his peak Horowitz had it all, heightened and amplified by a daredevil recklessness that infused every performance with an exhilarating, unabashed theatricality. . . .[He was] this most extraordinary of artists." Vladimir Horowitz's birth occurred in 1904 in Russia. He began to study piano with his mother at around age three. Within a few years he was seriously studying the instrument and by his late teens had already composed several songs. Other members of the family were also musical, especially Horowitz's sister, Regina, who also became a concert pianist, and an uncle who had studied composition with Scriabin and who arranged for Horowitz's concerts before the pianist left Russia.

Although Horowitz revealed talent at an early age, he was not considered a prodigy. He enrolled in the Kiev Conservatory in 1912, first studying with his mother's teacher, Vladimir Puchalsky, then Sergei Tarnowsky in 1915, and, finally, Felix Blumenfeld, a student of Anton Rubinstein, in 1919. Horowitz credited the last mentioned for his flat-fingered technique which resulted in a semi-staccato attack and produced a brilliant tone. Blumenfeld was to be Horowitz's last teacher, although he would have occasional lessons with Cartot in France. Throughout his conservatory years Horowitz usually practiced less than four hours a day, and this rather inefficiently, at least from a technical standpoint, preferring to play through operatic literature rather than work at the progressive lessons and exercises familiar to most pianists. From the beginning his intention had been to pursue a dual career as composer-pianist in the tradition of Liszt and Rachmaninoff. The Bolshevik takeover of Kiev in 1920, however, put an end to this plan, forcing him to concentrate on concerts as an efficient means to deriving an income. In the 1920's Horowitz gave 100 performances and earned a reputation as an explosive pianist capable of breaking piano strings with his thundering style.

During this period Horowitz met the famous German pianist Arthur Schnabel, who advised him to leave Russia, and shortly thereafter, in 1923, he found the means to do so through Alexander Merovich, his first manager. Horowitz's first European tour, as arranged by Merovich, included performances in Berlin and Paris; neither city accepted him without reservation. The rising anti-Semitism in Germany discouraged a Jewish musician who, moreover, did not play German music and who played in a romantic, high-flown style unacceptable to the German ideals of precision and strict adherence to the score. The French were as unreceptive to Horowitz's programming as the Germans, again preferring to hear music of their own composers.

Horowitz's New York debut took place on January 12, 1928, at Carnegie Hall, with Sir Thomas Beecham conducting the New York Philharmonic in the Tchaikovsky piano concerto. Although the passion and agility of Horowitz's playing amazed critics, the performance as a whole suffered from irreconcilable differences in interpretation and tempo between conductor and soloist.

A meeting with Rachmaninoff a few days before his New York debut marked the beginning of a friendship that would continue until Rachmaninoff's death in 1943. Equally important was his introduction to Toscanini in April 1932. In addition to the many fruitful collaborations that would take place between the two, Horowitz became further acquainted with Toscanini's daughter, whom he married in 1933.

The sensational qualities of Horowitz's playing soon established him at the forefront of the American concert scene. He found it increasingly difficult, however, to mediate between the public's and his manager's demands for brilliant showpieces and the more solid musicality of those around him, especially his father-in-law and mentor, Toscanini. This, along with the daily grind of a hectic concert schedule, a nervous constitution, and other personal problems, necessitated three extended absences from the stage and, partially, from recording. These occurred during the years 1936-1939, 1953-1965, and 1969-1973. Horowitz also became less interested in performing outside the United States, where he acquired citizenship in 1945. Between the years 1939 and 1986 he made only one tour of Europe, playing three London concerts in October 1951 and two recitals in Paris the following month. In 1986 he began a tour with a return to the Soviet Union—his first visit since leaving there 60 years before—for performances in Moscow and Leningrad in April. He then continued on to Hamburg, Berlin, and London.

Horowitz was undoubtedly one of the great pianists of the era and was compared to Franz Liszt in his total command of the instrument. He was most comfortable with Romantic works, especially Liszt and Rachmaninoff, and admitted a dislike for modern music that exploits the percussive, rather than lyrical, capabilities of the piano. Of the composers who can be admitted stylistically to the 20th century, Horowitz played only Debussy, Ravel, Scriabin, Prokofiev, and Barber. Acknowledging his affinity for their music, Prokofiev requested that Horowitz give the American premiers of his sonatas 6-8 (the *War Sonatas*), and Barber wrote the fourth movement fugue to his *Sonata, Op. 26* at the pianist's request for "something very flashy, but with content." In later years Horowitz tended away from these early moderns.

Among his many recordings, several deserve mention. Liszt's *Sonata in B Minor*, recorded in 1932 for RCA, shows Horowitz at the peak of his powers, especially in the clarity, evenness, and speed of his scale passages and octaves. A collaboration with Toscanini and the NBC Symphony Orchestra in a 1940 recording of Brahms' second piano concerto for RCA demonstrated the benefit of Horowitz's yielding control to the more solid formal instincts of the conductor. This recording also received praise for the comparatively life-like quality of the sound. Many consider Horowitz to be the foremost interpreter of Rachmaninoff, and especially of his third piano concerto. The first of Horowitz's three renditions of the work, a 1930 recording with Albert Coates and the London Symphony, is perhaps the preferred. Outside his usual repertory, Horowitz championed the works of two pre-Romantic composers, Muzio Clementi and Domenico Scarlatti, on two albums for RCA and Columbia, respectively.

Horowitz limited his teaching to only a few of the most talented prospects and later acknowledged only Byron Janis, Ronald Turini, and Gary Graffman as having studied with him. While Janis was typical in describing the difficulty of working with the strong personality of Horowitz, he ascribed his regard for pedaling according to varying acoustical situations to Horowitz's teaching. In 1995 and 1996, *The Private Collection I & II* were released based upon the private tapes owned by Horowitz.

Horowitz died of a heart attack on November 5, 1989 in New York City. "At his best," wrote Joah von Rhein in the *Chicago Tribune*, "Horowitz had a thunderous sonority and demonic daring that literally nobody in the world could match."

Further Reading

The most complete account of Horowitz's life is Glen Plaskin's *Horowitz* (1983). Thoroughly researched, meticulously documented, eminently readable, and impartial, it is a model of biographical writing. An abridged version of Chapter 10, describing Horowitz's introduction to the Toscanini family, appears in *Musical America* (March 1983). Shorter biographies are included in Harold Schonberg's *The Great Pianists* (1963) and in Wilson Lyle's *A Dictionary of Pianists* (1985). The May 5, 1986, issue of *Time* contains biographical material plus a description of his April 1986 return to Russia. The June 8, 1997 *Jerusalem Post* also had a fine feature on him, "The Fairy Tale Life of Vladimir Horowitz." □

Harry Houdini

Harry Houdini (1874-1926)—The Great Houdini—is a name that will forever define the term "escape artist." As the Budapest-born, American-bred performer would so often proclaim, "No prison can hold me; no hand or leg irons or steel locks can shackle me. No ropes or chains can keep me from my freedom."

No one before or since has so completely defined the art of escape as Harry Houdini, magician, actor, and stage personality. Old film footage and still photos recall Houdini as generations remember him—suspended upside-down high over the heads of the crowd, escaping from a straitjacket; plunging, manacled, into an icy river, only to reappear miraculously moments later; performing his signature Chinese Water Torture Cell illusion, in which audiences were invited to hold their breath along with Houdini as he made his escape from yet another watery coffin.

But there was a world of difference between what turn-of-the-century audiences saw, and what they *thought* they saw. Much of Houdini's escapes relied as much on myth and misdirection as they did on the magician's genuine physical and mental prowess. Likewise, Houdini made myth of his own life, elaborating details where he thought appropriate. Though in some documents Houdini claims to be born April 6, 1874, in Appleton, Wisconsin, this much is known: Erich Weiss, born March 24, 1874, in Budapest, Hungary, was the youngest of three sons of Rabbi Samuel

and Cecilia (Steiner) Weiss (the couple also had a daughter, Gladys).

The Making of a Magician

To escape persecution and find a better life, the Weiss family immigrated to Appleton—"perhaps April 6 was the date Samuel Weiss arrived in Wisconsin," remarked Ruth Brandon in her *The Life and Many Deaths of Harry Houdini*. Other moves took the Weisses to Milwaukee and, eventually, New York. But the family remained poor. Completely devoted to his mother to the point of obsession, the young Erich sought ways to ease her hardscrabble life. At one point, he took to begging for coins in the street. True to his illusionist ways, he hid the coins around his hair and clothing, then presented himself to Cecilia with the command, "Shake me, I'm magic." She did, and a flood of coins spilled out.

Magic was Erich's second obsession—indeed, "the abounding takes of his childhood magical exploits carry the mythic fuzz Houdini liked to generate," as Brandon wrote. After serving as a young circus acrobat (Eric, Prince of the Air) the teenager focused his attention on locks and lockpicking. He financed his hobby by working as a necktie cutter—the garment trade being one of the few occupations open to Jews at that time.

So it was with great dismay from his parents that Erich announced he was giving up the tie business for show business. At age 17 he took the stage name Houdini, after the nineteenth century French magician Robert-Houdin. "Harry" was an accepted Americanized version of Erich. By age 20 Houdini had married Wilhelmina Beatrice Rahner (known as Bess); she became his partner onstage as well.

As "Mysterious Harry and La Petit Bessie," the Houdinis played dime museums, medicine shows, and music halls, eventually working their way up to small billing at larger theaters. At one point, the couple toured with a circus. When escape tricks and magic didn't pan out, the pair billed themselves as a comedy act, cribbing old jokes from magazines, as Brandon noted in her book.

Typically, during these early years, Harry would perform his famed "Hindoo Needle Trick," in which he appeared to swallow 40 needles, then drew them from his mouth, threaded together. Bess became a well-prompted "mentalist," performing mind-reading routines based on an alpha-numeric code known to her and Harry. In 1895, in Massachusetts, Houdini first conceived the notion of escaping not from his own handcuffs, but from those of the local police. These stunts brought free publicity, which eventually led to the Houdinis' crack at the big time—a booking in the Hopkins Theatre, a top Chicago vaudeville house.

Houdini the Headliner

American tours were followed by smash appearances in Europe. Of course, with success came imitators; after all, anyone could buy a version of the Hindoo Needle Trick (Houdini himself had purchased the illusion). But Houdini clones fell by the wayside as long as the original toured. Still, "he was always edgy with his contemporaries, and saw younger magicians only as rivals, ready to push him into obscurity," wrote Brandon.

So, ever seeking the bigger and better illusion, Houdini escaped from every combination of straitjackets, jails, coffins, handcuffs, and leg shackles. At each performance, he invited police officials onstage to examine him and his props for authenticity. But even this was a ruse, as Brandon wrote: "Houdini's skill as a magician, which meant he could palm, misdirect attention, and hide his [lockpicks] in unlikely places, came in useful here. A favoured hiding place was his thick, wiry hair. When he had to strip naked, he sometimes hid a small pick in the thick skin on the sole of a foot—not a spot that would ordinarily be searched."

But "something new was needed," said Brandon, "and on 5 January 1908, it appeared. It was a galvanized-iron can shaped like an extremely large milk can—large enough to hold a man: Houdini." As she went on to say, the can held 22 pails of water. Handcuffed, Houdini would immerse himself inside, but not before asking the audience to hold their breath along with him. "At the end of three minutes, by which time the audience's lungs were bursting . . . Houdini appeared, dripping but triumphant. The can was revealed, filled to the rim, all its locks intact."

In 1918, the film industry was still in its infancy. But Houdini was not; at age 44 he was uncertain how much longer he could leap from bridges and squirm from straitjackets. So in June of that year the performer made his move into film with a character called the Master Detective. In this series of stories the detective, named Quentin Locke, fought peril and saved damsels through great stunts, and of course, great escapes.

"The plots were ludicrous and the acting wooden," Brandon reported of Houdini's films. Still, they showcased Houdini the way his public wanted to see him. And, importantly, each magic routine or stunt was shown as "real," with no camera tricks or editing to enhance the Master Detective's mastery. Other films followed, with varying degrees of financial and critical success.

The Spirit World Beckoned

Houdini's varied career would take another turn. "After the death of his mother in 1913," as Steve and Patricia Hanson related in a *Los Angeles* magazine article, the illusionist "became obsessed with 'making contact with those who had gone beyond.'" This venture brought the performer into contact with another notable figure of turn-of-the-century pop culture—Sir Arthur Conan Doyle, the creator of Sherlock Holmes.

The association—and eventual bitter breakup—of Houdini and Doyle began as far back as 1908, when as a publicity stunt Houdini wrote a letter to "Holmes," asking for help in catching scalawags who were stealing his tricks. By 1920 the two had formed a friendship that seemed connected not only by their talent but by their tragedies—just as Houdini had lost his beloved mother, Doyle lived in grief over the death of his son, Kingsley, a casualty of World War I. Each man sought to explore spiritualism as a way of making possible contact.

But at one point the friendship began to unravel. Houdini was much more the skeptic than Doyle, and indeed made something of a second career from debunking fraudulent mystics. As the Hansons noted in *Los Angeles,* "Houdini thought that there was an irrational part of Doyle's psyche that desperately wanted to believe contact with the dead was possible. Doyle thought Houdini's campaign against spiritualism was a 'mania.' Thus the feud between the two quickly escalated."

The Passing of a Legend

No evidence of real contact with Houdini's mother was ever recorded. But the specter of his mother's death followed the illusionist until the occasion of his own passing. Even that event has since been clouded by the mythology that always seemed to accompany the magician. For instance, a feature film of Houdini's life, released in 1953, had him perishing in one of his own watery coffins during a performance. One magic expert collected seven different versions of the death.

In reality, the magician, while on tour in Montreal, was relaxing backstage where some college students met him. Always proud of his physique, Houdini had often challenged people to punch him with all their strength in the abdomen. He agreed to let one of the students take a punch. But—reclining on a couch at the moment of contact—Houdini had not yet prepared his muscles for the blows. An injury to the appendix (or perhaps, as Brandon has asserted, an aggravation of an existing appendix problem) left untreated for some days, turned into an attack of peritonitis that struck down Houdini during a performance in Detroit. Rushed to a hospital where the city's finest doctor attended him, Houdini lingered for a few days, then died in the arms of his wife at 1:26 p.m., October 31, 1926—Halloween day.

Even in death, Houdini knew how to create publicity. His widow made headlines in announcing a yearly seance on the anniversary of Houdini's passing to try and make contact with his spirit. The ritual went on for some ten years, and though Bess once asserted that contact was made, she later recanted her story. While no longer among the living, Houdini lives on in a collective cultural imagination. After a lifetime of embodying mythic attributes, Houdini has become a myth himself.

Further Reading

Brandon, Ruth, *The Life and Many Deaths of Harry Houdini,* Random House, 1993.

Los Angeles, April 1989, p. 94. □

Charles Hamilton Houston

While with the NAACP, Charles Hamilton Houston (1895-1950) teamed with the American Fund for Public Service to direct a program of legal action and education aimed at the elimination of segregation.

Charles Hamilton Houston, a groundbreaking lawyer and educator, is credited with having recognized in the 1930s that the incipient black civil rights movement would achieve its greatest and most lasting successes in the courtroom. Endowed with a legal mind celebrated for its precision, Houston believed that the U.S. Congress and state legislatures, mired in the politics of race and beholden to constituencies that might be reluctant to disavow institutional discrimination against blacks, were more likely to frustrate the advances sought by civil rights leaders. In Houston's eyes, the courts, as ostensibly apolitical forums, would be more responsive to sound, analytical, legal arguments elucidating the nature and consequences of Jim Crow laws—which enforced discrimination against blacks after the Civil War—and state-sanctioned segregation.

Whether plotting strategy for the National Association for the Advancement of Colored People (NAACP), arguing cases before the U.S. Supreme Court, or retooling a second-rate law school into a first class institution that churned out generations of brilliant black lawyers, Houston helped focus politicians and courts in the United States on the patently unconstitutional foundation of racial inequality. Although he labored quietly and without self-promotion, his famous students and more flamboyant colleagues were always quick to point out that he effectively laid the groundwork for many of the century's milestone court decisions that progressively undid the knot of legal discrimination in the United States.

Unlike the more prominent civil rights leaders of the 20th century, Charles Hamilton Houston did not experience abject poverty or suffer the injurious tentacles of blatant discrimination as a child. He was born on September 3, 1895, in Washington, D.C., the only child of William, a lawyer, educator, and future assistant U.S. attorney general, and Mary, a public school teacher who abandoned her career for hairdressing and sewing in order to provide additional money for the family. The Houstons revered education, surrounding young Charles with books and encouraging his prodigious intellect. Legend had it that Houston's grandfather, a Kentucky slave, constantly provoked the ire of his illiterate master by reading books that had been smuggled onto the plantation. Largely insulated from the ways in which society denigrated blacks—including inadequate housing, lower wages for doing the same work as whites, and racial violence—Charles Houston attended what was arguably the best all-black high school in the country, from which he graduated as class valedictorian in 1911.

Excelled in School, Became Activist-Dean

Houston enrolled at Amherst College in Massachusetts, where he was elected to Phi Beta Kappa and was one of six valedictorians in 1915. Determined to be a lawyer like his father, Houston taught English for a couple of years back in Washington in order to save enough money to attend Harvard Law School. With an ever-sharpening analytical eye, Houston saw his choice of career validated when, while teaching, he came to see that blacks had not advanced meaningfully in the past 20 years and were becoming increasingly victimized by segregation in the public and private sectors.

After serving in the army during World War I, Houston entered Harvard Law School, where his intellectual zeal and worldly curiosity found a home. Author Richard Kluger wrote in his 1976 book *Simple Justice: The History of Brown v. Board of Education and Black America's Struggle for Equality,* "From the start, it was evident that [Houston] had a mind ideally contoured for a career at law. He relished the kind of abstract thinking needed to shape the building blocks of the law. He had a clarity of thought and grace of phraseology, a retentive brain, a doggedness for research, and a drive within him that few of his colleagues could match or understand."

After his first year, Houston was elected to the *Harvard Law Review,* a prestigious scholastic honor, and discovered a legal mentor in the eminent professor and future Supreme Court Justice Felix Frankfurter. Graduating with honors, Houston decided to obtain his doctorate degree in juridical science under Frankfurter, who taught his student not only the finer points of constitutional law but also the need to incorporate the lessons of history, economics, and sociology into a comprehensive, legalistic world view. These teachings, in combination with his own growing awareness of the second-class citizenship forced on blacks, forged in Houston the conviction of a social activist and the strategic thinking of a lawyer who understood the power of law to effect social change.

Returning from a one-year fellowship at the University of Madrid in Spain, Houston practiced law with his father, an experience that exposed him to the minutiae of case preparation and provided courtroom opportunities for him to exercise his blossoming forensic talents. In 1929 Houston was appointed vice-dean at the Howard University School of Law, a black institution that, despite glaring weaknesses, had produced nearly all the distinguished black lawyers in the country for two generations after the Civil War. Recognizing the need for blacks to thoroughly understand constitutional law with an eye toward dismantling the legal basis of segregation, and for black students to have higher education institutions on a par with those available only to whites, Houston set about reconstituting the law school. He shut down the night school, from which his father had graduated, toughened admissions standards, improved the library and curriculum, and purged from the faculty those he believed were not tapping the intellectual potential of the next generation's black lawyers and leaders.

By 1935, although there was still only one black lawyer for every 10,000 blacks in the country, Houston was optimistic. August Meier and Elliot Rudwick, writing in the *Journal of American History* in 1976, quoted Houston as saying at an NAACP convention, "The most hopeful sign about our legal defense is the ever-increasing number of young Negro lawyers, competent, conscientious, and courageous, who are anxious to pit themselves (without fee) against the forces of reaction and injustice.... The time is soon coming when the Negro will be able to rely on his own lawyers to give him every legal protection in every court."

Pursued Civil Rights as a Teacher and Lawyer

It was not only as an administrator that Houston advanced his cause. As a professor, he was empowered to directly shape the future of black law. His principal goal was to elucidate for his students—the future fighters for racial justice—the stark differences between the laws governing whites in American society and those governing blacks. In his book *Black Profiles,* George R. Metcalf wrote that Houston "called it making 'social engineers.' He had become dean in 1929 with but one purpose: to make Howard, which was then second rate, a 'West Point of Negro leadership' so that Negroes could gain equality by fighting segregation in the courts."

Of the students who braved Houston's intense mock court proceedings and military-style cerebral drillings, none would more successfully carry the torch that Houston had lit than Thurgood Marshall, who would ultimately be appointed to the Supreme Court. "First off, you thought he was a mean so-and-so," Marshall was quoted as saying in *Simple Justice.* "He used to tell us that doctors could bury their mistakes but lawyers couldn't. And he'd drive home to us that we would be competing not only with white lawyers but really well-trained white lawyers, so there just wasn't any point crying in our beer about being Negroes.... He made it clear to all of us that when we were done, we were expected to go out and do something with our lives."

In 1934 Houston was retained by the NAACP, then the dominant civil rights organ of the century, to chip away at segregation by leading a legal action campaign against racially biased funding of public education and discrimina-

tion in public transportation. One of his first cases, in which his legal artfulness was fully displayed, involved a black man from Maryland who wished to attend the University of Maryland Law School, the same school that years earlier had denied Thurgood Marshall admission on the grounds that he was black. Houston operated on the 1896 Plessy v. Ferguson Supreme Court decision, which validated separate but equal public education. University officials had told Donald Murray that because he was black he would not be admitted, but that he was qualified to attend Princess Anne Academy, a lackluster, all-black institution that was an extension of the university. Houston and Marshall set out to prove that Princess Anne Academy, without a law school or any other graduate programs, did not provide an education on a par with the University of Maryland, and therefore, the state had violated *Plessy.*

Houston and Marshall were victorious, not only in getting Murray into the University, but in showing that states that wanted to sustain separate but equal education had to face the onerous and expensive task of making black institutions qualitatively equal to white institutions. The courts, it became clear, were going to carefully scrutinize the allegedly equal education in states hiding behind *Plessy.* Segregation took on an impractical quality to those who tried to defend it on moral grounds. In subsequent pioneering cases, Houston would further lead the attack on segregated education by using the testimony of psychologists and social scientists who claimed that black children suffered enormous and lasting mental anguish as a result of segregation in public schools and the societal ostracism of blacks.

Argued Against Discrimination Before Supreme Court

Houston's first case before the U.S. Supreme Court involved a black man named Jess Hollins who had been convicted of rape in Oklahoma by an all-white jury and sentenced to death. Brandishing arguments he had used before in lower courts, Houston claimed that because blacks historically had been denied jury placements in Sapulpa, Oklahoma, only on the basis of their race, black defendants could maintain that they had been denied due process under the law. The Supreme Court, citing one of its recent decisions, concurred. Houston became the first black to successfully represent the NAACP before the highest court in the land.

During his tenure at the NAACP, Houston was praised not only for his legalistic virtuosity but for his prescience in picking cases that would collectively help erode segregation in the country. In his second major Supreme Court victory, he succeeded in guaranteeing that an all-white firemen labor union fairly represent in collective bargaining black firemen excluded from the union. Houston also persuaded the court that racially restricted covenants on real estate—such as deeds prohibiting blacks from occupying a house—were unconstitutional. In 1945 he argued and won a case involving a black woman from Baltimore who, on the basis of her skin color, had been denied entry into a training class operated by a public library and funded by tax-payer dollars.

Always trying to expand the scope and appeal of the NAACP, Houston suggested the establishment of satellite offices on college campuses and advised the association's officials to attend conferences of religious leaders as a way of better accessing black communities. As a native Washingtonian with many political contacts, he was also expected to comment on the racial consequences of legislation that was being considered by Congress, where he frequently testified before legislative committees. In 1944 Houston was appointed to the Fair Employment Practices Committee, created to enforce integration in private industries, but quit 20 months later, decrying what he viewed as a transparent commitment to racial equality on the part of the administration of President Harry S. Truman.

Houston died in 1950, four years before his star pupil, Marshall, succeeded in arguing before the Supreme Court that the separate but equal defense of segregated education was unconstitutional. The precedent set in *Brown v. Board of Education* was the culmination of decades of legal challenges, many of which had been masterminded and implemented by Houston. Although his name never would be as widely known as others in the civil rights community, many lawyers and activists who worked with him, including Marshall, have never strayed from their belief that Charles Hamilton Houston was one of the early, unsung heroes of the assault on segregation. Richard Kluger quoted Howard University Professor Charles Thompson in *Simple Justice* as saying, "[Houston] got less honor and remuneration than almost anyone else involved in this fight. He was a philanthropist without money."

Further Reading

Auerbach, Jerold, *Unequal Justice,* Oxford University Press, 1976.

Bardolph, Richard, *The Negro Vanguard,* Vintage Books, 1959.

Franklin, John Hope, and August Meier, editors, *Black Leaders of the Twentieth Century,* University of Illinois Press, 1982.

Kluger, Richard, *Simple Justice: The History of Brown v. Board of Education and Black America's Struggle for Equality,* Knopf, 1976.

Metcalf, George R., *Black Profiles,* McGraw-Hill, 1970.

Segal, Geraldine, *In Any Fight Some Fall,* Mercury Press, 1975.

Journal of American History, March 1976.

Additional information for this profile was obtained from papers housed at Howard University, Washington, D.C. □

Samuel Houston

Samuel Houston (1793-1863), American statesman and soldier, was the person most responsible for bringing Texas into the Union.

Sam Houston's life was controversial and colorful. It exemplified the opportunities that existed on the American frontier: he rose from humble origins to become governor of two states and to represent both in Congress.

Houston was born on March 2, 1793, in Rockbridge County, Va. Following the death of his father, he and his

mother moved to Blount County, Tenn., in 1807. Houston received less than a year and a half of formal education. In 1809, when farming and clerking proved distasteful to him, he ran away to live with the Cherokee Indians for 3 years. The Cherokee called him "The Raven." In 1812 he established a subscription school, where he also taught for a year.

Soldier and Lawyer

During the War of 1812 Houston enlisted as a private and rose to the rank of second lieutenant. He was severely wounded during the Battle of Horseshoe Bend, and Gen. Andrew Jackson, commander in the engagement, commended him for his coolness and courage. After the war Houston applied for a commission in the Regular Army and was assigned to Jackson's command at Nashville, where he also served as subagent to the Cherokee. Resigning his commission in 1818, he studied law and was quickly admitted to the bar. He established his practice at Lebanon, Tenn.

Entering politics in 1819 as a Jacksonian Democrat, Houston proved a colorful and magnetic orator and was elected attorney general of Tennessee. Two years later he was named major general of the Tennessee militia. In 1823 he was elected to Congress and reelected in 1825. He was elected governor of Tennessee in 1827 and probably would have been reelected in 1829 had not personal tragedy interfered. In January 1829 he had married Eliza Allen, but in April she left him. In response, Houston resigned his governorship and went to live with the Cherokee in the western part of Arkansas Territory.

Establishing himself near Ft. Gibson (in present Oklahoma), Houston opened a trading post and took a Cherokee wife, Tiana Rogers. Twice he represented the Cherokee in dealings with the Federal government. On the second trip, in 1832, Ohio representative William Stanberry charged him with misdealings with the Indians; enraged, Houston beat the congressman with a cane. Houston was tried by the House of Representatives, which issued a reprimand.

Career in Texas

In late 1832 President Andrew Jackson sent Houston to deliver peace medals to tribes of western Indians and to negotiate with them. After fulfilling this obligation, he decided to cast his lot with Texas, at this time a Mexican province, because of the land available there at reasonable prices. He established a law practice at Nacogdoches.

Houston was elected a delegate to the Convention of 1833, which advocated separate statehood for Texas within the Mexican Republic. He aligned himself with the militant faction of Texans, and when the revolution began in October 1835, he was elected commander in chief of the army. However, the volunteers refused to follow his lead during the winter of 1835/1836, and he spent his time with the Cherokee. Again, in 1836, he was named commander in chief of the Texan forces, this time by the convention that met to declare Texas independent.

Houston rallied a small army, drilled it briefly, then led it into battle. On April 21, 1836, he met the force commanded by Mexican president Antonio López de Santa Ana at San Jacinto. Houston's 783 men fought an estimated 1,500 Mexicans. The battle lasted 18 minutes and was a decisive defeat for the Mexicans. Santa Ana was later captured.

In 1836 Houston was elected the first president of the Republic of Texas. During his 2-year term he followed a conservative policy, seeking annexation to the United States, peace with the Indians and with Mexico, and minimum government spending. He served as president again from 1841 to 1844. His chosen successor, Dr. Anson Jones, concluded the annexation of Texas to the United States in 1845, and Houston became one of the state's first senators.

National Politics

Houston served Texas as a senator from 1845 to 1859. He was the only Southern Democrat to vote for the Compromise of 1850 and against the Kansas-Nebraska Act of 1854. Also, he frequently spoke for Indian rights. In 1859, fearing the drift toward Southern secession from the Union, he returned to Texas to campaign for the governorship. Despite charges of cowardice and treason, he was elected. He opposed secession and was able to force a statewide vote on the issue. When the vote favored secession, Houston refused President Abraham Lincoln's offer of troops to help him retain office. In March 1861 Houston was deposed from office for failure to take the oath of allegiance to the Confederacy.

Houston had remarried in 1840, following a Texas divorce. His third wife, Margaret Lea of Alabama, bore him eight children. They maintained a home at Huntsville, Tex.,

and there Houston died on July 26, 1863, having seen most of his predictions about the disaster of secession borne out. Proud to the point of being vain, Houston in later years had signed his first name with an "I" instead of an "S," so that his signature read "I am Houston."

Further Reading

Most of the known writings of Houston are contained, with adequate footnotes and introduction, in *The Writings of Sam Houston,* edited by Amelia Williams and Eugene C. Barker (8 vols., 1938-1943). A thorough and factual biography of Houston is Llerena Friend, *Sam Houston* (1954). Marquis James, *The Raven: A Biography of Sam Houston* (1929), is slightly more readable but very romanticized. □

Elias Howe

Elias Howe (1819-1867), American inventor, is credited with designing the first workable sewing machine, an invention which revolutionized garment and shoe manufacture.

Elias Howe was born in Spencer, Massachusetts, where his father operated a gristmill and sawmill. In 1835 Elias was apprenticed to a manufacturer of cotton machinery in Lowell, Massachusetts. Two years later he worked briefly in a machine shop in Cambridge, then apprenticed himself in Boston to a maker of watches and scientific instruments.

While working in this shop, Howe is said to have overheard the owner discussing the need for, and problems involved in making, a sewing machine. By 1844 Howe himself began trying to build a workable model. Even though he had acquired a family, he quit his job and, with financial support from his father, worked full-time on the invention. Later he was able to take in a partner, who provided more capital.

Howe had a sewing machine working as early as April 1845, and in September 1846 he obtained a U.S. patent for his second machine. One key to his success was the placement of the eye of the needle near the point, rather than at the opposite end as in a regular needle. Howe sent his brother to England to seek a market and there sold his third machine to a manufacturer of corsets, umbrellas, and shoes. This manufacturer saw the possibilities the sewing machine would have if it could be redesigned to sew leather for shoes. He asked Howe to come to England to work on the problem. The two soon quarreled, however, and Howe was forced to pawn his model and the patent papers to raise enough money to return home.

Upon his return Howe discovered that several manufacturers were developing a market in America for sewing machines. This appeared to infringe his patent. In a lawsuit that lasted from 1849 to 1854, he finally vindicated his claims to originality and priority and was able to extract a license fee for each machine produced by his rivals. At the height of his prosperity Howe received as much as $4,000 a week in royalties.

Howe's new wealth was but one measure of the success of the sewing machine. Within the decade of the 1850s it became a major trade item. In 1860 some 110,000 sewing machines were manufactured. In turn, there was a rise in the number of ready-to-wear garments. The sewing machine was applied to shoemaking with the same results.

Further Reading

There is no full biography of Howe. Facts on him must be gleaned from biographical collections and histories of technology. Egon Larson (pseudonym for Egon Lehrburger), *Men Who Shaped the Future: Stories of Invention and Discovery* (1954), has a profile of Howe. James Parton, *History of the Sewing Machine* (1872), discusses Howe and his major achievement. Frederick J. Allen, *The Shoe Industry* (1916), may be consulted for the application of sewing machines to shoe manufacture. See also Eric J. Hobsbawn, *The Age of Revolution, 1789-1848* (1962). ☐

Edwin Powell Hubble

The American astronomer Edwin Powell Hubble (1889-1953) established the scale of the universe and laid the observational basis for the cosmological theory of the expanding universe.

Edwin Hubble was born on Nov. 20, 1889, in Marshfield, Mo., where his father, a lawyer, was in the insurance business. Hubble received scholarship aid

to go to the University of Chicago. He chose law for a career, and after receiving his bachelor's degree in 1910, he went as a Rhodes scholar to Oxford University, England. In 1913 he returned to the United States, was admitted to the bar in Kentucky, and practiced law for about a year in Louisville.

Quite suddenly, Hubble decided that he would devote his life to astronomy, and in 1914 he left for the University of Chicago's Yerkes Observatory in Williams Bay, Wis. In 1917 he completed his doctorate and enlisted in the infantry. He served in France as a line officer in the American Expeditionary Force.

Early Work at Mount Wilson

As a student at Chicago, Hubble had attracted the attention of the well-known astronomer G. E. Hale, and after the war Hale offered him a staff position at Mount Wilson Observatory near Pasadena, Calif. Except for the period 1942-1946, when Hubble was with the Ordnance Department in Aberdeen, Md., he was connected with the Mount Wilson Observatory for the rest of his life.

Hubble's early observations at Mount Wilson were made with its 60-inch reflecting telescope and concentrated on objects within our own galaxy, for example, novae, nebulous stars, and variable stars. Gradually he began to observe more distant objects. To determine the distances of the spiral nebulae (galaxies), he used Cepheid variable stars. This method derived from Henrietta S. Leavitt's 1912 discovery that the period of variation in the intensity of these stars is directly related to their absolute magnitude, so that by measuring the former, one may easily determine the latter. By knowing the star's absolute magnitude and measuring its apparent magnitude, its (relative) distance may be readily calculated from the inverse-square law.

In 1923 Hubble definitely recognized a Cepheid variable in the Andromeda Nebula, known to astronomers as M31. Others were soon found in M31 and its companion nebula M33. To obtain his photographs, Hubble used Mount Wilson's 100-inch telescope. Once he had located the variables and determined their periods and apparent magnitudes, he used Leavitt's period-luminosity relationship to determine their distances. He concluded that the great spiral Andromeda Nebula is roughly 900,000 light-years away, a fantastically large distance, placing it clearly outside our own galaxy and proving that, in general, galaxies are islands in the universe. To allow for interstellar absorption, Hubble's distance estimate had to be later reduced to roughly 750,000 light-years, a figure that stood until shortly before Hubble's death.

Hubble continued to determine galactic distances and to study galactic characteristics. By 1925 he had enough observations to propose a scheme for their classification: he imagined concentrated, very luminous, spheroidal galaxies to merge into ellipsoidal ones, which in turn branched into "normal spirals" on the one hand, and "barred spirals" on the other. Hubble tended to avoid drawing evolutionary conclusions from his scheme, but it was clearly very suggestive in that direction. Furthermore, it proved invaluable in statistical studies of the universe. At the time of his death, Hubble was attempting to revise his scheme in order to make it more complete.

Expanding Universe

In the late 1920s Hubble laid the observational groundwork for the most spectacular astronomical discovery of this century: the expanding universe. V. M. Silpher had, over a period of years, made spectroscopic observations on tens of nebulae (galaxies) which indicated, on the basis of the Doppler shifts recorded, that these nebulae were receding from the earth at velocities between roughly 300 and 1,800 kilometers per second. Hubble realized the great importance of Silpher's observations for cosmological theories and organized a plan for measuring both the distances and (radial) velocities of as many galaxies as possible, down to the faintest ones detectable with Mount Wilson's 100-inch telescope.

While an assistant, M. L. Humason photographed galactic spectra and analyzed the observed Doppler shifts. Hubble photographed the galaxies themselves, searched for Cepheid variable stars, and computed the distances to the galaxies. By 1929 Hubble had distance data on Silpher's nebulae and announced what became known as Hubble's law: the velocity of recession of a galaxy is directly proportional to its distance from the earth. By the early 1940s this law had been confirmed for galactic velocities up to roughly 45,000 kilometers per second, corresponding to galactic distances up to roughly 220 million light-years.

During the 1930s Hubble became more and more cautious over the interpretation to be placed on the observed Doppler displacements, preferring to refer to them by the neutral (theory-free) term "red shifts." Thus, if at some future time these red shifts were found to be due, not to recessional velocity, but to some presently unknown physical law, the term "red shift" could still be retained as a description.

Postwar Work

After World War II Hubble devoted a great deal of time to planning the research program of the 200-inch Hale telescope at Mount Palomar; he was almost entirely responsible for conceiving and executing the National Geographic Society-Palomar Observatory Sky Survey carried out with the 48-inch Schmidt telescope. He received many honors, including a number of honorary degrees and medals, as well as membership in the National Academy of Sciences and other honorary societies. For his war research he received the Medal of Merit for 1946. In 1948 he was elected an honorary fellow of Queen's College, Oxford. He died of a coronary thrombosis in San Marino, Calif., on Sept. 28, 1953. In 1990, NASA launched the Hubble Space Telescope, which was named in his honor.

Further Reading

Hubble discusses his own work in *The Realm of the Nebulae* (1937) and *Observational Approach to Cosmology* (1937). For brief treatments of his life and work see Bernard Jaffe, *Men of Science in America* (1944; rev. ed. 1958); Otto Struve and Velta Zebergs, *Astronomy of the 20th Century* (1962); and Harlow Shapley, *Through Rugged Ways to the Stars* (1969). □

Howard Robard Hughes

Howard Robard Hughes (1905-1976) was a flamboyant entreprenuer who used an inherited fortune to achieve a national reputation in the motion picture and aviation industries, remaining in the news in later years because of his paranoid concern for privacy.

Howard Robard Hughes was born in Houston, Texas, on December 24, 1905, the only child of Howard Robard Hughes and Alene Gano Hughes. He attended private schools in California and Massachusetts, Rice Institute in Houston, and the California Institute of Technology. His mother died when Hughes was 16 and his father when he was 18, leaving him an orphan but with an estate worth $871,000 and a patent for a drill bit used in most oil and gas drilling that brought large revenues to the family's Hughes Tool Company that manufactured the bit. Hughes left school to take control of the company, using its profits to finance a variety of projects which he hoped would make him a legend in his own time. In 1925, when he was 20, Hughes married Ella Rice and moved to Los Angeles (they separated in 1928). In 1927 Hughes entered the motion picture business and produced such films as "Hell's Angels" (1930), "Scarface" (1932), and "The Outlaw" (1941). He discovered actors Jean Harlow and Paul Muni and made Jane Russell a well-known star.

In 1928 Hughes obtained a pilot's license. His interest in aviation led him to found the Hughes Aircraft Company in Glendale in 1932 and to design, build, and fly record-breaking airplanes. He set a world speed record in 1935, transcontinental speed records in 1936 and 1937, and a world flight record in 1938. Hughes was honored with the Harmon Trophy and a New York City ticker-tape parade after his world flight. He was awarded the Collier Trophy in 1939, the Octave Chanute Award in 1940, and a Congressional Medal in 1941.

In 1939 he began work on an experimental military aircraft, and in 1942 he received a contract to design and build the world's largest plane, a wooden seaplane, later nicknamed the "Spruce Goose," which was supposed to serve as a troop carrier in World War II. Hughes suffered a nervous breakdown in 1944 and was critically injured in the crash of his experimental military plane in 1946, but he recovered and flew the huge seaplane the next year, blunting the congressional investigation of his war contracts. As a result of these aviation activities, Hughes became a popular public figure because he seemed to embody the traditional American qualities of individuality, daring, and ingenuity. He was named to the Aviation Hall of Fame in 1973.

The Hughes Aircraft Company became a major defense contractor after World War II. As the profits of the company increased, Hughes became obsessed with avoiding taxes and in 1953 created the Howard Hughes Medical Institute as a sophisticated tax shelter to which he transferred the assets of the aircraft company. In 1956 Hughes loaned $205,000 to Richard Nixon's brother Donald in a successful effort to influence an Internal Revenue Service ruling on the medical institute. Hughes made secret contributions of $100,000 to the Nixon campaign in 1970 and was able to prevent enforcement of the Tax Reform Act against the medical institute. Hughes continued to use profits from the tool company for other ventures, including the creation of Trans World Airlines (TWA), in which he had begun investing in 1939.

In 1950 he went into seclusion, beginning a lifestyle which would ultimately turn him into a recluse, although he did marry actress Jean Peters in 1957, divorcing her in 1971. Hughes refused to appear in court or even give a deposition, and in a 1963 antitrust case over his ownership of 78 percent of TWA, his failure to appear resulted in a default ruling that led him to sell his holdings in 1966. The $566 million received from this sale was invested by Hughes in Las Vegas hotels, gambling casinos, golf courses, a television station, an airport, and land. In 1972 the Hughes Tool Division, the basis of the Hughes fortune, was sold. The holding company was renamed Summa Corporation and its headquarters relocated to Las Vegas, where Hughes had moved his residence.

From this point in his career, Hughes' accomplishments were minimal. His obsession to control every aspect of his environment turned him into a recluse seen by a few associates and isolated from the operations of his company. In 1970 he left the United States, abruptly moving from place to place—the Bahamas, Nicaragua, Canada, England, and Mexico. He always arrived unannounced in luxury hotels and took extreme precautions to ensure privacy. Hughes saw only a few male aides, worked for days without sleep in a black-curtained room, and became emaciated from the effects of a meager diet and the excessive use of drugs. His concern for privacy ultimately caused controversy, resulting in a scandal over his supposed memoirs by author Clifford Irving that sold for $1 million before being proven fraudulent. The Hughes conglomerate became involved with the Central Intelligence Agency (CIA), and in 1975 it built an undersea exploratory drilling ship which was actually for use by the CIA to attempt to recover a sunken Soviet submarine. The company retained a Washington, D.C., public relations firm that was also involved with the CIA, which led the Hughes corporation to become involved in the Watergate affair.

Hughes died, a hopeless psychotic, on April 5, 1976, on an airplane that was taking him from Acapulco, Mexico, to a hospital in Houston for medical attention. Hughes was controversial even after his death. Several wills appeared, one of which was found in the Mormon church in Salt Lake City, Utah, but all were declared to be forgeries after protracted litigation.

Further Reading

There are numerous books devoted to the controversial Hughes. The best biography is Donald L. Barlett and James B. Steele, *Empire: The Life, Legend, and Madness of Howard Hughes* (1979). John Keats, *Howard Hughes* (1972) is excellent on the qualities which made Hughes popular with Americans in the 1930s and 1940s. Noah Dietrich and Bob Thomas, *Howard: The Amazing Mr. Hughes* (1972) provide an insider's view of

Hughes' business affairs. James Phelan, *Howard Hughes: The Hidden Years* (1976) is the best book on Hughes' final years as a recluse. Michael Drosnin, *Citizen Hughes: In His Own Words—How Howard Hughes Tried To Buy America* (1985) is an example of studies which are extremely critical of Hughes' methods. ☐

Langston Hughes

American author Langston Hughes (1902-1967), a moving spirit in the artistic ferment of the 1920s often called the Harlem Renaissance, expressed the mind and spirit of most African Americans for nearly half a century.

L angston Hughes was born in Joplin, Mo., on Feb. 1, 1902. His parents soon separated, and Hughes was reared mainly by his mother, his maternal grandmother, and a childless couple named Reed. He attended public schools in Kansas and Illinois, graduating from high school in Cleveland, Ohio, in 1920. His high school companions, most of whom were white, remembered him as a handsome "Indian-looking" youth whom everyone liked and respected for his quiet, natural ways and his abilities. He won an athletic letter in track and held offices in the student council and the American Civic Association. In his senior year he was chosen class poet and yearbook editor.

Hughes spent the next year in Mexico with his father, who tried to discourage him from writing. But Hughes's poetry and prose were beginning to appear in the *Brownie's Book,* a publication for children edited by W. E. B. Du Bois, and he was starting work on more ambitious material dealing with adult realities. The poem "A Negro Speaks of River," which marked this development, appeared in the *Crisis* in 1921.

Hughes returned to America and enrolled at Columbia University; meanwhile, the *Crisis* printed several more of his poems. Finding the atmosphere at Columbia uncongenial, Hughes left after a year. He did odd jobs in New York. In 1923 he signed on as steward on a freighter. His first voyage took him down the west coast of Africa; his second took him to Spain. In 1924 he spent 6 months in Paris. He was relatively happy, produced some prose, and experimented with what he called "racial rhythms" in poetry. Most of this verse appeared in African American publications, but *Vanity Fair,* a magazine popular among middle- and upper-class women, published three poems.

Later in 1924 Hughes went to live with his mother in Washington, D.C. He hoped to earn enough money to return to college, but work as a hotel busboy paid very little, and life in the nation's capital, where class distinctions among African Americans were quite rigid, made him unhappy. He wrote many poems. "The Weary Blues" won first prize in 1925 in a literary competition sponsored by *Opportunity,* a magazine published by the National Urban League. That summer one of his essays and another poem won prizes in the *Crisis* literary contest. Meanwhile, Hughes had come to the attention of Carl Van Vechten, a white novelist and critic, who arranged publication of Hughes's first volume of verse, *The Weary Blues* (1926).

This book projected Hughes's enduring themes, established his style, and suggested the wide range of his poetic talent. It showed him committed to racial themes—pride in blackness and in his African heritage, the tragic mulatto, the everyday life of African Americans—and democracy and patriotism. Hughes transformed the bitterness which such themes generated in many of his African American contemporaries into sharp irony, gentle satire, and humor. His casual-seeming, folklike style, reflecting the simplicity and the earthy sincerity of his people, was strengthened in his second book, *Fine Clothes to the Jew* (1927).

Hughes had resumed his education in 1925 and graduated from Lincoln University in 1929. *Not without Laughter* (1930) was his first novel. The story deals with an African American boy, Sandy, caught between two worlds and two attitudes. The boy's hardworking, respectability-seeking mother provides a counterpoint to his high-spirited, easy-laughing, footloose father. The mother is oriented to the middle-class values of the white world; the father believes that fun and laughter are the only virtues worth pursuing. Though the boy's character is blurred, Hughes's attention to details that reveal African American culture in America gives the novel strength.

The relative commercial success of his novel inspired Hughes to try making his living as an author. In 1931 he made the first of what became annual lecture tours. He took a trip to Soviet Union the next year. Meanwhile, he turned out poems, essays, book reviews, song lyrics, plays, and short stories. He edited five anthologies of African American writing and collaborated with Arna Bontemps on another and on a book for children. He wrote some 20 plays, including *Mulatto, Simply Heavenly,* and *Tambourines to Glory.* He translated Federico Garcia Lorca, the Spanish poet, and Gabriela Mistral, the Latin American Nobel laureate poet, and wrote two long autobiographical works.

As a newspaper columnist, Hughes created "Simple," probably his most enduring character, brought his style to perfection, and solidified his reputation as the "most eloquent spokesman" for African Americans. The Simple sketches, collected in five volumes, are presented as conversations between an uneducated, African American city dweller, Jesse B. Semple (Simple), and an educated but less sensitive African American acquaintance. The sketches, which ran in the *Chicago Defender* for 25 years, are too varied in subject, too relevant to the universal human condition, and too remarkable in their display of Hughes's best writing for any quick summary. That Simple is a universal man, even though his language, habits, and personality are the result of his particular experiences as an African American man, is a measure of Hughes's genius.

Hughes received numerous fellowships, awards, and honorary degrees, including the Anisfield-Wolf Award (1953) for a book on improving race relations. He taught creative writing at two universities; had his plays produced on four continents; and made recordings of African American history, music commentary, and his own poetry. He was elected to the American Academy of Arts and Sciences and to the National Institute of Arts and Letters. His work, some of which was translated into a dozen languages, earned him an international reputation unlike any other African American writer except Richard Wright and Ralph Ellison. Forty-seven volumes bear Hughes's name. He died in New York City on May 22, 1967.

Further Reading

The chief sources of biographical data are Hughes's autobiographical *The Big Sea* (1940) and *I Wonder as I Wander: An Autobiographical Journey* (1956); Donald C. Dickinson, *A Bio-Bibliography of Langston Hughes, 1902-1967* (1967); James A. Emanuel, *Langston Hughes* (1967); Milton Meltzer, *Langston Hughes: A Biography* (1968); and Charlemae H. Rollins, *Black Troubadour: Langston Hughes* (1970). Hughes gets extensive critical treatment in Saunders Redding, *To Make a Poet Black* (1939); Hugh M. Gloster, *Negro Voices in American Fiction* (1948); John Milton Charles Hughes, *The Negro Novelist, 1940-1950* (1953); and Robert A. Boone, *The Negro Novel in America* (1958). Historical background is provided by Benjamin O. Brawley, *The Negro in Literature and Art in the United States* (1918); John Hope Franklin, *From Slavery to Freedom: A History of Negro Americans* (1947; 3d ed. 1967); and Vernon Loggins, *The Negro Author: His Development in America to 1900* (1959). □

Hubert Horatio Humphrey, Jr.

Hubert Horatio Humphrey, Jr. (1911-1978), the pharmacist turned politician, served different constituencies as mayor of Minneapolis, United States senator from Minnesota, and vice-president of the United States. He was an unsuccessful candidate for the presidency of the United States in 1968.

For 35 years, 1943-1978, Hubert Horatio Humphrey, Jr., held various public offices. At all times he was the liberal candidate for these public positions. Rather early Humphrey knew the meaning of the term "empirical collectivism," which, applied to government, meant providing answers to various *bona-fide* public problems that confronted the American people. When the people were faced with problems to which they could not find solutions individually or by group actions, they could call upon government to resolve those problems. On various occasions Humphrey proposed that government take over responsibility from the individuals or the groups.

Probably the experiences of his family and of neighbors and farmers in the state of South Dakota were responsible for Humphrey's proposals. The people of the state ran into problems of various kinds, including dust bowls, bank failures, farm failures, and depressed economic situations.

Hubert's father was a small businessman, a pharmacist and owner of several different drug stores in South Dakota, first in Wallace, then in Dorland, and finally in Huron. Actually, he was not successful before the 1930s. The Huron drug store succeeded, becoming the first Walgreen Agency in the United States. Before this there were ups and downs in the business which reflected economic conditions in South Dakota. They also affected the family and Hubert. For example, in 1927 Humphrey's father was forced to sell

their home to pay off debts of his business. The same thing had happened in 1932, when Humphrey was forced to withdraw from the University of Minnesota.

Education for Public Service

Humphrey was educated in the Dorland public schools and graduated from high school in 1929. He enrolled at the University of Minnesota in that year, remaining as a student for the next three years. Failure of his father's business forced Humphrey out of the university in 1932. In December of 1932 he was enrolled as a student at Capitol College of Pharmacy in Denver, Colorado. He graduated from this intensive program in six months. He then returned to the new drug store in Huron and was employed by his father. In Humphrey's words, "The drug store was my life and it seemed then it might always be." He remained as a druggist during the years 1933-1937. He was married to Muriel Buck in 1936, and they became a small town family. But Humphrey proved that he could do other things. Again he enrolled at the University of Minnesota in 1937 and received his Bachelor of Arts degree in 1939. He entered the master's program in political science at Louisiana State University and was awarded his graduate degree in 1940. He and his family returned to Minneapolis, and Humphrey did further graduate work at the University of Minnesota. He did not receive his Doctor of Philosophy degree because he did not complete his dissertation.

Other things were more important than becoming a professor of political science. From 1941 to 1945 Humphrey had various public service jobs, including state director of war production training and reemployment, assistant director of the War Manpower Commission, and mayor of Minneapolis. These positions served as stepping stones in his later political career.

Political Career

Humphrey's first attempt at elected public office occurred in 1943 when he attempted to win election as a mayoral candidate. He was narrowly defeated, but he benefitted from his loss. In 1945 he was elected mayor and won reelection in 1947.

Humphrey had his first chance to put at least one of his proposals into practice. He believed in the civil rights of all Americans, including African Americans. He successfully proposed to the city council that it adopt a fair employment practices ordinance. In 1948 Humphrey had an opportunity to do something about civil rights at the Democratic national convention. He and other liberal Democrats who were members of the platform committee were opposed to the proposed weak plank on civil rights. These liberals challenged the leadership of the party, and Humphrey gave a minority report before the convention. Among other things, he said, "There are those who say: This issue of civil rights is an infringement on State's rights. The time has arrived for the Democratic Party to get out of the shadow of State's rights and walk forth-rightfully into the bright sunshine of human rights."

The delegates were so excited at Humphrey's statements that they paraded around the convention floor and voted in favor of the stronger civil rights position set forth in the minority report. One of the consequences was that conservative Southern Democrats walked out of that convention and established a splinter party, the Dixiecrats. President Truman had to face the Republican candidate (Tom Dewey) and two splinter party candidates from the right (J. Strom Thurman) and the left (Henry A. Wallace) of the Democratic Party. He won reelection in part because of the victories of various strong senatorial candidates, including Guy Gillette of Iowa, Paul Douglas of Illinois, Estes Kefauver of Tennessee, Bob Kerr of Oklahoma, Matt Neely of West Virginia, and Hubert Humphrey of Minnesota.

Although the Democrats were in complete control of the Congress, no law guaranteeing the civil rights of African Americans could be passed. The first modern civil rights law was adopted in 1957 under a Republican president, Dwight Eisenhower. This law of 1957 was followed by other civil rights and voting rights laws in 1960, 1964, 1965, 1968, and 1972.

Civil rights was only one of the political goals of Hubert Humphrey. On other occasions he proposed the establishment of the Peace Corps, the creation of a Food for Peace program, and legislation favoring labor unions, farmers, and the unemployed. Humphrey was concerned about the bigotry confronting Jews, discrimination against African Americans, better working conditions for labor, economic protection for American farmers, and laws in the public interest.

Humphrey was in the Senate from 1949 to 1965 and from 1971 to January 1978. He was vice president from 1965 to 1969. During those years Humphrey had a number of opportunities to talk about his proposals. His reelections went hand in hand with his concerns about these various groups. The question was whether these groups would follow a two way street, maintaining their support for Humphrey and his political success.

Communists, Conservatives, and Liberal Democrats

Humphrey was challenged by, and in turn challenged, three major groups of foes at some time in his political life. During World War II, and especially in 1943 and 1944, Humphrey had trouble with the Communists and the extreme left wingers. He was chiefly responsible for the establishment of a non-communist liberal organization, Americans for a Democratic Society. During the same period of time Humphrey expressed concern over the two progressive parties in the State of Minnesota, the Democrats and the Farmer-Laborites. He had recognized that the left wing of the Farmer-Labor Party was controlled by the left, and he and others wanted to unify these two parties without any support from the radicals. Humphrey and others had gone to a state party convention in 1944, but they were forced to withdraw and establish a "rump convention" elsewhere. This was just one occasion when Humphrey was called a fascist and a war monger.

While Humphrey believed that he was an anti-communist, conservatives within the Democratic and Republican parties would not accept his claim. This was especially true within that period known as McCarthyism (1950-1954), when Humphrey and the liberal Democrats were accused of being "soft on Communism." It was at this time that the liberals under the leadership of Senator Humphrey proposed that Congress adopt the toughest anti-communist bill, the Communist Control Bill. What the liberals had done was to accuse the conservatives of being "soft on Communism," and they forced Congress to adopt this legislation. So many constitutional questions were present in this law, it was never enforced.

The conservatives and Humphrey challenged each other on other occasions. For example, as a freshman senator Humphrey had spoken about a conservative, Senator Harry Flood Byrd of Virginia, who was not present in the Senate. Humphrey was not concerned about the rules of the Senate nor the fact that he did not have the support of the inner circle in the Senate. Humphrey had made mistakes in this attack, and he decided thereafter to follow the Senate rules. He later became a member of the inner circle, as was demonstrated in 1961 when he was chosen the majority whip of the Senate.

Whenever Humphrey wanted to run for the presidency of the United States he was challenged by liberal Democrats, including Jack and Bobby Kennedy, Gene McCarthy, and George McGovern. In 1960 Humphrey entered several state presidential primaries. He did not have much money and had to campaign on a bus. Jack Kennedy flew from place to place and campaigned with the support of celebrities from Hollywood. In Humphrey's words: "I heard a plane overhead. On my cot, bundled in layers of uncomfortable clothes, both chilled and sweaty, I yelled, 'Come down here, Jack, and play fair.'"

Humphrey almost lost the 1960 presidential primary in Wisconsin and did lose the presidential primary in West Virginia. Immediately thereafter he withdrew from that presidential race and ran again for the United States Senate. He believed that he would spend the rest of his political life in the Senate. In 1964 this changed once again. President Lyndon Johnson selected Humphrey to be his running mate. While Johnson was overwhelmingly reelected, he still lost the confidence of the American people in the next four years as a consequence of increasing involvement in the war in Vietnam. Johnson almost lost the 1968 presidential primary in New Hampshire, and then he told the American people that he would not run for reelection.

Humphrey and other liberals—Gene McCarthy, George McGovern, and Bobby Kennedy—entered the 1968 primaries. Because Humphrey was part of the establishment and therefore responsible for the Vietnamese venture, he was opposed by many liberals, including McCarthy, McGovern, and Bobby Kennedy. Bobby Kennedy's effort ended in June when he was assassinated, but Kennedy's supporters would not join with Humphrey. Humphrey became the Democratic candidate for the presidency in 1968, but during the national convention the streets of Chicago were filled with anti-war rioters. At most Humphrey could only count on lukewarm support from McCarthy and McGovern. When Humphrey campaigned on college campuses and in major American cities he was heckled by anti-war activists. So many of these people refused to vote in that year that Humphrey lost the election to Richard Nixon.

Defeated and no doubt disappointed Humphrey returned to Minnesota and for the next two years served as a professor of public affairs at the university. This career did not last long, because in 1970 and again in 1976 Humphrey was reelected to the U.S. Senate.

In 1968 and again in 1977 doctors operated on Humphrey for cancer. In October 1977 Humphrey knew that his death was imminent and made his last trip to the Senate. On October 25 Humphrey was applauded by the senators and their guests, and several praised him in their speeches. On January 14, 1978, there was to be a tribute to Hubert Humphrey. Humphrey died the evening before. His Senate term was completed by his wife.

Further Reading

There are various books by Humphrey and about Humphrey and his ideas. There is an autobiography, *The Education of a Public Man* (1976), and a biography, *Hubert Humphrey: The Man and His Dream* (1978) by S. D. Engelmayer and R. J. Wagman. Humphrey was the author of *Beyond Civil Rights: A New Day of Equality* (1968), *Intergration vs. Segregation* (1964), *War on Poverty* (1964), and *Young American in the "Now" World* (1971). Humphrey was an able orator, and his notable statements were compiled by Perry D. Hall, *The Quotable Hubert H. Humphrey.* □

Lido Anthony Iacocca

After a 32-year career with Ford Motor Company, including eight years as president, Lido (Lee) Anthony Iacocca (born 1924) engineered one of business history's greatest comebacks at Chrysler Corporation. His success, coupled with appearances in television commercials and his best-selling book, made him one of the nation's best-known and most admired businessmen.

Lido (Lee) Anthony Iacocca was born October 15, 1924 in Allentown, Pennsylvania, the son of Italian immigrants Nicola and Antionette. Iacocca grew up in comfortable surroundings learning the nuts and bolts of business from his father. Nicola was an entrepreneur who taught his son about the responsibilities of borrowing money and the need for a hard-driving vision in order to build a thriving business. Nicola Iacocca worked as a cobbler, hot-dog restaurant and theater owner. He also ran one of the first car rental agencies in the country and passed on his love of the automobile to his son. Iaccoca was deferred during World War II because of having had rheumatic fever as a child. He earned his BS and MS degrees in engineering from Lehigh University and Princeton University, respectively. Even as a teenager, Iacocca decided that he was going to be an auto company executive and focused his studies in that direction. His degrees are in industrial engineering. He secured a coveted engineering trainee job at Ford in 1946, but deferred his start until he completed his masters degree at Princeton.

Joining Ford Motor Company as an engineering trainee in 1946, Iacocca soon entered the fast lane of sales. With the force of a muscle car and the maneuverability of a racing vehicle, in 1960, at age 36, he sped into the vice-presidency and general managership of the company's most important unit, Ford Division. In 1964, with others on his staff, he launched the Mustang, which, thanks to brilliant styling and marketing, introduced a new wave of sports cars, set a first-year sales record for any model, gave its name to a generation, and landed its creator's picture on the covers of *TIME* and *Newsweek* simultaneously.

In 1960 Iacocca was named Ford's vice-president, car and truck group; in 1967, executive vice-president; and in 1970, president. Pocketing an annual salary and bonus of $977,000, the flamboyant executive also earned a reputation as one of the greatest salesmen in U.S. history. Of Iacocca, it has been said that he was always selling, whether products, ideas—or himself.

From Ford to Chrysler

Iacocca was discharged from Ford Motor Company in June 1978 by Chairman Henry Ford II for reasons Ford never disclosed, but obviously relating to the chairman's distaste for having Iacocca succeed him. Though bitter at being dismissed from Ford, Iacocca was not out of the car business for long. Five months after his firing, Iacocca was named president of Chrysler (becoming chairman in 1979) and began transforming the number three automaker from corporate history's number one deficits manufacturer into a highly-profitable enterprise.

How was Chrysler turned around? By downsizing expenses to a much lower break-even point, by winning approval of $1.5 billion in federal loan guarantees, by selling off profitable units such as the tank division, and by introducing timely products. In addition, Chrysler welcomed, for the first time in U.S. corporate history, a union president to a board of directors. In 1984 the company posted profits of $2.4 billion (higher than in the previous 60 years combined), and in 1985 it bought Gulfstream Aerospace Corpo-

481

ration for $637 million and E. F. Hutton Credit Corporation for $125 million.

In the early 1980's Chrysler issued the K-car and what would later become its meal ticket—the minivan. Just as the Mustang re-established the sports car for Ford, the minivan would be loved by the young family in need of room and efficiency and revitalize Chrysler. In 1983, Chrysler paid the government back its loans and Iacocca became a star, a symbol of success and the achievement of the American Dream.

Along with spearheading Chrysler's resurgence, Iacocca assumed various civic responsibilities, most notably the chairmanship of the President's Statue of Liberty-Ellis Island Centennial Commission, set up to raise funds for and to oversee restoration of the two monuments. If Iacocca attained prominence through business stewardship, television commercials, and identification with the Statue of Liberty, he gained much additional exposure through his 1984 autobiography. *Iacocca: An Autobiography,* the best-selling nonfiction hard cover book in history, had two million copies in print by July 1985. Most readers seemed to accept the volume as near-gospel, while others ventured that Iacocca's achievements had lost nothing in the telling and that the author was overly vindictive toward Henry Ford II.

Folk Hero

By the mid-1980s Iacocca had achieved folk-hero status. Typically, the *Saturday Evening Post* described him as "the sex symbol of America"; the *Reader's Digest* as "the living embodiment of the American dream"; and *TIME* as "a

corporate capitalist with populist appeal, an 'eminence terrible' admired by working class and ruling class alike." Talk of Iacocca-for-President became increasingly widespread, and a 1985 poll of 1988 presidential preferences showed that the cocky industrialist trailed Vice-President George Bush by only three percentage points (41 to 38 points).

The late 1980s and early nineties were not as kind to Iacocca. His public image, like Chrysler's earnings, began to fall off. At a time when the American people, in the grip of a recession, renounced the huge paychecks of executives whose companies were ailing, Iacocca who had once achieved a publicity coup when, for a time, he only accepted one dollar a year from Chrysler, was paid a 1987 salary of $18 million. In addition, Iacocca, lambasted Japanese trading practices, blaming them for the ills that American car manufacturers had suffered. Critics cited that the American public believed that Japanese cars were superior and instead of criticizing the Japanese, Iacocca's car company should have been emulating them. At the end of 1992, Iacocca was forced to retire after he had bettered the position of the company for a merger or takeover. He remained a consultant to Chrysler (with a $500,000 a year salary and use of the company jet) until the end of 1994.

In 1995, Iacocca announced that he was suing Chrysler, claiming that it unlawfully blocked him from exercising $42 million in share options that he had earned while he was the chairman. Chrysler claimed that Iacocca's role as an adviser to Kirk Kerkorian, the investor who wanted to purchase the company, violated the share option plan agreement. Although Kerkorian's bid failed to materialize because he was unable to raise the financing, Chrysler agreed to pay Iaccoca $21 million to settle the lawsuit. Iacocca continued to work as Kerkorian's consultant.

Iacocca and Mary McCleary were married in 1956 and had two daughters, Kathi and Lia. Mary died of diabetes in 1983, and in her memory, Iacocca donated his book earnings to diabetes research. In 1986 Iacocca married Peggy Johnson (born 1950), an advertising executive from whom he was divorced in 1996.

Further Reading

The primary source of information about Iacocca is the executive's best-selling *Iacocca: An Autobiography* (1984), although critics say it was written mostly to stroke Iacocca's ego and to vilify Henry Ford II. David Abodaher's *Iacocca* (1982), written by an employee of Chrysler's advertising agency, ceaselessly praises the automaker while providing interesting anecdotal material. Perhaps the best of the numerous magazine and newspaper stories on the magnate are *New Republic*'s "What's So Great About Lee Iacocca?," July 16 and 23, 1984; *Newsweek*'s "Behind the Wheels," October 8, 1984; the *New York Times*'s "The Importance of Being Iacocca," December 23, 1984; and *Time*'s "A Spunky Tycoon Turned Superstar," April 1, 1985. *Detroit News,* "Retirement has been a rough ride for Iacocca," June 1996; *Automotive News,* June 1996. □

Washington Irving

Considered the first professional man of letters in the United States, Washington Irving (1783-1859) was influential in the development of the short story form and helped to gain international respect for fledgling American literature.

Following the tradition of the eighteenth-century essay exemplified by the elegant, lightly humorous prose of Joseph Addison and Oliver Goldsmith, Irving created endearing and often satiric short stories and sketches. In his most-acclaimed work, *The Sketch Book of Geoffrey Crayon, Gent.* (1819-20), he wove elements of myth and folklore into narratives, such as "Rip Van Winkle" and "The Legend of Sleepy Hollow," that achieved almost immediate classic status. Although Irving was also renowned in his lifetime for his extensive work in history and biography, it was through his short stories that he most strongly influenced American writing in subsequent generations and introduced a number of now-familiar images and archetypes into the body of the national literature.

Irving was born and raised in New York City, the youngest of eleven children of a prosperous merchant family. A dreamy and ineffectual student, he apprenticed himself in a law office rather than follow his elder brothers to nearby Columbia College. In his free time, he read avidly and wandered when he could in the misty, rolling Hudson River Valley, an area steeped in local folklore and legend that would serve as an inspiration for his later writings.

As a nineteen-year-old, Irving began contributing satirical letters under the pseudonym Jonathan Oldstyle to a newspaper owned by his brother Peter. His first book, *Salmagundi; or, The Whim-Whams and Opinions of Launcelot Langstaff, Esq., and Others* (1807-08), was a collaboration with another brother, William, and their friend James Kirke Paulding. This highly popular collection of short pieces poked fun at the political, social, and cultural life of the city. Irving enjoyed a second success in 1809 with *A History of New York, from the Beginning of the World to the End of the Dutch Dynasty,* a comical, deliberately inaccurate account of New York's Dutch colonization narrated by the fictitious Diedrich Knickerbocker, a fusty, colorful Dutch-American. His carefree social life and literary successes were shadowed at this time, however, by the death of his fiancée, Matilda Hoffmann, and for the next several years he floundered, wavering between a legal, mercantile, and editorial career. In 1815 he moved to England to work in the failing Liverpool branch of the family import-export business. Within three years the company was bankrupt, and, finding himself at age thirty-five without means of support, Irving decided that he would earn his living by writing. He began recording the impressions, thoughts, and descriptions which, polished and repolished in his meticulous manner, became the pieces that make up *The Sketch Book.* The volume was brought out under the pseudonym of Geoffrey Crayon, who was purportedly a good-natured American roaming Britain on his first trip abroad.

The Sketch Book comprises some thirty parts: about half English sketches, four general travel reminiscences, six literary essays, two descriptions of the American Indian, three essentially unclassifiable pieces, and three short stories: "Rip Van Winkle," "The Legend of Sleepy Hollow," and "The Spectre Bridegroom." Although only the last-named tale is set in Germany, all three stories draw upon the legends of that country. The book was published almost concurrently in the United States and England in order to escape the piracy to which literary works were vulnerable before international copyright laws, a shrewd move that many subsequent authors copied. The miscellaneous nature of *The Sketch Book* was an innovation that appealed to a broad range of readers; the work received a great deal of attention and sold briskly, and Irving found himself America's first international literary celebrity. In addition, the book's considerable profits allowed Irving to devote himself full-time to writing.

Remaining abroad for more than a decade after the appearance of *The Sketch Book,* Irving wrote steadily, capitalizing on his international success with two subsequent collections of tales and sketches that also appeared under the name Geoffrey Crayon. *Bracebridge Hall; or, the Humorists: A Medley* (1822) centers loosely around a fictitious English clan that Irving had introduced in several of the *Sketch Book* pieces. *Bracebridge Hall* further describes their manners, customs, and habits, and interjects several unrelated short stories, including "The Student from Salamanca" and "The Stout Gentleman." *Tales of a Traveller* (1824) consists entirely of short stories arranged in four categories: European stories, tales of London literary life, accounts of Italian bandits, and narrations by Irving's alter-ego, Diedrich Knickerbocker. The most enduring of these, according to many critics, are "The German Student," which some consider a significant early example of supernatural fiction, and "The Devil and Tom Walker," a Yankee tale that like "Rip Van Winkle" draws upon myth and legend for characters and incident. After 1824 Irving increasingly turned his attention from fiction and descriptive writing toward history and biography. He lived for several years in Spain, serving as a diplomatic attache to the American legation while writing a life of Christopher Columbus and a history of Granada. During this period he also began gathering material for *The Alhambra* (1832), a vibrantly romantic collection of sketches and tales centered around the Moorish palace in Granada.

Irving served as secretary to the American embassy in London from 1829 until 1832, when he returned to the United States. After receiving warm accolades from the literary and academic communities, he set out on a tour of the rugged western part of the country, which took him as far as Oklahoma. The expedition resulted in three books about the region, notably *A Tour on the Prairies* (1835), which provided easterners with their first description of life out west by a well-known author. Irving eventually settled near Tarrytown, New York, at a small estate on the Hudson River, which he named Sunnyside. Apart from four years in Madrid and Barcelona, which he spent as President John Tyler's minister to Spain, Irving lived there the rest of his life. Among the notable works of his later years is an extensive biography of George Washington, which Irving worked on determinedly, despite ill health, from the early 1850s until a few months before his death in 1859.

The Sketch Book prompted the first widespread critical response to Irving's writings. Reviewers in the United States were generally delighted with the work of their native son, and even English critics, normally hostile in that era to American authors, accorded the book generally favorable— if somewhat condescending—notice. Among the pieces singled out for praise in the early reviews were most frequently the three short stories, particularly "Rip Van Winkle." Critics found Irving's style pleasingly elegant, fine, and humorous, although some, including Richard Henry Dana, perceived a lack of intellectual content beneath the decorative surface. Dana also observed that in adopting the authorial persona of Geoffrey Crayon—with his prose style modeled after the eighteenth-century essayists—Irving lost the robustness, high color, and comic vigor of his previous incarnations as Jonathan Oldstyle, Launcelot Langstaff, and Diedrich Knickerbocker, an observation that was echoed by later critics. Subsequent "Crayon" works, such as *Bracebridge Hall, Tales of a Traveller,* and *The Alhambra,* while generally valued for their prose style, tended to prompt such complaints as that by the Irish author Maria Edgeworth that "the workmanship surpasses the work."

Beginning in the 1950s, however, critics began to explore technical and thematic innovations in Irving's short stories. These include the integration of folklore, myth, and fable into narrative fiction; setting and landscape as a reflection of theme and mood; the expression of the supernatural and use of Gothic elements in some stories; and the tension between imagination and creativity versus materialism and productivity in nineteenth-century America. Many critics read Rip's twenty-year sleep as a rejection of the capitalistic values of his society—ferociously personified by the shrewish Dame Van Winkle—and an embracing of the world of the imagination. Ichabod Crane, too, has been viewed by such critics as Robert Bone as representing the outcast artist-intellectual in American society, although he has been considered, conversely, as a caricature of the acquisitive, scheming Yankee Puritan, a type that Irving lampooned regularly in his early satirical writings.

Today, many critics concur with Fred Lewis Pattee's assertion that the "American short story began in 1819 with Washington Irving." Commentators agree, moreover, that in "Rip Van Winkle" and "The Legend of Sleepy Hollow," Irving established an artistic standard and model for subsequent generations of American short story writers. As George Snell wrote: "It is quite possible to say that Irving unconsciously shaped a principal current in American fiction, whatever may be the relative unimportance of his own work." In their continuing attention to the best of Irving's short fiction, critics affirm that while much of Irving's significance belongs properly to literary history, such stories as "Rip Van Winkle" and "The Legend of Sleepy Hollow" belong to literary art.

Further Reading

Bleiler, E. F., editor, *Supernatural Fiction Writers: Fantasy and Horror 2: A. E. Coppard to Roger Zelazny,* Scribners, 1985, pp. 685-91.

Bowden, Mary Weatherspoon, *Washington Irving,* Twayne, 1981.

Concise Dictionary of American Literary Biography: Colonization to the American Renaissance, 1640-1865, Gale, 1988.

Dictionary of Literary Biography, Gale, Volume 3: *Antebellum Writers in New York and the South,* 1979, Volume 11: *American Humorists, 1800-1950,* 1982, Volume 30: *American Historians, 1607-1865,* 1984, Volume 59: *American Literary Critics and Scholars,1800-1850,* 1987, Volume 73: *American Magazine Journalists 1741-1850,* 1988, Volume 74: *American Short-Story Writers before 1880,* 1988.

Harbert, Earl N., and Robert A. Rees, editor, *Fifteen American Authors before 1900: Bibliographic Essays on Research and Criticism,* University of Wisconsin Press, 1984.

Hedges, William L., *Washington Irving: An American Study, 1802-1832,* Johns Hopkins Press, 1965.

Leary, Lewis, *Washington Irving,* University of Minnesota Press, 1963. □

J

Andrew Jackson

Andrew Jackson (1767-1845), seventh president of the United States, symbolized the democratic advances of his time. His actions strengthened the power of the presidential office in American government.

When Andrew Jackson emerged on the national scene, the United States was undergoing profound social and economic changes as the new, postrevolutionary generation pushed forward in search of material gain and political power. Jackson was a classic example of the self-made man who rose from a log cabin to the White House, and he came to represent the aspirations of the ordinary citizen struggling to achieve wealth and status. He symbolized the "rise of the common man." So total was his identification with this period of American history that the years between 1828 and 1848 are frequently designated the "Age of Jackson."

Andrew Jackson was born on March 15, 1767, in Waxhaw country, which straddles North and South Carolina. His father, who died shortly before Andrew's birth, had come with his wife to America from Ireland in 1765. Andrew attended several academies in the Waxhaw settlement, but his education was spotty and he never developed a taste for learning.

After the outbreak of the American Revolution, Jackson, barely 13 years old, served as an orderly to Col. William Richardson. Following one engagement, Jackson and his brother were captured by the British and taken to a prison camp. When Jackson refused to clean an officer's boots, the officer slashed him with a sword, leaving a permanent scar on his forehead and left hand. Jackson was the only member of his family to survive the war, and it is generally believed that his harsh, adventuresome, early life developed his strong, aggressive qualities of leadership, his violent temper, and his need for intense loyalty from friends.

After the war Jackson drifted from one occupation to another and from one relative to another. He squandered a small inheritance and for a time lived a wild, undisciplined life that gave free rein to his passionate nature. He developed lifelong interests in horse racing and cock-fighting and frequently indulged in outrageous practical jokes. Standing just over 6 feet tall, with long, sharp, bony features lighted by intense blue eyes, Jackson presented an imposing figure that gave every impression of a will and need to command.

After learning the saddler's trade, Jackson tried schoolteaching for a season or two, then left in 1784 for Salisbury, N. C., where he studied law in a local office. Three years later, licensed to practice law in North Carolina, he migrated to the western district that eventually became Tennessee. Appointed public prosecutor for the district, he took up residence in Nashville. A successful prosecutor and lawyer, he was particularly useful to creditors who had trouble collecting debts. Since money was scarce in the West, he accepted land in payment for his services and within 10 years became one of the most important landowners in Tennessee. Unfortunately his speculations in land failed, and he spiraled deeply into debt, a misadventure that left him with lasting monetary prejudices. He came to condemn credit because it encouraged speculation and indebtedness. He distrusted the note-issuing, credit-producing aspects of banking and abhorred paper money. He regarded hard money—specie—as the only legitimate means by which honest men could engage in business transactions.

While Jackson was emerging as an important citizen by virtue of his land holdings, he also achieved social status by marrying Rachel Donelson, the daughter of one of the region's original settlers. The Jacksons had no children of their

485

own, but they adopted one of Rachel's nephews and named him Andrew Jackson, Jr.

When Congress created the Southwest Territory in 1790, Jackson was appointed an attorney general for the Mero District and judge advocate of the Davidson County militia. In 1796 the northern portion of the territory held a constitutional convention to petition Congress for admission as a state to the Union. Jackson attended the convention as a delegate from his county. Although he played a modest part in the proceedings, one tradition does credit him with suggesting the name of the state: Tennessee, derived from the name of a Cherokee Indian chief.

In 1796, with the admission of Tennessee as the sixteenth state of the Union, Jackson was elected to its sole seat in the U.S. House of Representatives. His voting record revealed strong nationalistic tendencies. The following year he was elected U.S. senator but he soon resigned to become judge of the Superior Court of Tennessee. His decisions as judge were described by one man as "short, untechnical, unlearned, sometimes ungrammatical, and generally right." He resigned from the bench in 1804 to devote himself exclusively to his plantation, where he later built a graceful mansion called the "Hermitage," and to his other business enterprises, including boatbuilding, horse breeding, and storekeeping.

Military Career

By the beginning of the War of 1812, Jackson had achieved the rank of major general of the Tennessee militia. He and his militia were directed to subdue the Creek Indians

in Alabama who had massacred white settlers at Ft. Mims. At the Battle of Horseshoe Bend (1814) Jackson inflicted such a decisive defeat that the Creek's power to wage war was permanently broken. During this engagement Jackson's men acknowledged his toughness and indomitable will by calling him "Old Hickory."

When the U.S. government heard rumors of an impending British penetration of the South through one of the ports on the Gulf of Mexico, Jackson was ordered to block the invasion. Supposing that New Orleans was the likeliest point of attack, he established a triple line of defense south of the city. After several minor skirmishes and an artillery bombardment, the British attacked in force on Jan. 8, 1815, and were decisively defeated. Over 2,000 British soldiers, including their commanding general, perished in the battle, while only 13 Americans were killed. It was a stupendous victory. Jackson became a national hero overnight, for he had infused Americans with confidence in their ability to defend their new liberty.

Florida Territory

When the war ended, Jackson returned to his plantation. However, he soon resumed military duty to subdue Indian raids along the southern frontier emanating from Spanish Florida. In a series of rapid moves he invaded Florida, subdued the Seminole Indians, extinguished Spanish authority, and executed two British subjects for inciting Indian attacks. Despite an international furor over this invasion, President James Monroe defended Jackson's actions and prevailed upon Spain to sell Florida to the United States for $5 million. Jackson served as governor of the Florida Territory briefly, but he was highhanded, was antagonistic to the Spanish, and tried to exercise absolute authority. He quit in disgust after serving only a few months.

These exploits served to increase Jackson's popularity throughout the country, alerting his friends in Tennessee to the possibility of making him a presidential candidate. First, he was elected to the U.S. Senate in October 1823. Then, the following year four candidates sought the presidency, each representing a different section of the country: Jackson of Tennessee, William H. Crawford of Georgia, John Quincy Adams of Massachusetts, and Henry Clay of Kentucky. In the election Jackson won the highest plurality of popular and electoral votes, but because he did not have the constitutionally mandated majority of electoral votes, the issue of selecting the president went to the House of Representatives. Here, on the first ballot, John Quincy Adams was chosen president. Adams's subsequent selection of Clay as his secretary of state convinced Jackson that a "bargain" had been concluded between the two to "fix" the election and cheat him of the presidency. For the next 4 years Jackson's friends battered the Adams administration with the accusation of a "corrupt bargain." In the election of 1828 Jackson won an overwhelming victory. During the campaign Martin Van Buren of New York and John C. Calhoun of South Carolina joined forces behind Jackson, and out of this coalition emerged the Democratic party. Supporters of Adams and Clay were now called National Republicans.

"Old Hickory" as President

Jackson's presidential inauguration demonstrated the beginning of a new political age as thousands of people swarmed into Washington to witness the outdoor inauguration, then poured through the White House to congratulate their hero, nearly wrecking the building in the process. Jackson appointed many second-rate men to his Cabinet, with the exception of Martin Van Buren, his secretary of state.

An initial estrangement between Jackson and his vice president, John C. Calhoun, soon grew worse because of their obvious disagreement over the important constitutional question of the nature of the Union. During a Senate debate between Daniel Webster of Massachusetts and Robert Y. Hayne of South Carolina, Hayne articulated Calhoun's doctrine of nullification (that is, the right of a state to nullify any objectionable Federal law). Although Jackson was politically conservative and a strong advocate of states' rights, he was also intensely nationalistic, and he regarded nullification as an abomination. At a dinner commemorating Thomas Jefferson's birthday, Jackson found the opportunity to express his feelings. When called upon to deliver a toast, he is said to have looked straight at Calhoun and said, "Our Federal Union. It must be preserved."

The final break between Jackson and Calhoun occurred when it was disclosed that, earlier, as secretary of war in James Monroe's Cabinet, Calhoun had sought to censure Jackson for his invasion of Florida. In self-defense, Calhoun gave his side of the controversy in a newspaper statement and ended by arguing that Van Buren had deliberately sought his downfall in order to eliminate him as a presidential rival. Van Buren there-upon resigned from the Cabinet, thus forcing the resignation of the remaining members, which gave Jackson the opportunity of reconstituting his Cabinet and ridding himself of Calhoun's friends. Later, however, when Jackson made Van Buren U.S. minister to Great Britain, confirmation of this appointment resulted in a tie vote in the Senate, and Calhoun, as vice president, gained a measure of revenge by voting against it. This action prompted Jackson to insist on Van Buren as his vice-presidential running mate in the next election.

Bank War

The presidential contest of 1832 involved not only personal vindication for Van Buren but also the important political issue of the national bank. The issue developed because of Jackson's prejudice against paper money and banks and because of his contention that the Second Bank of the United States (established in 1816) was not only unconstitutional but had failed to establish a sound and uniform currency. Moreover, he suspected the Bank of improper interference in the political process. Jackson had informed the Bank's president, Nicholas Biddle, of his displeasure in his first message to Congress back in December 1829. Following this, Biddle, at the urging of Henry Clay and other National Republicans, asked Congress for a recharter of the Bank 4 years before it came due. In this way the issue could be submitted to the people during the 1832 election if Jackson blocked the recharter.

Although the bank bill passed Congress rather handily, Jackson vetoed it in a strong message that lamented how "the rich and powerful too often bend the acts of government to their selfish purposes." This veto message broadened presidential power because it went beyond strictly constitutional reasons in faulting the bill. By citing social, political, and economic reasons, Jackson went beyond what all his predecessors had considered the limit of the presidential veto power.

In the 1832 election Henry Clay, running against Jackson on the bank issue, was decisively defeated. Jackson interpreted his reelection as a mandate to destroy the Bank of the United States. He therefore directed his secretary of the Treasury to remove Federal deposits and place them in selected state banks (called pet banks). Biddle counterattacked by a severe contraction of credit that produced a brief financial panic during the winter of 1833/1834. But Jackson held his ground, Biddle was finally forced to relax the pressure, and the Bank of the United States eventually collapsed. With the dispersal of government money among state banks and, later, with the distribution of surplus Federal funds to individual states, the nation entered a period of steep inflation. Jackson unsuccessfully tried to halt the inflation by issuing the Specie Circular (1836), which directed specie payments in the purchase of public land.

At the beginning of his second term, Jackson informed Congress of his intention to pay off the national debt. This goal was achieved on Jan. 1, 1835, thanks to income the Federal government received from land sales and tariff revenues. Jackson also advocated a policy of "rotation" with respect to Federal offices. In a democratic country, he declared, "no one man has any more intrinsic right to official station than another." He was accused of inaugurating the spoils system, but this was unfair for, actually, he removed only a modest number of officeholders. Jackson also advocated moving Native Americans west of the Mississippi River as the most humane policy the government could pursue in dealing with the Native American problem. Consequently he signed over 90 treaties with various tribes, in which lands owned by Native Americans within the existing states were exchanged for new lands in the open West. Jackson's veto of the Maysville Road Bill as an unwarranted exercise of Federal authority was widely interpreted as an expression of his opposition to Federal aid for public works.

Nullification Ordinance

Jackson also sought to modify tariff rates because they provoked sectional controversy. The North advocated high protective rates, but the South considered them a way of subsidizing northern manufacturers at the expense of southern and western purchasers. With the passage of the Tariff of 1832, South Carolina reacted violently by invoking Calhoun's doctrine of nullification. At a special convention in November 1832, South Carolina adopted the Ordinance of Nullification, declaring the tariffs of 1828 and 1832 null and void and warning the Federal government that if force were used to execute the law, the state would secede from the Union. In response to this threat, Jackson issued the Proclamation to the People of South

Carolina that blended warning with entreaty, demand with understanding. "The laws of the United States must be executed," he said. "Those who told you that you might peaceably prevent their execution deceived you. ... Disunion by armed force is *treason*."

Meanwhile a compromise tariff was hurried through Congress to reduce the rates schedule over a 10-year period, while another bill was passed giving Jackson permission to use the military to force South Carolina to obey the laws. The state chose to accept the compromise tariff and repealed its nullification ordinance, thereby averting a national crisis. Jackson's actions during the controversy were masterful. Through the careful use of presidential powers, by rallying the public to his side, alerting the military, and offering compromise while preparing for possible hostilities, he preserved the Union and upheld the supremacy of Federal law.

Foreign Affairs

Jackson also exercised forceful leadership in his relations with foreign nations, and he scored a number of notable diplomatic victories. He obtained favorable treaties with Turkey, Cochin China, and Siam (the first United States treaties with Asiatic powers), and he was also able to reopen American trade with the British West Indies. Furthermore, he forced France into agreeing to pay the debts owed to American citizens for the destruction of American property during the Napoleonic Wars. However, when the French chamber of deputies failed to appropriate the money to pay the debt, Jackson asked Congress to permit reprisals against French property in the United States. The French interpreted this as a deliberate insult, and for a time war between the two countries seemed unavoidable. The French demanded an apology, which Jackson refused to give, although in a message to Congress he denied any intention "to menace or insult" the French government. France chose to accept Jackson's disclaimer as an apology and forthwith paid the debt; thus hostilities were avoided.

At the end of his two terms in office, having participated in the inauguration of his successor, Martin Van Buren, Jackson retired to his plantation. He continued to keep his hand in national politics until his death on June 8, 1845.

Further Reading

The most scholarly, but not the most interesting, study of Jackson's life is John Spencer Bassett, *The Life of Andrew Jackson* (2 vols., 1911; new ed. 1916). More colorful is Marquis James, *The Life of Andrew Jackson* (1938), but its analysis of Jackson's character is superficial. James Parton, *Life of Andrew Jackson* (3 vols., 1860), is old but extremely valuable, particularly since it was researched among many people who actually knew Jackson. A brief biography is Robert V. Remini, *Andrew Jackson* (1966).

Arthur M. Schlesinger, Jr., is generally sympathetic to Jackson in *The Age of Jackson* (1945), while Glyndon G. Van Deusen in *The Jacksonian Era* (1959) and Edward Pessen in *Jacksonian America* (1969) are more critical. See also Harold Coffin Syrett, *Andrew Jackson: His Contributions to the American Tradition* (1953), and Leonard D. White, *The Jacksonians: A Study in Administrative History, 1829-1861* (1954). For the elections of 1828 and 1832 see Arthur M. Schlesinger, Jr., ed., *History of American Presidential Elections,* vol. 1 (1971). ☐

Jesse Louis Jackson

Civil rights leader Rev. Jesse Louis Jackson (born 1941), the most successful African American presidential candidate in U.S. history, received over three million votes in the 1984 election.

Jesse Louis Jackson was born on October 18, 1941, in Greenville, South Carolina, a city beset with the problems of racial segregation. From birth, Jackson faced his own personal brand of discrimination. As a young girl his mother, Helen Burns, became pregnant by her married next-door neighbor, Noah Robinson. The young boy was shunned and taunted by his neighbors and school classmates for being "a nobody who had no daddy." Instead of letting this adversity defeat him, Jackson developed his exceptional drive and understanding of those who are oppressed. His mother eventually married and became a successful hairdresser while his stepfather, a postal employee, adopted Jackson in 1957. With helpful advice from his maternal grandmother and his own desire to succeed, Jackson overcame his numerous childhood insecurities, finishing tenth in his high school class, even though he was actively involved in sports. His academic and athletic background earned Jackson a football scholarship at the University of Illinois in Chicago. Jackson, eager to get away from the Southern racial climate, traveled north only to find both open and covert discrimination at the university and in other parts of the city.

After several semesters Jackson decided to leave the University of Illinois, return to the South, and attend North Carolina Agricultural and Technical College (A&T) in Greensboro, an institution for African American students. Jackson again proved himself an able scholar and athlete. When his popularity on the campus led to his victory as student body president, Jackson did not take the responsibility lightly. As a college senior, he became a civil rights leader. Although he was not in Greensboro when the four African American freshman from A&T staged their famous Woolworth's sit-in in February 1960—the action which launched sit-down demonstrations throughout the South— Jackson actively encouraged his fellow students to continue their protests against racial injustice by staging repeated demonstrations and boycotts. Much of the open discrimination in the South fell before the onslaught of these student demonstrations.

Civil Rights Movement

In the spring of 1968 many of SCLC's officers— including Jackson—were drawn away from other civil rights protests by the Memphis, Tennessee, garbage collectors' strike. The situation in that city was especially tense because many African Americans who professed to be tired of passive resistance were willing and ready to fight. Tragically, King, in his attempt to prevent racial violence in that city, met a violent death by an assassin's bullet while standing on the balcony of his hotel room on April 4, 1968.

Some controversy surrounds the moments just after King was wounded. Jackson claimed on national television that he was the last person to talk to King and that he had held the dying leader in his arms, getting blood all over his shirt. The other men present unanimously agreed that this was not true, that Jackson had been in the parking lot facing King when he was shot and had neither climbed the steps to the balcony afterward nor gone to the hospital with King. Whatever the truth of the matter, Jackson's appearance on national television the next day with his bloodied turtleneck jersey vaulted him into national prominence. The image of Jackson and his bloody shirt brought the horror of the assassination into American homes. Jackson's ego, stirring oratory and charismatic presence caused the media to anoint him and not Ralph Abernathy, King's successor. Many observers believe that at this point, Jackson determined to become heir to King's position as the nation's foremost African American leader. In 1971, Jackson was suspended from the SCLC after its leaders claimed that he was using the organization to further his own personal agenda.

Operation PUSH

After his suspension from the SCLC, Jackson founded Operation PUSH (People United to Save Humanity), an organization which essentially continued the work of Operation Breadbasket without SCLC's sponsorship. Standing in front of a picture of Dr. King, Jackson promised to begin "a rainbow coalition of blacks and whites gathered together to push for a greater share of economic and political power for all poor people in America." Throughout the decade, Jackson relentlessly spoke out against racism, militarism and the

class divisions in American. He became a household name throughout the nation with his slogan "I Am Somebody".

By the mid 1970's, Jackson was a national figure. He realized that many of the problems plaguing the African American community stemmed from drug abuse and teen pregnancy and not simply economic deprivation. In 1976, Jackson created the PUSH-Excel, a program aimed at motivating children and teens to succeed. A fiery orator, Jackson traveled from city to city delivering his message of personal responsibility and self-worth to students: "You're not a man because you can kill somebody. You are not a man because you can make a baby. . .You're a man only if you can raise a baby, protect a baby and provide for a baby."

Jackson's support in the African American community allowed him to influence both local and national elections. Possibly the most important campaign in which he was involved was the election victory of the first African American mayor of Chicago, Harold Washington, in 1983. Washington's victory was attributed in part to Jackson's ability to convince over 100,000 African Americans, many of them youths, to register to vote. Jackson would also use his charisma to garner new voters during his 1984 campaign for the Democratic presidential nomination.

The Rainbow Coalition

Jackson's debut on the international scene occurred when President Jimmy Carter approved his visit to South Africa. Jackson attracted huge crowds at his rallies where he denounced apartheid, South Africa's oppressive system that prevented the black majority population from enjoying the rights and privileges of the white minority. Later in 1979, he toured the Middle East where he embraced Yassar Arafat, the then-exiled Palestinian leader. Jackson's embrace of a man considered a terrorist by the American government created yet another controversy. The result of these international excursions caused Jackson's fame and popularity to grow within the African American community.

As the 1980's began, Jackson moderated many of his political positions. He was no longer the flamboyant young man wearing long hair and gold medallions, but a more conservative, mature figure seeking ways to reform the Democratic party from within. He continued to advocate his "rainbow coalition" as a way for all Americans to improve the country.

After growing increasingly disenchanted with the existing political scene, Jackson decided that he would campaign against Walter Mondale and Gary Hart in the 1984 Democratic presidential primaries. His campaign centered on a platform of social programs for the poor and the disabled, alleviation of taxes for the poor, increased voting rights, effective affirmative action initiatives for the hiring of women and minorities, and improved civil rights for African Americans, poor whites, immigrants, homosexuals, Native Americans, and women. Jackson also took a stand on many world issues. He called for increased aid to African nations and more consideration of the rights of Arabs. His support for Arab nations and African American Muslims provoked much criticism, especially from Jewish voters. In early 1984, Jackson used his popularity in the Arab world to obtain the release of an American pilot, Lt. Robert Goodman, who had been shot down over Lebanon.

When he returned home, Jackson concentrated on securing the African American vote for his candidacy. He did not receive support from most senior African American politicians, who felt that Jackson's candidacy would cause disunity within the Democratic camp and benefit the Republicans. However, many poor African Americans enthusiastically supported him. Jackson received 3.5 million votes, and possibly 2 million of those voters were newly registered. He carried 60 congressional districts on a budget of less than $3 million. Although many Americans, both black and white, were decidedly opposed to Jackson, he earned grudging respect because his campaign fared better than most people had expected. When Jackson conceded defeat at the 1984 Democratic National Convention, much of America listened respectfully to his address. Although his campaign was unsuccessful, Jackson's powerful presence had broken new ground and involved more African Americans in the political process.

After the 1984 election, Jackson devoted his time between working for Operation PUSH in Chicago and his new National Rainbow Coalition in Washington DC. This national coalition was designed to be a force for reform within the Democratic party. It also provided Jackson with a platform from which to mount his 1988 presidential bid. Jackson's campaign received a much broader base of support than in 1984. His polished delivery, quick wit, and campaign experience helped him to gain many new supporters. Among the seven serious contenders for the Democratic nomination, Jackson finished second to Massachusetts Governor Michael Dukakis.

In 1990, Jackson was named one of two "shadow senators" to Congress from Washington DC to press for the district's statehood. Although the idea fizzled, it helped to keep Jackson in the public eye. In 1992, Jackson backed Democratic candidate Bill Clinton during the presidential campaign. He used his influence to urge African American voters to support Clinton. These efforts helped Clinton to win the election and return a Democrat to the White House for the first time in 12 years.

Critics often accuse Jackson of simply being a cheerleader of causes, a person who favors style over substance. Despite his unflagging energy and devotion to his causes, many felt that he was devoted only to his own self-aggrandizement. "This is the long-term pattern of Jackson's politics. He has always sought to operate and be recognized as a political insider, as a leader without portfolio or without accountability to any constituency that he claims to represent" wrote political critic Adolph Reed Jr. in the *Progressive*. "PUSH ran as a simple extension of his will and he has sought to ensure that the Rainbow Coalition would be the same kind of rubber stamp, a letterhead and front for his mercurial ambition."

Despite the criticism he has faced, Jackson continues to advocate for the rights of the downtrodden and challenge others to move beyond adversity. In 1995, Jackson wrote in *Essence* magazine, "People who are victimized may not be responsible for being down, but they must be responsible for getting up. Slave masters don't retire; people who are enslaved change their minds and choose to join the abolitionist struggle. . . . Change has always been led by those whose spirits were bigger than their circumstances . . . I do have hope. We have seen significant victories during the last 25 years."

Further Reading

Jackson's autobiography, *Straight from the Heart,* was published in 1987. There are a number of biographies of Jackson and several analytical studies of his presidential campaign. Two are Barbara A. Reynolds' sympathetic biography entitled *Jesse Jackson: America's David* (1985) and a critical work written by Thomas Landess and Richard Quinn, *Jesse Jackson and the Politics of Race* (1985). Several other biographies are Adolph L. Reed, *The Jesse Jackson Phenomenon,* a somewhat negative portrait (1986); Shield D. Collins, *From Melting Pot to Rainbow Coalition* (1986); and a children's book by Warren J. Halliburton, *The Picture Life of Jesse Jackson* (1984). Other works include *Jesse: The Life and Pilgrimage of Jesse Jackson;* James Haskins, *I Am Somebody! A Biography of Jesse Jackson,* and *Political Parties and Elections in the United States Vol. 1,* edited by L. Sandy Maisel. □

Michael Joe Jackson

One of the most popular singers in history was Michael Joe Jackson (born 1958). A performer since he was five years old, he was one of the few child stars ever to achieve greater success as an adult than as a child. Through his record albums and music videos he created an image imitated by his millions of fans, whose style of dressing and dancing was instantly recognizable all over the world.

Michael Jackson was born in Gary, Indiana, on August 29, 1958, the fifth of nine children. He was raised in a family that listened to music constantly and sang continuously, and regarded music as a ticket to success. Jackson's father ran a crane at a steel plant, but he dreamed of becoming a successful rhythm and blues musician. This dream eluded him, but relentlessly drove him to promote the careers of his children. The fact that he had marginal success with a group of his own caused him to attempt to exert control over his children's careers even after they were adults. The struggle for the control of the musical destiny of the Jackson family was a constant source of turmoil.

The Jackson 5 Is Born

The Jackson children were taught the gentler aspects of music by their mother, Katherine, who sang folk songs and spirituals to them. The boys sang along with her, and their joyful harmonizing took on a life of its own when the boys formed a family band that became a success at amateur shows and talent contests throughout the Midwest. From the age of five, Michael's amazing talent asserted itself; his dancing and stage presence caused him to become the focus of the group. The fame and popularity of the group spread until they were booked at the Apollo Theater in New York City's Harlem. While performing at the Apollo in 1968, they were discovered by Motown recording artist

Gladys Knight and pianist Billy Taylor. Later that year Diana Ross, who would become a crucial figure in Michael Jackson's life and career, became associated with the boys during a "Soul Weekend" in Gary, Indiana. With the support of Ross, the Jacksons signed a contract with Motown Records. Berry Gordy, the legendary Motown mogul, became the caretaker of the Jacksons' careers, which he nurtured zealously. As the lead singer, Michael took his brothers to the top of the charts with the group known as the Jackson 5.

Destined for Solo Stardom

Almost immediately, Gordy recognized Michael's special appeal and released solo albums of the child. These solo albums sold as well as those of the Jackson 5. Two years later, in 1970, the Jackson 5 were topping the charts and riding a wave of youth adulation with such hits as "ABC," "The Love You Save," and "I'll Be There," each selling over one million copies. However, the longer the Jackson 5 existed, the more apparent Michael's importance to the group's success became. The group managed to survive his voice change and a bitter break with Motown Records in 1976. The squabbles among the siblings and between them and their father might well have caused Jackson to withdraw from his family, even as he continued to live with his mother.

Having been successful in his appearances in a television variety show and as an animated cartoon character, it was not surprising to Jackson's fans that his appearance in the musical film *The Wiz* (1978) was the only distinguished aspect of this African American version of *The Wizard of Oz*. He sang the only hit to emerge from its soundtrack album ("Ease On Down the Road") in a duet with the film's star, Diana Ross. His success as the Scarecrow may also be seen as a preview of what was to come in his videos, for Jackson seemed to care most about dancing. He dedicated his autobiography to Fred Astaire, and its title, *Moonwalk,* refers to a dance that he popularized.

Emergence of a Pop Icon

Jackson's work in *The Wiz* was also notable in that it introduced Jackson to producer Quincy Jones, who arranged and conducted the film's score. In 1979, Jackson and Jones collaborated on Jackson's solo album *Off the Wall.* The album sold ten million copies and earned critical praise. In 1982, Jackson and Jones again collaborated on the blockbuster *Thriller* album. *Thriller* fully established Jackson as a solo performer and his trio of hit songs from the album—"Beat It," "Billie Jean," and "Thriller"—made him the major pop icon of the early 1980s. Jackson was also notable as a crossover performer. The spectacular success of the *Thriller* album and video enabled him to break the color barrier of album-oriented radio stations and the powerful music video channel, MTV. By 1983, Jackson had established himself as the single most popular entertainer in America.

Although Jackson's next two albums, *Bad* (1987) and *Dangerous* (1991), did not produce the phenomenal results of *Thriller,* Jackson remained in the entertainment spotlight throughout the 1980s and into the 1990s. In 1993, he was presented with the "Living Legend Award" at the Grammys and the Humanitarian of the Year trophy at the Soul Train awards. He also involved himself in many philanthropic efforts. In 1985, he reunited with Quincy Jones, this time on the vocal arrangement for USA for Africa's "We Are the World" to raise funds for the impoverished in Africa. In 1992, Jackson founded "Heal the World" to aid children and the environment.

Rocked By Scandal

Despite Jackson's popularity and philanthropic efforts, he became the subject of a major scandal. In 1993, a 13-year-old boy accused Jackson of sexually abusing him at the star's Neverland ranch. Jackson settled out of court, while always maintaining his innocence. The scandal cost Jackson his endorsement contract with Pepsi and a film deal. His sexual preference was called into question and his public image was severely damaged.

In 1995, Jackson was again the subject of scandal following the release of his new album *HIStory: Past, Present, and Future, Book I.* One of the songs on the album, "They Don't Care About Us", seemed to contain anti-Semitic lyrics. Jackson publicly apologized and changed the lyrics. He told the Associated Press that the song was supposed to "say no to racism, anti-Semitism, and stereotyping." He wrote a letter to Rabbi Marvin Hier, dean of the Simon Wiesenthal Center for Holocaust Studies, who had protested the lyrics, stating that "my choice of words may have unintentionally hurt the very people I wanted to stand in solidarity with. I apologize to anyone I might have hurt."

Hier replied, "It's the ambiguity I'm concerned of when it [the song] reaches 20 million buyers around the world."

Marriage and Fatherhood

In May of 1994, Jackson stunned the world when he married Lisa Marie Presley, daughter of the late rock legend Elvis Presley, at a private ceremony in the Dominican Republic. Many critics of Jackson speculated that the marriage was an attempt to improve his public image. In August of 1996, Jackson and Presley divorced. Many of Jackson's fans were shocked when he announced, in November of 1996, that he was to be a father. The child's mother was Debbie Rowe, a long-time friend of Jackson. They married later that month in Sydney, Australia. On February 13, 1997, their son, Prince Michael Jackson, Jr., was born at Cedars-Sinai Medical Center in Los Angeles. The couple had a second child, Paris Michael Katherine, born April 3, 1998, in Beverly Hills.

Despite the demands of fatherhood, Jackson continued to keep a busy schedule during 1997. He and his brothers were inducted into the Rock and Roll Hall of Fame in Cleveland, Ohio on May 6, 1997. He also attended the showing of his 40-minute musical *Ghosts* at the Cannes film festival on May 8, 1997. Another album, *Blood on the Dance Floor: HIStory in the Mix,* containing re-mixes of songs from *HIStory* plus five new songs, was released on May 29, 1997. The album received good reviews from both the *New York Times* and *Rolling Stone,* although the *New York Times* preferred the new songs, calling the re-mixes the "least interesting" music on the CD. *Village Voice* reviewer Armond White said of the new material, "His singing . . . has never been so tormented, or audacious". As the 20th century draws to a close, it seems likely that the world will continue to be fascinated by the talent and career of Michael Jackson.

Further Reading

Moonwalk (1988), Jackson's autobiography, is as good as any of the other books about him, perhaps better because it gives the reader insight into Jackson's "Peter Pan" image of himself; Dave Marsh, *Trapped: Michael Jackson and the Crossover Dream* (1985) is a most peculiar book. The author is highly critical of almost every aspect of Jackson's career and personality, yet he attempts to apologize to Jackson through open letters from himself to his subject. George Nelson, *The Michael Jackson Story* (1987) is a workman-like treatment of the basic biographical material. Jackson continued to be a mainstay of gossip columnists and was frequently featured in all sorts of periodicals from tabloids to newsweeklies in the 1990s. J. Randy Taraborrelli, *Michael Jackson: The Magic and the Madness* (1991) is a large (640 pages) unauthorized biography. A review of *HIStory* is in *Rolling Stone* (August 10, 1995). An interview with Jackson and Jackson-Presley is in *Jet* (July 3, 1995). □

Reginald Martinez Jackson

Baseball great Reggie Jackson (born 1946) was inducted into the Hall of Fame in 1993. Placed sixth on the all-time list for home runs, he also held the Major League record for strikeouts.

Former professional baseball player and Hall of Fame inductee Reggie Jackson's hard hitting, fleet footed style helped him lead two teams to five World Championships in only seven years. Called "the most theatrical baseball player of the last quarter century," by writer Mike Lupica in *Esquire,* Jackson made headlines with his egomaniacal remarks, hot temper, and flamboyant manner.

Reginald Martinez Jackson was born on May 18, 1946 in Wyncote, Pennsylvania. One of six children of African American and Spanish descent, he moved at an early age with two of his siblings to live with his divorced father in Cheltenham, Pennsylvania. His father, a once semi-pro baseball player in the Negro leagues who made a living running a small tailoring and dry cleaning business, encouraged his talented son in sports. By the time Jackson entered his senior year at Cheltenham High School he was an all star athlete: in track he ran the 100 yard dash in 9.7 seconds; on the football team he played halfback; in basketball he was a unparalleled player; and in baseball as a lefty player, he pitched three no-hitters and batted .550.

Jackson always felt he would be a professional athlete; the difficult part was deciding between football and baseball. College scholarships poured in and he ended up accepting a scholarship form Arizona State University in

Tempe. In his sophomore year he was a receiver on the football team, and was chosen to the All-American first team in baseball. His outstanding performance on the baseball team caught the attention of Charles O. Finley, owner of the Kansas City Athletics, who offered Jackson, a $95,000 bonus. Unable to refuse, he left college after his sophomore year and entered the world of professional baseball.

In 1966, Jackson was the second pick in the amateur draft. The New York Mets having the first pick chose another player, Steve Chilcott. Jackson played with the Kansas City Athletics farm teams for one and a half seasons. At the end of the 1967 season, he was called up to join the team in Kansas City, and in 1968 moved with the Athletics to their new home in Oakland, California.

In his first full season in the majors, he hit 29 home runs, and drove in another 74 runs. But he also made a dozen outfield errors and struck out a near record-breaking 171 times. The following season, in 1969, he again held a record number of strikeouts with 142, but hit a fantastic 47 home runs and led the American League in scoring 123 runs. Jackson credits then vice-president of the Athletics and Joe DiMaggio, the Hall-of-Fame center fielder of the New York Yankees, with developing his skills as a hitter.

The end of that glorious season was followed by a slump. The progressive pressures of trying to keep up with his own home run pace and the beginning of the eventual breakdown of his marriage to Jenni, his Mexican-American wife, contributed to his temporary decline. Further, he failed to negotiate successfully with Finley for a high increase in pay. The sour salary negotiations got the following season off to a bad start. Known for his hot temper, Jackson squabbled with teammates in the clubhouse, fought with Finley and often, after striking out, threw his bat in a rage. His average and his homers dropped and his continued poor performance caused him to be benched for a portion of that season.

In the Winter of 1970-71 he went to Santurce, Puerto Rico to work under an old idol, Frank Robinson. Robinson, a veteran player-manager, helped Jackson to ease up on himself and to put his own game into perspective. When he returned to the Athletics in Oakland he no longer felt the burdensome need to carry the team or to pressure himself for a hit every time he came to bat. Robinson's invaluable tutoring also helped him to cultivate his aggressive playing style while keeping his temper in check.

The following season saw him bouncing back to his high level of performance. Jackson helped lead the Athletics to the American League Eastern Division Title in 1971 with 32 home runs. But the Baltimore Orioles took the pennant at the playoffs. In 1972 the Athletics won the Western Division Title. In the playoffs, the Athletics beat the Detroit Tigers, with Jackson sliding into home plate to score the winning run in the final game. Tragically, during his slide he incurred an injury, a torn hamstring muscle, which forced him to sit out of the World Series. But as Jackson watched, the Athletics reigned victorious over the Cincinnati Reds.

Voted the American League's Most Valuable Player (MVP) in 1973, Jackson batted .293 and led the leagues in 32 home runs. That year the Atheltics defeated Baltimore to win the pennant. The team went on to win the World Championship over the New York Mets, with Jackson batting .310, driving in six runs, and hitting two home runs in the seventh game. Leading the league in runs, he was chosen MVP in the World Series. As sensational as the 1973 series was, it was not without its dark cloud. Anonymous death threats were sent to the Oakland office warning that Jackson would be killed if he played in the Championship games. During the playoffs and the World Series Jackson was under constant guard from both private and FBI agents. In the end, seemingly nothing resulted from the threats.

The Athletics won their fourth American League pennant in 1974, with Jackson hitting 29 homers for the season, and went on to defeat the Los Angeles Dodgers for their third straight World Series Championship. Finally, in 1975, after winning the American League Western Division Title and losing the pennant to the Boston Red Sox, Jackson, who had hit more homers and struck out more often than anyone on the team, ended his nine year stint with the Oakland Athletics. After unsuccessful contract negotiations, Finley traded Jackson to the Baltimore Orioles on April 2, 1976. The end of that season found Jackson a free agent, signed on with the New York Yankees for $300,000, and a five year contract, when Baltimore could not agree with Jackson's long term contract demands.

As a member of the New York Yankees, Jackson's ego and temper flared. He referred to himself as "the straw that stirs the drink," according to *Jet* magazine in a January 25, 1993 article. His comments and behavior antagonized his peers. Once again Jackson fought with teammates, his manager, Billy Martin, and the team owner, George Steinbrenner. And once again he led his team to the World Championship. The night of October 18, 1977 was one of Jackson's greatest triumphs. In the final game of the World Series, he hit three consecutive home runs, drove in five runs and brought the Yankees to victory over the Dodgers, winning 8-4. He had hit a Series record-breaking five home runs. "Maybe now, for at least this one night, I can feel like a real superstar," he was quoted in the *Lincoln Library of Sports Champions*. According to an article in *New York* written by Mike Lupica, Jackson had amazed himself on the day of the final game when during batting practice he hit 20 balls out of 40 into the seats. Amazingly enough, he had three more left to hit that night. He was named MVP of the World Series that fall and ended the season with 32 homers, 110 runs batted in (RBIs) and a .286 batting average.

Jackson followed that spectacular season with a second Series win against the Dodgers in 1978. He scored two runs, eight RBIs and batted .391. That year the first Reggie! chocolate candy bar appeared lasting only a short while as public interest waned. His walloping World Series hitting earned him the title "Mr. October," as he could always be counted on to pull his team to victory in a clinch.

1980 proved to be another fine season as Jackson hit a career high of .300 with 41 home runs and 111 RBIs. The Yankees won the American League pennant in 1981. In keeping with his fashion of coming through for the team, he hit his tenth and final Series home run that year. The California Angels signed Jackson on in 1982, and in a stunning achievement he reached the 500-homer plateau in 1984. Before retiring in 1987, he rejoined the Oakland Athletics for one last season. He was placed sixth on the all-time major leagues career home run list with 563 home runs during his 21 year baseball career. After retiring, Jackson worked briefly as a sports broadcaster for the Angels before moving on to coach for the Athletics. Dissatisfied with his coaching responsibilities he took a job with the Upper Deck Company handling sales of trading cards and sports collectibles.

The crowning achievement of his career came on August 1, 1993 when Reggie Jackson became the 216th inductee into the Baseball Hall of Fame—the only player to be so honored in that year. On his plaque he chose to be shown in the Yankee stripes, the uniform he found most fitting. Speaking of New York in the January issue of *Jet*, he said, "I feel this is the place that's really claimed me." His plaque lists him as sixth on the all-time list, ahead of such greats as Mickey Mantle, Ted Williams, and Lou Gehrig. His remarkable achievements run to both extremes: ten World Series home runs; five World Championships; 11 American League Championships with three different teams; and holding the major league record for lifetime strikeouts at 2,597. "Strung together, that's five years." Jackson quipped in Michael Angeli's article, "for five years I never touched the ball." At the induction, a passionate and eloquent Jackson spoke of the game he loved and his debt to the first Black Major League players, Jackie Robinson and Larry Doby. Quoting Lou Gehrig he ended by calling himself "the luckiest man on the face of the earth," as noted in *Jet*, August 16, 1993. The Yankees retired his number 44 baseball uniform and the Reggie! bar was reintroduced the year of Jackson's induction, packaged with a specially designed Reggie baseball card put out by Upper Deck.

During the Summer of 1993, George Steinbrenner announced that his former ballplayer was returning to the club in the capacity of special assistant and advisor to the Yankees general partners. Jackson continued his work in California for the trading card company and was made director of new buisness at a California-based computer company for which he was already a spokesman. However, Jackson still took on the added responsibility of evaluating players for the team, returning to New York one week out of each month. Given his celebrity status Jackson felt his presence was an asset to the ball club. Speaking of his fans to Mike Lupica in *Esquire* he noted, "If I walked out there right now, I could still stop the . . . place cold."

Jackson was emphatically disinterested in a career in sports broadcasting for the future. "I don't want to rip players," he stated in Angeli's article. "I don't want to talk on the air condescendingly about players. I know what it's like to try . . . and look like a bum." But he was open to the possibility of coaching for the Yankees down the road. "Never say never," he told Lupica. Going on to talk about his role with the ball club in the Angeli article, Jackson stated, "I'm very happy doing what I'm doing. I'm about as high as I can get here in this company without owning it. . . . I got it all."

Further Reading

Esquire, June 1993, pp. 69-71.

Jet, January 25, 1993, p. 46; May 1993, p. 47; August 16, 1993, p. 51; September 6, 1993, p. 51.

New York, April 19, 1993, pp. 158-160.

New Yorker, August 2, 1993, pp. 40-41.

Sports Illustrated, August 2, 1993, pp. 58-64. □

Thomas Jonathan Jackson

The American Thomas Jonathan "Stonewall" Jackson (1824-1863) was a Confederate hero and one of the outstanding Civil War generals.

Thomas Jackson was born on Jan. 21, 1824, at Clarksburg, Va. After the deaths of his father in 1826 and his mother in 1831, he was raised by his uncle. He went to local schools and then attended the U.S. Military Academy (1842-1846), graduating in time to join the 1st Artillery Regiment as a brevet second lieutenant in the Mexican War. Following service at the siege of Veracruz and at Cerro Gordo, he became a second lieutenant and transferred to a light field battery. While engaged in the fighting around Mexico City, Jackson received promotion to first lieutenant and later won brevets to captain and major.

Military Instructor

After the Mexican War, Jackson served at Ft. Columbus and at Ft. Hamilton. In 1851 he accepted a position as professor of philosophy and artillery tactics at Virginia Military Institute, where he proved a dedicated but inept instructor.

On Aug. 4, 1853, Jackson married Elinor Junkin of Lexington, Va., who died, with her baby, in childbirth in October 1854. After a tour of Europe in 1856, he married Mary Anna Morrison; they had a daughter. In December 1859 he commanded the cadet artillery at the hanging of abolitionist John Brown. He voted for John C. Breckinridge, the presidential candidate of the Southern Democrats in 1860, but hoped the Union would not be dissolved.

First Bull Run

When Virginia seceded from the Union in April 1861, Jackson traveled to Richmond with the cadet corps. The state government immediately commissioned him a colonel and sent him to Harpers Ferry. There he relinquished command to Joseph E. Johnston and became a brigade commander and brigadier general. At the First Battle of Bull Run on July 21, when Jackson's brigade reinforced the Confederate left to stem the Union attack, Gen. Bernard E. Bee rallied his men with the words, "There is Jackson standing like a stone wall." The Confederates drove back the Union advance, and Jackson won a new name.

Shenandoah Valley Campaigns

In October 1861 Jackson became a major general, and in November he received command of the Shenandoah Valley district of Virginia. On March 23 his attack on the

Federal army at Kernstown forced the diversion of troops intended to reinforce the Union army moving against Richmond.

Jackson attacked an enemy force at McDowell in May 1862 and then struck another Union army at Front Royal, driving it back to the Potomac. He withdrew and fought off converging Union armies at Cross Keys and at Port Republic. Thus, with 16,000 men he had diverted 60,000 Federal troops from the Richmond campaign.

Seven Days Battles

Jackson then joined his forces with those of Gen. Robert E. Lee outside Richmond and began the Seven Days Battles to defend the Confederate capital against Gen. George McClellan's army. Tired and unfamiliar with the country, Jackson moved slowly and failed to flank the enemy position at Beaver Dam Creek. His troops did participate in the successful attack at Gaines's Mill on June 27 and pursued the Union army to White Oak Swamp. There, because of personal fatigue, he again failed to press the Union retreat as expected. Some of his men were among those repulsed at Malvern Hill on July 1.

Second Bull Run

In mid-July of 1862 Lee detached Jackson and his men to meet the advance of a new Union army under Gen. John Pope in northern Virginia. At Cedar Run on August 9 Jackson defeated part of that command. He led his force around the Union right flank and destroyed its supply base at Manassas on August 27. He then withdrew to Groveton,

where he held off attacks while waiting for Lee. When Lee had reunited his forces, Jackson's men joined in a successful counterattack that drove the Union army from the field in the Second Battle of Bull Run on June 30.

Harpers Ferry, Sharpsburg, Fredericksburg

In September 1862 Lee advanced into Maryland and sent Jackson ahead with five divisions to capture the Union garrison of 11,000 men at Harpers Ferry. Jackson surrounded the town, which surrendered on September 15, then hurried north to help Lee beat off Union attacks at Sharpsburg on September 17. Lee withdrew into Virginia after the battle to recruit and reorganize his army. In October, Jackson received promotion to lieutenant general and became commander of the new 2d Corps.

In November 1862 the Confederate army moved east to meet a Union advance at Fredericksburg, Va. Lee placed his troops on the hills south of the town, with Jackson's corps on the right. On December 13 Gen. Ambrose Burnside attacked across the Rappahannock River with two columns, one aimed at Jackson's position. Though Burnside broke through a gap between two Confederate brigades, reinforcements drove the attackers back to the river. The entire Union assault was repulsed with heavy losses.

Chancellorsville and Mortal Injury

In late April 1863 Gen. Joseph Hooker decided to turn the Confederate left flank by crossing the Rappahannock River above Fredericksburg, while part of Lee's 1st Corps had been diverted to southern Virginia and North Carolina. Lee sent Jackson's corps around the Union position at Chancellorsville to strike it from the rear. Late in the afternoon of May 2, Jackson launched an attack that routed the Union right wing and drove it back almost to Chancellorsville. As Jackson returned with his staff from scouting Union lines, his left arm was broken by shots from his own men who mistook the riders for Union troops. The arm required amputation before Jackson was removed south to Guiney's Station, Va., for rest and recovery. There he developed pneumonia and died on May 10, 1863.

Stonewall Jackson was a masterful military strategist. He campaigned with aggressiveness and audacity; he moved rapidly; he was tenacious in defense and pursuit. His victories made him a hero in the Confederacy and won him the accolades of military historians, who consider him among America's greatest generals.

Further Reading

The most detailed analysis of Jackson's personal life and military campaigns is Lenoir Chambers, *Stonewall Jackson* (2 vols., 1959). The best one-volume biography is Frank E. Vandiver, *Mighty Stonewall* (1957). Of the older biographies, two are most useful: one by Jackson's chief of staff (in early 1862), Robert L. Dabney, *Life and Campaigns of Lieut.-Gen. Thomas J. Jackson* (2 vols., 1864-1866); the other by a British army officer, G. F. R. Henderson, *Stonewall Jackson and the American Civil War* (2 vols., 1898). □

Henry James

The American author Henry James (1843-1916) was one of the major novelists of the late 19th and early 20th centuries. His works deal largely with the impact of Europe and its society on Americans.

Henry James, the son of a theologian and the brother of the philosopher William James, was born on April 15, 1843, at Washington Place in New York City. His childhood was spent in the city and in Albany and then, between the ages of 12 and 17, in Europe. He was privately tutored in London, Geneva, and Paris. His American education began at school in Newport, R.I. James entered Harvard Law School in 1862, leaving after a year. In 1864 his family settled in Boston and then in Cambridge. That same year he published his first story and early reviews.

James's frequent appearances in the *Atlantic Monthly* began in 1865. Four years later he traveled again in England, France, and Italy, returning to Cambridge in 1870 and publishing his first novel, *Watch and Ward.* It concerned American life in a specifically American setting, the upper-class world of Boston, its suburbs, and Newport. At the age of 29 James was again in Europe, spending a summer in Paris and most of 1873 in Rome, where he began *Roderick Hudson.* For a year in New York City he was part of the literary world of the era. His criticism appeared in 1874 and 1875 in the *Nation* and the *North American Review.* Also in 1875, *Transatlantic Sketches, A Passionate Pilgrim,* and *Roderick Hudson* appeared. *Transatlantic Sketches* is a travel book, as is *A Passionate Pilgrim,* which anticipates the theme of the European impact on what James repeatedly identified as the "American state of Innocence." *Roderick Hudson* is fiction on the same theme, a response to the colony of American expatriates James knew in Rome.

His Expatriation

James's disengagement from America was a long process; he wrote: "I saw my parents homesick, as I conceived, for the ancient order, and distressed and inconvenienced by many of the more immediate features of the modern, as the modern pressed about us, and since their theory of a better living was from an early time that we should renew the question of the ancient on the very first possibility I simply grew greater in the faith that somehow to manage that would constitute success in life." Living in Paris during 1876, James wrote *The American.* At the time, he knew Ivan Turgenev, Gustave Flaubert, Edmond de Goncourt, Émile Zola, and others. His expatriation was complete by the end of that year, when he settled in London.

The impact of his short novel *Daisy Miller* (1879) brought James fame in Europe and the United States; it was his first popular success. He explained the novel this way: "The whole idea of the story is the little tragedy of a light, thin, natural, unsuspecting creature being sacrificed as it were to a social rumpus that went on quite over her head and to which she stood in no measurable relation. To deepen the effect, I have made it go over her mother's head as well." James repeated the same effect, and intention, in

several other novels and stories. In *The Portrait of a Lady,* for example, the effect is similar but more intricate. James mentioned his "Americano-European legends" as one of the central impulses of his work.

Between 1879 and 1882 James produced his first major series of novels. They were *The Europeans, Washington Square, Confidence,* and *The Portrait of a Lady.* Of the four, only *Washington Square* is about American life. By 1886 a 14-volume collection of his novels and tales was published. He wrote *The Bostonians* and *The Princess Casamassima* in 1886 while living in a flat in De Vere Gardens in London. Both are social dramas. "The Aspern Papers," the short novel *The Reverberator,* and "A London Life" appeared the following year. *The Tragic Muse,* one of his most ambitious novels, was serialized in the *Atlantic Monthly* in 1890.

James then entered a 5-year period in which he concentrated on writing drama. *The American* was produced as a play in London by Edward Compton. The effort ended in 1895, when he was jeered at the opening of his play *Guy Domville* at St. James's Theatre in London. He abandoned the stage. Almost never revived, his plays are included in two volumes, *Theatricals* and *Theatricals: Second Series.*

Later Career

A bachelor, James settled in Lamb House, Rye, in 1898, and continued his 20-year "siege" of English life and society. His schedule of concentrated work during the day and of relaxation at night produced in 1898 *The Two Magics,* a collection of stories that includes his novella "The Turn of the Screw" and the short novel *In the Cage.* What is frequently identified as his third and best phase began the following year with *The Awkward Age,* and between 1899 and 1904 he wrote *The Sacred Fount, The Wings of the Dove, The Ambassadors,* and *The Golden Bowl.* James himself described *The Ambassadors* as the "best 'all round'" of his novels. In his early, middle, and later periods he relied explicitly on "devices" and the "grammar" of fiction, on "point of view," "scene," "dramatizing," selection of incidents, structure, and perspective. It was through technique that he isolated values, and he insisted that the primary values were "truth" and "life."

In September 1904 James returned to the United States after a 20-year absence, passing the fall with his brother William in New Hampshire and, later, revisiting New York City. After a year of lecturing he returned to Lamb House in England and began revising his fiction and writing the critical prefaces to the definitive New York edition of his work. During 1909 he suffered from a long nervous illness and produced a series of stories that appeared as *The Finer Grain.* He was in New Hampshire when William died after a long illness. Before returning to England in 1911, he received an honorary degree from Harvard; he received another from Oxford the following year.

James's autobiographical memoirs, *A Small Boy and Others* and *Notes of a Son and Brother,* were completed shortly before the outbreak of World War I. The war's disruption greatly disturbed him. He began war work in various hospitals, writing for war charities and aiding Belgian refugees. On July 26, 1915, James was naturalized as a British subject. Later in the year his last illness, a stroke and pneumonia, began. Before his death on February 28, 1916, he received the Order of Merit from King George V. The funeral services were in Chelsea Old Church, London, and his ashes were buried in the family plot in Cambridge, Mass.

Further Reading

Critical and biographical material on James is extensive. The definitive biography is Leon Edel, *Henry James* (5 vols., 1953-1972). Other biographies are Van Wyck Brooks, *The Pilgrimage of Henry James* (1925), an early and influential book, and Quentin Anderson, *The American Henry James* (1957). F. W. Dupee, *Henry James* (1951; 2d ed. rev. 1956), is a critical biography. Millicent Bell, *Edith Wharton and Henry James: The Story of Their Friendship* (1965), contains correspondence of James to Mrs. Wharton and considerable biographical material. Oscar Cargill, *The Novels of Henry James* (1961), is an articulate introduction to his writing. Important critical studies of James are Joseph Warren Beach, *The Method of Henry James* (1918; rev. ed. 1954), and F. O. Matthiessen, *Henry James: The Major Phase* (1944). See also Christof Wegelin, *The Image of Europe in Henry James* (1958). Roger Gard, ed., *Henry James: The Critical Heritage* (1968), is a collection of reviews and articles on James and is useful in viewing responses to James's work from the late 19th to the early 20th century. □

Thomas Jefferson

American philosopher and statesman Thomas Jefferson (1743-1826) was the third president of the United States. A man of broad interests and activity, he exerted an immense influence on the political and intellectual life of the new nation.

Thomas Jefferson was born at Shadwell, Va., on April 13, 1743. His father had been among the earliest settlers in this wilderness country, and his position of leadership descended to his eldest son, together with 5,000 acres of land.

Jefferson became one of the best-educated Americans of his time. At the age of 17 he entered the College of William and Mary, where he got exciting first glimpses of "the expansion of science, and of the system of things in which we are placed." Nature destined him to be a scientist, he often said; but there was no opportunity for a scientific career in Virginia, and he took the path of the law, studying it under the tutelage of George With as a branch of the history of mankind. He read widely in the law, in the sciences, and in both ancient and modern history, philosophy, and literature. Jefferson was admitted to the bar in 1767; his successful practice led to a wide circle of influence and to cultivated intellectual habits that would prove remarkably creative in statesmanship. When the onrush of the American Revolution forced him to abandon practice in 1774, he turned these legal skills to the rebel cause.

Jefferson's public career began in 1769, when he served as a representative in the Virginia House of Burgesses. About this time, too, he began building Monticello, the lovely home perched on a densely wooded summit that became a lifelong obsession. He learned architecture from books, above all from the Renaissance Italian Andrea Palladio. Yet Monticello, like the many other buildings Jefferson designed over the years, was a uniquely personal creation. Dissatisfied with the first version, completed in 12 years, Jefferson later rebuilt it. Monticello assumed its ultimate form about the time he retired from the presidency.

His Philosophy

Jefferson rose to fame in the councils of the American Revolution. Insofar as the Revolution was a philosophical event, he was its most articulate spokesman, having absorbed the thought of the 18th-century Enlightenment. He believed in a beneficent natural order in the moral as in the physical world, freedom of inquiry in all things, and man's inherent capacity for justice and happiness, and he had faith in reason, improvement, and progress.

Jefferson's political thought would become the quintessence of Enlightenment liberalism, though it had roots in English law and government. The tradition of the English constitution gave concreteness to American patriot claims, even a color of legality to revolution itself, that no other modern revolutionaries have possessed. Jefferson used the libertarian elements of the English legal tradition for ideological combat with the mother country. He also separated the principles of English liberty from their corrupted forms in the empire of George III and identified these principles with nascent American ideals. In challenging the oppressions of the empire, Americans like Jefferson came to recognize their claims to an independent nationality.

Jefferson's most important contribution to the revolutionary debate was *A Summary View of the Rights of British America* (1774). He argued that Americans, as sons of expatriate Englishmen, possessed the same natural rights to govern themselves as their Saxon ancestors had exercised when they migrated to England from Germany. Only with the reign of George III had the violations of American rights proved to be "a deliberate, systematical plan of reducing us to slavery." Though the logic of his argument pointed to independence, Jefferson instead set forth the theory of an empire of equal self-governing states under a common king and appealed to George III to rule accordingly.

Declaration of Independence

The Revolution had begun when Jefferson took his seat in the Second Continental Congress, at Philadelphia, in June 1775. He brought to the Congress, as John Adams recalled, "a reputation for literature, science, and a happy talent for composition." It was chiefly as a legislative draftsman that he would make his mark. His great work was the Declaration of Independence. In June 1776 he was surprised to find himself at the head of the committee to prepare this paper. He submitted a rough draft to Adams and Benjamin Franklin, two of the committee, who suggested only minor changes, revised it to Jefferson's satisfaction, and sent it to Congress. Congress debated it line by line for 2 1/2 days. Though many changes were made, the Declaration that

emerged on July 4 bore the unmistakable stamp of Jefferson. It possessed that "peculiar felicity of expression" for which he was noted.

The Declaration of Independence crisply set forth the bill of particular grievances against the reigning sovereign and compressed a whole cosmology, a political philosophy, and a national creed in one paragraph. The truths declared to be "self-evident" were not new; as Jefferson later said, his purpose was "not to find out new principles, or new arguments . . ., but to place before mankind the common sense of the subject." But here, for the first time in history, these truths were laid at the foundation of a nation. Natural equality, the inalienable rights of man, the sovereignty of the people, the right of revolution—these principles endowed the American Revolution with high purpose united to a theory of government.

In Virginia

Jefferson returned to Virginia and to his seat in the reconstituted legislature. A constitution had been adopted for the commonwealth, but it was distressingly less democratic than the one Jefferson had drafted and dispatched to Williamsburg. He sought now to achieve liberal reforms by ordinary legislation. Most of these were contained in his comprehensive Revision of the Laws. Although the code was never enacted in entirety, the legislature went over the bills one by one. Of first importance was the Statute for Religious Freedom. Enacted in 1786, the statute climaxed the long campaign for separation of church and state in Virginia. Though Jefferson was responsible for the abolition of property laws that were merely relics of feudalism, his bill for the reform of Virginia's barbarous criminal code failed, and for the sake of expediency he withheld his plan for gradual emancipation of the slaves. Jefferson was sickened by the defeat of his Bill for the More General Diffusion of Knowledge. A landmark in the history of education, it proposed a complete system of public education, with elementary schools available to all, the gifted to be educated according to their ability.

Jefferson became Virginia's governor in June 1779. The Revolutionary War had entered a new phase. The British decision to "unravel the thread of rebellion from the southward" would, if successful, have made Virginia the crucial battleground. Jefferson struggled against enormous odds to aid the southern army. He was also handicapped by the weakness of his office under the constitution and by his personal aversion to anything bordering on dictatorial rule.

Early in 1781 the British invaded Virginia from the coast, slashed through to Richmond, and put the government to flight. Jefferson acted with more vigor than before, still to no avail. In May, Gen. Charles Cornwallis marched his army into Virginia. The government moved to safer quarters at Charlottesville. The Redcoats followed, and 2 days after his term of office expired but before a successor could be chosen, Jefferson was chased from Monticello. The General Assembly resolved to inquire into Jefferson's conduct, and months after the British surrender at Yorktown, he attended the legislature on this business. But no inquiry was held, the Assembly instead voting him resolution of thanks for his services.

Nevertheless, wounded by the criticism, Jefferson resolved to quit public service. A series of personal misfortunes, culminating in his wife's death in September 1782, plunged him into gloom. Yet her death finally returned him to his destiny. The idealized life he had sought in his family, farms, and books was suddenly out of reach. That November he eagerly accepted congressional appointment to the peace commission in Paris. He never sailed, however, and wound up in Congress instead.

During his retirement Jefferson had written his only book, *Note on the State of Virginia*. The inquiry had begun simply, but it grew as Jefferson worked. He finally published the manuscript in a private edition in Paris (1785). Viewed in the light of 18th-century knowledge, the book is work of natural and civil history, uniquely interesting as a guide to Jefferson's mind and to his native country. He expressed opinions on a variety of subjects, from cascades and caverns to constitutions and slavery. An early expression of American nationalism, the book acted as a catalyst in several fields of intellectual activity. It also ensured Jefferson a scientific and literary reputation on two continents.

Service in Congress

In Congress from November 1783 to the following May, Jefferson laid the foundations of national policy in several areas. His proposed decimal system of coinage was adopted. He drafted the first ordinance of government for the western territory, wherein free and equal republican states would be created out of the wilderness; and his land ordinance, adopted with certain changes in 1785, projected the rectilinear survey system of the American West.

Jefferson also took a leading part in formulating foreign policy. The American economy rested on foreign commerce and navigation. Cut adrift from the British mercantile system, Congress had pursued free trade to open foreign markets, but only France had been receptive. The matter became urgent in 1783-1784. Jefferson helped reformulate a liberal commercial policy, and in 1784 he was appointed to a three-man commission (with Adams and Franklin) to negotiate treaties of commerce with the European powers.

Minister to France

In Paris, Jefferson's first business was the treaty commission; in 1785 he succeeded Franklin as minister to France. The commission soon expired, and Jefferson focused his commercial diplomacy on France. In his opinion, France offered imposing political support for the United States in Europe as well as an entering wedge for the free commercial system on which American wealth and power depended. Louis XVI's foreign minister seemed well disposed, and influential men in the French capital were ardent friends of the American Revolution. Jefferson won valuable concessions for American commerce; however, because France realized few benefits in return, Britain maintained its economic ascendancy.

His duties left Jefferson time to haunt bookstores, frequent fashionable salons, and indulge his appetite for art, music, and theater. He toured the south of France and Italy, England, and the Rhineland. He interpreted the New World to the Old. Some of this activity had profound effects. For instance, his collaboration with a French architect in the design of the classical Roman Capitol of Virginia inaugurated the classical revival in American architecture.

About Europe generally, Jefferson expressed ambivalent feelings. But on balance, the more he saw of Europe, the dearer his own country became. "My God!" he exclaimed. "How little do my countrymen know what precious blessings they are in possession of, and which no other people on earth enjoy. I confess I had no idea of it myself. . . ."

Secretary of State

On Jefferson's return to America in 1789, President Washington prevailed upon him to become secretary of state. For the next 3 years he was chiefly engaged in fruitless negotiations with the European powers. With Spain he sought to fix the southern United States boundary and secure free navigation of the Mississippi River through Spanish territory to the Gulf of Mexico. With Britain he sought removal of English troops from the Northwest and settlement of issues left over from the peace treaty. In this encounter he was frustrated by the secretary of the Treasury, Alexander Hamilton, whose ascendancy in the government also checked Jefferson's and James Madison's efforts for commercial discrimination against Britain and freer trade with France. In Jefferson's opinion, Hamilton's fiscal system turned on British trade, credit, and power, while his own system turned on commercial liberation, friendship with France, and the success of the French Revolution. Hamilton's measures would enrich the few at the expense of the many, excite speculation and fraud, concentrate enormous power in the Treasury, and break down the restraints of the Constitution. To combat these tendencies, Jefferson associated himself with the incipient party opposition in Congress.

Developing Political Parties

As the party division deepened, Jefferson was denounced by the Federalists as the "generalissimo" of the Republican party, a role he neither possessed nor coveted but, finally, could not escape. When war erupted between France and Britain in 1793, the contrary dispositions of the parties toward these nations threatened American peace. Jefferson attempted to use American neutrality to force concessions from Britain and to improve cooperation between the embattled republics of the Atlantic world. In this he was embarrassed by Edmond Genet, the French minister to the United States, and finally had to abandon him altogether. The deterioration of Franco-American relations did irreparable damage to Jefferson's political system.

Jefferson resigned his post at the end of 1793, again determined to quit public life. But in 1796 the Republicans made him their presidential candidate against John Adams. Losing by three electoral votes, Jefferson became vice president. When the "XYZ affair" threatened to plunge the United States into war with France in 1798, Jefferson clung to the hope of peace and, in the developing war hysteria, rallied the Republicans around him. Enactment of the Alien and Sedition Laws convinced him that the Federalists aimed to annihilate the Republicans and that the Republicans' only salvation lay in political intervention by the state authorities. On this basis he drafted the Kentucky Resolutions of 1798, in which he elaborated the theory of the Union as a compact among the several states, declared the Alien and Sedition Laws unconstitutional, and prescribed the remedy of state "nullification" for such assumptions of power by the central government. Kentucky did not endorse this specific doctrine, but the defense of civil liberties was now joined to the defense of state rights. Though the celebrated resolutions did not force a change of policy, by contributing to the rising public clamor against the administration they achieved their political purpose.

President of the United States

Republicans doubled their efforts to elect the "man of the people" in the unusually bitter campaign of 1800. Jefferson topped Adams in the electoral vote. But because his running mate, Aaron Burr, received an equal number of votes, the final decision went to the House of Representatives. Only after 36 ballots was Jefferson elected.

Jefferson became president on March 4, 1801, in the new national capital, Washington, D.C. His inaugural address—a political touchstone for a century or longer—brilliantly summed up the Republican creed and appealed for the restoration of harmony and affection. "We have called by different names brethren of the same principle. We are all republicans: we are all federalists." Jefferson extended the hand of friendship to the Federalists and, although Federalists monopolized the Federal offices, he attempted to limit his removals of them. Even after party pressures forced him to revise this strategy, moderation characterized his course.

Reform was the order of the day. Working effectively with Congress, Jefferson restored freedom of the press; lowered the residency period of the law of naturalization to 5 years; scaled down the Army and Navy (despite a war against Barbary piracy); repealed the partisan Judiciary Act of 1801; abolished all internal taxes, together with a host of revenue offices; and began the planned retirement of the debt. The Jeffersonian reformation was bottomed on fiscal policy; by reducing the means and powers of government, it sought to further peace, equality, and individual freedom.

The President's greatest triumph—and his greatest defeat—came in foreign affairs. Spain's cession of Louisiana and the port of New Orleans to France in 1800 posed a serious threat to American security, especially to the aspirations of the West. Jefferson skillfully negotiated this crisis. With the Louisiana Purchase (1803), America gained an uncharted domain of some 800,000 square miles, doubling its size, for $11,250,000. Even before the treaty was signed, Jefferson planned an expedition to explore this country. The Lewis and Clark expedition, like the Louisiana Purchase, was a spectacular consummation of Jefferson's western vision.

Easily reelected in 1804, Jefferson soon encountered foreign and domestic troubles. His relations with Congress degenerated as Republicans quarreled among themselves.

Especially damaging was the insurgency of John Randolph, formerly Republican leader in the House. And former vice president Aaron Burr mounted an insurgency in the West; but Jefferson crushed this and, with difficulty, maintained control of Congress. The turbulence of the Napoleonic Wars, with American ships and seamen ravaged in the neutral trade, proved too difficult. France was not blameless, but Britain was the chief aggressor.

Finally there appeared to be no escape from war except by withdrawing from the oceans. In December 1807 the President proposed, and Congress enacted, a total embargo on America's seagoing commerce. More than an alternative to war, the embargo was a test of the power of commercial coercion in international disputes. On the whole, it was effectively enforced, but it failed to bring Britain or France to justice, and the mounting costs at home led to its repeal by Congress in the waning hours of Jefferson's presidency.

Active Retirement

In retirement Jefferson became the "Sage of Monticello," the most revered—by some the most hated—among the remaining Revolutionary founders. He maintained a large correspondence and intellectual pursuits on a broad front. Unfinished business from the Revolution drew his attention, such as revision of the Virginia constitution and gradual emancipation of slaves. But the former would come only after his death, and the failure of the latter would justify his worst fears. He revived his general plan of public education. Again the legislature rejected it, approving, however, a major part, the state university. Jefferson was the master planner of the University of Virginia in all its parts, from the grounds and buildings to the curriculum, faculty, and rules of governance. He died at Monticello on the fiftieth anniversary of American independence, July 4, 1826.

After his death, there was much historical speculation regarding Jefferson's involvement with Sally Hemings, a slave. The debate was finally laid to rest after extensive DNA testing proved that he indeed fathered a child by Hemmings, who had been Jefferson's companion for 36 years after the death of his wife.

Further Reading

There are several editions of Jefferson's writings: *The Writings of Thomas Jefferson,* edited by Paul Leicester Ford (10 vols., 1892-1899); *The Writings of Thomas Jefferson,* edited by Andrew A. Lipscomb and Albert Ellery Bergh (20 vols. in 10; 1905); and *Papers,* edited by Julian P. Boyd and others (17 vols., 1950-1965). The Boyd work, though complete only to November 1790, is the best edition; a good companion piece is *The Family Letters of Thomas Jefferson,* edited by Edwin Morris Betts and James Adam Bear, Jr. (1966).

The major biography is Dumas Malone, *Jefferson and His Time* (4 vols., 1948-1970), complete to 1805 and still in process. Less comprehensive is Merrill D. Peterson, *Thomas Jefferson and the New Nation* (1970). Accounts of Jefferson's elections are given in Arthur M. Schlesinger, Jr., ed., *History of American Presidential Elections* (4 vols., 1971). Jefferson as president is brilliantly, if not quite fairly, portrayed in the first four volumes of Henry Adams, *History of the United States of America during the Administrations of Jefferson and Madison* (9 vols., 1889-1891).

Other studies of Jefferson's life and thought include Fiske Kimball, *Thomas Jefferson: Architect* (1916); Roy J. Honeywell, *The Educational Work of Thomas Jefferson* (1931); Adrienne Koch, *The Philosophy of Thomas Jefferson* (1943); Karl Lehman, *Thomas Jefferson: American Humanist* (1947); Daniel J. Boorstin, *The Lost World of Thomas Jefferson* (1948); Edwin T. Martin, *Thomas Jefferson: Scientist* (1952); Caleb Perry Patterson, *The Constitutional Principles of Thomas Jefferson* (1953); Phillips Russell, *Jefferson: Champion of the Free Mind* (1956); Merrill D. Peterson, *The Jefferson Image in the American Mind* (1960); and Joseph Ellis, *American Sphinx: The Character of Thomas Jefferson* (1997). Merrill D. Peterson, ed., *Thomas Jefferson: A Profile* (1967), collects essays by historians of Jefferson's era as well as modern ones. Jonathan Daniels, *Ordeal of Ambition: Jefferson, Hamilton, Burr* (1970), an account of the intertwining political careers of these three, is part biography and part history. A large index of the Jefferson era can be found in David S. Brown, *Thomas Jefferson: A Biographical Companion* (1998). □

Steven Jobs

Computer designer and corporate executive Steven Jobs (born 1955) is cofounder of Apple Computers. With his vision of affordable personal computers, he launched one of the largest industries of the past decades while still in his early twenties and remains one of the most inventive and energetic minds in American technology.

Born in 1955, Steven Jobs was adopted shortly thereafter by a California couple, Paul and Clara Jobs. Jobs showed an early interest in electronics and gadgetry. As a high school student, he boldly asked William Hewlett, co-founder and president of the Hewlett-Packard computer firm, for some parts he needed to complete a class project. Hewlett was impressed enough to give Jobs the parts and offer him a summer internship at Hewlett-Packard.

Dropped Out of College

After graduating from high school in 1972, Jobs attended Reed College in Portland, Oregon, for two years before dropping out, partly to ease his family's financial burden and partly to find himself. He hoped to visit India and study eastern spiritualism, but lacking necessary funds, went to work part-time for Atari Computers. He was able to save enough money to finance a trip to India in the summer of 1974. While there, he practiced meditation, studied eastern culture and religion, and even shaved his head. But by the fall, he became ill with dysentery and was forced to return to the United States.

For a short time, Jobs lived in a California commune but soon became disenchanted with the lifestyle. In 1975, he began associating with a group of computer aficionados known as the Homebrew Computer Club. One member, a technical whiz named Steve Wosniak, whom Jobs had first met at Hewlett-Packard, was trying to build a small computer. Jobs became fascinated with the marketing potential of such a computer, and in 1976 he and Wosniak formed their own company. The team was content to sell circuit boards designed by Wosniak until the computer prototype was complete. That same year, Wosniak succeeded in de-

signing a small computer, and using Jobs's parents' garage, the two men worked to refine and market the product.

Cofounded Apple Computer Co.

Jobs saw a huge gap in the existing computer market, as no product was targeted for home use. Wosniak improved his initial computer while Jobs lined up investors and bank financing. Marketing manager A. C. Markkula eventually invested $250,000 and became an equal partner in the Apple Computer Company. With new capital, Jobs and Wosniak refined the prototype. The redesigned computer—christened the ''Apple II''—hit the market in 1977, with impressive first year sales of $2.7 million. In one of the most phenomenal cases of corporate growth in U.S. history, the company's sales grew to $200 million within three years. Jobs and Wosniak had opened an entirely new market, that of personal computers, bringing the computational speed of business systems into people's homes and beginning a new era in information processing.

By 1980, the personal computer era was well underway. Apple was forced to continually improve its products to remain ahead in a growing marketplace. Competitors such as Radio Shack, Commodore, and IBM were gaining sales from Apple's market. In 1980, Apple introduced the Apple III computer, and improved version of the Apple II, but the new model suffered technical and marketing problems. It was withdrawn from the market, but was later reworked and reintroduced.

Jobs continued to be the marketing force behind Apple. He admitted that mistakes were made with the Apple III, but looked for innovative ways to meet new and existing consumer needs. Early in 1983, Jobs unveiled Lisa, another new computer, aimed this time at business executives. Lisa was designed for people possessing minimal computer experience. The model did not sell well, however, because of its high price and increased competition from IBM personal computers. By 1983, it was estimated that Apple lost half of its market share to IBM.

Macintosh Falls, Jobs Resigns

Faced with a declining market share, Apple introduced the Macintosh in 1984. In designing the model, Jobs apparently paid more attention to appearances than function. Although the Macintosh had "user-friendly" software and on-screen displays, Jobs failed to equip it with either a letter-quality printer or a hard disk drive. Lacking these features, the Macintosh did not sell well to businesses. The failure of the Macintosh signalled the beginning of Jobs's downfall at Apple Computer Company. In 1985, following a highly publicized showdown at Apple, Jobs resigned from the company he had founded, though he retained his title as chairman of its board of directors.

It was not long before Steve Jobs resurfaced, however. Soon after leaving Apple, he hired some of his former employees to begin a new computer company. The company was called NeXT, and Jobs invested $7 million of his own money to get it started. For three years, Jobs and his employees worked to produce the first NeXT computer, which was aimed at the educational market. Late in 1988, the NeXT computer was introduced at a large gala event in San Francisco. Initial reactions were generally good; the product was user-friendly, with very fast processing speed, excellent graphics displays, and an outstanding sound system. Other innovations included an optical disk drive instead of floppy disks, and a special sound chip to provide the fidelity of a compact disc. Judging from initial reactions, many critics were convinced that Steve Jobs had brought another revolutionary product to American consumers.

Despite the warm reception, however, the NeXT machine never caught on. It was too costly, had a black-and-white screen, and couldn't be linked to other computers or run common software, Joseph Nocera wrote in a biting profile of Jobs in *Gentleman's Quarterly*. Nocera argued that Jobs's charisma and persuasive charm duped his employees, the press, and Jobs himself into believing he could not fail—despite strong evidence to the contrary. "Jobs started NeXT with an unshakable faith in his own press clips, in which his mistakes were always overlooked while his supposed triumphs were always wildly oversold," Nocera wrote.

Nocera said he also fell victim to the Jobs myth when he visited NeXT in 1986. He witnessed Jobs brutalize employees who worshipped him, obsess over mindless details, and indulge his expensive tastes—yet Nocera reported none of the contradictions. "The point is," he wrote in 1993, "my willingness to be seduced by Steve Jobs caused me to miss what I was seeing with my own eyes. Even in 1986, the evidence strongly suggested that lightning was not going to strike twice. The incongruities were too severe, the

dreams too farfetched. . . . You'd ask the people at NeXT how, exactly, their computer was going to change the world and they would lapse into gobbledygook; they really had no idea what they were trying to accomplish with this new machine."

Bought Pixar, Made *Toy Story*

NeXT was not, however, the end of Steve Jobs. Lightning, indeed, struck a second time. In 1986, Jobs paid filmmaker George Lucas $10 million for a small firm called Pixar that specialized in computer animation. "Over the next six years Jobs poured another $40 million of his own money into the company . . . as it set out to make the first-ever computer-animated feature film," *Time* magazine reported in February 1996. That film was *Toy Story*, a huge box office hit. Pixar's initial public stock offering was an enormous success. The share price climbed dramatically, and Jobs's 80 percent stake in Pixar suddenly was worth $1 billion.

"Jobs makes the point that Pixar, like other (initial public offering) overnight successes, was really anything but an overnight success," said the *Time* article. "'The things I've done in my life have required a lot of years of work before they took off,' he says. He and Wosniak started work on Apple in 1975. 'So it was really six years of work before we went public. And Pixar has been 10 years. . . . The thing that drives me and my colleagues . . . is that you see something very compelling to you, and you don't quite know how to get it, but you know, sometimes intuitively, it's within your grasp. And it's worth putting in years of your life to make it come into existence.'"

In December of 1996, Apple announced that it was purchasing Next Software for over $400 million. Jobs returned to Apple as a part-time consultant to CEO Gilbert Amelio. The following year, in August, Apple entered into a partnership with archrival Microsoft, in which the two companies, according to the *New York Times*, "agreed to cooperate on several sales and technology fronts." The alliance was an unprecedented one for the industry, but analysts predicted that Microsoft's support will ultimately save Apple, a company that had in the late 1990s come to serve a much more niche market than Microsoft. "We want to let go of this notion that for Apple to win, Microsoft has to lose," Jobs said. In September of 1997, Jobs was named interim CEO of Apple while a replacement for the ousted Amelio was sought.

Further Reading

Butcher, Lee, *Accidental Millionaire: The Rise and Fall of Steven Jobs at Apple Computer,* Paragon House, 1987.

Young, Jeffrey S., *Steve Jobs: The Journey Is the Reward,* Scott, Foresman, 1988.

Esquire, December, 1986, pp. 84-101.

Fortune, February 20, 1984, pp. 86-88.

Gentleman's Quarterly, October 1993, pp. 105-111.

Newsweek, January 30, 1984, pp. 54-57; September 30, 1985, pp. 46-50; October 24, 1988, pp. 46-51.

Rolling Stone, April 4, 1996, pp. 51+.

Time, February 15, 1982, pp. 40-41; January 3, 1983, pp. 25-27; January 30, 1984, pp. 68- 69; February 19, 1996, pp. 43-47.

Business Week March 17, 1997, pp. 116. □

Robert Joffrey

Dancer and choreographer Robert Joffrey's (1930-1988) trailblazing Joffrey Ballet, which he created in the 1960s, continues to be one of the most popular and respected dance troupes.

A dancer and choreographer, Robert Joffrey stormed onto the American ballet scene with his first company in 1953. Never intending to become a professional dancer, Joffrey turned simple medical advice into a phenomenal career. He elevated ballet, the "conservative" art form, to new heights that were never thought of or attempted before including the production of one of the first rock ballets. Joffrey viewed ballet as not only a theatrical art form, but an art form that was forever evolving. Operating from this credo, Robert Joffrey created one of the most respected and best-known ballet companies of the 1960s. Even after Joffrey's death in 1988, the reputation and ability of his company continues to amaze viewers of all ages.

Dancer Realized

Robert Joffrey was born in Seattle, Washington, on December 24, 1930, to an Afghan father and an Italian mother. He was given the name of Abdullah Jaffa Anver Bey Khan. During his childhood, Joffrey experienced multiple bouts with various illnesses, most notably asthma. He was confirmed as suffering from chronic asthma in his youth by his family's doctor. Based on the advice of his physician, Joffrey took to dancing. The doctor believed that the breathing exercises taught to the children would help alleviate some of Joffrey's asthmatic conditions thereby making the task of breathing a little easier and his overall childhood a little better.

Formal Study and Instruction

At the age of 12, Joffrey began serious study of dance under the auspices of Mary Ann Wells. Through her guidance and care Joffrey began to excel at dance. He performed locally on several occasions throughout his teens and even presented a solo recital of his own choreography in 1948. When Robert Joffrey turned 18, he traveled to New York City where he enrolled and began study at the School of American Ballet. Additionally, Joffrey studied under Alexandra Fedoroua. Joffrey studied modern dance techniques under May O' Donnell and Gertrude Shurr. Joffrey made his professional dance debut with Roland Petit's Ballets de Paris during that troupe's 1949-1950 New York season. Shortly after, Joffrey was invited to perform in O'Donnell's troupe between 1950 and 1953. Joffrey performed as a soloist in the troupe, Miss O'Donnell's, during the 1953 season of "American Dance" at the Alvin Theater in New York. Even while dancing under the guidance and protection of these greats, Joffrey longed to establish his own company. Joffrey knew his ambitions lied there since the companies he

worked with were either too restrictive or conservative in their approach to ballet. He continued, however, to study and master a variety of styles knowing that a successful company was dependent on successful dancers and an extensive repertoire of dances.

Student Becomes Teacher

During his early years, Joffrey earned a well-deserved reputation as not only a skilled dancer but an excellent teacher. He taught his students not only the dance technique but the interpretation as well. Between 1950 and 1955, Joffrey served as a faculty member at the High School of Performing Arts in New York City. He also served on the board and faculty of the American Ballet Theater School. Joffrey used his skills as a teacher to produce his first ballet. *Persephone,* Joffrey's first ballet, was produced utilizing students of the High School of Performing Arts. He also used the students to assist him in the production of his next two ballets as well. *Persephone,* was staged for the Choreographer's Workshop Program in 1952. His next two ballets, *Scaramouche* and *Umpateedle* were given in 1953 at Jacob's Pillow in Lee, Massachusetts, under the auspices of the Workshop as well. Joffrey's reputation as a consummate and creative professional was growing rapidly.

Professional Beginnings

Finally in 1953 Joffrey realized his long held dream. The Robert Joffrey Ballet Concert was formed in 1953 and first appeared at the YM-YWCA in New York City. Joffrey premiered two new ballets on that occasion, *Pas des Dees-*

ses and *Le Bal Masque*. The ballet company was well-received. In 1955 his company was invited back and again Joffrey used the opportunity to premiere another grouping of ballets. The two ballets premiered on that occasion were *Harpsichord Concerto* and *Pierrot Lunaire*. During these years, Joffrey undertook a variety of choreography assignments. One such assignment included the summer series at the Seattle Aquatheater from 1954 to 1956. Between 1957 and 1962, Joffrey became the resident choreographer for the New York City Opera. Additionally, Joffrey staged dances for the NBC-TV Opera Theater in 1956, 1957, and 1958. Joffrey accomplished all this besides his already heavy teaching load. However, Joffrey realized in order to keep his fledgling company afloat financially, this work was necessary. Joffrey launched his company to tour with six dancers, one of whom was longtime friend, co-founder and associate director, Gerald Arpino, and a borrowed station wagon in 1956. The group immediately set out on a 23 United States city tour. The music they used was prerecorded by another dancer in the group who also played the piano. A crowning achievement for Robert Joffrey and his company came just one year earlier in 1955. Joffrey had attracted enough media and dance world attention to become the first American choreographer invited to stage his works for the prestigious Ballet Lambert in England. Joffrey performed *Pas des Deesses* and *Persephone* while exhibiting there.

National Recognition and Sponsorship

The spring of 1962 brought changing fortune to Joffrey's company. He had renamed his company the Robert Joffrey Ballet and had already completed six national tours with no external financial assistance. Joffrey knew that he had to obtain money from some source as creativity could not be stifled due to lack of resources. His company had now grown to 38 members including a small orchestra. The ballet owned a repertoire of 21 ballets including some by the American choreographers Todd Bolender and Job Sanders. Perhaps the biggest change of fortune for the company came when they were taken under the wing of a wealthy arts patron, Rebekah Harkness Kean. Along with the Harkness Foundation which was founded by Mrs. Kean in 1959 to help American dance, Robert Joffrey was now able to freely work on his first love, choreography and dance. The Harkness Foundation also sponsored Jerome Robbins's Ballet USA which was an African tour by Pearl Primus as well as the late summer seasons of dance in Central Park's Delacorte Theater. The sponsorship and generosity of the Harkness relationship toward Joffrey and his company resulted in great things. They were invited to spend the summer of 1962 in the Harkness estate at Watch Hill, Rhode Island. Six choreographers—Joffrey, Arpino, Nault, Donald Saddler, Brian MacDonald, and Alvin Ailey created a variety of works during that summer. All dances were then previewed that fall and those which were deemed a success were added to Joffrey's company's repertoire complete with set and costumes courtesy of the Harkness Foundation. Additionally Joffrey's company toured the Middle East and Southeast Asia sponsored in part by the President's Special International Program for Cultural Presentations. His company was able to do work such as this due to ties within the

Foundation. Upon concluding a second summer at Watch Hill, the company appeared in a Ballet Gala program at the Harkness Dance Festival in Central Park.

In October of 1963, Joffrey's company was invited to perform at the White House by invitation of President John F. Kennedy. Shortly after, the company began a two-month tour of the Soviet Union sponsored in part by the State Department and the Harkness Foundation. This tour took the company to Moscow Leningrad, Donetsk, Kiev, and Kharkov. They were extremely well received up to the point of a 20 minute standing ovation after their debut in Leningrad. Unfortunately, for Joffrey's ballet though, the return to the United States meant significant changes.

End of Good Fortune

The Joffrey Ballet began a ten-week American tour once they returned to the United States. Near the end of the tour, March 16, 1964, came the news that stunned not only the dance world, but Joffrey's company as well. Rebekah Harkness announced that the Foundation was allocating more than one million dollars for the creation of the Harkness Ballet. Joffrey told the press that he was given an "ultimatum" to change the company's name while he retained artistic control. It was never clear as to how much control he would actually have let alone if he was really in real control over the direction of the company. Joffrey refused to rename his company and as a result he and his company were plunged into poverty. After two years, the relationship with the Harkness Foundation was over. This separation was crippling to the company. Most of the costumes, sets, and scores were owned by the Harkness Foundation even though they were created by Joffrey and his staff. Additionally, many of Joffrey's dancers were still under contract with the Foundation so it made performing for Joffrey's company very difficult, even impossible. Without equipment and dancers the Joffrey Ballet was all but finished.

Rebuilding a Career

Unlike other choreographers of his time, Joffrey possessed a certain resiliency and set about to re-build his company. By September of 1964 the Foundation for American Dance was chartered as a nonprofit, tax-exempt organization to support Joffrey's company. It was headed by a friend of Joffrey's who also served as the business manager during the Harkness years. The foundation immediately secured an emergency grant for thirty-five thousand dollars from the Ford Foundation. The re-organized company appeared at the June 1965 White House Festival of the Arts and then made its public debut in August at Jacob's Pillow. Additionally, Joffrey's company earned the opportunity to become the ballet in residence at the New York City Center when the New York City Ballet moved to the Lincoln Center of the Performing Arts. Though the financial troubles had not ended for Joffrey and his company, but the ballet's renewed eminence and prestige attracted help from important sources including a twenty-five thousand dollar grant from the New York State Council on the Arts which enable the company to revive the 1932 antiwar masterpiece, *The*

Green Table, by Kurt Joss. Additionally, the Ford Foundation provided a three year grant worth $500,000.

Death of a Dancer

Despite the setbacks and his extensive list of duties including artistic director of the City Center Joffrey Ballet and director of the American Ballet Center, Joffrey still found the time to enjoy leisure activities such as skiing and mountain climbing. Robert Joffrey also taught master classes, gave lecture-demonstrations and judged at master regional ballet festivals. He also pioneered the "crossover" ballet which included the rock classic ballet, *Astarte,* in 1967, and *Deuce Coupe,* in 1973. *Deuce Coupe* was developed in part with the modern dance choreographer Twyla Tharp. Joffrey also created *Rememberances* in 1973, *Beautiful Dreamer* in 1975, and *Postcards* in 1980. Robert Joffrey and his company have won many awards including those from the National Academy of Dance Masters at Chicago and from the Dance Masters of America. Robert Joffrey passed away on March 25, 1988, in New York due to ARC- Aids Related Complexes. These included liver and kidney aliments which resulted ultimately in respiratory arrest. However before passing on, Joffrey was able to prove his dictum that "ballet does not belong in the rarified realm of esoteric art, but . . . is a living, evolving form which is part of the 'theater' in its most comprehensive sense." The Joffrey Ballet, by which it is now known, has become one of America's major ballet companies. The company still performs annually based in both New York and Los Angeles. In true dedication, the company continues to pay tribute to their founder and dreamer, the remarkable Robert Joffrey. A man who, whatever the circumstances, never let the fire of his dreams become extinguished.

Further Reading

Holder, Christian, "A Rock Classic," in *Dance Magazine,* Vol. 68, August 1994, p. 28.

Hlibok, Bruce, *Silent Dancer,* Messner, 1981.

Solway, Diane, *A Dance Against Time,* Pocket Books, 1994. □

Jasper Johns

Jasper Johns (born 1930), American painter and sculptor, helped break the hold of abstract expressionism on modern American art and cleared the way for pop art. Versatile in several different artistic fields, he has given the world sculptures, lithographs, and prints, as well as paintings.

Jasper Johns was born in Augusta, Georgia, in the middle of the Great Depression, to Jean Riley Johns and her husband, Jasper, Sr. He was a year old when his mother left his alcoholic father. Shortly afterwards, he had yet another upset when his mother found herself unable to support him and left him with her father in Allendale, South Carolina. He was nine years old when he lost his grandfather, and thereafter, he was shuttled back and forth between his mother and various relatives on his father's side.

In Search of Focus

After graduating from high school in 1946, Johns drifted without noticeable focus for some time. He spent a desultory three semesters at the University of South Carolina, then moved on to New York, where he entered a commercial art school in 1949. Here he stayed until 1951, dropping out when told that his work did not merit a scholarship for which he had applied, but that it would nevertheless be granted to him on grounds of need. Completely on his own, he worked first as a messenger, then as a shipping clerk, and finally, after entering college for just one day, he got a job as a clerk in the Marlboro Bookstore.

In 1954, he was introduced to Robert Rauchenberg, an artist five years older than he was, and the two of them soon became firm friends. Both set up studios in the same building, and both supported themselves by doing collages, drawings and paintings for window displays used by luxury stores such as Tiffany and Bonwit Teller.

A Developing Artist

For the first time in his life, Johns was supporting himself with his art. This change from part-time painting and part-time clerking represented a profound change in the way he viewed his own profession and his own future. "Before, whenever anybody asked me what I did, I said I was going to become an artist," he told Michael Crichton, the author of his biography. "Finally, I decided that I could be going to become an artist forever, all my life. I decided to stop *becoming* and to *be* an artist." He was, in essence, reinventing himself, and as always when drastic measures are undertaken, there was both good and bad in his approach. One of the first things he did was to rip up and destroy every piece of his early work.. Fortunately, four paintings survived this action to give art-lovers an idea of his early creative years.

He began to develop a definite discipline and a method all his own. Intensely interested in experimentation, he learned to work with "encaustic" a method which combines pigments and hot wax before they are applied to the surface of a painting. Plaster casts of different types also began to appear on various paintings. The works most commonly associated with this period were his paintings of flags and of targets. The subjects he chose were oftentimes objects which are often seen, but are usually too commonplace to be closely noticed. Then, he proceeded to give them individuality by adding encaustic textures and other elements which both enhanced and lessened their familiarity at the same time.

In 1955, his painting *Green Target* was exhibited in the Jewish Museum as a part of the *Artists of the New York School: Second Generation* show. But this was not the only place Johns' paintings were to be seen. Along with other artists supplying pictures and drawings for Bonwit Teller's displays, he was invited to show two of his flag paintings in their windows. Johns had the first of many one-man shows in 1958. Paintings of flags, numbers and targets abounded, and all were sold, three of them to New York's Museum of Modern Art.

The year 1958 was noteworthy also for his first sculptures, called, *Flashlight* and *Lightbulb I.* But perhaps one of the year's most enduring achievements was a painting called *Three Flags,* which would be sold to the Whitney Museum in 1980 for the sum of $1 million.

Dada in Development

In 1959 Johns met the artist Marcel Duchamp for the first time. Duchamp, forty seven years Johns' senior, had long been one of the art world's most influential figures. He was a proponent of the school known as Dada, which, before dying out in 1923, had sought to destroy preconceived notions of what was or was not artistically acceptable. Duchamp himself had contributed to the movement, largely by depicting what he called "ready-mades," (utilitarian articles such as snow shovels and bottle racks) signing the resulting pictures, and presenting the result as objects of art rather than objects made for everyday use.

This was an idea that Johns embraced and modified. Like Duchamp he embellished his paintings with "devices," but shied away from Duchamp's spontaneity by making complex arrangements of the objects he used. His *Painted Bronze* consisting of a Savarin coffee can filled with paint brushes, is a perfect example of his careful arrangement.

By the middle of the 1970s, these ideas were joined by a technique called crosshatching. Johns was inspired to try this method after an automobile trip to the Hamptons, during which he saw a car covered with marks flash past in the opposite direction. Adapting it to his own purposes, he began to use it to convey a sense of something swiftly glimpsed, then turned into art.

By this time, Jasper Johns was well-known, and was expanding his interests to embrace new fields.

In 1967, for instance, he became artistic advisor to the Merce Cunningham Dance Company, for which he designed sets, costumes, and occasionally, posters. Cunningham's ballet *Second Hand,* produced in 1980, was just one work bearing the mark of Johns' creativity. Characteristically, he crystallized his experiences on canvas, with a picture called *Dancers on a Plane,* which he completed in 1980.

Another new direction was collaboration in the field of book illustration. In 1973 he started to create 33 etchings for a collection of short stories called *Foirades/Fizzles,* written by Nobel Prize winner Samuel Beckett. Unfortunately, as Johns biographer Richard Francis remarks, though the collection appeared on schedule in 1976 the two men could not compromise on interpretation. Despite their commonly held bleak view of life, the resulting work leaned more towards two parallel works, rather than one seamless one created by two artists working in unison.

The Legendary Jasper Johns

Over the years, the stylistic changes showing Jasper Johns' development as an artist have been seen by the public in so many exhibitions that they have been listed on a CD-ROM. Some of these have been retrospectives, in which the galleries responsible have tried to obtain works from each of his periods, so that earlier and later works can be compared and contrasted. In October 1996, the Museum of Modern Art held a Jasper Johns retrospective that stirred great interest in the art world. Occupying two floors of the museum, the exhibition featured 225 works arranged chronologically.

Johns rarely granted interviews. One friend, who remained anonymous, told the magazine *Vanity Fair,* ". . . he's terrified he might let slip something personal." This is why Johns was so incensed at the appearance of Jill Johnston's 1996 biography, *Privileged Information.* Currently a former friend who has known Johns for some 30 years, Johnston amazed Johns with her interpretation of some of his paintings, which she saw as coded references to his lonely childhood lurking behind the locked gate of his reticence. Because he believed her interpretations of his works to be inaccurate, as well as presumptuous, he forbade publisher Thames & Hudson to reproduce any of his paintings for the book. As always, his motto remained "privacy above all."

Further Reading

Max Kozloff, *Jasper Johns* (1968), is the largest and most recent monograph on the art of Johns; the catalog of the 1964 Jewish Museum exhibition has a fine essay by Alan Solomon. Leo Steinberg, *Jasper Johns* (1963), is a brief study; Mario Amaya, *Pop Art . . . and After* (1966), is recommended for general background.

Additional Sources

Crichton, Michael, *Jasper Johns,* Harry N. Abrams, 1977.

Francis, Richard, *Johns* Abbeville Modern Masters, 1983.

Johnston, Jill, *Jasper Johns: Privileged Information.*

Art in America, April, 1997.

Vanity Fair, September, 1996. □

Andrew Johnson

Andrew Johnson (1808-1875), seventeenth president of the United States, was the first president to be impeached.

Andrew Johnson was born on Dec. 29, 1808, in Raleigh, N.C. After serving an apprenticeship with a tailor, he moved to Greeneville, Tenn., where he opened a tailor shop in 1826. Johnson laboriously taught himself to read and write with the help of Eliza McCardle, whom he married in 1827. His business prospered, and Johnson entered the rough-and-tumble world of politics, becoming a formidable stump speaker.

A Jacksonian Democrat, Johnson moved up through local elective offices to U.S. senator in 1857. In the Senate he crusaded for a homestead law and was bitter when the South blocked its passage. Yet he supported Jefferson Davis's demand for a congressional guarantee of slave property in the territories and in 1860 backed the proslavery presidential candidate.

When the Southern states began seceding, however, Johnson was the only senator from the Confederate states to remain in Congress. In 1862 President Abraham Lincoln appointed him military governor of partly reconquered Tennessee with instructions to begin restoring the state to the Union. Johnson did a good job under trying circumstances. Converted by the Civil War to an antislavery position, he set in motion the machinery for a constitutional convention that abolished slavery in Tennessee (January 1865).

Accident President

In 1864 the Republicans, hoping to attract support from Unionist Democrats, nominated Johnson for vice president. When Lincoln was assassinated in 1865, heavy responsibilities fell upon Johnson. The new president indicated that he would impose severe punishment on "traitors," but his actual policy during 1865 was surprisingly lenient. He extended amnesty to all but the most prominent and wealthy Confederates and provided for the election (by white voters only) of delegates to the conventions to draw up new Southern state constitutions. Subsequently, Johnson granted thousands of pardons to Southerners exempted from the general amnesty.

Under their new constitutions the Southern states elected several prominent Confederates to high office. Some of the states passed "black codes" restricting the rights of freed slaves to a level little better than slavery. Republicans in Congress grew alarmed and feared that the South would regain by Johnson's leniency much of what it had lost in war; they sought a settlement that would provide Federal protection for freedmen and restrict the power of former Confederates. Congress passed a civil rights bill and

a Freedmen's Bureau bill in 1866, but Johnson vetoed both. Congress sent the 14th Amendment to the states for ratification, but Johnson influenced Southern states to reject it.

Impeachment Proceedings

Johnson's belief that "the people" supported his policies should have been shaken by the 1866 congressional elections, which gave the Republicans an overwhelming mandate. Nevertheless, he continued to force Congress to pass every Reconstruction measure over his veto. He tried to weaken enforcement of Reconstruction laws by appointing conservative commanders for some Southern military districts.

An exasperated and vengeful House of Representatives finally impeached Johnson on Feb. 25, 1868. The ostensible grounds were technical transgressions; in reality he was impeached for resisting Congress's will on vital national issues. At Johnson's trial before the Senate, his lawyers proved that he had committed no constitutional crimes or misdemeanors; the verdict for conviction fell one vote short of the necessary two-thirds majority. Johnson served out his term as a powerless president.

Six years later, in 1875, Johnson was elected to the U.S. Senate by Tennessee. However, he suffered a paralytic attack and died on July 31.

Further Reading

Pro-Johnson biographies include Robert W. Winston, *Andrew Johnson* (1928); Lloyd Paul Stryker, *Andrew Johnson* (1929); George F. Milton, *The Age of Hate: Andrew Johnson and the*

Radicals (1930); and Howard K. Beale, *The Critical Year: A Study of Andrew Johnson and Reconstruction* (1930). Recent scholarship is critical of Johnson; see Eric L. McKitrick, *Andrew Johnson and Reconstruction* (1960); LaWanda Cox and John H. Cox, *Politics, Principle, and Prejudice, 1865-66* (1963); and William R. Brock, *An American Crisis: Congress and Reconstruction, 1865-1867* (1963). A collection of essays that attempts balanced appraisal is Eric L. McKitrick, ed., *Andrew Johnson: A Profile* (1969). □

Earvin Johnson, Jr.

Joining the Los Angeles Lakers of the National Basketball Association in 1979, Earvin "Magic" Johnson, Jr. (born 1959) became one of basketball's most popular stars.

In November 1991, Magic Johnson stunned the sportsworld with his announcement that he was infected with the human immune deficiency virus (HIV), the virus that causes the disease acquired immune deficiency syndrome (AIDS). Johnson announced that he was retiring from professional basketball but returned in 1992 and again in 1996. He turned his enthusiasm and leadership skills to business. Among his successes, he developed movie theaters and shopping malls in poor and neglected sections of large cities where no one else would invest.

Johnson was born in 1959 in Lansing, Michigan. He first played organized basketball at Everett High School. In 1977 Johnson and the Everett team won the Michigan state high school championship. Johnson then attended Michigan State University. As a sophomore, he averaged 17.1 points per game and was named an All-American. In 1979 Michigan State won the national collegiate championship by defeating Indiana State University, a team led by future Boston Celtics star Larry Bird. Johnson scored 24 points and was chosen Most Valuable Player (MVP).

Johnson was selected first in the 1979 National Basketball Association (NBA) draft by the Los Angeles Lakers. In his first game for the Lakers he scored 26 points. He then became the first rookie to start in an NBA All-Star game. The Lakers won the 1979-1980 Pacific Division title and went on to play the Philadelphia 76ers for the championship. The Lakers defeated the 76ers for the NBA title, and Johnson became the youngest player ever to be named MVP of the playoffs.

Transformed Lakers into Champions

At 6 feet 9 inches, Johnson became the first big man to dominate play at point guard, a position usually reserved for smaller players. His passing, dribbling skills, and ballhandling technique won him the nickname "Magic." His magnetic personality made him one of the most popular players in the league.

During the 1981-1982 season Laker head coach Paul Westhead designed an offense that focused around center Kareem Abdul-Jabbar. The change upset Johnson, and he asked to be traded, a move that angered some Laker fans who felt that Johnson was selfish. Westhead was replaced

Magic Johnson (left)

by Pat Riley, who stressed the role of the point guard in his offense. Under Riley, Johnson matured into one of the best all-around players in the league. In his first season with Riley, Johnson had more than 700 rebounds and 700 assists, the first player since Wilt Chamberlain to do so. Johnson was again named MVP of the playoffs.

In 1985 the Lakers won their third NBA title, defeating the Boston Celtics and Larry Bird. The sports media liked to refer to the matchup between Bird and Johnson, but Johnson was a guard and Bird a forward. During that same season, Johnson averaged 23.9 points per game, 5 points above his career average. That season he became the first guard in league history to be voted MVP of the regular season. In 1987 the Lakers again defeated the Celtics for the championship, and Johnson was named MVP of the series.

During his 12 years with the Lakers beginning in 1979, John's team went to the playoffs eight times and won five championship titles. Johnson was chosen playoff MVP three times. He was a 12-time All-Star and the 1990 All-Star games' MVP. He scored a total of 17,239 points in 874 games, averaging 19.7 per game. He displayed his defensive skills by pulling down 6,376 rebounds and making 1,698 steals. During the 1990-1991 season he broke Oscar Robertson's assist record with 9,888, finishing the season with a total of 9,921. Not surprisingly, in October 1996, he was named one of the 50 greatest players in the history of the NBA.

Retires after Contracting AIDS

In November 1991, during a routine physical examination for an insurance policy, Johnson found out that he was a carrier of the HIV virus. Johnson admitted that his lifestyle as a sports celebrity included extensive heterosexual promiscuity. However, he never suspected that he might contact HIV, which he thought was limited to homosexual men. The Lakers team physician advised Johnson to quit basketball immediately in order to safeguard his threatened immune system. Johnson shared his discovery with the other players on the Laker team, then announced to the American people that he was HIV-positive.

Johnson's admission stunned his fans. Overnight the likeable player became a spokesman for AIDS awareness. "I want [kids] to understand that safe sex is the way to go, Johnson told *People*. Sometimes we think only gay people can get it [HIV], or that it's not going to happen to me. Here I am. And I'm saying it can happen to anybody, even Magic Johnson." President George Bush appointed Johnson to the National Commission on AIDS, but he resigned to protest what he considered to be the president's lack of support for AIDS research. Johnson continued to speak out and literally raised millions for research to combat the disease. He founded the Magic Johnson Foundation for HIV/AIDS education and coauthored *What You Can Do To Prevent AIDS*.

Retirement, Return, Retirement, and Return

In January 1992, two months after he had retired, Johnson was among the leaders in voting for the 1992 NBA All-Star game. He came out of retirement to play in the game, scoring 25 points, with nine assists, in 29 minutes. There was little surprise when Johnson was named the game's MVP.

In the summer of 1992, Johnson went to Barcelona, Spain, as a member of the United States' basketball team in the 25th Summer Olympics. Dubbed the "Dream Team," by sports journalists, the American entry also included NBA stars Michael Jordan, Larry Bird, John Stockton, Patrick Ewing, Karl Malone, Clyde Drexler, David Robinson, Charles Barkley, Scottie Pippen, Chris Mullen, and Duke University's Christian Laettner. The Dream Team easily won the gold medal. Fans were saddened, however, because they believed that the careers of both Magic Johnson and Larry Bird were over.

But Magic hoped that he still could have a future in basketball. He announced his return to the NBA shortly before the 1992 season began, but only played in five preseason games before retiring for the second time. Johnson cited the other players' concerns about the possibility of being infected while playing and his desire to stay healthy for his family.

Johnson remained active in the basketball world. He purchased five percent of the Lakers, and he formed a charitable—but competitive—basketball team that played exhibition games around the world. He became a vice-president in the Lakers organization and took over as interim head coach of the team for the last part of the 1992-93 season.

But Johnson really preferred playing to coaching. At the beginning of 1996, the rumors of his return proved to be true. Magic Johnson came back to the L. A. Lakers, this time as a power forward and not a point guard. By May 1996, however, Johnson, once again announced his retirement—this time for good. He had discovered that the current players on the team did not idolize him and would not give the ball exclusively to him.

Successful Business Ventures

Johnson showed the same all-star success as an entrepreneur. Like other star athletes, Johnson endorsed products, licensed use of his name, and gave corporate speeches for big fees. He led his Magic Johnson All-Stars round the world, playing exhibition games against foreign basketball teams for substantial profits. Since he lived in L.A, it was only natural for him to get involved in entertainment, possibly as host of of a late night talk show.

However, in a move less typical of a sports star, Johnson also became personally involved in large-scale property development. Among his successes were movie complexes and shopping centers in inner-city areas where no one else wanted to invest. In June 1995, Johnson partnered with Sony to open the 12-screen Magic Theatres multiplex in a predominantly black section of Los Angeles. The project became one of the top grossing movie outlets in America and helped boost sales and occupancy at the mall in which it was located. In 1997, Johnson opened another movie complex in southwest Atlanta. Magic movie marquees were under construction in Houston and Cleveland, and Johnson announced plans for 14 new multiplexes in 10 other cities. His company, Johnson Development went on to buy entire shopping centers in poor communties in Las Vegas and Los Angeles.

Johnson earned goodwill for helping spiff up and bringing jobs to the inner cities. His ventures also brought him great personal wealth. *Time* quoted him as saying "It's important to help the community, but the number one goal here is to make money. This is not charity."

Johnson's personal involvement in business affairs got its impetus early in his hoop career. He realized he had signed away his talents for too low a salary. And he also witnessed the fleecing of fellow Laker Kareem Abdul-Jabbar, who lost millions to unscrupulous financial advisers. In the mid-1980s, Johnson dumped his own advisers and demanded monthly statements from his new ones. By 1996, he had a net worth of more than $100 million.

Living with HIV

In September 1991, just before he learned he had HIV, Johnson wed longtime friend Earletha "Cookie" Kelly. The couple had a son in 1993 and adopted a daughter in 1995. Johnson also has a son from a previous relationship who spends the summers with him. Ever optimistic, Johnson believed that the right combination of medicine, diet, and exercise would help him to survive until a cure for AIDS was found.

Johnson's physicians announced in early 1997 that the AIDS virus in his body had been reduced to undetectable levels. They attributed the improvement to the use of powerful drugs, including protese inhibitors. His wife Cookie gave the credit to God stating, "The Lord has definitely healed Earvin. Doctors think it's the medicine. We claim it in the name of Jesus." The Johnsons attended the West Angles Church of God in Christ, to which he donated $5 million in 1995.

Further Reading

Two early biographies, *Magic* with Richard Levin (1983) and *Magic's Touch* with Roy S. Johnson (1989) are interesting but were written before the devastating discovery that ended Johnson's career. An important and well written biography is *Magic Johnson: My Life* (1992). Deeply moving, the book contains a message to young persons that shows Johnson's sincere concern for them. For more about the Olympic "Dream Team" readers should see *The Golden Boys* by Cameron Smith (1992).

Also see Blatt, Howard, *Magic! Against the Odds* (Pocket Books, 1996); "The Magic and the Money," *Forbes,* December 16, 1996, p. 264-266; and Monroe, Sylvester, "Post-game show," *Time,* March 17, 1997, p. 38-39. □

Jack Johnson

Jack Johnson (1878-1946) became the first African American heavyweight champion after winning the crown from Tommy Burns in Sydney, Australia on December 26, 1908. As a result of this victory, he became the center of a bitter racial controversy with the American public clamoring for the former white champion, Jim Jeffries, to come out of retirement and recapture the crown.

Jack Johnson, who became the first black heavyweight boxing champion in the world in 1908, was the preeminent American sports personality of his era, a man whose success in the ring spurred a worldwide search, tinged with bigotry, for a "Great White Hope" to defeat him. Handsome, successful, and personable, Johnson was known as much for his exploits outside of the ring as for his boxing skills. He married three white women in a time when such interracial unions resulted in denunciations of him from the floor of the United States Congress. He made big money, spent it lavishly, and lived grandly. And in doing so he gained admirers and detractors all over the world and became, quite simply, one of the best known men of the early twentieth century.

Johnson's autobiography, *Jack Johnson, In the Ring and Out,* remains the key source for information about his early life. In it he writes, "I am astounded when I realize that there are few men in any period of the world's history, who have led a more varied or intense existence than I." Like Muhammad Ali after him, Johnson was not shy about promoting himself or his exploits. Little is known of his early family life; Johnson writes that his three sisters and one brother had little effect on his life. His father was a janitor who was also known to have preached in local churches. He appears to have been closest to his mother, Tiny Johnson, and talks with pride of buying her a house with some of the purses he collected in his long boxing career.

When he was only 12 years old Johnson determined to leave his hometown of Galveston, Texas, and see the world, especially New York City. But getting to the city was difficult. He jumped a freight train, but was discovered, beaten, and thrown off. He jumped a boat, but ended up in Key West and worked as a fisherman. Finally, he hopped a freighter, worked as a cook on board, and reached New York. From there he went to Boston, where he worked in a stable, then hightailed it back to Galveston, where he became a dockworker at the age of 13.

Fought to Survive

Of his co-workers on the Texas waterfront, Johnson wrote, "To them, fighting was one of the important functions of existence. They fought upon every occasion and on any pretext. . . . Although I was one of the youngest in this rough and aggressive group, I had to do my share of fighting." After a series of street fights in Galveston, Johnson went to Dallas where he started to train as a boxer. Returning to Galveston, he began fighting his first series of bouts. After whipping a man named Pierson—known throughout Galveston as the toughest man in town—Johnson's reputation was firmly fixed. And he had a new nickname, one that he would carry throughout his life, "Lil' Arthur."

Johnson soon outgrew Galveston; he had fought every tough guy in town. So he travelled to Springfield, Illinois, and then to Chicago, fighting in hastily arranged bouts for food and lodging. He was 17 years old when he fought a man named "Klondike" and lost. Johnson claimed that the loss marked the time when he decided he could make a living as a fighter. From Chicago, he went to New York by way of Pittsburgh, fighting all the while. Then it was back to Texas, across the South, and finally out to Denver where he traveled about with a group of other boxers, taking on all comers in all weight classes.

Johnson had been married to a black woman, Mary Austin, since 1898, but in Colorado their marriage broke up, sending Johnson into a state of depression. They had a brief reconciliation, but Johnson writes in his autobiography that the troubles he had with women "led me to forswear colored women and to determine that my lot henceforth would be cast only with white women." In a United States where Jim Crow was the law of the land, that decision would get him into a great deal of trouble. In fact, after Johnson's marriage to the white woman, Etta Duryea, in 1911, a Georgia Congressman, Seaborn Roddenberry, was so incensed he tried to get passed a constitutional amendment banning racial intermarriage. His bill died.

Back in Colorado, Johnson continued to fight while serving as camp cook for the traveling stable of boxers. Eventually he moved west, won the world's light heavyweight championship from a boxer named George Gardiner and began to set his sights on the heavyweight championship of the world. That would prove to be an elusive goal. By the end of 1906, Johnson had fought in 56 official fights and lost only two. But no one would give him a shot at the title. "I had demonstrated my strength, speed and skill, but still faced many obstacles, the principle one of which was the customary prejudice because of my race," he wrote. To win the championship, he had to defeat the reigning champ, Tommy Burns, so Johnson began a two-year quest to get that match.

Champion of the World

Johnson fought in Australia and England and began to generate a worldwide following. The press began to criticize Burns for avoiding Johnson. Finally the fight was set for December 26, 1908, in Sydney, Australia. Thirty thousand people attended the bout; the purse was $35,000, of which only $5,000 went to Johnson. In another concession to get the bout underway, Johnson had to agree to let Burns's manager referee the fight. Even under that manifestly unfair condition Johnson won; the police stopped the fight in the 14th round and Johnson was declared champ.

"A new champion had arrived and that new champion was Jack Johnson," he wrote in his autobiography. "I had attained my life's ambition. The little Galveston colored boy had defeated the world's champion boxer and, for the first and only time in history, a black man held one of the greatest honors which exists in the field of sports and athletics—an honor for which white men had contested many times and which they held as a dear and most desirable one. . . . To me it was not a racial triumph, but there were those who were to take this view of the situation, and almost immediately a great hue and cry went up because a colored man was holding the championship."

Thus began the era of the "Great White Hope," the name given to the white man who could take the championship belt away from Johnson. Johnson wrote that he "regretted" the racial aspect of the search for a new contender but that he was willing to take on anyone, no matter their color. While the search went on, Johnson fought a few minor bouts and engaged in his second career: that of music hall performer. Throughout his professional life, Johnson was booked on the vaudeville and lecture circuit, singing and dancing, telling stories and giving boxing exhibitions. He performed across the United States and in Europe.

But the life of the stage was not what the public expected of Johnson. They expected him to fight and a good number of them, especially whites upset with Johnson's rich living style and his dating of white women, expected him to be "put in his place" by a white fighter. The ultimate White Hope was Jim Jeffries, the retired heavyweight champ. When Jeffries retired he had anointed Burns as his replacement. With Burns thoroughly beaten by Johnson, the pressure was on Jeffries to come out of retirement and defend the title, and his race. One of the prime movers behind the White Hope search was the novelist Jack London. In an *Ebony* magazine article about the Johnson-Jeffries bout, London is quoted as writing after the Burns fight, "But one thing now remains. Jim Jeffries must now emerge from his Alfalfa farm and remove that golden smile from Jack Johnson's face. Jeff, it's up to you. The White Man must be rescued!"

Finally, Jeffries agreed to come out of retirement. The fight was originally set for California, but the governor there intervened and banned the match. The match was then set for Reno, Nevada, on July 4, 1910. When they climbed into the ring, the 32-year-old Johnson was a trim 208 pounds, while the 35-year-old Jeffries weighed 230 pounds. At 2:45 pm the fight began in front of tens of thousands of people who had gathered under the hot sun. In the weeks preceding the fight, editorial writers had warned that a Johnson victory would give blacks the wrong ideas: that African Americans might get it into their heads to rebel against oppression with their fists like Johnson. There was fear of rioting no matter which way the fight decision went.

According to *Ebony*, crowds around the world gathered outside of telegraph offices to hear updates of the fight taking place in Reno. The fight itself was, by all accounts, a great one. Jeffries was known for his famous crouch, a bent-over way of boxing. But Johnson neutralized this strategy quickly and landed numerous blows to Jeffries' face. He also taunted the ex-champ, saying, "Let me see what you've got," or "Do something." Johnson recalled in his autobiography, "I recall that occasionally I took time during the exchange of these blows to suggest to telegraph operators what to tell their newspapers." Johnson was "trash talking" before it became fashionable and while some saw his words as evidence that he was in total control of the match, others—mainly whites—never forgave him for it.

In the *New York Times,* in an article that appeared the day after Johnson died in 1946, sports columnist Arthur Daley had little good to say about Johnson. He called Johnson's taunting of Jeffries an example of Johnson's "inherent meanness" and he talked about the "the stain that Lil' Arthur left on boxing and on his race." It seems that few people could forgive Johnson for what he had done in Reno that hot July day in 1910, when he knocked Jeffries out in the 15th round. In doing so, Johnson collected $60,000, as well as picture rights and bonuses that brought his total take to $120,000, a good sized sum in those days.

The predictions of violence in America came true: race riots erupted in many cities. Whites and blacks engaged in shoot outs and fistfights. As for Johnson, he took to the road to fulfill theatrical contracts, and when he had made some good money doing that, he traveled to London and Paris with his wife, Etta Duryea, who he had married in 1909. Johnson's vanity is evident when he describes his London trip, which occurred during the coronation of King George V: "Despite the fact that the King and his coronation were the center of attention, when my car traveled along London streets and it was announced that I was in sight, the attention of the crowds was turned upon me, and as long as I was in view the coronation ceremonies were forgotten while crowds milled and struggled for a glance at me."

When Johnson returned to the states, he opened a cabaret in Chicago. All races were welcome in his club. After about a year in Chicago, in September of 1912, Johnson's wife Etta committed suicide by shooting herself in the head. It was a great blow to the champ and his interest in boxing and business waned.

Exiled and a Questionable Defeat

Two months later Johnson would face an even greater personal challenge. He was arrested for violating the Mann Act, the statute prohibiting the transportation of women across state lines for unlawful purposes. The woman in question was Belle Schreiber, an old acquaintance of Johnson's. The problem with the charge is that Johnson and Schreiber were an item before the Mann Act became law in June of 1910. "It was a rank frame up," Johnson recalled in his memoirs. "The charges were based upon a law that was not in effect at the time Belle and I had been together, and legally was not operative against me."

That did not stop the courts from finding Johnson guilty in May of 1913, nor did it keep the judge from imposing a sentence of one year and one day in prison, and a fine of $1,000. In the meantime, Johnson had married Lucille Cameron, his 18-year-old white secretary. When the verdict was handed down, Johnson arranged for he and his wife to travel to Canada and, from there, to Paris. For the next seven years, Johnson was an exile from the United States, living in Europe, Mexico, and South America. His lifestyle overseas was lavish, and his exploits, including bullfighting, racing cars, performing on stage, and boxing, continued to receive worldwide attention. While in exile, his mother died, an event which saddened him very much.

On April 5, 1915, Johnson fought Jess Willard in Havana, Cuba. Willard won the bout, and the championship from Johnson, but Johnson would always claim that he threw the fight. He said that he was promised that he could return to the United States and avoid his year-and-a-day jail term if he would give up the championship to Willard, the latest in a line of White Hopes. Whether Johnson did indeed throw the fight, or whether he just got beat, has been a point of contention for many boxing observers since the fight ended by a knockout in the 26th round. "I could have disposed of him long before the final round," Johnson wrote of Willard. John Lardner in *Newsweek* recalled that Willard described his victory by saying, "I hit him [Johnson] a good uppercut." But Lardner goes on to write, "Very few people outside of Willard believe this, and maybe Jess doesn't either."

Whether fixed or fair, the bout cost Johnson the championship and did not end his exile. He wandered the globe for five more years before giving himself up to U.S. authorities in 1920. He served eight months in Leavenworth prison and became the physical director of the inmates, supervising track meets, baseball games, and fight training. While behind bars he continued to track his business interests and he used the time to think long and hard about the prison experience. Johnson came to believe that prison was good for the hardened criminal. But for the man who erred slightly in life, prison does nothing more than to arouse bitterness, Johnson felt. In any event, when he was released from Leavenworth, Johnson was met at the prison gates by a marching band and a horde of friends.

By 1921, Johnson had ended his exile, paid his debt to society, and began a new series of theatrical engagements. In 1924 he and his third wife were divorced and Johnson returned to boxing. He soon won a unanimous decision over a fighter named Homer Smith of Kalamazoo, Michigan. Two years later, at age 48, he beat a 24-year-old boxer named Pat Lester in Mexico.

In his autobiography, Johnson wrote, "I have always been an ardent motorist." He had cars when people were still riding bicycles and horses. Following his release from prison, the only run-ins with the law Johnson had came when he was behind the wheel of a car driving too fast. Five times cars rolled on top of Johnson and five times he survived. The sixth time he was not so lucky. According to the *New York Times* report of his death, Johnson was driving on Highway 1 near Raleigh, North Carolina, on June 10, 1946, when he lost control of his car, which hit a light pole and overturned. He died three hours later.

In the years before his death, Johnson had lectured at Hubert's Museum on Forty Second Street in New York. It was a seedy job that his friends and observers said allowed the great ex-champ to earn "bread and beer money." His last years were made enjoyable by his marriage to Irene Pineau in 1925. Johnson called her his true love.

The *Times* called Johnson, "One of the craftiest boxers known to the ring, recognized by many as one of the five outstanding heavyweight champions of all time." Johnson, who was cocky, confident, and talented, would not have disagreed. But as John Lardner wrote in *Newsweek* after Johnson died, the champ's interest in how he would be remembered ranged beyond boxing. "Whatever you write about me," Lardner remembered Johnson telling him, "just please remember that I'm a man, and a good one."

Further Reading

Johnson, Jack, *Jack Johnson, In the Ring and Out,* Proteus Publishing, 1977.

Ebony, April 1994, pp. 86-98.

Newsweek, June 24, 1946, p. 90.

New York Times, June 11, 1946, p. 1; June 12, 1946, p. 20. ☐

James Weldon Johnson

African American man of letters James Weldon Johnson (1871-1938) was also a teacher, politician, and lawyer. He is best known for his novel, *The Autobiography of an Ex-Colored Man,* and a book of poems, *God's Trombones.*

O n June 17, 1871, James Weldon Johnson was born in Jacksonville, Fla. His father, a restaurant headwaiter, was entirely self-taught; his mother was a musician and school teacher. After taking his bachelor of arts degree at Atlanta University in 1894, Johnson taught in the public school for blacks in Jacksonville. Meanwhile he studied law and helped establish the first daily African American newspaper in his native city.

In 1898 Johnson joined his older brother, J. Rosamond Johnson, in New York City. Collaborating with his brother, a skilled musician, he wrote such hits as "Tell Me, Dusky Maiden," "Nobody's Looking but the Owl and the Moon," and "Oh, Didn't He Ramble." Some of Johnson's early poetry was published in the *Century* and the *Bookman.* He took his master of arts degree from Atlanta University in 1904.

Returning from a European theatrical tour in 1904, Johnson joined Theodore Roosevelt's successful presidential campaign and was rewarded with the appointment as U.S. consul at Puerto Cabello, Venezuela, in 1907. Two years later he went to Nicaragua in this same capacity. There he wrote his only novel, *The Autobiography of an Ex-Colored Man.* First published in 1912, the book established Johnson's concern with the social problems that beset black people and his commitment to finding solutions. He had married Grace Nail in 1910.

In 1916 Johnson joined the staff of the National Association for the Advancement of Colored People (NAACP) and, becoming general secretary in 1920, continued there until 1930. He was a militant crusader for black Americans, demanding political and cultural equality. Though his fight for congressional passage of the Dyer Antilynching Bill was unsuccessful, it stirred the South to action to abolish lynching.

Johnson's *Fifty Years and Other Poems* was published in 1917, and in 1920 a book on politics, *Self-determining Haiti,* appeared. He presented the *Book of American Negro Poetry* in 1922. This was a pioneering anthology, like his *Book of American Negro Spirituals,* which, with piano arrangements by his brother, appeared in 1925. (The two volumes had their ninth printing in 1964). But the book that brought him national attention as a poet was *God's Trombones: Seven Negro Sermons in Verse* (1927). Here Johnson broke new literary ground by discarding Negro dialect, employing instead the "native idiom of Negro speech" without distortion. *Black Manhattan,* a kind of memoir, was published in 1930, the year Johnson became professor of

creative literature at Fisk University in Nashville, Tenn. He was also visiting professor of creative literature at New York University from 1934 until his death. His autobiography, *Along This Way* (1933), went through eight printings in 10 years. His last book, *St. Peter Relates an Incident* (1935), is a poetic satire on race prejudice.

Johnson won the W. E. B. Du Bois Prize for Negro literature in 1934, the Spingarn Medal twice, and the Harmon Award for distinguished achievement. He died in an automobile accident on June 26, 1938. In 1950 the James Weldon Johnson Memorial Collection of Negro Arts and Letters was founded in the Yale University Library.

Further Reading

Along This Way: The Autobiography of James Weldon Johnson (1933) is the best factual source. Johnson's *Black Manhattan* (1930) gives additional material. Sterling A. Brown, Arthur P. Davis, and Ulysses Lee, *Negro Caravan* (1940), and James A. Emanuel and Theodore Gross, eds., *Dark Symphony: Negro Literature in America* (1968), contain brief critical treatment. More extensive treatment is in Saunders Redding, *To Make a Poet Black* (1939).

Additional Sources

Egypt, Ophelia Settle, *James Weldon Johnson,* New York, Crowell 1974.

Johnson, James Weldon, *Along This Way: The Autobiography of James Weldon Johnson,* New York, Penguin Books, 1990. ☐

John Harold Johnson

John Harold Johnson (born 1918), an African American entrepreneur, turned a five hundred dollar loan into a multimillion-dollar business empire and became one of the richest men in the United States. He headed the most prosperous and powerful African American publishing company with such titles as *Ebony, Jet, Ebony Man, EM,* and *Ebony Jr.,* as part of his journalistic successes.

John H. Johnson was born in Arkansas City, Arkansas, on January 19, 1918. When he was six years old, his father died, so Johnson was raised by his mother and stepfather. He attended an overcrowded and segregated elementary school. Such was his love of learning, he repeated the eighth grade rather than discontinue his education, since there was no public high school for African Americans in his community. After a visit with his mother to the Chicago World's Fair, they decided that opportunities in the North were more plentiful than in the South. Facing poverty on every side in Arkansas during the Great Depression, the family made the move to Chicago, Illinois, in 1933 to try to find work and for Johnson to continue his education. Johnson entered DuSable High School while his mother and step-father scoured the city for jobs during the day. He looked for work after school and during the summer. Their attempts were un-rewarded. His mother was not even able to find any domestic work, the work that was generally available when all else failed. To support themselves the family applied for welfare, which they received for two years until Johnson's stepfather was finally able to obtain a position with the

Works Projects Administration (WPA) and Johnson himself secured a job with the National Youth Administration.

Johnson endured much teasing and taunting at his high school for his ragged clothes and country ways. This only fueled his already formidable determination to "make something of himself". Johnson's high school career was distinguished by the leadership qualities he demonstrated as student council president and as editor of the school newspaper and class yearbook. After he graduated in 1936, he was offered a tuition scholarship to the University of Chicago, but he thought he would have to decline it, because he could not figure out a way to pay for expenses other than tuition. Because of his achievements in high school, Johnson was invited to speak at dinner held by the Urban League. When the president of the Supreme Life Insurance Company, Harry Pace, heard Johnson's speech, he was so impressed with the young man that he offered Johnson a job so that he would be able to use the scholarship.

Johnson began as an office boy at Supreme Life and within two years had become Pace's assistant. His duties included preparing a monthly digest of newspaper articles. Johnson began to wonder if other people in the community might not enjoy the same type of service. He conceived of a publication patterned after *Reader's Digest.* His work at Supreme also gave him the opportunity to see the day-to-day operations of an African American-owned business and fostered his dream of starting a business of his own.

Once the idea of *Negro Digest* occurred to him, it began to seem like a "black gold mine", Johnson stated in his autobiography *Succeeding against the Odds.* Johnson remained enthusiastic even though he was discouraged on all sides from doing so. Only his mother, a woman with biblical faith and deep religious convictions, as well as a powerful belief in her son, supported his vision and allowed him to use her furniture as collateral for a $500 loan. He used this loan to publish the first edition of *Negro Digest* in 1942.

Johnson had a problem with distribution until he teamed up with Joseph Levy a magazine distributor who was impressed with him. Levy provided valuable marketing tips and opened the doors that allowed the new digest to reach newsstands in other urban centers. Within six months circulation had reached 50,000. This publication covered African American history, literature, arts, and cultural issues. After several decades of publication its name was changed to *Black World.*

Although that publication achieved some success and at its height had a circulation of more than 100,000, it could not be compared with Johnson's subsequent publication, *Ebony* magazine, which was so popular that its initial run of 25,000 copies easily sold out. The articles in *Ebony,* which were designed to look like those in *LIFE* or *Look* magazines, emphasized the achievements of successful African American. Photo essays about current events and articles about race relations were also included in the magazine. Initially focused on the rich and famous in the African American community, Johnson expanded the reporting to include issues such as "the white problem in America", African American militancy, crimes by African Americans against

African Americans, civil rights legislation, freedom rides and marches, and other aspects of segregation and discrimination. Trained historians were recruited for the magazine's staff so that the contributions of African American Americans to the history of the United States could be adequately documented. African American models were used in the magazine's advertisements and a conscious effort was made to portray positive aspects of African American life and culture. Everything in the magazine was addressed to the African American consumer. Johnson maintained that *Ebony*'s success was due to the positive image of African Americans that it offered.

In 1950, Johnson launched *Tan* magazine—a true confessions type magazine and in 1951, *Jet*—a weekly news digest. Later publications included *African American Stars* and *Ebony Jr.*—a children's magazine. Although all of the magazines achieved a measure of success, none was able to compete with *Ebony,* which in its 40th year of publication had a circulation of 2,300,000 and was the primary reason that Johnson was considered one of the 400 richest individuals in the United States. In 1972, he was named publisher of the year by the major magazine publishers in the United States.

Johnson expanded his business interests to areas other than his magazines. He became chairperson and chief executive officer of the Supreme Life Insurance Company, where he had begun as part-time office boy. He developed a line of cosmetics, purchased three radio stations, and started a book publishing company, and a television production company. He served on the board of directors of several major businesses, such as the Greyhound Corporation, and received numerous honors and awards for his achievements, including the National Association for the Advancement of Colored People's Spingarn Medal in 1966 for his contributions in the area of race relations.

In 1993, Johnson published his autobiography wherein he states "if it could happen to a Black boy from Arkansas it could happen to anyone". This publication celebrated the 50th anniversary of his publishing company.

In 1995, Johnson received the Communication Award for Communication on the occasion of Ebony magazine's 50th anniversary. Alfred C. Sykes, the chairman of the Center for Communication and president of Hearst Media Technology said "Mr. Johnson is a role model for many young people today, an example of how hard work, commitment and belief in oneself can lead to outstanding achievement. He rose from disadvantaged circumstances to achieve success in both business and national service during a time when great obstacles were placed in his path".

Because of his influential position in the African American community, Johnson was invited by the U.S. government to participate in several international missions. In 1959, he accompanied the vice president of the United States on a mission to Russia and Poland. He was appointed special ambassador to represent the United States at the independence ceremonies in the Ivory Coast in 1961 and in Kenya in 1963. Over the years Johnson had devoted a portion of several issues of *Ebony* to articles relating to African independence movements, but in August 1976 he dedicated an entire special issue to the subject "Africa, the Continent of the Future".

In 1996, President Bill Clinton bestowed the Presidential Medal of Freedom on Johnson and in 1997 Johnson was inducted into the Junior Achievement National Business Hall of Fame.

Further Reading

Johnson's autobiography *Succeeding Against the Odds* was published in 1989; biographical materials also appear in all of his publications *Ebony, Jet, Black World,*; other articles have appeared in *Black Enterprise, Chicago Tribune, Forbes, Fortune. Newsweek, LA Times, New York Post, Time, Printer's Ink, and Ebony Negro Almanac* (1976); some information about him is available in *The Shaping of African American America* (1975) by Lerone Bennett, Jr.; and in *African American Capitalism, Strategy for Business in the Ghetto* (1969) by Theodore L. Cross. □

Lyndon Baines Johnson

As the thirty-sixth president of the United States, Lyndon Baines Johnson (1908-1973) created new programs in health, education, human rights, and conservation and attacked the crushing 20th-century problems of urban blight and poverty with what he called the "War on Poverty."

Most commentators account Lyndon Johnson as one of America's most experienced and politically skilled presidents. He sponsored a flood of new legislation designed to better the quality of life among the disadvantaged and the dispossessed of the nation. In foreign policy he set about to strengthen regional arrangements of power so that new and small nations might develop their own form of political society without fear of intrusion from their more powerful neighbors. He inherited an American commitment in South Vietnam, and his determination to preserve the independence of that beleaguered country led to virulent attacks and, finally, his momentous decision not to seek reelection.

Lyndon Johnson was born on Aug. 27, 1908, near Johnson City, Texas, the small community founded by his forebears. Life was hard and plain in the Texas hill country at this time. Johnson's father struggled to raise his two sons and three daughters. His mother was a gentle woman, who encouraged her children to love books and gave them a sense of duty and responsibility. Johnson graduated from Southwest State Teachers College in San Marcos, Tex., with a bachelor of science degree, having combined his studies with a job teaching Mexican-American children.

Johnson's early teaching assignments were at Pearsall, Tex., and in the Houston high schools. In 1931, politics beckoned. He went to Washington, D.C., as secretary to Texas congressman Richard Kleberg. Almost immediately Johnson's talent for attracting affection and respect became visible. He was elected Speaker of the "Little Congress," an assembly of congressional secretaries on Capitol Hill.

On Nov. 17, 1934, an event occurred which Johnson always described as the most notable triumph of his life: he

married Claudia (Lady Bird) Taylor of Karnak, Texas. She became his partner, confidant, and counselor, and from her, Johnson drew strength and love and reserves of support that never faltered.

Johnson's ultimate destiny was beginning to take shape. At age 27, he was already exhibiting his characteristic traits of energy, intellect, and tenacity when he resigned as a congressional secretary in 1935 to become the Texas director of the National Youth Administration. The origins of the later Johnson can be located in his conduct of this office; he surrounded himself with bright, young men and invested his duties with a 24-hour torrent of activity.

Rising through Congress

In 1937, the congressman from Texas's Tenth District died suddenly. When a special election was called to select a successor, Johnson hesitated only slightly. His wife provided campaign funds from her inheritance, and Johnson leaped into a race crowded with eight opponents. The only candidate to support President Franklin Roosevelt's court-packing plan, he did so with such vigor that the eyes of the nation were drawn to the outcome, and none watched it with more intensity than Roosevelt himself. To the amazement of political veterans, the 28-year-old Johnson won the race.

President Roosevelt, in Texas on a fishing trip, was so elated that he invited Johnson to accompany him back to Washington, D.C. Thus, Johnson became his personal protégé. With the aid of the powerful House Speaker Sam Rayburn of Texas and the continuing support of the Presi-

dent, Johnson was brought into the councils of ruling establishmentarians of the House of Representatives.

In 1941, Johnson entered another special election, this time for a Senate seat made vacant by a death. Texans were surprised by the campaign he launched by helicopter. Nearly every community watched the tall, smiling Johnson alight from his helicopter. In a bitter campaign Johnson lost by 1,311 votes to that bizarre political phenomenon Governor W. Lee ("Pass the Biscuits Pappy") O'Daniel.

There was little time for Johnson to lick his wounds. That December he became the first member of Congress to enter active military duty. He joined the Navy and in 1942 received the Silver Star for gallantry in a bombing mission over New Guinea. When President Roosevelt ordered all congressmen back to the capital in 1942, Johnson reentered the House.

In 1948, Johnson's restless quest for higher office was finally successful. In a savagely fought senatorial campaign, he defeated a former governor of Texas by a celebrated margin of 87 votes. The elders of the Senate soon recognized that Johnson was no ordinary rookie senator. He did his homework, was knowledgable on every item that confronted the Senate, and was in instant command of all the nuances and subtleties of every important piece of legislation.

In January 1951, just 3 years into his first term, Johnson was elevated to Democratic "whip" (assistant minority leader). Regarding his age and tenure, no similar selection had ever been made in the history of the Senate. In 1953, when the post of minority leader in the Senate opened up Democratic senators without hesitation chose Johnson to take charge. With the congressional elections of 1954, the Democrats took command of both houses. And with this new alignment, Johnson again set a record as the youngest man ever to become majority leader.

The Johnson legend of leadership now became visible to the nation. Not since the early days of the republic had one man assumed such clear direction over the course and affairs of the Senate. Operating his office around the clock, intimately aware of all that transpired, and firmly fixed in his intent and design, Johnson was the "complete Senate leader." Now one voice spoke for the Democrats, as Johnson became the "second most powerful man in Washington, D.C."

The habits of work and discipline that would later confound the nation when Johnson became president were now on display in the Senate chamber. He handled the Senate with confidence and skill. The Republican opposition found it impossible to outflank this majority leader; legislation opposed by Johnson rarely found acceptance by the Senate. He encouraged new, young senators and found coveted spots for them on important committees.

Johnson led the first civil rights bill in 82 years through the Senate. He guided to final victory the first space legislation in the National Aeronautics and Space Act of 1958. In 1958, designated by President Dwight Eisenhower to represent the United States at the United Nations, he presented the resolution calling for the peaceful exploration of outer space. He exposed wastes in defense procurement during the Korean War and conducted defense hearings that were a model of accuracy and dispassionate scrutiny.

In 1960, Johnson briefly opposed John F. Kennedy for the Democratic presidential nomination; then Kennedy electrified the country by choosing Johnson as his vice-presidential running mate. While some Kennedy supporters grumbled, experts later agreed that Johnson's relentless campaigning in Texas and throughout the South had provided Kennedy with his winning margin.

Serving as Vice President

As vice-president, Johnson had important assignments. One of his principal tasks was the burgeoning space program, which was overshadowed by Russian triumphs with *Sputnik* and subsequent innovations that put the United States in an inferior role. Regarding civil rights, as chairman of the Equal Employment Opportunity forces, Johnson surprised many critics by putting uncompromising pressure on American industry. At the President's request, he made fact-finding trips to Berlin and to the Far East.

On Nov. 22, 1963, President Kennedy was assassinated in Dallas. Aboard the plane *Air Force One* at Love Field in Dallas, Johnson took the presidential oath of office on November 23. Giving orders to take off seconds later, the new president flew back to Washington to take command of the government, while the nation grieved for its fallen leader.

Filling the Presidency

Five days after taking office, President Johnson appeared before a joint session of the Congress. Speaking with firmness and controlled passion, he pledged "we shall continue." Important legislation submitted by President Kennedy to the Congress, currently bottled up and seemingly stymied in various committees of both houses, was met by Johnson's deliberate and concentrated action. The new president—meeting round the clock with staff, Cabinet, and congressmen—unbuckled key legislation, so that within a few short months the tax cut and the civil rights bills were passed by Congress and signed by the President.

Six months after assuming the presidency, Johnson announced his concept of the "Great Society." The areas he considered vital were health and education; the whole complex of the urban society, with its accompanying ills of ghettos, pollution, housing, and transportation; civil rights; and conservation.

Johnson took his innovative domestic programs to the nation in the election of 1964. Meanwhile, the American involvement in Vietnam, sanctioned by three presidents, became an issue. Senator Barry Goldwater chastised Johnson for his liberal approach to domestic problems and suggested a massive step-up in the bombing of North Vietnam. Johnson traversed the nation and convinced it that his leadership was of such caliber that the voters could not afford to drive him from office. He won by a margin of almost 16 million votes, more than 61 percent of the total vote, the widest margin in totals and percentage of any presidential election in American history.

Administration Achievements

Barely pausing, the President, reinforced by this clear mandate, began a legislative program which was rivaled in scope and form only by Franklin Roosevelt's New Deal a generation earlier. Between 1965 and 1968 more than 207 landmark bills were passed by the Congress.

In education, Johnson's administration tripled expenditures. By the end of 1968, 1.5 million students were receiving Federal aid to help them gain their college degrees; over 10 million people learned new skills through vocational education; and 19,000 school districts received special help under the Elementary and Secondary Education Act. More than 600,000 disabled citizens were trained through vocational rehabilitation programs. Head Start and other preschool programs brought specific assistance to more than 2 million children.

In the area of health, Johnson's administration increased Federal expenditures from $4 billion to $14 billion in 4 years. More than 20 million Americans were covered by Medicare, and more than 7 million received its benefits. About 31 million children were vaccinated against four severe diseases, reducing by 50 percent the number of children who suffered from these diseases, and more than 3 million children received health care under Medicaid in one year. Some 286 community mental health centers were built. More than 390,000 mothers and 680,000 infants received care through the Maternal and Child Health programs. Some 460,000 handicapped children were treated under the Crippled Children's Program.

Fighting poverty, the Johnson administration lifted more than 6,000,000 Americans out of the poverty depths. Over 100,000 young men and women completed Job Corps training; 2.2 million needy Americans were helped under the Food Stamp Program; school children benefited from the School Milk and School Lunch programs.

In the area of human and civil rights, the Voting Rights Act was passed in 1965, and within 3 years nearly 1 million Negroes registered to vote in the South. More than 98 percent of all the nation's hospitals agreed to provide services without discrimination. More than 28 percent of all Negro families by 1968 earned about $7,000 a year, doubling the 1960 figure. Some 35 percent more Negroes found professional, technical, and managerial jobs between 1964 and 1968.

In housing, in 4 years the Johnson administration generated the construction of 5.5 million new homes. Direct Federal expenditures for housing and community development increased from $635 million to nearly $3 billion. Two million families received Federal Housing Administration improvement loans. Federal assistance provided housing for 215,000 families earning less than $7,000 a year. Nearly $427 million was spent for water and sewage facilities in small towns. More than 3.5 million rural citizens benefited from economic opportunity loans, farm operation and emergency loans, and watershed and rural housing loans.

Most importantly, the Johnson administration presided over the longest upward curve of prosperity in the history of the nation. More than 85 months of unrivaled economic growth marked this as the strongest era of national prosperity. The average weekly wage of factory workers rose 18 percent in 4 years. Over 9 million additional workers were brought under minimum-wage protection. Total employment, increased by 7.5 million workers, added up to 75 million; the unemployment rate dropped to its lowest point in more than a decade.

In foreign affairs, where risk and confrontation stretched a perilous tightrope throughout the Johnson years, the President made significant achievements. In the Western Hemisphere, at Punta del Este, Uruguay, the Latin American nations agreed to a common market for the continent. Normal relations with Panama were restored and a new canal treaty negotiated. In Cyprus, at the brink of war, the President's special emissaries knitted a settlement that staved off conflict. A rebellion in the Congo, which would have had ugly repercussions throughout the continent, was put down with American aid in the form of transport planes. In the Dominican Republic, an incipient Communist threat was challenged by an overwhelming show of American force, with Latin American allies. Amid tangled criticism from sections of the press and some Latin American nations, the President persevered in the Dominican Republic, where democratic government and free elections were restored and U.S. troops promptly withdrawn.

An outer-space treaty was negotiated with the Soviet Union and a nuclear nonproliferation treaty was formulated and agreed to in Geneva. In June 1967 the President met with Premier Alexei Kosygin of the Soviet Union. Meanwhile, the North Atlantic Treaty Organization was successfully realigned after France withdrew, and the vast Western European alliance was restructured and strengthened.

It was the troubled Southeast Asian problem in South Vietnam to which Johnson devoted long, tormented hours. Presidents Truman, Eisenhower, and Kennedy had declared that the security of the United States was involved in deterring aggression in South Vietnam from an intruding Communist government from the North. However, there was much disagreement in the United States over this venture; some critics claimed the Vietnam war was a civil one, an insurrection, and not an invasion. When Johnson first became chief executive, 16,000 American troops were in Vietnam as advisers and combat instructors. In 1965 the United States decided to increase its military support of South Vietnam and authorized commitment of more American troops. By 1968 there was considerable disaffection over the Asian policy, and many critics in and out of the Congress determined to force the Johnson administration to shrink its commitment and withdraw U.S. troops.

Beginning in April 1965 with the President's speech at Johns Hopkins University, in which he set forth the American policy of reconstruction of the area and the promulgation of the Asian Development Bank as an instrument of peace building, the Johnson administration attempted to negotiate with a seemingly intransigent North Vietnam, whose troops were infiltrating into the South in increasing numbers. A 37-day bombing pause in December 1965 raised hopes for negotiation, but lack of response from the North Vietnamese blotted this out, and the bombing resumed.

Assaulted by fierce and growing criticism, yet determined to fix some course of action which would diminish the war and commence serious peace talks, the President startled the nation and the world on March 31, 1968, by renouncing his claim to renomination for the presidency. Johnson said that he believed that the necessity for finding a structure of peaceful negotiation was so important that even his own political fortunes must not be allowed to stand in its way. Therefore, he stated, he would not seek renomination, so he could spend the rest of his days in the presidency searching for negotiation without any political taint marring a possible response from the enemy.

On May 11, 1968, it was announced that peace talks would indeed begin in Paris, and in November 1968 the President declared that all bombing of North Vietnam would cease.

Johnson retired to his ranch near San Antonio, Texas, where he took a keen interest in the care and sale of his cattle, while nursing a serious heart ailment.

The tragic Vietnam War was in its last days in January, 1973 when a period of mourning was declared to mark the death of President Harry S Truman. Shortly after it began, it also marked the death of Lyndon B. Johnson.

On the afternoon of January 22, 1973, Johnson suffered a heart attack while lying down to take a nap. He was flown to a hospital by his Secret Service agents, but was pronounced dead on arrival at 4:33 pm. His body lay in state first at the Johnson Library in Austin, Texas, then, as is usual for American presidents, in the rotunda of the Capitol in Washington, D.C. until his burial on his beloved ranch.

Johnson's Influence

While historians search the record and evaluate its significance, there seems little doubt that Lyndon Johnson's impress on the form and quality of life in the United States will be seen to be large. In the fields of health, education, civil rights, conservation, and the problem of the elderly, his legislative achievements have left their clear mark. His insistence that the pledges of the four preceding presidents be upheld in Southeast Asia is a subject for debate. But it must be argued that his peace-keeping efforts in the Middle East, in the Near East, in Africa, and in Latin America were forceful, remedial, and worthy of praise; the results have proved his policies' merits.

Johnson belongs in the tradition of the "strong president"; he dominated the government with his energy and personality and invested his office with intimate knowledge of all government business. He was the target of intense and sometimes virulent criticism, just as all strong American presidents have found themselves ceaselessly and bitterly attacked.

Further Reading

Johnson's *The Vantage Point* (1971) presents his own perspectives on his White House years. Boothe Mooney, *The Lyndon Johnson Story* (1956; rev. ed. 1964) and Clarke Newlon, *LBJ:*

The Man from Johnson City (1964; rev. ed. 1966) offer journalistic biographies. Sam Houston Johnson's *My Brother Lyndon,* edited by Enrique Hank Lopez, is a superficial and undocumented account by the President's brother. Robert Dallek has produced the most comprehensive biography in a two volume work, *Lone Star Rising: Lyndon Johnson and His Times, 1908–1960* (1991) and *Flawed Giant: Lyndon Johnson and His Times, 1961–1973* (1998).

Aspects of Johnson's life and presidency are treated in William S. White, *Citadel: The Story of the U.S. Senate* (1957) and *The Professional: Lyndon B Johnson* (1964); Michael Amrine, *This Awesome Challenge: A Hundred Days of Lyndon Johnson* (1964); Rebekah Baines Johnson, *A Family Album,* edited by John S. Moursund (1965); Charles Roberts, *LBJ's Inner Circle* (1965); Theodore H. White, *The Making of the President* (1965); Rowland Evans and Robert Novak, *Lyndon B. Johnson, The Exercise of Power: A Political Biography* (1966); Philip Geyelin, *Lyndon B. Johnson and the World* (1966); Jim Bishop, *A Day in the Life of President Johnson* (1967); James Deakin, *Lyndon Johnson's Credibility Gap* (1968); Hugh Sidney, *A Very Personal Presidency: Lyndon Johnson in the White House* (1968); Tom Wicker, *JFK and LBJ: The Influence of Personality upon Politics* (1968); Eric F. Goldman, *The Tragedy of Lyndon Johnson* (1969); on Johnson's policies on Vietnam, Lloyd Gardner, *Pay Any Price* (1995); and Irving Bernstein, *Guns or Butter* (1995). Lady Bird Johnson's *White House Diary* (1970) is a record of the Johnson presidency as experienced by his wife; For the mid-century political background see James L. Sundquist, *Politics and Policy: The Eisenhower, Kennedy, and Johnson Years* (1968). □

Joshua Johnston

Though questions about his identity and whether or not certain works should be attributed to him remain, Joshua Johnston (ca. 1765-ca. 1830) is considered to be the first African American portrait artist of distinction.

Joshua Johnston may or may not have been the first African American artist of distinction, and conflicting evidence about his identity, race, and work continue to exist. Many unsigned late eighteenth-century and early-nineteenth century family portraits are attributed to him. Nonetheless, a man in post-colonial Baltimore named Joshua Johnson or Johnston was listed in directories of the time and who, on at least two occasions, advertised himself as a portraitist. This man has since been assigned credit for a body of work and is universally included in histories of African-American art.

The "Brass Tacks" Artist

The existence of Joshua Johnston was first suggested by J. Hall Pleasants, a retired doctor and a nationally recognized expert on Colonial artists from Maryland. In the 1940s, Pleasants began investigating long-circulating stories among prominent Maryland society that a slave had painted the portraits of several of their ancestors. The story had been passed down for several generations without any documentation. Many families said the painter had been black. According to one story, the slave had belonged to a well known artist of the period, and that his name was William Johnson. Pleasants searched old directories of Baltimore,

and although he didn't find any William Johnsons, he did find an 1817 listing for Joshua Johnston, described as a portrait painter in the section for "free householders of colour."

This information further piqued Pleasant's curiosity, since he thought he had known of all the painters of that period. Pleasants eventually concluded that Johnston was most likely the painter of a series of portraits that were stylistically similar, of which the artist had never been identified. Previously, the painter was referred to simply as the "brass tacks artist" because his paintings often featured furniture upholstered with brass tacks.

Portrait Featured in *Life* Magazine

Over the next several years, Pleasants identified 34 paintings he felt could be attributed to Johnston, and in 1942 he published an article in the *Maryland Historical Magazine* called, "Joshua Johnston, the First Black American Portrait Painter?" In 1940, *Life* magazine sparked furthered interest in Johnston when it published a portrait attributed to him. The publicity from that article led to the discovery of four more paintings believed to be Johnston's.

In 1948, the Peale Museum in Baltimore held an exhibition of 23 paintings attributed to Johnston, and by the time of Pleasant's death in 1957, he had "identified" 50 paintings done by the artist. Over the next two decades, the mystery of Joshua Johnston continued, and in 1973 an auction in Washington sold three paintings assigned to Johnston for $31,000. The high prices were a result of the belief that Johnston was black, making the works historically significant. In Baltimore, a prominent art historian and friend of Pleasants wrote an essay published in the *Baltimore Evening Sun* challenging anyone to prove that either Johnston was black or that he was, in fact, the artist of these works. Three years later, half of this challenge was answered: documentary evidence revealed that Johnston actually did paint the works attributed to him.

Race Remains a Mystery

The proof came with the discovery of a will from Mrs. Thomas Everette, the wife of a wealthy Baltimore businessman, who had a family portrait done by the brass tacks artist. In her will, she left the painting to her daughter, claiming that it had been painted by J. Johnson. With this documentation, art historians were able to establish which works of the Johnston canon were stylistically similar enough to be his. While the Everette will established that the brass tacks artist was Joshua Johnston, it did nothing to establish his race, which remains a mystery.

In the mid-1980s, the Abby Aldrich Rockefeller Folk Art Center began a major study of the issue of Johnston's race. Running the study was Carolyn Weekely, the curator of the center. Her study focused on the family stories that had first interested Pleasants nearly four decades earlier. The Weekely study focused on the idea that Johnston was West Indian. This theory would explain the racial ambiguity from the Baltimore directories that Pleasants had first uncovered. In one, Joshua Johnston is listed as a "free householder of colour." Yet in an 1800 census, Johnston is listed as a free white householder and that his household consisted of his immediate family and, importantly, a free black. An obvious conclusion would be that Johnston, if he was in fact black, was so light skinned that he could pass for white, and at times did. This further supports the West Indies theory, because in the West Indies, racial inter-mixing was far more common than in colonial America.

Employed by an Abolitionist

The study never uncovered any definitive documentation as to Johnston's race, but it did raise some interesting new possibilities, the most significant of which was that Johnston was a French-speaking slave inherited as a young boy by Charles Wilson Peale, a prominent Baltimore portraitist and outspoken abolitionist. According to this theory, for which there is almost no documentation, Peale may have inherited the young Johnston from his brother-in-law and employed him as his assistant. As such, Johnston would have been exposed to the art of portraiture as it was practiced at the time. The Weekely study went to great lengths to show that Johnston's style was very much similar to that of Peale's. This theory has detractors, though, who point out that Peales kept extensive diaries and never once mentioned a Joshua Johnston or any artist apprentice.

Adding to the Johnston mystery is that he managed to pass unknown into history in the first place. There is no mention of him by any of the many Baltimore artists of the time, about which a great deal is known. Pleasants himself knew nothing of Johnston, and he was the greatest living expert on Colonial Maryland artists. Had he not been a portrait artist, this anonymity might be explainable, but painting portraits is a socially oriented art; it is often mentioned, and requires, that an artist be well known among a wide circle of people. Surely, if Johnston had been a black man, mention of this would have been made by someone. Of course, research in this area has been limited to a very few studies and it is hoped that in the future the truth about Joshua Johnston can be uncovered.

Further Reading

Bearden, Romare, *A History of African American Artists, from 1792 to the present,* Pantheon Books, 1993.

Fine, Elsa Honig, "A Search for Identity," in *The Afro-American Artists,* Hacker Art Books, 1982.

Samella, Lewis, *Art: African American,* Harcourt Brace Jovanovich, 1978. □

Al Jolson

Al Jolson (1886-1950) was a vaudeville, theater, and radio singing performer and a film actor.

Al Jolson (Asa Yoelson) was born on May 6, 1886, in Srednike, Lithuania. Jolson's family immigrated to the United States in 1894. Several factors in Jolson's youth were to influence his career, including his religious Jewish upbringing, the death of his mother when he was ten, and his father's tradition-steeped profession of cantor.

Jolson may have acquired a love of singing from his father, but he did not want to use his voice in the synagogue. Instead, he and his brother Harry sang on street corners to earn money. Jolson also attended the theater whenever possible and discovered a deep desire to become a performer.

In 1900 Jolson left Washington, D.C., for New York. His first job on the stage was in Israel Zangwill's *Children of the Ghetto,* in which he played one of the mob. He also sang in a circus sideshow and finally teamed up with his brother to play vaudeville. They toured as Jolson/Palmer/Jolson (Palmer, a paraplegic, was the third member of the team) with an act called *The Hebrew and the Cadet.* At first Al Jolson played the straight man to his brother's comic Jewish man, but eventually Harry Jolson and Palmer took over the comedy and Al Jolson sang. Jolson was best on the stage when he was alone, when he could be spontaneous and not under the pressure of delivering lines. In this manner he could really relate to the audience he loved so much to please.

In order to develop his singing abilities Jolson left his brother's group and spent several years in San Francisco playing in small clubs. One day he decided he must liven up his act, and he went on stage in blackface and sang "Rosey My Posey" in Southern style. The makeup and his unique musical interpretation brought a sensitivity to the act that elicited three encores from the audience. Al Jolson's style was born.

In 1909 he was given a job as one of the minstrels in Dockstader's *Minstrel Show,* a successful touring production. It was here that Arthur Klein, who became his agent, spotted Jolson and convinced the powerful Broadway producer, Lee Shubert, to put him in his new show, *La Belle Paree* (1911). On March 20, 1911, the blackface singer went on stage and sang "I Want a Girl Just Like the Girl That Married Dear Old Dad." He was an instant hit. Jolson's singing and stage manner were different from anything the audience had seen. He took a song and applied to it a loose jazz/ragtime rhythm (this type of music had not yet been popularized). He wore blackface and rolled his eyes with a mischievous grin on his face. He also appealed to the emotions of the audience with his sentimental song deliveries interpolated with ad libbed dialogue.

Although Jolson did not receive star billing until 1914 in *Dancing Around,* the audiences clearly came to see *him.* The Shuberts knew this and signed Jolson for a seven year contract at the Winter Garden on Broadway. He played to overflowing houses in such shows as *Vera Violetta* (1911), *The Honeymoon Express* (1913), *Robinson Crusoe, Jr.* (1916), *Sinbad* (1918), and *Bombo* (1921). In most of these Jolson had no set script and no scheduled list of songs. He would come out on stage after the final act and talk to the audience and sing what pleased him. After each song he delighted the audiences with his standard retort, "You ain't heard nothing yet."

Jolson's renditions of songs were sung by people throughout the country, and he became known for songs like "Sonny Boy," "Swanee" (with this song Jolson introduced the composer George Gershwin), and most particularly "My Mammy." In "Mammy" the performer would go down on one knee with his hands in front of him as if in prayer. With tears in his eyes he would speak to "mother," telling her he'd "walk a million miles" just to see her. At the end he would get up and sing the last chorus with his hands spread wide and his face tilted upwards. After he introduced this song he was billed as "the greatest entertainer of all time." To his adoring audiences this was the truth.

Jolson's intense need to be constantly at work led him to do a six week tour of his own one-man show, in which he established the format for solo performance; then a vaudeville tour; a Sunday theater series for performers; and finally—Hollywood. On October 6, 1927, Warner Brothers presented the world's first talking-picture feature, *The Jazz Singer* . The story of Jakie Rabinowitz, the rabbi's son who turned actor against the wishes of his father, became a sensation and remains a motion picture classic. It starred Al Jolson. People came to associate the movie with Jolson's own life, a myth that he encouraged and had even contributed to early in his career with songs like "Mammy." This myth of the lonely man who had given up everything for the public was necessary for him—it was indeed reflected in his need for the audience's love.

Despite the overwhelming popularity of this film and its sequel, *The Singing Fool* (1928), Jolson did not succeed in film. He made several films afterwards, but his ultimate gift was his personal appeal to an audience. He was too big for the camera and could not convey his personality by way of screen. His career, in general, declined in the 1930s—

sentimentality was out and the audiences sought after a different type of singing.

Jolson filled his time by performing on radio and entertaining the troops in World War II. (He also did this in the early days of the Korean War.) He was a politically involved man, and he campaigned for several presidents by singing at rallies.

In 1946 Columbia Pictures presented *The Al Jolson Story,* in which Larry Parks impersonated Jolson and Jolson sang. The film was a fantasized version of his life and an immediate success. In 1949 they presented a sequel, *Jolson Sings Again,* another smash hit. These films not only brought the singer's career back to its heights but also immortalized this unique performer.

Jolson was married four times (his third wife was the actress Ruby Keeler), and he had three children. Al Jolson died of heart failure on October 24, 1950, the night before a planned radio taping with Bing Crosby.

Further Reading

Al Jolson: You Ain't Heard Nothin' Yet! by Robert Ober-first (1980) is a biography/dramatization of the central aspects of Jolson's work and personal life, with pictures. Jolson is listed in *Who's Who In The Theatre* (1939), edited by John Parker, and in *Famous Actors and Actresses on the American Stage,* Volume I (1975), by William C. Young. The latter book includes reviews of his work. Recordings of Al Jolson's songs and performances are still available. □

James Earl Jones

Award-winning actor James Earl Jones (born 1931) has acted on television, stage, and screen. He is, perhaps, best known for his sonorous bass voice.

Some people know him as one of the nation's finest stage actors, an artist who tackles the works of such playwrights as William Shakespeare and Eugene O'Neill. Others know his sonorous bass voice as the most menacing aspect of the evil Darth Vader in the blockbuster film *Star Wars.* Still others recognize him as a television star who brings depths of humanity to cliched character parts. James Earl Jones fits all these descriptions, and more: for more than 30 years he has been one of the most esteemed actors in the United States.

Jones has worked steadily for decades in a market that supplies little hope to black performers. Having first established himself as a serious dramatic actor, he has never balked at the so-called "low brow" pursuits of television and popular film. His resume includes *Othello* as well as television episodes of *Tarzan.* He has been laden with Tony, Emmy, and Obie awards, and yet he can be heard as the voice announcing "This is CNN" for Cable News Network. With film appearances ranging from the classic *Dr. Strangelove* to the forgettable *Conan, the Barbarian,* Jones admitted in the *Saturday Review* that he takes roles to surprise people—including himself. "Because I have a varied career, and I've not typecast myself, nobody knows what I'm going to do next. They don't know if I'm going to drop 20 pounds

and play an athlete. They don't know whether I'm ready to be a good guy or a bad guy."

Whatever Jones plays—villain or hero—he infuses each role with "enormous talent, range, courage, taste, [and] sensitivity," in the words of a *Newsweek* correspondent. During a career that began in the late 1950s, James Earl Jones has struggled to define himself not as a black actor, but simply as an actor. In an effort to resist stereotypes, he has opted for maximum variety, but each new part bears his particular, memorable stamp. In *Newsweek,* Jack Kroll called Jones "the embodiment of the living paradox that informs all great acting: his powerful persona is at once intimate and apart, friendly and heroic. He's right there in the room with you, but he's also in your mind, an electrifying double presence that only the strongest actors can create."

A Traumatic Boyhood

The only child of Robert Earl and Ruth Connolly Jones, James Earl Jones was born in Arkabutla, Mississippi, on his maternal grandfather's farm. Before his son's birth, James's father left the family to pursue a career as a prize fighter and later as an actor. Ruth Jones soon followed suit when she found tailoring work that kept her separated from her son for long periods of time. Born during the Great Depression, in 1931, Jones remarked in *Newsweek* that he realizes economic circumstances forced his parents apart. Still, he said, the abandonment hurt him deeply. "No matter how old the character I play," he concluded, "those deep childhood memories, those furies, will come out. I understand this."

Living on his grandparents' farm, Jones was afforded a measure of security. As a youngster he hunted, fished, and performed various farm chores. He also attended church, where he watched his grandmother's emotional displays of holy rapture. "There was a strong evangelistic aspect to her religion, and when she went to church and felt the spirit, she ended up behaving like a holy roller," Jones recalled in the *Saturday Review.* "There wasn't much touching in the family, but there was emotion."

Eventually Jones's grandparents formally adopted him, and took him north to rural Michigan. Jones acknowledged in *Newsweek* that the move north helped him to escape "a certain self-castration" common among Southern blacks at the time, but he did not adjust easily to his new surroundings. He developed a stutter and eventually found communication so difficult that at certain periods during grammar school he could talk only to himself or his immediate family. The problem followed him to high school, where one of his English teachers suggested he memorize speeches and enter oratorical contests. It seemed an unlikely way to cure a stutter, but it worked for Jones. Slowly, wrote Michelle Green in the *Saturday Review,* Jones "became such a skilled speaker that he began besting his voluble opponents."

Acting Beat out Other Careers

Jones attended the University of Michigan on a full scholarship, intending to study medicine. At first he took acting classes simply as a sideline, but he soon switched his major to theater. When he was 21 years old, and a junior at Michigan, he traveled east to New York City to meet his father. They had only spoken briefly on the telephone several times. The relationship was strained by the long years without communication, but Jones's father encouraged him to pursue a career in theater; James graduated from Michigan in 1953 with a bachelor's degree in drama.

The U.S. Army, specifically the Reserve Officers' Training Corps (ROTC), recruited Jones in 1953 for two years of compulsory service. He spent much of his stint in a rigorous ranger training program in the Colorado mountains and was set to reenlist in 1955 when his commanding officer suggested that he taste civilian life before making a long-term commitment to the armed services. So Jones moved to New York City and enrolled in further acting classes. Two things helped ease his decision: he knew he could return to the army if he did not find success as an actor, and his tuition at the American Theater Wing was paid for by the Army's G.I. Bill.

Jones lived with his father for a time, and the two supplemented their meager acting incomes by polishing floors in Off-Broadway theaters. In 1957 the younger Jones earned his first professional role in an Off-Broadway production of *Wedding in Japan.* He was rarely out of work after that, but his salary during the last years of the 1950s averaged $45 a week. He made ends meet by renting a cold-water flat on the Lower East Side. Even as a journeyman actor, Jones proved willing to try any role, no matter how small. In 1959 he began a long tenure with the New York Shakespeare Festival, carrying a spear in *Henry V.* Before long he was given more prominent roles, culminating in his 1963 performance as the lead in *Othello*—one of a staggering 13 plays he appeared in that year.

Fame Assured by The Great White Hope

Othello ran for a year Off-Broadway with Jones in the lead. The actor also found time to do television spots and to make one film appearance—as the bombardier in Stanley Kubrick's dark comedy *Dr. Strangelove.* In the mid-1960s Jones began augmenting his theater work with television parts. He took cameo roles in shows such as *The Defenders* and *East Side/West Side,* and he became the first black man to take a continuing role on a daytime serial when he portrayed a doctor on *As The World Turns.* The big break for Jones, though, came during a period when he was touring Europe as the lead in Eugene O'Neill's *The Emperor Jones.*

A copy of a play titled *The Great White Hope* landed in Jones's lap in 1967. A dramatization of the life of boxing champion Jack Johnson, *The Great White Hope* was slated for a possible Broadway run. Jones wanted the part desperately. He began to train at gymnasiums in order to build his muscles, working with boxing managers and watching old footage of Johnson's fights. He was ultimately awarded the part, and the show opened on Broadway on October 3, 1968.

The Great White Hope was a success, and its reception propelled Jones to stardom. "Fourteen years of good hard acting work, including more Shakespeare than most British actors attempt, have gone into the making of James Earl Jones," wrote a *Newsweek* reviewer who also concluded that "only an actor with the bigness and power of Jones" could make such a play work. Jones won a Tony Award for his contribution to *The Great White Hope,* and he was nominated for an Academy Award in 1970 when the play was made into a motion picture.

The instant celebrity brought Jones a new awareness of his limitations. The actor told *TV Guide* that his work in *The Great White Hope* did not prove to be the career boost he thought it would. "I thought with the Oscar nomination that several projects would be waiting for me immediately," he continued in *TV Guide.* "But then projects—very viable ones close to getting go-aheads—caved in under racism's insanity." One of those projects was a life story of civil rights activist Malcolm X, a version of which was finally scheduled for release by filmmaker Spike Lee in 1992.

Working for Love and Money

Jones returned to the stage, appearing in *Hamlet* in 1972, *King Lear* in 1973, and *Of Mice and Men* in 1974. He also performed in a series of minor films, including *The Man* and *The Bingo Long Traveling All-Stars and Motor Kings.* Jones's most notable movie role of the 1970s and early 1980s, though, was one in which only his voice was used. He gave a memorable level of malevolence to the half-man, half-machine villain Darth Vader in all three *Star Wars* films.

In 1982 Jones appeared on Broadway as Othello to standing ovations. He also portrayed the villain in the film *Conan, the Barbarian.* To critics who faulted him for taking roles in substandard films, Jones had a simple reply: movies

and television pay well, theater does not. "I can't afford to take a vacation unless I do some commercials when I'm in New York," he pointed out in the *Saturday Review.* "Money goes fast, and you can't get along doing only stage work. I've never minded doing commercials. . . . Commercials can be very exciting." In 1991 Jones lent himself to a string of TV ads for the Bell Atlantic Yellow Pages, his first on-air product endorsement.

Jones's work in the late 1980s and early 1990s was as varied as his early career. He played an enigmatic writer in the 1990 hit film *Field of Dreams,* a CIA chief in the 1992 screen adaptation of Tom Clancy's novel *Patriot Games,* and a judge in the 1994 film *Sommersby.* On televison he starred as an ex-convict private investigator in the award-winning series *Gabriel's Fire* and, in 1995, as a widowed police officer in the series *Under One Roof.* Not neglecting his onstage work, he earned yet another Tony Award in 1988 for his portrayal of a disenchanted Negro League baseball player in August Wilson's play *Fences.* Jones explained in the *Los Angeles Times* that he has taken so many minor film roles and so much television work simply because he likes to work. "Just as, on stage, I waited years for a role like Jack [Johnson] in *Great White Hope,* or a role like Troy in *Fences,* you do the same thing in movies," he said. "Unless you are among that handful of exceptions, the stars who have projects lined up, you don't wait, at least I didn't want to wait. . . . I don't think I've done many films that counted. What I'm getting at, rather than waiting for that wonderful role in a movie, I take 'off' jobs."

To quote *Los Angeles Times* correspondent David Wallace, those "off jobs" are often "memorable only for [Jones's] commanding presence [or] for the brevity of his appearance." That situation would change, however; in 1990 Jones announced that his age and health were forcing him to curtail his work in live theater. "After six months in a play, the fatigue factor begins to affect the quality of a performance," the actor conceded in the *Los Angeles Times.* "The audiences might not know it, but I do. My thing is serious drama, and usually the lead character has a heavy load to carry. I find that after six months, if you get four out of eight shows a week that work perfectly the way you want, you're lucky." Jones stressed that he did not plan to retire from the theater completely, but rather to cut back his live work in favor of other projects.

A shelf full of awards to his credit and contributions to every sort of mass media notwithstanding, James Earl Jones remains a modest man with a sense of adventure about his career. He and his second wife, actress Cecilia Hart, have one son, and Jones told the *Los Angeles Times* that he guards against appearing heroic to his child. "When I go home nobody is saying, 'Hi, can I have your autograph?' I'm me, that's reality. I'm an actor. That's something you do, not something you are, and I want my son to have a sense of reality." Looking toward the future, Jones sees no lack of opportunities in show business. "There are lots of wonderful cameos and a lot of good lead roles out there," he concluded in the *Los Angeles Times.* "There are a lot of things I can do."

In 1995, Jones played Neb Langston in the CBS drama *Under One Roof.* Langston is a retired police officer who is raising a foster child. In early 1996, Jones starred opposite Richard Harris in the apartheid movie *Cry, Beloved Country.* Jones plays the role of a preacher whose son is arrested for the murder of a prominent white man.

Further Reading

Chicago Tribune, May 26, 1990; May 5, 1991.

Ebony, April 1965; June 1969.

Los Angeles Times, September 2, 1990; August 26, 1991; September 26, 1991.

Newsweek, October 21, 1968; April 6, 1987.

Saturday Review, February 1982.

Time, April 6, 1987.

TV Guide, October 27, 1990.

Variety, September 23, 1991. □

Quincy Delight Jones, Jr.

A resume for Quincy Delight Jones, Jr. (born 1933), would read like a run-on sentence with too many hyphens: musician-composer-arranger-producer-film and television executive, just to name a few. He propelled not only his own stardom, but that of Michael Jackson, Oprah Winfrey, James Ingram, Donna Summer—again, just to name a few. For more than four decades, Jones left a permanent, unique mark on the world of entertainment.

Quincy Delight Jones, Jr., was born on the south side of Chicago on March 14, 1933. His parents divorced soon after his younger brother, Lloyd, was born, and the Jones boys were raised by their father, a carpenter, and his new wife. She had three children of her own, and three more with Quincy Jones, Sr. His birth mother, Sarah Jones, was in and out of mental health facilities, and it wasn't until his adult life that Quincy was able to enjoy a close relationship with her.

When Jones was 10 years old his family moved to Bremerton, Washington. The Seattle suburb was alive with World War II sailors on their way to the Pacific; the nightlife and its music were the backdrop for Quincy's early teens. Three years later he met a 15-year-old musician named Ray Charles. The two formed a combo and played in local clubs and weddings, and soon Jones was composing and arranging for the group. After high school and a scholarship at Boston's Berklee College of Music, Quincy was introduced to the life of a musician on the road, a road which started in New York and went around the world. He toured with Dizzy Gillespie in 1956, Lionel Hampton in 1957, and then made his base in Paris. He studied with Nadia Boulanger and Olivier Messiaen, was musical director at Barclay Disques, wrote for Harry Arnold's Swedish All-Stars in Stockholm, and directed the music for Harold Arlen's production "Free and Easy," which toured Europe for three months, ending in early 1960.

After a financially unsuccessful tour of the United States with a big band made up of 18 musicians from "Free

and Easy," Jones served as musical director at Mercury Records in New York. He became the first African American executive in a white-owned record company in 1964 when he was promoted to vice-president at Mercury. At the company he produced albums, sat in on recording sessions with the orchestra, and wrote arrangements for artists at Mercury as well as other labels. Jones wrote for Sammy Davis, Jr., Andy Williams, Sarah Vaughan, Peggy Lee, and Aretha Franklin, as well as arranged and conducted *It Might As Well Be Swing,* an album featuring Frank Sinatra and the Count Basie Band.

In 1969 Jones signed a contract as a recording artist with Herb Alpert's A&M Records, and Quincy's first album with that label, *Walking in Space,* won a Grammy for best jazz instrumental album of 1969. Quincy Jones was later nominated for 67 Grammys, and had won 25 going into 1997.

His first foray into Hollywood—another crossing of a racial barrier—came when he composed the score for *The Pawnbroker,* a 1965 film by Sidney Lumet. Two films released in 1967 featured music by Jones: *In Cold Blood* and *In the Heat of the Night.* Both scores won enough votes to be nominated for Academy Awards. Jones was advised not to "compete with himself," so he went with *In Cold Blood* and it was the other film that ended up winning the Oscars. It didn't stop him from going on to write the music for over 52 films.

Television, as well, has featured the music of Quincy Jones, starting in 1971 with theme songs for "Ironside," "Sanford and Son," and "The Bill Cosby Show" (the first one). In 1973 Jones co-produced "Duke Ellington, We Love You Madly," a special for CBS, featuring Peggy Lee, Aretha Franklin, Count Basie, Joe Williams, Sarah Vaughan, and a 48-piece orchestra conducted by Jones. The special was a project of the Institute for Black American Music, a foundation formed by Jones, Isaac Hayes, Roberta Flack, and other musicians with the intention of promoting recognition of the African American contribution to American music. Jones also wrote the score for the widely acclaimed 1977 television mini-series "Roots."

Burned out from producing film score after film score, Jones stopped working for Hollywood in 1973 to explore his own pop music career as a vocalist. His singing debut was with Valerie Simpson on an album called *You've Got It Bad, Girl*. The title song from the album stayed at the top of the charts for most of the summer of 1973. Jones's next album was an even bigger hit. *Body Heat,* released in the summer of 1974, contained the hit songs "Soul Saga," "Everything Must Change," and "If I Ever Lose This Heaven." The album remained within the top five on the charts for over six months and sold over a million copies.

In 1974 Jones suffered two aneurysms two months apart. He nearly died, but after a six-month recuperation he was back at work, touring and recording with a 15-member band. *Mellow Madness* was the first album by the new band, which included songs by George and Louis Johnson, Otis Smith, and Stevie Wonder ("My Cherie Amour").

His 1980 album, *The Dude,* featured a host of talent directed by Jones, earned 12 Grammy nominations, and won five awards. At the same time *The Dude* was released, Jones signed a deal with Warner Brothers Records creating his own label, Quest. It took Jones almost ten years to make his next album, *Back on the Block*. During that time he was focused on producing hit albums for other artists such as Donna Summer, Frank Sinatra, and James Ingram. In 1983 Michael Jackson recorded a Quincy Jones production, and at 40 million copies *Thriller* is still the best-selling album of all time. Quincy Jones also has the best-selling single of all time to his credit: the all-star choir on "We Are the World." Another triumph for Jones in the mid-1980s was his production of *The Color Purple,* the film adaptation of Alice Walker's novel, which featured the Oscar-nominated, debut film performance of Oprah Winfrey.

Jones's projects in the early 1990s included continuing work on an ongoing, mammoth project for which he'd been gathering material for decades, "The Evolution of Black Music." He was back in television, as well, with the Quincy Jones Entertainment Company producing the NBC situation comedy "Fresh Prince of Bel Air," as well as a weekly syndicated talk show hosted by Jones's friend the Rev. Jesse Jackson. Quincy Jones was also working on a film biography of the Black Russian poet Alexander Pushkin. The film was a co-production with Soviet filmmakers. Quincy Jones Broadcasting and Time Warner bought a New Orleans television station, WNOL, which Jones was to oversee.

The personal life of Quincy Jones was strained because of the pace of his professional endeavors. He was married and divorced three times (his latest wife was actress Peggy Lipton), and his six children have only recently been able to spend time with and come to know their father. The 1990 documentary "Listen Up: The Lives of Quincy Jones," produced by Courtney Sale Ross, contains poignant scenes in which Quincy confronts his difficult childhood, his mentally ill mother, and his strained past with his children. The film also contains testimonials from Frank Sinatra, Ella Fitzgerald, Michael Jackson, Miles Davis, Stephen Spielberg, Barbra Streisand, Oprah Winfrey, Ray Charles, Billy Eckstine, and others. They talk about an obsessed genius, a workaholic, and a man with a creative brilliance that has touched virtually every facet of popular entertainment since 1950.

In 1993 Jones announced that he was starting a magazine called *Vibe*. The magazine has been well received as an African American music journal. The album Jones released in 1995 was *Q's Jook Joint.* The album combined the talents of many of Quincy Jones's counterparts such as Stevie Wonder, Ray Charles, Sonny Bono and many others. The album was a celebration of his 50 years within the music industry. In 1996 Jones released an instrumental album entitled *Cocktail Mix.*

Further Reading

Two excellent in-depth and insightful interviews with Quincy Jones are in *The New York Times Magazine* (November 18, 1990) and *The Washington Post Style* section (October 6, 1990); Jones is the cover story of the October 22, 1990, issue of *Jet*. □

Robert Tyre Jones

Golf great Robert Tyre Jones (1902-1971) won his first match, a neighborhood tournament for kids, when he was only six years old. He went on from there to become America's greatest golfer.

Bobby Jones was born March 17, 1902, in Atlanta, Georgia. By the time he was 12 he was the Georgia state champion, and in 1921 he became the youngest member of the U.S. Walker Cup team when it journeyed to England. Between 1923 and 1930 he won five U.S. amateur titles, four U.S. Opens, three British Opens, and one British amateur title. He won the "Grand Slam"—four separate tournaments consisting of amateur and professional championships in the United States and England—in 1930. Meanwhile he earned a law degree from Emory University, following degrees from what is now Georgia Tech and from Harvard University.

After 1930 Jones gave up his amateur standing and made a series of instructional films. He practiced law, and in 1934 he founded the "Masters Tournament," a yearly event held in Augusta, Georgia, at the Augusta National Golf Club, which he had helped establish.

A spinal injury suffered in 1948 made it increasingly difficult for him to move about, but Jones continued to make yearly visits to the Masters to drape the green jacket, symbol of the event, around the shoulders of the winner.

In 1948 Bobby Jones was granted the "freedom of the burgh" of St. Andrew's, Scotland, traditional birthplace of

the game of golf and one of the world's most famous courses. The only other American to have been granted that honor was Benjamin Franklin.

When he died on December 18, 1971, he was known as the greatest player who ever lived. Good looking and well educated, he was the personification of the all-American boy.

Further Reading

No book about golf would be complete without considerable space devoted to Bobby Jones. The reader needs only to pick up a book about golf to read more about Bobby Jones. His biography, *Golf Is My Game,* was published in 1960. □

Scott Joplin

While Scott Joplin (1868-1917) is most noted for developing ragtime music, he also wrote music for ballet and opera.

As Johann Strauss is to the waltz and John Philip Sousa is to the march, so is Scott Joplin to ragtime: its guru, chief champion, the figure most closely associated with its composition. It was Joplin's short, hard-driving melodies—and the syncopated backbone he furnished them—that helped define the musical parameters of ragtime, a style that gave voice to the African American experience during the late 19th and early 20th centuries. According to David W. Eagle in the liner notes to *Scott Joplin: Greatest Hits,* "Ragtime, a type of written piano music, . . . was actually a hybrid of European and African musical traditions" consisting of "folk melodies (usually of black origin) and commercial music from minstrel shows . . . overlaid on West African cross-rhythms."

Sadly, for all his accomplishments in putting a new musical form on the map, Joplin spent his final years madly obsessed with a fruitless crusade to enter, if not conquer, another arena: opera, the staid, classical venue accepted by a white community that had for so long ridiculed ragtime as cheap, vulgar, and facile black music.

Many of the details of Joplin's life, like much of his music, have been lost to history. He was born November 24, 1868, in Texarkana, a small city straddling the border of Texas and Arkansas. Joplin's father, Giles, was a railroad laborer who was born into slavery and obtained his freedom five years before his son's birth. Florence Givens Joplin was a freeborn black woman who worked as a laundress and cared for her children. Like many in the black community, the Joplins saw in music a rewarding tool of expression, and the talented family was sought out to perform at weddings, funerals, and parties.

Scott, whose first foray into the world of scales and half notes came on the guitar, discovered a richer lyrical agent in his neighbor's piano. At first, Giles Joplin was concerned that music would sidetrack his son from a solid, wage-earning trade, but he soon saw the clear inventive genius in Scott, who, by the time he was 11, was playing and improvising with unbelievable smoothness. A local German musician, similarly entranced with Scott Joplin's gift, gave the boy free lessons, teaching him the works of European composers, as well as the nuts and bolts of musical theory and harmony.

Articulated Black Experience

In a move not uncommon for young blacks at the time, Joplin left home in his early teens, working as an itinerant pianist at honky-tonks and salons of the Midwest, South, and Southwest. Although some revisionist historians have placed the birth of ragtime at the feet of white composers, such as Irving Berlin, who published "Alexander's Ragtime Band" in 1911, the true origin of the music was to be found in these low rent musical halls. In explaining the black roots of the musical form, Rudi Blesh and Harriet Janis wrote in *They All Played Ragtime,* "Piano ragtime was developed by the Negro from folk melodies and from the syncopations of the plantation banjos. As it grew, it carried its basic principle of displaced accents played against a regular meter to a very high degree of elaboration." The signature fast and frenetic pace of ragtime reflected the jubilant side of the black experience—compared with the melancholy-heavy blues—and the music became, according to Blesh and Janis, America's "most original artistic creation."

In 1893 Joplin played cornet with a band at the World's Columbian Exposition in Chicago, where musicians from throughout the country displayed for one another the regional variations of ragtime and where Joplin was encouraged by pianist Otis Saunders to write down his original compositions. Joplin left Chicago leading a male vocal octet, the repertoire of which included plantation medleys,

popular songs of the day, and his own compositions. Ironically, Joplin questioned the staying power of ragtime, and his first two published pieces, "A Picture of Her Face" and "Please Say You Will," were conventional, sentimental, waltz songs.

After touring, Joplin settled in Sedalia, Missouri, which would later become known as the "Cradle of Classic Ragtime." Joplin attended music classes at the George R. Smith College for Negroes, played with local bands, and taught piano and composition to other ragtime composers, most notably Arthur Marshall and Scott Hayden. This nurturing side would forever buoy Joplin's reputation within the musical community. In several cases, to help the careers of his lesser known contemporaries, Joplin lent his big-money name to their compositions.

In 1899 Joplin issued his first piano rags, "Original Rags" and "Maple Leaf Rag," the latter named for a social club where he often played. A white music publisher, John Stark, had heard Joplin playing the "Maple Leaf" and, though he was concerned that its technical difficulty exceeded even the grasp of its composer, he gave Joplin a $50 advance and a royalty contract that would bring Joplin one cent per copy sold. Such an arrangement was a wild departure from the norm, which netted composers no royalties and advances rarely surpassing $25. According to Peter Gammond in his book *Scott Joplin and the Ragtime Era,* Joplin said after he had finished this tune, "One day the 'Maple Leaf' will make me King of Ragtime Composers." Although only about 400 copies were sold in the first year, it had sold nearly half a million copies by the end of 1909.

Made Ragtime Premier Musical Trend

With this financial cushion, Joplin was able to stop playing at the clubs and devote all his time to composition and teaching. Joplin's prolific output, including "Peacherine Rag," "A Breeze from Alabama," "Elite Syncopations," and "The Entertainer," made ragtime the premier musical trend of the time, with Joplin the ingenious trendsetter. His compositions—glossed over by some shallow-minded white critics as the so-called "music of brothels"—showcased his keen understanding of inner voices, chromatic harmonies, and the rich interrelationships of melody and rhythm. William J. Schafer and Johannes Riedel wrote in *The Art of Ragtime: Form and Meaning of an Original Black American Art:* "The secret of Joplin's ragtime is the subtle balance of polarities, continuity, and repetition of melody and rhythm, much the same combination of energy and lyricism as in the marches of his contemporary, John Philip Sousa."

Despite his material successes and the regal status bestowed on him by ragtime composers and aficionados, Joplin could not easily brush off the disparaging accent the white world gave the term "rag"; such condescension, according to Joplin, was a transparent means of discrediting the black music as an artless form of folk entertainment. He gave his compositions elegant names, such as "The Chrysanthemum" and "Heliotrope Bouquet," capturing the lyrical mood and seriousness of classical music. To educate the advanced music student about the intricacies of ragtime, Joplin wrote a series of études, *The School of Ragtime: Six Exercises for Piano,* published in 1908, when schools promising the quick learning of the music were popping up across the country. John Rublowsky, writing in *Black Music in America,* quoted Joplin's preface to the series: "Syncopations are no indication of light or trashy music, and to shy bricks at 'hateful ragtime' no longer passes for musical culture. To assist the amateur players in giving the 'Joplin Rags' that weird and intoxicating effect intended by the composer is the object of this work."

But Joplin was not satisfied with the composition of unconnected, short pieces, and his wish to explore the cultural context and functions of ragtime—in short, to explain the deeper meaning of ragtime to the white world—led to his *Rag Time Dance.* Published in 1902, it was conceived as a sort of ragtime ballet, combining folk dances of the period choreographed by Joplin, and a narrative written by him. Unable to find financial backers, Joplin put up his own money for an ensemble production of the piece. Although *The Rag Time Dance* proved Joplin's ability to write in extended, musical themes, it did not have the unifying and didactic effects for which he had hoped.

Undeterred and still courting the kind of exposure he believed his music needed, Joplin penned the first ragtime opera, *A Guest of Honor.* Unfortunately, the opera, which was performed once in a test rehearsal to gauge public sentiment, was never published and was lost. It was apparently Joplin's most inventive musical exercise, but, like *The Rag Time Dance,* its reception was a major disappointment to him. Blesh and Janis wrote, "The fate of *A Guest of Honor* is the story of what might have been, for the time was right for syncopated opera. It was certainly time for the romantic-costume idea of light opera as epitomized by the sentimentalities of Victor Herbert to be superseded by something more American, and there is no doubt that America itself was ready for it and that Joplin was the man equipped to write it."

Penned Opera, Suffered Disappointment

But this would be not be the last, nor the most consuming of Joplin's failures. Ever driven to push his own musical limits and to break the shackles in which he believed the white world had bound him, Joplin spent the final years of his life composing and maneuvering to produce a full-fledged opera. *Treemonisha* is a fable, a folk story about an orphaned girl (the title character), who, by virtue of having an education, is chosen to raise her people above ignorance, superstition, and conjuration to enlightenment. In *Treemonisha,* Joplin found a forum for the exploration of history and politics, a piece that would never allow the seriousness of his music and of his intellect to be questioned.

With words, choreography, and music by Joplin, *Treemonisha* was not a ragtime opera, but instead a complex work borrowing the phraseology and themes of some of the popular music of the day: Gilbert and Sullivan's sentimental show music, spirituals, plantation songs, brass band marches, and barber shop harmonies. Schafer and Riedel wrote that *Treemonisha* was Joplin's "greatest accomplishment as a composer," and that it, having been composed two decades before George Gershwin's *Porgy and Bess,* served as "the first demonstrably great American opera, for it speaks a genuine American musical idiom within the conventional forms of Western opera."

The world at that time, however, was not ready for Joplin's operatic alchemy, in some respects because Joplin's name, so closely associated with ragtime, had begun to fade from the popular mind as ragtime became absorbed by the derivative white tunes of Tin Pan Alley. There was a threadbare performance of *Treemonisha* in 1915, but without scenery, orchestra, costumes, or lighting, the piece that had been at the center of his musical and intellectual life for more than five years came across as thin and unconvincing. Some writers have suggested that when Joplin died in 1917, he did so brokenhearted, shattered that his entry into the most socially redeeming class of music—opera—had been a bust. "The death certificate said that he had died of 'dementia paralytica-cerebral' which had partly been brought on by syphilis," Gammond wrote, "but it didn't add that it had been hastened by a violent addiction to *Treemonisha.*"

Though Joplin died well after he had reached the heights of his popularity, his contributions to music, particularly in the popularization of an originally black musical form, have never been in question. The mesmerizing interplay of rhythm and melody influenced European composers Claude Debussy and Antonín Dvořák, and ragtime enjoyed a brief revival in the 1970s, when the film *The Sting,* starring Paul Newman and Robert Redford and featuring Joplin's

song "The Entertainer," reintroduced music lovers to Joplin's playful brilliance.

"The genius of Joplin was twofold," attested Blesh and Janis, "the tyrannical creative urge and the vision. With the first alone, even had he been, perhaps, the greatest of all the ragtime players, his most perfectly constructed pieces, unscored, would today be one with all the others, lost with a lost time. But his vision was the sculptor's, molding transitory vision into stone's indestructibility. He was at once the one who makes and the one who saves. Through the labor of this one 'homeless itinerant' the vast outcry of a whole dark generation can go on sounding as long as any music will sound."

Further Reading
Blesh, Rudi, and Harriet Janis, *They All Played Ragtime,* Oak Publications, 1971.

Gammond, Peter, *Scott Joplin and the Ragtime Era,* St. Martin's, 1975.

Rublowsky, John, *Black Music in America,* Basic Books, 1971.

Schafer, William J., and Johannes Riedel, *The Art of Ragtime: Form and Meaning of an Original Black American Art,* Louisiana State University Press, 1973.

New York Times, December 1, 1991.

Additional information for this profile was taken from liner notes by David W. Eagle to *Scott Joplin: Greatest Hits,* RCA Victor, 1991. □

Louis Jordan

Louis Jordan's (1908-1975) jazz-based boogie shuffle rhythms laid the foundation for rhythm and blues, modern electric blues, and rockabilly music.

At the height of his career, in the 1940s, bandleader and alto saxophonist Louis Jordan scored 18 Number One hit records. In the tradition of Louis Armstrong and Fats Waller, Jordan exhibited a brilliant sense of showmanship that, as music critic Leonard Feather explained in his book *The Jazz Years,* brought audiences first-rate entertainment "without any loss of musical integrity." Against the backdrop of house parties, fish fries, and corner grills, Jordan performed songs that appealed to millions of black *and* white listeners. Able to "straddle the fence" between these two audiences, Jordan emerged as one of the first successful crossover artists of American popular music.

Born on July 8, 1908, in Brinkley, Arkansas, Jordan was the son of Jim Jordan, a bandleader and music teacher. Under the tutelage of his father, Jordan began studying clarinet at age seven. After spotting a saxophone in a music store window, however, he "ran errands all over Brinkley" until he could raise the money to purchase the instrument. While on summer vacation at the age of 15, Jordan landed his first gig, with Ruby "Tuna Boy" Williams's Belvedere Orchestra, at the Green Gables in Hot Springs, Arkansas. His first professional engagement was with Fat Chappelle's Rabbit Foot Minstrels, playing clarinet and dancing throughout the South. At Arkansas Baptist College in Little Rock, Jordan majored in music and played on the school

baseball team. After school he played local dates with Jimmy Pryor's Imperial Serenaders.

On the Road

Moving to Philadelphia in 1930, Jordan worked with trumpeter Charlie Gaines's orchestra and tuba player Jim Winters's band. Two years later, Jordan traveled to New York with Gaines's group, where he took part in a recording session with pianist Clarence Williams's band. In New York he briefly worked with the bands of Kaiser Marshall and drummer Joe Marshall. His most important job, though, came in 1936 when he joined drummer Chick Webb's orchestra—a 13-piece ensemble that featured singer Ella Fitzgerald. A small, "hunch-backed" man whose physical deformity nonetheless failed to hinder his inventive drumming talent, Webb hired Jordan as a singer, sideman, and announcer. In 1937 Jordan recorded his first vocal with Webb's band, a song titled "Gee, But You're Swell." During his stint with Webb Jordan developed his skills as a frontman. "Louis would go out and just break up the show," recalled former bandmember Garvin Bushell in his autobiography *Jazz From the Beginning.* "Nobody could follow him."

In the summer of 1938, Jordan left Webb's orchestra to form his own, nine-piece, band; although Jordan enjoyed performing as part of large jazz ensembles, he embarked on a career as a bandleader and more general entertainer. "I wanted to play for the people, for millions, not just a few hep cats," explained Jordan in Arnold Shaw's *Honkers and Shouters.* Billing himself as "Bert Williams," Jordan played

shows at the Elk's Rendezvous at 44 Lenox Avenue, in Harlem. His long residency at the club eventually prompted him to name his group the Elk's Rendezvous Band. After playing various club dates on 52nd Street, he booked his band at proms and dances at Yale University and Amherst College. In 1939, this group recorded several sides for the Decca label.

That December, after changing the name of his band to the Tympany Five, Jordan reduced the size of the unit to six members (later it would number seven or eight). Invited to open for the Mills Brothers at the Capitol Theater in Chicago, Jordan played a ten-minute spot during the intermission between the featured performances. In no time, Jordan's energetic stage presence began to draw larger crowds than the headline acts, so Capitol's management decided to lengthen his performance to half an hour.

But the real turning point in Jordan's career came when he performed at a small "beer joint" called the Fox Head Tavern in Cedar Rapids, Iowa. Distanced from the demanding crowds of Chicago and New York, Jordan found he was freer to experiment with new material. At the Fox Head he assembled a large repertoire of blues and novelty songs. On his return to the Capitol Theater, Jordan became a sensation. In January of 1942 he hit the charts with a rendition of the blues standard "I'm Gonna Move to the Outskirts of Town."

King of the Jukeboxes

From 1942 Jordan was rarely absent from the *Harlem Hit Parade.* Over the following ten years he recorded more than 54 rhythm-and-blues best-sellers. Material for his band came from a number of black and white songwriters. As Jordan's manager, Berle Adams, told *Honkers and Shouters* author Shaw, "When we found something we liked, an arrangement would be made up, and we'd play it on one-nighters. The songs the public asked for again and again were the songs we recorded." Jordan soon produced a stream of hits, including "What's the Use of Getting Sober (When You're Gonna Get Drunk Again)," "Five Guys Named Moe," and "G.I. Jive," a boogie number intended for the entertainment of troops fighting in World War II.

Aside from the universal appeal of his material, the key to Jordan's success lay in his tight organization and the use of talented arrangers such as pianists Wild Bill Davis and Bill Dogget. Though he exhibited a casual manner, Jordan was a serious bandleader who demanded that his outfit be well dressed and thoroughly rehearsed. In *An Autobiography of Black Jazz,* saxophonist Eddie Johnson described how Jordan's penchant for "neatness" led him to require his band to "look right even down to their shoes." Jordan furnished bandmembers with six or seven uniforms, which displayed a post-zoot-suit style with multicolor designs.

In the mid-1940s, Jordan's Tympany Five drew thousands of listeners to white nightclubs and black theaters. Traveling by car caravan, the band toured constantly, playing shows at venues like Billy Berg's Swing Club in Hollywood, the Oriental Theatre in Chicago, the Apollo in Harlem, and the Paradise Theatre in Detroit. In black movie houses, Jordan's releases were featured in film shorts, many of which became so popular that the regular features often received second billing. Around this time Jordan also appeared in several motion pictures, including *Meet Miss Bobby Socks, Swing Parade of 1946,* and *Beware,* which was advertised as "the first truly great all-colored musical feature."

After World War II, when the big bands began to disappear, Jordan's small combo continued to find commercial success. "With my little band, I did everything they did with a big band. I made the blues jump," Jordan explained in *Honkers and Shouters.* The band became so popular, in fact, that Jordan toured with such sought-after opening acts as Dinah Washington, Ruth Brown, Sarah Vaughn, and Sister Rosetta Tharpe. Following his 1945 million-seller "Caldonia," Jordan and the Tympany Five continued to score hits, among them "Beware Brother Beware," "Boogie Woogie Blue Plate," "Nobody Here But Us Chickens," and "Open the Door Richard," a song adapted from a black vaudeville comedy routine popularized during the 1930s and '40s. In 1950, Jordan recorded a cover version of "(I'll be Glad When You're Dead) You Rascal You" with trumpeter-singer Louis Armstrong.

Obscured by the Sound He Helped Create

The following year Jordan changed course, disbanding the Tympany Five and forming a 16-piece big band. But this group did not live up to the sound or favor of the earlier unit. On leaving the Decca label in 1954, Jordan largely lost the steady stream of material, sidemen, and producers that had helped him maintain his national celebrity. Determined to keep up with the burgeoning rhythm and blues market, however, he signed with West Coast-based Aladdin Records. But after failing to score commercially, he moved to RCA's Victor X subsidiary. In the meanwhile, Jordan had recorded for more than a dozen labels in the U.S., including Mercury, Warwick, Tangerine, Pzazz, and Blue Spectrum. Despite his persistence, Jordan faced a new record-buying public dominated by teenagers who demanded rock 'n' roll lyrics, idol images, and heavy back-beat rhythms.

Health problems eventually forced Jordan to retire from one-night stands, which required that he drive hundreds of miles across the country. In 1946 he bought a home in Phoenix, Arizona, where he stayed for 18 years; he moved to Los Angeles in the early 1960s. During this period he devoted his time to playing occasional month-long engagements in Phoenix, Las Vegas, and New York. On a tour of England in 1962, Jordan performed and recorded with the Chris Barbers band. Two years later, he reformed the Tympany Five to appear at show lounges and music festivals. His performances in the Near East in 1967 and 1968 received enthusiastic responses. At the 1973 Newport Jazz Festival, too, crowds gave him a warm reception.

In October of 1974, Jordan suffered a heart attack while performing in Sparks, Nevada. After entering St. Mary's Hospital in Reno, he returned home to Los Angeles, where he died on February 4, 1975. His body was flown to St. Louis for burial at Mt. Olive Cemetery.

In 1987 Jordan was inducted into the Rock and Roll Hall of Fame. Though many had forgotten his contributions to popular music over the intervening years, this honor paid tribute to one of the performers most responsible for the development of rhythm and blues and rock and roll. As trumpeter Dizzy Gillespie related in his autobiography *To Be or Not to Bop,* "Rock n' roll had been with us a long time" and "Louis Jordan had been playing it long before Elvis Presley." Jordan helped shape the careers of rock and roll pioneers Chuck Berry, Fats Domino, Bill Haley, and countless others, though his music would later become obscured by evolving trends. In 1990 Jordan's work was celebrated in the hit stage production *Five Guys Named Moe,* a rollicking look at a man whose "whole theory of life" was to make audiences "smile or laugh." With the many reissues of Jordan's music on compact disc, one need only listen to realize the lasting sincerity of his commitment.

Further Reading

Bushell, Garvin, *Jazz From the Beginning: As Told to Mark Tucker,* University of Michigan Press, 1988.

Chilton, John, *Let the Good Times Roll: The Story of Louis Jordan and His Music,* University of Michigan Press, 1994.

Feather, Leonard, *The Jazz Years: Earwitness to an Era,* Quartet Books, 1989.

(With Al Fraser) Gillespie, Dizzy, *To Be or Not to Bop: Memoirs,* Doubleday, 1979.

Rusch, Robert D., *Jazztalk: The Cadence of Interviews,* Lyle Stuart Inc., 1984.

Shaw, Arnold, *Honkers and Shouters: The Golden Years of Rhythm and Blues,* Collier, 1978.

Simon, George T., *The Big Bands,* Schirmer, 1981.

Tosches, Nick, *Unsung Heroes of Rock n' Roll,* Scribner's, 1984.

Travis, Dempsey J., *An Autobiography of Black Jazz,* Urban Research Institute, 1983.

Down Beat, March 27, 1975.

Newsweek, April 20, 1992.

Pulse!, November 1992.

Variety, November 1990.

Additional information for this profile was obtained from liner notes by Peter Grendysa to *Just Say Moe! Mo' of the Best of Louis Jordan,* Rhino Records, 1992. □

Michael Jordan

Basketball superstar Michael Jordan (born 1963) is one of the most successful, popular, and wealthy athletes in college, Olympic, and professional sports history.

Michael Jordan was born on February 17, 1963. He did not make the high school basketball team as a sophomore in his native Wilmington, North Carolina, but did make the team as a junior. After high school he accepted a basketball scholarship to the University of North Carolina where he played under head coach Dean Smith. In his first season at Carolina he became only the second Tarheel player to start every game as a freshman and was named Atlantic Coast Conference (ACC) Rookie of the Year (1982). In his freshman year he played on the ACC championship team and made the clutch jump shot that beat Georgetown University for the championship of the Na-

Michael Jordan (left)

tional Collegiate Athletic Association (NCAA). He led the ACC in scoring as a sophomore in the 1982-1983 season and as a junior in the 1983-1984 season. The *Sporting News* named him college player of the year in 1983 and again in 1984. He left North Carolina after his junior year and was drafted by the Chicago Bulls of the National Basketball Association (NBA) as the third overall pick of the 1984 draft, behind Hakeem Olajuwon and Sam Bowie. Before joining the Bulls, Jordan was a member of the Summer 1984 United States Olympic basketball team that easily won the gold medal in Los Angeles, California.

Air Jordan Was Born

When Jordan was drafted by the Chicago Bulls they were a lackluster team, seldom drawing not much more than 6,000 fans to a home game. Jordan quickly turned that around. His style of play and fierce spirit of competition reminded sportswriters and fans of Julius Erving, who had dominated play during the 1970s. Jordan's incredible leaping ability and hang time thrilled fans in arenas around the league. As a rookie in his first season he was named to the All-Star team and was later named the league's Rookie of the Year (1985).

A broken foot sidelined him for 64 games during the 1985-1986 season, but he returned in rare form, scoring 49 points against the Boston Celtics in the first game of the playoffs and 63 in the second game, an NBA record. The 1986-1987 season was again one of individual successes, and Jordan started in the All-Star game after receiving a

record 1.5 million votes. He became the first player since Wilt Chamberlain to score 3,000 points in a single season. Jordan enjoyed personal success, but Chicago did not advance beyond the first round of the playoffs until 1988, when they defeated the Cleveland Cavaliers. The Bulls were then eliminated in the semi-final round by the Detroit Pistons. During the season Jordan had concentrated on improving his other basketball skills to the point where he was named Defensive Player of the Year (1988). He was also named the league's Most Valuable Player (MVP) and became the first player to lead the league in both scoring and steals. He was again named the MVP in that year's All-Star game.

The Bulls' management knew that they had a superstar in Michael Jordan, but they knew as well that they did not have a championship team. By adding such players as center Bill Cartwright, Horace Grant, and John Paxon to complement Jordan's skills they created a strong team that won the 1991 title by defeating the Los Angeles Lakers. The next year, the Bulls repeated as NBA champions by beating the Portland Trail Blazers.

In 1992 Jordan joined NBA stars Magic Johnson, Larry Bird, John Stockton, Patrick Ewing, Karl Malone, Clyde Drexler, David Robinson, Charles Barkley, Scottie Pippen, Chris Mullin, and Duke University's Christian Laettner to form the "Dream Team" that participated in the 25th Summer Olympic Games in Barcelona, Spain. The Olympic Committee had voted to lift the ban on professional athletes participating in the games. The team easily won the gold medal, winning their eight games by a 43.7 average margin of victory, scoring more than 100 points in each game.

1993—Personal Trials and Triumphs

In 1993, after a grueling semi-final playoff series with the New York Knicks, the Bulls met the Phoenix Suns for the NBA championship. When it was over, Jordan was again playoff MVP and Chicago had an unprecedented third straight title. Then, unexpectedly, tragedy struck. Jordan's father, James, was murdered by two men during a robbery attempt. Jordan was grief stricken, and that, combined with increasing media scrutiny over his gambling, left him feeling depleted and disenchanted with his life as a basketball superstar. Stating that he had nothing left to accomplish, he announced his retirement from professional basketball in October. By all accounts Jordan handled the personal tragedy of his father's death with great dignity. And while he felt the joy and challenge was gone from basketball, nothing could diminish what he had accomplished: three consecutive NBA titles, three regular season MVP awards, three playoff MVP titles, member of the All-Star team every year that he was in the league, and seven consecutive scoring titles. In just nine seasons he had become the Bulls all-time scoring leader.

In 1994 Jordan changed sports and joined the Chicago White Sox minor league baseball team. Professionally, the next 17 months proved to be mediocre at best, but the experience and time away from basketball provided a much needed respite and opportunity to regain his passion for basketball.

The Road Back Was a Slam Dunk

It had been a long time since anyone who knew Jordan thought—or dared ask—could he cut it. But when he returned to the Chicago Bulls during the 1994-1995 regular season, people wondered, "Could he do it again?" He played well, but inconsistently and so did the Bulls. The team was defeated in the playoffs by the Orlando Magic. After a summer of playing basketball during breaks from filming the movie *Space Jam,* he returned with fierce determination to prove any skeptic that he had what it took to get back on top. The 1995-1996 season was built on the type of playing on which records are made—the team finished the regular season 72-10, an NBA record that topped the 1971-1972 record established by the Los Angeles Lakers, and Jordan, with his shooting rhythm back, earned his eighth scoring title. He also became the tenth NBA player to score 25,000 career points, second only to Wilt Chamberlain in the number of games it took. The Bulls, with the Jordan, Pippen, and Dennis Rodman super combo, went on to win their fourth NBA championship in the decade, overpowering the Seattle Supersonics in six games. It was a moment few who watched will ever forget, as Jordan sank to his knees, head bent over the winning ball, in an emotional moment of bittersweet victory and deep sadness. The game had been played on Father's Day, exactly three years after his father's murder. It was the kind of moment both Jordans would have relished sharing.

The defending champions encountered a tougher playing field during the 1996-1997 season, but entered the playoffs as expected. Sheer determination took the Bulls to their fifth NBA championship. Illness, injury, and at times wavering mental focus plagued the team. In the fifth game Jordan almost single handedly delivered the winning score, despite suffering from a stomach virus. In the 1997-98 season the Bulls were again in the playoffs, and again they faced tough competition. As before, they were able to clinch the NBA championship and Jordan claimed his sixth NBA finals MVP award.

Jordan's other professional life as businessman and celebrity endorser was never off track. He co-starred with Bugs Bunny and the Loony Tunes gang in the live action/animation film, *Space Jam.* Megabuck endorsements for companies such as Nike and Wheaties, as well as his own golf company and branded products such as Michael Jordan cologne, which reportedly sold 1,500,000 bottles in the first two months on the market, made Jordan a multimillionaire. In 1997 Jordan was ranked the world's highest paid athlete, with a $30 million contract—the largest one-year salary in sports history—and approximately $40 million a year in endorsement fees. Jordan retired for a second time in 1999, ending his career on a high note just after the official end of the first ever NBA lockout. Many people saw him as the greatest basketball player ever, and his retirement was called the end of an era.

To top off his stellar professional resume, Jordan was regarded as an all around nice guy with moral courage, poise, *and* personal charisma. He credited his family and faith for his success. As the twentieth century came to a close, this African American hero was a cultural and sports icon around the world.

Further Reading

Hang Time, Jordan's biography, written with Bob Greene (Doubleday, 1992) and *Rare Air: Michael on Michael,* edited by Mark Vancil (Collins Publishers, San Francisco, 1993) are good general accounts of his life through 1992. *Taking to the Air: The Rise of Michael Jordan* by Jim Naughton (Warner Books, 1992) and *Hang Time: Days and Dreams with Michael Jordan* by Bob Greene (1992) are both good general biographies. For a critical look at Jordan see *The Jordan Rules* by Sam Smith (1992). For more on the Olympic "Dream Team" see *The Golden Boys* by Cameron Stauth (1992). See also *Second Coming: The Strange Odyssey of Michael Jordan—from Courtside to Home Plate and Back Again* by Sam Smith (HarperCollins, 1995). □

Percy Lavon Julian

As the inventor of synthetic cortisone, fire-extinguishing Aero-Foam, and drugs to treat glaucoma, Percy Lavon Julian (1899-1975) made life-enhancing and life-saving products more affordable. Despite facing racial prejudice and segregation at nearly every step of his career, Julian became the first African American to be named director of research at a white-owned firm, and he eventually founded his own Julian Laboratories and Julian Research Institute, where he continued as director until his death.

Percy Lavon Julian was born in Montgomery, Alabama, on April 11, 1899; his father was a railway mail clerk, and his grandfather had been a slave. He credited his strict father with providing the discipline and high standards necessary to his success. *Reader's Digest* reported that when as a young boy Julian proudly brought home a math test with a grade of 80, his father responded, "A son of mine must not be satisfied with mediocrity. After this make it 100!"

As a teenager, Julian moved with his family to Greencastle, Indiana, home of DePauw University. All six of the Julian children, including Percy, studied there. Although he was required to enter the university as a "sub-freshman," in 1920 he graduated Phi Beta Kappa, as class valedictorian. He hoped to continue his education and become a research scientist in the field of organic chemistry, but his mentors dissuaded him. Although one of his chemistry professors made inquiries to graduate schools on Julian's behalf, they all replied negatively. "Discourage your bright young colored lad," one school advised. "We couldn't get him a job when he was done, and it'll only mean frustration. Why don't you find him a teaching job in a Negro college in the South? He doesn't need a Ph.D. for that."

Despite his father's suggestion that he go into medicine, where he could be more independent, Julian persisted in chemistry. He went to Fisk University in Nashville, a school for African Americans, where he taught until 1923. The talent of his students encouraged him to pursue his own dream, and he applied for a research fellowship at Harvard. He earned his Master's degree in a year, finishing in the top

group of his class. Had he been white, Harvard would have rewarded him with a post as a teaching assistant, but, as they explained to Julian, they feared that white students from the South would not accept him as a teacher. He stayed at Harvard on minor research fellowships, then returned to the South to teach at all-black schools West Virginia State College and Howard University, where after one year he was appointed head of the chemistry department.

Invented Drug for Glaucoma

Julian's research at Harvard served him well later. He had begun to repeat the experiments of the Austrian chemist Ernst Spëth, who had learned to synthesize chemicals such as nicotine and ephedrine—rather than studying these compounds as they appeared in nature, Julian experimented on making these chemicals himself. With the financial backing of a wealthy Harvard classmate, he went to Vienna to study with Spëth. Spëth welcomed Julian into his household, initiating a father-son relationship and working closely together on synthesizing a variety of naturally occurring chemicals. Through his work with Spëth, Julian received his Ph.D. at the University of Vienna in 1931. With his Ph.D., he returned to Howard, and then went again to DePauw, where he both taught and researched, but was denied the title of professor because of his race.

Although he would make one of his most important discoveries at this time, Julian's students remembered him as a committed teacher. Chemist J. Wayne Cole recalled in *Ebony* magazine, "He was obviously involved in his laboratory work but was essentially an instructor—first and fore-

most. It was the shaping of the student that appealed to him the most. And believe me, he never tolerated laziness or disinterestedness."

While carrying his teaching load, Julian pursued the problem of synthesizing physostigmine, a chemical known to help in the treatment of glaucoma. Despite years of effort, chemists had not been able to make the chemical in the laboratory. With fundraising help from his former professor Dean William Blanchard, Julian's research progressed rapidly and attracted international attention as he reported his findings in the *Journal of the American Chemical Society*. When he finally succeeded, he was universally acknowledged as leader in the field of chemistry. Dean Blanchard moved to appoint Julian as the head of DePauw's chemistry department, to make Julian the first professor of chemistry at any traditionally white university in America, and to make DePauw, as *Reader's Digest* reported, "a chemical Mecca." Blanchard's colleagues refused, calling the appointment "inadvisable."

Soybean Research Enabled More Innovations

With his academic career apparently at a dead-end, Julian received a timely invitation from Chicago's Glidden Company to direct soybean research. While there, he developed a process for isolating and preparing soya protein, which led to a number of important inventions. Among the most highly praised was his "bean soup," commercially known as Aero-Foam, which the Navy used during wartime to put out fires; he also developed a soy protein for coating paper at a fraction of the cost of the previously used milk casein.

Even more important was his discovery of a technique by which he could mass-produce the hormones testosterone and progesterone. Testosterone was then touted as an anti-aging drug for men, while progesterone helped prevent spontaneous abortion in pregnant mothers. While these hormones were available in nature, they were difficult to get, with the supply limited to the brains and spines of cattle that had been slaughtered. Although German chemists had extracted hormones from soybean oil, the technique they used was expensive and could not provide them in commercial quantities. Julian discovered away to make the oil porous, enabling chemists to create mass quantities of the hormones.

The invention of Compound S, however, is considered Julian's biggest scientific achievement. Natural cortisone was a recognized treatment for rheumatoid arthritis and other illnesses causing muscle pain; to get it, however, the bile from nearly 15,000 oxen would be required to treat a single patient for a year. The limited supply of cortisone made it impractical as a treatment option. Again using soybean oils, Julian created a drug—Compound S—that could mimic the effects of natural cortisone in the body. His synthesized cortisone resembled natural cortisone in every way, except that it lacked an oxygen atom in a crucial position. Because the body itself could replace that atom when the drug was used, the therapeutic result was the same. Julian's discovery made the benefits of cortisone economically feasible for all patients.

Racial Discrimination Did Not Deter Him

Julian patented these and nearly 130 other chemical innovations, enabling him to earn make a living much larger than that available to most blacks. In 1950, shortly after he had been named "Chicagoan of the Year" in a *Chicago Sun-Times* poll, Julian moved into the white, middle-class suburb of Oak Park, Illinois. He purchased an ornate, 15-room house and planned extensive landscaping and improvements, but even before he and his family moved in, they received threats and were the victims of an attempted arson. The water commissioner refused to turn on their water, until the family threatened to go to court. Julian was compelled to hire a private guard to patrol the property 24 hours a day. He told *Time,* "We've lived through these things all our lives. As far as the hurt to the spirit goes, we've become accustomed to that."

Julian continued to confront racism in his professional life as well. In 1951, when the Research Corporation of New York City invited Julian, along with 34 other scientists, to hear a talk at the Union League Club of Chicago, the club's manager contacted the organization and informed them that Julian would not be permitted to enter the building. The *New York Times* reported that the club's directors had issued "explicit instructions" forbidding Julian's attendance. By 1956, he had become more actively involved in opposing racial injustice. He became the first black man to chair the General Council of Congregational Christian Churches' Council for Social Action. The council voted to raise litigation funds for a delegate who had been refused admission to an American Legion Post, and, according to the *New York Times,* called on members to "support nonsegregated practices in selling, buying, and leasing property."

In 1967, Julian and North Carolina Mutual Life Insurance Company president Asa Spaulding organized a group of 47 wealthy business persons and professionals to raise money for the NAACP Legal Defense and Educational Fund. The group, calling itself the National Negro Business and Professional Committee for the Legal Defense Fund, announced in the *New York Times,* "This means the Negro millionaire is coming of age and taking a responsible place in the community." The committee planned to raise $1 million a year for cases involving voting rights, school desegregation, and job discrimination. Julian had been connected with the NAACP since 1947, when he won their Spingarn Medal Award.

Founded His Own Laboratories

Julian's financial success also enabled him to leave Glidden in 1953 and found Julian Laboratories. In addition to his suburban Chicago laboratory, he established subsidiaries in Mexico and Guatemala, which studied the possible medical benefits of the Mexican yam. These pharmaceutical businesses were so successful that eventually Julian, approaching his mid-60s, found the pressure to be too much, and in 1961 he sold them for nearly $2.4 million. In 1964, he retired as president from Julian Laboratories, then became director of Julian Research Institute and president of Julian Associates.

In 1974, Julian became increasingly ill, and was diagnosed with cancer of the liver. Despite a lack of energy and a difficult schedule of treatment, Julian continued to work and give speeches. In November of that year, he was honored by Sigma Xi, a society of research scientists, with the Procter Prize for extraordinary service to science and humanity. As *Ebony* reported, in his acceptance speech he discussed the benefits and drawbacks of scientific advancements: "Many of these successes have been abused, he acknowledged, while others have been the subjects of material applications having little implication for the enrichment of the spirit; man has treasured them as weapons or employed them as gadgets." Despite this, he said, he "shares the humanistic faith in an ordered, purposeful and meaningful reality."

Shortly before his death, Julian announced that he was satisfied with his life's work. "I have had one goal in my life," he said, "that of playing some role in making life a little easier for the persons who come after me." He died in April of 1975. In addition to many academic honors and citations he received during his lifetime, he was honored in 1993 by the U.S. Postal Service with a postage stamp in the Black Heritage Series. He was also honored by the city of Oak Park, Illinois, which named a middle school after one of its first residents.

Further Reading

Contemporary Black Biography, vol. 6, Gale, 1994.

Ebony, March 1975.

Jet, June 3, 1985; January 29, 1990.

New York Times, January 18, 1950; July 19, 1951; June 28, 1956; March 20, 1967; April 21, 1975.

Reader's Digest, August, 1946.

Stamps, February 13, 1993.

Time, December 4, 1950.

"Percy Julian School," http://kato.TheRamp.net/julian/bio.html (March 20, 1998). □

NAME INDEX

OCCUPATION INDEX

Aviation Pioneer

Occupation Index

Occupation Index

Occupation Index

Occupation Index

Occupation Index